Ireland is as sweet as a new world, lapped by two expanses of water, and as fierce as a land that has withstood the onslaughts of the Atlantic for years. Its shores have already surrendered their weakest estates to the storms but men still wait with their small brightly colored boats in the shelter of a pier for the chance to bring in a meager catch. But Ireland's heart is not torn between the land and the sea: instead, it dances a jig in the pubs.

The Emerald Isle's mysterious stones embrace an incredible architectural variety (standing stones, stone circles, dolmens, like the one at Legananny ▲ *307*, or funerary chambers), and there is a sacred geography in the choice of their sites which binds mankind to the land and the gods.

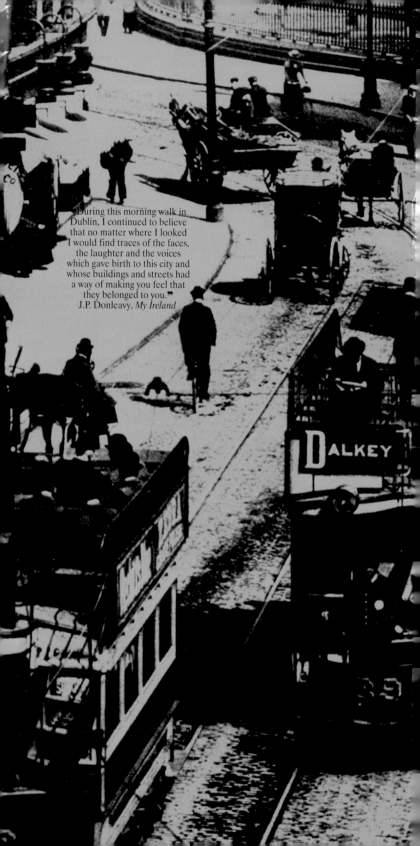

"During this morning walk in Dublin, I continued to believe that no matter where I looked I would find traces of the faces, the laughter and the voices which gave birth to this city and whose buildings and streets had a way of making you feel that they belonged to you."
J.P. Donleavy, *My Ireland*

I

THIS IS A BORZOI BOOK
PUBLISHED BY ALFRED A. KNOPF, INC.

Copyright © 1995 Alfred A. Knopf, Inc., New York

All rights reserved under International and Pan-American Copyright Conventions.
Published in the United States by Alfred A. Knopf, Inc., New York, and
simultaneously in Canada by Random House of Canada Limited, Toronto.
Distributed by Random House, Inc., New York.

Originally published in France by Nouveaux-Loisirs, a subsidiary of
Gallimard, Paris, 1994. Copyright © 1994 by Editions Nouveaux-Loisirs

Library of Congress Cataloging-in-Publication Data

Ireland. English
Ireland/ [Gallimard Editions].
p. cm.— (Knopf guides)
Includes bibliographical references and index.
ISBN 0-679-76203-5
1. Ireland — Guidebooks.
I. Gallimard (Firm) . II. Title. III. Series.
DA980.I553   1995
914.1504'824 — dc20
CIP 95-2426

First American Edition

NUMEROUS SPECIALISTS AND ACADEMICS HAVE CONTRIBUTED TO THIS GUIDE:

AUTHORS AND EDITORS: Frédéric Bony, Catherine Bourrabier, Paul Brennan, Jacques Briard,
Vincent Brunot, Mary F. Cawley, Stella Cherry, John De Courcy, Martine Denisot,
Philippe J. Dubois, Peadar Duignan, Seán Dunne, Éric Guillemot, Peter Harbison, Ian Hill,
Claude Jacquet, Pierre Joannon, Stephen Joannon, Raymond Keaveney, Pierre-Yves Lambert,
Patrick Léger, Bruno Lenormand, Vladimir Léon, Fiona McLaughlin, Béatrice Méneux,
Fidelma Mullane, Jean-Michel Picard, Philippe Pilard, Laure Raffaëlli, Sabine Rousselet,
James Scully, Odile, Simon, Peadar O'Dowd, Seamus O'Tuama, Éithne Verling,
Michael Viney, Patrick F. Wallace
ILLUSTRATORS AND ICONOGRAPHERS: Patrick Alexandre, Michèle Bisgambiglia, Anne Bodin,
Frédéric Bony, Suzanne Bosman, Olivier Brunot, Vincent Brunot, Philippe Canville,
Kristof Chemineau, Jean Chevallier, Élise Chleq, Denis Clavreul, Claire Cormier, Paul Coulbois,
Gismonde Curiace, François Desbordes, Bernard Duhem, Claire Felloni,
Martine Frouin-Marmouget (AFDEC), Eric Gillion, Jean-Marie Guillou, Gilbert Houbre,
Roger Hutchins, Jean-Marc Lanusse, Alban Larousse, Yvon Le Corre, Yann Leduc,
Dominique Mansion, François Place, Maurice Pommier, Claude Quiec, Pascal Robin,
Frédérique Schwebel, Catherine Totems, Tony Townshend
PHOTOGRAPHERS: Philippe Benet, Emmanuel Chaspoul, Sonia Dourlot,
Renata Holzbachova, Benoît Juge, John Murray, Dominique Zintzmeyer

WE WOULD ALSO LIKE TO THANK:
Seymourina Cruse, Patricia Deseine, Patricia Deseine (Northern Ireland Tourist Office), David Doyle,
Maura and Michael Duignan, Sylvie François, Claudine Hédin (Irish Tourist Office),
Desmond Kenny, Peter Murray, Brigitte Porte

WE WOULD LIKE TO GIVE SPECIAL THANKS TO:
Peter Harbison (Archeologist, Editor of *Ireland of the Welcomes* and member
of the Royal Irish Academy), Pierre Joannon (managing director of
Études irlandaises and president of the Ireland Fund de France)
and Fidelma Mullane (Údarás na Gaeltachta)

TRANSLATED BY SUE ROSE AND CORDELIA UNGER-HAMILTON.
PRACTICAL INFORMATION TRANSLATED BY YVONNE WORTH.
EDITED AND TYPESET BY BOOK CREATION SERVICES, LONDON.
PRINTED IN ITALY BY EDITORIALE LIBRARIA.

IRELAND

KNOPF GUIDES

CONTENTS

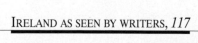

LEINSTER

MUNSTER

CONNACHT

ULSTER

▲ IRELAND

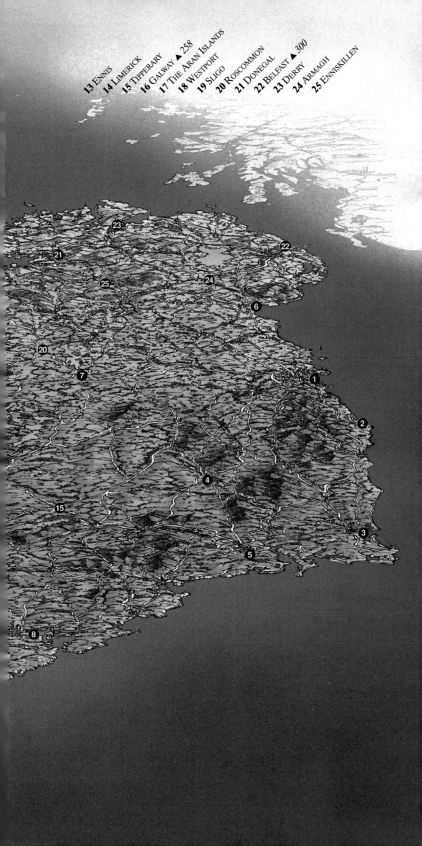

13 Ennis **14** Limerick **15** Tipperary **16** Galway ▲ 258 **17** The Aran Islands **18** Westport **19** Sligo **20** Roscommon **21** Donegal **22** Belfast ▲ 300 **23** Derry **24** Armagh **25** Enniskillen

THE IDENTITY OF IRELAND

"IRISH HOSPITALITY"

❝There is perpetual kindness in the Irish cabin – butter-milk, potatoes – a stool is offered or a stone is rolled that your honour may sit down and be out of the smoke, and those who beg everywhere else seem desirous to exercise free hospitality in their own houses. Their natural disposition is turned to gaiety and happiness . . . Pat's mind is always turned to fun and ridicule. They are terribly excitable, to be sure, and will murder you on slight suspicion, and find out the next day that it was all a mistake, and that it was not yourself they meant to kill, at all at all.❞
Sir Walter Scott, *Life of Scott,* 1838

Tricolor of the Republic of Ireland, symbol of the union (white) between the nationalists (green) and the unionists (orange), in front of the Union Jack of Great Britain.

STATISTICS

REPUBLIC OF IRELAND
Surface area: 85,058 square miles
Population : 3.5 million of which 46 percent are under 25 years old.
Capital: Dublin
Administrative division: 26 counties divided between 4 provinces : Leinster (12), Connacht (6), Munster (5), Ulster (3)
Language : English and Gaelic
Sovereign state: parliamentary democracy

NORTHERN IRELAND
Surface area: 16,967 square miles
Population : 1.5 million
Capital: Belfast

Administrative division: 6 out of the 9 counties of Ulster province
Language: English
Subordinate state: province of Great Britain

Donegal Bay

SLIGO
SLIGO

Achill Island
CASTLEBAR
Clew Bay
MAYO
ROSCOMMO

C O N N A C H T
ROSCOMMON
Lough Corrib
Lough Ree

GALWAY
GALWAY
Galway Bay
Aran Islands

E I
River Shannon
Lough Derg

CLARE
• ENNIS

TIPPERAR
Mouth of the Shannon
LIMERICK
LIMERICK
Tipperary •

• TRALEE
M U N S T E R

Dingle Bay

KERRY
CORK
Dungar

Lee
CORK

TOURISM

Peace has revived the tourist trade in Northern Ireland. In the Republic, where tourism has more than doubled since 1981, the annual three million tourists represent over a billion pounds a year for the tourist industry.

RELIGION

The transition from Celtic paganism to Christianity was a smooth one. More tragic is the division between Protestants and Catholics which has been the cause of much bloodshed. In the Republic 93 percent of the population are Catholic and 3.4 percent are Protestant; in Northern Ireland 38.4 percent are Catholic and 51 percent Protestant.

SYMBOLS

The shamrock ● 71
The celtic harp: symbol of an independent Ireland, it appears on the Leinster coat of arms.
The red hand: symbol of the province of Northern Ireland, it appears in the center of the Ulster coat of arms.

AGRICULTURE

This still constitutes an important part of the Irish economy in both the north and south, even though it represents less than 10 percent of their GNP. On either side of the border, livestock (largely cattle) and dairy products (mainly milk) are the most important elements of Irish agriculture. Joining the European Community has brought with it price guarantees and opened new outlets for Ireland's agricultural produce.

FISHING

A growing industry. Herring, cod, whiting, place, mackerel and shellfish are the main types of catch along the coasts. The rivers are packed with trout and salmon.

0   12   25   37 miles

―――― Regional boundaries
―――― County boundaries
―――― Waterways

INDUSTRY

Northern Ireland has been industrialized since the 19th century. Its economy was originally dominated by its shipyards, the textile industry and the construction industry. However the political problems changed this. In the Republic industry has expanded rapidly since 1960. Beverages, food and mechanical engineering are now the largest industries, while pharmaceuticals and electronics are still growing.

15

How to Use this Guide
(Sample page shown from the guide to Venice)

The symbols at the top of each page refer to the different parts of the guide.

■ Natural Environment

● Keys to Understanding

▲ Itineraries

◆ Practical Information

The itinerary map shows the main points of interest along the way and is intended to help you find your bearings.

The mini-map locates the particular itinerary within the wider area covered by the guide.

▲ CANNAREGIO

CHURCH OF SANTA MARIA DELLA SCALZA
CHURCH OF SAN GEREMIA
PALAZZO LABIA
GHETTO
PALAZZO MASTELLI DEL CAMMELLO
PALAZZO GIOVANELLI
CHURCH OF MADONNA DELL'ORTO
CHURCH OF SANTA MARIA DEI MIRACOLI
CHURCH OF SANTA SOFIA
CHURCH OF SANTI APOSTOLI
CHURCH OF SAN CANCIANO
UNIVERSITY OF SAN JOB
...

CHURCH OF SANTI GIOVANNI E PAOLO
CHURCH OF SAN GIOBBE
CHURCH OF SAN MARCUOLA
PALAZZO VENDRAMIN CALERGI
CHURCH OF SAN STAE
CHURCH OF SANTA MARIA MATER DOMINI
CHURCH OF SAN SIMEON PICCOLO
LUCIA STATION
CHURCH OF SAN GEREMIA
BUILT BRIDGE
PESCHERIA
FONDACO DEI TURCHI
TEATRO MALIBRAN
CHURCH OF SAN CASSIANO
CHURCH OF SANTA MARIA MATER DOMINI

▲ THE GATEWAY TO VENICE ★

Immediately outside the railway station lies Cannaregio, the first of the six sestieri of Venice. Situated at the north-west end of the city, this is the second largest sestiere after Castello ▲ 155, covering an area of 150 hectares. Nearly a third of the population of Venice is concentrated here, amounting to more than twenty thousand people. There are two theories about the origin of the name Cannaregio, according to one, it comes from Canal regio (the Royal Canal), meaning the broad waterway which once provided convenient access to the city from the main city which once provided convenient access to the city from the main city which once provided convenient access to Secundo hypothesis is that the word derives from the reeds and canes which used to abound in this area. In any case, a system of straight, parallel canals, with long fondamentas abutting southwards and linked by bridges, criss-cross this zone of the south, behind interspersed with magnificent palaces. To street known as the Strada Nuova was built at the end of the last century. Now pedestrianized, this street runs from the sestiere from one side to the Apostoli, crossing a number of different names as other and adopting, and it seems to have taken form only as it goes. Few people believed in the process of draining and 11th century, and the project as progressed. From the 15th gradually, as the province a definable quarter, though century onwards, Canaregio became manufacturing was the it was still peripheral to Venice proper. Before the railway bridge and the station were built, despite attempts to create a principal industry in the district, despite attempts to create a new area of growth with the Fondamenta Nuove. A similar project in the 16th century, the draining of the Sacca della Misericordia, was also never realized.

The gateway to Venice, after all, is neither the station nor the Grand Canal but the churned before the churned waters as a grippos, turbulent as a propellers.
Fernand Braudel, Hesse

Santa Lucia Station.

PONTE DELLA LIBERTÀ. Built by the Austrians 50 years after the Treaty of Campo Formio in 1797 ● 34, to link Venice with Milan. The bridge ended the thousand-year separation from the mainland and shook the city's economy to its roots as Venice, already in the throes of the industrial revolution, saw its dependence on the mainland grow out of all recognition. SANTA LUCIA STATION. The present station dates from 1955, but still bears the name of the Renaissance church demolished in 1861 to make way for it. Opposite is the green dome of the Church of San Simeone Piccolo.

Half a day

BRIDGES TO VENICE
The Venetians conceived a project for a bridge between Milan and Venice as early as 1834 but it was not until 1846 that construction of the Ponte della Libertà was finally begun. The span of this new viaduct was almost 11,500 feet, and it included 222 arches. On April 25, 1933, the Ponte della Libertà was opened. Built in less than two years by the engineer Umberto Fantucci, this bridge was intended for use by motor cars.

136

─────────────

●▲■◆
The symbols alongside a title or within the text itself provide cross-references to a theme or place dealt with elsewhere in the guide.

★ The star symbol signifies that a particular site has been singled out by the publishers for its special beauty, atmosphere or cultural interest.

At the beginning of each itinerary, the suggested means of transport to be used and the time it will take to cover the area are indicated:
🚤 By boat
🚶 On foot
🚲 By bicycle
🕐 Duration

─────────────

THE GATEWAY TO VENICE ★

PONTE DELLA LIBERTÀ. Built by the Austrians 50 years after the Treaty of Campo Formio in 1797 ● *34,* to link Venice with Milan. The bridge ended the thousand-year separation from the mainland and shook the city's economy to its roots as Venice, already in the throes of the industrial revolution, saw

🚶 Half a day

BRIDGES TO VENICE

NATURE

◼ CLIMATE

The humidity of the climate lends itself to the appearance of some spectacular rainbows, especially in the southwest of Ireland.

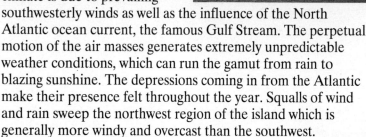

Ireland's temperate, humid climate is due to prevailing southwesterly winds as well as the influence of the North Atlantic ocean current, the famous Gulf Stream. The perpetual motion of the air masses generates extremely unpredictable weather conditions, which can run the gamut from rain to blazing sunshine. The depressions coming in from the Atlantic make their presence felt throughout the year. Squalls of wind and rain sweep the northwest region of the island which is generally more windy and overcast than the southwest. In winter, extremely violent storms can blow in from the ocean shores, lashing Ireland with the full force of their fury.

Although snow never lasts long in Ireland, it does settle in the country's central mountainous regions. It is unusual in the south.

As they pass over Ireland, the depressions generate first southwesterly and then northwesterly winds.

ATLANTIC OCEAN

Clew Bay

Galway Bay

Burren

Shannon

Boggerah Mountains

PECTORAL SANDPIPER
This North American shorebird turns up in small numbers (up to twenty or so) in Ireland each fall.

BUFF-BREASTED SANDPIPER
This is the second most likely North American wader to be blown off course to Ireland in fall.

During the last ice age, Ireland was almost entirely covered with ice. Geological deposits carried by the drifting glaciers formed a composite layer over the many different types of the island's former bedrock. When the glaciers retreated, small hills of stone and clay, called drumlins, were formed. In some fairly shallow bays, like Clew Bay ▲ 279, opposite, these small knolls formed islands.

"If you don't like the weather, wait a couple of minutes!" This saying illustrates the extremely changeable nature of the Irish climate, which sets the scene for some superb lighting effects.

Every winter, the storms carry salt water a long way inland. Due to the fierce westerly winds, the vegetation is flattened and even the trees are stunted.

STOAT
The stoat is one of the few species to have survived the ice age in Ireland where the subsequent severe rises in temperature and sea level were fatal to many animals.

Summer

Winter

The turning of the Earth deflects the winds westward over the Atlantic.

Warm air masses move up from the Gulf of Mexico along with the warm waters of the Gulf Stream (mauve arrows), causing fog and rain as they cool.

Donegal Bay

Sperrin Mountains

North Canal

Mourne Mountains

Shannon

Wicklow Mountains

IRISH SEA

Less than 30 inches
30 to 40 inches
40 to 50 inches
50 to 60 inches
60 to 80 inches
More than 80 inches

In winter, rain can cause floods. The mountains receive over 6 feet of water per year.

When the cold air coming down from the pole meets the tropical air rising northward, this creates depressions off the coast of Ireland. Before a depression, the weather is overcast and humid; afterward, it is colder and clearer, with showers and a northwesterly wind.

The Irish summer is generally cool. Thanks to warm air moving in from Europe, the island enjoys some long warm spells.

GANNET
This bird's busy, noisy colonies
are one of the finest natural
sights on the Irish coastline.

The high cliffs on the Atlantic coast afford a
superb vantage point, over a distance of
164 feet, for watching the slow advance of the waves which
teem with underwater life. In spring, plankton (tiny marine
plants and animals that drift with the currents) flourishes:
this is the staple source of nourishment in the food chain
for the pelagic species. From the west and south coasts,
you can see dolphins, whales and basking sharks, while the
comings and goings of the seabirds, at the height of their
migration season in the fall and spring, bring the coastline
to life.

There are countless shoals of mackerel,
herring and cod at the point where the cold
waters of the Atlantic meet the warm currents
of the Gulf Stream.

BOTTLE-NOSED DOLPHIN
During the breeding season,
in summer, this dolphin goes
hunting in pods for shoals of mackerel,
which is its favorite food.
Some bays have their own resident
group of dolphins.

BLUE SHARK
This impressive
predator of the deep
with nocturnal habits
is harmless. It comes
in close to the coast
in summer to feast on
shoals of fish.

GREAT SKUA
A passage migrant to Ireland, this powerful seabird forces other seabirds to regurgitate their prey, then snatches it from them.

MANX SHEARWATER
This shearwater, a notable long-distance migrant which travels out over the Atlantic in winter as far as Canada, South America and South Africa, nests on some of the same islets as the petrels.

STORM PETREL
Every night in summer, tens of thousands of these tiny seabirds come to sit on their eggs in holes situated on islands off the west coast.

F. Desbordes

◀ **COMMON SEAL**
This is an inhabitant of the estuaries and bays whose sandbards, cut off by the channels, offer it refuge at low tide.

Young gray seal with white coat

GRAY SEAL
This large powerful seal eats about 13 lbs of fish per day. Its numbers are steadily increasing along Ireland's Atlantic coast.

MINKE WHALE
The Irish waters are a favorite haunt for this small whale which grows up to about 33 feet long.

BASKING SHARK
This giant cruises along the coastline, its mouth gaping at water level as it devours the plankton. It can grow up to 33 feet long.

LEATHERY TURTLE
This is the largest species of turtle and can grow up to 6 feet long and weigh up to 1,000 lbs. Its nesting sites are scattered throughout the tropics, but it may wander great distances and occasionally reaches Irish waters.

21

RAVEN
Most of the cliffs have
their own resident pair of
this largest of crows. They
nest very early in the season.

SEA PINK
This plant decorates
the clifftop grass
with pinkish flower
heads which are
exposed to the wind
and salt.

BLADDER CAMPION
Bladder campion favors
bare environments,
growing in windy places
reminiscent of the
mountain areas which
are this type of plant's
original habitat.

SHAG
Unlike its close relative the
cormorant, from which it can be
distinguished by its jaunty crest in
the breeding season, the shag is
almost entirely marine.

PUFFIN
Unlike some seabirds, such as
gulls, this comical little member of
the auk family does not regurgitate fish
for its young, carrying it instead in its beak.

CHOUGH
Ireland's Atlantic shoreline is one of the few places in the British Isles that still provides a home for these acrobatic and handsome crows.

During the winter, waves lash Ireland's Atlantic coastline more fiercely than anywhere else in Europe. The eroded rocks rearing over the ocean are a spectacular sight. In spring and early summer, rocks jutting out from the steepest slopes are colonized by large numbers of nesting birds. Each species selects a favorite site where it will rear its young. The islands near the coastline are also home to large colonies of birds, which populate the clifftops or the crevices, avoiding the hustle and bustle of human life.

Cliffs of Moher

KITTIWAKE
Living far out to sea in winter, this dapper gull nests on the cliffs every spring. Its wingtips look as if they have been dipped in ink.

GUILLEMOT
Most abundant of the auks in Ireland, this bird breeds in dense noisy colonies on ledges of seacliffs, especially around the south and west coasts.

RAZORBILL
In spring, this relative of the guillemot likes to build its nest in nooks and crevices in the cliffs.

FULMAR
The first record of this Arctic petrel breeding in Ireland was in 1911, in Mayo; today there are about 32,000 breeding pairs.

Kittiwakes, clustered in colonies, build their deep nests with seaweed which they cement with their droppings to the steep ledges of the rock.

ROCKY STRAND

Despite being buffeted by the waves, the rocky shore is an extremely well balanced environment which provides permanent habitats for a wide variety of organisms.

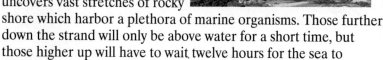

Twice a day, the ebb tide uncovers vast stretches of rocky shore which harbor a plethora of marine organisms. Those further down the strand will only be above water for a short time, but those higher up will have to wait twelve hours for the sea to submerge them once more. Each organism, however, is specially adapted to the length of time that the littoral zone where it makes its home is above water level. The diversity of locations is a result of the island's geographical position, in the area where the cold waters from the north meet the warm currents from the south.

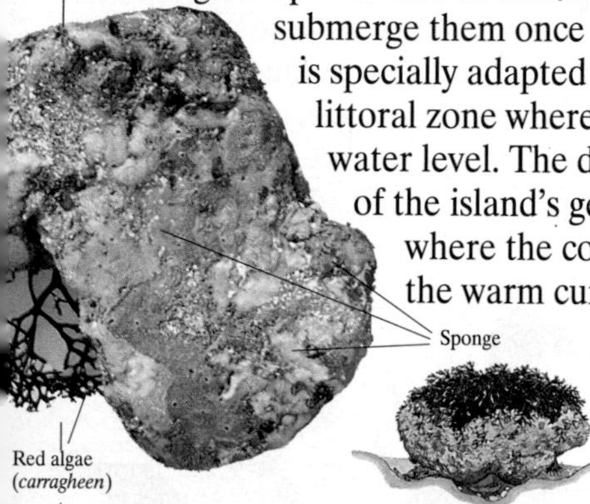

Sponge

Oyster catcher

Mussels

Red algae
(carragheen)

Under water, the top of the rocks is usually covered in different types of algae. Their underside, however, starved of light, is home to a variety of animal life.

GOBY
In small rock pools, this voracious predator clings to the rock using its joined ventral fins, which form suction discs.

Fucus serratus

Laver
(*porphyra umbilicalis*)

Calliblepharis ciliata

Caragheen
(*chondrus crispus*)

Cormorant

Sea urchin

Scallop

Oarweed
(*laminaria hyperborea*)

Velvet
swimming
crab

SUBLITTORAL ZONE
In the clear waters of the Atlantic, large brown seaweeds may grow as deep as 98 feet: their strong, flexible roots can withstand the pull of the waves. Many red seaweeds also grow here, forming water plant communities which provide shelter for fish and crabs.

VELVET SWIMMING CRAB
This crab's legs, which resemble paddles, enable it to move extremely fast.

EDIBLE CRAB
This summer visitor to rocky shores can be found in the deeper rock pools.

Common periwinkle

Flat periwinkle

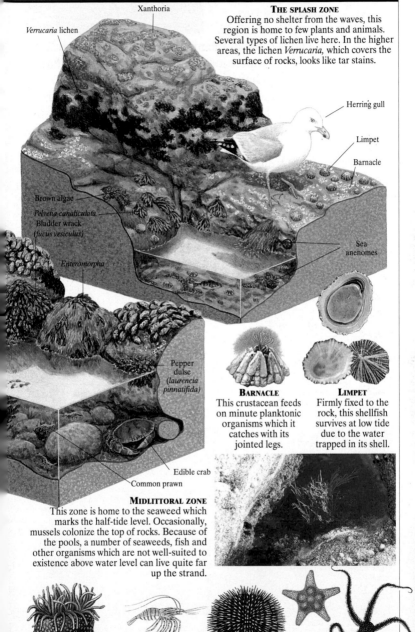

Xanthoria

Verrucaria lichen

THE SPLASH ZONE
Offering no shelter from the waves, this region is home to few plants and animals. Several types of lichen live here. In the higher areas, the lichen *Verrucaria*, which covers the surface of rocks, looks like tar stains.

Herring gull

Limpet

Barnacle

Brown algae

Pelvetia canaliculata
Bladder wrack
(*fucus vesiculus*)

Enteromorpha

Sea anemones

Pepper dulse
(*laurencia pinnatifida*)

Edible crab

Common prawn

BARNACLE
This crustacean feeds on minute planktonic organisms which it catches with its jointed legs.

LIMPET
Firmly fixed to the rock, this shellfish survives at low tide due to the water trapped in its shell.

MIDLITTORAL ZONE
This zone is home to the seaweed which marks the half-tide level. Occasionally, mussels colonize the top of rocks. Because of the pools, a number of seaweeds, fish and other organisms which are not well-suited to existence above water level can live quite far up the strand.

SEA ANEMONE
These predators unfurl their tentacles covered with stinging cells to paralyse their prey.

COMMON PRAWN
This is a scavenger in temporary rock pools; its fanlike tail enables it to escape backward.

EDIBLE SEA URCHIN
On the Atlantic coast, sea urchins use their spines to open up cavities in the rock.

STARFISH AND BRITTLE STARS
These carnivores feed on bivalves and can even open mussel shells.

25

WEXFORD BAY

Geese from Greenland and swans from Russia winter together in Wexford Harbour ▲ *181*.

Ireland possesses many wetlands which rank among some of the most important in Europe and provide a safe haven in winter for many waterfowl and shorebirds. These waterbirds, which have migrated from their breeding grounds in Canada, Greenland, Iceland, Northern Europe and Siberia, find abundant food in the estuaries and sounds which are sheltered from frost and always accessible. The nature reserve of Wexford Slobs provides a winter home for up to eight thousand white-fronted geese from Greenland (half of the world's population) which feed on cereals, unlifted potatoes, seeds and grass.

Young

Young

Adult

Adult

WHITE-FRONTED GOOSE
Birds from the population that breeds in Greenland winter in Ireland.

BEWICK'S SWAN
Breeding on the remote tundras of Arctic Russia, this wild swan winters in northwest Europe, arriving in Ireland in late fall.

Male   Female

Thousands of geese can be watched from the observation posts erected in Wexford.

WIDGEON
The most common wintering duck in Ireland can be found in large numbers on the banks of the River Shannon at the end of winter.

DUNLIN
This shorebird winters in large flocks, especially on the Shannon Estuary, Dundalk Bay, Strangford Lough, North Bull, Dublin and Cork Harbour.

BAR-TAILED GODWIT
This shorebird feeds on large worms, especially lugworms, in the ooze. In Wexford, when there are high spring tides it also forages for food in the flooded fields.

REDSHANK
Most redshanks that winter in Ireland once nested in Iceland. The largest numbers of this noisy shorebird occur in the autumn and spring migration peaks.

LAPWING
Large flocks of this atttractive shorebird winter in Ireland, particularly in the Wexford area.

BRENT GOOSE
This small sea goose, which is quite tame, sometimes frequents the roadsides in Dublin Bay, where it feeds.

SHORT-EARED OWL
This winter visitor is seen mainly on the east coast and hunts all kinds of rodents, mostly during the daytime.

PEREGRINE FALCON
This bird climbs to very high altitudes, then dives suddenly at great speed on small waders.

■ SANDY BEACHES

Sandhopper

SKATE'S EGG
Spotted dogfish eggs, commonly found
around the tide mark, are similar to skate's
eggs but darker brown in color.

The Irish coastline, although mainly rocky by nature, boasts
some fine sandy beaches. Some of these, which consist of grains
of quartz or granite carried by the rivers, are conducive to the
formation of dunes. Dunes cover a total of 466 miles of the
coastline. In Connacht, the beaches more often than not consist
of tiny shells or fragments of calcareous algae. Although the
Atlantic shoreline, which is particularly vulnerable to the wind

and the currents, is not very
hospitable to marine life, the
northern bays, whose beaches
are composed of finer deposits,
provide a home for a wide
variety of fauna.

Strands are long sandy beaches, bordered on
the landward side by dunes where maritime
plants, such as sea holly, grow.

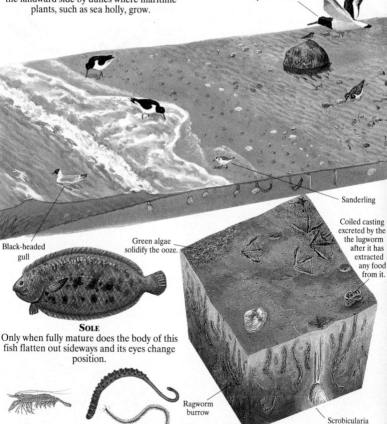

Oyster catcher

Sanderling

Coiled casting
excreted by the
the lugworm
after it has
extracted
any food
from it.

Black-headed
gull

Green algae
solidify the ooze.

SOLE
Only when fully mature does the body of this
fish flatten out sideways and its eyes change
position.

Ragworm
burrow

Scrobicularia

COMMON SHRIMP
This shellfish changes
color to blend in with
its surroundings.

**LUGWORMS AND
RAGWORMS**
These form the
staple diet of
waders.

The upper part of the ooze is home to many
micro-organisms. Deeper down, it becomes
darker in color due to the lack of oxygen.

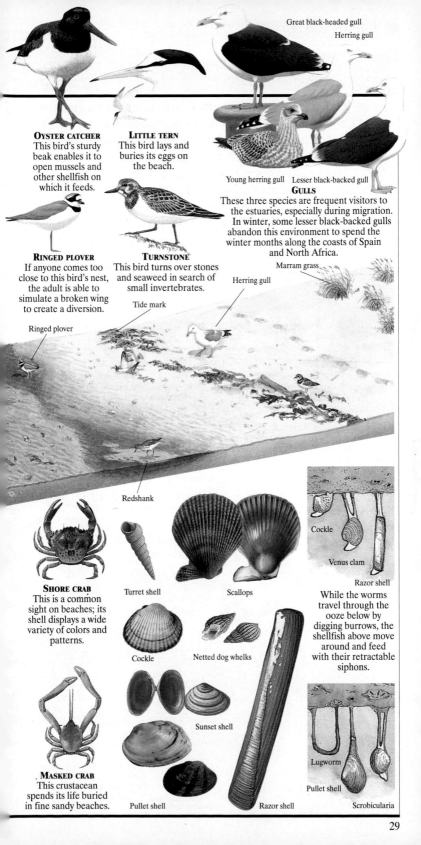

OYSTER CATCHER
This bird's sturdy beak enables it to open mussels and other shellfish on which it feeds.

LITTLE TERN
This bird lays and buries its eggs on the beach.

Great black-headed gull

Herring gull

Young herring gull   Lesser black-backed gull

GULLS
These three species are frequent visitors to the estuaries, especially during migration. In winter, some lesser black-backed gulls abandon this environment to spend the winter months along the coasts of Spain and North Africa.

RINGED PLOVER
If anyone comes too close to this bird's nest, the adult is able to simulate a broken wing to create a diversion.

TURNSTONE
This bird turns over stones and seaweed in search of small invertebrates.

Marram grass

Herring gull

Tide mark

Ringed plover

Redshank

SHORE CRAB
This is a common sight on beaches; its shell displays a wide variety of colors and patterns.

Turret shell   Scallops

Cockle

Venus clam

Razor shell

While the worms travel through the ooze below by digging burrows, the shellfish above move around and feed with their retractable siphons.

Cockle   Netted dog whelks

Sunset shell

MASKED CRAB
This crustacean spends its life buried in fine sandy beaches.

Pullet shell   Razor shell

Lugworm

Pullet shell

Scrobicularia

29

The Burren, in County Clare, resembles a giant rock garden. It is one of the largest natural rocky sites in Ireland. Although the erosion of the hills and limestone plateaus was aggravated by pre-Christian farmers who grazed their goats and sheep here, nature has mitigated this ecological disaster by carpeting the rugged fissures with unusual plants. From May onward, the plants flower luxuriantly in combinations which are unique in Europe. Arctic and Mediterranean flora flower together; woodland flowers thrive out in the open and alpine species bloom by the edge of the ocean.

RED FOX

The fox is a mainly nocturnal animal, hunting small mammals.

PINE MARTEN

The pine marten, Ireland's rarest mammal, climbs trees with great agility when hunting its prey. The Burren is one of its last strongholds in the British Isles.

Botanists flock to the Burren ▲ *242*, which has made a name for itself for its variety of plant communities. Flowers native to the Atlantic coast, as well as the Arctic, grow side by side with southern orchids in its cracked chalky soil.

Peacock butterfly

Hart's tongue fern
(asplenium scolopendrium)

Pine marten

Irish saxifrage
(saxifraga rosacea)

Squinancywort
(asperula cynanchica)

The roots of certain plants penetrate deep into cracks in the rock where organic matter has accumulated.

Hoary rock-rose
(helianthemum canum)

Maidenhair fern
(adiantium capillus veneris)

ALPINE BEARBERRY
This plant can be found on the warm hillsides of the Burren.

BLOODY CRANESBILL
The anthers at the center of this magenta flower are turquoise.

BEE ORCHID
More than twenty species of orchids bloom in the Burren.

BURNET ROSE
This rose flowers in early summer. In the fall, its leaves turn deep red.

Female   Male

HEN HARRIER
This handsome bird of prey patrols at low altitudes in search of the small birds and rodents which form its diet. Its population has greatly declined since the 1970's.

Fox   Blackthorn

SPRING GENTIAN
Originally an Alpine flower, this blooms from mid April to mid June.

MOUNTAIN AVENS
This Arctic plant carpets the limestone clifftops in May and June.

STONECHAT
This non-migrant bird is a common sight in the Burren. It occurs mainly along the coast.

Male wheatear   Female wheatear   Male wheatear in flight

WHEATEAR
This bird nests in summer in the crevices of rocks on moors and in the mountains and migrates to Africa for winter.

31

■ THE BOGS

Over four centuries the area covered by peat bogs has greatly diminished. Nevertheless, some bogs in the hills still survive intact.

One-seventh of the island is not green, but brown. Ireland's most inhospitable landscapes lie above peat. Heavy rainfall, poor, badly drained soil, and a cool climate are the three main conditions which have favored the development of two types of bog. Topographical bogs are situated on the marshy lowlands at the center of the country and climatic bogs occupy the mountainsides and long stretches of the west coast. These latter are either blanket bogs or raised bogs.

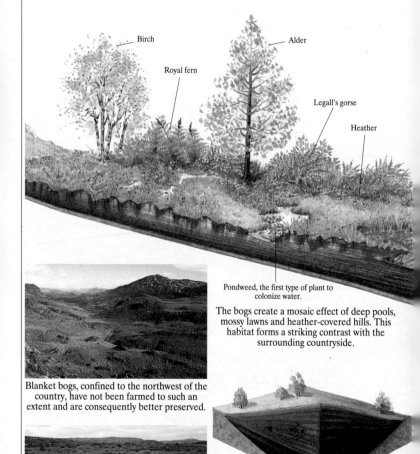

Birch

Alder

Royal fern

Legall's gorse

Heather

Pondweed, the first type of plant to colonize water.

The bogs create a mosaic effect of deep pools, mossy lawns and heather-covered hills. This habitat forms a striking contrast with the surrounding countryside.

Blanket bogs, confined to the northwest of the country, have not been farmed to such an extent and are consequently better preserved.

The prevailing humidity in the bogs favors the growth of the royal fern.

RAISED BOGS
These form on land which is waterlogged and sheltered, two qualities which slow down the bacterial decomposition of the plants. They accumulate and, compressed, form layers of peat which can be as thick as 33 feet.

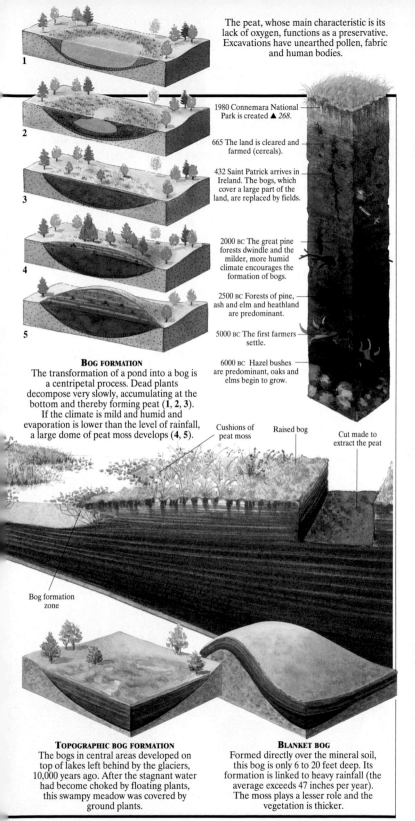

The peat, whose main characteristic is its lack of oxygen, functions as a preservative. Excavations have unearthed pollen, fabric and human bodies.

1980 Connemara National Park is created ▲ 268.

665 The land is cleared and farmed (cereals).

432 Saint Patrick arrives in Ireland. The bogs, which cover a large part of the land, are replaced by fields.

2000 BC The great pine forests dwindle and the milder, more humid climate encourages the formation of bogs.

2500 BC Forests of pine, ash and elm and heathland are predominant.

5000 BC The first farmers settle.

6000 BC Hazel bushes are predominant, oaks and elms begin to grow.

BOG FORMATION
The transformation of a pond into a bog is a centripetal process. Dead plants decompose very slowly, accumulating at the bottom and thereby forming peat (**1, 2, 3**).
If the climate is mild and humid and evaporation is lower than the level of rainfall, a large dome of peat moss develops (**4, 5**).

Cushions of peat moss

Raised bog

Cut made to extract the peat

Bog formation zone

TOPOGRAPHIC BOG FORMATION
The bogs in central areas developed on top of lakes left behind by the glaciers, 10,000 years ago. After the stagnant water had become choked by floating plants, this swampy meadow was covered by ground plants.

BLANKET BOG
Formed directly over the mineral soil, this bog is only 6 to 20 feet deep. Its formation is linked to heavy rainfall (the average exceeds 47 inches per year). The moss plays a lesser role and the vegetation is thicker.

■ PLANTS AND WILDLIFE OF THE BOGS

The white, fleecy tufts of cotton grass give the bogs an extraordinarily summery look.

The acidity of the peat, the lack of nutrients, a waterlogged subsoil, starved of air, and a dry topsoil in summer, make the bogs extremely inhospitable for most plants. Nonetheless, a wide variety of species can adapt to such extremes. Tufts of grass, sedge and rushes, as well as carnivorous plants, are concealed on the western hills which are thickly carpeted with peat moss. Few birds inhabit these areas, but some have a cryptic plumage which enables them to remain unseen when nesting on the ground.

BOG ASPHODEL
This plant carpets the bogs in thick clumps.

VIVIPAROUS LIZARD
As the name implies, Ireland's only lizard gives birth to fully formed young. It feeds on insects and spiders.

Spaghnum moss can store up to thirty times its weight in water.

BROWN HARE
This mammal, the most common on the bogs, browses on sedge and cotton grass.

Female

Male

RED DEER
Formerly a forest species, this can now be found in the vast bogs in the mountains, where it is protected.

Peat moss has no roots but absorbs the nutrients contained in rainwater. It stores water in the dead cells on its leaves.

CURLEW
The bogs provide a safe haven for this large shorebird with its beautiful wild, bubbling song. In winter, it frequents the estuaries.

KESTREL
A common sight in the bogs, this bird of prey hunts rodents, frogs and dragonflies by hovering.

Cotton grass

Cross-leaved heather

Bog pimpernel

LESSER BLADDERWORT
This carnivorous plant grows in boggy pools. Its leaves act like trapdoors to catch insects.

COMMON SUNDEW
This plant catches insects using the hairs on its leaves. These insects provide the nitrogen and phosphorus it needs.

FINE-LEAVED HEATHER
This grows in thick clumps on extremely dry soils.

HEATHER (LING)
The most common species of heather. Its frail stem offers little resistance to the wind.

In late summer, when the various plants are in full bloom, the bog becomes a kaleidoscope of magnificent colors.

The dead moss slowly decomposes and turns into peat.

FOUR-SPOTTED CHASER
This large species of dragonfly flies at high speed and in straight lines to catch insects in the bog.

EMPEROR MOTH
This attractive moth hovers over moorland and, in flight, displays the bold markings on its wings which resemble large eyes.

■ PEAT FARMING

Dry peat is used as a fuel called turf which is slow-burning and gives off an acrid smell.

For centuries, the Irish looked on the bogs as wild, damp areas, barely good enough for grazing. When the peat was cut, first on a small scale, then mechanized around 1930, it provided litter for cattle. It was also used in horticulture as an organic manure and, primarily, as an inexpensive fuel. From 1946, industrial cutting led to the drainage of this previously

uncultivated land. Although at first glance the number of bogs seems to have remained unchanged, protected ecosystems are becoming increasingly few and far between.

The donkey, the beast of burden best suited to working in the bogs.

Peat bricks cut with the *slean*.

OPENING A PEAT BED
The surface vegetation and roots are cut away with a spade. This uncovers the first strip of peat.

CUTTING THE PEAT
The peat bricks are cut from narrow strips of peat and laid out on top of the bog.

DRYING
The waterlogged bricks are spread out at intervals to dry in the sun and wind.

STANDING
When they are firm enough, the bricks are stood on end to speed up the drying process.

PILING
The dry bricks are piled up and occasionally covered with straw. They then spend the winter on the bog.

THE ROLE OF THE DONKEY
Before machine-cutting, donkeys carried the peat in wicker panniers.

THE SLEDGE
Commonly used when the ground was uneven, this pannier on a wooden platform was pulled by a horse.

Modern machines, operated with tractors, extract long strips of peat, then compress and dry them.

Stumps from the prehistoric forest have been found under the cut peat.

ROPE MADE OF "BOG WOOD"
This rope is made from pine trees salvaged from the bogs and has the advantage of being waterproof. It was used to moor boats and secure bundles of straw. It also served to burn as torches.

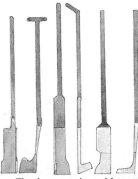

The compressed peat bricks manufactured by Bord na Mona are sold as fuel.

Co. Armagh Co. Antrim Co. Galway

Wicker basket

The *slean*, a spade used for cutting and extracting the peat, is comprised of a narrow blade and a piece of metal at the side to stop the peat brick falling off. Its shape varies from one area to another, depending on the type of peat and the methods of extraction.

The machines owned by the national company, Bord na Mona, extract the peat on a large scale. Powdered peat is used for fuel in the country's thermal power stations.

TRANSPORTING THE PEAT
Nowadays, most of the bogs can be reached by tractor. Formerly, the peat had to be carried as far as the road in a basket or pannier.

PEAT STACKS
Peat stacks stand behind many homes in the countryside. They are constructed so that rainwater simply runs off the sides without being absorbed by the peat.

37

■ GARINISH ISLAND

The formal design of this Italian garden ▲ 226 provides an ideal setting for the luxuriant plants and bushes.

◉

Created in the early 20th century by Joan Annan Bryce, the island's owner, and Harold Peto, architect and landscape designer, the garden on Garinish, has been state-owned since 1953. The island, which comes under the influence of the Gulf Stream, reaps the benefits of a particularly temperate, humid climate: the winters are not terribly severe and frost is virtually unheard of. Due to these exceptional conditions, in some ways reminiscent of subtropical regions, collections of flowers have been planted from all over the world.

CALLISTEMON
The flame-red hues of the various species of callistemon deck out the Italian garden in a cavalcade of color.

"YAKUSHIMANUM" RHODODENDRON
The island's soil is perfect for growing rhododendrons, including this miniature species from Japan.

"SINOGRANDE" RHODODENDRON
Originally from China and Tibet, this large species is covered with bell-shaped flowers.

"GOLDEN HORN" RHODODENDRON
This rhododendron ranks among the loveliest species and flowers in the section of the garden called "Happy Valley".

ROBIN AND BLACKBIRD
When the temperature is mild, the
air is filled with the song of these
non-migrant birds, even in the
depths of winter.

The island's pools are home to many types of
water lilies, which dapple the tranquil surface
of the waters with light and color.

"DICKSONIA ANTARCTICA"
This tree fern, native to New Zealand, has a
fibrous trunk and fronds, similar to a palm
tree. It can grow as tall as 33 feet.

"EXMOUTH"
MAGNOLIA
GRANDIFLORA
Like all magnolias,
this is frost-hardy. It
flowers early.

"ASHFORD RED"
ABUTILON
This shrub, native to
South America,
belongs to the mallow
family.

DATURA
This ornamental
species belongs to the
tomato and potato
family.

EMBOTHRIUM
COCCINEUM
Known as "the
Chilean fire bush", this
species flowers in early
summer.

■ HEDGEROWS AND DRY STONE WALLS

Near the sea, hedgerows and trees are few and far between so stone walls serve as havens for the fauna.

Thousands of miles of hedgerow wind their way across the farmland forming a leafy network of hawthorn bushes and tall grass, a sanctuary for birds and small mammals. On less fertile soil, in particular near the windswept west coast, the hedgerows are replaced by dry stone walls or earth and rubble embankments. The small enclosed fields, in part spared by pesticides and weedkillers, are home to countless wild flowers and insects. In Ireland, the roadsides are also of considerable ecological interest.

Male

YELLOW HAMMER
This bird is fond of building its nest in rough hedges.

LONG-TAILED TIT
This acrobatic passerine uses lichen, dry grass and feathers to build its extremely intricate nest.

SPARROWHAWK
The most common bird of prey in Ireland flies at low altitudes above the hedgerows hunting for birds such as finches and tits.

Jackdaw

BADGER
This member of the weasel family may dig its set beside the hedgerow at the side of quiet roads. It hunts for food at night.

Bank vole

HEDGEHOG
This insectivore lives discreetly in the hedgerows. When disturbed, it rolls itself into a ball of spines.

PYGMY SHREW
The smallest Irish mammal, this shrew feeds on beetles, spiders and woodlice.

BANK VOLE
This rodent feeds on bark, leaves and seeds.

RABBIT
This animal digs holes with secret exits in dry hedgerows.

LONG-TAILED FIELDMOUSE
In fall, this animal sometimes makes its home in abandoned bird nests.

Deep cavities in the walls sometimes contain enough soil for ferns and moss to grow side by side.

Ash

Willow warbler

Yellow hammer (male)

WREN
This bird slips like a mouse through the hedgerows, hunting for tiny insects and spiders.

Stoat

BLACKBERRY BUSH
Butterflies gather nectar from its flowers. In the fall, birds, as well as mice, foxes and other mammals feast on its berries.

RAGGED ROBIN
This plant's clusters of raggedly cut pink petals bring a splash of color to the marshy pastures near roadsides.

Hazel bush

Hedgehog

Fern

COMMON GORSE
This plant's spiny leaves are ideally suited to the dry, windy environment of the verges of Irish roads.

GIANT HOGWEED
This huge, stout-stemmed wildflower, which grows up to 16 feet tall at roadsides, attracts nectar-feeding insects.

Ireland is an archetypal stock farming country. Traditionally cattle from poor areas are reared side by side with top-class continental breeds. The counties of Galway and Donegal concentrate mainly on sheep, including some old breeds which are now in danger of becoming extinct. Last but not least, this country is renowned, and rightly so, for breeding both racing horses and draught horses, not to mention ponies for riding.

Fifty years ago, milk was still being churned by hand on Irish farms.

LANDRACE PIG
This pig is bred intensively to produce prolific stock and is more often battery-reared than free-range.

BURREN GOATS
There are goats running virtually wild in the most remote areas of Ireland's mountains, particularly in the Burren ▲ 242.

SAANEN GOAT
This Swiss breed has become very popular because a growing number of people in Ireland are developing a taste for its cheese and milk.

KERRY COW
The oldest breed of cow in Ireland, it is now protected in several herds. This hardy beast can still calve at the age of fourteen.

IRISH MOIL COW
Currently very few in number, this cow is now only found in Ulster. It has no horns.

At the country fairs of the past, the cattle boasted Hereford blood and still sported horns.

In Ireland, the donkey has traditionally been used as a beast of burden.

SUFFOLK SHEEP
Native to East Anglia (UK), this animal is currently being reared in Ireland for its prime quality meat and fine wool.

DOMESTIC DONKEY
This species from North Africa was imported on a large scale at the beginning of the 19th century, because the horses had been pressed into service by the British cavalry.

JACOB SHEEP
This multi-horned mountain sheep comes from Spain. Certain farmers breed it for its hard-wearing wool and its lean, tasty meat.

BLACKFACE SHEEP
This sheep, native to the Scottish Highlands, produces excellent lamb but its wool is of little commercial value.

CONNEMARA PONY
Introduced by the Celts, this pony, native to the Alps, has been crossbred with Arab and Spanish horses. This is an attractive, hardy breed.

IRISH HUNTER
The product of cross-breeding between a draught mare and a thoroughbred stallion, this is now the most popular horse in Ireland for riding and, particularly, jumping.

43

FRESHWATER FISHING

The adult salmon's ascent of fast-flowing rivers is a formidable ordeal.

Eels and salmon are migratory fish. The routes taken by eels span the entire north Atlantic as well as Arctic or subtropical seas, especially the Sargasso Sea.

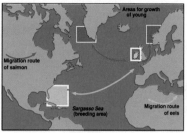

Although the Irish are not great fish-eaters, their country is renowned for the abundance and quality of its fish: 8,700 miles of river and 1,554 square miles of lakes have made fishing a true way of life. Remarkable catches of salmon or trout, naturally, but also of char and eels are not unusual here. Although river salmon and trout are usually caught by flyfishing, they are also industrially farmed, but the meat of farmed fish never equals the delicacy of that of their cousins in the wild.

SALMON
Salmon can be caught from February to April, when large salmon journey upstream to breed; or from June to the end of August, when the grilses or young salmon migrate in their turn.

At dawn, trout forage for food in the clear water.

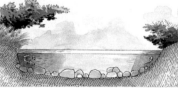

During the day, trout take refuge among the river's aquatic plants or under the overhanging banks.

Migration is a demanding ordeal, during which the fish rests sporadically in the still water of coves. They can also use drifting trunks and branches to protect themselves from the current and from predators.

THE TECHNIQUE OF FLYFISHING
The fisher is able to bait the fish, which thinks it is seeing a real insect alighting on the water, due to the swaying of the rod, the silk line and the lightness of the fly.

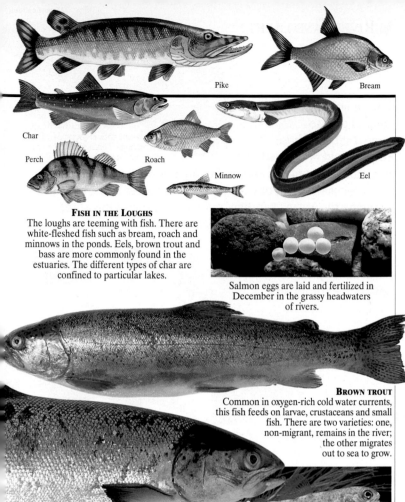

Pike

Bream

Char

Perch

Roach

Minnow

Eel

FISH IN THE LOUGHS
The loughs are teeming with fish. There are white-fleshed fish such as bream, roach and minnows in the ponds. Eels, brown trout and bass are more commonly found in the estuaries. The different types of char are confined to particular lakes.

Salmon eggs are laid and fertilized in December in the grassy headwaters of rivers.

BROWN TROUT
Common in oxygen-rich cold water currents, this fish feeds on larvae, crustaceans and small fish. There are two varieties: one, non-migrant, remains in the river; the other migrates out to sea to grow.

SALMON FLIES
Skilled craftsmanship is needed for the manufacture of flies used to bait salmon or trout.

Salmon have adapted to become small freshwater fish, but in the wild are extremely powerful sea creatures. The salmon fishing is the shortest of all the fishing seasons.

THE DEVELOPMENT OF THE SALMON
The young salmon (**1**) grow fast from April to July; at this stage they are called parrs (**2**). They then head out to sea, normally in April to May, aged between one and three years: these are smolts (**3**) and have a silvery skin. Their migration takes them west of Greenland and north of the Faroe Islands. Once they have become grilses (3 to 10 lbs) after a year, or salmon (6 to 60 lbs) after two to four years, they return to lay their eggs in the same river.

RIVERS AND LAKES

Mountain stream

Lough

Slow-moving river

Estuary

The geography of Ireland calls to mind a saucer whose edges would be formed by the granite mountains and cliffs. Most of the country's running water takes the form of wide alkaline rivers, or lakes, before rejoining the sea via winding, marshy estuaries. Only some waterways, which are more acidic, flow directly from the mountains into the ocean. Limestone-rich water is a particularly suitable environment for fish.

In the center of the country, carboniferous, limestone rock is covered by fields and bogs. This is where the rivers widen out, becoming tranquil loughs.

EUROPEAN MINK
This small nocturnal carnivore has now become extremely scarce throughout Europe.

CONNEMARA'S TORRENTIAL RIVER ▲ *264*
These limpid waters race down the limestone rocks before reaching wide rivers or alkaline lakes.

OTTER
An inhabitant of Ireland, this fish-eating carnivore was once widely hunted for its pelt.

Dipper

Otter

Brown trout

HISTORY

−9000	−6600	−4500	−2000		−500	0
First traces of man in Ireland	Mesolithic period	Megalithic civilization	Bronze Age		Celtic invasions	

PRE-CHRISTIAN IRELAND

FIRST INHABITANTS

Excavations at Mount Sandel near Coleraine (County Derry) and at Lough Boora (County Offaly) have yielded evidence of human habitation in Ireland as early as 9000 BC. These Mesolithic peoples were succeeded by Neolithic tribes (around 3500 BC); the megaliths, dolmens, and funerary chambers scattered at intervals along the Boyne ▲ 194 are attributed to them.

Between 2000 and 1700, a new wave of immigrants ushered in the Bronze Age, mining for copper in the counties of Cork and Kerry and working the gold that was extracted from the Wicklow Mountains.

THE CELTS

Around 500 BC, the Celts, or Gaels, invaded the island and subjugated its inhabitants. Their strong social, cultural, linguistic, artistic and religious identity set them apart, contrasting sharply with the political anarchy and violence endemic in Ireland (which had never been tempered by Roman invasion).

The island was bristling with small, warlike kingdoms governed by elected kinglets, or *Rí*, who were more inclined to fight than to unite in allegiance to an *Ard Rí* (High King). In the 4th century, they formed a federation of five main kingdoms corresponding, roughly, to the provinces of Ulster, Leinster, Munster, Connacht and the counties of Meath and Westmeath. The two politico-religious capitals of Gaelic Ireland were Emain Macha (Navan Fort ▲ 322), the seat of the kings of Ulster, and Tara ▲ 191, the seat of the kings of Meath and, later, of Ireland's *Ard Rí*.

CHRISTIAN IRELAND

"ISLAND OF SCHOLARS AND SAINTS"

Comgal and Finian founded wealthy, monasteries whose fame drew scholars, nobles and men of letters from the continent. These centers of worship and culture promoted the arts, particularly calligraphy and illumination ▲ 150. They trained missionaries who carried the Word of God into the world: Saint Fiacre near Meaux, Saint Kilian in Wurzburg, etc. The most famous was Saint Colombanus, the founder of Luxeuil Abbey.

Saint Patrick completed the island's evangelization in the 5th century. The patrician Church, originally episcopal and Roman, became Celtic and monastic in the 6th century. Columba (also known as Columcille), Ciarán, Brendan,

303–304 Persecution of the Christians (Rome)	455 Rome seized by the Vandals	800 Charlemagne crowned Emperor in Rome	1066 Battle of Hastings (England)	1099 First crusade and the storming of Jerusalem

300   **600**   **900**   **1000**   **1200**

5TH CENTURY Evangelism of Saint Patrick	550–650 Rise of Celtic monachism	795 First Viking raids in Ireland	1069 Norman invasion

VIKING INVASIONS

From 795, Scandinavian pirates plundered the islands and the settlements along the coast. These raiders became bolder: in 837, two fleets sailed up the Boyne and the Liffey. By the latter part of the 9th century, they had settled and founded fortified ports (at Dublin, Waterford and Cork, for example). The High King Brian Boru (right) tried to create a unified realm under his rule, crushing the Vikings and their Celtic allies at Clontarf in 1014. He was murdered immediately after the battle, however, and any possibility of a strong and united kingdom died with him.

REORGANIZATION OF THE CHURCH

Saint Malachy, Archbishop of Armagh, put an end to the Celtic particularism of the Irish church. The synods of Cashel (1101), Rath Breasail (1111) and Kells (1152) abolished local customs and set up the current Diocesan organization, placing the island's thirty-six bishops under the supervision of the four archbishops of Cashel, Tuam, Dublin and Armagh, the seat of Ireland's primate. The abbeys, brought under control once more, were handed over to the monastic orders ● 56.

CELTO-NORMAN IRELAND

AN UNFINISHED CONQUEST

In response to an appeal by the dethroned king of Leinster, Dermot MacMurrough, a company of Norman knights landed on the coast of Wexford in 1169, led by Richard FitzGilbert de Clare, Earl of Pembroke ("Strongbow"). A year later, Strongbow seized Dublin and assumed the crown of Leinster. In 1171, the Plantagenet king, Henry II, wary of Strongbow's ambitions, landed at Waterford (below) and made the Celtic leaders, Norman barons and princes of the Church acknowledge his suzerainty. For three centuries, Celts and Normans waged a bitter war: initially victorious, the Normans were gradually driven back by Aedh O'Connor, Art MacMurrough, Donald O'Neill and the Scotsman Edward Bruce.

1337 Outbreak of the
Hundred Years' War

1200   1300   1400

1366 Statutes of
Kilkenny

SOCIAL AND LEGAL REVOLUTION

The Normans built castles and fortified villages ● *100* throughout Ireland. Cottage industries and trade developed. A central government was set up with a viceroy at its helm, who convoked a two-chamber parliament to vote on taxes, and legislate in areas not covered by English law. The king of England was finally, legally, the king of Ireland.

Irish men-at-arms.

THE GREAT ANGLO-NORMAN HOUSES

Through their association with the Celts, the Norman invaders became increasingly Hibernized. In 1366, the colonial parliament passed the Statutes of Kilkenny, forbidding both intermarriage and the adoption of Irish names, dress, speech, and customs. Later, between 1394 and 1399, Richard II tried to bring down "the Irish enemies and English rebels", but ultimately failed. Power was now in the hands of three great families: the FitzGeralds of Desmond, the FitzGeralds of Kildare and the Butlers of Ormonde. Despite Poyning's Law (1494) which subjugated the Irish parliament to the Crown, Garret More, the eighth earl of Kildare, reigned supreme in Ireland from 1477 to 1513.

Richard II returning to England.

CONQUEST AND COLONIZATION

TUDOR MIGHT

In 1534, a revolt led by "Silken Thomas", Garret More's grandson, was put down by Henry VIII, who had Thomas beheaded in London. Having destroyed the influence of the FitzGeralds, Henry VIII tightened his grip on Ireland at the same time as he broke with Rome, dissolving the monasteries and setting himself up as the head of the Anglo-Norman Church (established as the Anglican Church of Ireland). Although Mary Tudor (right) was Catholic, she continued to appoint the Irish bishops and also supported the first attempts to colonize lands belonging to the O'Mores and the O'Connors, respectively re-named "Queen's County" and "King's County". Her half-sister, Elizabeth, who came to the throne in 1558, extended the Act of Supremacy to Ireland. Her reign was punctuated by violently suppressed revolts: the rebellion of Shane O'Neill in 1567, the double revolt of James FitzMaurice FitzGerald in 1579, and the uprising of Ulster in 1594, led by Hugh O'Neill, Earl of Tyrone, and Hugh O'Donnell, Earl of Tyrconnell. After their defeat at Yellow Ford in 1598, the English launched a campaign of systematic annihilation. In 1601, Lord Mountjoy crushed the Irish and their Spanish allies at Kinsale. O'Donnell emigrated while O'Neill was forced to sign the treaty of Mellifont in 1603, before his exile. The "Flight of the Earls" sealed Ulster's fate and sounded the knell on the old Gaelic civilization.

1453 Fall of Byzantium	1492 Columbus discovers America	1534 Henry VIII breaks with Rome, becomes head of the Church of England	1588 Defeat of the Invincible Armada	1598 Edict of Nantes	1618–40 Thirty Years' War	1649 Execution of Charles I
	1500			**1600**		**1700**
1494 Poyning's Law		**1541** Henry VIII acknowledged King of Ireland	**1558–1603** Elizabeth I suppresses Irish revolts		**1649–55** Cromwell colonizes Ireland	

Colonists massacred by the Irish in 1641.

JACOBITE AND CROMWELLIAN "PLANTATIONS"

ratified Cromwell's confiscations. James II, however, was less hostile toward them. Deposed in 1689 by his daughter Mary and his son-in-law William III of Orange, he attempted to reclaim his throne with the support of Louis XIV. He was defeated at the Battle of the Boyne in 1690 ▲ *194*. The Treaty of Limerick (1691) put an end to the war, although it did not prevent the defeated from being stripped of all their rights and property.

In May 1609, the Plantation Articles gave the colonists almost the whole of the province of Ulster which, it was hoped, would be transformed into a bastion of loyalty to the English crown. Although the dispossessed Irish citizens were not entirely driven out, this "planting" upset the physiognomy of the northeast of the island, which was never again at one with the rest of Ireland. The men of Ulster were quick to take advantage of the weakening of central power that occurred around the time of the English Civil War, rebelling and massacring a great many colonists. The military side of the revolt was organized by Owen Roe O'Neill, who crushed the English at Benburb (1646), and the political side by the Catholic Confederation of Kilkenny, a central government that was undermined by serious conflict from the start. In 1649, Charles I was beheaded and Cromwell landed in Ireland, mercilessly butchering the garrisons of Drogheda and Wexford. Violently quelling the rebellion, he tried to drive the Irish into the poor lands of the west ("to hell or Connaught"), and establish a military colonate in the rest of the country. Although this attempt to create a Puritan "plantation" failed, it nonetheless left the Irish more dispossessed and embittered than ever before. Their lot did not improve with the restoration of the Stuarts: Charles II

1776 Declaration of American Independence	**1789** French Revolution	**1815** Battle of Waterloo	**1837** Queen Victoria ascends the English throne
1775		1800	
1780–2 England grants Ireland free trade and parliamentary independence	**1798** Failure of the revolt by the United Irishmen	**1800** Act of Union passed	**1829** Catholic emancipation

THE PROTESTANT NATION

THE PENAL LAWS

Under William III, Queen Anne and George I, the penal laws effectively outlawed Catholics from society. They saw their clergy exiled, lands confiscated, professions closed, education and political rights suspended. As a consequence, their military elite swelled the ranks of the Irish regiments in the service of France and Spain, while their ecclesiastical counterparts made their escape to Irish colleges on the continent.

THE PATRIOT PARTY

Colonial Ireland was upheld by two pillars: the minor Ulster Protestants, radical and nonconformist, and the "Ascendancy", the Anglican landed gentry who were very powerful in the south of the island. Comfortable in their supremacy, they began to object to the authority of the parent state. A "Patriot Party", under the leadership of high-ranking figures such as Henry Grattan, Flood and Lord Charlemont, made its presence felt

at the Dublin parliament. The revolt of the American colonies and the levy of a corps of Irish volunteers enabled the party to wrest free trade from England in 1780 and legislative independence for Dublin in 1782. Such were the achievements of the Patriot Party, which was committed to boosting industry and trade, but which came up against the twin stumbling blocks of parliamentary reform and Catholic emancipation.

REVOLUTIONARY FERVOR

The French Revolution galvanized the Presbyterian workers in Ulster and the Catholic middle classes in the South, whose most radical contingent founded the Society of United Irishmen in Belfast and Dublin in 1791. This provoked a preventive crackdown

Defeat at Vinegar Hill.

instituted by the Castle ▲ *167,* and the mobilization of the Orange Order (supporters of Protestant supremacy); which, in turn, compelled the United Irishmen to seek aid from France. In 1798, part of Ulster and the Wicklow Mountains rose up in arms, before being hacked to pieces at Vinegar Hill ▲ *181.* The Protestant Theobald Wolfe Tone, the founding father of modern Irish Nationalism, won over the Directoire, which launched three unsuccessful expeditions. Captured and sentenced to death, Wolfe Tone slit his throat in prison. In 1800, the Act of Union between Ireland and Great Britain was passed, dealing the death blow to the Dublin parliament and creating the United Kingdom.

1861–5 American Civil War		**HISTORY OF IRELAND** ●
1850	1900	1913
1845–9 Great Famine	**1858** Birth of the Fenian movement	**1912** Protestant Ulster rebels against Home Rule

The great strike of 1913.

IRELAND UNDER THE UNION

THE LIBERATOR

Daniel O'Connell, nicknamed "the Liberator", enlisted the Church to fight under his banner, had himself elected to parliament (even though he was not eligible) and compelled the English parliament to pass a law in 1829 emancipating the Catholics. He organized mass meetings and attempted to bring about the repeal of the Union. At this point the government took action, and O'Connell and his followers were forced to back down.

REBELLIONS AND REFORMS

After O'Connell's death (1847), the torch of unrest was handed on to the romantic Young Ireland movement. This party stirred up a futile rebellion in 1848, while the island was struggling in the throes of the Great Famine ● 58. In 1858, the foundations of the Irish Republican Brotherhood (the Fenians) were laid, and the movement gathered support throughout the United States, England and Ireland. The failure of the Fenian rebellion of 1867 did not prevent this revolutionary movement from remaining active behind the scenes until shortly after World War One. From 1879 onward, the Protestant Charles Stewart Parnell took over at the helm of the reform movement. Skillfully embracing parliamentary debate, the agrarian demands of the Land League and the benevolent neutrality of the Fenians, he obtained the beginnings of land reform in 1881; but his campaign for self-government, or Home Rule, however, came up against the uncompromising hostility of both Presbyterian Ulster and the British Imperialist establishment. The ambitious land reform passed in 1903, twelve years after Parnell's death,

enabled Irish peasants to purchase the lands they were farming. At the same time, a great wave of cultural pride made itself felt, as evidenced by the Gaelic League ● 67, founded in 1893 by Douglas Hyde, by Sinn Féin, founded in 1905 by Arthur Griffiths, by the literary revival symbolized by William Butler Yeats ● 122 and by the advent of Irish trade unionism, set up by Larkin and Connolly (who were forced to deal with the lock-out of 1913 in Dublin).

Above right, James Larkin; left, James Connolly.

1914		**1914–18** World War One		**1931** The Statute of Westminster recognizes the freedom of the dominions within the Commonwealth	**1939–45** World War Two	
1914			1920	1935		1950

1916 Nationalist uprising in Dublin **1919–21** Anglo-Irish War of Independence **1922** Birth of the Free State of Ireland **1949** Proclamation of the Republic of Ireland in Dublin

WE SERVE NEITHER KING NOR KAISER, BUT IRELAND!

HOME RULE

At the resumption of the debate in favor of Home Rule, Protestant Ulster looked set to start a civil war. Westminster accepted the principle of separate treatment for the six counties making up Northern Ireland, and passed a Home Rule Bill in 1912, which was immediately suspended for the duration of the war. On Easter Monday 1916 ● *60*, a handful of rebels seized the nerve centers of Dublin. They held out for a week, despite being outnumbered fifteen to one. The execution of the leaders of the rebellion and the clumsy crackdown by the English paved the way for Sinn Féin to walk off with over two thirds of the Irish seats in the 1918 elections. The Anglo-Irish War of Independence broke out immediately afterward. Unable to "pacify" the country using strong-arm tactics, Lloyd George tackled the problem in two stages: in 1920, the six counties in the northeast were given home rule within the United Kingdom; and in 1921, the twenty-six

Nationalist counties became the Irish Free State.

Ulster volunteers on bikes, Irish volunteers on foot!

MODERN IRELAND

BUILDING THE STATE

The Irish Free State, which came into being in 1922, had to face a bitter civil war which raged until May 1923 ● *62*. The victorious government of William Thomas Cosgrave helped the country back on its feet and established its independence by joining the League of Nations and by negotiating increased powers of home rule for the dominions of the Commonwealth. In 1926, Eamonn De Valera, who had been defeated in the civil war, founded the Fianna Fáil party ("soldiers of destiny") and became the leader of the opposition; in 1932, he came to power. Apart from two short periods (1948–51 and 1954–7), he remained in power until 1959 when he became President. He severed the last constitutional links between Ireland and the Empire, stoically suffered the "economic war" of 1932–8, and in 1937 brought in a Catholic constitution, which was almost Republican. On the home front, he quelled any movements that challenged the authority of the State, played an active role within the League of Nations, and transformed Ireland's neutrality during World War Two into a true test of sovereignty.

ILLVSTRAZIONE DEL POPOLO

1955 Warsaw Pact		**1989** Fall of the Berlin Wall	**1991** Dissolution of the USSR	
	1975			**2000**
1969 London sends troops into Northern Ireland	**1972** The Republic of Ireland and the United Kingdom join the EEC	**1985** Signing of the Agreement of Hillsborough	**1993** Downing Street Declaration	

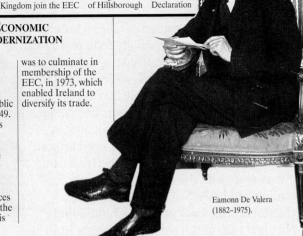

ECONOMIC MODERNIZATION

The postwar years were marked by a desire for political and economic change. The Republic was declared in 1949. Economic progress was boosted by industrialization, which involved the influx of foreign capital, the modernization of agricultural practices and the growth of the export market. This was to culminate in membership of the EEC, in 1973, which enabled Ireland to diversify its trade.

Eamonn De Valera (1882–1975).

THE NORTHERN IRELAND QUESTION

Northern Ireland, created by the English parliament and ratified by the 1925 border agreement, had within it various institutions whose discriminatory practices eventually triggered off a nonviolent campaign for civil rights. In 1969, however, this campaign fell foul of hostile Protestant extremists and local police. In 1970 the IRA rose again from its ashes and unleashed a terrorist offensive against the Northern Irish State and the English presence there. Protestant paramilitary groups were formed to meet violence with violence. In view of the deteriorating situation in Northern Ireland, Westminster sent in troops in 1969, suspended the local institutions in 1972 and imposed direct rule over the province, interrupted only by the brief interlude in 1973 when power was shared, in line with the Sunningdale Agreement. Since then, continuing Republican terrorism both in Northern Ireland, and on the mainland, and Loyalist sectarian attacks, the failure of crackdowns, however energetic, and the inability of Nationalist politicians and moderate Unionists to find any common ground, have forced the governments in London and Dublin to join forces to resolve the situation. In 1985, the Anglo-Irish Agreement, made at Hillsborough, institutionalized the Republic of Ireland's advisory role in controlling the crisis. At last, on December 15, 1993, a joint declaration, called the Downing Street Declaration, by the English and Irish prime ministers (below) recognized the Irish people's right to self-determination.

The spread of Christianity in western Europe initially took place in areas where the Romans had settled. Unlike Britain (where Christian communities had been established as early as the beginning of the 3rd century), Ireland had never been occupied by the Roman armies and did not discover Christianity until around the middle of the 4th century. The Irish came into contact with the new faith through trading and raids. Not only did the tribal chieftains bring back gold, silver and other personal treasures from their pillaging in Britain and on the continent, but they also took prisoners who were sold as slaves. Among their numbers were Christians who continued to practice their religion unhindered, and gained followers.

PALLADIUS
In 431, Pope Celestine I (above) sent a bishop, Palladius the Gaul, to Ireland to set up an episcopal organization to instruct and supervise people who had already become Christians. His activity seems to have been confined to the southern half of the island, where he certainly helped to familiarize its people with the practices of the Roman church.

SAINT PATRICK
(above and left) Patrick the Gaul (c. 415–93) was abducted at the age of sixteen by Irish warriors and sold as a slave. He spent six years in captivity in the Mayo area before managing to escape. He then made a career for himself within the church, possibly staying in Gaul before being ordained as a bishop.

Saint Patrick's Evangelization

Originally sent to Ulster, Patrick returned to western Ireland, without official permission, to preach to the peoples with whom he had been imprisoned. It was not until the end of the 6th century that Bishop Patricius began to be worshipped as an apostle of Ireland. Although at first he was venerated on the northeast coast, in the 7th century he became the patron saint of Armagh's powerful monastic organization, whose expansion was linked to the political fortunes of the dynasty of the Uí Néills, great kings of Ireland at Tara ▲ 191.

The Early Church

Although the transition from the old Celtic religion to the new Christian faith was not made without opposition, there was no bloodshed. The tribal chieftains forged close links first with the bishops, and later with the abbots of the large monasteries. By the 7th century, most of the members of the former learned classes, along with the most important tribal chieftains, had become Christians.

The Golden Age of Monasteries

The monastic movement, introduced in Ireland during Patrick's lifetime, had become the main method of structuring the Irish Church in the 8th and 9th centuries. Large monasteries (Armagh, Bangor, Iona, Kildare, Clonmacnois) were actual cities, centers of culture and trade. They also took over from the pagan necropolises in so far as the kings now chose to be buried within their holy walls. The intense lifestyle of these wealthy monasteries lent itself to the creation of some magnificent works of art in which Christian themes were integrated with motifs inspired by the Celtic style ▲ 151 or by Germanic gold and silver work.

Between 1845 and 1847, the potato harvests were ruined by the blight. A famine of great proportions descended on the peasantry whose sole means of subsistence was potatoes. The English government intervened halfheartedly before giving up at the enormity of the catastrophe. It is estimated that around one million Irish citizens died of starvation, typhus, scurvy and dysentery. Hundreds of thousands of emigrants took to the seas to escape the horror of a ravaged country: those who survived the crossing were confronted with poverty and the hostility of the indigenous population.

THE STATE'S RESPONSE

Robert Peel's Tory government tried to import maize, control prices and solve unemployment by starting some large public works projects. It was not enough. John Russell's Liberal cabinet, opposed to any interventionism, made the Anglo-Irish landowners

"CABBAGE GARDEN REVOLUTION"

Fired by aspirations for a new beginning for their people, the Nationalists in the Young Ireland Movement launched a revolt during the famine, but this came to an unfortunate end on July 29, 1848, in a Ballinary cabbage garden.

responsible for helping the people. Some went bankrupt; others mercilessly evicted their peasants. The soup kitchens and the aid distributed by the charities proved woefully inadequate.

DEPARTURE

The transportation of emigrants rapidly became an extremely lucrative business for shipowners.

THE IRISH DIASPORA

Braving storms, poverty, disease, hostility and exploitation, the Irish emigrated, putting down roots in all English-speaking countries. It is now estimated that seventy million members of the Irish diaspora are scattered throughout the world. An estimated forty-two million of these live in the United States alone.

IRISH AMERICANS

They helped to build roads and railways and, with the passing years, succeeded in controlling the American Federation of Labor, the Catholic Church, and the electoral machinery of the Democratic Party which was to make John F. Kennedy president.

A NEW AGE

The great famine bled dry Ireland's poor population. Between 1847 and 1857, it dropped from 8 to 6½ million inhabitants. It also swelled the wave of emigration which swept eight million Irish from their native land between 1801 and 1921, and it destroyed large-scale land ownership without improving the lot of the exploited peasants. Most importantly, it created a new Irish nation beyond the seas, strong and thirsty for revenge: a tragic birth for the Ireland of the modern era.

● Dublin's Easter Uprising

World War One forced back the specter of civil war by sending Orangemen and Nationalist militiamen to the front. Only a few diehards declared they would serve neither "king nor kaiser, but Ireland". On Monday, April 24, 1916 a secret military committee ordered around one thousand poorly armed rebels to storm Dublin's key buildings. It took no less than sixteen thousand soldiers supported by artillery to dislodge them after a week of street-fighting. All the leaders of the uprising were shot. At first hostile to this insane and violent takeover, the Irish people were rapidly won over by the wild daring of these men, and by their courage in the face of the English firing squads.

THE REBELLION
Taking advantage of England's other problems, the Irish Volunteers and the Citizen Army besieged the General Post Office and Dublin's other key buildings. Having failed to raise support in the province, however, and unpopular in Dublin, the rebels, isolated, ill-equipped and outnumbered in the fighting by twenty to one, had to give in. Dublin was in ruins!

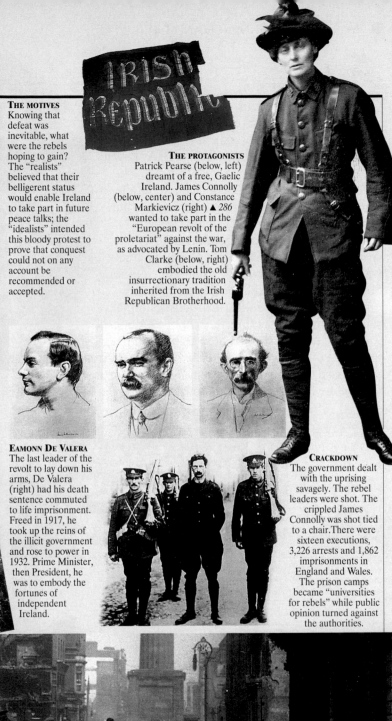

THE MOTIVES

Knowing that defeat was inevitable, what were the rebels hoping to gain? The "realists" believed that their belligerent status would enable Ireland to take part in future peace talks; the "idealists" intended this bloody protest to prove that conquest could not on any account be recommended or accepted.

THE PROTAGONISTS

Patrick Pearse (below, left) dreamt of a free, Gaelic Ireland. James Connolly (below, center) and Constance Markievicz (right) ▲ 286 wanted to take part in the "European revolt of the proletariat" against the war, as advocated by Lenin. Tom Clarke (below, right) embodied the old insurrectionary tradition inherited from the Irish Republican Brotherhood.

EAMONN DE VALERA

The last leader of the revolt to lay down his arms, De Valera (right) had his death sentence commuted to life imprisonment. Freed in 1917, he took up the reins of the illicit government and rose to power in 1932. Prime Minister, then President, he was to embody the fortunes of independent Ireland.

CRACKDOWN

The government dealt with the uprising savagely. The rebel leaders were shot. The crippled James Connolly was shot tied to a chair. There were sixteen executions, 3,226 arrests and 1,862 imprisonments in England and Wales. The prison camps became "universities for rebels" while public opinion turned against the authorities.

● WAR OF INDEPENDENCE AND CIVIL WAR

Signatures on
the 1921 treaty.

Sinn Féin won a landslide victory at the 1918 elections, established an Irish Parliament and declared independence. The IRA started the war of liberation.

Outflanked, London called out the veterans of the Great War to restore order, but their methods permanently alienated them from the people. Having partitioned off Northern Ireland, Lloyd George signed a treaty with the moderate factions of Sinn Féin, granting Southern Ireland Dominion Status. This was unacceptable to Republican extremists, and they rejected the agreement. In June 1922 a bitter civil war broke out which devastated Dublin before inflaming the whole province. The Free State's army suppressed the centers of resistance without further ado, forcing the Republicans to lay down their arms in May 1923.

THE ILLICIT PARLIAMENT
Having won 73 of the 105 Irish seats in the 1918 elections, Sinn Féin convoked its members of parliament at Mansion House in Dublin on January 21, 1919: they formed an Irish parliament (Dáil Éireann) with De Valera as President, proclaimed independence, launched an appeal to the free nations of the world and voted in favor of a democratic program. A provisional government was appointed.

THE IRA
When diplomacy failed, the Dáil Éireann's army opened guerrilla warfare on Dublin (where they deployed mobile commando units), and in the countryside with "flying columns", the most famous of which was Tom Barry's West Cork Column.

THE CRACKDOWN
Attached to the Royal Irish Constabulary, the Black and Tans and the Auxiliaries (all former officers and soldiers from the trenches) spread terror throughout the country, burning towns and villages. Well-armed, lacking in discipline, they traveled around in Crossley trucks or Austin armored cars.

MICHAEL COLLINS
He galvanized the IRA and neutralized enemy intelligence. A negotiator of the 1921 treaty, President of the Provisional Government and Commander-in-Chief of the national army, he died in an ambush in 1922.

CIVIL WAR
Civil war broke out on June 28, 1922, first in Dublin, devastated by another week-long bloodbath, then in the countryside, where the Free State's army hunted down the Republican "irregulars". Once Liam Lynch, the military leader of the rebellion had been been killed, De Valera ordered a ceasefire on May 24, 1923.

THE TREATY
The compromise treaty of December 1921 caused a rift between Sinn Féin and the IRA. The supporters of the agreement, led by Griffiths and Collins, were elected by plebiscite; their opponents, led by De Valera and Brugha, refused to admit defeat.

EASTER WEEK REPEATS ITSELF

THE I.R.A. STILL DEFENDS THE REPUBLIC

Divorced
from the rest of Ireland
and retained as a distinctive part of the
United Kingdom by an English act of 1920, Northern
Ireland comprises six of the nine counties in the historic
province of Ulster: Antrim, Armagh, Down, Fermanagh, Derry
and Tyrone. Here, the friction inherited from colonization has
been brought to fever pitch by partition. This is a divided
society: 60 percent of its inhabitants are Unionist Protestant and
40 percent Nationalist Catholic. Since 1969, armed
confrontations between the IRA, Loyalist paramilitary groups
and British peace-keeping forces have claimed three thousand
lives. For want of a consensus between the communities,
London and Dublin have combined forces to try and restore
peace in this trouble-stricken province.

A DIVIDED SOCIETY
Hostile to any
thought of
reunification, the
majority Unionist
party commandeered
the State machinery
and treated members
of the Catholic
minority as second-
class citizens. In the
mid-1960's, the latter
staged a peaceful
march, demanding
their rights. The
violence of the
Protestant response,
in the summer of
1969, helped
reactivate the IRA,
forcing Westminster
to take control of
administration and
introduce the
necessary reforms.

Republican terrorism,
official counter-
measures and Loyalist
paramilitaries plunged
the province into
chaos.

From top to bottom:
Hume, Paisley and
Adams.

SUMMER OF 1969
The Catholic ghetto of the Bogside in
Derry ▲ *318* was fortified and became a
"no-go area"; in Belfast, British soldiers
intervened. Westminster tried to outlaw
discrimination.

AN UNATTAINABLE CONSENSUS
No internal
negotiation has so far
been able to come up
with a universally
acceptable system of
government. John
Hume's mainly
Catholic SDLP
opposes James
Molyneaux's official
Unionist party and
Reverend Ian
Paisley's Democratic
Unionist Party
because it wants to
unite all of Ireland.
The Unionists suspect
that the cease-fire
ordered by the IRA
on August 31, 1994,
and by the Loyalist
paramilitaries six
weeks later, may lead
to the abandonment
of Northern Ireland
as a British province.
The spirit of
compromise still has
to triumph over
intransigence, as
much among the
IRA and Gerry
Adams' Sinn
Féin as
among the
Unionists.

A PAINFUL LEGACY
The problem of
Northern Ireland
remains the poisoned
fruit of many
centuries of
bitterness.

A CLIMATE OF COOPERATION
Most solutions presuppose a prior agreement
between Dublin and London. That was the
tenor of the Thatcher-FitzGerald agreements
(1985) and of the joint declaration by John
Major and Albert Reynolds (1993).

● THE IRISH LANGUAGE

Irish is sometimes referred to as "Gaelic", but so is the Scottish language. To be more accurate, the term "Irish Gaelic" should be used to describe the language spoken in Ireland. "Gaelic" is actually derived from the word "Gael", the name given to the Celts. The Irish word for their language is "Gaedhilge" ("Gaelige", after the spelling reform of 1945, which was designed to abolish a certain number of letters which were written but not pronounced).

ORIGINS

Irish is a Celtic language, and therefore has Indo-European roots. It has been used in Ireland since the 4th century. Since then the language has passed through several distinct linguistic periods: the proto-Irish of the ogham inscriptions (4th to 7th century), the Old Irish found in commentaries (8th to 9th century), Middle Irish (around 900–1200) and Modern Irish (since 1200). Old Irish is one of the earliest languages to appear in western Europe.

OGHAM STONES
The name of these strange standing stones dotted around Ireland bears close similarities to that of the Celtic god of writing, Ogmios. They probably marked the site of a grave. Dating, it seems, from the beginning of Christian times (4th century) to the 7th century, they were found primarily in the counties of Cork and Kerry. In oghamic writing, each letter is formed by using straight or oblique lines, appearing on either side of the stone's edge. Each letter is composed of between one and five strokes. The inscription is read from the top and, more often than not, it bears a person's name, as well as that of their father.

ANCIENT IRISH LITERATURE

The main body of ancient Irish literature is made up of epic legends which in many cases date back to the Old Irish period, at least as far as the written tradition is concerned. These legends speak of an aristocratic and warlike society in which the individual person was subordinate to the clan. In this society, the poet enjoyed a privileged status on a par with lawyers, doctors and musicians. The lives of the Irish saints also introduced a type of character similar to the epic hero.

IRISH ON THE WANE

FROM OLD IRISH TO MODERN IRISH

During the late Middle Ages, Ireland had a profound cultural influence on Great Britain and the continent. At the time of the Viking invasions (10th century), the Irish became more inward-looking, which led to a simplification of the language (Middle Irish). Although the Anglo-Norman invasions did not cause Irish to be eradicated, they brought about a fresh simplification (Modern Irish). Despite the attempts of English sovereigns (such as Henry VIII, for example) to oust the Irish language from the island, the whole of the Irish population was still speaking Gaelic until the Great Famine of 1845
● 58.

Douglas Hyde and Eoin MacNeill, founders of the Gaelic League.

DOUGLAS HYDE

A poet and man of letters, Hyde was born in Sligo in 1860. After studying at Trinity College ▲ *148*, he founded an Irish literary society in 1891 in London and became President of the one in Dublin the following year. This sensitized him to the importance of Irish as a ferment of national unity, and, in line with this principle, he founded the Gaelic League in 1893. He finally left the League in 1915 and started a political career which culminated in his becoming President in 1938.

GRADUAL DISAPPEARANCE

While the wealthy farmers of Ireland were becoming anglicized, among the poorer peasants, mortality and emigration were taking their toll; consequently the Irish language declined more quickly in the wealthiest areas. In 1800, it is estimated that half of the population (5 million people) still spoke Irish. Fifty years later, according to the census taken after the Great Famine, there were 1½ million Irish speakers; in 1911, only an eighth remained.

THE GAELIC REVIVAL

THE FOUNDATION OF THE GAELIC LEAGUE

Several learned societies sprang up during the 19th century in an attempt to check the decline of the language. The most active of these was the Gaelic League ("Conradh na Gaedhilge"), founded on July 31, 1893, under the presidency of the poet Douglas Hyde. From this time onward, some people linked the political movement for national liberation with the linguistic struggle for the "restoration" of the Irish language and Celtic culture. This idea gained a great deal of support, even from a number of Anglo-Irish Protestants and Dublin intellectuals. Many learned to speak Irish (like Synge ● *123*) and occasionally even wrote in Irish (such as Patrick Pearse, the future hero of 1916 ● *61*). This Nationalist movement was banned in 1915.

SUPPORT POLICIES

Since independence in 1921, the various governments have all enforced a policy of support for Gaelic (recognized as the first national language by Article 8 of the 1937 Constitution): used in official documents, Gaelic is a compulsory subject on the curriculum of primary and secondary schools and, until very recently, on that of state examinations, in particular for entrance to jobs in the civil service. This means that many English-speaking Irish people have a "smattering" of Irish and say that they speak it whenever a census is taken. This policy of support for the language has occasionally led to excesses; for example, money has been found to fund the translation of a great number of foreign books. In order to revive the Irish language for all occasions, some neologisms have had to be coined to make up for its cultural backwardness, and certain towns and villages that have long been anglicized have now had their original Gaelic name restored.

IRISH LANGUAGE MEDIA

Four radio stations (*Raidio na Gaeltachta*) broadcast throughout the country (92.6–94.4 FM). The major national channels, RTE Radio and Radio 2, and the television channels, broadcast very few programs in Irish, apart from a daily news bulletin. The written press is small and not widely available: four fairly specialized monthly publications, a weekly, *Anois* ("Now"), printed in Dublin, as well as a daily newspaper *Lá* ("Day"), printed in Belfast.

THE "GAELTACHT"

Irish is still spoken in the *Gaeltacht*, areas mainly encompassing parts of the counties of Cork, Kerry, Galway (Aran, Connemara), Mayo and Donegal. These remote regions are on the periphery economically. The people who live there now are encouraged to stay by a continued policy of social support and grants awarded for education and economic initiatives. Since 1956, there has been a *Gaeltacht* ministry, responsible for protecting the Irish-speaking areas.

THE "GAELTACHT"
After the 1991 census, there were 1,095,830 Irish-speaking people out of 3,367,000 inhabitants over three years of age. But the population of the *Gaeltacht* in 1981 was 58,000 inhabitants and again only 75 percent of the people in these districts were Irish-speaking.

Map of Irish-speaking areas in 1851 and 1981.

LINGUISTIC ASPECTS

TRADITIONAL WRITING

The Irish alphabet is derived from the medieval Irish scribal tradition. In fact, it is a product of so-called "Irish semi-uncial" writing, used in Latin manuscripts from Ireland. Several sets of "Gaelic" block letters were perfected in the 17th century.

But for some twenty years now, Irish has mainly been printed using the Latin alphabet. (The Irish alphabet is the same as the French or English alphabet, but does not include the letters j, k, q, v, w, x, y or z).

PHONETICS

There is a discrepancy between writing and pronunciation which may at first disconcert the uninitiated. The phonetic system contrasts palatal (front) consonants with non-palatal consonants. These are marked by a preceding vowel, *e* or *i*, which is not pronounced: *fáilte* ("welcome") is pronounced *fa:lt'e* (*l'*, *t'* are palatal consonants, as indicated by the *i*). The system also contrasts occlusive consonants and spirant consonants (indicated by an *h* or a superscribed dot in the *cló Gaelach* – the traditional written form). Moreover, the same word may start sometimes with an occlusive consonant or at others with a spirant consonant: nominative, *an Ghaeltacht* ("the Gaeltacht"); genitive, *Aire na Gaeltachta* ("the Gaeltacht Minister").

BILINGUALISM
Telefon (telephone) can be understood immediately by any non-speaker, but *bruscar* ("litter") poses a little more of a problem. Take care in the toilets not to confuse *fir* ("men") with *mná* ("women"). Road signs are usually bilingual. However, in the Gaelic-speaking areas of the *Gaeltacht*, the English translations are often painted over.

The important Irish holidays, in the North as in the South, are actually professions of faith and statements of identity which expose the contradictions and frictions that have been shaped by history. St Patrick's Day, March 17, is a day of rejoicing for the local Irish people as well as for the seventy million descendants of Irish blood scattered throughout the world. On this day, green (the national, or even Nationalist, color) is accorded particular pride of place. In Northern Ireland, on July 12, it is orange, the symbolic color of Unionism, which spreads like wildfire through the streets during this important holiday. "The Twelfth" is a celebration of the victory of William of Orange at the Battle of the Boyne.

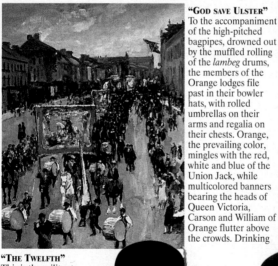

"GOD SAVE ULSTER"
To the accompaniment of the high-pitched bagpipes, drowned out by the muffled rolling of the *lambeg* drums, the members of the Orange lodges file past in their bowler hats, with rolled umbrellas on their arms and regalia on their chests. Orange, the prevailing color, mingles with the red, white and blue of the Union Jack, while multicolored banners bearing the heads of Queen Victoria, Carson and William of Orange flutter above the crowds. Drinking heavily, singing hymns and declaring their dogged determination to stay British, the Orangemen are probably trying as much to put their own minds at ease as to remind the outside world that peace is impossible without them.

"THE TWELFTH"
This is the militant Orangeman's day. Every year, the loyal "sons and daughters of Ulster" enthusiastically and flamboyantly celebrate their loyalty to "Crown and Constitution". Quite apart from its political and denominational angle, "The Twelfth" reflects a lasting attachment to local Northern-Irish traditions.

The shamrock (three-leafed clover) was used by Saint Patrick ● *56* to illustrate and explain the Holy Trinity – the mystery of one God divided into three coexisting, consubstantial and coeternal persons – to the Celts of Ireland.

"St Patrick's Day is an important symbol for all Irish people. It reconciles our many distinct cultural traditions and influences. It instils in us a feeling of hope and pride at the richness of our heritage."

Mary Robinson

ST PATRICK'S DAY

This day is not just the most important national holiday in Ireland, it is also a holiday for Irish people all over the world. This is the day when the United States turns green! In New York, parades create a holiday mood all day. On March 17, continuing a time-honored tradition, the *taoiseach* (Ireland's prime minister) goes to Washington to present a Waterford crystal dish filled with shamrocks to the president of the United States, who never fails to seize this opportunity to remember he has Irish blood in his veins! Back across the water in Dublin, where 350,000 people gather to celebrate the occasion, St Patrick's Day is an excuse for some jubilant, colorful reunions between Irish people who stayed at home and their expatriate friends and relatives, all marching together in close order behind brass bands. In this way, they can "return to their roots", and reassert an Irish identity that is not nearly as shaky as some might claim.

Bones

The famous English composer Arnold Bax (1883–1953) apparently declared that "of all the antiquities in the world Ireland possesses the most varied and beautiful music". This tradition is more alive today than ever before, and although the successors of the Gaelic bards are continuing to give Irish life a certain rhythm, even now, they have also been a source of delight for the rest of the world for over thirty years. The aim of the *Comhaltas Ceoltóirí Éireann*, an organization for Irish musicians founded in 1951, was to promote traditional music. And with countless musical events under its belt, it can pride itself on a mission accomplished.

THE CELTIC HARP

The Celtic harp, which has been around since the Gael period, is now the emblem of Ireland. It is the instrument played by the poets, the *filid*, who were admired both for their scholarship and their music. Stripped of their social role by the Normans, and persecuted by the English, the harpists survived various acts of repression to make a comeback at the festivals in Belfast in the late 18th century.

A HERITAGE REVISITED

In the early 1960's, the composer Seán O'Riada (1931–71) and his group, *Ceoltóirí Chualann*, popularized representative tunes and instruments such as the *uilleann* pipes, elbow pipes operated with the right arm (below); the fiddle, a violin without a chin rest played by bowing very quickly; and the *bodhrán*, a drum made of goatskin stretched over a beechwood frame.

Traditional groups also include different types of diatonic and chromatic accordions, concertinas (smaller than the accordion), tin whistles, metal pipes with six holes, transverse flutes, and even bones; nowadays spoons are also knocked against one another to produce a rhythm.

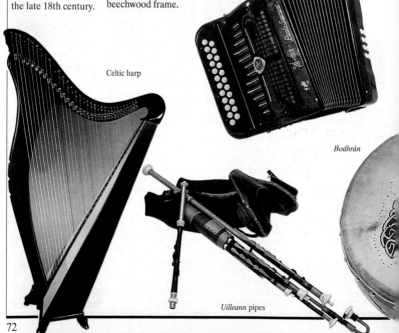

Celtic harp

Accordion

Bodhrán

Uilleann pipes

KEY VENUES

The success of traditional music led to the creation of many festivals, the most important of which, the *Fleadh Cheoil na hÉireann*, is held every year in a different village. But, above all, music is a sociable pursuit and so it can often be heard in the pubs or even in the street, coming into direct contact with the people.

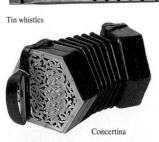

Tin whistles

Concertina

AND TRADITIONAL MUSIC BECAME FOLK . . .

In the 1970's, groups such as the *Chieftains*, the *Dubliners*, *Planxty*, *Dé Dannann*, *Moving Hearts* (with Christie Moore) and Van Morrison (below) took a fresh look at traditional music, adapted to more contemporary rhythms by *Clannad* (left).

AND FOLK BECAME ROCK . . .

The punk phenomenon contributed to the evolution of folk, and Irish rock made an appearance in the late 1970's. *U2* (above), the true ambassadors of "Celtic rock" today, have become one of the leading rock bands in the world. Other major figures on the current musical scene are Chris de Burgh, the *Pogues*, the *Hothouse Flowers*, Sineád O'Connor, *Frank and Walters* and *Divine Comedy*.

In Ireland, *Guinness* filling a glass is "liquid poetry" and knowing how to drink it is "a serious matter, which requires almost as much effort as staying sober" ◆ *346*.

The oldest pub in Ireland is said to be around eight hundred years old. Because of the advances made in agriculture, brewing and distilling in the 17th and 18th centuries, alcohol production escalated, ushering in a golden age of public houses in the mid-19th century (there were fifteen thousand licenses in 1850). Acquiring a public house in those days was one way of acquiring an education. This "licensed place of worship" (Flann O'Brien) contained a mishmash of all aspects of the country's life, whether poetic or polemic, cultural or political.

In former times, pubs frequently doubled as grocers' shops.

Typical pubs have a bar (at which you can stand) and a lounge (where you can sit down).

When closing time is imminent, the bartender will call out "Last orders, please!" to remind drinkers that it is time to order their last drinks and get ready to leave.

Tradition dictates that women do not drink in the bar, but times are changing.

When drinks are bought in rounds, everyone takes turns to pay.

In Dublin, it is said that the statue of Parnell points in the direction of the nearest pub.

Ireland is a country of story-telling, and pub raconteurs enjoy spinning a yarn.

The Romans despised beer, the vulgar "barley wine" which Christians associated for many years with the pagans lost in the cold and foggy reaches of the North. Nonetheless, the Christian monks were the first to brew beer. To get into the Church's good books, Ireland's first lay brewers cleverly chose a patron saint: Colombanus. As the legend goes, the latter introduced beer-making skills to many European monasteries during the 6th century. Today, Ireland is the world's thirtieth largest producer of beer . . . and the fifth largest consumer.

"WATER, MALT AND HOPS"
Barley, the best cereal for brewing, has to be malted so that the starch it contains can be converted into sugar, ready to be fermented and converted, in turn, into alcohol and carbon dioxide. The malt obtained in this way is ground into flour which, mixed with hot water in enormous vats (mashing), has its solid residue (mash) filtered out. The liquid obtained (wort) is heated with the hops at a temperature higher than 212ºF. Once it has been cooled, yeasts are added and it is left to ferment. The "green beer" then goes through a resting stage before being racked into barrels or bottled.

GUINNESS

Guinness, with its famous black and gold label, produces four million pints per day; and nearly eight million pints are drunk every day throughout the world. This international company also has interests in the whiskey, spirits and champagne industries.

THE SERVING OF STOUT

This is a true ritual, a favorite with the Irish: the pint is pulled very slowly and the glass is filled in two stages so that a creamy head is formed. Then the "most natural of drinks" is left to stand for several minutes before being quaffed.

STOUT, ALE AND LAGER

The manner of fermentation determines the type of beer. Top fermentation, the oldest method, produces full-bodied beers with a strong flavor. In Ireland these include ale, an English beer which is amber-colored (light or dark, as the case may be); and stout, also of English origin (formerly porter), but made famous in 1824 by the beer invented by Arthur Guinness, using strongly roasted malt. Bottom fermentation is used to produce the extremely popular lager beer. And Guinness created the harp label accordingly.

MURPHY'S, BEAMISH AND SMITHWICK'S

The two other Irish stouts, *Murphy's* (1792) and *Beamish* (1858), are proud to flaunt their southern origins. In Cork, local patriotism requires that you down a pint of *Murphy's* rather than *Guinness*, the capital's stout. *Smithwick's* (created in Kilkenny in 1710) is an ale produced by the Guinness group.

"Of all the wines, Irish is the best", maintained Peter the Great, Tsar of Russia. He was talking about Irish whiskey, "the blessed elixir of the gods", since it was the Irish monks, on their return from the Holy Land in around AD 600 who came up with the secrets of its distillation. The main ingredients of this drink, called *uisce beatha* ("water of life" in Gaelic), are pure water and barley. The drink was enthusiastically taken up by the Anglo-Norman invaders who anglicized its name to "whiskey" and helped popularize it on both sides of the Irish Sea.

MANUFACTURE

During malting, the germination of some of the barley is provoked, then halted when it is dried in a kiln. The barley, either malted or unmalted, is then ground and mixed with cooled boiled water, so that the enzyme diastase in the malt can convert the starch in the unmalted barley into fermentable sugar. This fermentation produces a brownish liquid called wash, which, after about three days, undergoes the first distillation in a pot still or column still. The vapor which is given off is condensed to produce low wines. Once these are distilled, they produce an alcohol called feints, which, when this in turn is distilled, finally results in Irish whiskey. This is matured in oak casks for at least three years, and often for twelve or fifteen years, before being blended and bottled.

" I suppose what makes Irish whiskey
and Irish Guinness so good, is the
curative properties of Liffey water. **"**
Brendan Behan

"SLÁINTE!" ◆ *346*
There are many ways
to drink Irish
whiskey. In cold
weather, order an
"Irish coffee", a
mixture of whiskey,
coffee and cream
invented by Joe
Sheridan in Shannon,
or a "hot Irish", made
with boiling water,
lemon, cloves,
cinnamon and brown
sugar. You can also
drink it in cocktails or
"on the rocks". But
the best way to savor
its velvety flavor is to
drink it at room
temperature, neat or
diluted with a little
still water. Whatever
the case, do not
ignore the tradition
of the round, which
still prevails here, and
which will prompt
you to take up the
chorus of the famous
song, *The Wild Rover*:
"I've been a wild
rover for many a year
and I spent all my
money on whiskey
and beer . . ."

DISTILLERIES

In the 18th century,
there were two
thousand stills in
operation in Ireland.
Everyone profited by
this except the
Treasury. So the
government decided
to grant licenses only
to the largest
distilleries. This was
the start of the
modern distilling
industry, which has
never completely
stamped out the illicit
stills that even today
produce *poteen*,
contraband whiskey
strong enough to fell
a herd of aurochs. It
was at this time that
the Irish whiskey
giants appeared:
Bushmills, the first
recorded distillery
which opened its
doors in 1608;
Jameson, founded by
John Jameson in
1780; Power, created
by James Power in
1791; Midleton,
which produces
Paddy, set up by the
Murphy brothers in
1825; Tullamore,
which started
production in 1829.
In 1966, these big
names merged to
create the Irish

Distillers group
which has
brought Irish
whiskey to the
fore.

The "tinkers" now live on the fringes of Irish society, often despised and usually ignored. Only a very few, divorced from their background, can be found dotted among the pages of Irish literature. They prefer the term "travellers" or "travelling people" to that of "tinkers", which they find insulting. These children of an Irish society that has long disappeared are no relation whatsoever to the gypsies on the continent. But, as is also the case with the latter, people have tried on occasion to romanticize their life . . . a life which is actually extremely hard. However, those who once traveled the country's roads in their thousands enjoyed a certain symbiotic relationship with the rural world. Since the mid-20th century, two phenomena have profoundly altered their way of life: rural depopulation and the urbanization of the countryside. This marginal, nomadic minority was once again deprived of its roots when it had to adapt to a sedentary life on the outskirts of towns.

ON THE ROADS

In the 19th century, the "travellers" abandoned ditches for tents, then tents for carts or wagons at the beginning of the 20th century. Before 1960, most still lived in groups of two to four families in brightly decorated horse-drawn caravans, now exchanged for mobile homes.

A SECRET LANGUAGE
The language of Shelta, derived
from Gaelic, and still spoken by
the elderly, enabled the
"travellers" to communicate
with each other without being
understood by outsiders.

ODD JOBS OF DAYS GONE BY
Descended from the wandering craftsmen of
olden times, from peasants evicted from
their lands or from poor people
reduced to begging, the
"travellers" went in search of
odd jobs, following a route
laid down by tradition.
Their role in society,
which was at that point
essentially rural, was
well-defined.

They would take on
all kinds of jobs:
repairing broken
objects, working tin
(the word "tinker"
originally described a
tinsmith), selling
horses, sweeping
chimneys, peddling
knick-knacks and
begging.

On November 1, 1884, in Thurles, Michael Cusack founded the Gaelic Athletic Association (G.A.A.) to revive the national sports that had been ousted by those "imported from abroad", and to boost national identity. Its impact was so great that every district now has its own division. Gaelic football and hurling teams (which now boast around 300,000 members, exclusively made up of amateurs), play for the glory of their county and the delight of the 70,000 spectators who attend the finals.

GAELIC FOOTBALL
A cross between football and rugby, Gaelic football is known for its high, accurate passes, its long kicks and its extremely violent tackles. Thirty players (fifteen players per team) join battle on a field measuring approximately 459 feet by 262 feet. The ball, smaller than a football, is dribbled by either hand or foot. The match falls into two thirty-minute halves. Each team has a goalkeeper, six defenders, two center-field players and six attackers. The goals are similar to those in rugby except that there is a net below the crossbar. The aim is therefore to score a goal, worth three points, by kicking the ball into the net below the crossbar, which is 10 feet above the ground, or to score a point by kicking the ball over the top of the crossbar.

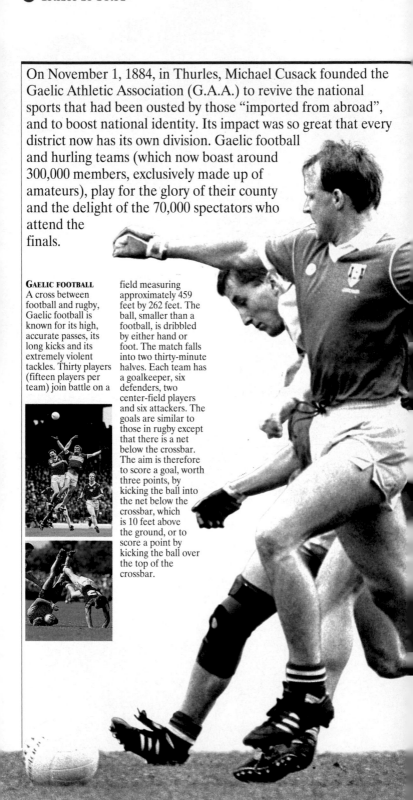

RUGBY

The Irish claim that they invented rugby and "who else but compatriots of Yeats, and Synge, O'Casey, Wilde and Shaw would have been crazy enough to invent . . . this game which bears such a strong resemblance to the windswept, rugged wastes of Connemara" (Jean Lacouture)! In the 1860's, the sport was played in the universities and the predominantly Protestant public schools, before ' becoming an established activity in Catholic schools in the 1900's. Nowadays, sportsmen from the Republic and from Northern Ireland will play on the same teams.

"ALL-IRELAND FINALS"

The finals of the hurling and Gaelic football championships take place in September, in Croke Park (Dublin), where the G.A.A. has its headquarters.

HURLING

Hurling is a type of hockey played on turf and is regarded as the most exciting field sport because of the skill and the strength it demands. Hurling has several points in common with Gaelic football: the number of players, the size of the pitch and the principle of goal-scoring. Each player uses a hurley (*camán*, in Irish), a flat stick made of ash with a wide base. The size of the hurley may vary depending on the height of the player, but is usually around 3 feet. The ball (*sliothár*), which is slightly larger than a tennis ball, has a cork center and is covered with well-sewn leather. It can travel as fast as 68 miles per hour. There is also a version of hurling for women: *camogie*, with teams of thirteen players on a smaller pitch.

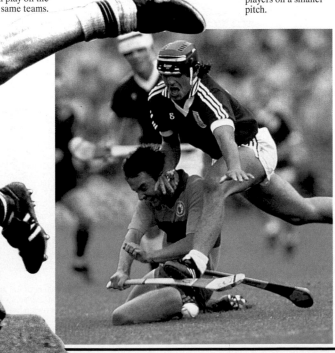

Irish cooking, which is wholesome and plentiful, uses prime quality products. The basic ingredient of Irish stew, the "national dish", used to be goat or kid, as no farmer would have sacrificed his young lambs. Today, Irish stew is prepared with free-range lamb, potatoes and onions. You can supplement these ingredients, to the horror of the purists, with carrots and swedes. Countless recipes agree on one point: a good Irish stew should be thick and creamy.

INGREDIENTS
2 lb neck of lamb, 8 onions, 1–1½ pints water, 2¼ lb potatoes, chopped parsley, thyme, salt and pepper. Optional: 1 lb swedes, 12 oz carrots, 1 *bouquet garni*.

1. Begin by boning the meat, cut into fairly large chunks and trim the fat.

4. Repeat the same procedure with the rest of the ingredients until the dish is full. Add the water and position the *bouquet garni*.

5. Cover with a sheet of foil and a lid. Cook in the oven at 250°F/Gas Mark 4 or leave to simmer over a low heat for around 2 hours. Stir occasionally to prevent the stew from sticking; add more water if it gets too dry.

SODA BREAD

8 oz/2 cups wheat flour, 1 lb/4 cups wholemeal flour, 1 teaspoon salt,
1 teaspoon bicarbonate of soda, 1 pint milk

1. Mix the dry ingredients in a bowl and make a hollow in the center. Pour in a little milk.

2. Stir gently with a wooden spoon. Continue adding the milk to obtain a loose dough which is not too sticky.

3. Sprinkle the work surface with flour and knead the dough to obtain a ball around 2 inches thick.

4. Place the ball on a board sprinkled with flour and, using a buttered knife, make a cross-shaped cut in the top of the bread. Bake in the oven for around 40 minutes at 400°F/Gas Mark 6.

Pierce with a skewer to check it is thoroughly cooked.

5. Leave to cool for 4 to 6 hours before cutting. It can also be enjoyed spread with salted butter.

2. Peel and slice the potatoes and onions into small rounds. Arrange a layer of potatoes at the bottom of a dish, add parsley, thyme, onions, and if required swedes and carrots.

3. Add the chunks of meat and season with salt and pepper.

6. An Irish stew can be prepared several hours beforehand. It often tastes better after reheating. Soda bread is the ideal accompaniment for this lamb stew.

● IRISH SPECIALTIES

SALMON
Salmon, whether smoked over oak or grilled, is the most prestigious dish served at the Irish table. It is always accompanied by brown bread spread with salted butter.

BEER
Ireland is a major producer of good-quality beers, many of them with an international reputation. They include *Guinness, Murphy's* and *Beamish* (stouts), *Smithwick's* (ale) and *Harp* (lager).

BLACK PUDDING
Black pudding is, with bacon and eggs, the main ingredient in the Irish breakfast.

WHISKEY
There are now more than ten brands of Irish whiskey, including: *John Power, Jameson, Bushmills, Tullamore* and *Paddy*. Last but not least, there are whiskey cream liqueurs such as *Bailey's* and *Irish Mist*.

JEWELRY
The silversmiths are above all famous for jewelry inspired by Celtic motifs. Lovers may be tempted to buy the Claddagh ring, an ancient symbol of fidelity.

TEA
The Irish drink a great deal of this "west-European nectar". *Barry's Tea* is the largest manufacturer.

GLASSWARE
Irish crystal is the best in the history of fine glassware (since 1715). The crystal glassworks at Waterford are now the largest in the world.

CLOTHING
Originally made in Donegal, tweed is a woven woolen cloth used for making jackets and the famous caps. Aran sweaters are knitted using undyed wool produced from Connemara sheep.

THE PRESS
The five national dailies, three evening newspapers and five weekend magazines published by the Irish press boast a weekly circulation of about five million copies.

MUSICAL INSTRUMENTS
Some of these are peculiar to Ireland such as the tin whistle, a pipe often tuned to D, and the *bodhrán*, a traditional drum.

ARCHITECTURE

● MEGALITHS

PORTAL TOMBS
Portal tombs, which date from between 4000 and
3500 BC, have an enormous roofing stone, often sloping
(like the one at Proleek ▲ *199*), supported by
several uprights.

You will find an incredible array of prehistoric
architecture in Ireland, which boasts in the
region of one thousand megaliths. Appearing
quite late, they rank among the finest in
Europe. Portal tombs, probably the most
ancient of them all, are the most widespread in the island. Court
cairns, wedge tombs and passage tombs are often grouped
together in vast necropolises, as in the Boyne Valley where the
famous Newgrange tumulus measures 305 feet in diameter
and 38 feet high.

NEWGRANGE
A 62-foot-long passage
leads to a corbeled
chamber 20 feet high,
framed by three small
lower chambers at the
sides. The monument
was once surrounded
by a circle of standing
stones, of which
only twelve
survive.

CARVINGS
Ireland is a treasure house of megalithic art.
The main motifs are spirals, diamonds, suns
and arcs, not to mention human feet
and bizarre "rib cages".

PASSAGE TOMBS
Passage tombs are the
finest examples of
megalithic
monuments, often
grouped together in
commanding
necropolises like the
one at Carrowkeel,
County Sligo (plan
right) and particularly
in the Boyne Valley at
Newgrange, Dowth
and Knowth. They
date from between
3300 and 2500 BC.

CARROWKEEL
These dolmens
have a central
chamber with three
side recesses and a
passage with stepped
capstones.

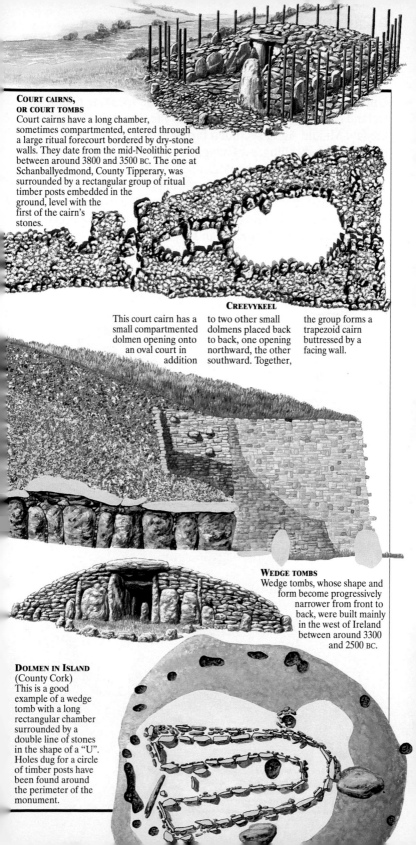

COURT CAIRNS, OR COURT TOMBS

Court cairns have a long chamber, sometimes compartmented, entered through a large ritual forecourt bordered by dry-stone walls. They date from the mid-Neolithic period between around 3800 and 3500 BC. The one at Schanballyedmond, County Tipperary, was surrounded by a rectangular group of ritual timber posts embedded in the ground, level with the first of the cairn's stones.

CREEVYKEEL
This court cairn has a small compartmented dolmen opening onto an oval court in addition to two other small dolmens placed back to back, one opening northward, the other southward. Together, the group forms a trapezoid cairn buttressed by a facing wall.

WEDGE TOMBS
Wedge tombs, whose shape and form become progressively narrower from front to back, were built mainly in the west of Ireland between around 3300 and 2500 BC.

DOLMEN IN ISLAND
(County Cork)
This is a good example of a wedge tomb with a long rectangular chamber surrounded by a double line of stones in the shape of a "U". Holes dug for a circle of timber posts have been found around the perimeter of the monument.

Different types of palisade.

Unlike the Mediterranean races, the Celtic-speaking peoples of Ireland never acquired a taste for city life. From the Iron Age to the late Middle Ages, secluded farmsteads were the most popular Irish dwelling. At Craggaunowen, Ferrycarrig and in the Ulster History Park, archeological excavations have given a much clearer picture of daily life during this period than has been obtained solely from visible remains. The two most common types of dwelling were the ring-fort (or *rath*, in Gaelic) and the *crannóg*, both circular in shape.

HOUSES
Inside the *crannógs*, houses were generally round, with trellis walls made of a mixture of wattle and daub, and probably a thatched roof, or a roof made of reeds. Within the ring-fort, houses were often made of stone and had weight-bearing walls: a single post, in the center, could be enough to support the roof.

"CRANNÓGS", ARTIFICIAL ISLANDS
Very popular around the 7th century, *crannógs* were built on lakes, usually not far from the bank, in shallow water. A layer of stones, tree trunks and branches was assembled, held in place by a rampart of posts driven into the bed of the lake. The platform created in this way was covered with a surface of earth and sand and protected by a wooden palisade.

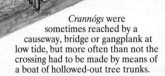

Crannógs were sometimes reached by a causeway, bridge or gangplank at low tide, but more often than not the crossing had to be made by means of a boat of hollowed-out tree trunks.

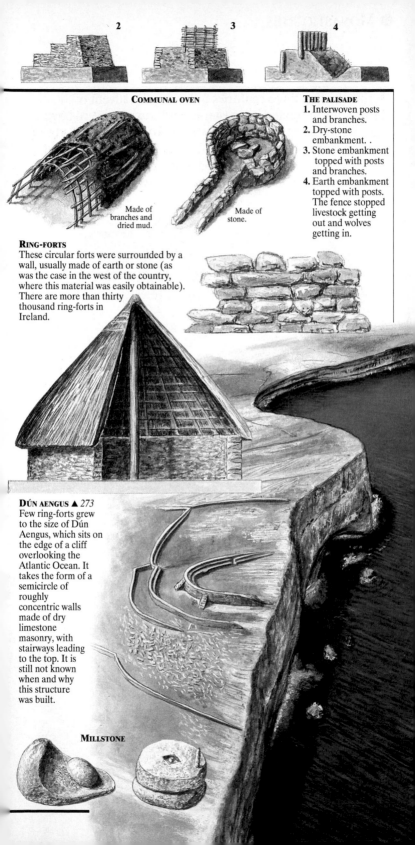

2   **3**   **4**

COMMUNAL OVEN

Made of branches and dried mud.

Made of stone.

THE PALISADE
1. Interwoven posts and branches.
2. Dry-stone embankment. .
3. Stone embankment topped with posts and branches.
4. Earth embankment topped with posts. The fence stopped livestock getting out and wolves getting in.

RING-FORTS
These circular forts were surrounded by a wall, usually made of earth or stone (as was the case in the west of the country, where this material was easily obtainable). There are more than thirty thousand ring-forts in Ireland.

DÚN AENGUS ▲ 273
Few ring-forts grew to the size of Dún Aengus, which sits on the edge of a cliff overlooking the Atlantic Ocean. It takes the form of a semicircle of roughly concentric walls made of dry limestone masonry, with stairways leading to the top. It is still not known when and why this structure was built.

MILLSTONE

During the first three centuries following the advent of Christianity in Ireland, monasteries and churches were largely built of timber. After 800, however, the Irish developed a taste for the grandeur and durability of stone structures, and used stone more and more, at least for churches and crosses, saving the timber for the monk's lodgings which were more temporary.

ORATORIES
The Oratory of Gallarus ▲ 238 is a good example of how the corbel principle, used in building the *clocháin* ("beehive huts", so-called because of their rounded shape) ▲ 236, was successfully applied to a rectangular plan.

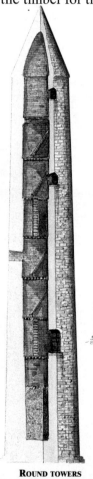

ROUND TOWERS
Constructed between 950 and 1200, these towers were probably useful for taking bearings. The door, between 7 and 10 feet above the ground, suggests that the tower may have been used for defense and also for storing treasure. However, its Irish name, *cloigtheach* ("bell house") implies a more peaceful purpose.

DOORWAY OF GALLARUS ORATORY
The door, swinging on a wooden hinge, was unusual in that it opened horizontally.

EARLY CHURCHES
Churches continued to be small as late as the 12th century, even when they were made of stone, probably because they were merely reproductions of the older wooden churches they had just superseded. The church on St MacDara's Island ▲ 265 (above) is a good example of this. It displays two of the typical features of early Irish churches: the antae, which prolong the south and north walls beyond the east and west gable-ends; and the stone roof, probably derived from shingle roofs.

MONASTERIES
The first monasteries, whose boundaries were demarcated by a circular earth embankment containing the church and the monks' huts, were not very extensive. Between the 8th and 9th centuries, a second enclosure, reserved for the laity connected with the monastery, was often added. Sometimes, as at Nendrum ▲ 306 (opposite), there was also a third enclosure, where the craftsmen lived and worked.

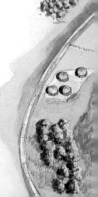

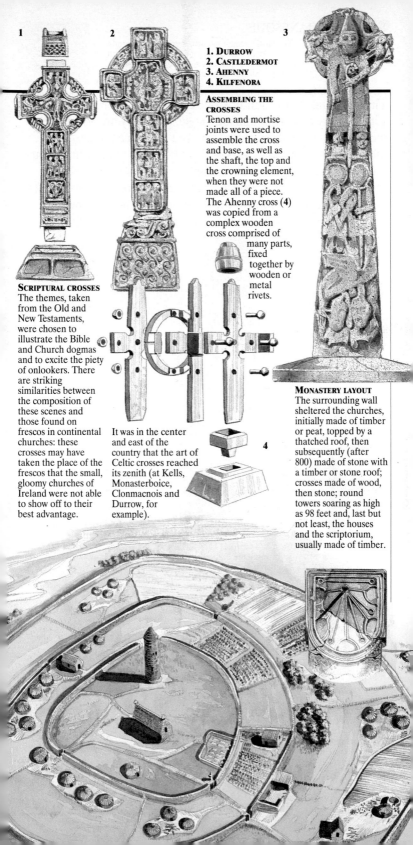

1. DURROW
2. CASTLEDERMOT
3. AHENNY
4. KILFENORA

ASSEMBLING THE CROSSES

Tenon and mortise joints were used to assemble the cross and base, as well as the shaft, the top and the crowning element, when they were not made all of a piece. The Ahenny cross (**4**) was copied from a complex wooden cross comprised of many parts, fixed together by wooden or metal rivets.

SCRIPTURAL CROSSES

The themes, taken from the Old and New Testaments, were chosen to illustrate the Bible and Church dogmas and to excite the piety of onlookers. There are striking similarities between the composition of these scenes and those found on frescos in continental churches: these crosses may have taken the place of the frescos that the small, gloomy churches of Ireland were not able to show off to their best advantage.

It was in the center and east of the country that the art of Celtic crosses reached its zenith (at Kells, Monasterboice, Clonmacnois and Durrow, for example).

MONASTERY LAYOUT

The surrounding wall sheltered the churches, initially made of timber or peat, topped by a thatched roof, then subsequently (after 800) made of stone with a timber or stone roof; crosses made of wood, then stone; round towers soaring as high as 98 feet and, last but not least, the houses and the scriptorium, usually made of timber.

The most widespread ornament is the palmette
(**2**), occasionally stylized and combined with
chevrons (**1**), which can also be found alone (**3**).
On the capitals, carved heads with plaited hair
are interwoven with zoomorphic motifs. **1**

There was no decoration in stone churches in Ireland until the
12th century. The Romanesque style, probably introduced by
the English, drew its sources from the French churches along
the pilgrims' route to Compostela. The relics of founding saints
drew the Irish pilgrims like a magnet, so it may have been for
them that the first Romanesque churches were built. With a few
exceptions, ornamentation was reserved for the windows, the
west porch and the chancel-arch separating the choir from
the nave.

EARLY ROMANESQUE
The early 12th-
century Cormac's
Chapel has three
porches (there is no
porch on the
western façade), as
well as bands of
blind arcading on
the outer side walls,
and two towers over
the arms of the
transept: distinctive
features that make
this building unique.
Its stone roof is
virtually the only
feature to be
imitated in Ireland.

LATE ROMANESQUE
Characteristic
features of
Romanesque
churches dating from
the end of the 12th
century included a
rectangular nave and
smaller choir without
a transept, decorated
porches, an
embellished chancel-
arch rising between
the nave and the
choir, and a small,
rarely ornamented,
east window. The
roof was usually
timber,
occasionally
thatched, but
hardly ever
stone.

Cormac's Chapel (1127–34) ▲ 253, at Cashel,
is probably the earliest genuine Romanesque
church in Ireland. It bears the stamp of
English (far more than continental)
influences.

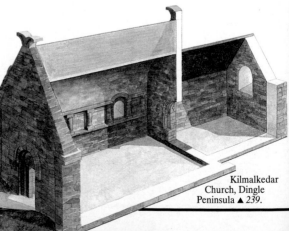

Kilmalkedar
Church, Dingle
Peninsula ▲ 239.

THE DOORWAY
The porch at Clonfert (*below*) has a doorway surrounded by engaged piers, crowned by an architrave flanked by a triangular gable.

THE ARCHES
The arches of the doorway and the chancel-arch are adorned with carvings of geometric motifs and interlacing animal ornaments which continue from one block of stone to another.

THE GABLE
This boasts two distinct styles: a blind arcade embellished by heads reminiscent of Celtic "severed heads", and a geometric motif suggesting a chevron ornament.

Jamb (detail): 15th-century statue of a saint.

Voussoir

Capital

95

THE GREAT ABBEYS

Religious architecture changed drastically during the 12th and early 13th centuries, when ecclesiastical orders from the continent arrived in Ireland. The small churches scattered here and there in monastic cities were replaced by monasteries, huge structures creating veritable religious cities in which the monastery buildings formed a whole with the church. This change was ushered in by the Cistercians, an order introduced in Ireland in 1142 by Saint Bernard of Clairvaux, at the request of Saint Malachy. They brought in new rules for monastic life and for the architecture of the establishments they set up.

FRANCISCAN PLAN

FRANCISCAN PLAN
In the 15th century, the foremost builders among monks were the Franciscans. They had, moreover, started to erect priories and convents as early as the 13th century. The long, narrow churches often had chapels or a single transept on the south side, as well as high, slender towers over the arms of the transept.

FRANCISCAN TOWER   **CISTERCIAN TOWER**

CISTERCIAN PLAN
(above)
Cistercian buildings are positioned around the square or rectangular courtyard of the cloister. The church, on the north side, is cruciform in plan (**1**) and, over the crossing of the transept, there is a wide, squat tower (**2**), sometimes added in the 15th century. Around the courtyard runs an arcade (**3**); the chapterhouse (**4**), perpendicular to the cloister, is on the east side; the refectory (**5**) is on the south side. The kitchens (**6**) and the storehouses (**7**) are located to the west of the refectory and are on the first floor, while the dormitory is on the second floor (**8**).

The purpose of the crenelations on monastery towers was more decorative than defensive.

Cistercian abbey at Greyabbey ▲ *306*.

FUNERARY MONUMENTS

In the 15th century, families who were privileged enough to bury their dead within the abbey walls erected large monuments in honor of their deceased relatives. The top of the tombs was often decorated with carvings, while figures of saints adorned the outside. At Kilconnell (County Galway), for example, two French saints (Denis and Louis) appear on the tomb of an unknown family.

THE LAVABO

The Cistercian Rule insisted that monks washed their hands before and after meals. The octagonal lavabo at Mellifont ▲ 198 was built for this purpose. Below its ogive vault, there would have been a spring fed by a nearby stream by dint of an underground system of pipes.

Tower house.

In 1169, the Normans landed in
Ireland. In order to enforce their dominion
over lands conquered by force of arms, they built fortifications
called "motte-and-baileys": wooden towers (*bretesche*) erected
on top of mounds of earth and, at their base, the lower
wards where the soldiers were billeted (and
probably the livestock was kept), the
whole area surrounded on occasion by
a fosse. Nevertheless, even before 1200,
the Normans were gradually replacing these fortifications with
strong stone castles which were often extremely large and
sometimes surrounded by a moat. It was not until the 15th and
16th centuries that the Irish erected their own type of
fortification: the tower house.

NORMAN CASTLES
When their motte-
and-baileys had fallen
into a state of
disrepair, the
Normans launched an
extensive building

campaign to replace
them: they built
stronger stone keeps
which were either

rectangular (Trim
▲ *190*), polygonal
(Athlone ▲ *208*),
or round (Dundrum
▲ *307*).

In the 17th century,
the entrance to
Limerick Castle was
flanked by two
sturdy machicolated
twin towers. In
those days, the
castle could be
reached by
means of a
drawbridge

**LIMERICK
CASTLE**
This is built
to the plan
favored by the
Normans in the
early 13th
century: a roughly
rectangular bailey
surrounded by
curtain walls and
defended by
cylindrical towers
erected at each
corner.

The northeast tower
was replaced in 1611 by
a rectangular bastion
capable of taking the
weight of five or six
pieces of artillery.

Bull's-eye window of a fortified tower.

The vault of the ceiling was often constructed over a brushwood trellis, which held the stones in place until the arch was completed.

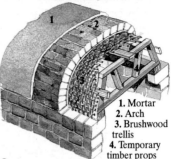

1. Mortar
2. Arch
3. Brushwood trellis
4. Temporary timber props

OPENINGS

Narrow windows protected the occupants from arrow-fire. Missiles could be hurled onto the attacking forces from additional defenses situated at roof level above the main entrance or at the corners.

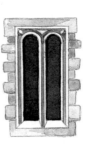

IRISH FORTIFIED TOWERS

These towers, smaller than a Norman castle, usually had three stories, linked by a spiral staircase just inside the main entrance. The tower was often surrounded by a high wall which kept the enemy out and meant that the livestock could be penned in at night.

TUDOR-STYLE MANOR HOUSES

(17th century) These buildings were intended more for comfort than defense, as can be seen by their many large windows. However, despite this, they still displayed some defensive features. At Portumna ▲ 200, there is a square tower at either corner of the main body of the building, from which cannon could be fired. The doorways were often decorated in the Renaissance style, but muskets could be fired on attackers through narrow loopholes concealed beside the door.

The present gates
of Derry.

After the 17th century, it was the English who built
fortifications in Ireland, in a bid to protect themselves from the
natives and to safeguard against the ever-present danger of
attack by sea: after all, the island could have served as a gateway
into England for France; but either these invasions did not take
place, or else they ended in failure.

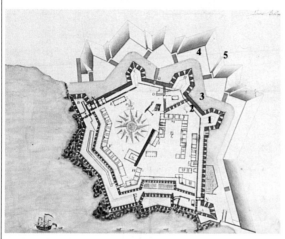

**FORTIFICATIONS
WITH BASTIONS**
From 1600, the
English revived the
defensive system of
fortified towns being
used in Europe; the
finest example of this
in Ireland is Charles
Fort ▲ *223*, protected
both by sea and by
land. The star-shaped
fort is comprised of
polygonal bastions
(**1**), designed to fire
from all sides, curtain
walls (**2**), separated
by a fosse (**3**) from a
covered way with
traverses (**4**) and a
glacis (**5**).

**URBAN
FORTIFICATIONS**
Throughout medieval
Europe, thick walls,
furnished with
variously shaped
bastions, were built
around the cities as a
defense against
cannonades. One of
the last towns to erect
fortifications of this
nature was Derry in
1613 ▲ *318*. Its city
walls were comprised
of an outer wall,
6 feet thick, which
stood in front of a
rampart made of
earth 13 feet thick.
These were protected
by eight bastions, two
platforms and four
gatehouses with
drawbridges,
indicating the new
town's cruciform axis:
four streets leading
from a central square
to the city gates.

THE SHANNON FORTIFICATIONS

To guard against possible attacks from the west, the English erected fortifications along the Shannon during the last two decades of the 19th century, including the Martello tower at Banagher ▲ *201* and the far more sophisticated defenses at Shannonbridge (right). This square battery on the Shannon was a variation on the Martello tower.

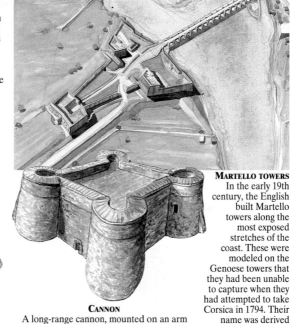

THE LOCATION OF MARTELLO TOWERS

Most of the Martello towers were built along the east coast, and in such a way that each one was in sight of the last.

CANNON

A long-range cannon, mounted on an arm able to swivel 360°, was installed on the roof of Martello towers.

MARTELLO TOWERS

In the early 19th century, the English built Martello towers along the most exposed stretches of the coast. These were modeled on the Genoese towers that they had been unable to capture when they had attempted to take Corsica in 1794. Their name was derived from a corruption of the name "Mortella" (a village in Corsica). The only entrance to these self-contained round towers with extremely thick walls was on the first floor, and they required very few men to defend them.

Straw or reeds made the best roofing materials. Rye, corn, oat and barley straw was widely used, but nowadays reeds are the most common material.

The traditional Irish house is a powerful symbol, a testament to past societies. Its characteristic size and shape have remained unchanged from the Neolithic period to the present day: one single story, a thatched roof, and a rectangular plan. It is built along precise lines, ensuring the sturdiness of the house, which may vary in length but not in breadth.

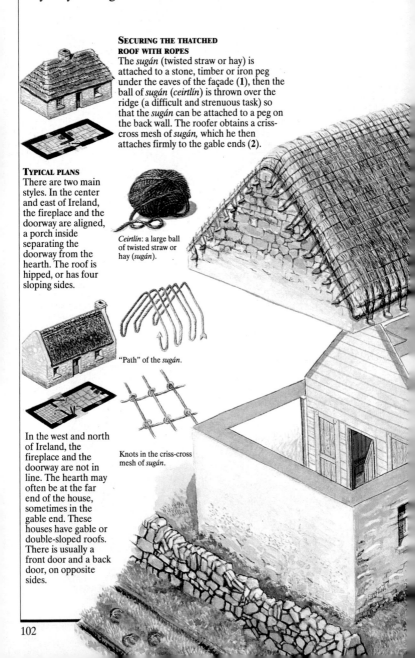

SECURING THE THATCHED ROOF WITH ROPES

The *sugán* (twisted straw or hay) is attached to a stone, timber or iron peg under the eaves of the façade (**1**), then the ball of *sugán* (*ceirtlín*) is thrown over the ridge (a difficult and strenuous task) so that the *sugán* can be attached to a peg on the back wall. The roofer obtains a criss-cross mesh of *sugán*, which he then attaches firmly to the gable ends (**2**).

TYPICAL PLANS

There are two main styles. In the center and east of Ireland, the fireplace and the doorway are aligned, a porch inside separating the doorway from the hearth. The roof is hipped, or has four sloping sides.

Ceirtlín: a large ball of twisted straw or hay (*sugán*).

"Path" of the *sugán*.

Knots in the criss-cross mesh of *sugán*.

In the west and north of Ireland, the fireplace and the doorway are not in line. The hearth may often be at the far end of the house, sometimes in the gable end. These houses have gable or double-sloped roofs. There is usually a front door and a back door, on opposite sides.

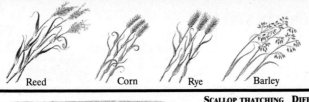

Reed · Corn · Rye · Barley

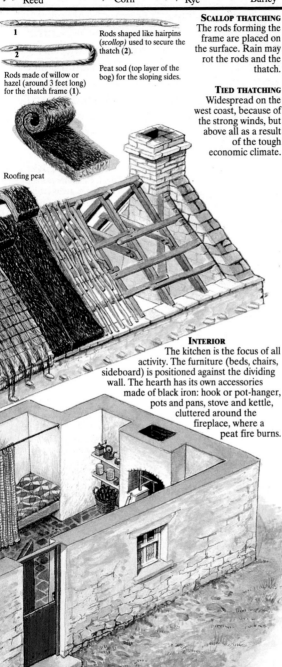

1

2

Rods shaped like hairpins (*scollop*) used to secure the thatch (**2**).

Rods made of willow or hazel (around 3 feet long) for the thatch frame (**1**).

Peat sod (top layer of the bog) for the sloping sides.

Roofing peat

SCALLOP THATCHING
The rods forming the frame are placed on the surface. Rain may rot the rods and the thatch.

TIED THATCHING
Widespread on the west coast, because of the strong winds, but above all as a result of the tough economic climate.

INTERIOR
The kitchen is the focus of all activity. The furniture (beds, chairs, sideboard) is positioned against the dividing wall. The hearth has its own accessories made of black iron: hook or pot-hanger, pots and pans, stove and kettle, cluttered around the fireplace, where a peat fire burns.

DIFFERENT TYPES OF ROOFING

SCALLOP THATCHING

TIED THATCHING

THRUST THATCHING
This is the best method, using high-quality straw or reeds.

SLATE ROOFS
Carboniferous limestone rock, like Liscannor stone from the north of County Clare ▲ *240*, makes excellent roofing.

The term "Georgian" covers a classical architectural style, fashionable in Ireland during the reigns of the three Georges between 1714 and 1820, at a time when country residences were being modeled on city styles. The type of Italian Renaissance villa built by Palladio served as a model for manor houses built between 1725 and 1750: a tall central building linked to smaller wing buildings by a short colonnade. Later on, the neoclassical style reigned supreme, deriving its colonnaded porticos and its liking for carvings from antiquity.

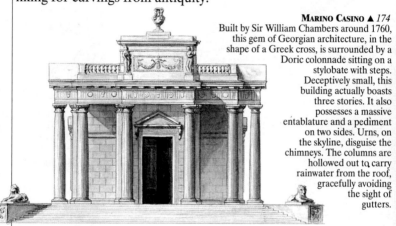

MARINO CASINO ▲ 174
Built by Sir William Chambers around 1760, this gem of Georgian architecture, in the shape of a Greek cross, is surrounded by a Doric colonnade sitting on a stylobate with steps. Deceptively small, this building actually boasts three stories. It also possesses a massive entablature and a pediment on two sides. Urns, on the skyline, disguise the chimneys. The columns are hollowed out to carry rainwater from the roof, gracefully avoiding the sight of gutters.

EMO COURT ▲ 182
James Gandon, the leading exponent of Irish neoclassicism in the late 18th century, who built the Four Courts ▲ 146 and the Custom House ▲ 144 in Dublin, designed Emo Court in the 1790's.

Its plan is rectangular and both façades are formed of a central block with three ornamental fronts linked by a balustrade to the buildings which jut out on either side and which are decorated by carvings depicting the arts. The central dome was not completed until 1860.

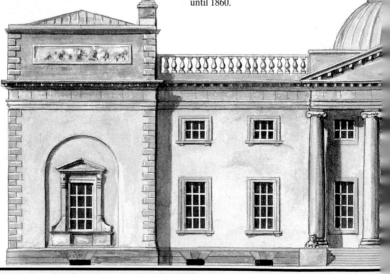

DOORWAYS

Dublin is renowned for its Georgian doorways. Made of wood, often paneled and painted in bright colors, they are surrounded by a classical doorcase, flanked by columns, occasionally topped by small windows. The style of the capitals varies greatly. The entablature is crowned by a semi-circular fanlight; the extent and lavishness of its decoration gives some measure of the owner's imagination.

RUSSBOROUGH HOUSE ▲ 184

Like a long stage set, its façade stretching for 787 feet, Russborough was designed by Castle and Bindon around 1740 in the style of the Irish Palladian villas. The central block, with its portico crowned by a pediment, is slightly set back from the two shorter buildings which are linked to it by a colonnade. A court at each end is entered through a tall arch made of rusticated stone.

BALCONIES

Many of the Georgian terraces had elliptical wrought-iron balconies, adorned with classical motifs which were generally geometric (Greek borders) or floral (garlands, lyres, etc).

TOWNHOUSES

In the Dublin of the 1740's, huge stone residences were built, ushering in the neoclassical style. Rather than these few isolated buildings, however, the houses which belonged to the minor nobility were more typical of urban Georgian style: redbrick, four-story buildings with recessed doorways and windows whose proportions gradually altered. These houses were built in terraces, sometimes forming a square around a central park. They were often copied, on a more modest scale, in country towns.

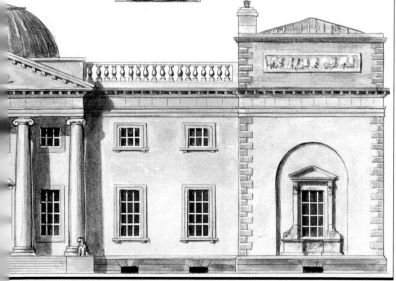

Georgian decoration is characterized by an abundance of ornaments, made of stone or wood for architectural embellishment and stucco for interiors. Stuccowork, already being practiced as early as 1620, reached the height of its popularity in the 18th century, with high-reliefs depicting human figures, festoons, garlands and other *putti*, introduced by the Swiss Lafranchini brothers. In the middle of the century, Robert West nudged stuccowork toward a Rococo style, teeming with fruit, flowers, and birds. Later, Michael Stapleton returned to more understated bas-reliefs: dancing figures for friezes, garlands, urns and cameos.

Wooden furniture was often carved with naturalistic floral motifs.

Oval cameos were also extremely popular and depicted portraits or full-length figures inspired by mythology. They were flanked on either side by garlands, thereby forming a continuous motif, extremely popular in the 1770's.

Georgian ornamentation displayed countless details borrowed from classical architecture: Greek borders, palmettes, rosettes linked by garlands and bucraniums.

Bas-relief human figures often depicted mythological subjects.

Rococo stuccoworkers liked to use swirling plant-like volutes for high-reliefs.

Among the most characteristic motifs of the Georgian style were lion heads, with drapery, rosettes and all types of garlands.

IRELAND
AS SEEN BY PAINTERS

The "English landscape" was invented in the 18th century: important landowners, no longer satisfied with building and restoring their houses, wanted to shape the countryside around them in equal measure. If painters were supposed to imitate nature, then landscape gardeners were supposed to imitate art. Influenced by Edmund Burke's theories of esthetics, GEORGE BARRET (1728/32–84) produced works reflecting both the sublime: *Stormy Landscape*; and the beautiful: *The Waterfall at Powerscourt* (1760) (3). PHILIP HUSSEY (1713–83) was reputedly a sailor before he became a painter, learning his second trade while working on the figureheads for sailing ships. His *Interior with members of a family* (around 1750) (2) depicts the salon of a bourgeois house, probably belonging to a family of the Ascendancy. The painting is directly related to the "conversation piece" genre: the portrait of a family or group of friends practicing the art of conversation in a salon or garden (as seen in the works of Francis Hayman and the young Gainsborough), especially in *The Grosvenor Family*. This is a group portrait for which everyone poses as if for a photograph a century or so later. This blend of social ostentation and outward simplicity can also be found, but in a more intense

form, in *The Vere Foster Family* (1), painted by WILLIAM ORPEN (1878–1931) around 1907. The artist is unequivocally, and not without humor, quoting Gainsborough and the *Portrait of Mr and Mrs Andrews*: the hunting rifle held by the male protagonist is as much a social symbol as a realistic object. Unlike Gainsborough, however, Orpen only suggests the landscape. According to Bruce Arnold, his biographer, the work was unfinished and, indeed, the Foster family do seem to be posing in front of a studio backdrop. Orpen, gifted and worldly, spent more of his time living in London than in Ireland and, like Sir John Lavery, was carrying on the tradition, in the 20th century, of gaining a reputation as an artist by painting portraits of influential people in society. In 1902, in his play *Cathleen Ni Houlihan*, William Butler Yeats personified Ireland as an old beggar-woman transformed into a radiant young beauty when she finds a man who is prepared to die for her. Twenty years later, SIR JOHN LAVERY (1856–1941) painted a romantic picture of Cathleen ● *107*, lending her the features of his wife, Hazel, who was born in Chicago. The idea of using an American beauty to personify Ireland was rather controversial: however, it was given the official stamp of approval when she appeared on the bank notes of the Free State.

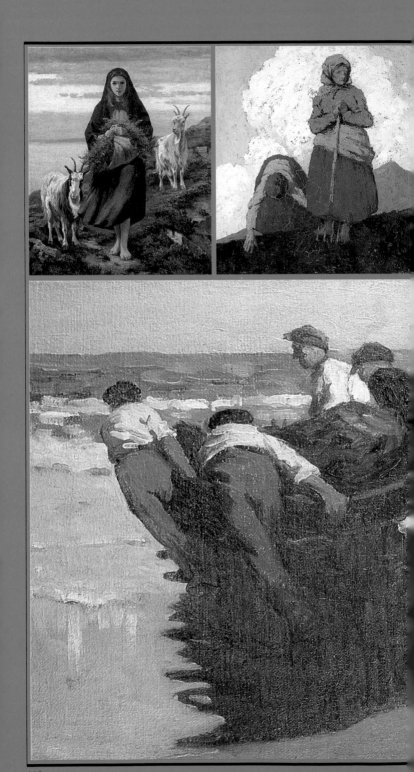

> **"ANYONE WHO HAS NOT LIVED FOR WEEKS AMONG THESE GREY CLOUDS AND WATERS CANNOT UNDERSTAND MY DELIGHT IN LAYING EYES ON THE RED GARMENTS WORN BY THE WOMEN."**
>
> J. M. SYNGE

William Butler Yeats was fond of declaring that an artist's work must have a homeland. In painting *A Connemara Girl* (**1**), AUGUSTUS BURKE (1849–91) had, in his way, anticipated this belief. Possibly influenced by French painting, which throughout the 19th century had developed a rural theme (in the work of painters as different and as ill-matched as Rosa Bonheur, Jules Breton, Jules Sébastien-Lepage and above all Jean-François Millet and Camille Pissarro), Burke depicted the innocent beauty of a young girl with her goats, set against the backdrop of a sunset and a tranquil ocean. A vision? This painting shares similarities with the work of Puvis de Chavannes. The work of PAUL HENRY (1876–1958) evokes a completely different mood. Painting at the same time as Jack Butler Yeats, he devoted several sets of canvases to daily life in the west: *Launching the Currach* (**4**), *The Potato Pickers* (**2**), and *Connemara Landscape* (**3**) create strong, simple images. Too simple, in the eyes of his critics.

1	2	3
4		

JACK·B·YEATS

One might be tempted to say of Jack Butler Yeats (1871–1957), son of John, the portrait painter (1839–1922), and younger brother of William (1865–1939) ▲ *284*, that he was in an ideal position to depict "Irishness" in art. For Jack, like Synge ▲ *123*, "Irishness" was to be found on the northwest coast. Jack exhibited his drawings of *Life in the West* in 1899 and Synge published *The Aran Islands* in 1907. Portraits of peasants, fishermen, scenes in the grocer's, or in court; pen-and-ink drawings, often enhanced by ~~watercolors.~~ . . . *Life in the West of Ireland* (1912) (**4**) contains a collection of pictures that must have seemed extremely exotic in Belfast or Dublin. In 1913, G.A. Birmingham published *Irishmen All* which Jack illustrated with a dozen or so portraits, executed in oils, of Irish "types"such as the priest, the politician, the publican, the pastor (**3**). The bold outlines of the characters and objects were set in representative landscapes. However, Yeats was not just concerned with producing an eye-witness account of reality. He made many sketches and placed great emphasis on the role of memory and imagination in his creative work. In the 1920's, Yeats' painting style became more flowing, his strokes became broader and the outlines disappeared, as can be seen, for example, in *The Island Funeral* (1923) (**2**). He gradually abandoned subjects taken from the west and focused his attention on Dublin, as can be seen in *The Liffey Swim* (1923) (**1**).

G. Courbet

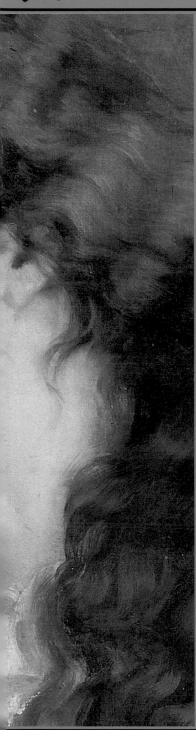

In Trouville, in 1865, GUSTAVE COURBET met Johanna Hefferman, mistress of the Anglo-American painter, James Abbott McNeill Whistler, who had painted her in 1863 in *The White Girl*, now owned by the National Gallery of Art in Washington. *La Belle Irlandaise* (**1**, **2** detail) was given various titles: *Portrait de Jo, Femme irlandaise, Femme d'Irlande*. Ireland comes up every time: the young woman's beauty, like her red hair, whose luxuriance is emphasized by the gesture of her right hand, seems quintessentially "Irish". A woman at the mirror. Vanity? Anxiety? More metaphorically, searching for an identity? Several months later, Courbet painted his scandalous *Sommeil*: two naked women, intertwined. One woman is a brunette, the other a redhead. The "beautiful Irishwoman" again shows her face.

LUCIAN FREUD (born in 1922) is one of the leading names of London's art world. Herbert Read, the historian and art critic, has summed up this artist as being steadfastly representational, "the Ingres of Existentialism": a description that encapsulates both the artist's technical mastery and the atmosphere of anxiety exuded by his works. In *Two Irishmen* (**3**), two men strike a pose. Although this composition has an apparent solidity, it still knocks us off-balance: the man sitting down is painted from above, while the man standing up seems to be viewed from below, creating an off-center effect. One of them is looking straight at us, the other is not. An almost photographic view of the city can be seen through the window. Energy, melancholy, solitude. Terseness is also one of the characteristic features of Lucian Freud's art.

LOUIS LE BROCQUY (born in Dublin in 1926) has won international acclaim after several decades of unflagging work on a sequence of portraits of legendary Irish writers, including William Butler Yeats, James Joyce (above) and Samuel Beckett. An aggrieved contingent will protest that Irish painting is still taking a back seat to its literature. What is undeniable is that Le Brocquy's "surreal" portraits stay with the observer. The art critic Richard Kearney has rightly called attention to the "insomniac" quality of this painting. And the poet John Montague has contributed the observation that, in its hypnotic whiteness, the canvas becomes a modern "Saint Veronica's veil". It is no longer a portrait, it has become an apparition.

IRELAND
AS SEEN BY WRITERS

HISTORY

THE TUATHA DE DANAAN

There is a rich tradition of storytelling amongst the Celtic peoples of Ireland. Many have never been written down but are passed from generation to generation by word of mouth in the long, dark winter nights.

❝Long ago the Tuatha De Danaan came to Ireland in a great fleet of ships to take the land from the Fir Bolgs who lived there. These newcomers were the People of the Goddess Danu and their men of learning possessed great powers and were revered as if they were gods. They were accomplished in the various arts of druidry, namely magic, prophecy and occult lore. They had learnt their druidic skills in Falias, Gorias, Findias and Murias, the four cities of the northern islands.

When they reached Ireland and landed on the western shore, they set fire to their boats so that there would be no turning back. The smoke from the burning boats darkened the sun and filled the land for three days, and the Fir Bolgs thought the Tuatha De Danaan had arrived in a magic mist.

The invaders brought with them the four great treasures of their tribe. From Falias they brought Lia Fail, the Stone of Destiny. They brought it to Tara and it screamed when a rightful king of Ireland sat on it. From Gorias they brought Lugh's spear. Anyone who held it was invincible in battle. From Findias they brought Nuada's irresistible sword. No one could escape it once it was unsheathed. From Murias they brought the Dagda's cauldron. No one ever left it hungry.

Nuada was the king of the Tuatha De Danaan and he led them against the Fir Bolgs. They fought a fierce battle on the Plain of Moytura, the first one the Tuatha De Danaan fought in a place of that name. Thousands of the Fir Bolgs were killed, a hundred thousand in all, and among them their king, Eochai Mac Erc. Many of the Tuatha De Danaan died too, and their king, Nuada, had his arm severed from his body in the fight.

In the end the Tuatha De Danaan overcame the Fir Bolgs and routed them until only a handful of them survived. These survivors boarded their ships and set sail to the far-scattered islands around Ireland.

When the Fir Bolgs had fled, the Tuatha De Danaan took over the country and went with their treasures to Tara to establish themselves as masters of the island.❞

MARIE HEANEY, *OVER NINE WAVES*
A BOOK OF IRISH LEGENDS,
PUB. FABER AND FABER, LONDON AND BOSTON, 1994

ON THE IRISH

Strabo (c. 63 BC–after AD 21), the Greek geographer, historian and philosopher, never actually visited Britain but gleaned his information from the writings of Caesar.

❝Besides some small islands round about Britain, there is also a large island, Ierne, which stretches parallel to Britain on the north, its breadth being greater than its length. Concerning this island I have

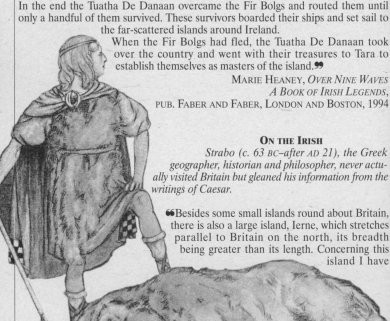

nothing certain to tell, except that its inhabitants are more savage than the Britons, since they are man-eaters as well as heavy eaters, and since, further, they count it an honourable thing, when their fathers die, to devour them, and openly to have intercourse, not only with the other women, but also with their mothers and sisters; but I am saying this only with the understanding that I have no trustworthy witnesses for it; and yet, as for the matter of man-eating, that is said to be a custom of the Scythians also, and in cases of necessity forced by sieges, the Celti, the Iberians, and several other peoples are said to have practised it.**

STRABO, *GEOGRAPHY*, TRANS. H.L. JONES,
LONDON AND NEW YORK, 1930

THE IRISH DIET

English traveler Fynes Moryson (1526–1617) was horrified by the standard of food he encountered.

Touching the Irish dyet, Some Lords and Knights, and Gentlemen of the English-Irish, and all the English there abiding, having competent meanes, use the English dyet, but some more, some lesse cleanly, few or none curiously, and no doubt they have as great and for their part greater plenty then the English, of flesh, fowle, fish, and all things for food, if they will use like Art of Cookery. Alwaies I except the Fruits, Venison, and some dainties proper to England, and rare in Ireland. And we must conceive, that Venison and Fowle seeme to be more plentiful in Ireland, because they neither so generally affect dainty foode, nor so diligently search it as the English do. Many of the English-Irish, have by little and little been infected with the Irish filthinesse, and that in the very cities, excepting Dublyn, and some of the better sort in Waterford, where the English continually lodging in their houses, they more retaine the English diet. The English-Irish after our manner serve to the table joynts of flesh cut after our fashion, with Geese, Pullets, Pigges and like rosted meats, but their ordinary food for the common sort is of Whitmeates, and they eate cakes of oates for bread, and drinke not English Beere made of Mault and Hops, but Ale. At Corck I have seene with these eyes, young maides starke naked grinding of Corne with certaine stones to make cakes thereof, and striking of into the tub of meale, such reliques thereof as stuck on their belly, thighes and more unseemely parts. And for the cheese or butter commonly made by the English Irish, an English man would not touch it with his lippes, though hee were halfe starved; yet many English inhabitants make very good of both kindes. In Cities they have such bread as ours, but of a sharpe savour, and some mingled with Annisseeds, and baked like cakes, and that onely in the houses of the better sort.

FYNES MORYSON, *AN ITINERARY, VOLUME III*,
PUB. JAMES MACLEHOSE AND SONS, GLASGOW, 1908

A WELL-EATEN CHILD IS BETTER THAN TWO UNDERFED

Born in Ireland of English parents, Jonathan Swift (1667–1745) departed for England following his ordination. Forced to return to Ireland in search of a better situation he finally accepted a position at St Patrick's Cathedral, Dublin. Forerunner of Joyce for his love of words and creative use of the English language, Swift is one of the great satirists. His novel "Gulliver's Travels" was published in 1726. The administration of Ireland by the English provided a perfect target and in the following extract Swift offers blackly ironic solutions to the problems of poverty and overpopulation in Ireland following the famine.

**I have been assured by a very knowing American of my acquaintance in London, that a young healthy Child well Nursed is at a year Old a most delicious nourishing and wholesome Food, whether Stewed, Roasted, Baked, or Boiled; and I make no doubt that it will equally serve in a Fricasie, or a Ragoust.

I do therefore humbly offer it to publick consideration, that of the Hundred and twenty thousand Children, already computed, twenty thousand may be reserved for

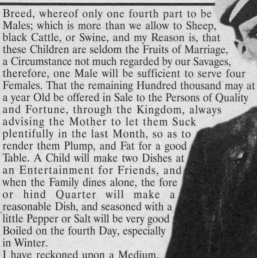

Breed, whereof only one fourth part to be Males; which is more than we allow to Sheep, black Cattle, or Swine, and my Reason is, that these Children are seldom the Fruits of Marriage, a Circumstance not much regarded by our Savages, therefore, one Male will be sufficient to serve four Females. That the remaining Hundred thousand may at a year Old be offered in Sale to the Persons of Quality and Fortune, through the Kingdom, always advising the Mother to let them Suck plentifully in the last Month, so as to render them Plump, and Fat for a good Table. A Child will make two Dishes at an Entertainment for Friends, and when the Family dines alone, the fore or hind Quarter will make a reasonable Dish, and seasoned with a little Pepper or Salt will be very good Boiled on the fourth Day, especially in Winter.

I have reckoned upon a Medium, that a Child just born will weigh 12 pounds, and in a solar Year, if tolerably nursed, encreaseth to 28 Pounds.

I grant this food will be somewhat dear, and therefore very proper for Landlords, who, as they have already devoured most of the Parents seem to have the best Title to the Children. **99**

JONATHAN SWIFT, *SATIRES AND PERSONAL WRITINGS*, PUB. OXFORD UNIVERSITY PRESS, LONDON, 1958

JAMES JOYCE'S IRELAND

A GENTLE APOCALYPSE

James Joyce (1882–1941) is one of the most important writers of our times. He revolutionized the form and structure of the novel and pushed language to extreme limits. Although he left Dublin in 1902, only returning sporadically thereafter, Ireland remained his major inspiration. "Dubliners" is a collection of short stories which did not appear until 1914 because the publishers were worried about potential libel actions. "Ulysses", first published in 1922, was immediately hailed as a work of genius.

66A few light taps upon the pane made him turn to the window. It had begun to snow again. He watched sleepily the flakes, silver and dark, falling obliquely against the lamplight. The time had come for him to set out on his journey westward. Yes, the newspapers were right: snow was general all over Ireland. It was falling on every part of the dark central plain, on the treeless hills, falling softly upon the Bog of Allen and, farther westward, softly falling into the dark mutinous Shannon waves. It was falling, too, upon every part of the lonely churchyard on the hill where Michael Furey lay buried. It lay thickly drifted on the crooked crosses and headstones, on the spears of the little gate, on the barren thorns. His soul swooned slowly as he heard the snow falling faintly through the universe and faintly falling, like the descent of their last end, upon all the living and the dead.**"**

JAMES JOYCE, DUBLINERS,
PUB. ALFRED A. KNOPF INC.,
NEW YORK, 1991

"I was thinking of so many things he didnt know of Mulvey and Mr Stanhope and Hester and father and old captain Groves and the sailors playing all birds fly and I say stoop and washing up dishes they called it on the pier and the sentry in front of the governors house with the thing round his white helmet poor devil half roasted and the Spanish girls laughing in their shawls and their tall combs and the auctions in the morning the Greeks and the jews and the Arabs and the devil knows who else from all the ends of Europe and Duke street and the fowl market all clucking outside Larby Sharons and the poor donkeys slipping half asleep and the vague fellows in the cloaks asleep in the shade on the steps and the big wheels of the carts of the bulls and the old cattle thousands of years old yes and those handsome Moors all in white and turbans like kings asking you to sit down in their little bit of a shop and Ronda with the old windows of the posadas glancing eyes a lattice hid for her lover to kiss the iron and the wineshops half open at night and the castanets and the night we missed the boat at Algeciras the watchman going about serene with his lamp and O that awful deepdown torrent O and the sea the sea crimson sometimes like fire and the glorious sunsets and the

figtrees in the Alameda gardens yes and all the queer little streets and pink and blue and yellow houses and the rosegardens and the jessamine and geraniums and cactuses and Gibraltar as a girl where I was a Flower of the mountain yes when I put the rose in my hair like the Andalusian girls used or shall I wear a red yes and how he kissed me under the Moorish wall and I thought well as well him as another and then I asked him with my eyes to ask again yes and then he asked me would I yes to say yes my mountain flower and first I put my arms around his yes and drew him down to me so he could feel my breasts all perfume yes and his heart was going like mad and yes I said yes I will Yes. **"**

JAMES JOYCE, ULYSSES,
PUB. EVERYMAN'S LIBRARY,
LONDON, 1992

IRISH LANDSCAPES

THE LAKE ISLE OF INNISFREE

W.B. Yeats (1865–1939) was born and brought up in Dublin and remained an ardent Irish nationalist throughout his life. He was a senator of the Irish Free State from 1922–8, and in 1923 he was awarded the Nobel Prize for literature.

❝I will arise and go now, and go to Innisfree,
And a small cabin build there, of clay and wattles made:
Nine bean-rows will I have there, a hive for the honey-bee,
And live alone in the bee-loud glade.

And I shall have some peace there, for peace comes dropping slow,
Dropping from the veils of the morning to where the cricket sings;
There midnight's all a glimmer, and noon a purple glow,
And evening full of the linnet's wings.

I will arise and go now, for always night and day
I hear lake water lapping with low sounds by the shore;
While I stand on the roadway, or on the pavements grey,
I hear it in the deep heart's core.❞

W.B. YEATS, "THE LAKE ISLE OF INNISFREE"
FROM "THE ROSE", *THE POEMS*, PUB.
EVERYMAN'S LIBRARY, LONDON 1992

DRUMCLIFF CHURCHYARD

Although he died in the south of France, Yeats' body was brought back to Ireland for burial in Drumcliff. Heinrich Böll (1917–85) visited Ireland during the mid 1950's and went in search of his grave.

❝As the train entered Sligo it was still raining; kisses were exchanged under umbrellas, tears were wept under umbrellas; a taxi driver was asleep over his steering wheel, his head resting on his folded arms; I woke him up; he was one of those pleasant people who wake up with a smile.

'Where to?' he asked.
'To Drumcliff churchyard.'
'But nobody lives there.'
'Maybe,' I said, 'but I'd like to go there.'
'And back?'
'Yes.'
'All right.'
We drove through puddles, empty streets; in the twilight I looked through an open window at a piano; the music looked as if the dust on it must be an inch thick. A barber was standing in his doorway, snipping with his scissors as if he wanted to cut off threads of rain; at the entrance to a movie a girl was putting on fresh lipstick, children with prayer books under their arms ran through the rain, an old woman shouted across the street to an old man: 'Howya, Paddy?' and the old man shouted back: 'I'm all right – with the help of God and His most blessed Mother.'
'Are you quite sure,' the driver asked me, 'you really want to go to Drumcliff churchyard?'
'Quite sure,' I said.
The hills round about were covered with faded ferns like the wet hair of an aging red-haired woman, two grim rocks guarded the entrance to this little bay: 'Benbulbin and Knocknarea,' said the driver, as if he were introducing me to two distant relations he didn't much care about.
'There,' said the driver, pointing to where a church tower reared up in the mist; rooks were flying round the tower, clouds of rooks, and from a distance they looked like black snowflakes. 'I think,' said the driver, 'you must be looking for the old battlefield.'
'No,' I said, 'I've never heard of any battle.'
'In 561,' he began in a guide's mild tone of voice, 'a battle was fought here which was the only one every fought in all the world on account of a copyright.'
I shook my head as I looked at him.
'It's really true,' he said; 'the followers of St. Columba had copied a psalter belonging to St. Finian, and there was a battle between the followers of St. Finian and the followers of St. Columba. Three thousand dead – but the king decided the quarrel; he said: 'As the calf belongs to every cow, so the copy belongs to every book.' You're sure you don't want to see the battlefield?'
'No,' I said, 'I'm looking for a grave.'
'Oh yes,' he said. 'Yeats, that's right – then I expect you want to go to Innisfree too.'
'I don't know yet,' I said; 'wait here, please.'
Rooks flew up from the old gravestones, circled cawing around the old church tower. Yeats' grave was wet, the stone was cold, and the lines which Yeats had had inscribed on his gravestone were as cold as the ice needles that had been shot at me from Swift's tomb: 'Cast a cold eye on life, on death. Horseman, pass by!' I looked up; were the rooks enchanted swans? They cawed mockingly at me, fluttered around the church tower. The ferns lay flat on the surrounding hills, beaten down by the rain, rust-colored and withered. I felt cold.
'Drive on,' I said to the driver.
'On to Innisfree then?' 'No,' I said, 'back to the station.'
Rocks in the mist, the lonely church, encircled by fluttering rooks, and three thousand miles of water beyond Yeats' grave. Not a swan to be seen.**

HEINRICH BÖLL, *IRISH JOURNAL*, TRANS. L VENNEUITZ, PUB. SECKER & WARBURG, McGRAW-HILL BOOK CO., NEW YORK, 1967

THE ARAN ISLANDS

John Millington Synge (1871–1909) went to the Aran Islands following a suggestion by Yeats, in order to write about the peasant lifestyle there. He visited annually from 1898 to 1902 and his book on the islands was first published in 1907.

**The rain has cleared off, and I have had my first real introduction to the island and its people.

I went out through Killeany – the poorest village in Aranmor – to a long neck of sandhill that runs out into the sea towards the south-west. As I lay there on the grass the clouds lifted from the Connemara mountains and, for a moment, the green undulating foreground, backed in the distance by a mass of hills, reminded me of the country near Rome. Then the dun top-sail of a hooker swept above the edge of the sandhill and revealed the presence of the sea.

As I moved on a boy and a man came down from the next village to talk to me, and I found that here, at least, English was imperfectly understood. When I asked them if there were any trees in the island they held a hurried consultation in Gaelic, and then the man asked if 'tree' meant the same thing as 'bush', for if so there were a few in sheltered hollows to the east.

They walked on with me to the sound which separates this island from Inishmaan – the middle island of the group – and showed me the roll from the Atlantic running up between two walls of cliff.

They told me that several men had stayed on Inishmaan to learn Irish, and the boy pointed out a line of hovels where they had lodged, running like a belt of straw round the middle of the island. The place looked hardly fit for habitation. There was no green to be seen, and no sign of the people except these beehive-like roofs, and the outline of a dun that stood out above them against the edge of the sky.

. . . In spite of the charm of my teacher, the old blind man I met the day of my arrival, I have decided to move on to Inishmaan, where Gaelic is more generally used, and the life is perhaps the most primitive that is left in Europe.

I spent all this last day with my blind guide, looking at the antiquities that abound in the west or north-west of the island.

As we set out I noticed among the groups of girls who smiled at our fellowship – old Mourteen says we are like the cuckoo with its pipit – a beautiful oval face with the singularly spiritual expression that is so marked in one type of the West Ireland women. Later in the day, as the old man talked continually of the fairies and women they have taken, it seemed that there was a possible link between the wild mythology that is accepted on the islands and the strange beauty of the women. **99**

J.M. SYNGE, *THE ARAN ISLANDS*,
PUB. MAUNSEL & ROBERTS LTD,
DUBLIN AND LONDON, 1921

RELIGION

IRISH PROTESTANTISM

George Bernard Shaw (1856–1950) was a freethinker, whose unorthodox views mingled with his humor and love of paradox, made him an institution in his lifetime. He wrote over fifty plays and a number of essays and criticisms, and was awarded the Nobel Prize for literature in 1925.

❝I believe Ireland, as far as the Protestant gentry is concerned, to be the most irreligious country in the world. I was christened by my uncle; and as my godfather was intoxicated and did not turn up, the sexton was ordered to promise and vow in his place, precisely as my uncle might have ordered him to put more coals on the vestry fire. I was never confirmed; and I believe my parents never were either. Of the seriousness with which English families took this rite I had no conception; for Irish Protestantism was not then a religion: it was a side in political faction, a class prejudice, a conviction that Roman Catholics are socially inferior persons who will go to hell when they die and leave Heaven in the exclusive possession of Protestant ladies and gentlemen. In my childhood I was sent every Sunday to a Sunday-school where genteel little children repeated texts, and were rewarded with cards inscribed with them. After an hour of this we were marched into the adjoining church (the Molyneux in Upper Leeson Street), to sit round the altar rails and fidget there until our neighbors must have wished the service over as heartily as we did. I suffered this, not for my salvation, but because my father's respectability demanded it. When we went to live in Dalkey we broke with the observance and never resumed it.

What helped to make 'church' a hotbed of all the social vices was that no working folk ever came there. In England the clergy go among the poor, and sometimes do try desperately to get them to come to church. In Ireland the poor are Roman Catholics (Papists my Orange grandfather called them). The Protestant Church has nothing to do with them. I cannot say that in Ireland in my time there all the Protestants were the worse for what they called their religion. I can only answer for those I knew.**❞**

GEORGE BERNARD SHAW, *SIXTEEN SELF SKETCHES*,
CONSTABLE AND COMPANY LTD, LONDON, 1949

A WEDDING AND A FUNERAL

Edna O'Brien was born in Tuamgraney, County Clare, in 1932, and her novels are imbued with a nostalgic and lyrical image of her homeland. Her male characters are often treacherous but the abused heroines retain a warmth and sense of celebration that is intrinsically Irish.

❝There was much speculation about the wedding. No one from the village had been invited but then that was to be expected. Some said that it was to be in a Register Office in Dublin but others said that the bank clerk had assured the Parish Priest that he would be married in a Catholic church, and had guaranteed a huge sum of money in order to get his letter of freedom. It was even said that Miss Amy was going to take instruction so as to be converted but that was only wishful thinking. People were stunned the day the bank clerk suddenly left. He left the bank at lunchtime, after a private talk with the Manager. Miss Amy drove him to the little railway station ten miles away, and they kissed several times before he jumped on to the moving train. The story was that he had gone ahead to make the plans and that the Connor girls and their father would travel shortly after. But the postman who was a Protestant said that the Major would not travel one inch to see his daughter marry a Papist. . . . **99**

66The funeral was to an island on the Shannon. Most of the people stayed on the quay, but we, the family, piled into two rowboats and followed the boat that carried the coffin. It was a jolty ride with big waves coming in over us and our feet getting drenched. The island itself was full of cows. The sudden arrivals made them bawl and race about, and I thought it was quite improper to see that happening, while the remains were being lowered and buried. It was totally desolate, and though my aunt sniffled a bit, and my grandmother let out ejaculations, there was no real grief and that was the saddest thing.

Next day they burned his working clothes and threw his muddy boots on to the manure heap. Then my aunt sewed black diamonds of cloth on her clothes, on my grandmother's and on Joe's. She wrote a long letter to her son in England, and enclosed black diamonds of cloth for him to stitch on to his effects. He worked in Liverpool in a motor car factory. Whenever they said Liverpool I thought of a whole mound of bloodied liver, but then I would look down at my watch and be happy again and pretend to tell the time. The house was gloomy. I went off with Joe who was moving hay and sat with him on the moving machine and fell slightly in love. Indoors was worst, what with my grandmother sighing, and recalling old times, such as when her husband tried to kill her with a carving knife, and then she would snivel and miss him and say 'The poor old creature, he wasn't prepared. . .'**99**

EDNA O'BRIEN, "THE CONNOR GIRLS" AND "MY MOTHER'S MOTHER" FROM *RETURNING*, PUB. PENGUIN BOOKS, LONDON, 1983

THE FEAST OF CORPUS CHRISTI
Born in County Monaghan, Patrick Kavanagh (1905–67) worked as a farmer for several years before he became established as a poet and journalist. His theme is often the discrepancy between the idealized view of the Irish peasant and the reality.

66The Catholic Church of Dargan was a building like a barn – a common rectangle, with a square belfry at the north gable; the church was scaling its mortar rough-casting and its pink wash was almost faded white. The roof span was wide and the roof timbers rotten so that only people with a strong faith in God's goodness-to-His-own would risk sitting in the centre aisle. The centre aisle was always packed, which proved that both faith and piety abided in the parish of Dargan. Standing on a rise in the middle of a weedy graveyard above the village with its shops and new dance hall the

church looked shabby, but God would surely over-look this apparent disrespect in the blaze of the people's devotion. There were faith and piety and all the richness of human character that goes with a deep faith in the Hereafter. Father Daly said first Mass on the Feast of Corpus Christi. The chapel was crowded, for as well as being a Feast day of importance, on which the Faithful were exhorted to receive Holy Communion, this day was also the big summer fair day in the neighbouring town, and many of the congregation had business in the town and by coming to early Mass were able to serve both God and Mammon. The doors and windows were open, but still the place was stuffy with that morning closeness which comes before people are acclimatised to summer. Outside the door a group of men stood whispering while the less solemn parts of the Mass were being said. These men stared about them at the rolling country of little hills and commented on the crops, the weather, the tombstones or whatever came into their dreaming minds.

'Very weedy piece of spuds, them of Mick Finnegan's.'

'He doesn't put on the dung, Larry: the man that doesn't drive on the dung won't take out a crop.' A pause, 'nothing like the dung.' **99**

PATRICK KAVANAGH, *TARRY FLYNN*, PUB. THE PILOT PRESS LTD, LONDON, 1948

IRISH CHARACTERS

FAMILY
John McGahern was born in Dublin in 1934 and brought up in the west of Ireland.

66 I came by train at the same time in July as I'd come every summer, the excitement I'd always felt tainted with melancholy that it'd probably be the last summer I would come. . . . All the meadows had been cut and saved, the bales stacked in groups of five or six and roofed with green grass. The Big Meadow beyond the beeches was completely clean, the bales having been taken in. Though I had come intending to make it my last summer at the hay, I now felt a keen outrage that it had been ended without me. Rose and my father were nowhere to be seen.

'What happened?' I asked when I found them at last, weeding the potato ridge one side of the orchard.

'The winter feeding got too much for us,' my father said. 'We decided to let the meadows. Gillespie took them. He cut early – two weeks ago.'

'Why didn't you tell me?'

My father and Rose exchanged looks, and my father spoke as if he was delivering a prepared statement.

'We didn't like to. And anyhow we thought you'd want to come, hay or no hay. It's more normal to come for a rest instead of just to kill yourself at the old hay. And indeed there's plenty else for you to do if you have a mind to do it. I've taken up the garden again myself.'

'Anyhow, I've brought these,' I handed Rose the box of chocolates and bottle of scent, and gave my father the watch.

'What's this for?' He had always disliked receiving presents.

'It's the watch I told you I'd get in place of the old watch.'

'I don't need a watch.'

'I got it anyhow. What do you think of it?'

'It's ugly,' he said, turning it over. . . .

I went idly toward the orchard, and as I passed the tar barrel I saw a thin fishing line hanging from a part of the low yew branch down into the barrel. I heard the

127

ticking even before the wrist watch came up tied to the end of the line. What shocked me was that I felt neither surprise nor shock.

I felt the bag that we'd left to steep earlier in the water. The blue stone had all melted down. It was a barrel of pure poison, ready for spraying.

I listened to the ticking of the watch on the end of the line in silence before letting it drop back into the barrel. The poison had already eaten into the casing of the watch. The shining rim and back were no longer smooth. It could hardly run much past morning.**

JOHN MCGAHERN, "THE GOLD WATCH"
FROM *HIGH GROUND*, PUB. FABER AND
FABER LTD, LONDON, 1985

MRS FITZGERALD

Virginia Woolf (1882–1941) stayed at the Dunraven Arms Hotel in Adare on May 3, 1934, and she described the character of the landlady in her diary, as follows:

**I wd like to describe the perfection of Irish conversation, which was Mrs FitzGerald's last night. She is exactly the great French lady – only living in a black jersey on an Irish bog. After dinner she came in, ostensibly to lend us a paper & offer advice, in fact to indulge her genius for talk. She talked till 11, & wd. willingly be talking now: about hotel keeping, about frigidaires, about her grandmother sitting on a chair in the kitchen & saying Thats done that wants another 2 minutes & so on, never stirring herself but somehow getting it done. We have the name of being good housekeepers. Then on about bogs, she has bought several fragments because now there may be money in it. However I can give no notion of the glowing, yet formed sentences, the richness & ease of the language; the lay out, dexterity & adroitness of the arrangement. There was the story of old Julia the cook, who had gone off home in a huff jealous of the young maids; had her daughter & the London husband on her, bought them gramophone records, & now wont own that she has wasted her savings. Mrs F. is one of those bluntnosed parted haired Irishwomen with luminous brown eyes & something sardonic and secretive in her expression. Talk is to her an intoxicant, but there is as Mr Rowlands said, something heartless about the I[Irish]: quite cold indifferent sarcastic, for all their melody, their fluency, their adorable ease & forthcomingness. She was very much on the spot, accurate, managing, shrewd, hard headed, analytic. Why arent these people the greatest novelists in the world? – with this facility, this balance, this fundamental . . . But why isn't Mrs F. a great novelist? Certainly the salon survives at Glenbeith, the lust for talk, & finishing one's sentence – only with complete naturalness. For instance, explaining the bogs, 'saturated, now whats the opposite word?' Dessiccated, L. suggested, & she adopted it with pleasure. She said one could never understand the Irish: one had to live as they did. They sit in their cottage talking about politics: they dont dance much; they have no amusements. They at once started to poach on her bog merely because she had bought it – otherwise it had been let alone for centuries. The bogs are full of trees, cant be self planted, so orderly, but now who has planted them? And they burn in a resinous way – go up – puf! – in a flash, like petrol. Suddenly she became severe and thought me a fool 'What does this good lady mean?' Her grandmother was an innkeeper; she herself went away for 25 years; Oh, as my grandmother said, one becomes able to read peoples characters before they step over the door, & ones never wrong one way or the other. Her quickness was amazing. This morning the talk began & L. very slightly put out his hand. ' Oh I know that means you wanting to be off' – & so

we parted from the last representative of the French salon of the 18th Century, this strange mixture of county lady, peasant, & landlady.**

The Diary of Virginia Woolf, Volume Four 1931–1935, ed. Anne Olivier Bell, assisted by Andrew McNeillie, pub. Harcourt Brace Jovanovich, New York and London, 1982

MOTHER

Brian Friel, playwright and short-story writer, here has one of his characters, Eamon, describing their mother.

She was an actress. Did you know that? No, you didn't – that little detail was absorbed into the great silence. Yes; travelling round the country with the Charles Doran Company. Spotted by the judge in the lounge of the Railway Hotel and within five days decently wed and ensconced in the Hall here and bugger poor aul' Charles Doran who had to face the rest of rural Ireland without a Colleen Bawn! And a raving beauty by all accounts. No sooner did Yeats clap eyes on her than a sonnet burst from him – 'That I may know the beauty of that form' – Alice'll rattle it off for you there. Oh terrific stuff. And O'Casey – haven't they told you that one? – poor O'Casey out here one day ploughterin' after tennis balls and spoutin' about the workin'-man when she appeared in the doorway in there and the poor creatur' made such a ramstam to get to her that he tripped over the Pope or Plato or Shirley Temple or somebody an smashed his bloody glasses! The more you think of it – all those calamities – Chesterton's ribs, Hopkins's hand, O'Casey's aul' specs – the County Council should put up a sign outside that room – Accident Black Spot – shouldn't they? Between ourselves, it's a very dangerous house, Professor.

Brian Friel, *Aristocrats*, pub. Gallery Press, 1983

JARS OF PORTER

Brian O'Nolan (1911–66), alias Flann O'Brien, worked for the Irish civil service in Dublin. "At Swim-Two-Birds", his first novel, published in 1939, mixes Irish folklore and farce with a realistic portrayal of lower-middle-class life.

**It was only a few months before composing the foregoing that I had my first experience of intoxicating beverages and their strange intestinal chemistry. I was walking through the Stephen's Green on a summer evening and conducting a conversation with a man called Kelly, then a student, hitherto a member of the farming class and now a private in the armed forces of the King. He was addicted to unclean expressions in ordinary conversation and spat continually, always fouling the flowerbeds on his way through the Green with a mucous deposit dislodged with a low grunting from the interior of his windpipe. In some respects he was a coarse man but he was lacking in malice or ill-humour. He purported to be a medical student but he had failed at least once to satisfy a body of examiners charged with regulating admission to the faculty. He suggested that we should drink a number of *jars* or pints of plain porter in Grogan's public house. I derived considerable

pleasure from the casual quality of his suggestion and observed that it would probably do us no harm, thus expressing my whole-hearted concurrence by a figure of speech.

Name of figure of speech: Litotes (or Meiosis).

He turned to me with a facetious wry expression and showed me a penny and a sixpence in his rough hand.

I'm thirsty, he said. I have sevenpence. Therefore I buy a pint.

I immediately recognized this as an intimation that I should pay for my own porter. The conclusion of your syllogism, I said lightly, is fallacious, being based on licensed premises.❞

Flann O'Brien, *At Swim-Two-Birds*,
pub. MacGibbon & Kee, London, 1966

The thinking Irish

Brendan Behan (1923–64) is the controversial, nationalist enfant terrible of Irish literature. He was arrested in 1939 for his involvement with the IRA and describes his period in Borstal in "Borstal Boy" (1958). In the following speech, his character, Cronin, condemns English and American prejudice against the Irish.

❝My wife tries to cheer me up by saying that girls like me – that she loves me. But then she is my wife. I mean, I don't mean that she just loves me because a wife is supposed to love her husband. Ah no! My wife is a very, very, exceptional person, and she is very kind to everyone, and particularly to me.

But I'll tell you something for nothing. There's a lot of nonsense given out by the English and Americans about our attitude to women. They say it just to flatter themselves. Some old Jesuit in America attacks the Irish for not screwing early and often enough. A hundred years ago screwing and having kids was out of fashion and Paddy was being lambasted because he got married too soon, and had too many kids. It's like saying all Jews are capitalists because Rothschild is a capitalist, and all Jews are Reds because Karl Marx was a Jew – if they don't get you one way they get you another. If they don't get you by the beard they get you by the balls.

The English and Americans dislike only *some* Irish – the same Irish that the Irish themselves detest, Irish writers – the ones that *think*. But then they hate their own people who think. I just like to think, and in this city I'm hated and despised. They give me beer, because I can say things that I remember from my thoughts – not everything, because, by Jesus, they'd crucify you, and you have to remember that when you're drunk, but some things, enough to flatter them.❞

Brendan Behan, *Richard's Cork Leg*,
pub. Eyre Methuen, London, 1973

Grieving women

The plays of Sean O'Casey (1880–1964) deal with the dangers of Irish nationalism. When "The Plough and the Stars" was performed at the Abbey Theatre in 1926, it provoked riots. In the following speech from "Juno and the Paycock", his character has just heard of the shooting of her Republican son Johnny.

&&Me home is gone now; he was me only child, an' to think that he was lyin' for a whole night stretched out on the side of a lonely counthry lane, with his head, his darlin' head, that I ofen kissed an' fondled, half hidden in the wather of a runnin' brook. An' I'm told he was the leadher of the ambush where me nex' door neighbour, Mrs. Mannin', lost her Free State soldier son. An' now here's the two of us oul' women, standin' one on each side of a scales o' sorra, balanced be the bodies of our two dead darlin' sons. (*Mrs. Madigan returns, and wraps a shawl around her.*) God bless you, Mrs. Madigan . . . . (*She moves slowly towards the door*) Mother o' God, Mother o' God, have pity on the pair of us! . . . O Blessed Virgin, where were you when me darlin' son was riddled with bullets, when me darlin' son was riddled with bullets! . . . Sacred Heart of the Crucified Jesus, take away our hearts o' stone . . . an' give us hearts o' flesh! . . . take away this murdherin' hate . . . an' give us Thine own eternal love!&&

SEAN O'CASEY, *JUNO AND THE PAYCOCK*,
PUB. MACMILLAN LONDON LTD, LONDON, 1972

THE STRAND AT LOUGH BEG
Seamus Heaney was born in County Derry in 1939. His poems combine a strong physical sense of the environment with wider social and political concerns.

&&Leaving the white glow of filling stations
And a few lonely streetlamps among fields
You climbed the hills towards Newtownhamilton
Past the Fews Forest, out beneath the stars –
Along that road, a high, bare pilgrim's track
Where Sweeney fled before the bloodied heads,
Goat-beards and dogs' eyes in a demon pack
Blazing out of the ground, snapping and squealing.
What blazed ahead of you? A faked road block?
The red lamp swung, the sudden brakes and stalling
Engine, voices, heads hooded and the cold-nosed gun?
Or in your driving mirror, tailing headlights
That pulled out suddenly and flagged you down
Where you weren't known and far from what you knew:
The lowland clays and waters of Lough Beg,
Church Island's spire, its soft treeline of yew.&&

SEAMUS HEANEY, "THE STRAND AT LOUGH BEG" FROM *FIELD WORK*,
PUB. FABER AND FABER LTD, LONDON AND BOSTON, 1979

FIRST LOVE
Samuel Beckett (1906–89) was born at Foxrock, near Dublin, but spent most of his life in France. His plays and novels feature a distinctive, despairing tone with sharp use of black humor, and his work was enormously influential on English theater in particular.

&&I met her on a bench, on the bank of the canal, one of the canals, for our town boasts two, though I never knew which was which. It was a well situated bench, backed by a mound of solid earth and garbage, so that my rear was covered. My flanks too, partially thanks to a pair of venerable trees, more than venerable, dead, at either end of the bench. It was no doubt these trees one fine day, aripple with all

131

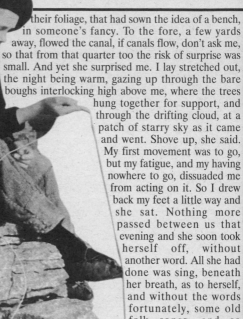

their foliage, that had sown the idea of a bench, in someone's fancy. To the fore, a few yards away, flowed the canal, if canals flow, don't ask me, so that from that quarter too the risk of surprise was small. And yet she surprised me. I lay stretched out, the night being warm, gazing up through the bare boughs interlocking high above me, where the trees hung together for support, and through the drifting cloud, at a patch of starry sky as it came and went. Shove up, she said. My first movement was to go, but my fatigue, and my having nowhere to go, dissuaded me from acting on it. So I drew back my feet a little way and she sat. Nothing more passed between us that evening and she soon took herself off, without another word. All she had done was sing, beneath her breath, as to herself, and without the words fortunately, some old folk songs, and so disjointedly, skipping from one to another and finishing none, that even I found it strange. The voice, though out of tune, was not unpleasant. It breathed of a soul too soon wearied ever to conclude, that perhaps least arse-aching soul of all. The bench itself was soon more than she could bear and as for me, one look had been enough for her. Whereas in reality she was a most tenacious woman. She came back the next day and the day after and all went off more or less as before. Perhaps a few words were exchanged. The next day it was raining and I felt in security. Wrong again. I asked her if she was resolved to disturb me every evening. I disturb you? she said. I felt her eyes on me. They can't have seen much, two eyelids at the most, with a hint of nose and brow, darkly, because of the dark. I thought we were easy, she said. You disturb me, I said, I can't stretch out with you there. The collar of my coat was over my mouth and yet she heard me. Must you stretch out? she said. The mistake one makes is to speak to people.**99**

SAMUEL BECKETT, FIRST LOVE, PUB. CALDER & BOYARS,
LONDON AND NEW YORK, 1973

RUNNING AWAY

The novels of Roddy Doyle (b. 1958) are set in contemporary Dublin.

66I got my atlas out of my bag. We hadn't used it much, only for learning the counties of Ireland so far. Offaly was the easiest one to remember because it was the hardest. Dublin was okay just as long as you didn't mix it up with Louth. With Fermanagh and Tyrone it was hard to remember which was which. I stared at the map of Ireland from the top to the bottom. There was nowhere I wanted to run away to, except maybe some of the islands. I was still going to do it though. You couldn't run away to an island; you had to sail or swim part of the the way. It wasn't like a game though; there were no rules you had to stick to. An uncle of mine had run away to Australia. I opened the map of the world in the middle of the atlas. There were places right in the middle that I couldn't read properly because the pages wouldn't flatten fully for me.

There were plenty of other places though.

I was serious. **99**

RODDY DOYLE, *PADDY CLARKE HA HA HA*, PUB. SECKER & WARBURG, LONDON, 1993

A JOURNEY
AROUND IRELAND

▲ A restaurant in Galway.   ▼ Greengrocer's in Athlone (Co. Westmeath).

▼ Housefront, Mallow (Co. Cork).

▲ Coffeeshop in Kilkenny.

▼ Butcher's shop in Galway.

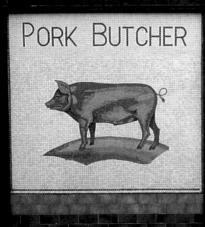

▼ *Dan Foley's* pub, Annascaul (Co. Kerry).

▲ Countryside, Co. Cork.   ▼ Traditional turf cutting.

▼ Connemara Lough (Co. Galway).

▲ Tower house, Castlecove (Co. Kerry).   ▼ Roundstone in the heart of Connemara (Co. Galway

▼ Wicklow Mountains (Co. Wicklow).

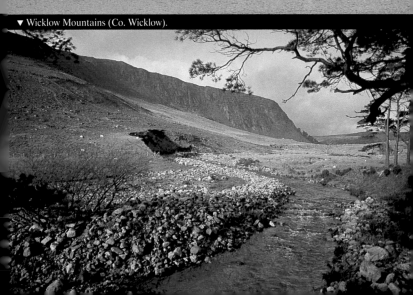

▲ Giant's Causeway (Co. Antrim).

▼ Glens of Antrim (Co. Antrim).

▼ Antrim Coast (Co. Antrim).

LEINSTER

▲ LEINSTER

DUBLIN-WEXFORD ▲ 176
1 DUBLIN ▲ 142
2 POWERSCOURT
3 WICKLOW MOUNTAINS
4 GLENDALOUGH
5 WICKLOW
6 ENNISCORTHY
7 WEXFORD
8 ROSSLARE HARBOUR
9 JOHNSTOWN CASTLE
DUBLIN-WATERFORD ▲ 182
10 KILDARE
11 RUSSBOROUGH HOUSE
12 CARLOW
13 KILKENNY
14 JERPOINT ABBEY
15 NEW ROSS

DUBLIN

▲ LEINSTER
DUBLIN – HISTORY

1 PHOENIX PARK 2 HEUSTON STATION 3 GUINNESS BREWERY 4 FOUR COURTS 5 CHRIST CHURCH 6 ST. PATRICK'S CATHEDRAL 7 DUBLIN CASTLE 8 PARNELL SQUARE

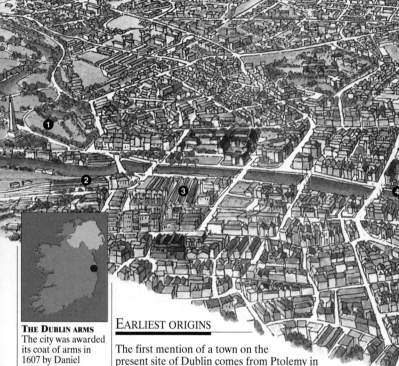

THE DUBLIN ARMS
The city was awarded
its coat of arms in
1607 by Daniel
Molyneux, Ulster
King of Arms and
principal herald of
all Ireland. The shield
is decorated with
three castles, symbol
of the city since the
Middle Ages, and
held on either side
by female figures
(Law on the left and
Justice on the right).
The flowers beneath
their feet symbolize
hope and joy. The
arms bear the motto
*Obedientia Civium
Urbis Felicitas*
("Happy the city
whose citizens
obey"). A modified
version of the
Lord Mayor's
arms, including
the sword and
mace used for
official
ceremonies,
appears on many
Dublin street
lamps.

EARLIEST ORIGINS

The first mention of a town on the
present site of Dublin comes from Ptolemy in
the year 140, who knew of it as Eblana. It is generally
accepted, however, that today's city has its origins in the small
Viking encampment established on the spot in 841. The tiny
village from which Dublin has developed was set overlooking
a lake, near the confluence of the Liffey and Poddle rivers,
and the dark turf-colored waters gave the town its present
name (derived from the Gaelic *dubh linn*, or "black water").

ANGLO-NORMAN INVASION

In 1170 the Vikings relinquished control of the city. Dublin
was besieged by Dermot MacMurrough, King of Leinster, and
Richard FitzGilbert de Clare, Earl of Pembroke, known as
"Strongbow" ● *49*. Henry II confirmed his claim to
sovereignty, and for the next 750 years Dublin was to remain
under British rule, with the castle ▲ *167* as the seat of power
and symbol of the crown.

UNDER THE STUARTS

Dublin bloomed under
Stuart rule, following the
Restoration. The Protestant
aristocracy began a
successful development of
the city's industries, and
many ambitious building
projects were launched.

OBEDIENTIA·CIVIUM·URBIS·FELICITAS

RECENT HISTORY

The 18th century was Dublin's Golden Age. The *Ascendancy* ● *52* was at its height. English architect James Gandon designed many Georgian buildings and the city's elegant squares appeared. After the Act of Union ● *52* Dublin went into decline, although a century later it revived to become the center of a growing Nationalist movement and a literary renaissance ● *67*, which encouraged the awakening of consciousness to the idea of an independent nation. At the end of the Civil War ● *63* came the historic moment when

"Fort of the Dane, Garrison of the Saxon, Augustan capital Of a Gaelic nation, Appropriating all The alien brought."
Louis MacNeice

Dublin, seen from Phoenix Park.

143

Dublin is capital of the Irish Republic and accounts for one third of its entire population. The city is prosperous, unpretentious and young in spirit. Pubs proliferate: there are said to be more than six hundred, including some frequented by James Joyce (and his heroes), as well as other eminent literary figures ◆ *347*. The city is divided in two by the dark waters of the River Liffey. On the north side lay the ancient city, while to the south the charitable institutions, the barracks and the prisons were found. Along the banks of the river stand the impressive buildings of James Gandon.

THE O'CONNELL STREET MONUMENTS The wide street contains many statues. Along with O'Connell himself there are also monuments to William Smith O'Brien (1804–64), leader of the Young Ireland movement ● *58*, the trade unionist James Larkin (1876–1947) ● *53*, and Father Matthew, 19th-century advocate of the temperance movement. Further on stands the astonishing statue of Anna Livia, Joyce's personification of the Liffey, known to Dubliners themselves as "the Floozie in the Jacuzzi" because of the foaming fountain that pours over her. She was erected in 1988 on the site of the Nelson Pillar that was blown up in 1966. At the far end of the street is the monument dedicated to Charles Stewart Parnell (1846–91), upon which are carved his unforgettable words "No man has a right to fix the boundary to the march of a nation."

CUSTOM HOUSE

The building was designed by James Gandon. It is a masterpiece of Georgian design (1781–91), extending 375 feet alongside the Liffey, not far from Butt Bridge and in the shadow of the metal railway bridge. The attic storey of Custom House is adorned with a number of statues based on allegorical themes (such as Navigation, Industry, and Wealth), while the copper dome is crowned with a statue of Commerce. The building was set on fire by Republicans in 1921 ● *62*, but has since been restored to its original splendor. Today it houses government offices.

ABBEY THEATRE. W.B. Yeats ● *122* and Lady Gregory ▲ *247* wanted to create an Irish national theater and in 1904 they founded the Abbey. Not all new works went down well: in 1907 the public gave a poor reception to the premiere of Synge's *Playboy of the Western World*, shocked by its realism and anti-heroic attitude. In 1951 the theater went up in flames. It was not rebuilt until the 1960's.

O'CONNELL STREET

O'CONNELL BRIDGE. The bridge was rebuilt in 1880 and is unusual in being almost as wide as it is long. When it was first erected, between 1794 and 1798, it made O'Connell Street (first named Gardiner Mall, then Sackville Street) the most important street in Dublin.

Dublin's tribute to her errant son seems to stand guard at the entrance to Earl Street North as it crosses O'Connell Street.

O'CONNELL STREET. A STATUE OF DANIEL O'CONNELL stands at the entrance to the street, work of sculptor John Henry Foley and unveiled at the reopening of the bridge in 1882. Erin (Ireland) is handing O'Connell a copy of the 1829 Act of Emancipation. The four winged Victories (some with clearly visible bullet holes from the 1916 Rising) symbolize Courage, Fidelity, Eloquence and Patriotism, the virtues attributed to O'Connell "the Liberator". Further up the street is the GENERAL POST OFFICE (G.P.O.), the last major public building to be constructed by Francis Johnston, completed in 1818. During the Easter Rising of 1916 ● *60*, the G.P.O. was used as the rebel headquarters and was seriously damaged, although the Ionic portico remained intact. Inside is a statue dedicated to the victims of 1916 depicting the death of Cú Chulainn, hero of Irish legend. On the base is the text of the Proclamation of the Irish Republic ● *54*, first read from the steps outside. Not far from the G.P.O. is ST MARY'S PRO CATHEDRAL (1815, John Sweetman), a Greco-Doric structure.

PARNELL SQUARE

Parnell Square, originally named Rutland Square, lies at the elegant former heart of Dublin; the city center later moved south of the river. In the middle of the square is the Garden of Remembrance, dedicated to all those who gave their lives in the struggle for Irish independence ● *54*.

ROTUNDA HOSPITAL. The first maternity hospital in the entire British Isles was created through the generosity and determination of Doctor Mosse, who was distressed by the conditions in which poor women had to give birth in Dublin. The hospital was ready for its first patients only five years after works began in 1752. The ROTUNDA ROOM, from which the hospital took its name, dates from 1764. The PILLAR ROOM, which was once a sumptuous ballroom, has now been incorporated into the modern teaching department. The gem of the hospital is the CHAPEL ★, with a delightful Baroque interior in the Bavarian or Austrian style, making it one the most exceptional places of worship in all Dublin. This marvelous hospital building is admired throughout the world for the elegant restraint and harmony of its architectural design.

FIRST MATERNITY HOSPITAL
In 1745 Doctor Bartholomew Mosse, an obstetric surgeon horrified by the terrible conditions in which poor women were forced to give birth, founded a little hospital in an old theater in George's Lane, now Fade Street. A little later Mosse realized that more space was needed. He bought four acres of land north of the Liffey and entrusted Richard Castle with the building of a new hospital. The architect based his design on a modified version of the Leinster House ▲ *160* plans, and the first stone was laid in 1752.

The Writers' Museum.

PRELUDE TO THE CIVIL WAR
In 1922, when Republicans hostile to the 1921 Anglo-Irish Treaty occupied the Four Courts, Michael Collins ● 63, ▲ 224 resorted to

force. He shelled the building from the opposite bank. By the time the rebels retreated, the building was on fire and a quantity of documents were burnt.

DUBLIN WRITERS' MUSEUM. Opened in 1991 at nos. 18–19 Parnell Square this little museum houses a collection of letters, first editions, photographs and memorabilia of the capital's great authors.
MUNICIPAL ART GALLERY. The gallery, founded in 1908 by the wealthy art collector Sir Hugh Lane (nephew of Lady Gregory ▲ 247), is housed in the former home of the first earl of Charlemont (built in 1762 using the Scottish architect Sir William Chambers). Sir Hugh Lane went down with the *Lusitania*, the boat torpedoed by the Germans on May 7, 1915 off the Irish coast ▲ 224. He had left his collection, mainly of paintings by French Impressionists such as Manet, Monet, Renoir, Courbet and Corot, to the "nation". But which nation? Ireland had not yet gained independence. After decades of bitter wrangling, the two governments eventually reached agreement in 1960, dividing the paintings equally and exchanging them every five years. The Municipal Gallery has also extended its collection with the addition of works by more recent Irish painters such as Jack B. Yeats, Paul Henry and Louis Le Brocquy ● 116.
MOUNTJOY SQUARE. In 1770, a substantial building project was begun at North Great George's Street. The fine town houses of Mountjoy Square were erected between 1772 and 1818. These residential squares north of the Liffey are justly famous; their Georgian splendor is now faded and neglected, but they have lost nothing of their grandeur.

NORTHEAST OF THE RIVER

FOUR COURTS. From the south bank of the Liffey there is a marvelous view of James Gandon's second great work (1786–1802). As its name suggests, the building once housed four courts: Exchequer, Common Pleas, King's Bench and Chancery. Today the building is the seat of Ireland's High Court and Supreme Court.

ST MICHAN'S CHURCH (Church Street). The present church was built in the 17th century on the site of a Viking shrine (1095) and still retains a tower from the earlier building. There is a fascinating crypt and a lovely early 18th-century organ, still with its original gilding, upon which Handel played during his visit to Dublin.

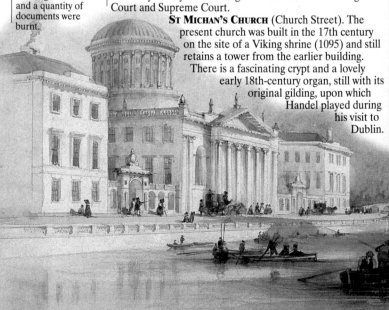

THE FOUR COURTS

JOHN JAMESON & SON L^{TD}

THE CRYPT OF ST MICHAN'S CHURCH
The walls of the crypt absorb humidity and as a result corpses within do not decompose. The skin turns brown but remains supple. Among the mummies that lie here are the Sheares brothers, executed for their part in the 1798 rebellion ● *52*, ▲ *171*.

WHISKEY CORNER. This area, once redolent of Jameson ● *79*, has sadly lost its heart since the giant Bow Street distillery closed its doors in 1972. Since 1980, the old warehouse has been converted into the company headquarters. Behind the old warehouse there is a museum to visit, Whiskey Corner, where the different stages of manufacture of this famous national beverage ● *78* are described.

FRUIT AND VEGETABLE MARKET (7, St Michan's Street). The market building was erected in 1892 to replace the many grubby market stalls that then traded in courtyards all over the city. Spencer Harty was the architect of the handsome construction in red and yellow brick. Over the main entrance on Mary's Lane there is an immense Dublin coat of arms ▲ *142*.

ST MARY'S ABBEY. Founded in the 12th century, St Mary's was one of the most important monasteries in the region. It also housed a number of different institutions in a city that always lacked adequate public buildings, including the State Treasury and the National Archives. In the 16th century it was the seat of royal authority in Ireland and it was here that the Crown's representative, "Silken Thomas" FitzGerald ● *50*, denied royal authority and began his failed rebellion against Henry VIII. Today the chapterhouse is virtually all that remains of the old abbey.

HENRY STREET AND MARY STREET. The two pedestrian streets are at the lively heart of commercial north Dublin. On MOORE STREET the lilting accents of street vendors fill the air. Their fruits, vegetables and flowers are generally displayed on overladen prams.

KING'S INNS. Looking along HENRIETTA STREET, King's Inns, designed by Gandon in 1795, stands at the end of a marvelous perspective of Georgian façades. Built to house the Dublin inns of court, it was eventually completed in 1817 by Henry Aaron Baker and Francis Johnston.

MOORE STREET MARKET
This depiction of the market is characteristic of the "stained-glass" effect particular to Michael Joseph Healy (1873–1941), a painter specializing in street scenes. On his return to Dublin from Florence in 1901, he joined Sarah Purser's group An Túr Gloine ("the glass tower") and perfected this style of recreating everyday scenes with great warmth of color and feeling.

147

COLLEGE GREEN

The site of this important crossroads and key Dublin landmark was once a Viking meeting place and burial ground. Today statues of two outstanding figures in Irish history look down upon the place: Thomas Davis (1818–45), poet and founder of the Young Ireland movement ● *58*, and the famous parliamentarian Henry Grattan (1746–1820).

BANK OF IRELAND. This was once the seat of parliament and the center of government until the passing of the Act of Union ● *52*. Having lost its former purpose, the building was sold to the Bank of Ireland for the modest sum of £40,000. It was designed in the Palladian style by the young Edward Lovett Pearce and begun in 1729. The prostyle Ionic portico on the southeast façade faces a square courtyard flanked by two semicircular wings. When Westmoreland Street was created James Gandon added a new Corinthian portico to the eastern façade, attached to Pearce's building by a circular windowless structure. The oak-paneled Lords' Chamber is open to visitors; in it hang tapestries illustrating the Battle of the Boyne ▲ *194* and the Siege of Derry ▲ *318*.

TRINITY COLLEGE. In 1591 Queen Elizabeth I decided to found a university in order to "civilize" the Irish and to protect them from "papist" influence. The great Protestant families began to send their sons there, rather than to England. The stern visages of two former graduates, Edmund Burke (1729–97), statesman and philosopher, and Oliver Goldsmith (1728–74), poet and dramatist, look down upon the students of Trinity as they strive to emulate such and other illustrious predecessors, who include Jonathan Swift ● *119*, Wolfe Tone ● *52*, Bram Stoker (1847–1912), author of *Dracula*, J.M. Synge ● *123*, and Samuel Beckett ● *131*. The LIBRARY was built between 1712 and 1732 by Thomas Burgh, and was the first of a number of grand building projects undertaken in the 18th century. Originally the library had three floors, but in 1857, Benjamin Woodward had the ceiling removed from the middle floor in order to create the magnificent LONG ROOM, 209 feet in length, with a high barrel-vaulted ceiling, in which were placed the *Books of Durrow*, *Kells* and *Armagh*, the most precious treasures in Trinity ▲ *150*. This old library building also holds 200,000 of the total of 3,000,000 books now in the Trinity College

BRIAN BORU'S HARP
The magnificent instrument is on show in the Long Room and known as "Brian Boru's harp". In fact it was made in the 15th century, about four centuries after Boru's death (he was murdered shortly after the Battle of Clontarf in 1014 ● *49*). The harp appears on Irish coins and also on the national coat of arms.

THE LONG ROOM
In addition to Brian Boru's harp, a copy of the 1916 Proclamation of Independence is kept

Library, which has been a Copyright Library since 1801. There are several important Greek and Latin manuscripts, Egyptian papyri, Irish works dating from the 16th and 17th centuries, and a Shakespeare first edition. The university buildings are a good illustration of Dublin architecture over the centuries: Burgh's library represents the 18th; from the 19th century there is Woodward's Museum Building (one of the most inspired Victorian buildings in the country); and recent additions are the New Library (1964–7) and the Arts Block (which houses the Douglas Hyde Modern Art Gallery, one of the rare innovative artistic centers in the city), designed by Paul Koralek.

in the Long Room. The room is decorated with a series of writers' busts in marble, and the names of the library's benefactors engraved in gold letters. The book conservation center is also in here.

THE HEART OF COMMERCE

GRAFTON STREET. Dear to Dubliners and a popular symbol of the city is Molly Malone, whose statue can be seen wheeling its barrow with determined stride along Grafton Street, one the smartest and also the prettiest shopping streets in Dublin. There is music to be heard at all hours of the day and night, from old Irish airs to hard rock ● 73. With changing tastes, many of the old cafés have disappeared, while others have been assimilated into the modern face of Dublin. BEWLEY'S COFFEE HOUSE has stood the test of time. It was founded by a family of Quakers respectful of the old traditions of trade (correct measures, reasonable prices and good quality), and in its time has been frequented by many famous writers (Yeats, Shaw, Beckett, O'Casey, Wilde, Joyce and Behan ● 117). Bewley's is still a much-loved meeting place ◆ 366.
POWERSCOURT TOWNHOUSE (South William Street). A pleasant and extremely popular shopping center recently created around a glassed-in courtyard behind the house once occupied by the Viscount Powerscourt, and built in 1771 by Robert Mack.

MOLLY MALONE
"She died of a fever, No one could relieve her." It is said that the ghost of Molly Malone, itinerant fish seller, still haunts the streets of Dublin.

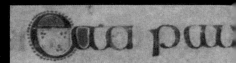

The earliest Irish manuscripts that survive today date from around the year 600. During the 5th and 6th centuries, scribes in Ireland had created their own script and particular style, apparently inspired by examples from Gaul, Spain, Italy and even as far away as North Africa. The scriptorium, where the writing and decoration was done, was an important place within a monastery. Scribes were trained from an early age and first practiced their art on waxed tablets or slates. The finest scribes continued to work until they were very old, as long as their eyesight remained good enough.

WRITING MATERIALS
The most important tool was the quill pen, taken from a goose, crow or swan, which would be cut with a chisel edge so that contrasting downstrokes and upstrokes could be made. The inkhorn held black ink, made from oak gall or from a solution of soot.

The pigments used for decoration were made from minerals and vegetable-matter crushed to powder and bound with resin or egg-white and water. Manuscripts were written on vellum made from prepared skins of sheep, cow or goat.

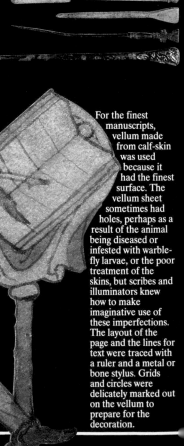

For the finest manuscripts, vellum made from calf-skin was used because it had the finest surface. The vellum sheet sometimes had holes, perhaps as a result of the animal being diseased or infested with warble-fly larvae, or the poor treatment of the skins, but scribes and illuminators knew how to make imaginative use of these imperfections. The layout of the page and the lines for text were traced with a ruler and a metal or bone stylus. Grids and circles were delicately marked out on the vellum to prepare for the decoration.

IRISH MAJUSCULE SCRIPT

The style known as "Irish majuscule" is basically a Latin half-uncial script incorporating shapes derived from Roman cursive script. The bold Irish majuscule is seen in the Gospel manuscripts, the *Book of Durrow* and the *Book of Kells*.

MINUSCULE

For works of lesser importance, which might be smaller in size or written in Gaelic, a minuscule script was used which made it possible to get more text onto each sheet. It is also used in the *Book of Armagh*, a masterpiece of calligraphy.

SAINT COLUMBA'S MANUSCRIPT ▲ 192
The first example of a decorated manuscript is a Latin psalter generally attributed to Saint Columba of Ireland and Scotland, who died in 597. The ornamentation is quite rudimentary. There is no interlace design, but many of the elements that were to become typical of Irish illuminated manuscripts are already in evidence. There are large decorated initials followed by a diminuendo bringing the letters down to normal size. The initials are outlined with red dots, Coptic in origin, and there are triangles with curved sides, Celtic spirals, Germanic zoomorphic forms and the Christian motif of a fish or dolphin carrying a cross.

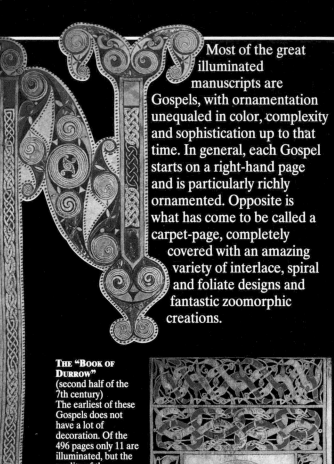

Most of the great illuminated manuscripts are Gospels, with ornamentation unequaled in color, complexity and sophistication up to that time. In general, each Gospel starts on a right-hand page and is particularly richly ornamented. Opposite is what has come to be called a carpet-page, completely covered with an amazing variety of interlace, spiral and foliate designs and fantastic zoomorphic creations.

THE "BOOK OF DURROW"
(second half of the 7th century)
The earliest of these Gospels does not have a lot of decoration. Of the 496 pages only 11 are illuminated, but the quality of the decoration is exceptional. Apart from black, the colors are limited to red, yellow, green and brown. These are combined to create an exuberant fantasy of spirals, knots, curved patterns descended from "La Tène" Celtic designs and, on one page only (f° 192v), animals showing a Teutonic influence.

8TH- AND 9TH-CENTURY GOSPELS

The range of decorative motifs expanded early in the 8th century, as can be seen from the *Lindisfarne Gospels* (c. 700), the *Book of Lichfield* and the *Echternach Gospels*. The largest of these is the *Book of MacRegol* (14 inches by 11 inches), made at Birr ▲ *201* before the year 822. There is a certain roughness in the decoration, but it is marvelously bold, both in its script and in its colors: brilliant red, golden yellow, apple green and a vivid purple. Apart from these especially elaborate Gospels there were also smaller, more functional books such as the *Saint Gall Gospels* and the *Book of Dimma*, which has remarkable stylized portraits of the Evangelists. Even in the *Stowe Missal* (c. 800) and the *Book of Armagh* (807), books that are not specifically collections of the Gospels, it is always the first pages from the Gospels that have been decorated.

The *Book of Kells* is the most splendid of all these great manuscripts, perhaps the most beautiful of all medieval manuscripts in the Western world. It was probably begun on the Hebridean island of Iona in the second half of the 8th century, and brought to Kells by monks fleeing the Viking raids.

TEAMWORK
Four illuminators and at least three scribes worked on the book. The skins of 170 cattle were needed to provide the vellum for its pages. There are over two thousand decorated large initials, each one different, and about forty pages are entirely covered with illuminations. Here the artists indulged their skill and imagination to the full. The decoration is not entirely abstract. There are also fine and sensitive portraits of the Evangelists and characters from the Gospels, some of them reminiscent of Byzantine icons and mosaics. The artists of the *Book of Kells* did not confine themselves to the traditional design; they accompanied the text with numerous animals and scenes from everyday life, depicted in minute detail.

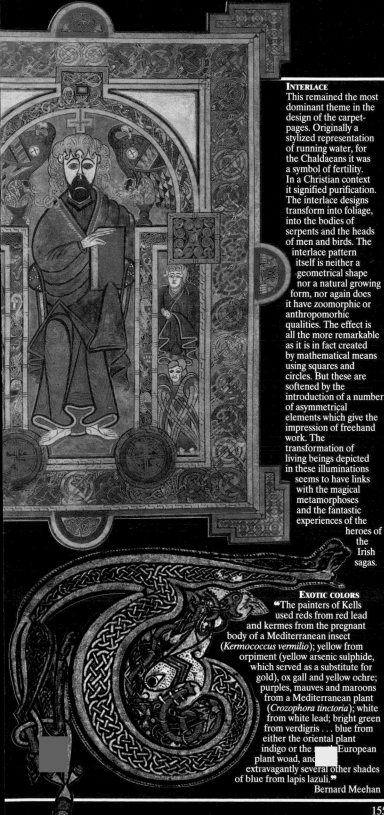

INTERLACE

This remained the most dominant theme in the design of the carpet-pages. Originally a stylized representation of running water, for the Chaldaeans it was a symbol of fertility. In a Christian context it signified purification. The interlace designs transform into foliage, into the bodies of serpents and the heads of men and birds. The interlace pattern itself is neither a geometrical shape nor a natural growing form, nor again does it have zoomorphic or anthropomorhic qualities. The effect is all the more remarkable as it is in fact created by mathematical means using squares and circles. But these are softened by the introduction of a number of asymmetrical elements which give the impression of freehand work. The transformation of living beings depicted in these illuminations seems to have links with the magical metamorphoses and the fantastic experiences of the heroes of the Irish sagas.

EXOTIC COLORS

"The painters of Kells used reds from red lead and kermes from the pregnant body of a Mediterranean insect (*Kermococcus vermilio*); yellow from orpiment (yellow arsenic sulphide, which served as a substitute for gold), ox gall and yellow ochre; purples, mauves and maroons from a Mediterranean plant (*Crozophora tinctoria*); white from white lead; bright green from verdigris . . . blue from either the oriental plant indigo or the ■■■ European plant woad, and ■■■ extravagantly several other shades of blue from lapis lazuli."

Bernard Meehan

155

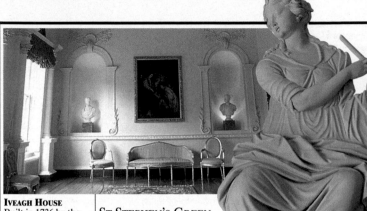

IVEAGH HOUSE

Built in 1736 by the architect Richard Castle, the house was acquired by the Guinness family in 1856. In 1919 the grandson of Arthur Guinness, who had become first Earl of Iveagh, renamed the house. He later gave it to the State.

Since then the foreign affairs department has been based in the house, which is closed to the public. Behind the austere façade are rooms decorated with stucco, wood bas-reliefs and sculptures. A Victorian ballroom was later added. The monumental staircase is an amalgam of 18th-, 19th- and 20th-century styles.

ST STEPHEN'S GREEN

Public gardens were laid out at St Stephen's Green in 1880, on what until 1663 was a piece of common land. Sir Arthur Guinness ▲ 170, the Dublin brewery owner, funded the project. The leafy paths make a delighful place to stroll or sit (see below), and it is much loved by all, from students to grandparents. Along the north side of the square ran what was known in the 18th century as "Beau Walk", an elegant place to stroll, see and be seen. Opposite stands the ever fashionable SHELBOURNE HOTEL (1867), the epitome of high-class gentility and still claiming to be "the best address in Dublin". It is worth peeping through the front doors for a glimpse of the delicate stucco decorations, some Rococo and others in the more classical Robert Adam style ● 106.

ROYAL COLLEGE OF SURGEONS. The building stands on the west side of the square. During the 1916 Easter Rising it was the headquarters of the Irish Citizens' Army, whose second-in-command was Constance Markievicz ▲ 286.

UNIVERSITY COLLEGE (NEWMAN HOUSE) (No. 86). The city's Catholic university has among its former graduates Pearse ● 61, De Valera ● 61 and Joyce ● 120. It was founded by Cardinal Newman to counterbalance the influence of Trinity College. The APOLLO ROOM is the most impressive: it is elaborately decorated with stuccos by the Lafranchini brothers, depicting Apollo and the nine muses (above). The UNIVERSITY CHURCH stands next to the College, an incredibly ornate Byzantine extravaganza, with an interior decorated in rich colored marble.

HARCOURT STREET AND DAWSON STREET

Two gracious Georgian thoroughfares lead from St Stephen's Green: Harcourt Street, which has a famous Gaelic bookshop at no. 6 (An Siopa Leabhar), and Dawson Street, where the best bookshops in Dublin are to be found.

Y SIOP LLYFRAU CELTAIDD

AN
SIOPA LEABHAR

CELTIC BOOKSHOP

MANSION HOUSE. The building was designed by Joshua Dawson (after whom the street was named) in 1710. It is decorated with massive Victorian cast-ironwork. Since 1715 the Mansion House has been the residence of the Lord Mayor. It was in the Round Room here, on January 21, 1919, that the Declaration of Irish Independence was ratified ● *62*.

ROYAL IRISH ACADEMY (19 Dawson Street). The academy was created in 1785 with the aim of encouraging science and learning. It is one of Europe's great scholarly institutions. The Ardagh Chalice, the Tara Brooch and the Cross of Cong were among the Academy's treasures, before they were donated to the National Museum ▲ *158*.

GEORGIAN DUBLIN

It was the English who gave Dublin the stately architectural flavor that it retains today. In the 18th century, they created the elegant squares and built graceful terraces of Georgian houses. The most fashionable districts developed to the south of the Liffey as a result of the influence of the Duke of Leinster.

KILDARE STREET CLUB. Benjamin Woodward built the premises between 1858 and 1861. For years the Club was the bastion of Dublin conservatism. Today a part of the building has been purchased by the State to house the Genealogical Office, conserving documents dating back to 1552 that were moved here in 1981 from Bedford Tower in Dublin Castle ▲ *167*. Here, too, is the State Heraldic Museum, where thousands of people come every year to trace their family origins.

NATIONAL LIBRARY. The library has a fine collection of first editions, old manuscripts, and works by Irish authors (Swift ● *119*, Goldsmith, Yeats ● *122*, Shaw ● *125*, Joyce ● *120* and Beckett ● *131*). There are also occasional exhibitions held here on native authors and their works.

NATIONAL MUSEUM ▲ *158*. Some of the greatest treasures of ancient Ireland are to be found here. The collection includes Celtic jewelry and Christian artefacts such as reliquaries and chalices. Two rooms are given over to a dramatic account of the events of 1916.

LEADEN BULLA
A heart-shaped lead bulla is conserved in the National Museum, one of five known in Ireland. Its origin and use remain a mystery, but it is known to date from the 8th century BC. It is a lump of lead, visible through scratches in its covering of gold leaf. Its design is a complex pattern of chevrons, triangles, crossed lines and concentric circles. Also in the museum is the Cross of Cong, an ancient and famous reliquary enclosing a fragment of the Holy Cross. The wooden center is covered with silver and gilt bronze engraved with animals, highlighted in gold.

The cross was kept at Cong until 1839, when it was brought to the museum.

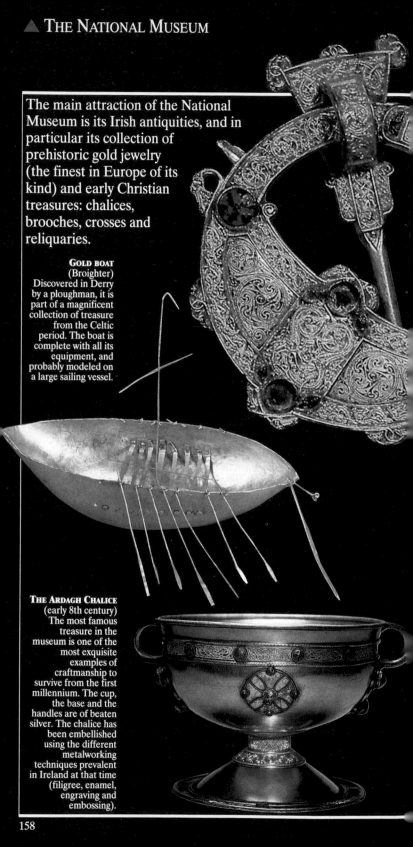

The main attraction of the National Museum is its Irish antiquities, and in particular its collection of prehistoric gold jewelry (the finest in Europe of its kind) and early Christian treasures: chalices, brooches, crosses and reliquaries.

GOLD BOAT
(Broighter)
Discovered in Derry by a ploughman, it is part of a magnificent collection of treasure from the Celtic period. The boat is complete with all its equipment, and probably modeled on a large sailing vessel.

THE ARDAGH CHALICE
(early 8th century)
The most famous treasure in the museum is one of the most exquisite examples of craftmanship to survive from the first millennium. The cup, the base and the handles are of beaten silver. The chalice has been embellished using the different metalworking techniques prevalent in Ireland at that time (filigree, enamel, engraving and embossing).

NECKLACE FROM GLENINSHEEN, County Clare, c. 800 BC.

"BREACH MAEDOG" (early 12th century) Three women saints are depicted on a tiny panel of this reliquary. Their appearance tells us much about the garments and hairstyles of the period.

THISTLE FIBULA (10th century) The silver fibula takes its name from the resemblance of the decoration to thistle flowers. It is probably an example of a style of art developed to please the Vikings, who supplied the local artisans with metal.

LISMORE CROSIER (c. AD 1100) The crosier-shrine is made from sections of gilded bronze covering a wooden cane. Pieces of blue glass decorated with red and white motifs are set into the bronze and there are also panels of zoomorphic interlace design, separated by inlays of millefiori glass. The ridge is formed by three fanged beasts.

THE TARA BROOCH (c. 8th century) The brooch was found on the seashore at Bettystown, south of Drogheda. It is the most superb example of a penannular brooch: a large, richly decorated brooch worn on the shoulder with the pin pointing upward. It is of white bronze decorated with gold filigree and studded with amber and colored glass. On the face there are elaborate filigree interlace designs, with birds and beasts, while on the reverse there is intricate chasing, mainly of spiral patterns. Fixed to the side of the ring is a silver cord with a hinged and pivoting attachment decorated with the heads of wild beasts.

GOLD TORQUE (Broighter, 1st century BC) The wide necklace is the finest example of the Irish goldsmiths' art, and a product of the "La Tène" period of Celtic civilization ▲ *151*. It is unique in Europe, with a complex symmetrical design based on a floral motif. Similarities can be noted with the torque of the *Dying Gaul* in the Capitoline Museum in Rome.

A NEW FASHION
When James FitzGerald decided to build his house on the south side of the city he had many critics. But the Duke made a bold prediction that others would follow him. He was right: soon the aristocracy were all building their elegant Georgian residences in his preferred area.

They were to become the architectural pride of Dublin.

MERRION SQUARE
The square is lined with Georgian houses, and on one side stands the National Gallery. It is

now known as one of Dublin's finest squares, but it has not always enjoyed such a reputation. During the Famine ● 58 the central gardens were the site of one of Dublin's busiest soup kitchens.

LEINSTER HOUSE. In 1745 James FitzGerald, Earl of Kildare and future Duke of Leinster, asked the architect Richard Castle to build him the largest private residence in Dublin. The site he chose for his townhouse was on the southern outskirts of the city, virtually in the country. Today, Leinster House is the seat of the Dáil Éireann (Parliament) and of the Seanad Éireann (Senate).

NATURAL HISTORY MUSEUM. An amazing, old-fashioned museum containing fascinating skeletons of the Irish elk, a creature that became extinct ten thousand years ago.

NATIONAL GALLERY ▲ *162.* The country's principal art collection has a wide range of works from the Irish school, giving a good overview. There are also a number of fine works by old masters (particularly Dutch and Italian). A new wing (1995) has now been added to the National Gallery, allowing many more works to be shown.

MERRION SQUARE. A colorful square, striking for its perfect architectural harmony. It is one of the finest groups of Georgian buildings in Dublin. The rich red brick, painted front doors, decorative fanlights and lacy wrought-ironwork have made it one of the sights of the city. Viscount Fitzwilliam of Meryon, eager to emulate the new fashion for elegant construction set by the Duke of Leinster with the building of his fine house, constructed a row of Georgian houses on Merrion Street. The charm of the district continued to attract newcomers, and over the years many well-known people have lived here: George Russell (no. 84), W.B. Yeats (nos. 52 and 82), Daniel O'Connell (no. 58), Sir William and Lady Wilde – the parents of Oscar – (no. 1: note the particularly delicate wrought-ironwork). Today the houses in the square have mainly been converted into offices.

EARLSFORT TERRACE. This building, begun in 1863, is in the classical style. Behind, in Coburg Gardens, is an amazing glass and metal structure originally intended as only temporary. It was built to house the Winter Garden opened for the International Exhibition of May 1865 where the latest scentific and artistic achievements of the age were on show. In 1908, after University College regained possession of the

building, R.M. Butler altered it to give it its present appearance. When most of the university departments moved further south to Belfield, in 1974, the government decided to alter the interior to make a concert hall.

GEORGIAN SQUARES AND DOORS

In 1757 the Wide Streets Commission was set up, the first example of organized urban planning in Europe. Its role was to define practical and esthetic rules for building development. Other commissions were later given the responsibility for street paving and lighting. It was from this time that some of Dublin's grandest public buildings were erected, along with the stately Georgian squares. Close to Merrion Square, with its elegant fanlights and decorative door knockers, are Ely Place and Fitzwilliam Square (the smallest square in Dublin and, in 1825, the last to be built). They too have lovely Georgian architecture. Today the great families who once rivaled each other in the design and embellishment of their townhouses have moved out of the center of town. The Georgian houses were first divided into apartments and are now mostly converted into offices for the professions.

161

The fantastic success of the art exhibition mounted as part of the Irish Great Exhibition of 1853 was the catalyst for the creation of the National Gallery. At its opening in 1864 it had only 125 paintings. Today there are more than 13,000 works in all: 3,000 oil on canvas, 5,000 watercolors and drawings, and a great many prints, sculptures and other works of art. The range and quality of the collection of Old Masters, considering the meager funds available to the gallery, is proof of the generous donations that have been made. Sir Hugh Lane ▲ *146* (1875–1915) who was the director of the gallery until his death, bequeathed it works by Titian, El Greco, Chardin and Van Dyck. More recently the museum received a donation from Sir Alfred Beit of seventeen paintings by Gainsborough, Goya, Velazquez and Vermeer, and the Irish Jesuit Fathers donated a painting by Caravaggio (*The Arrest of Christ*). The National Gallery also has a vast collection of works by Irish artists (18th and 19th century).

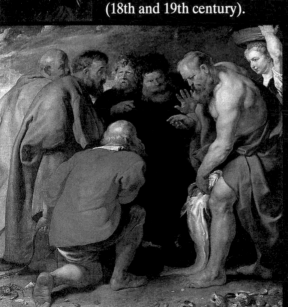

PETER PAUL RUBENS
(1577–1640)
Paying Tribute
c. 1618
(**1**, detail) and (**5**)

CARAVAGGIO
(1573–1610)
The Arrest of Christ
c. 1602 (**2**)

PAOLO UCCELLO
(1397–1475)
Virgin and Child
c. 1440 (**3**)

FRANCISCO DE GOYA
(1746–1828)
Doña Antonia Zárata
c. 1805 (**4**)

1
2

3	4	5

REMBRANDT VAN RIJN
(1606–69)
Rest on the Flight into Egypt
1647 (**1**, detail) and
(**4**)

JAMES BARRY
(1741–1806)
Self-portrait as Timanthes
c. 1780 (**2**)

JOHANNES VERMEER
(1632–75)
Woman writing a letter
c. 1665 (**5**)

THOMAS GAINSBOROUGH
(1727–88)
The Cottage Girl
1785 (**3**)

PROJECT ARTS CENTRE
(East Essex Street). This recently-opened center in the heart of Temple Bar favors work of experimental and politically committed work. It stages plays, concerts and exhibitions. Jim Sheridan, director of the films *My Left Foot* and *In the Name of the Father*, worked here ◆ *333*.

TEMPLE BAR

HA'PENNY BRIDGE ★. A charming footbridge, and one of Dublin's popular landmarks. It was built in 1816 and given the official name of Liffey Bridge, but it soon gained its nickname from the halfpenny toll that had to be paid to cross it. The fine old metal structure has recently received the rather exaggerated embellishment of old-fashioned lamps.

TEMPLE BAR ★. The narrow street passing beneath Merchant's Arch leads into Temple Bar. This is now a fashionable district, but in the 1980's it was threatened with the ball and chain to make way for a vast bus terminal. Fortunately, the area has been improved instead, streets cobbled and the 18th-century houses saved. Temple Bar is now full of artists, designers and enthusiastic fledgling businesses, restaurants and cafés. The atmosphere is further enlivened by the colorful musicians, jugglers, acrobats and other street artists and entertainers who perform here.

THE MEDIEVAL CITY AND THE LIBERTIES

The Liberties are the oldest part of Dublin and are so named because they were built outside the city wall (a portion of which still remains). There are now granite stones set out to show the course of the old wall.

DAME STREET. The Dublin banking and business world has its center in this street of sturdy Victorian buildings. The only exception is Sam Stephenson's 1978 design for the Central Bank, which makes a striking contrast.

CITY HALL. The building was once the Royal Exchange and was the work of Thomas Cooley (1769). It is built in the Corinthian style, and is particularly impressive seen after dark, when it is illuminated. The twelve frescos that decorate the rotunda illustrate old legends of the city as well as episodes from the country's ancient history. The first Lord Mayor, Sir Daniel Bellingham, elected in 1665, gave Dublin the ceremonial mace and sword that are on show here.

DUBLIN CASTLE. The original castle was built by the Normans in the 13th century and for nearly seven and a half centuries it was the seat and symbol of English power in Ireland. Originally it stood on the southeast corner of the city's fortifications, surrounded by ramparts and a moat. This meant that the castle could be defended from an enemy attempting to take the town, as was the case with "Silken Thomas" in 1534 ● *50*. After two disastrous fires in 1670 and 1680 which destroyed a medieval hall on the west side of the courtyard, the castle was entirely rebuilt in the classical style between 1730 and 1800. As a result the UPPER YARD looks Georgian. Early in the 19th century the castle again underwent alterations, along with the BERMINGHAM TOWER on the southwest corner, this time in neo-Gothic style. The two north towers were only revealed during archeological excavations within the last decade, so they have fortunately remained unaltered. From the POWDER TOWER, which joined the castle to the city walls, it is now possible to visit earth fortifications from the Viking era. At the entrance to the castle stands the BEDFORD TOWER, its dome and sculptures being later embellishments by Van Nost. Today it leads into a conference center added in 1988. The south façade of the courtyard is mainly taken up by the state apartments, once the residence of the Viceroys, representatives of the British Crown in Ireland until independence ● *62*. Groups are taken round the rooms, but they can be closed if important guests of state are being received. ST PATRICK'S HALL has a ceiling painted by the Italian Vincent Waldre. Other rooms are decorated in strong colors such as blue, yellow and green, and have a wealth of 18th-century stucco taken from Georgian houses in the city. The viceroy and the castle staff used to worship in the ROYAL CHAPEL (1807–14), which stands to the west of the RECORD TOWER. This is an elegant neo-Gothic construction designed by Francis Johnston. The exterior sculptures as well as most of the stucco inside were made by the Dubliner Edward Smith and his son John. At the main entrance to the castle stands a memorial to insurgents who died attacking the castle on Easter Monday 1916 ● *60*.

TEMPLE BAR
The area considers itself to be at the forefront of cultural activity in Ireland today. *U2*, Ireland's internationally famous rock group, have bought up a number of buildings and turned them into theaters, concert halls, pubs and nightclubs.

"What counts for the visitor is the Dublin we bring to Dublin in our heads. We put that personal Dublin like a template over the real one and are more or less satisfied. . . . To hell with Dublin being Paris. Dublin has enough on its plate being the city of our imaginations.**"**
Thomas Keneally

167

STRONGBOW'S TOMB
Although said to contain Strongbow, leader of the Norman knights who came to conquer Ireland in the 12th century, the tomb dates from the 1340's.

WOOD QUAY
No less than nine quays have been uncovered along the stretch of river between Wine Tavern Street and Fishamble Street. Some are very primitive moorings, but two are certainly of Viking construction, both defensive. Also discovered dating from the same period (around 1100) is part of a stone wall that probably encircled the town. A description of Dublin given at the time of the Norman invasion of 1170 describes a city wall with at least two gates, a castle and a keep. Finds from excavations made between 1962 and 1981 at Christ Church Place, Wine Tavern Street and Wood Quay, are on show in the National Museum Annexe. The sophistication of these artefacts are proof of a highly civilized society: boxes, combs carved from bone and deer antlers, scales with sets of weights and iron swords.

ST WERBURGH'S CHURCH. This 18th-century church is closely bound up with the history of the FitzGerald family ● 50: Lord Edward, who was wounded during his arrest for leading the 1798 rebellion ● 52, is buried in the crypt. Ironically Major Henry Sirr, who defeated him, is buried in the churchyard of St Werbugh's.

CHRIST CHURCH CATHEDRAL. In 1038, Sitric Silkenbeard, the first Christianized Danish king to rule in Dublin, built a simple wooden church within the city walls, calling it Christ Church of the Holy Trinity. With the arrival of the Normans, the building was replaced by a more substantial stone church. By the end of the 19th century the cathedral had fallen into such disrepair that drastic renovation work was needed. A large part of the medieval stonework had to be replaced, under the direction of George Edmund Street, and at the expense of the whiskey distiller Henry Roe. Further repairs were made in the 1980's. Fascinating details of the original Viking construction are still visible in the vaulted ceilings of the 12th- and 13th-century CRYPT (above). This is the most unusual and striking part of the building, unique in the entire British Isles for extending the length of the cathedral. There are a few remains of the Norman church, the city's most ancient stone building. Among them are the late Norman arches in the west bay of the chancel, resting on capitals carved with human figures and animals, and certain portions of the transept. In this cathedral the kings of Ireland came to pay homage to Richard II in 1394; James II stopped to hear mass on his way to the Battle of the Boyne ▲ 194, and William of Orange gave thanks afterward for having defeated him.

WOOD QUAY. The important archeological finds made in and around Christ Church make it clear that this was the heart of Viking and medieval Dublin. Sadly, despite bitter arguments, this did not prevent two tower blocks designed by Sam Stephenson being built here in 1986.

THE BRAZEN HEAD ◆ 366. The pub opened in 1688 and was the headquarters of Wolfe Tone's Society of United Irishmen ● 52 in the 1790's. Fifteen people were arrested here in one year. The desk of Robert Emmet, leader of the 1803 rising, is kept in the pub.

ST AUDOEN'S CHURCH. This medieval church has within its 12th-century tower the three oldest bells in Ireland (1423). There is a way into the church through the one remaining gate of the old city wall, on the corner of Cork Street.

TAILORS' GUILD HALL. The only guild hall left in Dublin was built in 1706. It has an assembly room with a musicians' gallery from which, in the 1790's, Wolfe Tone and Napper Tandy addressed the "Back Lane Parliament". Today Tailors' Hall is the headquarters of An Taisce, a national society dedicated to the preservation and restoration of old buildings.

ST PATRICK'S CATHEDRAL. Hostility toward the Christ Church authorities led Archbishop Henry de Londres to raise the nearby church of St Patrick's to the status of cathedral in 1213. In this rather unconventional way Dublin came to have two cathedrals. De Londres chose the Gothic style for the rebuilding of St Patrick's (1225–54). It is 330 feet in length, making it the longest medieval church in Ireland, and much of the stone carving was done by masons from the southwest of England. Part of their work can still be seen in the chancel. In the 19th century the building was in such a poor state that restoration was imperative; the money was provided by the brewer Sir Benjamin Guinness – inspiring Henry Roe to do the same for Christ Church. Guinness also commissioned his own statue to stand at the southwest porch. St Patrick's is now the cathedral of the Protestant Church of Ireland. It is famous also for having had Jonathan Swift (1667–1745) ● *119* as dean from 1713 to 1745. He is buried in the cathedral, at the foot of the second column on the right on entering the main doors, lying beside his beloved "Stella" (Esther Johnson).

MARSH'S LIBRARY ★. A delightful little library, still with three "cages" to enclose those who wished to study rare books. It was founded by Archbishop Narcissus Marsh, built in four years by Sir William Robinson, and opened in 1705 as the first public library in Ireland.

THE BRAZEN HEAD
The oldest pub in Dublin. It is claimed that a Viking inn once stood here.

BOYLE MONUMENT
(St Patrick's Cathedral) Richard Boyle, Earl of Cork, had the

monument erected in 1632 to the memory of his wife, Catherine. It is decorated with painted figures, members of her family. Among the couple's children, bottom row, is the infant Robert Boyle (1627–91), physicist, later to formulate Boyle's Law on the pressure and volume of gases.

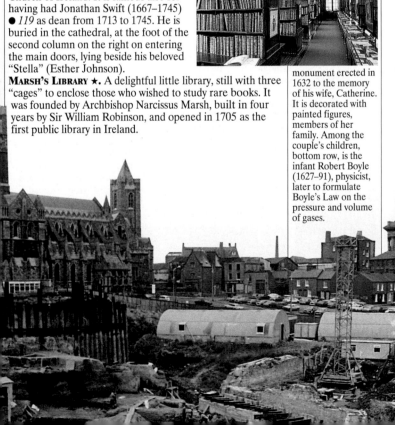

SIR ARTHUR GUINNESS (1725–1803)
On December 31, 1759, thirty-four-year-old Sir Arthur Guinness ● *156*, a confident young brewer, paid Mark Rainsford III £100, signed his name to a thousand-year lease at a rent of £45 a year and entered St James's Gate, his fate sealed. One of the world's great beers was about to be brewed for the first time.

The brewery he had just leased consisted of a cooper's shop, a boiler, a mill, a malthouse, stabling for twelve horses and a loft for 200 tons of hay.

GUINNESS BREWERY
● *76.* The heavy, sweet smell of brewing has hung in the air around St James's Gate since 1759. It comes from the Guinness Brewery. Stout is one of the great Irish institutions, a smooth dark beer topped with a thick creamy band of foam. Its popularity never wains, and the brewery, one of the most famous in Europe, produces four million pints a day and exports more beer than any other brewery in the world. The factory covers 64 acres south of the Liffey and employs four thousand people. Adjoining it is a small museum where a film of the making of *Guinness* is shown, followed by the offer of a pint. Since it is said that *Guinness* doesn't travel well, this must be the best place in the world to drink it.

NATIONAL COLLEGE OF ART AND DESIGN. The college was founded nearly 250 years ago, but moved in the early 1980's from its old home in Kildare Street to John Power's abandoned distillery in Thomas Street. The buildings have been beautifully converted and the students have fitted in happily here, bringing some new life and enthusiasm to the district.

TOWARD PHOENIX PARK

KILMAINHAM HOSPITAL. Viceroy James Butler, Duke of Ormonde, representing King Charles II, initiated the building of the Kilmainham Royal Hospital in 1680. It was a military institution intended to take in wounded and veteran soldiers. It is an impressively simple and harmonious building fronted with colonnades around a central courtyard. Well restored between 1980 and 1984, in 1991 it was converted to house the Irish Museum of Modern Art.

The inner courtyard of Kilmainham prison.

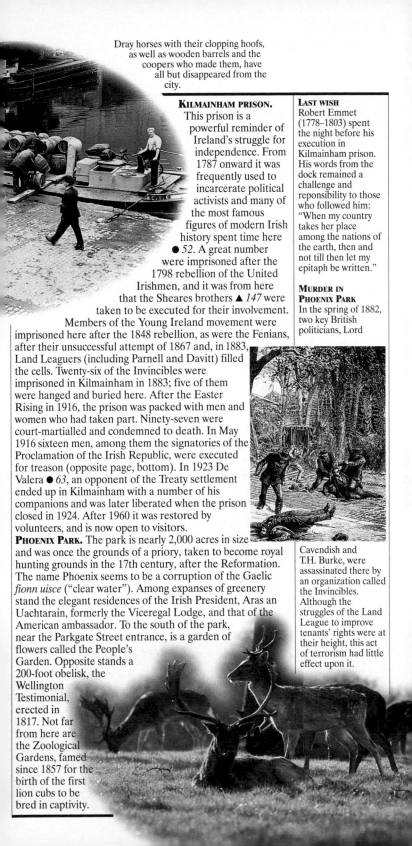

Dray horses with their clopping hoofs, as well as wooden barrels and the coopers who made them, have all but disappeared from the city.

KILMAINHAM PRISON. This prison is a powerful reminder of Ireland's struggle for independence. From 1787 onward it was frequently used to incarcerate political activists and many of the most famous figures of modern Irish history spent time here ● *52*. A great number were imprisoned after the 1798 rebellion of the United Irishmen, and it was from here that the Sheares brothers ▲ *147* were taken to be executed for their involvement. Members of the Young Ireland movement were imprisoned here after the 1848 rebellion, as were the Fenians, after their unsuccessful attempt of 1867 and, in 1883, Land Leaguers (including Parnell and Davitt) filled the cells. Twenty-six of the Invincibles were imprisoned in Kilmainham in 1883; five of them were hanged and buried here. After the Easter Rising in 1916, the prison was packed with men and women who had taken part. Ninety-seven were court-martialled and condemned to death. In May 1916 sixteen men, among them the signatories of the Proclamation of the Irish Republic, were executed for treason (opposite page, bottom). In 1923 De Valera ● *63*, an opponent of the Treaty settlement ended up in Kilmainham with a number of his companions and was later liberated when the prison closed in 1924. After 1960 it was restored by volunteers, and is now open to visitors.

PHOENIX PARK. The park is nearly 2,000 acres in size and was once the grounds of a priory, taken to become royal hunting grounds in the 17th century, after the Reformation. The name Phoenix seems to be a corruption of the Gaelic *fionn uisce* ("clear water"). Among expanses of greenery stand the elegant residences of the Irish President, Aras an Uachtarain, formerly the Viceregal Lodge, and that of the American ambassador. To the south of the park, near the Parkgate Street entrance, is a garden of flowers called the People's Garden. Opposite stands a 200-foot obelisk, the Wellington Testimonial, erected in 1817. Not far from here are the Zoological Gardens, famed since 1857 for the birth of the first lion cubs to be bred in captivity.

LAST WISH
Robert Emmet (1778–1803) spent the night before his execution in Kilmainham prison. His words from the dock remained a challenge and reponsibility to those who followed him: "When my country takes her place among the nations of the earth, then and not till then let my epitaph be written."

MURDER IN PHOENIX PARK
In the spring of 1882, two key British politicians, Lord Cavendish and T.H. Burke, were assassinated there by an organization called the Invincibles. Although the struggles of the Land League to improve tenants' rights were at their height, this act of terrorism had little effect upon it.

Below left, Killiney Bay
(south of Dún Laoghaire).

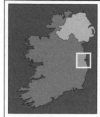

THE SOUTHEAST

THE GRAND CANAL. Two canals were dug from Dublin in the late 18th century, the Royal Canal, which runs north of the city center, and the Grand Canal. The latter leads west to join the River Shannon ▲ *200* and south to join the River Barrow, so providing a means of transport for passengers and goods right across the country, to Limerick in the west and Waterford in the south. It was in commercial use until 1960. The Waterways Visitors' Centre, situated on the Grand Canal basin, recounts the history of the Irish inland water transport system.

CHESTER BEATTY LIBRARY (Shrewsbury Rd). The Oriental art and manuscripts in the library and gallery are among the finest in the world. It is, needless to say, one of the most important collections in Dublin. Alfred Chester Beatty (1875–1968) was an American who settled in the city in 1950, and was later made Ireland's first honorary citizen. He spent his large, self-made fortune on manuscripts, paintings, prints, scrolls, Korans and rare books (often with exquisite bindings) and furniture. His treasures came from Europe, India, the Middle East, China and Japan and the collection was left to the State. He also bequeathed some important canvases by painters of the Barbizon school, now hung in the National Gallery ▲ *162*.

CHESTER BEATTY LIBRARY
By 1905 Alfred Chester Beatty was already collecting 17th- and 18th-century Chinese snuff bottles. Today some nine hundred of them are on display in the Far Eastern section of the New Gallery, alongside jade books, rhinoceros-horn cups and two Chinese imperial robes. On the first floor is the Islamic collection,

including 270 Persian, Egyptian and Turkish Korans, some illuminated by great masters of calligraphy. The Garden Library, near the entrance, displays items from Western Europe, with prints by Dürer, Holbein and Piranesi, and also some precious illuminated works. Other items in the vast and varied collection are Babylonian clay tablets and Egyptian papyri.

DÚN LAOGHAIRE. The town (left), pronounced "Dunleary", is named after an ancient fortress built here in the 5th century by Laoghaire (Leary), King of Ireland. From a small fishing village it grew to become a busy port in the 18th century, through the growth of trade with England. From 1821 until 1920 it was called "Kingstown" in honor of George IV, who set sail from here in 1820. Today Dún Laoghaire is a popular residential district and seaside resort, as well as remaining an important terminal for ferries to Great Britain. As the main yachting center in Ireland, it has an attractive and lively harbor with plenty of shops and

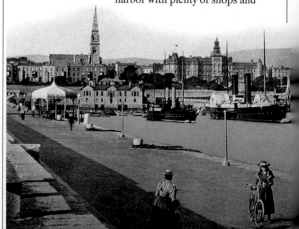

restaurants. Behind the ROYAL MARINE GARDENS, in the Moran Public Park, is the the former residence of the harbor captain. From here, in 1898, Marconi transmitted one of his earliest outdoor communications: a commentary on a sporting event. The National Maritime Museum, in the old Mariners' Church on Haigh Terrace, gives a good account of Irish shipping history from its most primitive origins.

SANDYCOVE. Sandycove is probably best known for its Martello tower ● *101* (1804). The English built a series of these towers along the coast when fearing invasion by Napoleon. The small, round fort with walls nearly 40 feet high is also called JAMES JOYCE'S TOWER, because in 1904 the writer spent a short time here and subsequently described it in the first chapter of *Ulysses* ● *120*. In 1962 Sylvia Beach, who had first published the novel in Paris, started the James Joyce Museum here. Letters, documents, memorabilia, rare copies and first editions are on show.

THE NORTHEAST

NATIONAL BOTANIC GARDENS. The property once belonged to the family of the poet Thomas Tickell. The Royal Dublin Society bought the estate and, in 1795, founded the Botanic Gardens. Thomas Tickell's house is now the director's residence. The celebrated essayist Thomas Addison may also have lived in the area: certainly there is a yew walk called "Addison's Walk". The Botanic Gardens cover some 50 acres and contain a number of rare species of tree, shrub and other plants. The Palm House was built by Richard Turner ▲ *302*, a Dublin ironfounder who also made the greenhouses at Kew Gardens. The property came into state ownership in the late 19th century, and the gardens are run by the Office of Public Works.

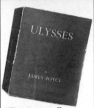

"BLOOMSDAY"
On June 16 each year Dublin celebrates Bloomsday, Leopold Bloom's day of peregrination, as described by James Joyce in *Ulysses* ● *120*. On June 16, 1954, when Joyce was still much disapproved of in Ireland, some writers (among them Flann O'Brien, Patrick Kavanagh and Tom Joyce) inaugurated Bloomsday. Their idea was to make a sort of pilgrimage in the footsteps of the novel's characters.

The story goes that they were in the end unable to carry out their good intentions in full because a number of the obligatory stops were Dublin pubs. Bloomsday has become a big event in literary tourism, with people dressed in Edwardian costume wandering the city, bearing their copy of *Ulysses*.

DUBLIN BAY PRAWNS
These are often enjoyed in a Dublin Bay prawn cocktail: cooked and peeled, they are steeped in white wine, covered in a well-peppered,

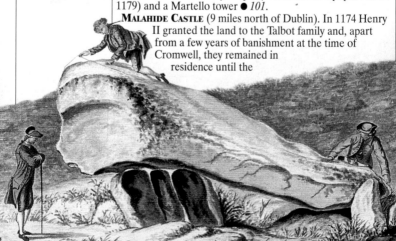

creamy sauce and surrounded by fresh, crisp lettuce.

MARINO CASINO ● *104.* An exquisite, miniature neoclassical villa (▲ *173,* top) designed by Sir William Chambers for the Earl of Charlemont, who laid the first stone in 1762. The attractive rooms within are beautifully proportioned. The gracious urns that decorate the roof are a disguise for chimneys. There are also some interesting underground passages. The influence of this building can be seen in the Customs House in Dublin ▲ *144* designed twenty years later by James Gandon, Chambers' pupil.

HOWTH. From Howth Head, at the end of the Howth Peninsula, there are views of Dublin and also the nearby village of Howth, with its steep streets and fine harbor. This is a popular place with Dubliners, and plenty of yachts lie alongside the busy fleet of fishing boats. A walk along the high cliff gives a breathtaking view of Dublin Bay and Lambay Island. The gardens of HOWTH CASTLE are particularly famous for their rhododendrons, which are a mass of purple flowers in May and June. Lady Emily St Lawrence, who planted them in 1850, had to have earth brought in to cover the slopes before putting them in. The species, *R. Ponticum,* is less popular now than other more colorful varieties, but it is one of the most hardy. Also in the gardens of the castle is an interesting TRANSPORT MUSEUM. A short walk further on is a CROMLECH, a Neolithic tomb dating from about 2000 BC. The huge stone slab is some 8 feet high and has been calculated to weigh 70 tons. Not surprisingly, it has gradually subsided over the ages.

IRELAND'S EYE. Just over a mile offshore from Howth Harbour (above right) lies a tiny rocky islet which has been made into a bird reserve. Excursions to Ireland's Eye leave from Dublin. On the islet can also be seen the restored remains of a 7th-century chapel (mentioned in a papal bull of 1179) and a Martello tower ● *101.*

MALAHIDE CASTLE (9 miles north of Dublin). In 1174 Henry II granted the land to the Talbot family and, apart from a few years of banishment at the time of Cromwell, they remained in residence until the

> **"DELIGHTFUL TO BE ON THE HILL OF HOWTH, VERY SWEET TO BE ABOVE ITS WHITE SEA; THE PERFECT FERTILE HILL, HOME OF SHIPS, THE VINEGROWN PLEASANT WARLIKE PEAK."**
> ANON. 14TH-CENTURY (?) IRISH POEM TRANS. KENNETH HURLSTONE JACKSON

mid 1970's. The Honorable Rose Talbot then had to sell the house, the 250 acres of land and most of the furniture and paintings that had been in her family for centuries. Fortunately, when Dublin County Council acquired the property they bought as much furniture as possible, to enable the visiting public to see the castle as it had been when the Talbots lived there. Over centuries of occupation the castle had been much altered. In the second half of the 18th century twin towers and a rampart were added. Today it is hard to tell that this was once a 15th-century defensive tower house. The interior, too, was redesigned in the 18th century, with Baroque-style plasterwork by Robert West and mantelpieces by the famous Italian craftsman Bossi. One of the rooms on the first floor, the Oak Room, still has its dark wood paneling dating from the 17th century, enlivened by some Dutch or Flemish pieces depicting the *Holy Virgin* and *Adam and Eve.* Irish paintings from the 18th century hang in the second-floor reception rooms, which have decoration from the Georgian period. Many of the works of art in the castle, particularly those in the medieval Great Hall, are portraits on loan from the National Gallery of Ireland ▲ 162. There are thirty-one Talbot family members alone. The last Lord Talbot, Milo, left the property to his sister Rose. He was a diplomat but also a great gardener, and he brought many species of plant back from Tasmania where the family had another property. They can be seen in the gardens today.

NEWBRIDGE DEMESNE (North of Malahide, on the western edge of Donabate). The 320-acre estate has been a County Dublin regional park since 1986. The hillside pastures, gentle valleys, streams and woodland are delightful. NEWBRIDGE HOUSE itself is a fine neoclassical residence built in about 1737 for Rev. Charles Cobbe, who became archbishop of Dublin in 1746. The possession of such an agricultural estate in the 18th century would have permitted almost total self-suffiency. The Cobbe family archives going back to this period survive. They give a detailed picture of the day-to-day administration, incomings and outgoings of such an estate in Ireland at the time. There also survives a fascinating family Museum of Curiosities.

THE LEGENDS OF MALAHIDE CASTLE
Malahide Castle has the only medieval great hall still to exist in Ireland today. On the walls is an impressive collection of family portraits. It is said that fourteen Talbot cousins had breakfast here together before leaving for the Battle of the Boyne ▲ 194. None of them returned. Another story concerns the carved Flemish panel of the *Coronation of the Virgin* in the Oak Room which supposedly disappeared when the Talbots were banished and mysteriously reappeared on their return to the castle.

FRY MODEL RAILWAY
A vast room has been constructed at Malahide Castle to accommodate the Fry Model Railway, a unique and detailed O-gauge layout (1:43). The miniature trains are reproductions of those dating from 1834 up to the present day, and there are also boats, trams and cars. They have taken Cecil Fry many years of dedicated enthusiasm to make.

175

PRETTY AS A PICTURE
Many films have been shot in the stunning and varied scenery of this county so convenient to Dublin. The ruined tower at Killincarraig (between Delganny and Greystones) appears in the opening scenes of Stanley Kubrick's *Barry Lyndon*. Part of John Boorman's *Excalibur* was filmed around Bray, Enniskerry and the Wicklow Mountains (Lough Tay); and the combat between Arthur and Lancelot was shot at Powerscourt waterfall.

The "Garden of Ireland", County Wicklow, is remarkable for the beauty and variety of its landscape. The stark outlines of the Wicklow Mountains contrast with rich, abundant woodlands and lush green fields, at times ordered into the geometrical shapes of a country-house garden. These hidden valleys, wild gorges, dark lakes and dizzy waterfalls have barely changed since Celtic and early Christian times.

SOUTH OF DUBLIN

BRAY. A Victorian seaside resort modeled on the English town of Brighton. Handsome pastel-colored houses line the seafront, which ends in the shadow of BRAY HEAD. From the top there is a view over mountains, valley and sea. A path leads along the cliff to Greystones, a similar resort.

POWERSCOURT DEMESNE ★. On the edge of the picturesque village of Enniskerry lies this magnificent estate, named after the Norman knight Eustace de la Poers. In 1609, James I granted the property to Sir Richard Wingfield. A grand house was built between 1731 and 1740, designed by Richard Castle and modeled on the Palladian Villa Pisani near Venice. Powerscourt is famed for its gardens, first laid out in the 18th century and probably designed by Richard Castle. Their formality is accentuated by the view over the

valley to the wild Great and Little Sugar Loaf mountains. Daniel Robertson designed the upper terraces. In 1974 the owners decided to open the house to the public and interior renovations were carried out. During a lunch party to celebrate these renovations a chimney caught fire; it was thought the fire had been extinguished but later that night it took hold and the owners narrowly escaped with their lives. The entire top story was destroyed and only the walls remain.

WICKLOW MOUNTAINS

The massive granite outcrops, eroded over the centuries, are wild and beautiful. J.M. Synge wrote: "I passed through a narrow gap with high rocks on either side of it and fir trees above them, and a handful of jagged sky filled with extra-ordinarily brilliant stars. In a few moments I passed out on the brow of the hill . . . and smelt the fragrance of the bogs."

SALLY GAP. Passing through Glencree, join the old Military Road leading past the deep lakes of Bray at the foot of Mount Kippure to Sally Gap, a crossroads set between Djouce Mountain to the east and Mullaghcleevaun to the southwest. (There are now two possible routes to Glendalough.)

VIA ROUNDWOOD. Pass Lough Tay, where the valley sides descend sharply to the deep waters, and the narrow Lough Dan. The two are linked by the Cloghoge river. Roundwood is the highest village in Ireland (768 feet). Stop at Roundwood Inn ◆ 370 before setting off up the Annamoe Valley.

VIA GLENMACNASS VALLEY. This carries along the Military Road, alongside the spectacular Glenmacnass waterfall.

THE MILITARY ROAD
The English forged this route into the Dublin hinterland to pursue rebels from the 1798 rebellion, who had taken refuge in the Wicklow Mountains. The 50 miles of road led across the rugged hills connecting a series of military posts whose ruins are still visible (at Glencree, Glenmalure, Laragh, Drumgoff). It is a good route by which to explore Wicklow, leading from the outskirts of Dublin to Aghavannagh.

GLENDALOUGH ★

Set in a lonely valley beside two dark lakes, the monastic site of Glendalough (from the Irish, Gleann da Loch, meaning "Valley of the Two Lakes") was founded in the 6th century by Saint Kevin. Over nearly eight centuries the monastery was a flourishing religious center, surrounded by a large number of dependent dwellings, scriptoriums, an infirmary and a farm. Now only ruins remain, but Glendalough has lost none of its spiritual power. There is a Visitors' Centre which provides a good explanation of the site, and which also displays ancient crosses (including the 12th-century Market Cross) and tombstones that have been found there.

LOWER LAKE. The main buildings lie to the east of the Lower Lake, reached through a fortified gateway that was once two stories high (most unusual for its period). The ROUND TOWER, well over 100 feet high, probably dates from the 11th century. It is far taller than the other buildings and was a good landmark for approaching pilgrims as well as being a useful refuge in times of danger (as were the church and watch towers). The roof of the tower was reconstructed in 1876 using the original materials. ST MARY'S CHURCH and the CATHEDRAL are typical of early Irish churches: the former consists only of nave and chancel, the latter, which precedes it in date, has an unusual north doorway and a fine ornamental east window. The tiny PRIEST'S HOUSE has an exterior Romanesque arch and a carved lintel whose central figure is thought to be Saint Kevin. Priests were buried here during the

St Kevin's Church.

THE TWO SAINTS OF GLENDALOUGH
Kevin (d. c. 618) was born into the royal House of Leinster but retired as a hermit to Glendalough. He had many disciples and he later founded what was to be an important monastery in the valley, becoming its abbot from 570. Despite being pillaged and burnt during the 9th and 10th centuries, the monastery remained a key religious and scholastic center. It was given a new lease of life in the 12th century by Laurence O'Toole (1128–80) who later became archbishop of Dublin, returning on occasion to Glendalough and the solitude of St Kevin's Bed. He was canonized in 1226.

Pilgrimage to Glendalough.

suppression of Catholicism, hence its name. ST KEVIN'S CHURCH, also called St Kevin's Kitchen, has a steep corbeled stone roof and, making it unique in Ireland, a small round tower in addition. TRINITY CHURCH (near to the Laragh road) was once the same, but its tower collapsed in a storm in 1818. There is another interesting Romanesque church among the trees, ST SAVIOUR'S (to the east, on Green Road), possibly built by Saint Laurence O'Toole. Note the decorations on the capitals of the chancel arch, including a serpent, a dragon and two crows holding a human head in their beaks.

UPPER LAKE. Along the walk between the car park and REEFERT CHURCH are five boundary crosses. The shrines around the Upper Lake were much revered, and a pilgrimage continued to be made here until 1862. The name Reefert comes from *rí fearta* ("tomb of the kings") because the kings of Leinster were buried here. Nearby are the remains of the Church of the Rock, or Teampull na Skellig, an ancient oratory mentioned in accounts of Saint Kevin's life.

TOWARD WICKLOW

DEVIL'S GLEN. The valley is steep and wooded. Through it the River Vartry rushes down a rocky bed to flow into the huge Devil's Punch Bowl. There are signed footpaths making it possible to admire the glen on foot.

MOUNT USHER GARDENS. Not far from Ashford is one of the finest parks in Ireland, Mount Usher Gardens (right). The gardens are famed for their immense variety of trees and exotic plants (more than four thousand species). On a nearby road stands Hunter's Hotel, one of the country's oldest coaching inns. Travelers have been welcomed here for over two hundred years.

WICKLOW. The county town is also a popular seaside resort overlooking a huge crescent-shaped bay. In Market Square stands a memorial honoring the Wicklow men who fought in the 1798 rebellion ● *52*. On a cliff to the east of the town are the scant remains of BLACK CASTLE, dating back to the Norman invasion.

ACROSS THE VALLEYS

GLENMALURE. From Laragh, the Military Road leads to Glenmalure, the wildest valley in Wicklow and surrounded by mountains. Highest of all is Lugnaquillia, which at 3,039 feet is the tallest peak in the county. A nine-mile walk leads through the deep glen to Baravore.

VALE OF CLARA. Southwest of Glendalough a pretty road follows the Avonmore river to the village of Rathdrum, at the entrance to the Vale of Avoca.

TEMPTATION OF SAINT KEVIN
St Kevin's Bed is a deep ledge partly dug by hand into the rock face and set some 5 feet above the Upper Lake. It is said that the saint took refuge here to avoid the attentions of a young woman. One morning, finding her there beside him, he threw her into the lake.

"WICKLOW": THE ORIGIN OF THE NAME
"Wicklow" is derived from the Danish *Vikingalo* ("Viking field"), a strategically important 9th-century Viking encampment. The Irish name *Cill Mhantáin* refers to the church founded by Saint Mantan, who was said to be a disciple of Saint Patrick ● *56*.

CHARLES STEWART PARNELL (1846–91)
Born to a Protestant family, in 1875 Parnell became Member of Parliament for County Meath giving his support to the cause of Home Rule. His leadership was most effective until the scandal broke of his liaison with Kitty O'Shea. Divorce proceedings instituted by her husband ruined Parnell's political career, and he died soon after, a broken man. Today he is celebrated as one of the heroes of Irish nationalism.

VALE OF AVOCA

AVONDALE HOUSE. The house is neoclassical in style and dates from the 18th century. It is filled with souvenirs of the politician Charles Stewart Parnell ● *53*, born here in 1846. The house is now a forestry school (set up by the English in 1904), and also contains Forestry Service offices. This would have pleased the former owner Samuel Hayes, who in 1794 wrote one of the first treatises on arboriculture and who planted the estate with trees native to Ireland. Today the forest has species from all over the world.

MEETING OF THE WATERS. The confluence of the the Avonbeg and Avonmore, joining their waters in the River Avoca, has a magic that inspired the poet and composer of songs Thomas Moore to write the poem *The Meeting of the Waters* in 1807.

ARKLOW. The town was founded by the Vikings. It has lost its former importance as a port, and consequently its prosperity, but it retains its old reputation for yacht-building. There is a maritime museum, and visitors also come from Dublin to enjoy the beaches of Brittas Bay, to the north.

TOWARD WEXFORD

FERNS. The ruins of the imposing Anglo-Norman castle dating from the 12th and 13th centuries dominate the town, which was once the seat of the kings of Leinster. In one of the towers is a 13th-century chapel. Around the church of St Aidan are the remains of a 6th-century abbey.

ENNISCORTHY. The town has a history stretching back to the 6th century, when Saint Senan founded a church here. The 13th-century Norman castle, later rebuilt, overlooks the River

Slaney. It houses the County Museum, a collection of photographs, documents and varied objects mainly relating to Enniscorthy's part in the 1798 rebellion and the 1916 Easter Rising ● *60*. The neo-Gothic cathedral of St Aidan was designed by Augustus Welby Pugin.

FERRYCARRIG ● *90*. The Irish National Heritage Park (left) gives an overview of nine thousand years of history through a number of reconstructions of ancient settlements and religious sites (*crannog, rath,* monastery, Norman castle). A round tower was built here in 1857 in memory of those who died in the Crimean War.

WEXFORD. The capital of County Wexford stands on a site once occupied by a Belgian clan, and later by the Vikings (from the 9th to the 12th centuries) who founded the flourishing port of Waesfjord. The town was taken by Normans in 1169. Today it is known internationally for its Opera Festival, held annually in October. Near to Westgate Tower, the only one of five fortified gateways to remain, lie the ruins of SELSKAR ABBEY, scene of some important events: a treaty was signed here with the English in 1169; in 1172 Henry II did

WOODENBRIDGE GOLD RUSH
In the 18th century the village of Woodenbridge, five miles northwest of Arklow, was swamped by a rush for gold. Over a few months 2,600 ounces were found on Croghan Mountain. The largest nuggets are displayed in the National Museum, Dublin ▲ *158*.

> **"SWEET VALE OF AVOCA! HOW CALM COULD I REST IN THY BOSOM OF SHADE, WITH THE FRIENDS I LOVE BEST, WHERE THE STORMS THAT WE FEEL IN THIS COLD WORLD SHOULD CEASE, AND OUR HEARTS, LIKE THY WATERS, BE MINGLED IN PEACE."**
>
> THOMAS MOORE

penance here after the murder of Thomas Becket; Strongbow's daughter married Raymond le Gros in Selskar in 1175. Cromwell destroyed the abbey in 1649 and massacred two hundred citizens of Wexford.

WEXFORD WILDFOWL RESERVE ■ 26. For eight months of the year a large proportion of Greenland's white-fronted geese find peace on mud flats about 3 miles north of Wexford.

AROUND WEXFORD

JOHNSTOWN CASTLE. The estate belonged to the earls of Desmond in the 18th century. The vast 19th-century neo-Gothic building is now an agricultural college, and in the grounds is the Irish Agricultural Museum.

ROSSLARE. The town is a busy port, but also a popular seaside resort with a long and beautiful beach. There are ferries to Fishguard, Le Havre and Cherbourg.

TACUMSHIN. The village is encircled by Tacumshin Lake and Lady's Island Lake, lagoons surrounded by rich vegetation and renowned for their birdlife. There is a working windmill (below) dating from 1846.

KILMORE QUAY. A charming and genuine fishing village of thatched and white-walled cottages. *Guillemot*, an old lightship now moored along the quay, has been turned into a museum of the maritime history of Wexford.

SALTEE ISLANDS. The two uninhabited islands are Ireland's largest bird reserve, sheltering more than 220 of the 380 species known in the country. These include puffins, guillemots, razorbills, and gulls. The islands can be reached by boat from Kilmore Quay.

A PARTISAN COUNTY
The memory of the 1798 rebellion is still alive in County Wexford. Sites of victory are marked (Battle of Duffry Gate), and even more so those of defeat. At Vinegar Hill, near Enniscorthy, an encampment of some twenty thousand held out for nearly a month. The rebels were eventually overcome, and many of them, unarmed, were massacred in cold blood. The leaders were hanged.

JOHNSTOWN CASTLE PARK
The park covers nearly 50 acres, and has over two hundred species of tree and shrub set around the three lakes. There are also lovely walled gardens and greenhouses.

Scenes from the Irish Derby,
run on the famous
Curragh racecourse.

T he country roads that lead southwest from Dublin cross the peaceful counties of Kildare, Carlow and Kilkenny, passing huge dolmens, Norman castles, monasteries, celtic crosses, medieval towns and fine country houses. Other precious but little visited sites are to be found on the borders of the three coastal counties of Wicklow, Wexford and Waterford.

TOWARD KILDARE

IRISH NATIONAL STUD (Tully ◆ *350*) In 1943 the British National Stud (once the stud of Colonel Hall Walker, and given to the State in 1915) became the Irish National Stud. A museum traces the history of the horse in Ireland, and includes among its display items the skeleton of Arkle, one of the greatest racehorses of the 20th century. Hall Walker, later Lord Wavertree, was considered fairly eccentric: he was not interested in a foal unless its star chart was favorable. Perhaps the nearby Japanese gardens that he had laid out in 1904 were also intended to have a positive effect on his youngstock.

CASTLETOWN HOUSE. At the foot of the Wicklow Mountains ▲ *177* stands the magnificent Castletown House, the first Palladian villa to be built in Ireland. It was constructed between 1722 and 1732 and designed by the Florentine architect Alessandro Galilei (1691–1737) and Englishman Edward Lovett Pearce ▲ *148* for "Speaker" William Conolly, Speaker of the Irish House of Commons from 1715. In 1967 it was bought by Desmond Guinness and later, in 1979, by the Irish Georgian Society who undertook its restoration and provided replacement Irish furniture and paintings for any originals that were missing. The central block of the house is flanked by two rounded and colonnaded wings. The rooms are as they were in the 18th century: the BROWN ROOM has pine paneling and an unusual grooved ceiling, and the LONG GALLERY ★ (left) is decorated in a vivid blue Pompeian style. The Rococo stucco on the staircase walls was made by the much-admired Lafranchini brothers ● *106*.

NAAS. The town was once the capital of the kings of Leinster and is at the center of a region famous for its horse-breeding ◆ *350*. Much horseracing takes place in the vicinity, in particular at PUNCHESTOWN, 3 miles southwest of the town. Races here in 1868, graced by the presence of the Prince of Wales, drew a crowd of 150,000 people. The meetings continue to be popular.

KILDARE. The town grew up around a monastery founded in the 5th century by Saint Brigid. It is said that she kept a sacred fire burning in her church. It remained alight through the Viking raids, but was extinguished at the beginning of the 13th century on the orders of the archbishop of Dublin. Shortly afterward the fire was relit, to burn until the Reformation. ST BRIGID'S CATHEDRAL dates from the 13th century but it was much restored in the 19th. There is an interesting primitive font in the nave.

EMO COURT DEMESNE ● *104.* The estate belongs in part to the Forest Service and has on it a house built in the classical style (1790) by James Gandon for the Earl of Portarlington. A magnificent avenue of sequoias, over one hundred years old, runs through the gardens. There are also glorious cypress trees, cedars, pines and spruces, some more than 100 feet in height. Along the path leading to the lake four Greek statues representing the Seasons stand on the lawns.

THE HORSE

In the pre-Christian era Ireland's Knights of the Red Branch already rode on horseback. The steeplechase was invented in Ireland in 1752, with the first race being run between two church steeples. For centuries the Irish have been justly proud of their horses. The two best-known breeds are the Connemara pony ▲ 266 and the Irish Draught, a heavy working horse. The latter is crossed with the thoroughbred to produce marvelous Irish Hunters, originally bred for the hunting field but, for many years now, successful as showjumping horses too. There are a number of local horse fairs in Ireland, always well attended, as are the numerous race meetings held on the country's twenty-seven racecourses. Each course has a unique atmosphere, but most famous is the Curragh, home of the Irish Derby.

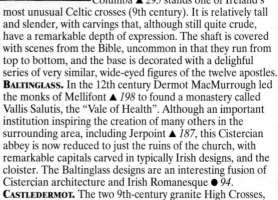

THE TIMES

Saturday April 27 1974

No 59,075   Price 6p

Irish gang seize Vermeer and 15 other paintings in world's biggest art robbery

Old masters worth at least £8m were stolen last night in a seven-minute armed raid on a house near Dublin. It was the world's biggest art robbery. The gang, led by a woman with a French accent, who selected the paintings to be taken, tied up the owner, Sir Alfred Beit, and his wife. Among the stolen pictures were Jan Vermeer's "Love letter", said by police to be worth £3m. As in the Kenwood robbery earlier this year, political motives are not being discounted.

THE BEIT COLLECTION
This includes works by the Dutch and Flemish masters (Rubens, Jan Steen, Frans Hals), paintings

by Goya, Murillo and other Spanish artists, views by Guardi and portraits by Gainsborough and Raeburn.

TOWARD KILKENNY

RUSSBOROUGH HOUSE ● 105.
Brewer Joseph Leeson, later Earl of Milltown, employed the architect Richard Castle to build Russborough. He began the Palladian-style country house in 1741; it was finished ten years later by Francis Bindon. Inside is remarkable Rococo stuccowork by the Lafranchini brothers ● 106. The decoration of the staircase, probably by Irish pupils of the brothers, is so extravagant that one viewer ascribed it to a "raving lunatic". The property was bought in 1952 by Sir Alfred Beit, whose uncle, also Alfred Beit, made his fortune from the South-African diamond mines. He spent it on marvelous paintings, amassing his collection late in the 19th century. His nephew bought Russborough House to house the paintings but, in 1974, members of the IRA stole sixteen of them for ransom. They were caught and the paintings recovered. It did not prevent the Beits from opening the house to the public, while still in residence. In 1986 the best paintings were stolen once again in mysterious circumstances. By 1992 only one had been recovered.

MOONE ▲ 206. On the site of a Franciscan abbey associated with Saint Columba ▲ 295 stands one of Ireland's most unusual Celtic crosses (9th century). It is relatively tall and slender, with carvings that, although still quite crude, have a remarkable depth of expression. The shaft is covered with scenes from the Bible, uncommon in that they run from top to bottom, and the base is decorated with a delightful series of very similar, wide-eyed figures of the twelve apostles.

BALTINGLASS. In the 12th century Dermot MacMurrough led the monks of Mellifont ▲ 198 to found a monastery called Vallis Salutis, the "Vale of Health". Although an important institution inspiring the creation of many others in the surrounding area, including Jerpoint ▲ 187, this Cistercian abbey is now reduced to just the ruins of the church, with remarkable capitals carved in typically Irish designs, and the cloister. The Baltinglass designs are an interesting fusion of Cistercian architecture and Irish Romanesque ● 94.

CASTLEDERMOT. The two 9th-century granite High Crosses, the Romanesque doorway of a long-gone chapel, and the 10th-century round tower were all part of a monastery founded by Saint Dermot in 812. In the 14th century there was a Franciscan friary here, now also reduced to a few ruins. Once a walled town, Castledermot was also of great military significance. Edward Bruce was defeated here in 1316 by Sir Edmund Butler, and in 1499 a Parliament was held here.

CARLOW. The remains of William Marshal's CASTLE, along with the town's other ruins, are a forceful reminder of the battles endured by the inhabitants. Carlow was a prized position, set strategically on the confluent of the rivers Barrow and Burren. One of the bloodiest episodes in its history occurred in 1798. Six hundred Nationalist rebels tried

to take the town and were massacred by the English. To the west of town, toward Graiguecullen, are the stone quarries where 417 of them lie buried. About 3 miles beyond stands Killeshin Church ★ where, despite the advancing brambles, a remarkable carved Romanesque doorway is to be admired, one of the most interesting in Ireland. Two miles northwest of Carlow, in the Browne's Hill demesne, is one of the largest dolmens in Europe. It is four thousand years old and the covering slab is calculated to weigh 100 tons.

KILKENNY ★

The county town of Kilkenny, set on the banks of the river Nore, is justly proud of both its castle and cathedral. It has some fine medieval buildings, handsome old houses, narrow streets and vaulted passageways. The delightful shopfronts add character and color to the town, while the sixty-eight licensed premises contribute much to its flavor.

HISTORY. The city developed around a monastery founded in the 6th century by Saint Canice, from which came the name "Cill Chainnigh". Strongbow built a fortress here late in the 12th century and, because of its strategic position, Kilkenny remained important in Anglo-Irish affairs. A number of parliaments were held here, and in 1366 the famous Statutes of Kilkenny were passed ● 50. The town reached its peak of

THE KILLESHIN DOOR
This Romanesque doorway owes its unusual appearance to the different-colored stones used for the four arches of its archivolt. It was probably originally brightly painted, which would have made the capitals stand out. They are great carved heads with hair and beards entwined into Celtic

importance between 1642 and 1648 after the founding of an independent parliament known as the Confederation of Kilkenny ● 51. It then became weakened by internal dissent, and in 1650 Cromwell was able to take control after five days' siege. Kilkenny has long had a strong nationalist tradition and was active in the fight for independence early in this century. Sinn Féin member William Thomas Cosgrave was elected to Parliament for the city of Kilkenny, and in 1922 became the first president of the Irish Free State ▲ 54.

patterns in a manner that has been likened to Byzantine sculpture.

185

TOMBS IN ST CANICE'S
The sepulchral monuments that were the main decoration of the cathedral in the 16th century have suffered the ravages of time, not to mention those inflicted by Cromwell's troops. Some were reconstructed from fragments, not always from the same tomb. The largest monument (right), in the south transept, has probably retained its original appearance. It is the tomb of the eighth Earl of Ormonde and his wife Margaret FitzGerald, dating from 1539. In the north transept are some recumbent figures with hauntingly memorable faces.

KILKENNY CASTLE. William Marshal built the castle late in the 12th century on the site of his father-in-law Strongbow's original fort. In 1392 it came into the possession of the earls of Ormonde, the Butler family. They made many alterations to the castle over the centuries and it remained their residence until 1935. In 1967 it was given to the State. The veneer of French elegance given by 17th-century alterations does not disguise the massive features of the medieval castle (left), which overlooks the River Nore. Three sides of the original quadrangle remain, with round towers and curtain walls. The PICTURE GALLERY, built between 1858 and 1862 by Benjamin Woodward, has an interesting collection of family portraits, and an incongruous hammer-beam roof painted by John Hungerford Pollen. The tea rooms benefit from a charming setting in the old kitchen, still with massive cooking ranges and gleaming copper pans: a good place to pause before setting off to explore the grounds. The 18th-century stables are converted into workshops for the KILKENNY DESIGN CENTRE, a government-subsidized craft center encouraging innovative work in traditional mediums (such as weaving, pottery, jewelry-making).

ST CANICE'S CATHEDRAL ★. The lovely cathedral was built in the 13th century. It stands on the site of St Canice's

monastery, founded in the 6th century, of which nothing remains but a tall, round tower. It is possible to climb to the top for a fine view of the town and surrounding countryside. The light and spacious cathedral was built in a pure Gothic style and has escaped almost entirely from subsequent alterations. It contains a number of Ireland's finest funerary monuments, some of them extremely old, such as that of Henry de Pont de Lyra's son (1285).

ROTHE HOUSE ★. The only Tudor merchant's house to survive in Ireland is a fascinating complex consisting of three buildings and two courtyards, erected in 1594 for the wealthy John Rothe Fitzpiers. It was once the headquarters of the Gaelic League ● *67*, and today it houses the museum and library of the Kilkenny Archeological Society.

KYTELER'S INN ♦ *368* (27 St Kieran Street). The inn occupies one of the oldest houses in Kilkenny, once the home of Dame Alice Kyteler, born in 1280. She was the widow of four rich husbands, and suspected also of their murder. When condemned to death for witchcraft, she escaped, leaving her servant Petronilla to be burnt at the stake in her place.

DUNMORE CAVES (5 miles north of Kilkenny). Those keen on speleology should visit these limestone caves with their impressive stalagmites and stalactites. The story goes that the monster Luchtigern, the "Lord of the Mice", was killed at the giant MARKET CROSS stalactite. These caves are one of three places of darkness and evil in Irish legend. The reputation may be based on fact: in 1967, the bones of over a thousand people were discovered here, victims of a Viking raid in 928.

TOWARD WATERFORD (VIA NEW ROSS)

In the 12th century the newly arrived Normans were drawn to County Kilkenny by its fertile and wooded countryside. This explains the number of medieval buildings in the county.

GOWRAN ★. The massive square tower and chancel of the original Collegiate Church of St Mary (1275) have been incorporated into the more recent Protestant church. It contains some fine sepulchral monuments and an effigy of the first earl of Ormonde in armor, on the floor of the nave.

JERPOINT ABBEY ● *96* **★.** The abbey (above) is one of the most remarkable historic sites in County Kilkenny. It was founded around 1160, probably by Donal MacGillapatrick, Lord of Ossory, and it is laid out in the Cistercian cruciform plan with two square chapels in each transept. The south side of the nave has now disappeared, but there are some magnificent capitals on the north side, probably made by the same masons who worked at Baltinglass ▲ *184*. The ancient barrel vault over the choir still remains, and above is the 15th-century tower with Irish battlements. There are tombs in both transepts and also in the choir, which had a dividing wall to separate monks and lay-brothers during services. The most striking monument here is the tomb of Felix O'Dullany (first abbot of Jerpoint and founder of Kilkenny cathedral), with a serpent gnawing the end of his crozier. What makes Jerpoint unique among Irish Cistercian abbeys is the cloister which, like the tower, was added in the 15th century. It is decorated with carved figures including Saint Margaret standing on a dragon, Saint Christopher, a knight, and an intriguing monkey-like creature.

CELTIC CROSSES
Among the crosses in southern Kilkenny (Kilree, Kilkieran), the 8th-century High Crosses at Ahenny (above) have the most intricate carved patterns. Only on the base do human figures feature. Those on the more northerly cross would seem to be: *Adam and the animals* (east side), *Christ surrounded by six apostles* (west side) and *David leaving for battle on a chariot and returning with the head of Goliath, the giant's body being dragged by a horse* (the other two sides).

SMITHWICK'S BREWERY ● *77*
The visit includes a chance to taste the famous "Kilkenny" beer, but also gives a history of local brewing. Monks at the now ruined St Francis' Abbey (1234) were making beer in the 14th century.

DUISKE ABBEY
The church, founded in 1204 by William Marshal, has suffered the ravages of time. Much of the nave has disappeared: the octagonal tower fell in 1774 with three of the supporting arches, burying many sculptured monuments under tons of stone. Over the centuries the floor level has risen owing to accumulated rubble from the crumbling structure. Despite this, the church is still a fine example of early English Gothic, with some beautifully carved capitals.

Graiguenamanagh Cross.

INISTIOGE. A tree-lined square and old stone bridge give great charm to this unpretentious village of pretty 18th- and 19th-century houses. Of the Augustinian priory founded in 1210 only the ruins of the nave, tower and chapel remain.

GRAIGUENAMANAGH, "THE GRANARY OF THE MONKS". An ancient religious center, now a prosperous market town set on the banks of the River Barrow, beneath Brandon Hill, and grown up around the ruins of the 13th-century Cistercian abbey of DUISKE. Despite the abbey's former importance, little of its history remains apart from details of its debts to Italian bankers in the late 13th century, or the last abbot's gift of a silver cross brought back from a pilgrimage to Santiago de Compostela in 1504 which disappeared at the monastery's dissolution, under Henry VIII. The exterior is now sadly changed, although the inside retains recognizable features.

ST MULLINS. The village has ruins of a 7th-century monastery founded by Saint Moling; its plan appears in *The Book of Moling*, an ancient manuscript conserved in Dublin. Close by, among ruins of several churches, stand a truncated round tower, a small oratory and a cross.

NEW ROSS. The town, which sprawls along the River Barrow, was founded by Isabella, daughter of Strongbow and wife of William Marshal. It was an important garrison and later became a thriving market town. In the cemetery are the ruined choir and transept of St Mary's Abbey (13th century), possibly the largest parish church in medieval Ireland. From here it is possible to visit the John F. Kennedy Memorial Park, 250 acres planted with six hundred species of trees. The late President's family came from County Wexford.

TOWARD WATERFORD (VIA CARRICK-ON-SUIR)

KELLS PRIORY. A circle of high walls and supporting towers surround the vast Augustinian priory founded in 1193. The church (14th and 15th century) looks tiny in the middle of this 5-acre enclosure, but it was considered quite large when it was built.

An 18th-century view of Waterford.

CARRICK-ON-SUIR. Nestling in the Suir Valley, the town straddles the border between County Tipperary ▲ *251* and County Waterford. It was founded by the Butler family. In the 16th century Thomas Butler, tenth Earl of Ormonde, known as "Black Tom", built the superb Elizabethan MANSION in expectation of a visit from Elizabeth I, who in fact never came. Two towers from the family's former castle still stand behind the manor.

WATERFORD AND WATERFORD HARBOUR

THE CITY. Waterford stretches along the south bank of the Suir. Behind the long riverfront quays are narrow streets that must have run there since medieval times. The town was a Norman stronghold established in the 12th century on the site of a Viking encampment. Commerce increased and by the 16th century Waterford had developed into a thriving port. There are some rare remains of the medieval town. The 12th- or 13th-century REGINALD'S TOWER (right), where Strongbow was married now houses the town museum. The central tower of BLACKFRIARS (1226), a Dominican priory, stands almost intact. There are also ruins of the FRENCH CHURCH (1240), so called because it was used by refugee Huguenots from France in 1695. But Waterford has a great many more Georgian buildings, some by John Roberts, including the Protestant CHRIST CHURCH (1770–9) and the Catholic HOLY TRINITY CATHEDRAL (1793–6). The latter possesses a collection of holy vestments discovered during the construction of Christ Church and presented by the Protestant bishop to his Catholic counterpart.

WATERFORD HARBOUR. There are a number of places of interest along the estuary that leads from Waterford to the sea. Cistercians founded DUNBRODY ABBEY in the 11th century on the east bank of the Barrow. The Gothic church was built in the 12th century and additions were made in the 15th century. The ruins have a graceful purity of style often found in Cistercian buildings. The walls of Duncannon Fort still stand proud upon their promontory, erected in 1588 to protect the region from attack by the Armada ▲ *316*. At the end of Hook Head stands HOOK TOWER, one of the oldest lighthouses in Europe. It was built by Raymond le Gros in the 12th century. Southwest of Garrycullen stand the ruins of TINTERN ABBEY, a Cistercian abbey founded by William Marshal after surviving a shipwreck on the coast in 1200.

WATERFORD CRYSTAL The glassworks were founded in 1783 but, after reaching a peak of success, closed in the 19th century. Reopened in 1947, today Waterford's is the largest crystal factory in the world.

The Valley of the Boyne, crossing the fertile plains of County Meath, was a land of pagan legend and Celtic kings, where later Saint Patrick was welcomed with his news of Christianity. All the more tragic, then, that it should have been the site of the great battle between Protestant William of Orange and Catholic James II. Some of the most important historic monuments in Ireland are to be found in the valley, illustrating its long and eventful history.

TRIM

The town of Trim stood on the outer edge of the Pale, the territory around Dublin under Anglo-Norman control.
KING JOHN'S CASTLE. The Norman baron Hugh de Lacy established the original fortress in 1173. It was destroyed by Roderick O'Connor, who was considered by some as the last of the Ard Rí ● *48*. The fortress was rebuilt around 1204, and came into the possession of John Lackland. It has continued to be called after the English king, although only five years later he returned it to the Lacy family. A moat was created by redirecting the waters of the Boyne, and an outer curtain wall built, defended by ten semicircular towers. By the mid-13th century, King John's Castle was one of the most important Anglo-Norman strongholds. In the 14th century it was returned to the possession of the English Crown; two hundred years later it was in ruins. The confederates repaired the castle but it was taken in 1649 by Cromwell's troops. Later it became the property of the Plunket family who sold it to the State in 1993: today it is Ireland's largest Anglo-Norman castle.
YELLOW STEEPLE (Across the river). The 14th-century tower was once part of the Augustinian Abbey of St Mary. It was severely damaged by Cromwell's army, as was the town's defensive wall, little of which remains apart from SHEEP GATE, where sheep brought in for the great fairs were taxed. TALBOT CASTLE is an early 15th-century fortified manor built on the site of the abbey. In the 18th century it was converted into a school where Arthur Wellesley, later Duke of Wellington, was a pupil. ST PATRICK'S CHURCH was built on the site of a church founded by the saint in the 5th century.

WELLINGTON (1769–1852)
Although born in Dublin, Arthur Wellesley, Duke of Wellington, took no pride in his native land. When once described as "Irish", he replied that had he been born in a stable, it wouldn't have made him a horse. He represented Trim in Parliament and was Chief Secretary for Ireland before becoming Prime Minister. Despite his attitude, the "Iron Duke" gave O'Connell his way, passing the Act of Catholic Emancipation in 1829.

> **"THE FEIS OF TEMUR EACH THIRD YEAR,**
> **TO PRESERVE LAWS AND RULES**
> **WAS THEN CONVENED FIRMLY**
> **BY THE ILLUSTRIOUS KINGS OF ERIN."**
>
> (POEM DATED 984)

BECTIVE ABBEY

On the left bank of the Boyne lie the quiet ruins of one of County Meath's most impressive abbeys. It was founded for the Cistercian order in 1150 by Murchad O'Meleghlin, King of Meath, and grew rapidly in importance through its influential abbot, who was a Lord of Parliament. The main features of the ruins are a fortified tower and an elegant cloister (right) dating from the 15th century when, like other abbeys, Bective was fortified ● *96*. The road along the river toward Drogheda, past Oldbridge, leads to the site of the Battle of the Boyne ▲ *194*.

HILL OF TARA

The immense importance of this low hill is not obvious to the uninformed visitor. The grassy mounds are of little help to the imagination in evoking its legendary past. The Interpretative Centre offers good explanations and is a great aid to understanding the extraordinary site and bringing it to life. **ANCIENT HISTORY.** The oldest part of the site, the MOUND OF THE HOSTAGES, is a Bronze Age passage grave. Later Tara became an important place of pagan worship, and its very name evokes memories of the great heroes of Celtic legend such as High King Cormac MacAirt, whose daughter Gráinne eloped with the warrior Diarmait ▲ *289* on the eve of a wedding to another and High King Laoghaire who is said to be buried upright in his armor, ready to confront his enemies. **TARA OF THE KINGS.** Tara was the seat of the High Kings of Ireland and the source of royal power. Every three years the country's leaders would meet here to make laws and dispense justice. It was thought that these *feis* were held in the part of the site identified as the BANQUET HALL (right, a document showing a seating plan). The two parallel earthworks are now thought to have been a ceremonial entrance. The High Kings were crowned on a stone called the CORONATION STONE (Lia Fáil) which was said to sound if it approved the new leader.

THE MEETING OF TARA
During the 1798 rebellion ● *52* thirty-two people were killed on the hill of Tara. In August 1843 O'Connell deliberately chose the ancient Gaelic site for one of his great meetings protesting against the Act of Union ● *52*. Nearly one million people were there.

THE "BOOK OF KELLS" ▲ *154*
Most experts agree in dating the book from around 800. Opinions differ, however, as to where the astonishing illuminated manuscript was made. Some think it originated in Kells itself, others suggest Pict territory, in the east of Scotland, while the majority believe it to have been made at the monastery of Saint Columba on the Hebridean Isle of Iona. It was stolen from Kells in 1006, but found less than a year later, without the gold shrine that enclosed it. Since 1661 it has been kept in Trinity College, Dublin.

CHRISTIANITY ARRIVES. Tradition has it that Saint Patrick drove the Celtic druids from Tara. It is not known whether he actually converted the kings, but he won the population over to his faith, and the growing strength of Christianity ● *56* brought with it the decline of Tara's importance. The last pagan festival took place in the 6th century, and by the 8th century the kings no longer lived there. The site was finally abandoned c. 1022.

NAVAN

At the point where the green valleys of the Boyne and Blackwater rivers meet stands Navan, the capital of County Meath and, in far distant history, capital of Ulster for more than a thousand years. The most interesting monuments are outside the town. The noble LISCARTAN CASTLE, two square towers joined by a central hall, was held by William Talbot in 1633. DONAGHMORE CHURCH has a fine 12th-century round tower. Above its unusual doorway is a carving of *Christ on the Cross*, and there is a face carved on either side of the architrave. The church is said to stand on the site of Saint Patrick's first monastery.

KELLS (CEANANNUS MOR) ★

THE MONASTERY. Early in the 9th century the monks of Iona became so fearful of Viking attack that they fled to a monastery founded by Saint Columba ▲ *151* in the 6th century and set on the banks of the Blackwater. Whether they achieved their desired peace seems doubtful: Kells was invaded by Viking warriors five times between 807 and 1019.
THE "BOOK OF KELLS". The village of Kells is famed for an illuminated manuscript of the Gospels, stolen in 1006. The monastery was built on a circular plan (imitated later by the Norman defensive walls and, even today, preserved in the road pattern). At its center was the church from which the book was taken. The 19th-century building contains facsimiles and photographs of objects linked with the history of Kells. The ROUND TOWER served as a watchtower and place of safekeeping. It is known to predate 1076, when the son of the king of Meath was assassinated there.

Slane Castle.

SOUTH CROSS. The cross probably dates from the 9th century, and owes its other name, the Cross of Saint Patrick and Saint Columba, to the scarcely legible Latin inscription that runs around the base. Among the many carvings on the cross are (east face) *Adam and Eve*, *Cain and Abel* and the *Sacrifice of Abraham*, and (west face) the *Crucifixion* and the *Last Judgement*.

WEST CROSS. Not far away is another cross, now broken. It was certainly one of the finest in Ireland. Water seems to be the predominant theme in the carvings, which include the apocryphal scene of the *Bathing of the Infant Jesus*, a possible representation of the *Wedding at Cana*, and, focusing on the sacrament of baptism itself, a depiction of the *Baptism of Christ*.

EAST CROSS. South of the church is an unfinished cross with a carving of the *Crucifixion*.

SAINT COLUMBA'S HOUSE ★. Just north of the churchyard is a steep-roofed stone oratory probably built to house the precious relics of Saint Columba brought from Iona. Possibly once linked to the graveyard by a tunnel, the only other entrance used to be high up, going into the upper floor where there are three small cells. These are now reached from within by a ladder. (Before heading for Slane by the N51, it is possible take the road to Oldcastle, northwest of Kells, and visit Loughcrew.)

LOUGHCREW. A vast burial site lies on Slieve na Caillighe ("Hill of the Witch") in the Loughcrew Hills. Tumuli cover gallery tombs in which pieces of pottery dating from 2500 BC have been found. Note the many slabs with chevron and spiral designs.

SLANE

The hill above Slane offers a view up and down the valley that descends from Trim to Drogheda. There are remains of a famous monastery and church built in the 16th century on the site of a sanctuary founded by Saint Patrick. According to legend the saint lit a paschal fire here in 433, in defiance of the druids who were celebrating across the hilltops at Tara. Below is SLANE CASTLE (1785–1821), the work of numerous architects including James Gandon and Francis Johnston.

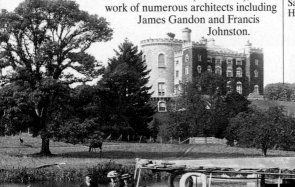

MARKET CROSS
The cross stands in the center of the village where the east door of the original monastery once was. In 1798 it was used as a gallows to hang local rebels. Among many interesting carvings there is a particularly fine *Hand of God* high up on one side of the shaft.

Saint Columba's House.

▲ THE BATTLE OF THE BOYNE

Louis XIV

Not so much a battle as a skirmish followed quickly by retreat, the Battle of the Boyne, which took place a few miles from Drogheda, seems to have marked the end of James II's ambitions to regain the English throne that he had lost to his son-in-law William of Orange. This dynastic quarrel was also important in larger terms: James was supported by Louis XIV of France and William by the King of Spain, two major forces struggling for domination in Europe. The achievements of the relatively tolerant William of Orange were later twisted by history. His 1691 Treaty of Limerick was infringed, and he was taken as the figurehead of the fervently Protestant Orange movement, which spread the myth of the Battle of the Boyne as the triumph of Protestant over Papist.

JAMES II
He ascended to the English throne in 1685. His tyranny and fervent Catholicism alarmed his subjects. The birth of an heir in 1688 brought matters to a head, and a faction invited his son-in-law, William, Prince of Orange, to take the throne. James II went into exile, and in 1689 Parliament ruled that he had abdicated.

WILLIAM III
Son-in-law and nephew of James II, William, Prince of Orange, was welcomed into England with open arms. He and his wife Mary were made king and queen. After bringing Scotland to heel he landed in Ireland on June 11, 1690, and quickly defeated James II's followers there, and their allies. The Protestant nation had triumphed in Ireland.

THE FLIGHT OF JAMES II
James II fled the field of battle and set sail for France from Waterford. Louis XIV gave him shelter, but he died a bitter man in exile. The Jacobites did not give up hope. Their activities continued with little success until well into the 18th century. The defeat of the "Young Pretender", Charles Edward Stewart, at Culloden, Scotland (1746) eventually put an end to their ambitions.

THE BATTLE
On July 1, 1690 (July 12 by the modern calendar), the 25,000 strong Jacobite army met William of Orange's 37,000 experienced soldiers at the River Boyne. The latter concentrated their attack at the hamlet of Oldbridge, where they crossed the river and forced the Irish back. James II, who did not use all his troops in the battle, fled. It was not a battle of great importance, but it gave William encouragement and eleven days later, at Aughrim, he gained the definitive victory.

THE TREATY STONE
It is said that the Treaty of Limerick was signed here on October 30, 1691, setting the seal on Protestant supremacy in Ireland.

THE ORANGE ORDER
Founded in 1795 "to maintain the laws and peace of the country and the Protestant constitution", it became increasingly influential in Northern Ireland.

The Newgrange
tumulus encloses a
passage grave 66 feet
long supported by
forty-three uprights.
It leads to a main
chamber with an
extraordinary
corbeled vaulted roof
20 feet high. Opening
from here are three
side chambers, each
with a polished and
decorated stone
trough in which
offerings were placed.
The grave is
positioned so that the
rising sun on the
winter solstice shines
through a slit directly
into the chamber.

VALLEY OF THE BOYNE ★

Within the Valley of the Boyne can be found one of the most
extraordinary megalithic sites in the world, both for the
number, grandeur and state of preservation of the remains
and for the beauty of every detail. The huge mounds of
Dowth, Newgrange and Knowth, lying low in the valley, are
proof not only of the skill and vision of their builders, but also
of their unshakeable religious faith.

DOWTH. The Dowth tumulus has suffered damage on a
number of occasions, including a Viking raid and pillaging for
stones as late as 1857. The mound encloses a number of
passage graves and funeral chambers which are still being
excavated. The main passage grave is cruciform with two side
chambers. It is entered by a metal stairway and lined with
stone uprights, while massive lintels form the roof. Fallen
blocks within the chamber make viewing difficult. When
reparations were made in 1847, "Within the chamber, mixed
with the clay and dust which had accumulated, were found a
quantity of bones consisting of heaps as well as scattered
fragments of burned bones, many of which proved to be
human."

NEWGRANGE ● 88. This is the most famous passage grave in
Ireland. The massive mound (290 feet in diameter and 36 feet
high) is partly constructed of huge stones brought from the
river. It was encircled by standing stones possibly more recent
in origin, but only twelve remain of a probable thirty-six.
Around the bottom of the cairn are ninety-seven kerb stones,
some with carved patterns. The famous threshold stone, just
below the entrance, is covered with marvelous spiral and
lozenge decorations. Carbon-dating shows Newgrange to be a
relatively late grave, from around 2500 BC. It was not
thoroughly restored until 1962. Some aspects of the grave are
unusual, especially the great wall of white quartzite stone
embossed with granite pebbles at surprisingly regular
intervals. The restoration was based on knowledge passed
down by word of mouth.

KNOWTH. The third of the valley's giant tumuli has been
undergoing painstaking reconstruction since 1960. Two big
passage graves have been found. The first, as at Newgrange,
has a corridor that widens out into the main chamber. The
carvings found at Knowth are particularly striking, both on

the kerb stones around the outside of the mound (lozenges, squares and sun symbols), and in the chambers where there are lozenges, triangles and zigzags as well as concentric arcs (also found in Brittany). There are unusual stones with a dotted pattern similar to some discovered in Neolithic temples on Malta. Around Knowth are about twenty satellite tumuli, at least sixteen of which contain passage graves. From the remains of dwellings and tunnels that have been found, it is evident that the cairn had a variety of occupants over the centuries including Vikings and early Christians. (Before continuing to Drogheda, take the road to Dunleer, then to Ardcath, to visit the interesting passage grave on Fourknocks hill.)

FOURKNOCKS. On the hill is another huge grave (2200–1800 BC). A short passage leads to the main chamber, which was once uncovered, but is now surmounted by a dome that is pierced with holes giving ample light to study the extraordinary decorations. The chamber opens onto three niches with zigzag motifs on the lintels. Among the stones on the ground is one of particular interest, showing a strange carving of a human face.

DROGHEDA TO DUNDALK

DROGHEDA. Of the many Parliaments that sat at Drogheda, the most famous is that of 1494, which brought in Poyning's Law. The town was once surrounded by a wall punctuated by ten gateways. The only one to remain is ST LAWRENCE'S GATE, an imposing 13th-century barbican with two round towers. Drogheda was the first town to suffer Cromwell's attack when he arrived in 1649 to subdue Ireland after the 1641 rebellion ● 51. MAGDELENE TOWER, all that remains of a Dominican monastery founded in 1224, still shows the scars of Cromwell's cannon, while the Protestant ST PETER'S CHURCH conserves a few fragments of a medieval church burnt by Cromwell to be rid of some one hundred men who had taken refuge in the tower. The Catholic ST PETER'S CHURCH has become a place of pilgrimage in reverence to the severed head of archbishop and martyr Oliver Plunket ▲ 199 which is embalmed and enshrined here.

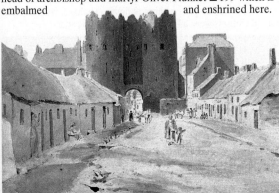

THE SYMBOLISM OF NEWGRANGE
The Neolithic decorations of the outer stones at Newgrange, and those lining the chamber, are among the richest in Ireland. The chevrons, spirals, lozenges, zigzags and waves are similar to patterns found on ancient monuments in Brittany, France, but their symbolism continues to puzzle experts and remains little understood. It is possible that the spirals are a symbol of the labyrinthine path to the underworld. The concentric circles could be connected with sun worship. The arcs perhaps represent the great Earth Mother, protectress of the dead, and goddess of harvests and fruitfulness. The waves, snake patterns and zigzags may stand for the sea of the living world, an important force, but they may also evoke the celestial sea of religious meditation.

St Lawrence's Gate, Drogheda.

MUIREDACH'S CROSS
On east side are seen, from bottom to top: *Adam and Eve* and *Cain and Abel* (on the same panel), *David and Goliath*, *Moses striking water from the rock* and the *Adoration of the Magi* (of whom there are four); in the center of the cross, the *Last Judgement* with, below, *Saint Michael weighing souls*. On the west side, from bottom to top, are: the *Taking of Christ*, *Christ arisen*, and *Christ giving Saint Peter the keys and Saint Paul the Gospels*; in the center is the *Crucifixion*, with the *Resurrection* on the right arm and, below, the *Ascension*. At the ends of the arms are scenes from the Passion: *Pilate washing his hands* (south arm), and what may be the *Taking of Christ* with, below, *Saint Paul and Saint Anthony in the desert.*

MONASTERBOICE. The ruins here are those of a monastery founded in the 5th century by Saint Buithe, disciple of Saint Patrick ● *56*, making it one of the earliest in Ireland. It was occupied for a time by the Danes until they were chased out by the king of Tara in 968. The precious manuscripts kept in the tower have disappeared, probably destroyed by fire in 1097. The three crosses that stand in the graveyard are of greatest interest. Like all crosses carved with scriptural scenes, their main purpose was to instruct the faithful, showing episodes from both the Old and New Testaments ▲ *204*. MUIREDACH'S CROSS (the nearest to the entrance) takes its name from a 9th-century abbot (there is an inscription low on the west side) and is topped by a carved church. The WEST CROSS, or Tall Cross, the highest in Ireland (21 feet), has suffered much damage from the elements, and the carvings are harder to decipher. The NORTH CROSS, badly damaged perhaps by Cromwell's troops, has a carving of the Crucifixion on one side and an interlace design on the other.

MELLIFONT ● *97*. On his way to Rome, Saint Malachy, bishop of Armagh ▲ *322*, stopped at Clairvaux in France in 1139 to meet Saint Bernard, a founder of the Cistercian Order. On his return to Ireland, Malachy began founding Cistercian communities, starting with the Mellifont Abbey (Fons Mellis), in 1142, and continuing with eight others, all following Clairvaux's rule, including Bective ▲ *191* and Boyle ▲ *289*. Little remains of the vast, stark and severe Mellifont Abbey buildings, except the foundations, some of the cloister arches and part of the elegant octagonal lavabo (below), whose finely carved capitals were a foretaste of the Gothic style.

Details of
carved capitals at
Mellifont Abbey.

ARDEE. It is well worth stopping in the main street of this little village to see ARDEE CASTLE, a 13th-century fortified tower once used as a tribunal, and HATCH'S CASTLE (private), a rare example of a round-cornered tower. Two miles southwest lies KILDEMOCK with its curious little church, known as Jumping Church because of the startling angle at which one of its walls leans. It is said to have rocked forward to exclude an excommunicated man who had been buried within.

DUNDALK. The town's strategic position on the route from the north brought it under repeated attack over many centuries. The Scotsman Edward Bruce was among many who took Dundalk, having proclaimed himself King of Ireland from a nearby hill in 1316. Between 1560 and 1650 the town was besieged no less than six times. In the 18th century its fortifications were dismantled. Today Dundalk is a prosperous industrial town and capital of County Louth. Only two of the ancient monuments still remain: the bell tower of ST NICHOLAS' CHURCH which dates back to its foundation in 1207, and a 15th-century TOWER from a Franciscan monastery built in 1240. An old mill still stands in Seatown, and here too is KINCORA HOUSE where the arctic explorer Admiral Sir Francis Leopold McClintock (1819–1907) was born. Dundalk has two patron saints: Saint Brigid (also the patron saint of Ireland), who is said to have been born at Faughart (about 4 miles north) and who remains the object of veneration and pilgrimage, and Oliver Plunket, of whom there is a reliquary in the old church of Ballybarrack (2 miles south).

COOLEY PENINSULA

To visit Ballymascanlon and the famous PROLEEK DOLMEN ● *88* (over 11 feet high and with a capstone weighing more than 40 tons) is to venture into the land of the legendary epic of the *Táin Bó Cuailnge*. The Cooley Peninsula is a rocky finger of land between Dundalk Bay and Carlingford Lough, with magnificent views of the east coast and down onto the historic small town of Carlingford. This old port is set on the lough and faces the Mourne Mountains over the waters. The town is said to have once had thirty-two fortified castles. Among the few remains are the massive ruins of KING JOHN'S CASTLE, built on the king's orders at the lough's edge to defend the harbor.

OLIVER PLUNKET (1629–81)
Plunket was born into an influential Anglo-Norman family and ordained a priest in Rome in 1654. In 1669 he returned to Ireland to become archbishop of Armagh and primate of the land. He struggled against constant persecution to defend the Church in Ireland, but he was arrested and accused of taking part in the "Popish Plot" to spread the Catholic religion. Brought to London in 1681, he was convicted on absurd evidence, and hanged, drawn and quartered at Tyburn. Plunket was beatified in 1920 and canonized in 1975. His head, returned to Ireland in 1721, is enshrined in a reliquary at Drogheda.

King John's Castle, Carlingford.

Between Lough Ree and Lough Derg the river regularly overflows. This has created wetland pastures known as "callows" along the banks. They have never been of much use for cultivation and have therefore been little drained or treated; just a crop of hay is taken each summer. This old-fashioned and gentle farming has preserved a great variety of wild plants and has made the wetlands a sanctuary for nesting birds. However, with changing methods and intensifying production, the wildlife is now beginning to suffer.

The River Shannon rises on the slopes of Cuilcagh Mountain, County Cavan, in what is called Lug Na Sionainne, the "Shannon Pot". It makes its way 213 miles to the Atlantic Ocean. It is the longest river in the British Isles. The Shannon basin covers over 4,500 square miles, 20 percent of the surface area of Ireland. Edmund Spenser's "spacious Shannon spreading like a sea" is a gentle river descending gradually between marshy banks. It takes a lazy course that frequently opens out into large lakes, the first being Lough Allen. The river has long been a means of transport and communication, providing a way into the thickly forested lands of central Ireland, but more important has been its role as a natural defense, as it is a particularly difficult river to cross. A project was begun in the 1840's to make the Shannon navigable and today more than 150 miles of the river are open. In addition, the recent reopening of the canal from Ballinamore to Ballyconnell has linked the Shannon to the network of the River Erne, in Northern Ireland ◆ *359*.

PORTUMNA TO BALLINASLOE

PORTUMNA. The village of TERRYGLASS and the town of Portumna face each other across the northeast end of Lough Derg. Terryglass has many pretty houses, a delightful park on the banks of the water, a new marina, and a Norman castle. One of its two churches (1910) looks rather strange, surrounded by identical tombstones at the orders of its patron. Portumna is a pleasant town with a busy marina, bordered by a splendid park containing the ruins of a Dominican priory (13th–15th century). The PORTUMNA CASTLE estate is now a wildlife reserve. The castle itself is

the remains of a 17th-century fortified mansion, now being restored.

MEELICK. Although so apparently isolated, Meelick provided an important crossing point over the Shannon. Near to the 15th-century Franciscan priory is Victoria Lock, the biggest lock on the Shannon. A small fort was built here by the English, defended by nine cannons. It was intended to halt a French expeditionary force that was expected to advance to Dublin from the west coast ● *101*.

BIRR. The spacious layout and elegant houses of Birr make it one of Ireland's most beautiful provincial Georgian towns. It is best known, however, for its castle, which has been the seat of the earls of Rosse since the 17th century. The splendid GARDENS ★ (above) are open to visitors. Designed by the second earl, they now contain well over a thousand varieties of tree and shrub and they are a mass of blossom in the spring. The beech and maple trees make the autumn equally spectacular. In the formal gardens, the box hedges are reputed to be the highest in the world. Also in the gardens is the structure that housed the Rosse telescope, built in the 1840's by the third earl and used by the fourth to first measure the heat of the moon and to observe spiral nebulae. For seventy years the "Leviathan of Parsonstown" (Birr was formerly called Parsonstown) was the largest telescope in the world; it is now in the London Science Museum.

KINNITTY, a few miles west, is a good place from which to explore the SLIEVE BLOOM MOUNTAINS, where forest paths lead up to stretches of turf bog ■ *32*.

BANAGHER ● *101*. Archeological finds have shown evidence of human habitation along this stretch of the river as far back as the Bronze Age, four thousand years ago. Bridges built across the water had to be defended, and along the banks lies a series of fortifications from different periods: Cromwell's Castle, Fort Falkland, Fort Elisa and a Martello tower. Together with Shannonbridge further north, Banagher was one of the most important strongholds on this part of the Shannon. The main street has buildings in various styles including the Georgian Crank House, which stands with its eye-catching pink façade in among traditional shopfronts and licensed premises (*Hough's, Lyons*). Anthony Trollope lived in Banagher when he was first sent as Post Office surveyor to Ireland, and Charlotte Brontë spent her honeymoon nearby.

SHANNON HARBOUR ★. The village was built in 1804, on the completion of the Grand Canal from Dublin, to service the river and canal traffic. Now the hotel is ruined and the bridge, the warehouses, the locks and basins, and the police station are silent. But the little harbor where the Shannon and the canal meet is full of colorful narrowboats and other craft.

CALLOWS BIRDLIFE
The callows are one of the rare spots in Ireland where species becoming increasingly rare elsewhere remain common. Among the waders, the most numerous are the grebes, marking their territory in the spring with a noisy call and airborne diving display. Other waders to breed here are the redshank, curlew and black-tailed godwit (below). Many species of duck make their nests here too, including the mallard, shoveler duck and teal. There are swans, dabchicks and great-crested grebes, coots and moorhens (above), all happy nesting in the thick reeds; and on warm, still evenings from late May until early July, the rasping sound of the corncrake can be heard, the rarest bird of all.

A year after the Protestant victory at the Battle of the Boyne ▲ *194*, a second battle was fought, at Aughrim. French troops under General Saint-Ruth had been sent by Louis XIV to aid the Irish Jacobites. On July 21, 1691 the two armies met in Bloody Hollow at the foot of Aughrim Hill. Saint-Ruth was killed trying to block

CLONFERT CATHEDRAL ★, ● *95*. The monastery of Clonfert was founded in the 6th century by Saint Brendan the Navigator ▲ *239*, who, according to legend, sailed to America nearly one thousand years before Christopher Columbus. Around the year 1200 a beautiful and ornate doorway dedicated to the saint was inserted into an existing church wall. It is considered by many to be the finest Hiberno-Romanesque doorway of all. The capitals are highly sculptured, showing grotesque human and animal heads; the entire surface of the doorway shows an extraordinary combination of interlaced patterns, and a variety of carving executed with great skill and ingenuity. The columns, "instead of representing an element of calm and repose in the overall composition . . . are so covered with carving that their surface seems alive, almost sparkling, and the decorations continue irrepressibly on to the outer piers" (Françoise Henry). The cathedral is cruciform in shape, unusual for a Romanesque church in Ireland. The chancel, with a lovely window at the east end that should be viewed from both within and without, dates from around 1200. The slender tower and south transept, the latter now without a roof, were added in the 15th century. On the inner wall of the choir is the carving of a siren, a symbol of vanity, or it could be a creature met by Brendan on one of his famous voyages.

SHANNONBRIDGE ● *101*. The village gets its name from the lovely bridge, which is an extension of the main street at its western end across the Shannon. It was built around 1750, and in Napoleonic times fortifications were constructed on

William of Orange's troops on the road west. This, along with a determined cavalry charge led by Ruvigny, routed the Jacobite army. The Orangemen marched on into Galway that same day, and later that year the Catholic armies surrendered. In Aughrim, a cross commemorates the Irish and French dead.

the west bank, remains of which are still prominently visible today.

CLONTUSKERT PRIORY ★, ◆ *381*. The priory was an Augustinian institution built on the site of a 9th-century monastery. Its doorway is decorated with the figures of Saint Michael, Saint Catherine and Saint John the Baptist, surrounded by mythical beasts.

BALLINASLOE. A horse fair has been held here every October since the 18th century ◆ *337*. The village is linked to the Shannon by the River Suck, now made navigable and

INDEPENDENT SPIRIT Clonmacnois was one of the most independent monasteries of early times. While many religious institutions chose their abbots from the founding family, Clonmacnois always appointed superiors for their personal qualities, rather than their family origins or social status. By the height of the Middle Ages Clonmacnois had become one of the most important centers of learning, art and craftsmanship in Ireland. There were scriptoria, a school for historians, metal workshops and, as is clear from the surviving portions of the ancient monastery, a flourishing tradition of stonemasonry.

replacing a section of the Grand Canal which was in use from 1820 to 1960. In the village of Aughrim, west of Ballinasloe, there is an exhibition on the battle that took place in 1691, one of the bloodiest in the history of Ireland.

CLONMACNOIS ★

AN IMPORTANT CROSSROADS. Very near to Clonmacnois was the meeting place of two main routes of primitive Ireland. Here the east–west road, Eiscir Riada, met the north–south artery, the Shannon, making Clonmacnois a key crossing point. It is known that during the life of Saint Ciarán (512–45), and probably before, merchants from Gaul would travel up the river to sell wine. Three centuries later the Shannon brought less welcome visitors: Danes, led by their chief Turgesius, whose wife Ota would proclaim oracles at the high altar of the cathedral.

HISTORY OF THE MONASTERY. Ciarán founded his monastery here in 545, but unfortunately he did not live to see it prosper, dying later that same year. The saint continued to be revered, his grave became an object of pilgrimage, and the monastery flourished for many centuries. In the 16th century, however, English troops attacked and plundered the institution. It was never to be restored. Today the ruins of Clonmacnois monastery command a great sense of peace and serenity, and many still make them an object of pilgrimage.

CARVED STONES. A remarkable number of what may be ancient tombstones have been found at Clonmacnois (8th to 12th century), which can now be seen in the Visitors' Centre. They are carved with crosses of different designs, and often bear an inscription seeking prayers for the person whose name is on the stone. It has not been proved that these are tombstones, however, and a recent theory proposes that they marked the completion of a pilgrimage by the person whose name is inscribed.

CROSS OF THE SCRIPTURES

From an incomplete inscription at the bottom of the shaft it is known that the cross was carved by a man called Colman for the High King Flann Sinna (879–916). On the east face the only scene clearly recognizable is that of Christ, seated, handing the Keys to Saint Peter and the Gospels to Saint Paul. It has been suggested that the two panels below show either Joseph interpreting the pharaoh's dreams, or an Irish king helping Saint Ciarán to build his church. The *Last Judgement* is to be seen at the top. The west face of the cross depicts, from bottom to top, the *Watching over the Tomb*, the *Arrest*, the *Betrayal* and the *Crucifixion*. Although very worn, it is possible to follow the Passion on the lower part of the base, from Palm Sunday to Easter Sunday (above, Christ is seated with the Apostles). The Passion continues on the south face with the *Kiss of Judas*. The hunting scenes, also on the base, are difficult to explain, as are the panels on the narrow sides of the cross, apart from the one on the south side showing David playing his harp.

THE CROSSES. The three crosses of Clonmacnois have been recently moved into the Visitors' Centre. Copies of two of them show where they used to stand. The most important is the CROSS OF THE SCRIPTURES, which has fine elegant proportions, arms slanting slightly upward and the ring carved proud of the face. It is probably the cross mentioned in documents of 957, and later in 1060, at which time it marked the site of a shrine. The biblical scenes are hard to interpret. On the South Cross an inscription also found at the base of the shaft would seem to imply that it was carved at least seventeen years earlier for Maelsechnaill, father of Flann and son of Maelruanaid (846–62), the first true king of all Ireland. This cross is covered with panels with interesting geometric and zoomorphic motifs, but apart from a possible image of Adam and Eve on the base, the only biblical scene recognizable is the Crucifixion on the shaft. Only the shaft remains of the North Cross, with a strange cross-legged figure on its south side. Some think this may be the Gallic god Cernunnos.

THE TOWERS. Standing some distance from the other buildings is O'Rourke's Tower, partly rebuilt in the 12th century after being struck by lightning. The cone-shaped stone roof is missing, but must have resembled that of the smaller tower attached to the remains of a small Romanesque church, Teampull Finghin.

THE CATHEDRAL. Much of the structure probably dates back to the 10th century. However, the Romanesque west door was added later, as was the Gothic north door which was opened up in about 1460 by Dean Odo, with statues of Saint Francis, Saint Patrick, and Saint Dominic placed above. The vaulted ceiling in the eastern part of the building was added in the 15th century. This is the burial place of the last High Kings of Ireland ● *48*, Turloch Mór O'Conor and his son Rúairí.

> "AND IN CLONMACNOIS THEY LAID THE MEN OF TEFFIA,
> AND RIGHT MANY A LORD OF BREAGH;
> DEEP THE SOD ABOVE CLAN CREIDE AND CLAN CONAILL,
> KIND IN HALL AND FIERCE IN FRAY." T.W. ROLLESTON

THE SEVEN CHURCHES. The seven churches on the site may symbolize the seven hills of Rome and their churches, which would have been seen by Irish pilgrims. The smallest, TEAMPULL KIERAN, is also in its way the most important, since Saint Ciarán is thought to be buried there. It is known that in 1684 the church still had its roof and the faithful were still coming there to worship a relic of the saint's hand. To the west are the foundations of TEAMPULL KELLY. South of the cathedral are the two joined churches of TEAMPULL DOOLIN and TEAMPULL HURPAN (17th century); southwest stands a third, TEAMPULL RI (c. 1200), and to the north is TEAMPULL CONOR, which has been maintained and used by the Protestant Church of Ireland since 1780. TEAMPULL FINGHIN is at the north edge of the enclosure. The only structure to have been built at a distance from the walled monastery complex is the NUN'S CHURCH (c. 1166). It is about half a mile away to the east and can be reached along the old paved pilgrims' road. It is a typical Hiberno-Romanesque church, both in size and appearance. The roof is gone, but the doorway and the chancel arch retain fine decoration representative of the period ● *94.*

THE CASTLE. On the riverside pastures to the west of the Visitors' Centre some ruins stand on a grassy mound. These are the remains of a Norman castle built early in the 13th century. They are a reminder that the Shannon was a natural frontier, across which the Normans fiercely defended the land that they had conquered. The collapsed state of the castle largely results from the action of Cromwell's troops in the 17th century, although it had probably long lost its strategic importance by then. The castle, built around the year 1210 at Athlone, 9 miles further north, which guarded a key crossing place on the Shannon at the lower end of Lough Ree, was to become the prominent stronghold. From there, the Normans began their conquest of Connacht in 1235.

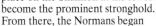

> "Clonmacnois still feels austere. The young men must have looked about them wildly sometimes, over the reedy, golden land and across the cold Shannon water...[this] was a school for saints and ascetics, this 'dewy hillside', beneath which so many of them sleep unmentioned."
> Kate O'Brien (1897–1974)

The stone crosses bound with a circular wheel that stand today as monuments to an intense Christian belief combined with a more general Celtic spirituality were erected by monks, by kings and by warriors. There are about one hundred crosses and High Crosses in all, but those at Ahenny, Clonmacnois and Cashel are particularly impressive because of the beauty and richness of their carvings. The High Crosses are a reminder of the religious spirit that has always remained strong in Ireland. Standing tall amid the ruins they are a precious treasure from the past and a powerful omen for the future.

1   **2**   **3**   **4**

STONE SLAB AT KILNASAGGART (1) On it is carved a Latin cross and the name of a priest, Ternoc, who died in 714.

NORTH CROSS AT AHENNY (2) belongs to the group of Ossory carved crosses dating from the 8th or 9th century.

THE CASHEL HIGH CROSS (4), 12th century, has a carving representing a crucifix with Christ in high-relief on one side.

THE CROSS AT MOONE is particularly interesting and unusual, with its clear detail and strong, simple figures. Like many Celtic crosses, it is carved with scenes from both the Old and New Testaments, as here: *Daniel in the Lions' Den.*

MUIREDACH'S CROSS (3) at Monasterboice is the best preserved of all the carved crosses. The panel of the *Taking of Christ*, just above the base, is in almost perfect condition.

THE BASE The Ahenny cross has a base carved with secular subjects: here a procession with a horse and dog. They are a contrast to religious subjects and abstract motifs.

Designs often include combinations of spirals, interlacing, animals' heads and Greek patterns.

CONSTRUCTION

The Celtic High Cross was set on a base that tapered toward the top. It was either carved from one block of stone or from several pieces fixed together with tenon and mortise joints. The basic Latin cross was bound by a wheel surrounding

the center, giving a more dramatic and decorative appearance. Ornamental carving was of interlace and serpentine designs, biblical scenes, or sometimes local stories. These crosses represent some of the finest medieval art to have been produced in Ireland.

THE CROSS OF THE SCRIPTURES AT CLONMACNOIS

The carvings are accomplished. The purity of their design shows the skill of the craftsmen who worked on these early carved crosses. Patterns and figures blend with a remarkable grace of line and form.

POWER OF THE CROSS

Celtic crosses have withstood the vicissitudes of history and the violence of successive invaders better than many other Irish religious monuments. The artistic power of these 8th- and 9th-century crosses has lost none of its fascination: their decoration, an inspired mixture of ornamental design and narrative drama, still expresses the potency of the mythical world that obsessed those who made them. Many subsequent works of art have been influenced by these complex and enthralling monuments of early Irish belief.

Detail from the *Last Judgement*, a scene carved on the Clonmacnois Cross of the Scriptures.

STYLIZED BEASTS

The incorporation of creatures from the Bible, often the serpent, into the carved interlacing is one of the most common decorative traditions on Irish medieval High Crosses.

THE SHRINE

The top of the cross, representing a shrine open to the sky, seems to symbolize Christ's ascension.

McGahern was born in Dublin in 1934 and has come to be respected as one of the leading writers of his generation. In the 1960's, however, the Irish authorities seized and banned his second novel, *The Dark* (1965), the story of a young man confronted by near-incestuous scenes with his father and homosexual advances from a priest. McGahern lost his job as a school-teacher and left the country. He spent time in London, Paris, Spain and the United States. He has now returned to live in Ireland. In his novellas (*Nightlines*, 1971, *High Ground*, 1985) and his novels (*The Barracks*, 1963; *The Leavetaking*, 1974; *The Pornographer*, 1978; *Among Women*, 1990) John McGahern reveals the abyss that lies thinly concealed behind the banal exterior of ordinary people's lives.

FROM ATHLONE TO CARRICK-ON-SHANNON

In 1183 Giraldus Cambrensis of Wales visited Ireland and in his survey he wrote that the Shannon "rightly holds the chief place among all of the rivers of Ireland, whether old or new, both on account of the magnificence of its size, its long meanderings, and its abundance of fish". The peaceful river is familiar to many Irish people and precious to all. The author John McGahern, who now lives in County Leitrim, has described how Republican prisoners would relieve their boredom and distress by describing imaginary walks along the banks of the river, each trying to remember details that the others missed out.

ATHLONE. JOHN'S CASTLE is Athlone's most impressive monument: a massive medieval structure, much changed and repaired, which has stood guard over the bridge at the southern end of Lough Ree for nearly eight

hundred years. Today the castle houses an Exhibition Centre and the Castle Museum; the present bridge dates from 1844. The old part of town lies around the castle, with some good old-fashioned pubs (*Higgins', The Palace, Séan's,* and *The Castle*). Just upstream is a fine railway bridge built in the 1850's. Athlone was the birthplace, in 1884, of the tenor John McCormack. A bronze bust in his memory stands in the town center. The CHURCH OF STS PETER AND PAUL is a modern building (1937) with some fine stained glass by Harry Clarke ▲ *214*. The town was besieged twice during the war between James II and William of Orange. The military camp on the west bank, Custume Barracks, is named after a hero of the second siege in 1691.

RICHMOND HARBOUR. Richmond Harbour stands at the end of the Royal Canal, which was built to link the Liffey and the Shannon. It has been closed since 1961, but thanks to an energetic campaign it will be reopened in a few years.

CARRICK-ON-SHANNON. The largest town on the upper reaches of the Shannon is a busy and prosperous holiday boating resort, and also the county town of County Leitrim. In the

center is one of the world's smallest churches (roughly 15 feet by 12 feet). It is called the COSTELLO CHAPEL, and is the mausoleum of Edward Costello and his wife. Beyond Lake Drumharlow, northwest of the town, lies WOODBROOK HOUSE, the setting of David Thomson's novel *Woodbrook*. On the banks of Lough Key is LOUGH KEY FOREST PARK. Take a stroll through the forest with its bog gardens ■ *34,* or simply enjoy the views.

CORK

▲ MUNSTER
CORK

1 BLARNEY CASTLE
2 UNIVERSITY
3 CORK MUSEUM
4 ST FINBARR'S CATHEDRAL
5 CRAWFORD GALLERY
6 ST MARY'S CATHEDRAL
7 ST ANNE'S CHURCH
8 HOLY TRINITY CHURCH

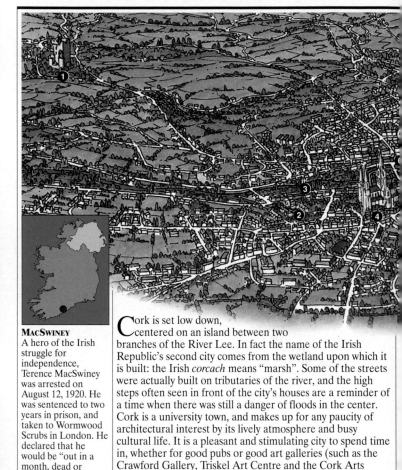

MACSWINEY
A hero of the Irish struggle for independence, Terence MacSwiney was arrested on August 12, 1920. He was sentenced to two years in prison, and taken to Wormwood Scrubs in London. He declared that he would be "out in a month, dead or alive", and went on hunger strike. Despite high-level attempts at intervention, as well as fervent prayers and masses, the British government would not relent.

Cork is set low down, centered on an island between two branches of the River Lee. In fact the name of the Irish Republic's second city comes from the wetland upon which it is built: the Irish *corcach* means "marsh". Some of the streets were actually built on tributaries of the river, and the high steps often seen in front of the city's houses are a reminder of a time when there was still a danger of floods in the center. Cork is a university town, and makes up for any paucity of architectural interest by its lively atmosphere and busy cultural life. It is a pleasant and stimulating city to spend time in, whether for good pubs or good art galleries (such as the Crawford Gallery, Triskel Art Centre and the Cork Arts Society Gallery).

HISTORY

EARLY TIMES. The city's history goes back to the 7th century, when Saint Finbarr ▲ 226 built a lonely monastery on the marshes where St Finbarr's Cathedral ▲ 214 stands today. The monastery prospered and the Vikings soon arrived, settling in Cork in the 10th century. The Normans came in their turn; in 1172 they took over from the Vikings. Henry II established a garrison and gave the city its first charter.

A REBELLIOUS CITY. Cork is a city that has always been quick to support a rebel cause. In 1491 the inhabitants welcomed the adventurer Perkin Warbeck, who claimed to be the son of Edward IV. In 1649 it supported the

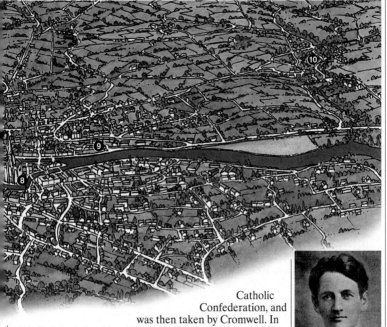

Catholic Confederation, and was then taken by Cromwell. In 1690 Cork took the side of James II, then to be brought to order by John Churchill, later Duke of Marlborough. The Fenians ● *53* were active here in the 19th century. In 1920 the Lord Mayor of Cork, Thomas MacCurtain, was shot dead by the police; his successor, Terence MacSwiney, starved himself to death in an English prison, and the city center was burnt by the Black and Tans in reprisal for an ambush. In 1922, after the withdrawal of English troops, Cork was occupied by Republicans hostile to the Treaty and had to be brought to order by troops of the Irish Free State.

Terence MacSwiney died on October 25, 1920 after seventy-four days refusing nourishment. The sacrifice of the Lord Mayor of Cork made the headlines worldwide. It did serious damage to the reputation of England, losing the British much support.

THE CITY CENTER

Cork did not achieve much architectural distinction until the 19th century. The Pain brothers, pupils of John Nash of London, designed a number of handsome buildings, the finest of which are HOLY TRINITY CHURCH (Father Matthew Quay) and the COURT HOUSE (Washington Street). The heavy scent of brewing from the Beamish Brewery ● *77* hangs in the air around the elegant spire and classical portico of these imposing buildings.

GRAND PARADE AND PATRICK STREET. The two main shopping streets of Cork are lined with curved façades of fine late 18th-century houses. In the covered market, called the English Market, the stalls are filled with delicious and often unusual produce, including local specialties such as *cruibins* (pigs' feet), and *drisheen* (a glistening black pudding). Behind Patrick Street is the old Huguenot district which is now full of bookshops, art galleries, little cafés and restaurants, and shops selling specialty and luxury goods.

The increasing size of the English Market, where some traders have had their stalls for generations, is a sign of the growing agricultural prosperity of County Cork.

213

Frank O'Connor.

WRITERS
Two famous writers
who come from Cork
are Sean O'Faolain
(1900–91) ◆ *303*,
whose work suffered
under the censor, and
Frank O'Connor
(1903–66), arguably
as great a storyteller
as Chekhov or
Maupassant. Both
Irishmen found
inspiration in the
work of Daniel
Corkery (1878–1964),
writer and
Professor of
English
Literature at
University
College,
Cork (*The
Hidden
Ireland*,
1925).

CRAWFORD MUNICIPAL ART GALLERY ★ (Emmet Place). The gallery has been housed since 1884 in an elegant building of warm orange brick designed by the well-known Cork architect Arthur Hill. It has a good collection of works by Irish painters of the 19th and 20th centuries (such as Daniel Maclise, Nathaniel Grogan and Walter Osborne); *Minerva* (1822) and other works by Hogan, a local sculptor; and also plaster copies of Roman statues done under the direction of Canova. Next to the Crawford stands the new OPERA HOUSE, built in the 1960's by Michael Scott to replace the former building (above), destoyed by fire in 1955.

SOUTH CORK

ST FINBARR'S CATHEDRAL. A three-spired cathedral built in early French pointed Gothic style between 1867 and 1879, on what is thought to be the site of the monastery founded by Saint Finbarr. It was designed, in typically flamboyant spirit, by the London architect William Burges. It is the Church of Ireland cathedral, and was funded by the city's Protestant families.

UNIVERSITY COLLEGE. Cork has been a seat of learning since Saint Finbarr founded his school here, and University College has as its motto "Where Finbarr taught, let Munster learn". The college was opened by Queen Victoria during a visit to Cork in 1849, and for a time it was called Queen's College. She knighted the architect, Thomas Deane, with whom Benjamin Woodward worked for a time. A statue was erected to the queen to commemorate the occasion (now tucked away in a corner). The HONAN COLLEGIATE CHAPEL (1915) is exquisite. It was designed by James F. Macmullen. The stained-glass windows were made by Sarah Purser and Harry Clarke in Art Nouveau style and include images of the eleven Irish saints in especially vivid

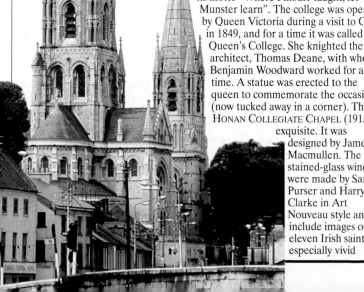

GOLD BIRD FROM GARRYDUFF
A little piece of jewelry found during excavations of the ring-fort at Garryduff in 1945. Comprising a thin sheet of beaten gold decorated with filigree spiral designs, the piece has been dated at between 570 and 660 BC, but some believe it to be even older.

colors. One of University College's earliest professors was the mathematician George Boole (1815–64), a pioneer of modern symbolic logic and the early theories leading to the development of computer technology.

CORK MUSEUM. A few hundred yards away, along Mardyke Walk, lies FITZGERALD PARK, the most pleasant and spacious of Cork's all-too-few parks and gardens. Housed in a Georgian mansion in the park is the PUBLIC MUSEUM, opened in 1945. On display are collections illustrating various aspects of the city and its history, encompassing geology, archeology and natural history, social and industrial history, and local crafts and traditions. Among the most interesting exhibits are Irish elk antlers dating back to the Iron Age, the little gold bird from Garryduff, pieces of silver and glassware made in Cork, and lace from Youghal ▲ 220. In addition, there is a section on Cork in medieval times, and another on its role in the events of 1916 to 1922 ● 54, 60, 62.

NORTH CORK

BUTTER EXCHANGE. Next to ST MARY'S CATHEDRAL (1808) is the Shandon Craft Centre. The building was formerly occupied by the Cork Butter Exchange, an institution founded in 1730 that organized sales and guaranteed the quality of Cork butter until 1925.

ST ANNE'S ANGLICAN CHURCH. The church of St Anne, Shandon, has a conspicuous pepper-pot steeple and is the most prominent building on the north side of the city. The Shandon district has become well known through paintings, songs and poems. Most famous is *The Bells of Shandon*, a poem by the 19th-century writer Francis Sylvester Mahony, under his pen-name Father Prout.

THE SURROUNDING AREA

ROYAL GUNPOWDER MILLS (Ballincollig). Charles Henry Leslie began manufacturing gunpowder here in 1794, in order to supply the British army. The mills finally closed in 1903, and today it is possible to visit them and see how the gunpowder was produced.

DUNKATHEL HOUSE (near to the village of Glanmire). The Georgian country house built in the 18th century by the wealthy businessman and Member of Parliament Abraham Morris is worthy of Palladio. It has a strikingly elegant staircase and there is also some interesting stuccowork along with superb watercolors by Beatrice Gubbins.

RIVERSTOWN HOUSE (5 miles northwest of Cork). The Protestant bishop of Cloyne ▲ 220, Dr Jemmett Brown, built the magnificent Riverstown House in 1745. It is a perfect example of all that was fine and elegant in the Georgian period. There are splendid Rococo-style stucco panels by the Swiss brothers Paul and Philip Lafranchini ● 106.

TOWN FESTIVALS
Cork has a large number of cultural events during the year. The Film Festival (October) has gained a reputation for its eclectic program and its encouragement of young Irish film makers. The Cork Festival (September) is a great gathering of lovers of traditional music, while there is also the Jazz Festival in October. The Cork Choral Festival is held in the spring, bringing together choirs from all backgrounds to compete in a city proud of its long musical tradition.

County Cork is a prosperous agricultural region. Traditionally it produced large quantities of butter which, up until World War One, was exported to Europe and America.

Rococo plasterwork in Riverstown House.

215

Blarney Castle ◆ *374* was built in 1446 by Dermot Láidir MacCarthy. It stands on a rock high above the River Martin most probably on the site of a Norman fortress, its massive walls 18 feet thick and the tower 83 feet high. As the MacCarthy stronghold, it was besieged several times, taken by Cromwell, and finally lost to the troops of William of Orange. Blarney Castle is a magnificent building set in lovely grounds, and has breathtaking views from the top, but it is the Blarney Stone that has made it the most famous tourist site in the Cork region.

A QUEEN VEXED BY THE BLARNEY
Cormac MacCarthy, Lord of Blarney in the reign of Queen Elizabeth I, claimed to be loyal to the Queen, but "with fair words and soft speech" avoided coming to agreement with her or her Lord Deputy over taking the tenure of his lands from the Crown. Exasperated, the Queen declared: "This is all Blarney! What he says he never means." And so, it is said, the phrase was coined.

ORIGIN OF THE BLARNEY STONE
According to one story, Cormac MacCarthy received half of the Stone of Scone in gratitude for his support of Robert Bruce's troops at the Battle of Bannockburn in 1314. It was set into the castle keep just below the battlements and came to be called the Blarney Stone. There is no mention of its magical properties until early in the 19th century.

GIFT OF ELOQUENCE
It is said that anyone who kisses the Blarney Stone will receive the gift of eloquence. There is generally a queue to perform this feat, although to do so involves hanging head-first over the castle wall, the legs firmly held by two strong men. The origin of the legendary power of the stone is a mystery. One tale tells of a king of Munster who saved a witch from drowning. In return she promised that if he kissed the stone he would have such a persuasive tongue that his subjects would obey his every command.

> **"T**HERE IS A STONE THAT WHOEVER KISSES,
> O, HE NEVER MISSES TO GROW ELOQUENT.
> 'T**IS HE MAY CLAMBER TO A LADY'S CHAMBER,
> O**R BECOME A MEMBER OF PARLIAMENT.**"**
>
> F. S. MAHONY

BLARNEY HOUSE

Attached to the massive keep are the remnants of a Gothic-style Georgian manor house built in the early 18th century by James St John Jefferyes. In the grounds there is also Blarney House, built in the Scottish baronial tradition late in the 19th century. It is lived in by the Colthurst family, descendants of the Jefferyes.

ROCK CLOSE

These gardens, planted around a number of standing stones said to mark a druidic site, have a magical atmosphere. There is a rock that looks like a witch, and steps that must be descended backward with the eyes shut for a wish to be granted. In the "Fairy Glade" the sun's first rays shine between the rocks onto the sacrificial stone; the ancient trees and massive stones blend to create a truly enchanted dell.

BLARNEY VILLAGE

At the end of the 18th century the village began to attract many visitors, among them Arthur Young, curious to see the prosperous and peaceful community created here by James Jefferyes. He had built a model village of ninety houses set around thirteen mills; each little house had its narrow garden behind. The industry went into decline, however, and the mills closed early in the 19th century. In 1824 Martin Mahony founded the Blarney Woollen Mills, bringing new life to the village and soon making it famous. Both the British and, later, the Irish soldiers of the two World Wars wore Blarney tweed.

The county of Waterford in the southeastern corner of
Ireland is one of the mildest and wettest in the country.
It is a popular holiday area with some pleasant seaside
resorts. The road along the coast runs beside extensive sandy
beaches, little harbors and pretty fishing villages, and offers
some spectacular views over the wide and picturesque bays.

FOTA ISLAND

Once privately owned, Fota Island is set in the mouth of Cork
Harbour and can now be visited. On it is a wildlife park. It is
also possible to visit the arboretum attached to Fota House,
filled with rare species imported by the Smith-Barry family in
the 19th century that have flourished in the mild climate.

COBH ★

QUEENSTOWN. Cobh is the Irish rendering of the Cove of
Cork. In 1849, when Queen Victoria landed here, the
sheltered port was renamed Queenstown. It remained so until
resuming its original name in Gaelic form in 1922.
LAST PORT BEFORE AMERICA ● 59. The Queenstown Project, a
permanent exhibition and heritage center, has been installed
in the old Victorian railway station. It tells the story of the
port from which so many set sail to start new stories of their
own.

The port of Cobh.

ANNIE MOORE
On January 1, 1892,
her fifteenth birthday,
Annie Moore was the
first of seventeen
million emigrants
who were to pass
through the Ellis
Island immigration
office on arrival at
New York. There is a
statue of her with her
two brothers in front
of the museum.

From 1845 to 1960, several million Irish people left Ireland from Cobh to sail to America, Australia and New Zealand. During the Famine the crafts on which the desperate refugees traveled came to be known as "coffin ships". Under better circumstances emigrants set sail aboard the many steamers that called at Cobh. After the success of the *Sirius*, the first steamship to cross the Atlantic, which left Cobh on April 14, 1838 and reached New York eighteen days later, many companies had begun to build bigger, faster and more comfortable boats to transport passengers, mail and freight. After World War Two transatlantic crossings called less and less frequently at Cobh, unable to compete with rapidly improving air services. The heritage center has a section on the *Titanic*, which made its last stop at Cobh on April 11, 1912, and on the sinking of the *Lusitania*, torpedoed by a German submarine on May 7, 1915, off Old Head, Kinsale ▲ *224*. Only eight hundred of the two thousand passengers survived, and many of them victims are buried near Cobh. A memorial to them stands in Casement Square.

THE VILLAGE. Cobh has a second museum, housed in an old Presbyterian church and concentrating on local history. The steep streets of the little town lead up toward its crowning glory, the French Gothic cathedral of ST COLMAN (1868–1919). From here there are views over Haulbowline Island, where there is a dockyard and naval headquarters, and Spike Island, once a prison from which many left for Botany Bay. In WEST VIEW a line of twenty-three identical houses has earned the nickname of "the pack of cards".

FAIRBARN'S PADDLEWHEEL
The massive iron wheel of the *Midleton* distillery (1852) remained in use until 1975. It is well over 20 feet in diameter and was used to produce energy for the works. When the water level was too low, steam engines were used to boost the power.

THE ROYAL CORK YACHT CLUB
The exclusive club, founded in 1720 as the Cork Harbour Water Club based on Haulbowline Island, claims to be the oldest yacht club in the world. It transferred its base to Cobh shortly afterward, and the name was changed in 1828. In 1854, the architect Anthony Salvin (1799–1881) was instructed to build a new headquarters for the club. His Italianate structure was built behind Westbourne Place, overlooking Cobh Harbour, which was used until 1969.

MIDLETON ★

Before going on as far as Midleton, the famous whiskey town ● *78*, there is an agreeable stop to be made at BARRYSCOURT CASTLE, near the village of Carriguohill. A pleasant little restaurant is just next to the castle.

A PRECIOUS HERITAGE. In 1825 the Murphy brothers bought some old wool-producing premises in Midleton and founded a distillery that was soon to be one of the most successful in the south of Ireland. In 1867 it merged with four Cork distilleries, and a century later this new company joined forces with the Dublin distillers John Jameson and John Power & Son. Today *Midleton* and *Bushmills* ▲ *314* are the two largest whiskey producers in Ireland. A part of the old distillery buildings now houses the Jameson Heritage Centre, where the long process of making whiskey is explained. There is a chance to taste the product afterward. (Take the R629 to Cloyne.)

CLOYNE

Cloyne includes among its famous inhabitants the bishop and philosopher George Berkeley, who came here in 1742, and the more recent hero, Christy Ring, Cork star of hurling ● *83,* who is honored with a statue in the town center. The CATHEDRAL dates from the 13th century, but lost much of its beauty during restoration. The west door still has some interesting primitive carvings of pagan symbols. Before continuing along the coast road to Youghal, lined with delightful little beaches and villages such as Ballycotton (above), it is worth stopping at Shanagarry to visit BALLYMALOE HOUSE ◆ *374,* a restaurant and cookery school. The nearby ruined castle belonged to the Penn family and was the birthplace of the Quaker William Penn, founder of Pennsylvania.

GEORGE BERKELEY (1685–1753)
After studying at Trinity College ▲ *148,* Berkeley took holy orders and taught Greek, Hebrew and theology. His study of John Locke inspired him to write his *Treatise Concerning the Principles of Human Knowledge* (1710), and his most famous doctrine was "Esse is percipi" ("to

be is to be perceived"). He traveled in France, Spain and Italy, and returned in 1721, became Dean of Derry in 1724, but then spent time in America to pursue his project to found a Christian college in the Bermudas (which eventually failed). In the 1730's he became Bishop of Cloyne, and there is a monument to him in the cathedral. The city and university of Berkeley in California are named after him.

YOUGHAL ★

Youghal (meaning "yew wood" and pronounced "Yawl") is set at the mouth of the River Blackwater, one of the country's most unspoilt rivers. Since the last century Youghal has been a popular seaside resort with a grand, sandy beach, but the happy holiday-makers distract attention from some unexpectedly interesting buildings.

MAIN STREET. The tall CLOCKGATE TOWER (1771) spans the street. The building was once a prison, where condemned men were hanged from the windows, but it now houses a museum. A little further on is the striking façade of the RED HOUSE, a large brick-built town house designed around 1710 by a Dutch architect for the Uniacke family. Opposite is TYNTE'S CASTLE, a 15th-century fortified tower, now in ruins (left). At the corner of Church Street are some 17th-century ALMSHOUSES.

COLLEGIATE CHURCH OF ST MARY. The church dates back to the 13th century, but was badly restored in the 19th. It still contains some magnificent and fascinating tombs and effigies including that of Richard Boyle in the south transept.

FIRST POTATOES
Few historians give their support to the story, but it is said that Sir Walter Raleigh brought back the first potato plants from the New World to Youghal. The fateful importance of this foreign tuber in the history of Ireland, however, cannot be denied.

In 1619 he had a gigantic mausoleum built in the fashionable Italian style; but it was his brother John Boyle, the bishop of Cork, Cloyne and Ross, who was to be buried there a year later. In the graveyard lies the writer and journalist Claud Cockburn, who lived in Youghal and later Ardmore, where he died in 1981. Among other works he wrote an exuberant autobiography, *I, Claud*, as well as the novel from which the film *Beat the Devil* was made, starring James Cagney. Behind the church is a section of 13th-century town wall.

MYRTLE GROVE. This Elizabethan house is thought to date partly from the mid-15th century, and to be one of the oldest houses in Ireland. It was part of an estate confiscated from the FitzGerald family in the 1580's and presented to Sir Walter Raleigh, but there is no firm evidence that he spent time here.

LISMORE CASTLE. Before continuing along the coast, the road follows the wooded valley of the River Blackwater, famous for its salmon and trout, to reach Lismore. The castle, which overlooks the river, owes its present-day appearance to alterations made in the 1850's. It is a private house, but the gardens are open to the public and well worth a visit, with a yew-walk of trees almost a thousand years old. To get a feel of the wilder inland landscape, go and see the CISTERCIAN MONASTERY OF MOUNT MELLERAY (1832), over 600 feet up in the Knockmealdown Mountains. The views of the mountains and river valley are thrilling.

ARDMORE

Ardmore is another town popular with holiday-makers. It has one of the finest round towers in the country, still with its original conical stone roof, and decorative courses to mark the stories.

THE CATHEDRAL ★. Now a ruin known as St Declan's Church, the cathedral may stand on the site of the 6th-century monastery founded by Saint Declan. It is unique in Ireland for having a western façade covered with Romanesque reliefs. Inside are two ogham stones ● *66*. Next to the cathedral is the tiny ST DECLAN'S ORATORY, probably dating from the 8th century and restored in the 18th, in which the saint is thought to be buried.

ARDMORE CATHEDRAL ARCADING
Six of the thirteen bas-reliefs carved on the upper row of blind arcading date from the Romanesque period (late 12th century). They are similar in style and subject to scenes found on Celtic crosses ▲ *206*.

"MOBY DICK"
John Huston's film of Melville's novel was shot in Youghal in 1955. Some were unkind enough to criticize the masts that appeared over the roof tops for being so still when real masts would have moved with the wind and water. The waterfront pub, *Moby Dick's* ◆ *374*, has pictures of the filming taking place.

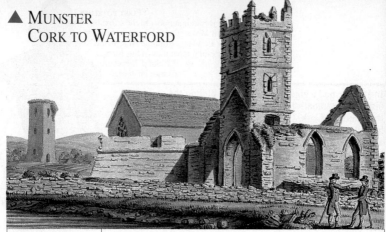

The Abbeyside ruins.

DYSERT CHURCH
Half a mile from the tower and cathedral in Ardmore are the ruins of a church probably built on the site of the *desertulum* ("little hermitage") of Saint Declan. Next to

it is St Declan's Well, where pilgrims used to bathe.

FAMINE VICTIMS
Not far from Dungarvan, on the road to Waterford, a sign marks a place where victims of the Great Famine ● *58*, particularly terrible in this area, lie buried. There is a cross in memory of the Irish who died during this dreadful time.

ST DECLAN'S STONE. Legend has it that this sacred stone carried the bell and garments of the saint over the waters from Wales, shortly after Declan visited Ardmore. The stone lies at the end of the long sandy beach and rests, rather like the stone slab of a dolmen, on two small rocks. It is said both physical distress (rheumatism) and spiritual ills can be cured by sliding beneath the stone on July 24, St Declan's Day.

DUNGARVAN

KING JOHN'S CASTLE. The town of Dungarvan lies on the banks of the River Colligan, and is set prettily around a spacious central square. It looks across the wide bay to Helvick Head. The ruins of its castle, built by King John and much damaged by Cromwell in 1649, have now been partly converted into a restaurant.
ABBEYSIDE. On the east bank of the Colligan are the peaceful ruins of an Augustinian priory dating from the late 13th century. Take a walk from the graveyard toward the sea to enjoy a wonderful view over the bay of Dungarvan and Helvick Head.
AN RINN. A few miles from Dungarvan is a little village where Gaelic is still spoken and where eager students come to listen and learn. An Rinn lies at the heart of a Gaelic-speaking area ● *68*, and a number of traditional Irish-language singers have their roots here (Nicolas Toibin, Aine Ni Cheallaigh).

TRAMORE

The road to Tramore runs along a coast bordered with quiet sandy beaches and beautiful seaside landscapes such as Clonea Bay. It passes through the villages of Stradbally, Bunmahon and Annestown. In some places copper mines make it dangerous to go onto the cliffs. In contrast, Tramore itself has one of the busiest beaches in Ireland. Children who have had enough of sea and sand can learn about the great Irish myths and legends at the Celtworld theme park ◆ *377*. The main road (N52) leads on to Waterford, with recommended stops at KILMACTHOMAS (where the grandfather of Hollywood star Tyrone Power was born), and at KILMEADEN, a little town now known for the cheese that bears its name. After Waterford there is a ferry at Dunmore East to take cars over to County Wexford ▲ *180*.

Thackeray found it very hard to describe the beauty of Ireland. Words seemed to lack the delicate nuances required to convey the range of colors and variations of light playing over land and ocean. Elizabeth Bowen captures these extreme changes of mood: "On fine days the view was remarkable, of almost Italian brilliance, with that constant reflection up from the water that even now prolonged the too-long day. Now, in continuous evening rain, the winding wooded line of the further shore could be seen and, nearer the windows, a smothered island with the stump of a watch-tower." Ireland is a challenge for painters too, especially the striking contrasts of landscape in the southwest.

THE COAST ROAD

KINSALE. Kinsale is jokingly referred to as the capital of the Irish Côte d'Azur, so it is no surprise to find it twinned with Antibes-Juan-les-Pins. The port is set around one of the most sheltered bays on the southern coast of the island, at the mouth of the River Bandon. It is a pretty town, well cared-for, buzzing with activity and happy to welcome its many visitors. It is a popular yachting center and also a favorite haunt of fishermen, especially those in pursuit of the blue shark ■ *20*. The town attracts almost equal numbers in search of good food: for an Irish town, Kinsale boasts an incredible number of restaurants. The annual Gourmet Festival has now been expanded to include an International Food Forum, bringing in food-lovers from far and wide. The narrow streets wind up from the harbor to reach the fields of Compass Hill. The church of ST MULTOSE dates from the 13th century and despite later alterations retains the feeling of great age. It is one of Kinsale's finest buildings, but there are a number of others to be seen. The early 18th-century Court House is now restored and houses the Kinsale Regional Museum. The Desmond Castle, a 15th-to-18th-century tower house, is also known as the French Prison (as it was so used). Many inmates died in a fire on January 27, 1747.

CHARLES FORT ● *100*. The star fort overlooking the sea beyond Summercove, 2 miles outside Kinsale, is a piece of military architecture in perfect Vauban style. It is the largest such construction from the 17th century to survive in Ireland.

THE BATTLE OF KINSALE
The Spanish fleet invaded in 1601 and held the town, aided by the Irish Earl of Tyrone. When the English regained Kinsale it was to mark the defeat of Gaelic Ireland; the "Flight of the Earls" to Europe was to follow. Kinsale became an English town, where the Irish were not allowed to live, until the late 18th century.

With the repeal of the Edict of Nantes in 1685, French Huguenots settled in the region and started a flourishing textile industry. In 1689 the French fleet landed the exiled King James II at Kinsale with a Franco-Irish expeditionary force: James wanted to regain his crown and Louis XIV wanted William of Orange out of the British Isles where he posed too much of a threat ▲ *194*.

Le Petit Journal illustré

MICHAEL COLLINS (1890–1922) ● 63
The leader of the Irish Liberation Movement became Minister of Finance in De Valera's Republican Ministry. He helped to get De Valera out of Lincoln prison, and organized Republican activity in the south. He was one of the negotiators of the Anglo-Irish Treaty, chairman of the Provisional Government, and commander of the IRA during the Civil War. The little farm of Woodfield where Collins was born on October 16, 1890, was burnt down in April 1921 by Black and Tans and he was murdered in an ambush nearby on August 20, 1922.

IRA volunteers during the war for independence.

Originally there was a small outpost on the site, destroyed when the Spanish fleet captured Kinsale in 1601. The English realized that such a strategically important harbor needed serious fortifications. They began by building James Fort (1602–4) whose ruins can still be seen on the opposite side of the inlet. The construction of Charles Fort was begun in 1678, in preparation for a Dutch seaborne attack. It was named after King Charles II. In 1681 the massive edifice was completed with fortifications on the landward side. In the 1690's John Goubet and Rudolph Corneille, Huguenot builders working for King William, made some modifications to the fort, and the main structure has remained virtually unaltered since. The barracks inside date from the 18th and early 19th century. The English evacuated Charles Fort in 1921. It was then occupied by Republicans hostile to the Treaty who were subsequently removed, with some damage to the fort, by the army of the Free State.

OLD HEAD OF KINSALE ★. On the craggy, wind-blown headland, surrounded by wild seas, stand the ruins of the De Courcy castle and a lighthouse. The *Lusitania* sank off Old Head in 1915 ▲ *219*.

TIMOLEAGUE. The village stands at the head of the Argideen estuary and incorporates the ruins of a 13th-century Franciscan abbey destroyed by Cromwell's troops in 1642.

CLONAKILTY. This part of West Cork saw much IRA guerilla action during the war for Irish independence. The events of this period are commemorated and recorded at a number of places, especially the WEST CORK REGIONAL MUSEUM in Clonakilty, and the MICHAEL COLLINS MEMORIAL CENTRE at Sam's Cross.

DROMBEG STONE CIRCLE. Between Rosscarbery and Glandore is one of Ireland's finest stone circles, consisting of seventeen regularly spaced standing stones (153 BC–AD 127). Dating from the same period, 200 feet away, are the remains of a kitchen hearth. There is a well and a trough where water was heated by throwing in hot stones that kept their warmth for about three hours.

CÉIM HILL MUSEUM ★. The little cottage in the middle of nowhere does not look at all like a museum. Yet the owner has packed three small rooms with an amazing mixture of exhibits, including prehistoric finds, memorabilia from the war of independence and various local artefacts.

CASTLETOWNSHEND. An old stronghold of the Ascendancy ● *52* that has been made famous by the

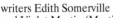

Baltimore Lighthouse.

FASTNET
A yacht race has been held every other year since 1925, starting at Cowes on the Isle of Wight, passing the Fastnet Lighthouse and returning to Plymouth. The 1979 race was marked by terrible storms, claiming the lives of fifteen contestants.

writers Edith Somerville and Violet Martin (Martin Ross) ▲ *267*, who set their "Irish R.M." stories here. They are both buried in the St BARRAHANE churchyard. There are many prehistoric remains in the area, but they can be quite hard to reach. KNOCKDRUM STONE FORT, an easily accessible one, stands on high ground in a field at the edge of the village. It has a round stone wall and some other remains.

BALTIMORE. A poem by Thomas Davis relates how in 1631 the little port of Baltimore was pillaged by Algerian pirates who took two hundred inhabitants into slavery. On the point stands a medieval lighthouse called LOT'S WIFE. Just offshore is SHERKIN ISLAND. Since 1975 it has been the site of the Marine Research Station, an institution responsible for keeping checks on the marine environment. There are a natural history museum and vivarium to visit. The east coast of the island, facing Baltimore, has deep waters where boats and yachts find good moorings. To the south can be seen the wild and rocky outline of CLEAR ISLAND, the most southerly in Ireland. Its bird observatory is well known for its study of migrating species, and the whole isle is a delight for birdlovers. In summer, puffins can be seen here on the cliffs, and out to sea there may be whales and dolphins ■ *20*. (Now proceed to Bantry by the N71, or continue to the southernmost tip of Ireland, Mizen Head.)

BANTRY ★. Bantry stands on an immense bay overlooking the Beara Peninsula. The bay was of great strategical importance in the past, and some dramatic events took place here, but today it is a vast and peaceful expanse of water, with a mild and sheltered climate that encourages lush vegetation. The town of Bantry has one of the finest houses in Ireland, BANTRY HOUSE, which overlooks the bay and the mountains beyond. The original long brick structure, three stories high, was built by the Hutchinson family around 1710. In the 18th century two wings were added, and in 1845 Richard White,

A FRUITLESS EXPEDITION
On December 15, 1796, a fleet of forty-three ships (16,000 troops) left Brest to come to the aid of the United Irishmen, whose leader Wolfe Tone ● *52* was on board. A storm blew many ships off course, including that of the commander, General Hoche, and only sixteen arrived in Bantry Bay. The second-in-command pressed on with the attack but it was prevented by gales, sleet and snow. Finally, the French ships returned home. It was a lucky escape for the English, since Bantry was very poorly defended. The wreck of the frigate *Surveillante* was raised in the 1980's.

ARCHEOLOGICAL REMAINS
The area around Bantry is full of ancient secrets. There is a circle of standing stones at Kealkil. At Kilnaruane the cross remains a puzzle to experts: the figures carved on the shaft seem to be of Saint Anthony and Saint Paul, while

other carvings include a boat and some obviously Celtic designs.

second Earl of Bantry, had the house completely redesigned and surrounded by gardens in the Italian style. Bantry House contains a varied collection of fine works of art from all over Europe, and has been open to the public since 1945. Today the two wings of Bantry House have been refurbished to accommodate tourists. More than 48,000 visitors come each year to view the house and permanent exhibition: "1796 Armada Trust".

THE INLAND ROUTE

The River Bandon runs through unspoilt countryside, perfect for walking. Each bend in the river reveals another lovely view, and the ever-changing weather transforms the mood and atmosphere of the landscape from one hour to the next.

BANDON. The town was founded early in the 17th century by Richard Boyle, Earl of Cork. Kilbrogan Church, one of Ireland's first Protestant churches, was built here in 1610. At this time the town was populated with English and Scottish settlers, and Catholics were not permitted to live here. Bandon long continued to have a strong anti-Catholic reputation.

GOUGANE BARRA ★. Saint Finbarr, the founder of Cork ▲ *212*, was born in Gougane Barra. The legend goes that he lived in a hermitage here, at a place now marked by a cross (left), having rid the lake of Gougane Barra of a dreadful monster. The lake, surrounded by forests and mountains, has provided romantic inspiration for many writers and poets. The National Park nearby is very good for walking, with well-marked paths including one leading to the source of the River Lee.

BEARA PENINSULA

The climate is mild, the vegetation abundant and seals are often seen sunning themselves on the rocks at Glengarriff.

The Beara Peninsula is a wild and mountainous finger of land stretching out toward the Atlantic Ocean between the bays of Bantry and Kenmare. It remains a mysterious place, especially the little-visited inland areas. There are a number of small loughs, and in the center of the peninsula run the Caha and the Slieve Mickish mountains. The coast road, bordered with lush vegetation, makes its way west around creeks and inlets, past beaches and bays and through tiny fishing villages. The inland road is extremely narrow and remote, leading between the sparsely covered mountain ridges.

GLENGARRIFF ★. The town stands at the entrance to the Beara Peninsula, and at the head of Bantry Bay. The Gulf Stream gives it a mild climate that has permitted an amazing number of Mediterranean plants to take root and flourish here in abundance, especially on south-facing slopes and beaches. In the bay just off Glengarriff lies GARINISH ISLAND ■ *38*, transformed into an exotic garden by its owner John Annan Bryce. For his

Gougane Barra.

ambitious project he brought tons of earth over from the mainland to cover the rocky land, and employed the well-known landscape gardener Harold Peto to design an Italian garden, certainly one of the most unusual and enchanting in Ireland. Before continuing to Kenmare over the HEALY PASS, a road cut through the Caha Mountains in the early 1930's, it is pleasant to spend some time on the Beara Peninsula discovering the traces of its ancient past. These include the tallest ogham stone in Ireland (17 feet), which stands overlooking the ocean at BALLYCROVANE.

CASTLETOWNBERE. On the outskirts of the village, surrounded by woods, is the ruined DUNBOY CASTLE, once the stronghold of O'Sullivan Bere and destroyed during a siege in 1602. Also to be found here are the remains of PUXLEY CASTLE (c.1866). This unusual building, half-French château, half-Italian villa, belonged to the Puxley family, who owned the Allihies copper mines. It was burned down by the IRA in 1921.

DURSEY ISLAND. The island is just off Crow Head, at the furthest end of the peninsula and emerges high and rocky from the sea, edged by steep cliffs. There is a cable-car trip to the island and many birdwatchers visit because it is a haven for seabirds ■ 21. On the north side of the peninsula toward Kenmare, north of the village of Lauragh lies DERREEN HOUSE. Its gardens contain rhododendrons, azaleas, eucalyptus trees and New Zealand tree ferns.

BERE ISLAND. The long, narrow island lies sheltered along the south coast of the peninsula, just over a mile offshore from Castletownbere. In World War One it was a Royal Navy base but was relinquished by the British government in 1938. Today Bere Island is enjoyed by those who like fishing and sailing.

THE ALLIHIES COPPER MINES
Copper was discovered on the Beara Peninsula in 1810. Two years later it began to be exploited. At the height of their activity the Allihies mines employed 1,300 miners, some from Cornwall, and brought prosperity to the region. They also made the fortune of the Puxley family, on whose story Daphne Du Maurier based her novel *Hungry Hill*. The mining stopped for good in 1962.

**DANIEL O'CONNELL
(1775–1847) ● 53**
Son of a small
landowner, Daniel
O'Connell was
adopted by a rich
uncle and brought up
in France. He was
called to the Irish Bar
and campaigned for
the emancipation of
Catholics.

At fifty-three he
was elected
Member of
Parliament for
County Clare
▲ 245. O'Connell
continued to fight
for the Repeal of
the Union, making
"Irish popular

County Kerry is renowned for its beauty, which is all the more dramatic because it combines so many different kinds of natural splendor. The coastline can vary from enchantingly peaceful to wild and rugged, while inland the landscape includes homely farms with walled fields and small streams, as well as powerful, dark-watered rivers, spectacular upland torrents, and craggy mountains, including the tallest in Ireland, Mount Carantouhil (3,414 feet) on the Iveragh Peninsula. The mild climate has also created pockets of dense and lush vegetation, particularly south of Killarney. There is a panoramic route leading around the Iveragh Peninsula known as the Ring of Kerry. The winding road passes through a succession of magnificent landscapes, and has long been one of the favorite sightseeing tours of Ireland.

KENMARE TO WATERVILLE

KENMARE. The small town (left) lies on the Kenmare River estuary and was founded in the 17th century by Sir William Petty, an economist whom Cromwell instructed to carry out a general survey of Ireland. He amassed the Lansdowne estate and, in 1775, his

opinion a force in
British politics for the
first time" (Robert
Kee).

descendant the Marquis of Lansdowne, came to live in the town and started its first market and its first inn. Among many ancient remains in the area is the mysterious circle of stones called the DRUID'S CIRCLE, standing near the town center beside the river.
PARKNASILLA. The house once belonged to the Bland family, but was converted to become the Great Southern Hotel, with George Bernard Shaw as its most famous guest. He is said to

> "BLUE SKY, ROARING WATER, HERE BLACK AND YONDER FOAMING OF A DAZZLING WHITE; ROCKS SHINING IN THE DARK PLACES, OR FROWNING BLACK AGAINST THE LIGHT."
>
> WILLIAM MAKEPEACE THACKERAY

GARINISH ISLAND
The little island lying off the coast near Sneem (not to be confused with that in Bantry Bay) was once the property of the earls of Dunraven. In 1865 the third earl was converted to Catholicism and thus discovered that his fellow parishioners had to practise their faith in dreadful conditions. He consequently built a new Catholic church in the Italian style, dedicated to Saint Michael.

THE "NUN OF KENMARE"
In 1861 a convent was founded in Kenmare. The nuns began a small lacemaking industry to help local girls earn a living. The lace soon gained a good reputation, winning several prizes. One of the nuns, Mary France Cusack, became known in the 19th century for her writings on religious subjects and social matters. She came to be called the "Nun of Kenmare" and herself became the subject of a number of pious writings, which tended to draw a veil over her more radical opinions.

have completed his play *Saint Joan* in what is now called the Shaw Library.

SNEEM. The village, through which the Ardsheelaun River rushes to the sea, is a popular stopping place. Winning a number of prizes for its tidy charm, it has made every effort to beautify itself for visitors; its pieces of modern sculpture in particular make it an interesting town. They include James Scanlon's curious pyramids, as well as the white *Peaceful Panda* (1986), symbolizing the peaceful relationship between Ireland and China; a metal tree given to the town in 1985 by the President of Israel; and Alan Hall's monument to commemorate General de Gaulle's stay nearby in 1969.

STAIGUE FORT ★. The fort lies less than 3 miles inland from Castlecove, in peaceful countryside. The massive circular dry-stone walls are 90 feet in diameter and remain in astonishingly good condition. They are 13 feet thick and up to 16 feet high, tapering toward the top. There is an intriguing system of diagonal runs of steps leading up to the top of the wall, which was probably surmounted by a palisade ● *91*. As usual there is a teasing legend to enliven the visit: it is said that the Iron Age fortress was built in a day and a night.

CAHERDANIEL. The town, whose name comes from CATHAIR DONAILL, a pre-Christian fort similar in construction to Staigue Fort, stands close to the lovely beach at Derrynane Bay. Just outside the village is DERRYNANE HOUSE, from 1825 the home of Daniel O'Connell (1775–1847), and now a museum. Sean O'Faolain gave this picture of O'Connell there: "He would breakfast on the hills, going quickly but intently through his letters, strewing the grass with The Times, The Universe, letters from France or America, reports from Dublin."

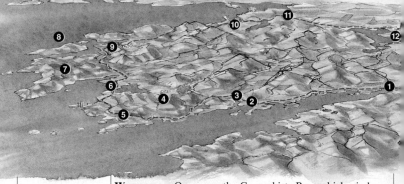

THE FIRST TRANSATLANTIC CABLE
Valentia Island, the most westerly point in Ireland, was chosen as the European end of the first transatlantic cable, laid to Newfoundland. The first message was transmitted on August 5, 1858,

WATERVILLE. Once over the Coomakista Pass, which winds up to 700 feet, there is a magnificent drive down toward Waterville with views over Ballinskellig Bay and the Skellig Islands. Waterville itself sits between the bay and Lough Currane, famous for brown trout and salmon fishing. All around are lovely beaches and fine walks.

WATERVILLE TO VALENTIA ISLAND

CHURCH ISLAND. The island in Lough Currane has the ruins of a 6th-century oratory and a 7th-century church. Nearby stand *clocháin* ▲ *236* (beehive huts), one of which is reputed

to have been the cell of Saint Finan. In clear weather, when the water is still, it is possible to look down into the lake and see the submerged ruins of a castle.

BALLINSKELLIGS. The village of Ballinskelligs is set on a lovely beach where the first Celts are thought to have landed. This is a Gaelic-speaking community, and many come here to learn the language. Near to the water are the wind- and sea-worn ruins of an Augustinian monastery. There is also a ruined 16th-century castle built by the MacCarthys to rebuff attacks by pirates and other invaders. For those who enjoy mountain scenery there is a road to Portmagee, where the bridge crosses to Valentia Island, over Coomanaspig Gap (1,080 feet). Otherwise, the coast road past ST FINAN'S BAY has equally spectacular views.

sending "Glory to God and peace on earth to men of goodwill". The station was in constant use from 1865 to 1965.

Above, the Augustinian monastery at Ballinskelligs, and St Finan's Bay.

Ballinskelligs.

VALENTIA ISLAND. At the western end are the rocky cliffs around Bray Head, and to the northeast lies the little village of KNIGHTSTOWN, named after the Knights of Kerry, a branch of the Anglo-Norman FitzGerald family, whose ancestral seat is at Glanleam. Here too are the subtropical gardens of Lord Mounteagle, flourishing in the warmth of the Gulf Stream climate. Visitors can learn more about the life of the islanders

at the Valentia Heritage Centre. Many also enjoy the Skellig Experience Visitor Centre which gives a history of the Skellig Islands.

CAHIRCIVEEN TO KILLARNEY

CAHIRCIVEEN. Daniel O'Connell was born here at CARHAN HOUSE, which today is an ivy-covered ruin. The Catholic church, the O'CONNELL MEMORIAL CHURCH, is the only one in the world to have been dedicated to a layman. Nearby there are two interesting ring-forts. LEACANABUAILE FORT is a massive construction with a single entrance to the east side. One of its three beehive huts

was occupied in the 9th and 10th centuries. CAHERGAL FORT is similar to Staigue Fort. It has two dry-stone constructions within, a beehive hut and a rectangular structure.

GLENBEIGH. The road leads back to the sea on Dingle Bay and descends into the valley of the River Beigh. This ends to the south with the circle of hills known as the Glenbeigh Horse Shoe. The village is a popular resort because of the nearby beach, lying along the sandy spit called Rossbeigh Strand that reaches out into Dingle Bay. The mud flats situated at the eastern spit of land offer some excellent birdwatching. The fishing is also good, and the seafood restaurants are notable. The road continues toward LOUGH CARAGH, a long curved lake extending nearly 4 miles and well known for its salmon and salmon trout.

KILLORGLIN. The town stands on the wide River Laune and the salmon fishing is good nearby. But Killorglin is chiefly famous for its Puck Fair , a three-day festival which takes place the second weekend in August.

"PUCK FAIR"
The fair at Killorglin lasts for three days, from August 10 to 12: Gathering Day, Fair Day, and Scattering Day. The emblem of the fair is a male wild goat, the "Puck", caught in the mountains. He is carried through the town in a procession, displayed on a high platform. The livestock on sale at the fair is varied, and includes horses, ponies and cows. Deals are celebrated with drinking, step-dancing and songs until the early hours. The fair is said to predate Christian times, and some claim it to be the oldest commercial event in the world, but more likely it celebrates the stampede of a herd of wild goats that warned the town of an English attack. It is one of the most popular fairs in Ireland, and was long a great meeting place for the traveling community, whose caravans would line the roads into town.

The craggy islands rise dramatically from the wild ocean, 10 miles off the western point of the Iveragh Peninsula. Little Skellig is now a bird reserve, while Skellig Michael (also called Great Skellig) is still a vivid reminder of the austerity of early monastic life in Ireland. The remote monastery on the Skelligs was the westernmost outpost of Christianity in the old world, and was once considered to be the end of the world itself. The rocky cliffs of the island rise 700 feet above the sea, steeper and more impregnable than any walls. Nevertheless, in the 9th century the Vikings dared to attack.

Puffin

A MAGNIFICENT SETTING
The tiny monastic settlement consists of two oratories, six beehive huts, a church and a graveyard, surrounded by a dry-stone wall. Over six hundred steps cut into the rocks by the monks lead up to it.

SKELLIG MICHAEL
Like so many holy sites perched on high rocks, the monastery is dedicated to the Archangel Michael, who is said to have helped Saint Patrick chase the snakes out of Ireland.

LITTLE SKELLIG
The isle is a nature reserve, and nearly twenty thousand gannets nest here each year. This flourishing colony was in great danger of dying out early in the century, but it is now protected. Landings on the island are strictly controlled.

THE MONASTERY
Saint Finan is said to have founded the monastery in the 6th century, and this is borne out by the style of construction. The monks left in the 12th century, taking refuge at Ballinskelligs ▲ 230.

PILGRIMAGE
Large numbers of the faithful have made the journey to Skellig Michael, one of the most holy spots in Ireland. After visiting the ruins, penitent pilgrims would make the hazardous climb up to the summit, Needle's Eye, to kiss the standing stone.

Manx shearwater

Razorbill

Gannet

Storm petrel

THE "CLOCHÁIN" ▲ *236*
Six cells in the form of beehive huts remain.
These *clocháin*, are dry-stone constructions,
rounded towards the top to create the roof,
which is finished with flat stones. They measure
15 to 25 feet in diameter. The exterior protruding
stones were probably for keying a covering of lime.

HORSE-DRAWN VEHICLES
In Killarney and at the gates of Muckross House there are "jarveys" waiting with their "jaunting cars" ready to take tourists for a ride. Passengers sitting back-to-back can take a relatively safe horse-drawn tour of the hills and lakes. Charlotte Brontë had a more unsettling horseback experience in the Gap of Dunloe in 1854: "A sudden glimpse of a very grim phantom came on us in the Gap. The guide had warned me to alight from my horse as the path was now very broken and dangerous – I did not feel

afraid and declined ... suddenly ... [the mare] seemed to go mad – reared, plunged – I was thrown on the stones right under her."

Muckross House.

KILLARNEY AND SURROUNDING AREA

Coming from the bare, windswept Atlantic coast of Kerry, the richness of vegetation around Killarney is a surprise. There are immensely tall trees, impenetrable rhododendron groves, and a feeling of fertile, green profusion that can be almost sinister. This region gives real meaning to the name Emerald Isle.

KILLARNEY. The town has made efforts to gratify the tourist trade since its development in the 19th century, but it has little in the way of architectural splendor. St Mary's Catholic Cathedral, a neo-Gothic structure by A.W. Pugin built between 1842 and 1855, is the only building of interest in the town. Its interior was stripped to bare stone in the 1970's. The Church of Christ, Prince of Peace, was erected at Fossa, just outside Killarney, in 1977. A number of well-known Irish artists were involved in the project including John Behan, Patrick Pye and Imogen Stuart. The window behind the altar must have the finest view of any church in Ireland.

KILLARNEY NATIONAL PARK. Twenty-three square miles of lakes and forest around Muckross House, southwest of Killarney, are now a protected area. There are many walks, some more strenuous than others, along which to explore the magnificent, romantic landscape. Tourists also enjoy the park by bicycle and on horseback. The area is of particular interest to botanists because the many patches of virgin oak wood are typical of that which once covered most of Ireland. Many other species abound, including birch, holly, bilberry and the red-barked arbutus or strawberry tree. The mosses and lichens are vigorous and varied. From the Aghadoe Heights there is an extraordinary view over the mountains and the three lakes: Upper Lake, Middle Lake, and Lower Lake.

MUCKROSS ABBEY. Half-hidden amid oaks, sycamores and ash trees are the peaceful ruins of a Franciscan monastery. The abbey was destroyed by Cromwell's soldiers in 1652. The buildings are typical of the 15th century, particularly the Gothic windows with interlace pattern and the impressive square tower ● 96. Finest of all are the cloisters, with pointed and round-topped arches, set around a dark yew tree. This symbol of mourning seems to honor

The Gap of Dunloe is a shadowy and rocky pass between MacGillycuddy's Reeks and the Purple Mountain, past lakes to a wonderful view over the Upper Lake. Kate Kearney's Cottage (below), a place to stop for refreshment on the road to the Gap, has lost its terror now that Kate is no longer there to curse all who enter the establishment.

three Kerry poets buried in the abbey: Geoffrey O'Donoghue (d. 1677), Egan O'Rahilly (1670–1728), whose poems denounced the disappearance of the old Gaelic order crushed by colonization, and Owen Roe O'Sullivan (1748–84), whose lyrical accounts of ancient legends have been assimilated into Irish folklore. A fourth poet, the betrayed chieftain Piaras Ferriter, is said to be buried in the graveyard outside the abbey. He was hanged on the nearby Hill of Sheep in 1643.

MUCKROSS HOUSE. The neo-Gothic mansion, where Queen Victoria stayed in 1861, was built in 1843 by William Burn. Some of the beautifully furnished rooms can be visited, with views over well-tended gardens to the magnificent lake and hills beyond. In the grounds, the Kerry Country Life Experience has recreated a farm as it would have been early in the century.

ROSS CASTLE. On the banks of Lower Lake stands a castle dating from around 1500, and probably built by a local chieftain, O'Donoghue Ross. According to an ancient prophecy, it was to fall to a warrior come from over the sea. The story is told that, as a result, in 1649, when Cromwell's General Ludlow approached the castle, it was abandoned. In fact, Lord Muskenny's troops fled under fire from Ludlow's cannons.

INNISFALLEN ISLAND. There are over thirty islands in the Lower Lake. From a landing stage below Ross Castle boats leave for Innisfallen Island, described by Macaulay as "not a reflex of heaven, but a bit of heaven itself". Two little chapels remain from a 7th-century monastery where in the 13th century an important manuscript was produced called the *Annals of Innisfallen*. It is now kept in Oxford.

TORC WATERFALL. The road winds past the lakes. On the wooded slopes opposite, the Torc river drops in a dramatic 60-foot waterfall. Tennyson's poem, set to music by Britten, captures the haunting beauty of the place: "Blow, bugle, blow, set the wild echoes flying, Blow, bugle, answer, echoes dying, dying, dying." Further along the road is Ladies View ★, a vantage point from which to survey the lakes and the far-off Gap of Dunloe. The name has various explanations: one is that Queen Victoria's ladies-in-waiting were enraptured by the view in 1861.

Meanwhile, at Kate Kearney's Cottage in the Gap of Dunloe...

They say you're a bit of witch, Kate?!

Don't anyone dare say that! I'll turn them into a toad! Heh! Heh!

ROMANTIC MUSE
Since the 18th century the special beauty of the landscape around Killarney has fascinated travelers, among them the philosopher George Berkeley ▲ 220, and many writers such as Scott, Tennyson, Thackeray and Shelley. There has long been a tourist industry catering to this image, but it has not managed to destroy the romantic magic of the place.

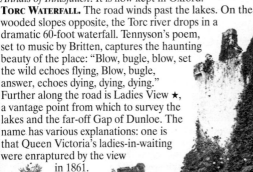

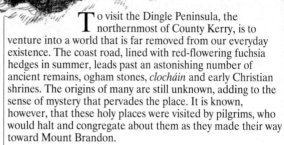

THE "CLOCHÁIN"
● 92
It has proved difficult to date the beehive huts with any accuracy, and some are perhaps quite recent. But the oldest of the round, dry-stone structures were often monks' cells, and were later used by shepherds. There are a good number of huts on the Dingle

To visit the Dingle Peninsula, the northernmost of County Kerry, is to venture into a world that is far removed from our everyday existence. The coast road, lined with red-flowering fuchsia hedges in summer, leads past an astonishing number of ancient remains, ogham stones, *clocháin* and early Christian shrines. The origins of many are still unknown, adding to the sense of mystery that pervades the place. It is known, however, that these holy places were visited by pilgrims, who would halt and congregate about them as they made their way toward Mount Brandon.

DINGLE TO DUNQUIN

BALLINTAGGART. Ogham stones ● 66 are perhaps the most remarkable pre-Christian remains in Ireland. The script on these stones is a primitive alphabet of twenty letters, representing the earliest phase of Gaelic. There are nine of them in the circular graveyard at Ballintaggart (2 miles southeast of Dingle). Three of the standing stones have incised crosses.

DINGLE. Dingle is one of the westernmost towns in Europe and lies at the welcome end of a long and winding road. Here is a fine, natural harbor with its curve of sandy beach. The sheltered port lies below the 2,050 foot high peak of Ballysitteragh. During the 14th and 15th centuries Dingle was the leading port of the peninsula and a major trading center having strong links with Spain, but the troops of Elizabeth I and Cromwell between them destroyed the town walls

Peninsula, resembling structures found in the Vaucluse, the Rhone Valley in France, and others elsewhere in Europe. Some of the Dingle huts are not officially indicated. When on private land they may be signposted at the farm or cottage gate. In such circumstances, although their date may be uncertain, they are particularly astonishing.

and other buildings. Dingle is thought to have operated for a while as a center for smuggling and, in the 18th century, to have even minted its owns coins. Today the lively town is the most important on the Dingle Penisula and has benefited from the growing tourist trade, while retaining a small fishing fleet. There are plenty of bars and restaurants. A pleasant evening can be spent in the *Café Liteartha* ◆ 375 which, in addition to the restaurant, has an interesting bookshop. In 1983 a bottlenosed dolphin was first sighted in the harbor. Nicknamed Fungi by the local fishermen he has become the star of Dingle and an international celebrity. He has inspired poems and television documentaries, and is now one of Dingle's main tourist attractions. (If not continuing west, there is a route straight back toward Tralee over the impressive Conor Pass with its view of the three dark lakes of the Owenmore Valley.)

VENTRY. The narrow neck of land separating Dingle and Ventry harbors is traditionally said to have been the last territory occupied by the Danes in Ireland. The town of Ventry is at the center of many of the area's legends. Here is the "White Strand" of the hero Finn MacCoul's battle with the "King of the World", a savage struggle lasting a year and a day. At this time, too, the beautiful Cael decided to give her hand to the man who composed the best poem in praise of her house. The fortunate winner, Crede, was not so lucky in combat. He died during the Battle of Ventry.

DÚN BEG FORT. The prehistoric fort stands on a narrow promontory at the very edge of the cliff. Its four outer stone walls contain the remains of a house and a beehive hut. An underground passage from the center of the fort to the outer defensive walls permitted escape in the event of a surprise attack.

FAHAN. Between Ventry and Slea Head, on the lower slopes of Mount Eagle, is an extended site of four hundred *clocháin* ● 92. The best of them are at Fahan.

SLEA HEAD ★. The little road winds out toward Slea Head passing beneath Mount Eagle and leading at last to the headland. Over the blue waters to the south lie the Iveragh peninsula and the Skellig Islands, and to the west are the Blasket Islands.

DUNMORE HEAD. A little further east, beyond the tiny village of Coomeenoole and its pretty beach, lies Dunmore Head. At the highest point is an ogham stone with a long inscription.

DUNQUIN (DÚN CHAOIN). A pocket of Gaelic culture surrounds this land's end hamlet, and it has become another center of *Gaeltacht* ● 68. Irish can be heard spoken everywhere, a thing rare in all but a few westcoast communities. Those who wish to learn the language can take summer courses at schools in Dingle, Ventry, Dunquin and Ballyferriter. Dunquin preserves a number of disappearing traditions, and *currachs* ▲ 276, or *naomhógs*, beautifully made old boats, can be seen in the harbor. From Dunquin there are magnificent views of the Blasket Islands and the impressive cliffs to the north

"RYAN'S DAUGHTER"
♦ 333 (above).
In 1969, David Lean shot the exterior scenes of his epic film on Coomeenoole beach and in a reconstruction of an old village near Dunquin. The love story was set against the backdrop of the 1916 Rising ● 60. It has considerably increased the number of summer visitors to Dingle.

The rusting wreck still to be seen on the Dingle coast is a reminder of the dangerous seas and rocks off Slea Head.

THE BLASKET ISLANDS

A LOST WORLD
A number of books have helped to preserve, in writing at least, the life of the Blasket islanders. There are autobiographies by Maurice O'Sullivan (1904–50), *Twenty Years A-Growing*, Peig Sayers (1873–1958), *Peig*, and perhaps most fascinating of all, *The Islandman* by Tomás Ó'Criomhthain (1854–1937). He describes the simple existence of fishing, seal hunting and farming, and remembers the events that affected the islanders' lives. Once a brown substance was salvaged in cases from a wreck and used by women as dye. Later they discovered it was an unknown stuff called tea later to become one of their greatest luxuries. The three books were written in Gaelic in the 1930's and translated much later.

"This is a crag in the midst of the great sea, and again and again the blown surf drives right over it before the violence of the wind, so that you daren't put your head out any more than a rabbit that crouches low in his burrow in Inishvickillaun when the rain and salt and spume are flying. Often would we put to sea at the dawn of the day when the weather was decent enough, and by the end of the day our people on land would be keening us, so much had the weather changed for the worse." At the end of *The Islandman* Tomás Ó'Criomhthain tried to explain why the inhabitants finally left the island of GREAT BLASKET, many to try their luck in the United States ● 59. Brought near to starvation by several disastrous seasons of fishing, the last twenty-two islanders were settled on the mainland by the government in 1953. Seen from the road to Slea Head, or from the top of Mount Eagle, the six islands hold a powerful fascination; not only the rocky silhouettes of the Blaskets themselves, however, but also the treacherous stretch of water, Blasket Sound, that separates them from the Dingle Peninsula. Two ships of the Armada sank here in a storm in 1588: the *San Juan de Ragusa* and the *Santa María de la Rosa* ▲ 316. Today there are boats from Dunquin and Dingle to take visitors across. There is an Interpretative Centre near Dunquin providing an informative survey of the islands' archeological past and more recent social history.

BALLYFERRITER TO TRALEE

Oratory of Gallarus.

Before reaching Ballyferriter, the road runs along the cliffs of Clogher Head, with a fine view of the cliff ridge of SYBIL HEAD. Turning inland it goes through a pretty gorge below Croaghmarhin. Far off can be seen the outline of Mount Brandon.

BALLYFERRITER. A few miles from the village, at REASK, are some varied and interesting ancient remains. There are beehive huts alongside tombs and a ruined stone oratory, as well as a magnificent standing stone called the REASK PILLAR STONE, with remarkable circular carvings. Those keen on archeology will also want to visit the Heritage Centre at Ballyferriter, which has a collection of ogham stones ● 66.

ORATORY OF GALLARUS ★ ● 92. At Ballynana is a building erected using the same method as a for a beehive hut, but adapted to form a rectangular structure. The Oratory of Gallarus is the only structure of its type to remain standing today, owing to the excellent skill of its drystone construction. There are no interior decorations to help with the dating of the oratory, but it is thought to have been built at some time between the 9th and the 12th centuries. Despite the number of visitors who come here, there is a feeling of spiritual calm around this perfect and utterly simple monument.

KILMALKEDAR ★. The 12th-century church of Kilmalkedar is on the pilgrim way to Santiago de Compostela, and is in the Romanesque style that is typical of the monuments along this holy route. The decoration on the doorway and chancel arch is true to the Hiberno-Romanesque style ● *94*. Note the strange creature on the door. There is a blind arcade on the interior wall of the nave, apparently copied from Cormac's chapel in Cashel ▲ *253*. The stone roof of the chancel is also typical of style and period (also seen at Glendalough ▲ *178*, Kells ▲ *192*, Cormac ▲ *253*).

ROSE OF TRALEE ★ ◆ *337*. The town of Tralee, well-positioned just inland from Tralee Bay and north of the Dingle Peninsula, is the capital of County Kerry. It is probably most famous for an annual competition held to celebrate the qualities of its womenfolk now scattered over the face of the planet. The contest honors the poet William Mulchinock (1820–64) and his lament written for a disdainful sweetheart. At the end of August each year, girls claiming Tralee origins come from near and far in the hope of being judged the most charming and beautiful: the Rose of Tralee. The festivities include a colorful carnival and other events to amuse the visitors, such as horse-races, Gaelic music, and poetry recitals. Pub life is also animated.

ARDFERT. Five miles northwest of Tralee is Ardfert, made an episcopal see by Saint Brendan and the site of one of his monasteries. Only part of the west façade of the original 12th-century Romanesque church remains. It was replaced in the 13th century by a cathedral, as it was probably too small to accommodate the large number of pilgrims. The ruined early Gothic cathedral with elegant lancet windows stands near two smaller churches, Teampull-na-Hoe and Teampull-na-Griffin.

PILGRIMAGE TO MOUNT BRANDON
The mountain is dedicated to Saint Brendan, one of Ireland's three most popular saints. He is said to have made a retreat here before leaving on a seven-year voyage in search of the Land of Promise. Brendan, patron saint of sailors, became well-known in the Middle Ages through a 10th-century tale, the *Navigatio Brendani*, a mixture of fact and myth.

F or a long time County Clare saw few tourists compared to its better-known neighbors Kerry, to the south ▲ *228*, and Galway, to the north ▲ *258.* Today Clare's unspoiled natural beauty is highly prized, and its dramatic coastline entices many visitors. It has also been discovered by lovers of Irish music. The genuine traditions of singing and playing have remained widespread, both in pubs and during festivals.

KILRUSH AND SCATTERY ISLAND

DIARMAIT AND GRÁINNE'S ROCK
The rock sticking up out of the sea just off Loop Head was the refuge of the famous warrior Cú Chulainn, trying to escape the amorous pursuit of a witch called Mal. When she joined him on the rock in one

bound, he was so horrified that he leapt back to shore. She tried to follow once more, but fell at the foot of the cliffs, bleeding so profusely that the waves all along the coast were red with her blood. This tale explains the nearby place names of "Mal Bay" and "Hag Head".

The main street of KILRUSH, lined with Georgian houses, is where the coastal route begins, and leads on to the port of Cappa. From here it is possible to see the ISLAND OF SCATTERY, out beyond Hog Island. Legend has it that Saint Senan, who founded the first monastery on the island, in the 6th century, delivered Scattery of a monster that lived there. Successive monasteries were destroyed by invaders and the ruins of the five churches that can now be seen there date from the 12th and 13th centuries. The well-preserved round tower is unusual in that its door is at ground level rather than the more usual position between 12 and 15 feet above the ground ● *92.*

LOOP HEAD ★

CASTLE. On the edge of the village of Carrigaholt, overlooking the Shannon estuary, there is a fortified tower built by the MacMahons late in the 15th century. It was a stronghold of the O'Briens ▲ *245* and it was they who had the fireplace (1603) and most of the windows installed. The castle was occupied by the English and used as a garrison for Cromwell's troops. At the end of the 17th century Lord Clare, an O'Brien loyal to the Jacobite cause, raised and trained a regiment of the "Wild Geese" here, Irish Catholic Irish troops who fought in the service of France.

GALE-FORCE WINDS. The strength of the Atlantic winds have forced cottagers to devise a method of securing their thatched roofs with a grid of ropes ● *103.* The constant erosion of the coast by the wind and the sea can be seen at BRIDGE OF ROSS, a good place to set out on a walk along the cliffs. After you are exhausted by squalls and sea air, a visit to the church of Moneen proves restful. Here there is a portable altar used by Catholics for secret masses during times of prohibition ● *52.*

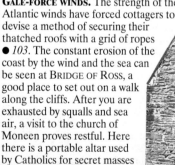

Right, the church at Kilkee.

THE "WILD GEESE"
After defeat at the Battle of the Boyne
▲ *194*, the Irish Jacobite regiments joined
Louis XIV's army and formed the famous
Irish brigade of "Wild Geese" which was to
make a significant contribution to the French
victory at Fontenoy in 1745.

St Brigid's Well.

WEST CLARE RAILWAY
A railway was built
along the coast
between Ennis and
Milltown Malbay, and
opened in 1887. In
1892, it was extended
as far as Kilkee and
Kilrush. It was a
delightful way for
visitors to travel (in
carriages weighted to
resist violent squalls),
but the line was closed
in 1961.

Another peaceful conclusion to an exploration of Loop Head
is the seaside resort of KILKEE, with its sheltered, sandy beach
on Moore Bay.

John Philip Holland.

TO LISCANNOR BAY

QUILTY. The church, whose architecture was inspired by Celtic
art, was funded by the crew of a wrecked French boat, saved
by the villagers in 1907. The abundance of seaweed along the
coast is a reminder that it was once an important resource,
and vital during the Great Famine ● *58*.

MILLTOWN MALBAY. In July the population of the village
triples for the annual William Clancy School of Music, named
for one of County Clare's greatest pipers ● *72*. It is a week of
intensive music-making, often continued late into the evening
by unofficial "classes" held in pubs. Near to the village is a
power station fueled by turf. To the southeast is the mountain
of SLIEVE CALLAN (1,282 feet). On its slopes is a dolmen
known as DIARMAIT AND GRÁINNE'S BED. Like other
megaliths associated with the names of Diarmait and Gráinne
▲ *289* (an Irish legend similar to that of Tristan and Isolde),
the stone is reputed to have aphrodisiac qualities and to cure
sterility.

LISCANNOR BAY. The opening of the West Clare Railway in
1887 led to the development of the seaside town of Lahinch.
ENNISTYMON, whose pretty and colorful main street is
particularly lively on market and fair days, stands beside the
gentle cascades of the River Cullenagh. LISCANNOR has a
plaque in its harbor in recognition of the fact that it was the
birthplace of John Philip Holland (1840–1914), inventor of
the first submarine in America. On the
edge of the village toward the coast
stands the square 15th-century tower of
LISCANNOR CASTLE. Not far from
O'BRIEN'S MONUMENT, erected in 1853
by local landowner Cornelius O'Brien in
his own honor, is ST BRIGID'S WELL, one
of many springs in Ireland whose reputed
powers of healing have their roots in
ancient Celtic culture. A pilgrimage is
made here on the last weekend of July.

**THE INVINCIBLE
ARMADA**
Although Spanish
Point is the only place
name to recall the
episode, the whole
coast of County Clare
witnessed the dramatic
sinking of the Armada
in 1588 ▲ *316*. Ships
went down at
Doonbeg, Tromra and
Doolin, and survivors
were for the most part
hanged. At Liscannor,
the villagers gathered
around the castle to
prevent the crew of
the galley *Zuñiga*
landing and
negotiating for
supplies.

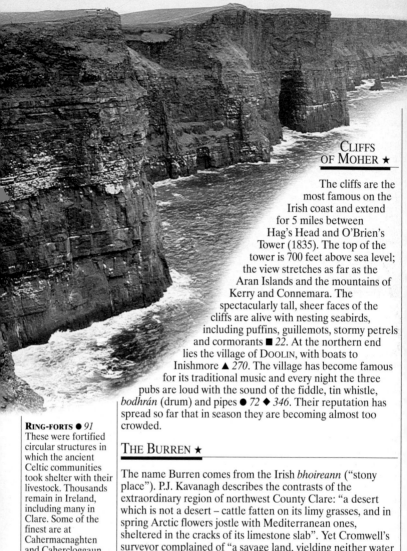

CLIFFS OF MOHER ★

The cliffs are the most famous on the Irish coast and extend for 5 miles between Hag's Head and O'Brien's Tower (1835). The top of the tower is 700 feet above sea level; the view stretches as far as the Aran Islands and the mountains of Kerry and Connemara. The spectacularly tall, sheer faces of the cliffs are alive with nesting seabirds, including puffins, guillemots, stormy petrels and cormorants ■ *22*. At the northern end lies the village of DOOLIN, with boats to Inishmore ▲ *270*. The village has become famous for its traditional music and every night the three pubs are loud with the sound of the fiddle, tin whistle, *bodhrán* (drum) and pipes ● *72* ◆ *346*. Their reputation has spread so far that in season they are becoming almost too crowded.

THE BURREN ★

The name Burren comes from the Irish *bhoireann* ("stony place"). P.J. Kavanagh describes the contrasts of the extraordinary region of northwest County Clare: "a desert which is not a desert – cattle fatten on its limy grasses, and in spring Arctic flowers jostle with Mediterranean ones, sheltered in the cracks of its limestone slab". Yet Cromwell's surveyor complained of "a savage land, yielding neither water enough to drown a man, nor a tree to hang him, nor soil enough to bury".

LISDOONVARNA. The town was developed as a spa in the 19th century, and has become a popular seaside resort. It is now best known for its September Matchmaking Festival, when bachelors flood the town in search of a wife, along with many others who come just to enjoy the fun. Northwest of the village is BALLYNALACKAN CASTLE, a well-preserved example of a 15th-century fortified tower ● *99*. There is a road leading around the coast to Ballyvaughan past the beach at FANORE, BLACK HEAD and the 16th-century GLENINAGH CASTLE, overlooking the bay. It is also possible to take a closer look at the Burren on the Green Road footpath that

RING-FORTS ● *91* These were fortified circular structures in which the ancient Celtic communities took shelter with their livestock. Thousands remain in Ireland, including many in Clare. Some of the finest are at Cahermacnaghten and Cahercloggaun, northeast of Lisdoonvarna, Caher Balliny, on the Green Road toward Ballyvaughan and Cathair Scribin.

Dolmen at Poulnabrone.

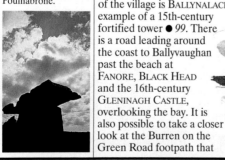

crosses barren stretches of the strange landscape and climbs the lower slopes of Slieve Elva (1,109 feet).

BALLYVAUGHAN. Most visitors come to the village because it is near the AILLWEE CAVE, the Burren cave that is the most easily accessible to the public. There are many megalithic sites in the surrounding area, although some are easily mistaken for piles of old stones. This is certainly not the case with the Neolithic POULNABRONE DOLMEN (on the road south to Corofin), whose striking, leaning silhouette has become the symbol of the Burren. South of Ballyvaughan is NEWTOWN CASTLE, an unusual round tower set back from the Corkscrew Road, the steep and winding road up to Corkscrew Hill. From the top there is a fine view over the region.

CORCOMROE ABBEY ★. The Cistercian abbey dating from the early 13th century is built to a cruciform plan. It is the most beautiful monument in the Burren. There are magnificent capitals in the choir and transept chapels, carved with human heads (right) and floral motifs of medicinal plants used by the monks (perhaps linked in some way with the Latin name of the monastery: St Mary of the Fertile Rock). There are some interesting tombs including that of Conor O'Brien, King of Thomond, who died in 1267. The eastern window embrasure still has traces of color and there are remains of drawings incised in the plaster of the choir (depicting an embarcation) and the south chapel (a lion). Northwest of the village of Burren is MOUNT VERNON LODGE, which belonged to Lady Gregory (1852–1932) ▲ *247*, and where she entertained W.B. Yeats ▲ *122* and George Bernard Shaw ▲ *125*.

Detail of capital at Corcomroe Abbey.

CAVES IN CLARE
The largest network of caves is around Slieve Elva, including the Pollnagolum, Cullaun, Coolagh River and Doolin caves, and also, in the valley, Pol an Ionain with an incredible 23-foot stalactite. At Kilshanny there is a center where lessons in speleology are given, and equipment may be hired.

KINVARRA

DUNGUAIRE CASTLE overlooks the bay close to Kinvarra (County Galway). It is a 16th-century tower house ● *99*, a fortified dwelling once belonging to the Martyn de Tulira family ▲ *247*. Medieval banquets are now organized here.

BUNRATTY
The banqueting hall in the keep is decorated with tapestries and furnished with medieval cupboards

and chests from France. In one of the window recesses is an example of a *sheela-na-gig*, a primitive carving of a naked woman in an immodest position. Nothing is known for sure of their significance, and numerous explanations have been offered. The hall and the chapel beside it have some rare examples of Irish stuccowork from the 17th century.

The Franciscan abbey at Quin.

NORTH BANK OF THE SHANNON TO ENNIS

BUNRATTY. The castle was built by the MacNamaras in 1450 on a site that had been fortified since Viking times. A century later it fell into the hands of the O'Briens. In the 1960's Bunratty Castle was restored and the great hall is now used for medieval banquets enjoyed to the music of harps. These lighthearted occasions are a far remove from the bloody battles of the past. Beside the castle, the FOLK PARK recreates a rural Ireland of the 19th and early 20th centuries. There are additional features illustrating much earlier periods, such as the little 8th-century watermill. Fishermen's and workmen's cottages have been reconstructed accurately, based on those found in County Clare and Limerick in the 19th century. The peasant homesteads have tools, furniture and everyday household items of the time. Nearby is a typical late 19th-century Irish village with post office, grocer's shop, printer's, school and doctor's surgery.

CRAGGAUNOWEN. The original 15th- to 16th-century fortified tower was extended by the former owners, art historian John Hunt and his wife Gertrude, with the addition of a medieval-style hall to house their collection of works of art. Most of the collection (prehistoric objects, Greek antiquities, holy art from Ireland, including some lovely crucifixes) is now displayed in the Hunt Museum in Limerick ▲ 248. Hunt also initiated a number of projects to construct replicas of ancient Irish structures. In the grounds are a *rath* and a *crannóg* (above) ● 90, both based on archeological evidence combined with Hunt's own intuition. Since his death in 1975 the museum has grown and now has a *fulacht fiadh* (prehistoric oven) and the *currach* ▲ 276 that the young Tim Severin used to cross the Atlantic in order to prove that Brendan the Navigator ▲ 239 could have reached the New World before the Danes.

QUIN. One of the best-preserved examples of Franciscan architecture in Ireland is the abbey at Quin. It was built in 1433 within what remained of a Norman castle (there are still the ruins of some of its towers). The cloister is exceptional ● 96. St Finghin's Church (1278–85), with fine ogival windows, stands at the other side of the stream. The 16th-century Knappogue Castle is another venue for medieval banquets.

> "THE STONE-MASON WAS AWFULLY GOOD AT DRIP-STONES
> ... AND WHEN HE CAME TO DO THE ST FRANCIS HE CHOSE THE
> NEAREST APPROPRIATE DRIP-STONE HEAD, AND THEN ATTACHED
> A BODY TO IT. HE WASN'T TOO GOOD AT BODIES."
>
> FRANK O'CONNOR VISITING ENNIS FRIARY

O'BRIEN

**COUNTY CLARE,
LAND OF THE
O'BRIENS**
The O'Brien family
goes back to King
Brian Boru ● 49. The
three lions that
decorated the
standards and were
worn by the soldiers
at the Battle of
Clontarf were those
of the O'Brien
armorial bearings.
The family built or
occupied most of the
strongholds of the
region and were key
figures in its political
history. Napoleon's
general, Marshal
MacMahon, belonged
to one branch of the
family.

ENNIS

The capital of County Clare has benifited enormously in
commercial terms by its proximity to Shannon airport, but
Ennis has little to detain the visitor. Some eminent people
were born here: Harriet Smithson (1800–54), Shakespearean
actress and wife of Hector Berlioz, and William Mulready
(1786–63), designer of the "Mulready envelope", the first
postage stamp (1840).

POLITICS. Ennis has also played an important part in the
political history of the nation. In 1828 the town voted by a
huge majority for Daniel O'Connell ▲ 228 to become
Member of Parliament for Clare. As a Catholic he
was prevented from taking his seat at Westminster,
but the Roman Catholic Relief act, passed by the
British government in 1829 and granting Catholic
emancipation, finally made him eligible. O'Connell
is commemorated by a monument on the spot where
he was first selected at a public meeting. He was
succeeded in 1830 by Cornelius O'Brien who won
the praise of Lord Palmerston for being the best
Irish parliamentarian ever: "He hasn't opened his
mouth for twenty years." Eamonn De Valera ● 54,
▲ 224 future Prime Minister and then President of
Ireland, was elected MP for County Clare in 1917, and
continued to represent the seat until 1959.

FRIARY. The Franciscan monastery was founded in Ennis in
1242, but the buildings were subsequently much altered and
most of the ruins are 14th century. There are some
remarkable carvings, including a *St Francis with stigmata* in
the nave, and the MacMahon tomb with fine panels depicting
the Passion.

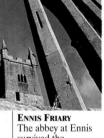

ENNIS FRIARY
The abbey at Ennis
survived the
dissolution of the
monasteries ● 50
thanks to its
protection by
Murrough O'Brien,
but in 1651
Cromwell's troops
ransacked it. The
Franciscans made a
brief return during
the reign of
Charles II before
disappearing for
good at the end of
the 17th century. In
1969 it was once
more handed back
to the Franciscans.

TOWARD THE BURREN

DYSERT O'DEA ★. There is a great
feeling of tranquility around the ruins at
Dysert O'Dea. The 8th-century saint Tola
(a hermit who has recently given his
name to a local goats' cheese) founded
the abbey and made it a place of prayer.
However, in 1318 it was also the scene of
a terrible battle when the Normans were
forced out of Thomond. Beside a

RED MARY
In Leamaneh Castle
lived Mary O'Brien,
known as Red Mary
for the color of her
hair. When her
husband, Conor
O'Brien, returned
mortally wounded
from the battle of
Inchicronan (1651),
she is said to have
shouted from the
window "We don't
need dead men
here!" She nursed
him until his dying
breath. To protect the
estate, her son's
inheritance, she
offered to marry an
enemy officer, Cornet
J. Cooper. He had no
time to enjoy the

pleasures of his
marriage bed,
however. Mary was so
infuriated by his
insults about her
dead husband that
she threw him out of
a window of the
castle.

Kilmacduagh.

truncated 11th-century tower stands a
Romanesque church (much altered in the 17th
century). The doorway is decorated with carved
heads. Their striking Mongolian features may have
been copied from French Romanesque churches
seen by the Irish when making pilgrimages to
Compostela. In a field a little to the east of the
church is a HIGH CROSS dating from the 12th
century. It has interlaced, geometrical and
zoomorphic designs that can be traced in their
inspiration to Scandinavian art, although the
influence of the Danes was by this time
much reduced in Ireland. Narrative biblical
scenes, as found on 9th-century High
Crosses ▲ 204, had not been entirely abandoned in the 12th
century. Here there are depictions of *Adam and Eve* and
Daniel in the Lions' Den on the lower panels of the
monument. On the cross itself are a *Crucifixion* and a figure
of a bishop or abbot thought to be Saint Tola. Not far away is
Dysert Castle, housing an ARCHEOLOGICAL MUSEUM.

COROFIN. The village is surrounded by lakes and is much
enjoyed by both walking and fishing enthusiasts. Overlooking
Lough Inchiquin, said to be the lake richest in fish, stands a
castle built by the O'Briens in 1459. An old legend warns that
if a swan on the lake is killed, a villager will die. The Clare
Heritage Centre gives an interesting picture of life in the west
of Ireland in the 19th century. It also provides a service to
help people investigate their genealogy.

KILLINABOY. There are two ruined churches in the village.
One, founded around 1200, has a double cross on its western
end and a *sheela-na-gig* in the arch over the south doorway,
probably dating from the 15th century when the church was
much altered.

LEAMENEH. A castle looms on the horizon on the way to
Kilfenora. It consists of a 15th-century fortified tower with a
Tudor-style manor (1640) ● *99* built on to it. Over the
imposing door is the O'Brien coat of arms.

KILFENORA. The Burren Display Centre, created in 1975, has
exhibits and audiovisual presentations explaining the unique
geological and botanical features of the region. Behind stand
the ruins of a small CATHEDRAL (13th–15th century), part of it
now a parish church. In the old chancel, now without a roof,
there is a magnificent east window with carved pillars and two
ecclesiastical figures (one being Saint Fachtnan, who founded
a monastery here in the 6th century). Most impressive of all
are the 12th-century CROSSES standing around the ruins. The
DOORTY CROSS, west of the cathedral, has particularly
interesting carvings.

KILMACDUAGH ★. On the road from County Clare to County Galway, going toward Gort, are the ruins at Kilmacduagh, founded as an episcopal see in the 7th century. The eye is drawn to the ROUND TOWER, probably pre-1200, which leans at a distinct angle. The CATHEDRAL has a remarkable doorway with an immense lintel-stone, typical of early Irish churches ● *92*. This doorway was closed up in the 15th century when the building was much enlarged, and a new one was opened in the south wall. Nearby are the 13th-century bishop's residence, and O'HEYNE'S CHURCH, built of limestone with remarkable carved capitals, fine windows (1200) and a ruined cloister.

GORT

The town of Gort probably served as the model for Lady Gregory's town of Cloon, which features in a number of her works including *Hyacinth Halvey*, *The Full Moon* and *The Jackdaw*. The memory of so many of Ireland's great writers who spent time here, in a period of burgeoning literary revival, brings many to visit the area.

THOOR BALLYLEE ★. Yeats ● *122* discovered the dilapidated 17th-century tower (*thoor* in Gaelic) while staying with Lady Gregory at Coole House (above). He bought it in 1916, made it habitable, and spent time there in the 1920's, finding inspiration for a number of his works. It was restored in 1961 and opened to the public along with the museum in 1965, the hundredth anniversary of the poet's birth.

COOLE PARK. Lady Gregory's house was demolished (now just a stone outline remains), but the grounds are cared for and open for visitors to enjoy the woods and admire the lake. A moving reminder of Coole Park's literary past is the autograph tree, where Lady Gregory asked her friends to carve their initials (Shaw, Yeats, O'Casey, Synge ● *117*). The road continues north past TULIRA CASTLE, home of the writer Edward Martyn (1859–1923).

> "The trees are in their autumn beauty,
> The woodland paths are dry,
> Under the October twilight the water
> Mirrors a still sky;
> Under the brimming water among the stones
> Are nine-and-fifty swans."
>
> W.B. Yeats

> "I, the poet William Yeats
> With old millboards and sea-green slates
> And smithy work from the Gort forge
> Restored this tower for my wife George.
> And may these characters remain
> When all is ruin once again."
>
> *Lines to be inscribed on a stone of Thoor Ballylee*

County Limerick is a fertile stretch of land bordering the south bank of the Shannon estuary. Life here is focused on the busy city of Limerick, a place that tourists have tended to avoid, nervous of its reputation as a rough, industrial center. Now its historical and architectural interests are being discovered. To the east lies Tipperary, Ireland's largest inland county. This is an agricultural region, which produces much of the country's milk. Most of the towns lie along the banks of the River Suir and its tributaries. They remain little known or visited. The most famous spot in the county by far is the Rock of Cashel ▲ *252*.

LIMERICK

HISTORY. Limerick was founded by the Danes in the 10th century, and later destroyed by the troops of Brian Boru after the Battle of Clontarf ● *49*. It became the residence of the kings of Munster after being rebuilt, but eventually fell into Anglo-Norman hands, and King John erected his castle in 1210. Now two towns developed side by side, an English and an Irish town. In 1651 Cromwell's troops under Ireton, his son-in-law, took the town from Hugh O'Neill after a six-month siege. Another long siege took place when the Jacobites, under Patrick Sarsfield, withdrew to Limerick after defeats by William of Orange and bravely defended the city. Eventually they capitulated and signed the Treaty of Limerick ▲ *195* which the English broke after a matter of months. The Catholics were once more savagely persecuted. A spirit of anger and rebellion seethed in the city right up until the early 20th century, manifested by the general workers' strike staged in protest at English rule. In historical terms the town center can be divided into three sectors: Irish Town, English Town and Newtown Perry.

IRISH TOWN. When Anglo-Norman domination was assured the native Irish were barred from the walled city, so from the 13th century a quarter began to develop outside the walls, across the Abbey River. The most interesting building in Irish Town today is the Georgian CUSTOMS HOUSE designed in 1769 by a Sardinian architect, Davis Ducart.

THE INTERIOR OF ST MARY'S ★
Most fascinating of all are the 15th-century misericords in the choir: human

figures and weird beasts are carved on the oak choir-stalls. They are extremely rare in Ireland and unique for being pre-Elizabethan. There are also some interesting tombs, including that of Galway-Bulting fort dating from the 15th century, and chapels financed by wealthy families of the town.

Patrick Sarsfield (1650–93).

ENGLISH TOWN. The English Town lies on the site of what was originally the walled city. It is the oldest part of Limerick. ST MARY'S CATHEDRAL was founded at the end of the 12th century by the great church-builder Donal Mór O'Brien. Despite having been severely altered and restored, it retains the allure of a 13th-century Gothic church. There are some Romanesque features still in evidence, such as the west door, but also many 15th-century additions. KING JOHN'S CASTLE ● *98* was begun early in the 13th century and was the most formidable of all the Anglo-Norman citadels in the west of Ireland. It is a five-sided structure with round towers joined by curtain walls and a tower on either side of the main gateway. There are still signs of the bombardment by the troops of William of Orange in 1690. Archeological excavations have uncovered interesting remains of Viking dwellings which are now sheltered within the unlovely structure of the Interpretative Centre. On the other side of the River Shannon, at the western end of Thomond Bridge, the TREATY STONE stands on a plinth. On this stone the Treaty of Limerick was signed ▲ *195*.

NEWTOWN PERRY. South of Irish Town lies a district dating from the 18th century, with lovely streets of red-brick Georgian houses. These were built as the plain but elegant and comfortable homes of well-to-do citizens.

HUNT MUSEUM (2 miles out of town, just off the Dublin Road). John Hunt's art collection ▲ *244* is well displayed in the premises of the National Institute of Higher Education. It features Irish and European antiquities from the Bronze Age to the Middle Ages, with many early Christian items.

THE SOUTH BANK OF THE SHANNON

ADARE. The village is often referred to as the prettiest in Ireland. Its charm was created by the Earl of Dunraven who had the thatched cottages built in the 19th century. The neo-Gothic ADARE MANOR (below) dates from the same period

THE LIMERICK "SOVIET"
In April 1914, Bobby Byrne, local Republican trade-union leader, was killed when Irish Volunteers ● *54* attempted to free him from prison. At his funeral fifteen thousand people were present. For Sinn Féin, it was an opportunity to show their strength. As a protest against the martial law that was imposed in certain parts of the city, workers called a general strike and set up a "soviet", soon supported by many thousands of trade-unionists. On April 24, the strike was broken by the British militia.

The picturesque village of Adare typified what the 19th-century English imagined as the "rustic idyll". It was in fact created by the Earl of Dunraven (1812–71) as a part of his project to improve his estate. There is no denying the charm of the place, and today Adare has an architectural interest as an ensemble of neo-Gothic buildings.

and is now a hotel ◆ *376*. The village has a much longer history, however. Beside the River Maigue stands DESMOND CASTLE, built by the Normans around 1200 and partially rebuilt in the 14th century. There is also a FRANCISCAN PRIORY (1464) with an interesting *sedilia* (the seat for the celebrants of the mass) and the remains of two abbeys: BLACK ABBEY (founded in 1325 by the Augustinians) and TRINITARIAN OR WHITE ABBEY, now the Catholic church.

CASTLE MATRIX ◆ *376*. The castle dates from the 15th century and was once the property of Sir Walter Raleigh ▲ *221*. It has been sumptuously restored and is filled with fine furniture, old arms and other antiques.

GLIN CASTLE. The Knight of Glin, together with the White Knight and the Knight of Kerry, form the three different branches of the powerful FitzGerald House of Desmond, which dates back to the 12th century. Glin Castle ◆ *376* is well worth visiting for its interior decoration – the Adam-style front hall ceiling, the flying staircase lit by Venetian windows, the family portraits, landscape paintings, and also for the impressive collection of 18th- and 19th-century Irish Georgian furniture, which renders the castle a cradle of Irish art and crafts at its very best. The richness of the interior and the preservation of the whole building is no doubt due also to Desmond FitzGerald, present Knight of Glin, the 29th in direct succession, who is fervently involved in conservationism, and is an eminent writer on Irish architecture and the decorative arts.

SPENSER, GUEST AT CASTLE MATRIX
The poet Edmund Spenser (1522–99) stayed in the castle in 1580, as secretary of Lord Grey de Wilton. Grey was instructed to quell the Irish rebellions but used such brutal methods that he was recalled to England.

Spenser wrote his own *View of the State of Ireland* in 1598 (published in 1663). Even then he was searching for possible reasons to explain the state of agitation to be found there. His own solution was quite uncompromising: exterminate the population by an organized famine. There is a terrible irony in his proposition when remembering the behavior of Lord Mountjoy two centuries later.

LOUGH GUR

The horseshoe-shaped Lough Gur is surrounded by marshy land and guarded by two fortified towers, BOURCHIER'S CASTLE (15th century) and BLACK CASTLE (13th century). Excavations made around the lake have revealed the presence of a busy community here in Neolithic times. Beside the road from Limerick is a circle of thirteen standing stones. Axe heads, arrow heads and blades were discovered inside the circle, along with some vessels. The precise significance and function of these circles, which date back to 4000 BC, is still not certain. The slopes of Knockadoon Hill rise from the lough, the site of dwellings and circular enclosures from 3500 to 100 BC. There is an Interpretative Centre with models of the dwellings, giving some idea of life here during Stone Age times.

KILMALLOCK

The village of Kilmallock was once the third most important town in Ireland. It grew up around an abbey founded in the 7th century by Saint Mocheallóg. From the 14th to the 17th century it was the seat of the earls of Desmond. There are a number of fine Norman monuments to be seen in Kilmallock. KING'S CASTLE is a

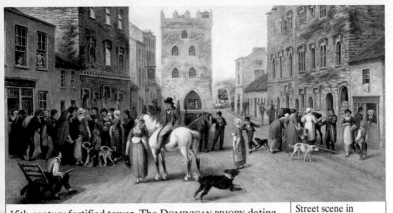

15th-century fortified tower. The DOMINICAN PRIORY dating from the 13th and 14th centuries was partly destroyed when the town fell to Cromwell in 1640. There is a fine stone-built medieval house of the type erected by wealthy merchants and landowners. ST JOHN'S TOWER castle was once at the heart of the city's defences, and BLOSSOM GATE is all that remains of the old town wall.

Street scene in Kilmallock.

TIPPERARY

Tipperary is comfortably set in the fertile Golden Vale. The town was founded by the Anglo-Normans and late in the 12th century it stood in the shadow of the castle built here by King John. Like Limerick, from early on Tipperary was known for its rebellious attitude to the English occupation, the growing resentment that would eventually lead the War of Independence ● 62. There was much involvement in the activities of the Land League in the 19th century. Visitors should note the gateway of a 13th-century Augustinian friary, the bronze statue of Charles Kickham (1826–82) the poet, novelist and patriot, and the memorial to the Manchester Martyrs, Allen, Larkin and O'Brien, Fenians executed at Manchester in 1867 ● 53.

"IT'S A LONG WAY TO TIPPERARY"
The name of the town became famous when the song was taken up by thousands of troops marching to battle in World War One. The two men who composed the song in 1912, Jack Judge and Harry Williams, are said to have chosen the name just for its sonority. A scurrilous version has it that Tipperary was the name of a London brothel.

CAHIR

Along the road coming from Tipperary, following the River Suir, are ruins of an AUGUSTINIAN PRIORY (below) founded around 1220 by Galfrid de Camvill. Cahir is a pleasant town, on a major crossroads, with several Georgian houses and a lovely park. The dominating monument is Cahir Castle, best-preserved and most imposing of all the late medieval Irish castles to survive.

Rock of Cashel.

CAHIR CASTLE
The outer ward is defended by a substantial curtain wall with *chemin de ronde*, and two circular towers. Inside is Castle Cottage, built in 1840 by the Earl of Glengall. There is a well-defended gateway to the middle ward, which is small and dominated by the huge three-story keep, constructed around a 13th-century fortified gateway.

The inner ward is on the highest part of the rock and is surrounded by another wall, probably on 13th-century foundations. There are two square towers, of which the northeast has some remains of the 13th-century stronghold. Apart from the keep, it is the most imposing and strongly fortified of the castle.

THE BUTLERS. Cahir Castle was built by the Butlers, earls of Ormonde, a family of Norman origin but who earned the epithet "more Irish than the Irish". The immense castle they built illustrates their massive family pride. It was far larger than other 15th-century fortified structures, and engulfed the previous 13th-century stronghold built here by Conor O'Brien. The tall outer walls defend three wards, with four towers and a keep. The castle was said to be impregnable, because of its position on a rock at the edge of the river, however the Earl of Essex led Elizabeth's troops to take it in 1599, thanks to their cannon, whose balls remain in the walls. In fact, this was almost the only success Essex was able to claim in Ireland. Cromwell took the castle in 1650, and it was here that a treaty was finally signed with Cromwell's generals ● 51.

SWISS COTTAGE. A few miles from Cahir is a hunting lodge with a thatched roof. It was designed by John Nash early in the 19th century and later he designed another for Windsor Castle park.

ROCK OF CASHEL

The tall and ancient buildings rise from the rocky spur of Cashel, overlooking the plains of the Golden Vale. They are the most beautiful group of medieval monuments in Ireland, and among the finest in Europe.

"CITY OF THE KINGS". As early as the 4th or 5th century Cashel was capital of the kingdom of the Eoghanacht, descendants of the hero Eoghan. One of them, Conall Corc,

built the first fortress here. Brian Boru was crowned here in the 10th century and it remained the seat of the kings of Munster until 1101 when King Murtagh O'Brien gave the Rock to the Church.

DOMINION OF THE CHURCH. In 1127 Bishop Cormac MacCarthy, King of Desmond, began the building of the chapel that still bears his name. The first cathedral was built in 1169, but it has completely disappeared. In the 13th century work began on a new cathedral. The Hall of the Vicars Choral dates from between 1404 and 1440, as does probably the fortified Bishop's Palace. The shrine remained Catholic until 1729, when a first

According to tradition, Saint Patrick came to Cashel in the year 450 and converted King Angus and his family. Here too he is said to have picked a shamrock leaf and

made his well-known comparison to the Trinity.

Protestant service was held here. Twenty years later the cathedral roof was removed, and it was abandoned for good. Restoration work was carried out from 1874 to 1876, and again in 1975.

THE ROUND TOWER. The oldest building on the site is the 92-foot-high round tower, standing at a corner of the north transept of the cathedral. It dates from the 11th or early 12th century.

CORMAC'S CHAPEL. The most beautiful of all the buildings is Cormac's Chapel, which stands up against the cathedral on the south side. It is the most elaborately decorated of all surviving Irish Romanesque churches ● *94*, and has survived in miraculously good condition. Noticeable from the outside are the twin towers on either side of the nave and chancel, replacing a transept. These are unique. There is blind arcading on the exterior walls, and also within. Unlike other churches of its period, the door is not on the west. The ornate north doorway, now blocked by the cathedral, was the original entrance. Today the south doorway is used. Above each is a tympanum, possibly indicating Norman influence. The carving over the north door shows a beast being attacked by a centaur while holding another creature in its grip. The barrel vaulting of the nave supports the steep stone roof, as seen at Glendalough ▲ *178*.

CORMAC'S CHAPEL
The ceiling of the chancel is almost Gothic in style, and is separated from the nave by a decorated arch. Above it are fragments of the only 12th-century frescos in Ireland. They appear to include a depiction of the *Baptism of Christ*, and a fortified town that might be the New Jerusalem. In the chapel is a sarcophagus, said to be King Cormac's. It has superb interlace patterns in the Norse style, and was once decorated with a 12th-century cross, now in the National Museum, Dublin ▲ *158*.

Rock of CASHEL

ST PATRICK'S CROSS
▲ *204*
The 12th-century
High Cross is unlike
any other because it
has vertical supports
(only one of which
remains) on either
side of the main shaft.
It may have been
made on the model of
an older wooden

THE CATHEDRAL. The cathedral was built between 1235 and 1270. The lancet windows that light the interior are characteristic of Irish churches of the period. The massive square central tower was probably completed in the 14th century; there are spiral staircases up to the roof. On entering via the 15th-century doorway, there is a view of the nave, with fine capitals carved with heads and leaf patterns; the carved heads in the transept can also be seen and, most impressive of all, the tombs. There is a monument on the south side of the chancel to the perfidious Myler MacGrath (c.1621), who managed to be a Catholic and a Protestant archbishop simultaneously. In the north transept are 16th-century tombs decorated with saints, animals and geometric patterns. The massive fortified tower that is the 15th-century Bishop's Castle stands square across the end of the nave, curtailing the original plan.

THE MUSEUM. Access to the Rock of Cashel is now through the Hall of the Vicars Choral. This was built in the 15th century for the use of those in charge of cathedral music. Today the building is a museum. Its most interesting item is St Patrick's Cross. This was moved here from outside, and a copy placed on the original site.

HORE ABBEY. (Half a mile from the Rock.) First a Benedictine monastery, the abbey was later rebuilt by Cistercian monks from Mellifont ▲ *198*. The central tower was added in the 15th century.

ATHASSEL PRIORY ★. A few miles from the Rock are the ruins of a vast Augustinian priory founded in 1192. There is a magnificent doorway and tomb with an effigy of the founder.

cross. Some believe
the supports
represent the crosses
of the thieves
crucified beside
Christ. It is over 7
feet high and has a
Crucifixion on one
side and a picture of a
bishop (probably
Saint Patrick) on the
other, with his feet
resting on the head of
an ox. The base is
decorated with
crosses, squares and
interlaced designs.

Holycross Abbey was
so named because a
piece of the True
Cross was kept here.

HOLYCROSS ABBEY

The Cistercian abbey was founded in the 1180's by Donal Mór O'Brien, King of Thomond. It was almost entirely rebuilt in the 15th century thanks to the generosity of the many pilgrims who came to venerate its relic, a piece of the True Cross. In 1975 it was given a new roof and the cloister was restored. The church is cruciform, and is a fine example of late Gothic architecture, with particularly remarkable stonework, well-preserved in the hard limestone of the region. The chancel has a magnificently carved triple-arcaded *sedilia*. In the transept is a mural of a hunting scene (such late medieval frescos are extremely rare in Ireland) and in one of the chapels can be found a curious structure with arches and twisted columns, which probably once displayed the holy relic.

▲ CONNACHT

GALWAY

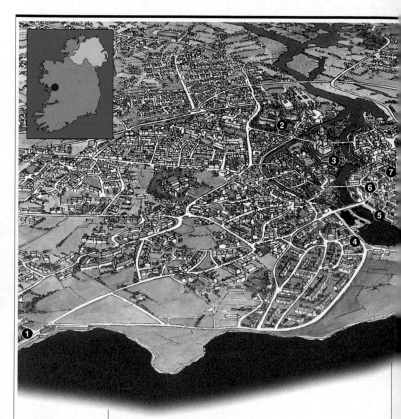

Scholars, idlers, tourists and men of business all feel at home in the relaxed atmosphere of Galway city. There are shops, pubs and restaurants for all tastes, and time flows by in an easy, cheerful manner.

Galway has grown faster than any other town in Europe in recent years, but it still has a medieval flavor that many other towns lost when they were developed in Georgian times. The old limestone buildings blend well with newer additions, and there is a whiff of the past around every corner.

HISTORY

Galway is a city on the water and its history is bound up with the sea, both in legend and in fact.

THE CITY'S FOUNDATION. The medieval city was founded on the east bank of the river where a fort built by the Anglo-Norman Richard de Burgo had stood. It was named after Galvia, a princess of the Firbolg tribe who was borne away by the waves. The city's university was founded in 1345. Galway was strategically placed on the estuary of the River Corrib, between Lough Corrib and the huge bay. It soon grew to become Ireland's third maritime port. The waters of the bay lapped against the city walls and, brought by favorable winds, Spanish ships arrived in ever greater numbers to discharge cargos of wine onto the stone quays. By the time Christopher Columbus arrived on a trade mission in 1477, Galway was on the way to becoming the linchpin of the Irish wine trade.

GALWAY'S SONS
Two figures familiar to the inhabitants of Galway have been given their place in the park in Eyre Square, the writer Padraig O'Conaire (1882–1928) and Liam Mellows, a prime mover in Galway's 1916 Rising ● *54*, subsequently killed in the Civil War ● *63*. O'Conaire, or Sean Phádraig ("Old Padraig"), is Galway's most famous writer in the Irish language (above). His carved figure is bent over a stone book, impervious to the busy throng around him. He wrote more than fifty novels and many short stories and articles before his death aged forty-six. He is buried in New Cemetery, half a mile away, along with William Joyce, better known as Lord Haw Haw, fervent admirer of Hitler and spokesman for Nazi ideas, who broadcast in English on Berlin radio. He was executed for collaboration following World War Two.

THE TRIBES OF GALWAY. The city was dominated by fourteen extremely successful merchant families: "the fourteen tribes of Galway". In the 16th and 17th centuries their wealth and influence reached a peak and they built themselves fine dressed-stone mansions.

DECLINE. The prosperity did not survive the religious disputes of the Reformation. Galway was besieged twice, once by Cromwell's troops in 1652, and later by those of William of Orange in 1691. Maritime trade dwindled and the town went into decline.

EYRE SQUARE

Today Eyre Square is the heart of the city, the center of Galway life. The small park was once a practice ground for armed combat, set at the foot of the old town walls. Young men prepared for battle here until, in 1710, Edward Eyre gave the land to the city. Since then it has been a place for recreation. It is still known by its old name, although

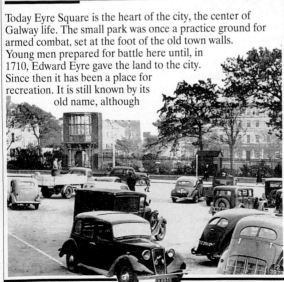

**"KENNY'S
BOOKSHOP"**
The bookshop and art
gallery ◆ 380 is a
world in itself, and
offers hours of
excitement and
discovery to its
customers. The
exploration can
continue through

the garden is now
officially the John F.
Kennedy Memorial Park in
memory of the American president, who was made an
honorary citizen of Galway in 1963. In the center of the
square there is a fountain with an iron sculpture evoking the
sails of a Galway hooker ▲ 277, erected in 1984 for the city's
five-hundredth anniversary. The sculpture symbolizes the
maritime history of Galway, a city whose coat of arms shows a
galleon, sails furled, with a shield bearing a sleeping lion
hanging from the mast.

BROWNE DOORWAY. On the northwest
side of Eyre Square stands a magnificent
example of 17th-century craftmanship
and a proof of the wealth of the "Galway
tribes". It is the beautifully carved
doorway of the Browne family house,
which once stood in Lower Abbeygate
Street. The house itself is long gone. The
coats of arms are those of Martin Browne
and his wife, Marie Lynch, who had the
house built in 1627. The doorway was
erected in Eyre Square in 1905 and was
the entrance to the park until the fences
were removed.

TOWN WALL. Galway's medieval past has
been brought to the fore in the Eyre
Square shopping center, west of the
square. A section of the wall, built to
protect the inhabitants many centuries
ago, has been restored and incorporated into the busy
modern commercial complex. Two towers, Penrice and
Shoemaker, also returned to their former glory, are almost all
that remain of fourteen towers that once stood at intervals
along the old ramparts.

THE MEDIEVAL CITY

everal floors of old
oks, prints, maps,
tings and
ture. The Kenny
has had the
p since 1940,
f the six
Maureen
Des
ere.

ofs

LYNCH'S CASTLE ★. The medieval townhouse dating from the
late 15th or early 16th century is considered the finest in
Ireland. It stands at the crossroads of the two main streets of
old Galway, Shop Street and Abbeygate Street, and it was the
home of the Lynch family, the most powerful of all the
"tribes". There are carved gargoyles and other pieces of
decorative stonework, including the arms of King Henry VII
and those of the Lynch family on the Shop Street side, and on
the Abbeygate Street façade those of the Earl of Kildare,
victor at the Battle of Knockdoe in 1504. Lynch's Castle now
houses a branch of the Allied Irish Bank.
COLLEGIATE CHURCH OF ST NICHOLAS. The old parish church
of Galway is dedicated to Saint Nicholas of Myra, the patron

GALWAY'S MANY FESTIVALS ◆ 337

Galway hosts a number of festivals and events. The A.T. Cross Literature Festival takes place in April, the Arts

saint of sailors. The church was founded in 1320, during the period when the Normans were consolidating their westernmost positions in the province of Connacht. The church was altered, embellished and enlarged over the centuries, often with money from the wealthy merchant families. It is said that Christopher Columbus came here to pray in the Chapel of the Virgin in 1477. In 1484, the Church of St Nicholas was elevated to the status of a collegiate church. It was much damaged during the siege and occupation of Galway by Cromwell's troops in 1651–2, but in the 1950's the church was finally restored, and it has regained much of its former character. Such interest in the old church has also prompted further research into its history, revealing its importance in the story of Galway and its inhabitants. Eminent townspeople have been buried here since the 13th century. At the juncture of the choir and south transept is an early FRENCH TOMBSTONE with a floriated cross. There is also a lovely example of medieval craftsmanship in a capital depicting two young apprentices. The nave was widened in the 16th century and the transepts extended. This work was made possible by the generosity of local patrons whose tombstones are also much in evidence, carved with their armorial bearings and competing with one another in their magnificence. Other interesting features in the church are the LEPERS' GALLERY, with finely carved statues, the baptismal fonts, the holy water stoup, some late medieval tombstones marked with symbols of craft guilds, and some more recent war memorials.

Festival in July. The latter was started in 1978 and has achieved an international reputation, with plays, concerts, children's shows, and street theater. The *Film Fleadh* is held at the same time. Other events include the Galway Races (July) and the Galway Oyster Festival (September).

LYNCH MEMORIAL WINDOW ★. The story is often told of the mayor of Galway, James Lynch, who condemned his own son to death in 1493 for the murder of a Spaniard with whom he had quarrelled over his lady. The mayor is said to have hanged the young man with his own hands from this medieval window in Market Street (right). During the 19th century a plaque was attached to the house to record the event, although no written record has ever been found to show that the story is true.

THE OLD MARKET. The only medieval remnant in modern Galway life is the market, still held every Saturday morning

261

The seaside town of
Salthill in the 19th century.

"THE QUIET MAN"
It was O'Máille's
establishment,
opened in Dominick
Street in 1938, that
made the costumes
for John Ford's film
The Quiet Man, shot
in the village of Cong

▲ *269*, ◆ *332*. The
shop now stocks an
enormous selection of
Aran sweaters.

beside the Church of St Nicholas. Town and country folk,
residents and outsiders, gather to buy and sell a wide variety
of local foodstuffs and other products. During this lively and
picturesque occasion it is not uncommon to hear a voice
declaiming in Gaelic above the general hubbub.

NORA BARNACLE'S HOUSE. The smallest house in Bowling
Green dates from the 19th century and was for a time the
home of Nora Barnacle, wife and muse of the Irish literary
giant James Joyce ● *120*. It is known
that the writer and his son Giorgio
had already come here to visit Annie
Barnacle, mother of Nora, by 1909.
In 1912 the Joyce family spent part
of their vacation here, and Annie
Barnacle continued to live in the
house until her death in 1940.
Mary and Sheila Gallagher, who
have owned the house since 1987,
have restored it and opened it to
the public.

SALMON WEIR BRIDGE. The first stone of the handsome
bridge was laid on July 29, 1818 and it was finished sixteen
months later. This meant that sentenced men could once
again go from the Court House, built in 1815 on the east bank
of the Corrib, to the prison built in 1810 on the other side.
The site of the old prison is now that of the new Catholic

Interior of Galway's
modern cathedral.

CATHEDRAL OF ST NICHOLAS, built in 1965. During
the spawning season it is possible to watch the
salmon leaping up a specially constructed staircase
over the flood barriers to make their way back
upriver.

SPANISH ARCH. A remnant of the old town wall
remains below the Claddagh Bridge. It dates from
1584 and was once part of the port's fortifications.
Now, however, a municipal museum is attached to it
containing a number of items linked with the city's past. The
façade and some of the stonework of the building came from
the Athy family house, dating from 1577.

CLADDAGH

On the west bank of the River Corrib stood a fishing village of
fewer than four hundred thatched cottages. It was far older
than Galway and had a strongly independent community. In
the 1930's the entire village was condemned as a health
hazard and demolished, although the villagers have retained
their close links and Claddagh is remembered in many of
their songs.

SALTHILL

BLAKE'S CASTLE
Facing Spanish Arch
is Blake's Castle. Like
Lynch's Castle, it is a
fine example of the
tower houses ● *99*
built as residences by
the wealthy merchant
families ("tribes")
during the 15th and
16th centuries.
Blake's Castle has
been recently
restored and has a
remarkable pointed
doorway with
traditional corbeling
above: an entirely
Irish architectural
feature.

Not long ago Ireland's busiest seaside resort was a quiet
suburb of Galway and a seaside spa. Only 3 miles from the
city, it is now surrounded by Galway's spreading housing
developments, but its center and long seafront promenade
retain a certain period charm. There are sandy beaches, a golf
course and pleasant public gardens, combining their
attractions with those of hotels, pubs, discotheques and
amusements to draw in the vacationers.

BLESSING OF THE BAY
In August every year
a fleet of old boats
such as hookers
▲ 277, leaves the old
quays of Claddagh to
take part in the
traditional blessing
performed by a
Dominican priest.
The boats form a
circle on the water
just as they used to
when the fishermen
prayed for clement
weather and an
abundance of herring.

THE CLADDAGH RING
The emblem of
Claddagh is world-
famous. The heart
and the two hands
symbolize Love, Faith
and Honor. The ring
is worn with the point
of the heart toward
the fingertip when
engaged, and reversed
when
married.

Before setting off into Connemara it is best to prepare for a slackening of pace. No one is in a hurry here, and there is no need to be. The narrow winding roads, frequently shared with wandering cattle and sheep, have a phenomenal number of potholes, one of Ireland's enduring features.

SAINT MACDARA
The fishermen used to lower the sail three times on passing the island. Although they no longer have sails, their respect remains undiminished.

Describing the landscape of Connemara, Kate O'Brien captured its unreal quality: "There is often an illusion that all is afloat, an uncertainty between hill and sky, an interchange of water and stone which the indescribably clear light seems paradoxically to exaggerate." Connemara remains the wildest, the most secretive and the most romantic place in Ireland. The original old Irish region of Conmhaicne Mara referred only to an area around Ballynahinch. Today the name covers almost all of County Galway, the section of land that juts out between Galway Bay, to the south, and Killary Bay. The west is bordered by the far Atlantic horizon, while Loughs Corrib and Mask form a natural frontier to the east. It is an area of mountains, loughs, heath and bog. Sun, rain and wind bring changing moods, patterns and colors. There are greens: the bright bracken against the dull, close-cropped turf; there are greys: lichen-patterned walls and steep rocky hillsides; there are rich browns in the turf bogs and rusty heathers, the lipstick-red of fuchsia hedges, and everywhere the gleaming silver lakes. The monuments, too, have a stern, proud beauty.

COASTAL ROUTE FROM GALWAY TO CLIFDEN

SPIDDAL (AN SPIDÉAL). Today artists, painters and craftsmen are particularly attracted by Spiddal, but its most lasting reputation has been as an important center of *Gaeltacht* ● 68. When Martin O'Cadhain (1906–70) was born here, the village was already a place where people came to learn the language and traditions of old Ireland from the local countryfolk. He became one of the writers who did most to make Irish a living language once more.

COSTELLOE (CASLA). The road leads through Rossaveal (Ros an Mhíl), the biggest fishing village in the county and the departure point for boats to the Aran Islands ▲ *270*, to reach Costelloe, the village from which *Raidió na Gaeltachta* ● *67* broadcasts programs in Irish to an enthusiastic audience all over the west of Ireland. Down the rocky peninsula to the south is CARRAROE (An Cheathrú Rua), home of the great Irish painter Charles Lamb (1893–1964). He never tired of looking out over the reefs and tiny islets scattered along this coast, so ragged it resembles lace.

ROSMUCK. At Gortmore (An Gort Mór) a little road on the left leads to the Pearse Memorial Cottage. Here the writer and nationalist Patrick Pearse came to work, and refresh his energies. He was shot by a British firing squad for his part in the 1916 Easter Rising ● *60*.

CARNA. The road leads around Kilkieran Bay to reach Carna where there is a maritime research center and fishermen make a living from catching lobsters. On July 16 each year there is a pilgrimage to ST MACDARA'S ISLAND ● *92*, where there is a 12th-century oratory and a saint's cell which has been recently restored. On the tongue of land adjoining is the single tower of Ard Castle. Just over the water is MASON ISLAND where the *Concepción*, a galleon of the Spanish Armada, was sunk ▲ *316*.

CASHEL. On the far side of Bunnahown, leave the main road to explore the beautiful Bay of Cashel, which is named after a burial mound on the hill above.

ROUNDSTONE (CLOCH NA RON). Follow the BRANDY AND SODA ROAD, so named for the intoxicating purity of the air, along the shores of Gurteen Bay and Dog's Bay, lined with long white strands. At the foot of Mount Errisberg, from which there is an all-round panorama hard to match elsewhere in Ireland, lies the fishing village of Roundstone (above). The tiny port of white cottages was built by Alexander Nimmo early in the 19th century. In the pubs congregate a fascinating crowd of lobster fishermen, artists in search of inspiration, instrument makers and botanists drawn to the area to study the local flora. Out to sea on the island of Inishlackan there are the ruins of a Franciscan monastery.

IRISH HOLIDAY
After retiring from his duties as President of France in 1969, General de Gaulle spent a month in Ireland. He stayed for a few days at Cashel House, a

secluded mansion surrounded by magnificent gardens on the Bay of Cashel. At the end of his holiday he declared: "At this difficult time in my life I have managed to do what I had to do here: come face to face with myself. Ireland made this possible in the most discreet and friendly manner."

BALLYCONNEELY. The village lies on the isthmus that separates Ballyconneely Bay and Mannin Bay. Its prosperity comes from the magnificent Connemara Golf Club whose eighteen holes are spread over the end of the peninsula that stretches west of the village into the ocean ◆ *355*. There is a road leading off to the right to BUNOWEN. Here are the remains of a castle built by Richard Geoghegan, descendant of a Cromwellian who remained in Ireland, using material from an older building that had been the property of the pirate queen Grace O'Malley ▲ *278* and Donal O'Flaherty.

DERRYGIMLAGH BOG. The road toward Clifden runs alongside a stretch of bog where on June 15, 1919 John Alcock and Arthur Whitten-Brown were forced to land after making the first non-stop east–west transatlantic flight. It had taken them 16 hours and 12 minutes. On the spot, a monument of an airplane wing pointing skyward records their feat.

THE CONNEMARA PONY

Intelligence and stamina are the great qualities of this hardy breed. The Connemara can be gray, bay, black, roan, or chestnut. It is an animal that is now appreciated and bred in many countries. The difficult terrain, rough climate and sparse vegetation have given the Connemara its attributes: the ponies are good jumpers and "good doers". The breed was originally evolved by crossing native ponies with pure-bred Arabs that arrived with the Armada and on the Spanish ships that came to the port of Galway with goods to trade ▲ *258*. A Connemara can be up to 14.2 hands high. A pony of this height can be ridden out hunting by an adult, but its gentle and sensible nature will permit it to be ridden by a child too.

CLIFDEN. The market town, port and, now, busy holiday resort was founded in 1812 by John D'Arcy. It is the capital of Connemara, and the great annual event, the Connemara Pony Show ◆ *352*, is held in mid-August. On the showground children in traditional costume dance jigs and reels, while the proud owners and breeders trot out their sturdy Connemaras in the different show classes. Plenty of buying and selling goes on, bringing in a mixed and noisy crowd of horse-dealers, along with many who just come to look over and admire the ponies. All about the town, up and down the streets of gaily painted houses (above), around the stalls that fill the pavements, and along the ropes of the show-ring can be heard languages from all over the world and accents from all four corners of Ireland.

THE INLAND ROUTE

This route leads over mountains, along rivers and loughs, through forest and bog ■ *32* and across empty plains dotted with granite rocks. On leaving Galway it follows the River Corrib, passes through the village of MOYCULLEN and runs beside Ross Lake. On the bank stands Ross House where

Violet Martin was born. Better known by her pen-name Martin Ross, she wrote, together with her cousin Edith Somerville, two of the masterpieces of Anglo-Irish humor: *Stories of an Irish R.M.* and *The Real Charlotte* ▲ *224*.

EYRE CONNAUGHT. In this region lived the ferocious clan of the O'Flahertys. Their raids terrorized the population of Galway, who were known to pray: "From the ferocious O'Flahertys, Good Lord deliver us!" Two miles south of Oughterard is the impressive square keep of AUGHNANURE CASTLE, the 16th-century castle of the O'Flahertys. This was their most imposing fortress, which had a strong position over Lough Corrib.

OUGHTERARD. The lively market town of Oughterard is best known by fishermen who come here from far and wide when the fly-fishing season opens in May ◆ *357*. Golfers have a good eighteen-hole course, and for walkers there is the Western Way footpath toward Curraun (opposite the Hill of Doon) which leads along Lough Corrib, dotted with islets of lush vegetation, and eventually reaches Leenane. The road runs on between lakes through a magnificent and deserted landscape. When the Comte d'Avèze visited Connemara in 1847 he wrote: "Not forty years ago Connemara, separated from the rest of Ireland by a natural barrier, was but little accustomed to the English rule of law; it was a huge ungoverned hideaway where bandits, smugglers and all kinds of outlaws could find refuge." The wrongdoers have been replaced by sheep, but it is easy to understand how this place remained so long beyond the rule of law.

MÁAM CROSS (AN TEACH DOITE). The village nestles between lakes and mountains, at the foot of Mount Leckavrea. It is situated at the meeting of two of the major roads that traverse Connemara, from which it derives its name, and it also has a thriving animal fair.

BALLYNAHINCH. The road follows the wooded bank of Lough Ballynahinch. Reflected in its still waters are the heights of Benlettery, one of the group of mountains known as the Twelve Bens. From the summit there is a view over the whole of northern Connemara.

"THROUGH CONNEMARA IN A GOVERNESS-CART"
"'[Oughterard] is the best village for its size this side of Galway,' said my cousin. . . And the place has improved so wonderfully. For instance there's the Widows' Almshouse. It isn't so very long ago that an old woman said to my grandmother, 'That's the Widdies Almshouse, and sorra widdy in it but one little owld man, and now it's simply bursting with widows – at least, I mean'."
Somerville and Ross

Lough Ballynahinch.

GUGLIELMO MARCONI (1874–1937)
It was on the turf bog of Derrygimlagh (left) that the Italian inventor (whose mother was Irish) set up his first station to transmit transatlantic telegraph messages.

"HUMANITY DICK" MARTIN (1754–1834)
The most remarkable member of the Martin family was a colorful and eccentric figure. He was a Member of Parliament, a philanthropic landowner, a supporter of Catholic emancipation and one of the founders of the Royal Society for the Prevention of Cruelty to Animals.

BALLYNAHINCH CASTLE stands on the south bank of the lough, a lovely 18th-century mansion. It belonged to the Martin family and was the home of "Humanity Dick" Martin. In 1926 the house was bought by Ranji, Jam Sahib of Nawanagar, an Indian prince and well-known cricketer. Since 1945 it has been a high-class hotel patronized by fishermen.

FROM CLIFDEN TO CONG, VIA LEENANE AND MAAM

THE "SKY ROAD". Going north out of Clifden and taking the little "Sky Road", the desolate ruins of John d'Arcy's castle can be seen. There are magnificent views over the Atlantic Ocean from the little peninsula between Clifden Bay and Streamstown Bay.

CLEGGAN. The tiny fishing village with lively pubs is also the departure point for boats to the island of Inishbofin. On the island are some religious remains and a Cromwellian fort, a reminder that persecuted Catholic priests and monks were kept prisoner here.

LETTERFRACK. The main entrance and Visitor Centre for the Connemara National Park are in Letterfrack. The park covers 49,400 acres and includes part of the Twelve Bens, Diamond Hill (2,385 feet), and vast stretches of bog and heathland. Those who prefer literary pursuits may visit the RENVYLE Peninsula, and Renvyle House at its further end. Before becoming a hotel it was the home of the doctor, writer and humorist Oliver St John Gogarty, immortalized by James Joyce as Buck Mulligan in the first pages of *Ulysses* ● *120*.

Top, the fjord that separates Clifden and Streamstown bays. Above, Kylemore Abbey. It has a neo-Gothic church with an ornate, marble-floored interior.

KYLEMORE ABBEY. The abbey (left) stands beside a small lake surrounded by thick rhododendron groves and fuchsia hedges, wedged between the Twelve Bens and the Doughruagh Mountains, Altnagaighera and Garraun. It is an immense, Victorian, neo-Gothic castle built by a rich Liverpool businessman. French Benedictine nuns took over the establishment and opened a girls' boarding school at the

Detail from
Cong Abbey.

end of World War One. A standard
wrenched from the hands of the English
by the Irish Brigade fighting for France at
the Battle of Fontenoy (1745) is a prized
possession here.

LEENANE (LIONAN CINN MHARA). The
road follows a 10-mile-long fjord-like
inlet that stretches from Killary Harbour
to Leenane, a pretty fishing village.
Leenane is featured in Jim Sheridan's
film *The Field* (1989) ◆ *333.* (Take left
fork toward Maam.)

JOYCE COUNTRY. The R336 crosses the
picturesque Maam Valley and leads
through the heart of Joyce Country. It
follows the River Joyce winding between
the Partry Mountains, on the left, and the
Maamturk Mountains. The steep rocky
sides are grazed by black-headed sheep,
which make up a large part of the
population of Connemara.

LOUGH CORRIB. The R345 to Cornamona runs along the
narrow northwest end of Lough Corrib, the largest
lough in the Republic of Ireland. It is 30 miles
long and covers 44,000 acres, stretching from
north of Galway ▲ *258* to the borders of
County Mayo. It has 365 islands. On one,
close to shore, is HEN'S CASTLE.
According to legend it was built in one
night by a witch and her hen, which,
together with the castle she gave to
O'Flaherty, would suffice to keep them
alive if they were ever besieged. The pirate
queen, Grace O'Malley ▲ *278*, wife of an
O'Flaherty, also used the castle.

CONG (CONGA). The village stands on the border between
Galway and Mayo. It is surrounded by magnificent woodland,
with Lough Corrib to the south and Lough Mask to the north.
The ruins of Cong Abbey are to be found here, including a
very elegant cloister. The Augustinian abbey was founded by
King Turlough O'Connor in 1137. The road out of the village
leads past the towers of ASHFORD CASTLE
(above), once owned by the Guinness family
▲ *170* and now converted into a luxurious
country-house hotel ◆ *382.* The gardens
extending down to the lough are open to
the public, and there is a boat to the little
island of INCHAGOILL, which has some
Romanesque ruins and other remains.

"THE QUIET MAN"
◆ *332*
In 1951 John Ford
(whose real name was
Sean Aloysius
O'Fearna) set up his
cameras in the little
village of Cong to
make his much-loved
film *The Quiet Man*
(below). John Wayne,
Maureen O'Hara,
Victor McLaglen and
Barry Fitzgerald
played out their roles
in a story-book
Ireland, where the
charms of rural life,
the funny situations
and the larger-than-
life characters were
all exploited to the
full.

Some were less than
pleased by this
stereotyping of
Ireland and the Irish.
The critic Hilton
Edwards stated in
1953 in *The Bell* that
he saw no relation at
all between the film
and the Ireland he
knew.

▲ CONNACHT
ARAN ISLANDS

1 ROCK ISLAND   2 BRANNOCK ISLANDS   INIS MÓR   3 DÚN AONGHASA   4 KILMURVEY   5 GORT NA GCAPALL   6 DÚN EOCHLA   7 CILL RÓNÁIN   8 KILLEANY   9 AIRPORT

BIRTH OF TOURISM
With easier access provided by the new steamer in 1891, the Aran Islands became a place of pilgrimage for numerous learned men. Archeologists and sociologists, botanists, politicans and nationalists (above all Patrick Pearse ● *61*, who was determined that the English flag should not fly over Inis Meáin), painters, film-makers, linguistic experts and writers (Hyde, MacNeill, Synge) were all enraptured by the haunting beauty of these islands that lay unspoilt, awaiting their exploration.

The Aran Islands lie in the ocean like a school of whales surveying Galway Bay. Geologically they are a ridge of carboniferous limestone, an extension of the Burren ▲ *242*. The land is stony, scored with rocky valleys, and has almost no soil cover at all. Crops have had to be scratched from the dry, ungenerous surface of the islands, divided up into the tiny stone-walled fields known as "gardens". Nowadays the fourteen thousand inhabitants are able to improve their meager living with ever-growing tourism. This and fishing are their main sources of income. They remain Gaelic-speaking and immensely proud of their ancient island traditions. The impressive dry-stone forts (*dúns*) are the sturdiest, although perhaps not the earliest, testament to human life on the islands. The islanders are known to have been converted to Christianity early in the 6th century. Their courageous approach to the incredibly harsh island existence has inspired a number of writers, in particular John Millington Synge, who stayed here for long months at the turn of the century. They were also inspiration for the American film director Robert Flaherty, maker of *Man of Aran*. A visit to the Aran Islands is a chance to see some unique and magnificent landscape, but also to step into a past world. The people seem hewn out of rock, wind and water: survivors from another age. In his poem "Lovers on Aran" Seamus Heaney expresses the ancient thrill of the islands: "Did sea define the land or land the sea . . . Each drew new meaning from the waves' collision. . . . Sea broke on land to full identity."

INIS MÓR (INISHMORE)

(From the jetty to the southern tip of the island.) Before coming to Cill Rónáin, there is a beach on the left called Tra na bhFrancach ("beach of the French"). A French ship sank here with all hands. A reminder of a happier event is the monument to mark the 1966 Atlantic crossing made in a rowing-boat by Ridgeway and Blythe.

CILL RÓNÁIN (KILRONAN). A Celtic cross has stood near the harbor since the late 19th century. It was carved by the father of Patrick Pearse ● *61* in honor of one of the island's curates, between 1881 and

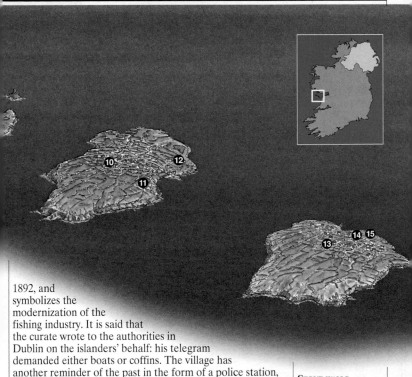

1892, and
symbolizes the
modernization of the
fishing industry. It is said that
the curate wrote to the authorities in
Dublin on the islanders' behalf: his telegram
demanded either boats or coffins. The village has
another reminder of the past in the form of a police station,
now in ruins, once occupied by the British police. There is still
a police station on the island, but now the police wear a
different uniform. The
Protestant church is also
ruined, as no one has
worshipped there since the
1930's.

**TEAMPULL BHEANÁIN
(ST BENEN'S CHURCH).**
Standing on a headland in
Killeany Bay are the ruins of
CAISLEAN AIRCIN (Arkyn Castle). It replaced a 16th-century
fortification and was probably built by Cromwell's supporters
in 1652–3. Not far from Killeany, set on the side of a hill, are
the foundations of the only ROUND TOWER on the island. On
top of the hill is one of the smallest churches in Ireland,
TEAMPULL BHEANÁIN. It was named after Saint Benen, one of

STONE WALLS
The islands are a like
a checkerboard,
criss-crossed with dry-
stone walls enclosing
fields often not much
bigger than a pocket
handkerchief. In
order to grow any
crops at all, over
generations the
islanders put down
layers of rotted
seaweed to fill out the
almost non-existent
soil.

271

ARAN SWEATERS
The famous pullovers, knitted with homespun sheep's wool (*báinín*) have an amazing variety of intricate patterns. The significance of different stitches and designs relates to the life of the islanders. The cables are fishing

Saint Patrick's youngest disciples. It has proved impossible to date the church accurately as there is no decoration, only a tombstone at the southeast corner inscribed with the letters "CAR". The church and round tower would have served as landmarks for the fishermen in their *currachs* ▲ 276, boats which are still used by the islanders today. Other surrounding ancient buildings were raided for stone to build Arkyn Castle. They included a 15th-century FRANCISCAN MONASTERY.

ST ENDA'S CHURCH. It was with Saint Enda, who died in 530, that the islands made their first appearance in history. The saint first entered a monastery in Scotland before coming to Inis Mór, where he was the first to teach the Irish the rules of monastic life. The island became "the capital of the Ireland of the saints". Disciples left to found other monasteries, centers of learning that were to kindle the flame of Irish literature and art. Killeany means "church of Saint Enda" and there is a shrine called Teaghlach Einne ("House of Saint Enda") near to the water's edge, on what was once the site of the monastery. This is the most holy and venerated place on the Aran Islands. There are 125 saints, including Enda, said to be buried here. In the church are the remains of one or two High Crosses from the 12th

ropes and the diamonds are the nets. The honeycomb is in honor of the hardworking bee, the trellis represents the stone-walled fields, marriage lines are the ups and downs of married life and Trinity stitch brings in the strong Christian thread of island life.

century, incorrectly restored, with interlaced carving, and the figures of Christ, a cleric and a horseman. (Going northward on Inis Mór.)

MONASTER KIERAN (ST KIERAN'S CHURCH). The church is named after Saint Ciarán, thought to be the founder of the monastery at Clonmacnois ▲ 203. It is built of the same austere, bare limestone as other churches on the island, but the windows suggest that the church dates from about 1200. Around it are some interesting pillars decorated with crosses, some ancient tombs and the remains of what must have been a sundial.

Dún Eochla (Dún Oghil), a fort with two concentric walls, lies near to the village of Eochaill (Oghil), halfway between Kilronan and Kilmurvey.

GORT NA GCAPPAL. Liam O'Flaherty (1896–1984), author of *The Informer* and *Skerrett*, was born in this village. Literary talent ran in the family, as his nephew Breandán Ó hEithir (1930–90), also a native Aran islander, is known for his writings in both Gaelic and Irish. Máirtín Ó Direáin (1911–88), who came from Inis Mór, is considered by many to be one of the finest contemporary poets in the Gaelic language.

KILMURVEY HOUSE. The house was the residence of the island's biggest landowner. He was famous for his cruelty and unjust evictions. Máirtín Ó Direáin wrote a poem about him, *O Morna,* and Liam O'Flaherty made the events the subject of his novel *Land*. It tells how, during the time of the Land League agrarian revolt, the islanders got their revenge on the landowner by leading his cattle blindfold over the cliffs.

TEAMPULL MACDUAGH. The church is dedicated to Colman MacDuagh, founder of Kilmacduagh. It was originally a plain rectangular building with antae (square pilasters forming the corners of the building). The choir, undecorated, was probably added at the end of the 12th century, with a crenelated parapet (a 15th-century embellishment).

DÚN AONGHASA (DÚN AENGUS) ★ ● 91. The 19th-century archeologist George Petrie described Dún Aengus as "the most magnificent barbaric monument now extant in Europe". The vast and rugged semicircular stone fort, set right on the edge of a sheer cliff that drops 300 feet to the ocean, is the most extraordinary site on the Aran Islands. There are three concentric walls. The well-preserved inner wall has flights of steps and conceals various chambers. Outside the middle wall is a circle of *chevaux de frise*, a mass of pointed rocks bristling from the ground, to deter attackers from the seaward side. There is a natural raised platform of stone at the center of the fort. This may indicate that it was a place where public sacrifices were held. Recent excavations in the thin soil that covers the rock here have not helped determine the purpose of Dún Aengus any further. They did permit a more accurate dating of the site, however, estimating it to have been occupied at the end of the Bronze Age, around 900 BC, or earlier. (Return to Kilmurvey.)

DUN EOGHANACHTA. The small circular fort has marvelously preserved walls, very similar in construction to Dún Aengus, with sets of steps on the inside running up to the parapets. It stands on a natural shelf overlooking one of the most lovely monuments on Inis Mór, Teampull Bhreacáin.

THE MYSTERY OF THE ARAN FORTS
Local folklore is surprisingly unhelpful in explaining these forts. Many others have been ready to speculate, however. The latest theory, the most fantastic of all, is that they were built by refugees from Atlantis! It is also believed that the defenses were built by the chiefs of the Firbolgs, ancient inhabitants of Aran. As to how the Firbolgs came to be on Aran, it used to be

told that this tribe, assimilated to the Belgae, were subjugated by Julius Caesar, and escaped to the Aran Islands to avoid Roman taxes.

"MAN OF ARAN"
◆ 332
The American film director Robert Flaherty, who was of Irish origin, made the remarkable documentary *Man of Aran* in the 1930's after spending two years on the Aran Islands. It was awarded the Venice Film Festival Grand Prix in 1934. Flaherty

TEAMPULL BHREACÁIN (ST BRECÁN'S CHURCH). Curiously, one of the most important religious buildings on the island stands at its westernmost and least accessible end. Saint Bhreacáin was the grandson of the first Christian prince of Thomond. The richly carved shaft of a cross, standing west of the church, marks his grave. It was opened in the 19th century by George Petrie to reveal a skull. The little church has a choir and nave, divided by a semicircular arch, all much rebuilt and restored. A number of tombstones surround the building, inscribed with exhortations to the passer-by to pray for the deceased. Fragments of some large 12th-century crosses include one with a primitive carving of the Crucifixion. Another piece of cross lies fenced-off in a field northeast of the church. A stone slab with the inscription VII ROMANI could refer to seven Irishmen who went on a pilgrimage to Rome, although it was long interpreted as proof that Romans made the pilgrimage to Aran. The Aran Islands, where Saint Brendan the Navigator ▲ *239* had so often landed, were of great religious importance in the 12th century and large numbers of people made pilgrimages here. It is known that late medieval buildings on the site were used to shelter pilgrims who came here to venerate the saint. Many of the plundered churches of the Aran Islands, few of them earlier than 12th-century, were used (as was Teampull Bhreacáin) as chapels for pilgrimages. During the 15th and 16th centuries the islands again became an important center of Christianity. The remains of numerous little churches are proof of a long and fervent history of worship.

dramatizes the desperate struggle of the islanders against storm and sea. He is one of many to find artistic inspiration in life on the Aran Islands (in particular J.M. Synge and Liam O'Flaherty). Those who have seen the film and were moved by the spectacular storm scenes will want to visit the spot where they were filmed, between Inis Mór and the Brannock Islands. Easier to reach is a little cottage built for the film, now open as a restaurant. Any who have not seen *Man of Aran* can attend a showing in Cill Rónáin during the tourist season.

Above, a *currach* on the beach.

INIS MEÁIN (INISHMAAN)

The narrow strait that separates Inis Mór from Inis Meáin
(Middle Island) is called Sunda Ghriora ("Gregory's Sound")
after Saint Gregory. Despite his desire to be buried on Aran,
Gregory was interred in Rome. According to legend, his
coffin rose up in rebellion from Roman earth and set off for
the islands. J.M. Synge's stay on Inis Meáin made a great
impression on its inhabitants. He stayed every summer from
1898 to 1902 in the MacDonnchas' house. It has been known
ever since as SYNGE'S COTTAGE, and even jokingly as Ollscoil
na Gaeilge, "the Gaelic University", because of the number of
intellectuals who gathered under its roof. Even today you can
sit on Cathaoir Synge, "Synge's Chair", the cliffside place
where the writer liked to gaze out over the sound.

DÚN CHONCHÚIR (DÚN CONOR). The large oval fort is set on
the side of a narrow valley, facing west. According to myth,
Conor was the brother of Aengus, the legendary chief of the
Firbolgs.

DÚN FEARBHAI (OR DÚN MOHER). The smaller D-shaped fort
stands to the east of the island on a low mound, looking out
over the village of Baile an Mhothair.

CILL CHEANANNACH. The stone oratory, or "canons' church"
dates from the 11th or 12th century. It has walls 2 feet thick
(one stone block measuring 18 feet long) and a massive lintel.
O'Donovan, the 19th-century Irish collector, thought it
Ireland's most perfect primitive church.

INIS OÍRR (INISHEER)

TEAMPULL CHAOMHÁIN (ST CAVAN'S CHURCH). Next to the
landing strip, in the midst of the dunes, lie the ruins of a little
church dedicated to
Saint Kevin, the
island's patron
saint. It dates from
around 1200, or
possibly later.
Each year the
ruins are gradually
covered by the sands, to be

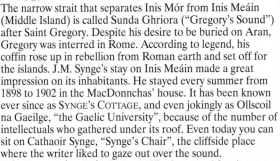

cleared in time for the annual pilgrimage, June 14, when the
islanders pay homage to Saint Kevin, probably a brother Saint
Kevin of Glendalough ▲ *178*.

O'BRIENS' CASTLE. The O'Flahertys of Connacht and the
O'Briens of Munster vied for control of the Aran Islands in
medieval times, but the O'Briens dominated Inis Oírr (East
Island). The ruins of the 14th-century castle are testament to
their power, built from the stones of a prehistoric fort Dún
Formna, but destroyed by Cromwell's troops in 1652.

CILL GHOBNAIT (ST GOBNET'S CHURCH). The little 11th- or
12th-century church is dedicated to Saint Gobnet, patron
saint of apiculture.

**JOHN MILLINGTON
SYNGE** ● *123*
For J.M. Synge,
periods spent on the
Aran Islands between
1898 and 1902 were
important for his
contribution to the
Irish cause and for his
writing. His affinity
with the islands was
expressed in his book
The Aran Islands
(1907), and provided
material for several
plays, including
Riders to the Sea
(1904) and *Playboy of
the Western World*
(1907). "The
continual passing in
this island between
the misery of last
night and the
splendour of today,
seems to create an
affinity between the
moods of these
people and the
moods of varying
rapture and dismay
that are frequent in
artists, and certain
forms of alienation.
Yet it is only in the
intonation of a few
sentences or some old
fragment of melody
that I catch the real
spirit of the island."

Left, abandoned
cottage on Inis Oírr.

Men of Aran
photographed by
Synge.

The first inhabitants of Ireland may have reached the island from Britain in boats of stretched hide, not unlike the *currachs* of today. Boat-making began in the Bronze Age, with the hollowing-out of tree trunks. These were clumsy craft, however, and could not put to sea in all weathers. Then the technique of making boats from tanned animal skins developed. Such craft are still in use in a few areas elsewhere in the world (China, Greenland and Alaska).

THE FIRST "CURRACH"

Improvements were gradually made to the simple Irish *currach*. The first coracle was very small, made with animal skins stretched over a wicker frame. Oars replaced paddles and the first masted and sailed *currachs* probably made their appearance in the early days of Christianity.

THE MODERN "CURRACH"

Today a *currach* is built from a frame of wooden laths, onto which are stretched strips of tarred canvas. It has no keel, and slides over the waves rather than ploughs through them. The boats are very light and can land without need of a sheltered harbor. There are several types of *currach*, adapted to the climatic conditions of different regions. The Aran *currach* is about 17 feet long and can have up to three oarsmen.

THE HOOKER

The hooker seems to have first appeared in County Cork in around 1700, although there is still doubt as to whether it originated in Spain or in the Low Countries. The Galway hooker is stronger than that of Kinsale, the craft most commonly used until 1900. Originally the hooker was a fishing boat, but by the 19th century it was being used to transport goods and passengers from island to island and along the coast.

THE CAPACITY OF THE "CURRACHS"

It is estimated that the Galway *currachs* were able to transport two cows and twenty-one sheep; and that the first *currachs* with oars, in early Christian times, could travel over 90 miles per day with nine or ten people on board, in fair weather. About 140 years ago, a man and his wife put their furniture and horse into a small paddle *currach* to go from Aranmore to Burtonport, nearly 2 miles away on the coast of Donegal.

▲ CONNACHT
COUNTY MAYO

County Mayo is the jutting northwest corner of the province of Connacht. Lough Corrib and the Killary fjord form its southern boundaries, while to the west and north is the Atlantic Ocean, rounding the points of Erris Head and Benwee Head and pushing inland into the Bay of Killala. Leading south from here the county's eastern border roughly traces the route of General Humbert and his small French army who landed in 1798 and gave the county its nickname, "French Mayo".

THE SOURCE
Ballintober Abbey ▲ *282*, south of Westport, was the starting point of the pilgrimage to Croagh Patrick (bottom). It had its roots in a pagan festival honoring the Celtic god Lug. Ballintober was dedicated to the Irish patron saint, and Cathal Grovdearg, king of Connacht, had an abbey built there in

1216 for the Augustinians. The church is cruciform, but the nave has no aisles. Much of the nave is Gothic, while there is fine Romanesque decoration at the base of many capitals and around the three blocked windows over the altar. At the junction of nave and transept is an elaborate altar-tomb. On the pediment five remarkable figures remain, most likely part of a row of ecclesiastics. Within the sacristy, added in the 17th century, is the mausoleum of the viscounts of Mayo

Above, Westport House.

THE MURRISK PENINSULA AND CLEW BAY

KILLARY HARBOUR. Leaving Leenane ▲ *269* the route leads past the rushing waterfall at Aasleagh where the River Erriff tumbles into the waters of Killary Harbour. Turning left off the main road, follow the steep northern bank of the fjord-inlet before bearing right and heading inland to the DELPHI fishing lodge. The Delphi Valley was given its name by Lord Sligo, because its peace reminded him of Apollo's shrine in Greece. Passing along the silent banks of dark DOO LOUGH, the road climbs up to a pass leading out of the valley. Here stands a stone recording that this lake and mountain wilderness was one of the "congested districts" of Ireland in the 19th century. (Before reaching Louisburgh there is a road on the left to Roonah Quay where boats cross to Clare Island.)
CLARE ISLAND. The largest island in Clew Bay was the family seat of the pirate-queen Grace O'Malley. She is thought to be buried in the ruined Carmelite abbey founded by her family in 1224. Queen Elizabeth I offered to confer honors on her, but Grace O'Malley refused them disdainfully, declaring that she was a queen in her own right: Queen of the West. Her island fortress is a massive square tower, overlooked by Mount Knockmore and protected to the northwest by spectacular cliffs scattered with warrior and monastic remains. It is an extraordinarily wild and beautiful place.
LOUISBURGH. The village stands on the moors, built in the 18th century on the banks of the Bunowen river. It has a small museum with displays relating both to Grace O'Malley and to the ancient sites of the surrounding area. These include ring-forts, the megalithic stone alignment at ASKILLAUN, the early church at THALLAGHBAWN, and KILGEEVER ABBEY.
LECKANVEY. In the village itself there is a MEMORIAL CROSS, recording the emancipation of

"Saint Patrick stood bell in hand, and every time he rang it he flung it away from him . . . and every time it thus hastily was rung, thousands of toads, adders, and noisome things went down, tumbling neck and heels one after the other."

Thomas Otway

1829, when Catholics in Ireland were at last accorded the status, in theory at least, of full British citizens. Not far from the village is a long stretch of beach backed by dunes, into which thousands of rabbits have burrowed their warrens.

CROAGH PATRICK. The road toward Westport runs along the base of Croagh Patrick: the "rick" of Saint Patrick (2,513 feet). The saint fasted here for forty days and nights, beseeching God to take care of the Irish. Here, too, he destroyed all the snakes and toads in the land, ringing his bell and flinging it into the abyss. His faithful follower Calvus Totus is buried on the hill. On the last Sunday in July thousands of barefoot pilgrims climb the stony slopes of Mayo's holy mountain, starting from the remains of the 15th-century Murrisk Abbey and making their way up to the chapel on top. The view from the summit is extremely good if the day is clear. Fields, villages and bogs stretch away to the horizon, and islands stand like sentinels along the ocean's edge.

WESTPORT. Westport is a pleasant town designed by James Wyatt, one of the great architects of the Georgian era. THE MALL has an aristocratic air, shaded by lime trees whose branches are reflected in the serene waters of the Carrowbeg river. WESTPORT HOUSE, the Marquess of Sligo's family seat, is a mansion designed in 1730 by Richard Castle, embellished by Thomas Ivory, and completed by James Wyatt around 1778. Both Thomas De Quincey, author of *Confessions of an English Opium-Eater*, and William Makepeace Thackeray spent time here.

NEWPORT. The village is renowned for its good fishing, both in Clew Bay and in the loughs that lie inland on either side. Two miles northwest of Newport are the ruins of BURRISHOOLE ABBEY, all that remain of a Dominican priory founded by Richard Burke in 1469. A little further on is the sturdy, square tower of CARRIGAHOOLEY, also called ROCKFLEET CASTLE, where Grace O'Malley fought off an English attack in 1574.

MULRANY. Sitting on the isthmus between Clew Bay and Blacksod Bay, Mulrany has a microclimate that has fostered the growth of rhododendrons and giant fuchsias. The superb beaches of fine sand and lovely views over the wild landscape of the Curraun Peninsula make this a popular holiday region with the Irish.

Many artists have found peace and beauty on Achill Island. Painters like Paul Henry ● *110* (above, *A Lake in the West*), Desmond Turner and Camille Souter have been inspired by the landscape. Poets and writers have sought refuge and replenishment here, including Thomas Carlyle, J.M. Synge ● *125*, ▲ *270*, Louis MacNiece, Ernie O'Malley, Graham Greene and Derek Mahon. The German Nobel prize-winner Heinrich Böll had a

cottage at Dugort and often came to stay between 1954 and 1983.

Bennee Head.

ACHILL ISLAND

The island covers 55 square miles and is the largest off the coast of Ireland. It was joined to the mainland in 1888 by the Michael Davitt swivel bridge. This crosses from the Curraun Peninsula to reach the village of Achill Sound. Achill Island is a magical and unspoilt region, covered with moorland and heather. There are impressive mountain peaks reaching well over 2,000 feet in height, some descending to sheer sea-cliffs and others sloping down to end in fine sandy beaches. The inhabitants of Achill have always had an extremely hard existence, often depending on the generosity of departed family members to survive.

THE NORTH COAST. The little village of Dugort, at the foot of Mount Slievemore, withstood the siege of a Protestant mission which began on August 1, 1834, when the Church Missionary Society leased the island. The Reverend Edward Nangle arrived to found "The Settlement", near Dugort, and tried to win the islanders away from their Catholic faith. He started free schools, an orphanage and a newspaper, and provided cottages and allotments at low rents, as well as a soup kitchen for the needy in hard times. Although he ended up owning a large part of the island, the mission was a failure. Nangle left Achill in 1852. The climb up Mount Slievemore provides an opportunity to see a number of ancient remains, and also a sad, deserted village. It is probably the one described by Heinrich Böll: "The skeleton of a village, cruelly distinct in its structure, neatly laid out on the sombre slope, as if for an anatomy lesson. . . . The main street, a little crooked like the spine of a labourer". From the beach at POULAVADDY there are boat trips to see amazing seal caves in the cliffs. A magnificent view can be had over the tall cliffs from Saddle Head, the tip of the promontory on the extreme northwest end of the island.

THE SOUTH COAST. The village of Dooagh, set on a bay renowned for its abundant fish, had a famous resident at CORRYMORE HOUSE: Captain Boycott ▲ *283*. From the next village east, KEEL, the smooth sands of Trawmore beach extend for 2 miles to end abruptly with the Menawn Cliffs. They rise to tower nearly 800 feet above the sea. The picturesque road that leads round Achill Island, called Atlantic Drive, continues from DOOEGA and winds around the southern tip of land to end at Achill Sound. It passes another stronghold of Grace O'Malley, the 15th-century KILDOWNET CASTLE. There are fine views over to the mainland. Not far away are the restored remains of a small 15th-century church, with Gaelic Stations of the Cross.

Fishermen at Inishglora, on the Belmullet Peninsula.

BELMULLET PENINSULA

A little further north is Belmullet Peninsula, or the Mullet, roughly 15 miles long and 9 miles wide. It is an area of outstanding beauty, famous for its bird life, with a large number of interesting ancient remains including cairns, megalithic tombs, stone huts, pillar stones, churches and ruined forts.

ERRIS HEAD. The headland juts out at the western end of Broad Haven, the bay north of the Mullet. Spectacular rocky cliffs extend for nearly 14 miles along this stretch of coast. The promontory fort at DOONAMO has a circle of *chevaux de frise* very similar to that seen at Dún Aengus on the Aran Islands ▲ *273*.

INISHGLORA. The bare island nearly 3 miles off the west coast from Binghamstown is of significance in Ireland's Pagan and Christian past. In Celtic legend the children of Lir were buried here, having become mortals again after being changed into swans for thrice three hundred years ▲ *311*. There are also an interesting chapel and monastery founded here by Saint Brendan, who died in 577 ▲ *239*.

BLACKSOD BAY. The bay lies protected by the Belmullet Peninsula, south of the isthmus that separates it from the mainland. Here, on September 7, 1588 the *Rata* sank. She was the largest galleon of the Spanish Armada, commanded by Don Alonso de Levya. From Belmullet to Belderrig the road runs along vast and desolate areas of bog. This coast, battered by Atlantic winds, seems forsaken by both God and man.

SHARK FISHING
Of all the seventy-three species of fish that live off the Irish coast, the shark remains the most glorious catch for any fisherman. The Irish used to brave storms in their fragile *currachs* ▲ *276* to harpoon basking shark, harmless fish that can weigh several tons. Today deep-sea fishing, between June and September, still requires stamina and courage, but the boats now measure from 25 to 60 feet and are motor-powered.

THE FRENCH LANDING
On August 22, 1798 three frigates dropped anchor off Kilcummin Head. Under the command of General Humbert, 1,067 French soldiers landed and took the town of Killala, shortly followed by Ballina. Local men loyal to Wolfe Tone's United Irishmen came to swell the ranks of the French, but the nationwide movement soon fell apart, as they had no real support. At Castlebar, on August 5, the tiny army managed to rout an English force of five thousand infantry and one thousand cavalry. But Lord Cornwallis and General Lake moved their best troops west to surround them at Ballynamuck, County Longford. Outnumbered, Humbert was forced to surrender.

INLAND THROUGH COUNTY MAYO

KILLALA. Killala, taken by the French in 1798, is a pleasant seaside and cathedral town. Saint Patrick founded the episcopal see here, and the town is named after his original church, which he entrusted to Saint Muiredach. Killala has the finest round tower in County Mayo (left), as well as a Protestant cathedral built in 1670 on the ruins of a Catholic one. The French are said to have held the bishop and his family, and treated them with courtesy throughout. There is a monument to the landing on Kilcummin Head.

FOXFORD. The town is set among delightful scenery, on the River Moy, near to the loughs of Conn and Cullin. Foxford is proud to have among its sons Admiral William Brown, "father of the Argentinian navy". In 1892, the Reverend Mother Agnes Morrogh Bernard created the Providence Woollen Mills here, to stem the flow of local people abroad. They remain in business today, and can be visited.

STRAID. Michael Davitt is buried here in the village where he was born to a peasant family. He was the founder of the Land League, in 1879, and worked with Parnell. Thanks to him tenants saw the first reforms in the Irish land system.

CASTLEBAR. The county town of Mayo is the site of the battle of 1798 (below) in which the French put the English into headlong flight (the "Castlebar Races"). There is a monument to the 1798 Rebellion in the shady, tree-lined Mall, beside the tomb of John Moore, president of the short-lived Republic of Connacht. On nearby FRENCH HILL there is a memorial to the French who fell at Castlebar and in the town church a tablet to the dead of the Fraser Fencibles, the best English regiment present at the debacle.

BALLINTOBER ▲ 278. About 8 miles along the road leading to Ballinrobe lies BALLINTOBER ABBEY, thoroughly restored between 1964 and 1966. It is the only abbey in Ireland where Mass has been celebrated without interruption since its foundation in 1216. Near to CARROWNACON, on the east bank

Cliffs at Downpatrick.

of Lough Carra, are the lonely ruins of Moorehall, John Moore's mansion and birthplace of Irish novelist George Moore (1852–1933). He spent time in Paris, where he became a close friend of Manet; he was also one of the leading lights of the Irish literary revival, and was involved in the founding of the Abbey Theatre ▲ *144*.

LOUGH MASK HOUSE. Southwest of Ballinrobe, Lough Mask House was the home of Captain Charles Boycott, land agent for Lord Erne. His poor treatment of the tenantry made him, in 1880, the first victim of Parnell's sending to "Moral Coventry" by supporters of the Land League. He was "left severely alone" and forced to use Orange farm workers from the north, protected by English soldiers. His name has become part of the English language.

KNOCK. On the plains 7 miles east of Claremorris stands

Knock, one of the most important centers of Catholic pilgrimage today. On August 21, 1879, the Blessed Virgin, Saint Joseph and Saint John appeared, with a lamb, on the gable wall of the Church of St John the Baptist. The visions recurred, and an enquiry was held which concluded that they were genuine. Since then Knock has been the destination for hundreds of thousands of pilgrims every year. The pilgrims gather to pray at the church dating from 1828. Nearby a basilica has been built, consecrated in 1976 to the Blessed Virgin. Capable of holding twenty thousand people, it has a circular ambulatory supported by thirty-two pillars, one for each county in Ireland. On September 30, 1979 Pope John Paul II came to Knock during the first papal visit to Ireland. An international airport was opened just outside Charlestown in 1986.

CÉIDE FIELDS
(On the north coast, west of Ballycastle, Downpatrick Head.) Recent excavations in the turf bogs of northern County Mayo have revealed long stretches of stone wall, set wide apart. They seem proof of a highly advanced state of social cohesion and community organization. Discovery has also been made, under layers of turf, of megalithic tombs and dwellings dating from the Stone and Bronze ages. All information on the excavations is available in the little pyramid-shaped museum at Céide Fields, the name that has been given to the site.

So often were the green and wooded valleys, the lofty mountains and the sandy beaches of County Sligo evoked in the poetry of W.B. Yeats and in the paintings of his brother Jack, that a part of the county has come to be known as Yeats Country. The outlines of megalithic monuments guarding their ancient secrets stand out starkly from the vast expanses of bog, heather and broom.

SLIGO

WILLIAM BUTLER YEATS (1865–1939)
As a child, he and his brother Jack ● *113* spent many holidays with their maternal grandparents at Ballisodare and Sligo. His first poems were inspired by folk-tales and Gaelic legends. Winner of the Nobel prize in 1923, in his work Yeats remained faithful to the land that nurtured his vocation.

The town stands on the Garavogue, the river linking Lough Gill to the Atlantic. The name "Sligo" comes from the Gaelic *sligeach*, meaning "shelly river". It grew up around a Dominican abbey founded in 1252, when the Anglo-Norman knights were taking over the northern territory of Connacht. Its fortunes oscillated until the second half of the 18th century, when Sligo prospered with the growth of trade with England and the New World. The ornate façades of the banks in Grattan Street and Stephen Street are proof of the resulting prosperity.

SLIGO ABBEY. The oldest building in Sligo is the abbey. It was badly damaged by fire in 1414, and rebuilt only to be ransacked during the Ulster rebellion in 1642. The eight pointed windows in the choir, widely splayed on the inside, are original. The window in the east wall and the high altar date from the 15th century, as do the three sides of the cloister that remain. Along the south wall of the choir is the richly carved MONUMENT TO O'CONOR SLIGO and his wife, and in the north wall of the nave is the TOMB OF CORMAC O'CREAN (1506), member

of a wealthy merchant family. The Dominicans left the abbey early in the 18th century, when penal laws were made forbidding the Catholic clergy to practice in Ireland ● *52*. **MUNICIPAL ART GALLERY AND COUNTY MUSEUM** ◆ *383*. Along with collections of local interest and the fiddle of Michael Coleman, one of Ireland's greatest folk players, a section is devoted to the Yeats brothers. There are paintings and drawings by Jack, and William's letters, along with first editions and other memorabilia.

LOUGH GILL ★

PARKE'S CASTLE. The tranquility of Lough Gill inspired Yeats, although in the past its calm must have been disturbed over

several centuries by life at the two castles that succeeded each other on its north bank. Excavations made within the walls of the present-day Parke's Castle have revealed that the high outer walls once surrounded a fortified tower built in the 15th or 16th century. It is suggested that this may have been Brian O'Rourke's fortress, possibly where he gave refuge to Captain Francisco de Cuellar of the Spanish Armada ▲ *316*. De Cuellar managed to get back to his homeland safe and sound, and left a thrilling account of his adventures. It appears that when Robert Parke built his castle in the 1620's, he dismantled the tower and reused the stones. Parke was an "entrepreneur", arriving in Ireland when the "plantation" of English and Scottish settlers was arranged early in the 17th century ● *51*. They brought with them their language, their culture and their architecture. Parke's Castle is one of the few "planters' castles" in Ireland.

HAZELWOOD DESMESNE ◆ *383*. Richard Castle designed the Palladian mansion in 1731. Today it is the headquarters of a Korean company. Nearby is Half Moon Bay, where a large park is laid out with modern sculpture by Irish and foreign artists.

DEERPARK. The monument has the Gaelic name of "Leact Chon Mhic Ruis", and has also been called the "Irish Stonehenge" because of its pillars traversed by lintels that recall the famous monument on Salisbury Plain. It is in fact a fine example of a court tomb ● *89*, with a 50-foot-long oval court flanked by standing stones. Below the main site are ruins of other graves and a small fortified enclosure with an underground passage.

PARKE'S CASTLE
In contrast to the tall O'Rourke Tower that stood within the walls before, Parke's Castle is a long, single-story edifice adjoining the ramparts. The interior has been restored recently and exhibitions are held here. A visit to the castle includes an audio-visual presentation. The outer defensive wall is well-preserved, and now encloses stables and a forge rebuilt on their original site.

"THE ISLE OF INNISFREE"
In 1890 William Butler Yeats, "exiled" in London, wrote the nostalgic poem dreaming of his native land, Lough Gill, and the "lake isle of Innisfree" on its southern bank. "I will arise and go now, for always night and day, I hear lake water lapping with low sounds by the shore; While I stand on the roadway, or on the pavements grey, I hear it in the deep heart's core."

COUNTESS MARKIEVICZ (1868–1927)
Constance Gore-Booth met the Polish Count Casimir DuninMarkievicz, her future husband, when she was a student at the Beaux Arts in Paris. She was condemned to death for her part in the 1916 Easter Rising, but her sentence was commuted to life imprisonment in June 1917. In December 1918 she was elected for Dublin as the first woman member of the British House of Commons, but did not take her seat. Liberated in 1919, she was later made a minister in the first government of the Irish Republic.

DROMAHAIRE. This was the ancient capital of the O'Rourkes, kings of Breffni. On the banks of the Bonet River are remains of the royal castle. Adjoining are the ruins of "Old Hall", a manor built in the 17th century by the English settler Edward Villiers, who had been granted the lands confiscated from the O'Rourkes. On a hill across the river from Dromahaire is CREEVELEA ABBEY, a Franciscan monastery founded in 1508. The remains are in a reasonable state of repair, and there are some plain but very lovely carved reliefs of Saint Francis.

TOWARD DONEGAL

DRUMCLIFF. Yeats died in the south of France in 1939, but it was not until 1948 that he was finally buried, near the Protestant church at Drumcliff, where his grandfather had been rector. He wrote his own epitaph: "Cast a cold eye, On life, on death. Horseman, pass by!" In the 6th century Saint Columba founded a MONASTERY here, but there is little left apart from the foundations of a round tower. On the walls of the Catholic cemetery are an 11th-century High Cross carved with scenes from the Old and New Testaments.

LISSADELL HOUSE. The estate and house, built in 1834 in an austere neoclassical style, belonged to the Gore-Booth family. Yeats was pleased to be a guest at Lissadell and much admired Constance and her sister Eva, the poetess. "Two girls in silk kimonos, both Beautiful, one a gazelle." Between Carney and Lissadell there is a nature reserve where barnacle geese from Greenland spend the winter.

STREEDAGH POINT. Three ships of the Spanish Armada went down here in 1588. The story only survives in the account of the Captain Francisco de Cuellar. Those who managed to get ashore were massacred by the local inhabitants.

CREEVYKEEL. Just east of the village of Cliffony is a court tomb ● *88*, dating back to 2500 BC. The site at Creevykeel has been recently restored and is one of the finest examples of this type of ancient grave in Ireland. It has a large oval court, with the entrance on the eastern side. This leads to a chamber traversed by a central wall. There are two smaller dolmens in the sides of the mound, perhaps of a later date. The monument is surrounded by stone slabs. In the Middle Ages the court was used by a blacksmith who installed a forge.

INISHMURRAY. The Island of Inishmurray lies 4 miles off the coast of Sligo and can be reached by boat from the little port of Mullaghmore. On it are remarkable monastic remains, with the main buildings grouped inside a *cashel* reminiscent of

some forts on the Aran Islands ▲ *273*. It is not known if these fortifications are contemporary with, or pre-date, the monastery founded by Saint Molaise (bottom right) in the 6th or 7th century. The oval enclosure is in almost perfect condition and divided into three sections. The structures within include an 11th- or 12th-century church, a late medieval "Church of Fire", "Saint Molaise's house" (a stone-roofed oratory that may also be the tomb of the founder), and a beehive hut, known as Tory Bhrenell in honor of Saint Brendan ▲ *239*. There are also three carved pillar stones and three altars, the largest of which has curious stones on its surface. The stones are used, according to ancient custom, for cursing. Until early in the 20th century an annual pilgrimage used to be made to Innishmurray. The faithful would make

CURSING STONES
According to an old custom, he who turns a stone can put a curse on anyone who has done him harm. However, if the grievance is not justified, the curse will turn back on him. It is told that an Englishwoman came here especially to turn a stone against Adolf Hitler.

their way around the island from east to west, following the Stations of the Cross, which can still be seen. (Return to Cliffony and continue to Grange where the road left, heading inland, will lead to the scenic Glenliff Horseshoe.)

GLENLIFF HORSESHOE LOOP DRIVE ★. The little road leads through magnificent landscapes, with views of Benwiskin, King's Mountain and Truskmore. The area is sparsely populated, although there is some pastureland.

GLENCAR LOUGH. A little further to the south is a small lough famous for its trout and salmon fishing ■ *44*. At the eastern end is a waterfall which cascades down 1,000 feet from the plateau above, to a final 50-foot drop into the lough. It has been described by Yeats in his poem *The Stolen Child*: "Where the wandering water gushes From the hills above Glen Car". In Gaelic the cascade is called *Sruth-i-naghaidhan-áird* ("torrent going back upward") because gusts of wind often blow the water in sprays back to the top of the cliff.

SLIGO TO ROSCOMMON

Carrowmore
and Carrowkeel.

KNOCKNAREA. West of Sligo rises Knocknarea ("hill of executions"), crowned by an enormous tumulus. It has been claimed that this is the tomb of Maeve, the legendary queen of Connacht. In fact the cairn probably covers a passage grave, as yet untouched, and Maeve is believed to lie at Rathcroghan.

CARROWMORE. The huge burial site, on a low hill near to Knocknarea, still has about fifty megalithic remains in all, despite much destruction by quarrying. A number of dolmens are in a good state of preservation. The earliest graves date from about 5000 BC, and many were surrounded by stone circles. Piles of charred bones found here are likely testimony to the mass cremations that probably took place at Carrowmore.

COLLOONEY. The road leading to this village passes through BALLYSADARE, known for its salmon fisheries ■ *44*. At the entrance to Collooney stands a statue raised late in the 19th century to Captain Bartholomew Teeling. He fought side-by-side with the French general Humbert to force back Colonel Vereker's Limerick militia on September 5, 1798 ● *52*.

South of the village is MARKREE CASTLE, built in the 18th century but with 19th-century additions and alterations in neo-Gothic style. The crenelated gateway at the entrance to the estate was designed by the London architect Francis Goodwin in 1830. Markree is now a hotel.

BALLYMOTE. Before reaching Ballymote, the road leads through KESHCORRAN where there are hillside caves. One legend has it that Cormac MacAirt, Ard Rí of Ireland ● *48*, was raised here by a she-wolf. Richard de Burgo built a massive castle at Ballymote in 1300, at a period when the Anglo-Normans were consolidating their hold over north Connacht. Although the fortress, abandoned in the 17th century, has not been greatly restored, the vast ruins leave no doubt as to its massive strength. *The Book of Ballymote* (left), an important codex giving a key to the ogham alphabet ● *66*, was compiled in the 15th century in the Franciscan friary at Ballymote, whose ruins also remain.

CARROWKEEL ● *88*. The slopes of the Bricklieve Mountains, overlooking lovely Lough Arrow, are covered in wild heathland and bog, in places dangerous to cross. This is the

site of a superb group of passage graves. Some of the cruciform graves have corbeled vaults. There are also wedge dolmens ● *89*. Neolithic pottery has been discovered here dating from 2500 to 2000 BC. Carrowkeel was also used as a site for individual burials during the Bronze Age, until 1500 BC. A number of the dolmens are in a dangerous condition, but one of the roofed tombs has been made safe for the public to visit. On the northern slopes are the remains of a prehistoric village.

CURLEW MOUNTAINS. The Curlew Mountains, a striking and unspoiled range of hills, separate the counties of Sligo and Roscommon. From the southern slopes there is a view over the pastures of Roscommon and Lough Key. At the foot of the hills, entering the town of Boyle, are the remains of a 12th-century Cistercian monastery.

BOYLE ABBEY ★. The MacDermots founded the abbey around 1160 and the church is an interesting illustration of the development of building techniques and architectural styles from the time of its foundation to 1220. The choir and transepts are the oldest part, with recessed chapels in both north and south transepts. On the south side of the nave are solid rounded arches in the English Norman style, with scalloped capitals (c. 1180); while on the north are three early pointed Gothic arches with exquisite moldings forming the corbels of the vaulting arches (c. 1200). At the intersection of the tower there are three segmental arches, and above is a

tower added in the 13th century along with the three lancet windows in the west gable. The cloister was seriously damaged in the 17th century when the monastery was used as a barracks. The porter's lodge and other buildings on the southern side of the monastery are from the 17th century.

LOUGH KEY. The huge wooded Lough Key National Park was once part of the estate of Rockingham House, property of the

DIARMAIT AND GRÁINNE
Keshcorran is also associated with the legend of Diarmait and Gráinne. The daughter of Cormac MacAirt agreed to marry Finn MacCoul, chief of a mythical army called the Fianna. But Finn was much older than Gráinne and she fell in love with Diarmait, one of Finn's soldiers. She eloped with him, and Finn pursued them across Ireland in vain. Diarmait was eventually to die on the slopes of Benbulben after being wounded by a wild boar, but for several years he and Gráinne spent happy times at Rath Ghrainne, near Keshcorran, where they had four sons and a daughter.

289

Barrow at Rathcroghan.

SCOTTISH MERCENARIES
The warriors in long coats of chainmail, grasping their swords, are two of the eight figures on the tomb

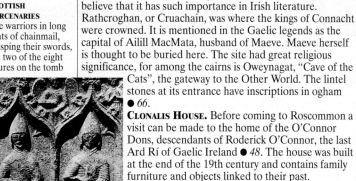

of Felim O'Conor in the nave of Roscommon Abbey. Such professional soldiers came from Scotland in the 15th century. They were hired as bodyguards by local barons, or taken into the best army regiments.

Church of the Sacred Heart, Roscommon.

King Harman family. The house has gone, but interesting features are a bog-garden ■ *34*, temple and ice-house.

RATHCROGHAN. The significance of this ring-barrow, northwest of Tulsk, can easily elude the visitor. It is hard to believe that it has such importance in Irish literature. Rathcroghan, or Cruachain, was where the kings of Connacht were crowned. It is mentioned in the Gaelic legends as the capital of Ailill MacMata, husband of Maeve. Maeve herself is thought to be buried here. The site had great religious significance, for among the cairns is Oweynagat, "Cave of the Cats", the gateway to the Other World. The lintel stones at its entrance have inscriptions in ogham ● *66*.

CLONALIS HOUSE. Before coming to Roscommon a visit can be made to the home of the O'Connor Dons, descendants of Roderick O'Connor, the last Ard Rí of Gaelic Ireland ● *48*. The house was built at the end of the 19th century and contains family furniture and objects linked to their past.

STROKESTOWN HOUSE. At the eastern end of the elegantly planned Strokestown stands the house of the Mahon family. In the 1730's, Richard Castle seems to have redesigned the residence in Palladian style at the request of Thomas Mahon. The two-story central block contained the family apartments; the more modest wings were outbuildings. The mansion has been carefully restored and furnished with pieces of the period. It also contains a museum on the subject of the Great Famine ● *58*.

ROSCOMMON. The town's name, "Coman's Wood", comes from that of Saint Coman who founded a monastery here in the 6th century. The monastical remains, however, are from a later 13th-century DOMINICAN PRIORY. They lie near the Abbey Hotel (N63). The tomb of its founder, Felim O'Conor, King of Connacht, is carved with his effigy (14th century) and watched over by eight armed figures (late 15th century). On the west side of town are the ruins of a CASTLE built in 1269 by the Royal Justiciar of Ireland, Roger d'Ufford. The building was badly damaged by Cromwell's men in 1652, but the four round towers still stand at its outer walls, as does the fortified gateway to the east, and the postern gate to the west. The mullioned windows were added in 1578.

ULSTER

▲ ULSTER

DONEGAL ▲ *294*
1 DONEGAL
2 SLIEVE LEAGUE
3 GLENCOLUMBKILLE
4 GLENTIES
5 DUNGLOE
6 ARANMORE ISLAND
7 GWEEDORE
8 TORY ISLAND
9 HORN HEAD
10 ROSGUILL
11 FANAD
12 RATHMULLAN
13 LETTERKENNY
14 GLENVEAGH
15 INISHOWEN
16 GRIANAN OF AILEACH

DERBY TO ARMAGH ▲
35 DERRY
36 DUNGIVEN
37 BANAGHER
38 STRABANE
39 ULSTER AMERICAN FOLK PARK
40 SPERRIN MOUNTAINS
41 NAVAN FORT
42 ARMAGH
43 ARDRESS HOUSE
44 LOUGH NEAGH

BELFAST

PILGRIMAGE TO STATION ISLAND
The island on Lough Derg, southeast
of Donegal, is the object of fervent
and well-attended pilgrimages on
June 1 and August 15 each year. Here
Saint Patrick had a vision of Purgatory
and chased demons out of a cave.

Donegal remains far less familiar to tourists than other areas. It has remained unspoilt and little explored. Some consider it the most beautiful county in Ireland, with varied landscapes and a long and magnificent coastline that boasts more beaches than any other Irish county. The many ancient remains are an added fascination. As early as the 5th century the northern part of Donegal was occupied by the O'Neills. The south was under the domination of the Conaill and the Eoghain families (Cenel Conaill and Cenel Eoghain), and two main regions are named after them: Inis Eoghain (the Eoghain Peninsula) and Tír Chonaill (Conaill Country).

DONEGAL TO GLENTIES

Doe Castle,
County Donegal.

The dizzy heights
of the Slieve
League cliffs.

DONEGAL. Donegal lies in the deep recesses of Donegal Bay, at the mouth of the River Eske. It is a pleasant and lively town, at the crossroads of three main routes. One road leads round the west coast, another goes east toward Derry ▲ *318*, and the third south to Sligo ▲ *284*. Donegal was founded by the Vikings, and its name means "fortress of the foreigners" (Dún na nGall), but it rose to importance as the stronghold of the O'Donnell clan. The two major monuments, DONEGAL ABBEY and DONEGAL CASTLE, were built in 1475, by Nuala O'Brien, and in 1505 by her husband, Red Hugh O'Donnell. In 1595, however, Hugh O'Donnell, the last prince of Tyrconnell, set fire to the castle rather than leave it to the English. It was a futile gesture, and the city fell to his enemies after the "Flight of the Earls"(1607) ● *50*, and was restored as part of the plantation scheme ● *51*. Captain Basil Brooke, in charge of replanning Donegal, built a stately, fortified Jacobean manor ● *99* into the remains of the castle.
SLIEVE LEAGUE ★. Along the coast to the east is the port of

KILLYBEGS, boasting just over fifteen hundred inhabitants. It is surprising to learn that this is one of the most important fishing ports in the country, along with Greencastle ▲ *299* and Inishowen ▲ *298*. From here to the little village of KILCAR the road descends with spectacular views. Kilcar is famous for its tweed, as is CARRICK nearby. Carrick marks the start of a Gaelic-speaking area, and it is also the starting point for boat excursions to see the formidable Slieve League cliffs, the highest in Europe (nearly 2,000 feet). They are best seen from the sea or from BUNGLASS POINT.

GLENCOLUMBKILLE. The Glen Valley, bordered on one side by mountains and on the other by a wild and rocky coast, was a place of retreat and prayer for Saint Columba (also known as Saint Columcille, *c.* 521–97) and his disciples. Each year on June 9 a pilgrimage is held in honor of the saint, locally called the Turas ("journey"). The barefoot pilgrims make their way past some fifteen Stations of the Cross spread over 3 miles. Along the way are stone crosses and the cell oratory, the bed, the well and the chair of Saint Columba. The village of Glencolumbkille, set in the Glen Valley, is where Father James McDyer decided to "save the West". He formed a market-gardening co-operative with the aim of relieving the poverty of his parishioners. The FOLK MUSEUM ◆ *387* was another of his ideas: three thatched cottages illustrate the life of peasants in Ireland at different periods of history. (The steep road crosses uninhabited hills and leads over the wild Pass of Glengesh, before descending to Ardara.)

GLENTIES. Playwright Brian Friel comes from this pleasant town, and used it as the setting for his play *Dancing at Lughnasa*. There is a handsome 19th-century COURT HOUSE, and nearby is ST CONNELL'S MUSEUM, with a collection of local items. ST CONAL'S CHURCH is modern, designed by Liam McCormick. Around the coast to the west are more good beaches, well worth exploration.

DUNGLOE TO RAMELTON

THE ROSSES. The soil in this area is so poor that it is virtually impossible to grow anything. Until late in the last century 75 percent of the population of The Rosses spoke Irish ● *68*; now the proportions are reversed, which still makes it one of today's strongest areas of *Gaeltacht*. The region is welcoming more and more visitors, however. Dungloe is usually their base for exploration of the wild, windbeaten landscape to the north and west, scattered with tiny lakes and studded with granite rocks. (From Burtonport, there is a regular ferry service to Aranmore Island.)

ARANMORE ISLAND. Although the island has an aura of calm, the 750-foot cliffs on the west coast are battered by powerful

SAINT COLUMBA AND THE "BATTLE OF THE BOOK" ▲ *151*
Saint Finian claimed possession of the copy Columba had made of his illuminated Latin psalter, called the *Cathach* ("battler"). The High King of Tara pronounced judgement: "as to every cow belongs its calf, so to every book belongs its copy". Columba, whose other Christian name, it should be remembered, was Crimthan ("wolf"), provoked a bloody battle at Cooladrummon, in 561, between his followers and those of Finian and the High King. Three thousand men were killed, and Columba was banished to Scotland to expiate his sins.

Above, carts in the Glencolumbkille Folk Museum.

TORY ISLAND SCHOOL OF PRIMITIVE PAINTING

The English painter Derek Hill (born 1916) first came to Tory Island in the 1950's, and rented a small house there. Some years later, a local man called James Dixon stood watching him paint and remarked that he could do better. Hill immediately supplied him with brushes and tubes of paint. Other inhabitants soon became interested in discovering their talents, and the Tory Island primitive school came into being. Some islanders are still painting. There is a permanent exhibition of work in the Community Hall.

Atlantic waves. The lighthouse was the first to be built in Donegal (1798), and it sweeps the seas with the most powerful beam of any along the Irish coast. Aranmore is inhabited all year round, but only comes to life in summer, when fishing and tourism are at their height.

ERRIGAL MOUNTAIN. Toward Errigal Mountain the landscape becomes wilder and more rocky. The cone-shaped quartzite peak, whose outline is strangely reminiscent of Mount Fuji, is the highest in Donegal (2,466 feet). From the top, on a clear day, one can see as far as Scotland and the peaks of Connacht. At the foot of Errigal Mountain lies the village of DUNLEWY, on Lough Lacung. Its Church of the Sacred Heart (1877) has splendidly colorful marble decoration. The nearby village of GWEEDORE, also set against the mountain backdrop, became known for its hotel (now closed). The far-sighted and philanthropic landlord Lord George Hill started the establishment to draw tourists and help relieve the poverty of the local people.

TORY ISLAND. Tory Island can be seen 8 miles offshore from BLOODY FORELAND (so-named after the gory colors of the sunsets that

can be seen from the point). According to legend the island was given to Saint Columba, and the ancient remains at the village of West Town may be those of a monastery he founded here. They consist of a ROUND TOWER, the 6-foot-high cross, a rare TAU CROSS of Saint Anthony (bottom left), and a church, TEAMPULL NA MUIRISEAR ("Church of the Seven"), named after seven pilgrims that Columba resuscitated in order to administer last rites. To the east of the island are the remains

Donegal seen from the island of Aranmore.

The harbor at Bunbeg.

of a fort, DÚN BHALOIR, a reminder that in legend the island was a stronghold of the Fomoriens, a race of giant pirates. Their chief, "Balor of the Evil Eye", had a single eye in the middle of his forehead. There are boats to the island from Magheraroarty and Bunbeg (above right). About 130 people live on Tory Island, making their living mainly from fishing. Derek Hill, an English painter, spent time here and inspired the start of the island's school of primitive painting.

HORN HEAD. The scenery is magnificent along the road west, which leads between the foothills of Muckish Mountain and the sea. It passes through Falcarragh, the last outpost of *Gaeltacht* ● 68. From the 800-foot cliffs of Horn Head, a favorite place for many varieties of sea bird, it possible to see how the Atlantic Ocean has torn away at the coast, leaving a few islands (Inishbofin, Inishdooey, Inish Beg and Tory) and a confusion of narrow sea channels and ragged bays.

ROSGUILL PENINSULA. A road known as Atlantic Drive leads around the peninsula, passing Carrigart and the nearby seaside resorts of Rosapenna and Downings. It runs above sea level until it reaches Tranarossan Bay, after which it descends to follow the wooded shores of a narrow estuary called Mulroy Bay, with sandy coves and tiny islets along its edge. Milford stands at the southern end of the bay, a good base for fishing on the River Lennon and Lough Fern.

FANAD PENINSULA. There are two routes signposted around the peninsula, but only the Fanad Peninsula Scenic Tour goes as far as Fanad Head, the curved headland at the entrance to Lough Swilly. The lough is in fact a sea inlet separating the Fanad Peninsula from the Inishowen. The name Swilly may come from a legendary former inhabitant of the bay, Suileach. This was a monster with one hundred eyes, killed by Saint Columba. The other route, the Knockalla Coast Road, follows the schist and heather-covered hills of Knockalla Mountain.

RATHMULLAN. The PRIORY in the center of the town was built for the Carmelites in 1516 by Owen Roe MacSweeney. In the tower of the stone fort standing on the sea front is a permanent exhibition on the region's history, and in particular the departure of the earls of Ulster for France in 1607, the crucial event known as the "Flight of the Earls" ● 50.

DOE CASTLE
The stronghold is well positioned, deep within the bay of Sheep Haven that separates Horn Head from the Rosguill Peninsula. Doe Castle was built early in the 16th century by the MacSweeney family. It was attacked many times by rival northern clans, and used to be protected by a moat hewn out of the rock and crossed by a drawbridge. In the graveyard beside the castle, where there was a Franciscan monastery founded by the MacSweeneys, many chiefs of the Donegal clans lie buried. There is a tombstone in the wall carved with a fine cross, the family coat of arms and mythological figures.

LETTERKENNY TO GLENVEAGH

LETTERKENNY. This rapidly growing town is now the largest in Donegal. It has the COUNTY MUSEUM, which is worth visiting for its broad collection of objects. ST EUNAN'S CATHEDRAL was built at the turn of the century. It is decorated with Celtic designs and stained glass. The carved throne is the work of a Dublin company owned by the father of the poet and hero of 1916, Patrick Pearse ● *61*.

COLMCILLE HERITAGE CENTRE. Gartan, birthplace of Saint Columba, or Saint Columcille, is now the site of the Colmcille Heritage Centre. It stands not far from various sites linked with the saint: the stone on which Saint Columba's mother is said to have given birth, ST COLMCILLE'S ORATORY, the monastery founded by the saint (of which only two crosses and a ruined church remain) and, to the northeast, Kilmacrenan, where he was brought up and built his first church. The museum tells the story of the missionary saint and has a section on early illuminated manuscripts ▲ *150*.

GLENVEAGH. The NATIONAL PARK covers 36 square miles of countryside around Lough Beagh, and includes GLENVEAGH CASTLE ♦ *387* and gardens. This Victorian castle was built in 1870 by the American John Adair and his wife Cornelia to designs by J.T. Trench. The granite building with its battlements and towers is set against a dramatic backdrop of rugged mountains. The narrow, barrel-vaulted entrance hall has a black and white Victorian tiled floor. The main drawing room is filled with Irish Chippendale

GLEBE HOUSE AND GALLERY
A 19th-century vicarage in the quiet parish of Gartan (near to the Colmcille Heritage Centre) was purchased in 1953 by the English painter and theater designer Derek Hill. Donegal was important to Hill: discovering it had filled him with new inspiration, and he eventually gave Glebe House to the State in 1981. The house illustrates the energy, and wide tastes and interests of its owner. Drawings by William Morris are to be seen alongside prints brought back from Japan and embroidery from Boukhara. There is an eclectic collection of paintings (Pasmore, Hokusai, Picasso, Kokoschka, and Tory Island primitives).

furniture. The round tower contains a music room lined in green tartan and decorated with antlers. In 1938 the property was bought by Henry McIlhenny, President of the Philadelphia Museum of Art. He transformed the grounds, creating a spectacular garden first with the help of Jim Russell and then Lanning Roper. The magnificent Gothic Revival conservatory was designed by Philippe Jullian. Glenveagh is now owned by the state and open to the public.

INISHOWEN PENINSULA ★

The peninsula lies between the deep sea-loughs Lough Swilly and Lough Foyle, and is bounded by the Atlantic to

the north. The land is rocky and mountainous, rising to the central peak of Slieve Snaght, 2,019 feet high. The peninsula forms a rough triangle, the three points being Inishowen Head, Dunree Head, and Malin Head, the most northerly place in Ireland (above). There are some sites of architectural interest on the peninsula (O'Dochertys' Keep at BUNCRANA, DUNREE FORT and GREENCASTLE FORT, and the resorts of MOVILLE and BALLYLIFFIN), but it is really for the superb scenery and archeological sites that visitors come here.

GRIANAN OF AILEACH ★. The most impressive ancient monument in the county. The massive circular fort stands on a hill 800 feet above sea level, with views over loughs Swilly and Foyle. The walls are 17 feet high and 13 feet thick at the base, and they surround a space 79 feet in diameter. Around the main fort are three earth ramparts, now only partly discernible. Like Staigue Fort ▲ *229*, the site is probably pre-Christian. It was the seat of the O'Neill dynasty, kings of Ulster, from the 5th to the 12th century, and it was twice destroyed, in 676 and in 1101. The Grianan of Aileach was restored in the 1870's. At the foot of the hill is ST AENGUS CHURCH, built in 1967 by Liam McCormick and Una Madden.

CROSS OF CARDONAGH. A remarkable cross (below) stands against the wall of the Protestant church, dating from the 8th or perhaps 7th century. It is carved with human figures and interlace designs. Most unusual are the two smaller stones standing on either side, also decorated. There is another standing stone in the graveyard showing a *flabellum* (a fan-shaped liturgical object) which must have been copied from one of the relics of Saint Columba.

CLONCA. The church probably dates from the 17th century and was built on the site of a monastery founded by Saint Buodan. Inside is the tombstone of Magnus MacOrristin, a Scot, on which are carved a sword and a hurley ● *83* along with an inscription in Scottish Gaelic ● *66*. In a field to the west is a Celtic cross. On the east face is the *Miracle of the Loaves and Fishes* and, on the other side, a depiction of two men, who could be Saint Paul and Saint Anthony in the desert.

COOLEY. Inland from Moville is Cooley where Saint Finian is said to be buried in the GRAVEYARD. There are also the remains of two churches and a burial place called the SKULL HOUSE. On the other side of Lough Foyle from the Inishowen Peninsula lies Northern Ireland. The nearest town over the border is Derry ▲ *318*.

GRIANAN OF AILEACH
The word *grianan* means "house of the sun". Neither the name nor the fort's original purpose have yet been fully explained. The walls curve in slightly towards the top, and within they are terraced. On each side of the entrance gate are passages inside the thickness of the wall extending half way round the fort. Their entrances are at the northern and southern ends. When Murtogh O'Brien, King of Munster, defeated the O'Neills here in 1101, he ordered the fort to be dismantled and many stones were carried away.

1 QUEEN'S UNIVERSITY   **2** BOTANIC GARDENS   **3** GRAND OPERA HOUSE

The tall cranes of the *Harland & Wolff* shipyards, founded in 1862, builders of the doomed Titanic.

The city of Belfast lies on low land between green hills, at the mouth of the River Lagan where it flows into Belfast Lough. Its name comes from "Béal Feirste" ("sandy ford"). Around it are mountains that continue along the northwest bank of the lough, a long, wide inlet from the North Channel. Belfast is the second largest city in Ireland and grew rapidly in the 18th and 19th centuries because of its busy port, shipbuilding yards, and linen industry. It is the industrial capital of Northern Ireland. Many of the old quarters of Belfast were bombed in the Blitz, and others pulled down by planners in the 1960's. However, the city has friendly pubs, some remarkably ornate churches and a number of impressive buildings erected during its heyday. The Anglo-Irish novelist and short-story writer William Trevor wrote: "When the sun shines on this city, and when its people smile, there is a warmth that does you good to be close to."

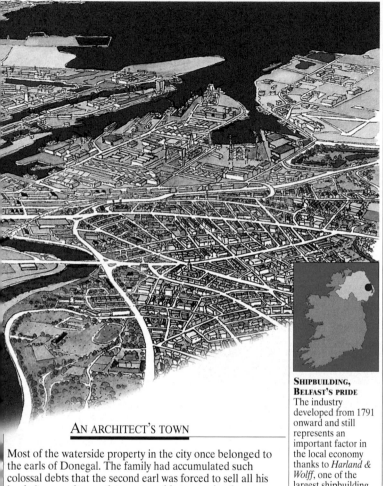

AN ARCHITECT'S TOWN

Most of the waterside property in the city once belonged to
the earls of Donegal. The family had accumulated such
colossal debts that the second earl was forced to sell all his
land. As a result speculators were able to acquire the green
and undeveloped banks of the Lagan. The greater the
instability of financial institutions became in the 19th
century, the more important it was to have an impressive
building exuding wealth and dependability. They employed
architects to give them this ring of confidence. Of the
fifty banks registered in Belfast
at the end of the
century, not one
remained forty years
later. The 19th-
century architects
who put their mark
on Belfast were
Sir Charles Lanyon
(1813–89), W.H.
Lynn (1829–1915)
and William J. Barre
(1830–67).

**SHIPBUILDING,
BELFAST'S PRIDE**
The industry
developed from 1791
onward and still
represents an
important factor in
the local economy
thanks to *Harland &
Wolff*, one of the
largest shipbuilding
and repair yards in
the United Kingdom
and *Short Brothers*,
the second largest
company in Belfast in
terms of employees.

QUEEN'S UNIVERSITY
The university,
founded in 1845 as
"Queen's College",
was associated with
the two other
universities of that
name (in Cork and
Galway), that in 1908
became part of the
National University of
Ireland. Queen's
College then became
the independent
Queen's University.
Today 8,500 students
attend courses. Every
year in November the
university plays host
to the Belfast Festival,
one of the major arts
festivals in the British
Isles.

LANYON, FATHER AND SON. The Englishman Charles Lanyon
was a ruthless property speculator, an engineer, an architect,
a Conservative politician and a "ladies man" who married the
boss's daughter and became Mayor of Belfast. He brought
with him an architectural language new to the people of
Belfast, who previously had little conception of what a
building could be. Under his influence, banks became castles
protecting the wealth of the linen manufacturers: examples
can still be seen, such as the NORTHERN BANK (Waring St) and
the FIRST TRUST BANK (Victoria St). The apparently
indestructible NEW HOUSE OF CORRECTION (now the Crumlin
Road prison) was a fearful warning to wrongdoers, and the
COURT HOUSE, to which it is linked by an underground
corridor, was an equally intimidating symbol of law and order.
And the churches soared skyward to evoke yet higher powers.
Among those that Lanyon built is the SINCLAIR SEAMAN'S
CHURCH (near the docks), of all the most spectacular. The
throne is made of a bowsprit and the figurehead from the
prow of the *Mitzpah*; the organ is decorated with port and
starboard lights; there is the gleaming copper bell of the
World War Two vessel *HMS Hood*, and the collection is taken

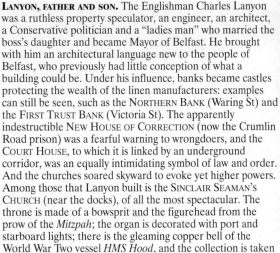

in miniature model lifeboats. The
University quarter (south Belfast) is also
strongly marked by the work of Charles
Lanyon. The mock-Tudor ● *99* buildings
of QUEEN'S UNIVERSITY (University Rd)
are of a warm red brick that blends
admirably with the style. Nearby are the
famous BOTANIC GARDENS. The Tuscan
Doric ASSEMBLY'S COLLEGE (east of the
university) was for a short time the seat
of parliament, and today houses the
Union Theological College. CUSTOMS HOUSE (Queen's Sq.),
containing a collection of paintings on a maritime theme, is
also by Lanyon. His son designed the imposing medieval-style
JENNYMOUNT MILL (North Derby St), and also BELFAST
CASTLE (Antrim Rd) which imitates the Scottish baronial
tradition. The latter was built for the Earl of Donegal before
all the money was gone.

W.H. LYNN, "AN ECLECTIC AMONG ECLECTICS". Lanyon's
partner W. H. Lynn gave Belfast some varied
and original buildings. On Donegall Square
North stands the LINEN
MERCHANTS' WAREHOUSE
that he built in 1869, now
converted to house

BOTANIC GARDENS
The gentle slopes
leading down to the
banks of the River
Lagan were laid out
as gardens in 1827 by
the Belfast
Horticultural and
Botanical Society. The
Palm House (below) is
one of the oldest such
greenhouses; its
elegant curves were
designed by Charles
Lanyon. It was built
between 1839 and
1852 by the Dublin
ironfounder Richard
Turner.

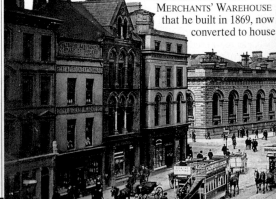

a branch of Marks & Spencer. It is on a street near a much older building, the LINEN HALL LIBRARY (1781), named after the hall that used to stand in the center of the square. It is an excellent library, open to the public, containing a collection of documents on the recent political troubles ● *64.* As access to this section is limited, lots are drawn to decide who can enter. There is a second building by W.H. Lynn at nos. 4–10 May Street. It is built in a mixture of Venetian and Gothic styles and is decorated with an eye-catching design of red, white and blue bricks. This once housed the YOUNG MENS' SOCIETY of the Church of Ireland. Another example of his work is the HARBOUR OFFICE (Corporation St).

WILLIAM J. BARRE, COMPETITION WINNER. Although Barre's designs were often chosen over those of Lanyon in architectural competitions, he did not have the same friends in high places. His lack of useful contacts meant that he was seldom able to raise the funds necessary for his projects. A number did come to fruition, however. They are the ULSTER HALL (Bedford St), built in 1860, now used for concerts by the Ulster Orchestra, the ALBERT MEMORIAL CLOCK TOWER (Queen's Sq.), which is not impressive enough to make it a real tourist attraction, the METHODIST CHURCH (University Rd), built in 1864 in the Lombardo-Venetian style, the FIRST TRUST BANK (Royal Ave), built in the same year, and a small hospital (116, Great Victoria St).

A TOWN OF PUBS AND CHURCHES

THE PUBLIC HOUSES ◆ *385.* Near the Europa Hotel, which has the uneasy reputation of being the European hotel most exposed to the danger of bombs, there is an amusing piece of sculpture dedicated to the women of easy virtue who used to people the streets of Belfast after nightfall. There is even a story, almost certainly invented, that a passage led under Great Victoria Street to take the girls from the Opera House directly to another no less baroque establishment: the thoroughly Victorian, tiled and mirrored, CROWN LIQUOR SALOON ★, even today lit by gas, where they could enjoy Guinness and oysters with their young men in the snugs.

"CROWN LIQUOR SALOON"
This is the haunt of actors, journalists, art students and tourists. The building was once the Ulster Railway Hotel (where Sarah Bernhardt spent the night), and was opened by Patrick Flanigan in 1885, who was inspired by the many railway hotels in which he had stayed while traveling in

Spain and Italy. The interior is Victorian and highly ornate, with brightly colored glass and tiles that are reflected in the polished mirrors behind the long counter. Over the entrances of the individual wood-paneled snugs are carved heraldic beasts.

ROADSIDE PORTRAIT GALLERY
When passing no. 10 Donegall Square South, look up. Some famous men are staring down at you: Humboldt, Jacquard, Washington, Galileo, Columbus, Newton, Stevenson, Moore, Watt, Michelangelo, Homer, Shakespeare and Schiller. The busts that cover two stories of the façade are the work of Charles Lanyon.

**BELFAST AND
THE STAGE**
Of all the theaters in the city the Grand Opera House (Great Victoria St) is the favorite of both artists and public alike. It offers an impressive program of opera, ballet, drama and variety. Part of its charm is the theater interior itself, sumptuously decorated with velvet, extravagant gilded molding, and the odd Renaissance-style touch. The Lyric Theatre (Ridgeway St) specializes in Irish drama and the classics, while the Arts Theatre (Botanic Ave) puts on musical comedies and modern plays. The Group Theatre (Bedford St) specializes in plays from Ulster.

ROBINSON'S, almost next door, is a pleasing reproduction which imitates the great Irish institution of the "spirit grocer", a grocer's shop that also provides customers with drinks at a small bar. Spirit grocers are still found in some country areas. MORRISON'S (Bedford St) is similar. The MORNING STAR (Pottinger's Entry) is one of Belfast's famous old oyster houses. In the city's oldest pub, KELLY'S CELLARS (Bank St), there is still something of the conspiratorial atmosphere that must have reigned at the time of the United Irishmen ● *52,* when Henry Joy McCracken was forced to hide behind the bar to escape the pursuit of English soldiers. DU BARRY'S, named after Louis XV's favorite, and where the painter Stanley Spencer's brother used to play the piano, is now closed. It was a shady place of secret assignations. The KITCHEN BAR and BITTLE'S BAR do their best to cheer up gloomy Victoria Square, once the heart of theatrical life in the city. They are among the rare traditional pubs to have survived in the center. Further south, toward the university, and marooned amid cafés and fast-food restaurants, is LAVERY'S GIN PALACE, a flourishing establishment in the 19th century which now retains a distinctly 1960's atmosphere. On the road to the docks is the ROTTERDAM BAR. It stands on the spot where orphaned and destitute girls were once handcuffed for transportation to Van Diemen's Land (now Tasmania). Today, the bar is known for good music from such far-flung places as Eastern Europe and South America, as well as from Ireland.

THE CHURCHES. ST GEORGE'S CHURCH (High St) offers more measured enjoyment. The sobre building is Corinthian in

style. It was built in 1811 on the former site of the CHAPEL OF THE FORD (1306), an important monument in Belfast's history, since the first written mention of the founding of the city is linked to the chapel. It stood on a tributary of the River Lagan called the Farset, which now runs underground. Until early in the 19th century choirboys from the chapel came to fish for salmon. However, archeologists have discovered flint arrowheads dating from the Stone Ages, affording the site an altogether more ancient history. The perfect lines of the First Presbyterian Church (Rosemary's St) are the work of Roger Mulholland. It dates back to 1781, making it not only the first Presbyterian church in the city but also the oldest. The Catholic ST MALACHY'S CHURCH (Alfred St) is interesting inside because of the construction of the vaults. The Protestant ST ANNE'S CATHEDRAL was designed by Sir Thomas Drew in 1899 to the plan of a basilica in a style imitating Hiberno-Romanesque architecture. The cathedral underwent alterations in 1981. Inside there are a number of beautiful mosaics by Gertrude and Margaret Martin, and carving by Morris Harding.

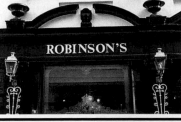

ROBINSON'S

The divine Sarah Bernhardt and the inimitable Anna Pavlova both played at the Grand Opera House.

OTHER PLACES OF INTEREST

CITY HALL (Donegall Square). The huge City Hall (below) was completed in 1906 to the design of Sir Brumwell Thomas, its dome inspired by St Paul's Cathedral. It stands on the site of the 18th-century White Linen Hall. The Renaissance-style building has a WHISPERING GALLERY in the dome and on the main landing is a mural (1951) by John Luke, which today appears somewhat naive. It is a romanticized portrayal of the great old industries of Belfast (rope-making, linen and shipbuilding), trades which may have brought wealth to some but offered many others little more than a hard life spent in poor, overcrowded sectarian ghettos. Outside the City Hall a STATUE OF QUEEN VICTORIA overlooks Royal Avenue. To the east side of Donegall Square note the line of GEORGIAN HOUSES in Chichester Street (nos. 7–11). Better still are those in Joy Street (nos. 14–26), built twenty-six years later: the finest example of Georgian architecture in the city.

ULSTER MUSEUM (Botanic Gardens). On display here are the incredible treasures salvaged from the wreck of the Spanish galleon *Girona*, the pride of the Armada, sunk in October 1588 along the rocky northern coast of the province ▲ *315*. The jewels, of inestimable value, and other objects were found by the Belgian archeologist Robert Sténuit and acquired by the museum in 1972. Dazzled visitors will come across the odd curiosity, such as a thin gold ring belonging to a Spanish officer that has *"No tengo mas que dar te"* ("I have nothing more to give you") engraved inside. A room on the third floor gives detailed information on the country's flora and fauna. On the fourth floor are paintings by many artists from Ireland and from elsewhere in Europe. Among the most striking in the collection are the images of the Giant's Causeway ▲ *312* by Andrew Nicol and Susannah Drury, some brilliant post-Impressionist works by George Campbell and Gerard Dillon, and William Conor's portrayal of the Belfast poor.

STORMONT (About 4 miles east of Belfast). The grand building in the classical style by A. Thornely was built in the early 1930's at the expense of the British government to be the Parliament and seat of government for Northern Ireland. So it remained until 1972. Today it houses the Northern Ireland Office.

STATUE OF VICTORIA
In the gardens of Donegall Square, Queen Victoria stands on a pedestal. At her feet are bronze figures symbolizing weaving and shipbuilding.

Bronze plaque with enamelwork and millefiori (Armagh, 8th century BC).

GIANT'S RING
Southwest of Belfast lie the woods and pastures of the Lagan Valley Regional Park, where the Giant's Ring dolmen stands. Surrounding what

was probably a place of worship is a circular earth rampart nearly 600 feet in diameter, 12 feet high and with a base 60 feet wide. The original dry-stone structure has long been overgrown, and has disappeared beneath earth and grass. At the center is the dolmen, under which a burial site has been discovered.

Cathedral of Downpatrick.

COUNTY DOWN

ARDS PENINSULA. East of Belfast, a long arm of land extends southward, separating Strangford Lough (below) from the Irish Sea. The narrow, winding road leading along the banks of the lough is of more interest than the eastern side of the peninsula. It leads through quiet countryside, between fuchsia hedges, passing waterside villages, castles and ruined abbeys. Before setting off, there are a number of things worth seeing. The fascinating ULSTER FOLK AND TRANSPORT MUSEUM ◆ *389* is at Cultra. Bangor has a marina, Donaghadee is a charming seaside resort, and BALLYCOPELAND has one of only two working windmills left in Ireland, dating from 1780. From NEWTOWNARDS, a market town known for its town hall and for the ruins of a Dominican priory, go west to the SCRABO COUNTRY PARK. This was designed by Charles Lanyon in 1857 for the Mountsteward family from Londonderry. On a hill is Scrabo Tower, with a climb of 125 steps to one of the finest views in the region. Crossing by causeway to Mahee Island, the remains of NENDRUM MONASTERY ● *92*, founded in the 5th century, lie within three concentric wards. There are the ruins of a church and a round tower from the 10th or 11th century, as well as a grand sundial. At the southern end of Strangford Lough is CASTLE WARD HOUSE (1762), built for Mr Bernard and Lady Anne Ward. The house is a masterpiece of architectural compromise. The front façade is classical, according to the tastes of Mr Bernard, and the rear is neo-Gothic, the choice of his wife Anne. The rooms also follow the two styles; the architect is unknown. The house and grounds (now a nature reserve) have been preserved and are administered by the National Trust. There are also farm buildings, a slaughterhouse, grain mill and laundry to visit. Concerts and recitals are held here during the summer. From the village of STRANGFORD there are boats to PORTAFERRY, a delightful harborside village which now has the Exploris Sea Aquarium. On the east bank of the lough lie the vast of GREYABBEY (1193) ● *96*. The church, in Early English style, consists only of a simple nave with no aisles. MOUNT STEWART HOUSE ★ was the Irish family seat of the Marquess of Londonderry; Viscount Castlereagh, the early 19th-century politician was born here. He is

said to have brought the twenty-two chairs (now in the dining room) used at the Congress of Vienna; each is embroidered with the coat of arms of the delegate and the country he represented (Wellington, Metternich, Talleyrand . . .). The house was built in two stages during the first half of the 19th century, on the site of a former family residence. London architect George Dance designed the west façade (1804–5), but the main part of the building was built to the neoclassical design of William Vitruvius Morrison, for the third marquess of Londonderry. The interior was redecorated by Edith, wife of the seventh marquess, who also created the gardens.

St Patrick's Country. In the graveyard of DOWNPATRICK CATHEDRAL , at the end of elegant English Street, a stone marks the possible burial place of Saint Patrick. On the other side of the River Quoile lie the ruins of INCH ABBEY, founded by John de Courcy in 1180 for a Cistercian order. At the center of the ruins the three breathtaking pointed windows of the chancel rise up. Further south, toward Ardglass, known for its herring fisheries and its "seven castles", the road crosses the source of the STRUELL, whose waters are said to possess strange powers. At Saintfield, to the northeast, lie the gardens of ROWALLANE, famous for their azaleas. Southwest is DUNDRUM CASTLE, a link in the powerful chain of defense created by the Norman John de Courcy. From the hill the imposing castle with circular keep overlooks the port of Dundrum, its defenses reinforced by a moat cut into the rock.

Mourne Mountains (below right). The prettiest landscape in County Down is provided by the Mourne Mountains, sloping gently toward the sea and the town of NEWCASTLE, on Dundrum Bay. Newcastle was a fashionable seaside resort but it now owes its reputation to the fame of its golf course. The Royal County Down Golf Club is considered to be one of the ten best courses in the world ◆ 354. This region of mountain and forests is marvelous for walking. Near to the summit of Slieve Croob, the highest of a range of mountains near Dromara, is the LEGANANNY TRIPOD-DOLMEN (above), the most remarkable in Ulster. Between Banbridge and Rathfriland is an area known as BRONTË COUNTRY, where Patrick, father of the writers, was born, worked and preached.

IRISH LINEN
When the Huguenots arrived in the Belfast region, they brought with them new weaving techniques. In 1698 the Huguenot Louis Cromelin, was asked by the king to improve and expand the Irish linen industry. His solution was to create a model weaving center at Lisburn, now virtually a suburb of southwest Belfast. The town became one of the centers of the Irish linen trade and during the 19th century was producing half the country's output. The Irish Linen Centre in Lisburn provides plenty of information.

TEMPLE OF THE WINDS
On a promontory east of Mount Stewart is the Temple of the Winds (1782–95), the only building in Ireland designed by James "Athenian" Stuart (1713–88). He was among the first architects in Europe to adopt the neoclassical style.

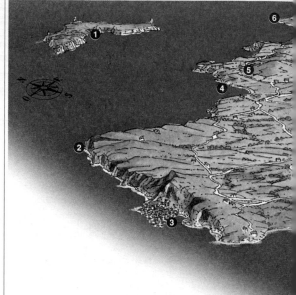

A MUCH-COVETED STRONGHOLD
Over a period of five hundred years Carrickfergus Castle was taken a number of times. First, John Lackland's siege subjugated his unruly barons. A little over a century later the Scottish soldiers of Edward Bruce spent a year wearing down the English defenses. Late in the Middle Ages the fortress was being used more for administrative purposes and fell into disrepair, until Schomberg took it for William III. It was from here that William began his campaign of 1690 ▲ *194*. The last action seen at the castle was in 1760 when it fell to Captain Thurot, leader of a French

expeditionary force, after a desperate resistance during which the defenders even resorted to tearing off their trouser buttons to use as amunition. A final episode in the history of Carrickfergus came in 1778, when it witnessed the engagement between John Paul Jones, founder of the American navy, with the British ship *HMS Drake*.

The long coast road offers spectacular views over the Irish Sea. It is bordered by red sandstone rocks worn by the sea, and white chalk cliffs, rich in fossils. Rising above are the Antrim Mountains, wind-blown and heather-covered moorland heights where grouse live in fear of buzzard and crow. To the north is the moonscape of the Giant's Causeway, stepping from the sea up to the cliffs, and the ancient territories of Sorley Boy MacDonnell with his romantic castle of Dunluce defying the seas and the elements that work daily to crumble the cliffs beneath its walls.

CARRICKFERGUS CASTLE

ON THE ROCK OF FERGUS. Carrickfergus Castle ◆ *384* stands on a rocky base that juts out from the north bank of Belfast Lough. It is the best-defended castle in Ulster and, along with Trim Castle ▲ *190*, one of the best-preserved Norman strongholds in Ireland. For centuries it has controlled traffic in and out of the lough, and it was of prime importance in the Norman conquest of Ulster led by John de Courcy, who first fortified the site between 1178 and 1204.
BEHIND THE RAMPARTS. De Courcy built the keep, which has its entrance on the first floor. The Great Chamber, on the second floor, has a fireplace, and was for the use of those of highest rank or station, while de Courcy probably occupied the third floor, which has a roof dating from the 16th century. The keep stood surrounded by wards and protected by high walls. The defenses were improved in the 13th century by the addition of a further rampart flanked by two solid towers on the northern side.
CHURCH OF ST NICHOLAS. In peacetime the soldiers would leave the castle to attend the Church of St Nicholas, in the town. Built from the 12th to the 16th century, the different phases of construction can be easily distinguished.

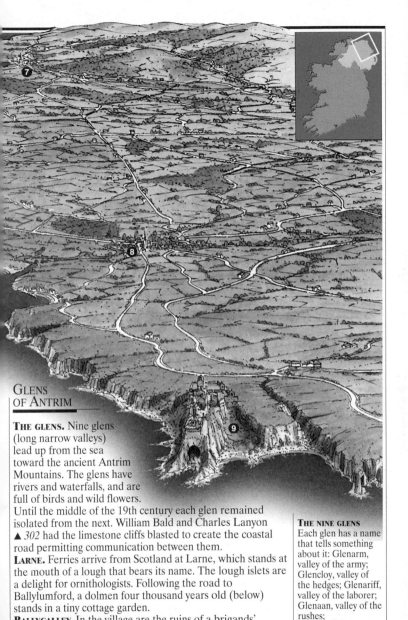

GLENS OF ANTRIM

THE GLENS. Nine glens (long narrow valleys) lead up from the sea toward the ancient Antrim Mountains. The glens have rivers and waterfalls, and are full of birds and wild flowers. Until the middle of the 19th century each glen remained isolated from the next. William Bald and Charles Lanyon ▲ *302* had the limestone cliffs blasted to create the coastal road permitting communication between them.

LARNE. Ferries arrive from Scotland at Larne, which stands at the mouth of a lough that bears its name. The lough islets are a delight for ornithologists. Following the road to Ballylumford, a dolmen four thousand years old (below) stands in a tiny cottage garden.

BALLYGALLEY. In the village are the ruins of a brigands' stronghold, a lovely beach and a castle. The latter is a Scottish baronial residence built in 1625 by James Shaw of Greenock and typical of the style favored by the Scots who came over to colonize the province in the early 17th-century "plantations". It is now a hotel, with a bar in the ancient keep (haunted, of course).

THE NINE GLENS
Each glen has a name that tells something about it: Glenarm, valley of the army; Glencloy, valley of the hedges; Glenariff, valley of the laborer; Glenaan, valley of the rushes; Glenballyeamon, Eamon's valley; Glencorp, valley of the slaughterer; Glendun, brown valley; Glenshesk, valley of the sedges; and Glentaisie, Taisie's valley (seductress of Rathlin Island, fought over by Vikings and natives).

Waterfall in Glenariff.

THE FLAVORS OF BALLYCASTLE
Dulse (an edible seaweed, to be chewed once it has been dried) and "yellow man" (a hard toffee) are two of the gastronomic treats to be sampled during the *Ould Lammas Fair* in Ballycastle.

GLENARM. Despite its coastal setting, dust fills the air of Glenarm, the oldest village in the glen. This comes from the adjacent limestone quarries. Glenarm Castle was the seat of the earls of Antrim. It is a peculiar and not very successful mixture of many styles, which can be entered by a bridge and mock-medieval gateway that was built in 1825.

CARNLOUGH. A charming little port at the lower end of Glencloy with an old posting inn inherited by Winston Churchill, the LONDONDERRY ARMS ◆ *384*. Over the road is a white stone bridge built for the railway that until the 1960's transported limestone from the quarries above down to the port. A little further north stands GARRON TOWER, a castellated mansion built in 1848, which would look more at home on the Rhine. It is the venue for a week-long summer seminar devoted to the literary traditions of the North.

GLENARIFF ★. In Glenariff Forest Park, which is bisected by the A43, is the enchanting woodland waterfall known as Ess na Larach.

RED BAY ★. The long bay curves round beyond Garron Point. It owes its name to the water that rushes down into it, which is colored by the surrounding sandstone hills. The distinctive outline of LURIGETHAN (1,150 feet), with steep sides and a flat top, can be seen in the distance.

CUSHENDALL. A delightful village at the bottom of three glens that has charmed many travelers. Thackeray noted that he dined well here on fish and beer. There is a red sandstone tower (1809) built to be "a place of confinement for idlers and rioters", and to the west, further up Glenaan, are ancient stone remains that have been wrongly called Ossian's Grave. Ossian was the warrior bard, son of Finn MacCoul ▲ *312*. Certainly, the contemporary poet John Hewitt (1907–87), who loved Cushendall best of all, wished it to be his burial place.

CUSHENDUN. Clough William-Ellis, architect of the Welsh seaside village of Portmerion (where the television series *The Prisoner* was filmed), designed a large part of Cushendun. The village is now listed and protected. The English poet John Masefield courted and married a young girl of Huguenot descent whose family owned CUSHENDUN'S CAVE HOUSE, which can be entered through a cave 200 feet long.

MURLOUGH BAY ★. The view over sloping green meadows down to the waters of Murlough Bay is idyllic, and the little white cottage that nestles beside the water must be the dream

of everyone who sees it. Halfway down to the bay, amid the grass and buttercups, is a memorial to Sir Roger Casement, a man decorated for his humanitarian work, but eventually stripped of all honors and hanged for treason.

FAIR HEAD. The spectacular promontory, known for the good trout fishing offered by its loughs, is at the extreme northeast of Ireland, ending in 600-foot-high cliffs looking out to the Scottish islands. There are traces of prehistoric dwellings (in particular a *crannóg* ● *90*), around Fair Head. The cliffs can be reached either by a narrow road winding between fuchsia hedges, or else by Grey Man's Path, which leads walkers over broken rocky surfaces that seem to have been shattered by a giant's footsteps.

BONAMARGY. The ruins of a friary, founded in the year 1500 and once thatched, lie to the east of Ballycastle. In a vault in the church are buried Sorley Boy MacDonnell and his descendants, the earls of Antrim.

BALLYCASTLE. The two valleys of Glenshesk and Glentaisie meet at Ballycastle, an agreeable port with boats to Rathlin Island. Marconi's assistants received the first radio messages here from the lighthouse on Rathlin Island, later to be used to inform insurance companies of the safe passage of ships. In June every year Ballycastle hosts the *Fleadh Amhráin Agus Rince*, three days of traditional music and dancing, and at the end of August the *Ould Lammas Fair* takes place, the oldest fair in Ireland ◆ *337*.

RATHLIN ISLAND. One hundred people live on the L-shaped island. Puffins and guillemots crowd onto the ledges of its high cliff, near the lighthouse at the western end, to nest and breed. The reedy loughs offer plenty of brown trout, and wild flowers sparkle in the pastures. There is a guest house, a restaurant, a pub and a social center ready to welcome and entertain visitors, whether their arrival is intended or forced upon them by stormy seas. Robert Bruce (1274–1329), crowned King of Scotland in 1306, exiled himself to Rathlin Island after his defeat at the hands of the English at Methven. It was here that a determined spider, trying again and again to make her web on the slippery wet walls of his cave inspired him to find courage to take up arms again.

CHILDREN OF LIR
A legend recounts how the four children of Lir, the sea god, were changed into swans by their stepmother. In one

version they were forced to swim in the rough waters of the sea of Moyle, between the Irish coast and Rathlin Island.

SIR ROGER CASEMENT
Casement grew up in the region, and was knighted for his humanitarian work in the Belgian Congo and Putumayo, Peru. He was arrested on the Kerry coast during World War One, after landing in a German submarine. He had hoped to bring the Kaiser's support to Sinn Féin and the Nationalist cause. His diaries, which also describe homosexual practices, were long suppressed, and their authenticity is still in question.

311

It comes as no surprise to learn that the Giant's Causeway has been included in a list of World Heritage Sites since 1987: it is one of the wonders of the natural world. According to legend, it was made by a giant; it is now known that sixty million years ago underground volcanic explosions sent up molten basalt that solidified into these polygonal columns of rock.

GIANT-SIZE STORIES
One well-known legend has it that Finn MacCoul built the causeway to bring over his love, a giantess, from the Hebrides. In another version the giant was involved in a long-distance quarrel with a Scottish giant called Fingal. Unable to settle their differences, the two were preparing for battle, but had not yet met. They began by emitting hostile roars at one another over the Irish Sea. Finn constructed the causeway, certain that his enemy had begun his on the other side (there are, in fact, similar rock formations on the Hebridean islands of Iona, Staffa and Mull). He ventured forward but when he heard the heavy tread of Fingal's approach, he retreated in fright to Antrim. His wife, Oonagh, helped him to make a huge cot in which he disguised himself as a baby. Fingal arrived and saw the size of what he thought was Finn MacCoul's child and, imagining how big the father must be, he quickly made his way back home across the causeway. Finn grasped a sod of earth, leaving a crater that formed Lough Neagh ▲ *324*, and threw it after his retreating opponent. The clod missed, fell into the sea, and remained there as the Isle of Man.

A GEOLOGICAL PHENOMENON

There are about forty thousand columns of basalt fitting together so perfectly that only the thinnest cracks remain visible between them. They form cliffs and irregular surfaces, and the molten basalt continues beneath the sea. It was on these reefs that the Spanish galleon *Girona* sank in 1588 ▲ *315*.

TOURISM

Naturally enough the causeway has always held a fascination for local people, but it was not until the 18th century that large numbers of travelers as well as scientists began to visit, among them Sir Walter Scott and Thackeray. In 1883 the new railway from Belfast increased tourism further still.

NAMES

The causeway's different geological formations have come to be known by special names, usually linked with legend: "Giant's Organ", "Giant's Well", "Giant's Cannon", "Chimney Point", "Wishing Chair", "Giant's Gateway", "Lord Antrim's Parlour" and "Lady's Fan".

Although he didn't like being hounded as a tourist when he visited the causeway, Thackeray was still impressed: "When the world was moulded and fashioned out of formless chaos, this must have been the *bit over* – a remnant of chaos." (*The Irish Sketchbook*, 1843)

BETWEEN SEA AND SKY
West of Dunineny Castle, the coast road passes a path leading to the Carrick-a-Rede rope bridge, which crosses a gap of 65 feet over an 80-foot chasm between the cliff and a basalt pillar. It is in place between April and September and is used by salmon fishermen for their nets.

Sir John Perrot, reputed to be the son of Henry VIII.

CAUSEWAY COAST

DUNINENY CASTLE. Remains of the castle where Sorley Boy MacDonnell lived until his death in 1590 are scattered over the cliffs west of Ballycastle. His brother Colla's stronghold, the castle of Kinbane ("white head"), set high above the sea, is a more picturesque and impressive ruin.

BALLINTOY. The road to Ballintoy, a bright and breezy little port, passes a most eccentric house built by an artist determined to have unrivaled views. At PORTBRADDAN is the tiny church of St Gobhan (not alone in its claim to be the smallest in Ireland). It sits huddled at the cliff base, west of the crescent of sand that borders White Park Bay.

DUNSEVERICK CASTLE. Ireland's oldest love story is about Deirdre who ran away with Naoise, the bodyguard of King Conor, her betrothed. She was tricked into returning to Dunseverick; her lover was betrayed and assassinated, and she killed herself. The present-day ruins, which can also be reached by footpath from the Giant's Causeway, only date from the 16th century.

BUSHMILLS ● *78.* West of the causeway is the small village of Bushmills. Through it runs the River Bush, known for its good fishing. The village itself has established a reputation for its marvelous peat-flavored whiskey, and the air is sweet with its fumes.

The first license to distill whiskey was accorded in 1608 to Sir Thomas Phillips, but the earliest records of distilling go back to 1276.

DUNLUCE CASTLE ★ ◆ 384. The romantic ruins of Dunluce Castle cling to the top of a rocky promontory, above cliffs that drop 100 feet to the water below. The castle is cut off from land by a vast cave that runs beneath the promontory, making access only possible by bridge. The cave can be visited by boat. It may have been the MacQuillan family who first took advantage of the natural defensive position and fortified it. In the 16th century it fell into the hands of the MacDonnells, a clan of Scottish origin who had obtained large amounts of land in the region. In 1584, during Sorley Boy MacDonnell's occupation, the castle was taken by Sir John Perrot after a lengthy siege, but the crafty Sorley Boy got one of his men to infiltrate the castle staff and used baskets to get his soldiers onto the cliffs where they were able to take control of the fortress once again. The earls of Antrim, descendants of MacDonnell who had subsequently made peace with the English, abandoned the castle in 1690 after the Battle of the Boyne, because they had donated their fortune to the cause of James II. The security of its position encouraged the building of an elaborate and relatively luxurious castle. It once had four ROUND TOWERS joined by an outer wall, two of which have survived. The one that looks out over the sea (Maeve's Tower) is said to have sheltered a fairy. The style of the towers and gables of the fortified gateway to the southeast leave no doubt as to the Scottish origins of the MacDonnells. The fortifications facing toward land made it possible to scrutinize visitors before permitting them to enter over what was then a drawbridge. A Renaissance-style LOGGIA is an unusual feature, and the only one in Ireland of this type of structure. At the right-hand corner is a Great Hall with three mullioned windows in the west wall that appear to date from the 17th century.

PORTBALLINTRAE. At this seaside resort, and also in its more crowded and noisier neighbor Portrush, one of the most exciting expeditions available is a deep-sea fishing trip in a hired boat, or else a tour of the caves around the Giant's Causeway, Portcoon and Runkerry.

PORTSTEWART. The peaceful resort lying on the eastern bank of the Bann estuary is an alternative to the brashness of Portrush.

DOWNHILL. Buildings along the cliff were erected by Frederick Augustus Hervey, whose estate was here. This Anglican Bishop of Derry ▲ 319, who became Earl of Bristol, was immensely wealthy. On the edge of the cliff is MUSSENDEN TEMPLE, built by Hervey in 1785 in honor of his cousin Mrs Mussenden: it became her memorial. The eccentric bishop allowed the local Catholic priest to say mass in it weekly. It is possible to walk along the sand dunes all the way to MAGILLIGAN POINT where there is a Martello tower ● 101.

The three *Bushmills* whiskey labels.

DISASTER
On the seaward side of the promontory on which Dunluce Castle stands is a court surrounded on three sides by buildings once occupied by servants. Apparently, in 1639, the northern end of the promontory crumbled into the sea, taking the kitchens and seven servants with it.

DANGEROUS ROCKS
Having rounded Ramore Head, the captain of the Spanish galleon *Girona*, escaping after the humiliating defeat of the Armada, mistook the chimneys of the Giant's Causeway ▲ 313 for those of Dunluce Castle, where he hoped to find refuge. The ship sank off Port na Spanniagh late in the summer of 1588. The Belgian archeologist Robert Sténuit held underwater searches for the wreck and succeeded in bringing up its treasure and other remains, now on display in the Ulster Museum, Belfast ▲ 305.

In 1588 Philip II of Spain sent an Armada of 130 vessels to invade England. After a number of engagements in the Channel, in which they were outdone by Elizabeth's ships and failed to land a single man on English soil, the Spanish fleet fled north to round Scotland and Ireland and regain the Atlantic. Between September 16 and October 26 violent storms sank twenty-seven ships off the coast of Ireland. Far from welcoming the Spaniards as allies, the Celtic chieftains killed the shipwrecked sailors and took all they could from the capsized galleons.

TREASURE OF THE SPANISH GRANDEES
They lost all their riches in the wrecks: a fabulous collection of gold and silver objects.

CARNAGE
On September 18, George Carew was able to assure Sir Francis Walsingham that the three thousand men who had swum to shore had all been massacred and two thousand had drowned between Loughfoyle and Dingle.

The galleons were powered by sail and oars, and had a formidable battery of arms.

SPAIN HUMILIATED

What Philip II of Spain (below) had envisaged as a second Lepanto ended in utter disaster. On learning of the sinking of his ships he is said to have remarked that he had sent them to do battle with the English, not the elements.

BITTER RIVALRY

The emnity between the two countries involved both religion and politics. The Catholic Philip II of Spain and the Protestant Elizabeth I of England (above) were struggling for control of the Atlantic, which was of strategic importance to both countries. Spain wanted to protect the routes to its colonies, while England wanted to remove all obstacles to its flourishing maritime trade.

"RULE BRITANNIA"

The defeat of the Armada resulted in an enormous expansion in the English economy, to Ireland's cost.

D erry lies on the gentle slopes that
descend to the banks of the River
Foyle. It still has well-preserved 17th-
century town walls, but is deeply marked
by a turbulent past. The city was founded
in the 6th century, and is today the second
largest in Northern Ireland.

HISTORY

THE MAP OF DERRY
In the old center of
Derry the streets are
laid out on a grid, a
common feature of
twenty-three other
towns in the province
which goes back to

the "plantations".
Roads radiate from a
central square called
the Diamond,
crossing each other at
right-angles and
leading to four gates
in the city walls.
Philadelphia was also
laid out on this plan,
which was originally
inspired by the
French town of Vitry-
le-François.

THE SIEGE OF DERRY
In 1689, behind the
unbreached walls of
the town, seven
thousand people died
of hunger in the
longest siege in Irish
history. The
Protestant inhabitants
managed to resist the
Jacobite army until a
boat carrying
provisions, the
Mountjoy, managed to
break through the
blockade on the
River Foyle, thereby
saving the town.
The memory of the
siege is perpetuated
in the Loyalist
political slogan
"No surrender",
which was used then
for the first time.

CELTIC AND CHRISTIAN ROOTS. In legend,
the tribe of the Tuatha Dé Dannan, so fair that they
could not bear the sight of their own reflection, took
refuge in the bowels of the earth. The entrance
was at the mouth of the River Foyle, where
Derry stands today. What is known for certain is
that Saint Columba ▲ *295* came in around 546 and
founded a monastery at the heart of the *diore*, the
oak wood that covered the hillside. The wood gave the town
its name, and Columba is its patron saint. The monastery
flourished for two hundred years, until the arrival of the
Vikings.
THE "PLANTATIONS" ● *51.* James I came to the throne in 1603
and gave new impetus to the colonization of Ulster with the
"plantations". Not averse to using either flattery or force, he
persuaded members of the London craft guilds (such as
drapers and vintners) to set up business in Derry along with
their workers. This is why in 1613 it was rebaptized
Londonderry.
THE SIEGE. After holding out against Royalist troops for
twenty weeks in 1649, the city was relieved. In 1688 Derry, a
garrison town, was threatened with a regiment of Catholic

troops. The town
did not dare declare
open opposition to
King James II, but
in the December a
handful of
apprentice boys
closed the city
gates. In March of
the following year
James II's troops besieged Derry and did not retreat until
July, after 105 days of siege.
THE "TROUBLES" ● *64.* In 1968 Derry was witnessing a
growing civil rights movement, demanding equal treatment,
both political and social, for the Catholics in a city where the
Protestants were dominant. The first demonstration march
was felt by the authorities to be provocation, so they refused
permission for it to take place within the city walls. As a result
the outlying district of the BOGSIDE, Catholic and working-
class, was the setting for what deteriorated into a riot. The
Bogside became a "no-go area" and was barricaded from
1969 to 1972 as a reaction to assaults on police and Loyalists.
But January 30, 1972, Bloody Sunday, is the day most deeply
engraved on the memory of the Catholic community of Derry
(center, top). Murals at the bottom of Westland Street honor
the memory of the thirteen people who died, killed by British
paratroopers. On a housefront in the Bogside the words

Bishop's Gate.

painted during the 1969 riots remain as a monument: "You are now entering Free Derry."

VISITING THE TOWN

ST COLUMBA'S LONG TOWER CHURCH. (Outside the walls.) This was the first Catholic church to be built after the Reformation and the "plantations", and has superb neo-Renaissance decoration. It was built on the site of the great Teampull Mor ("big church") which dated from 1164 and was mostly destroyed in the 17th century. Only its tall tower stood for longer, from which this church takes its name.

THE WALLS ● 100. Derry was the last fortified town to be built in Ireland and it has the best-preserved old walls of any town in Europe. A walk around them provides lovely views of the city, the River Foyle estuary, and the surrounding countryside. The way up is at SHIPQUAY GATE, a dour three-arched gateway, and from there the wall can be walked as far as FERRYQUAY GATE, which is decorated with the carved busts of heroes of the siege. On the other side of Artillery Street and St Columba 's Cathedral is BISHOP'S GATE. This was rebuilt as a triumphal arch in honor of William of Orange in 1789.

BISHOP'S STREET. On this street stand the COURT HOUSE (1817) and the MASONIC HALL. The latter was once the Bishop's Palace, rebuilt by Bishop Frederick Augustus Hervey, fourth earl of Bristol, and a man so rich and enamored of travel that across the whole of Europe businessmen renamed their hotels *Bristol* in the hope of increasing their clientele ▲ *315*.

ORANGE PARADES
The Battle of the Boyne ▲ *194* intensified religious antagonism in Ireland, and all the weight of collective memory can be felt during the annual Orange marches held on July 12, "The Twelfth" ● *70*, commemorating the Battle of the Boyne, and August 12, the Apprentice Boys' March. Over recent years the two events have been the

occasion of some violent and dreadful demonstrations, and there is no doubt that tensions between the Catholic and Loyalist communities are always heightened at these times. Murals in the mainly Protestant Waterside district show the victory of King Billy (William of Orange).

The gentle curves of the Sperrin Mountains (formed of schist and gneiss) that lie southwest of Derry. The highest peak is Mount Sawel (2,240 feet).

The tower of the Protestant cathedral of St Columba has a spire that was added in the 19th century.

"Singing pub" ◆ 346 in Strabane.

"DANNY BOY"
The notes of the "Londonderry Air" were taken down by Miss Jane Ross when she heard it played by a traveling violinist at Limavady, 16 miles east of Derry. It is not known why Irish emigrants to the United States took up this song in particular, which was a special favorite at funerals.

ST COLUMBA'S CATHEDRAL. Behind the Court House stands the first specifically Protestant cathedral to have been erected in Ireland after the Reformation (1633). The pure, well-balanced style of which it is an excellent example came to be known as "Planter's Gothic". It has remarkable stained-glass windows and the locks and keys of the original town gates are kept here, as well as souvenirs of the siege.

SHIPQUAY STREET. On the far side of the Diamond, the central square, Shipquay Street climbs steeply uphill. Off it are some of the loveliest streets within the walls, and in one is the DERRY CRAFT VILLAGE. There are Georgian housefronts to admire and, near to the top of the hill, the BELFAST TELEGRAPH BUILDING, which was once the Wesleyan Chapel.

THE TOWER MUSEUM. The little museum has audiovisual displays explaining the history of Derry. A new center, "The Fifth Province", opens in 1995, exploring the role of the Celtic peoples in the history of civilization.

THE GUILDHALL. The neo-Gothic building (1912) stands alongside the river and was once the town hall. The stained-glass windows telling the history of Derry are worth studying.

AROUND DERRY

AMELIA EARHEART COTTAGE. Three miles from the town is a little cottage with a museum dedicated to the woman known as Lady Lindbergh, the first woman to make a solo flight across the Atlantic (1932). (Take the A6.)

DUNGIVEN PRIORY ★. The 12th-century Augustinian priory has an intricately carved tomb against the south wall of the church. On it can be seen an armed man (probably one of the O'Cahan chiefs, Cooey-na-Gall, who died in 1385) along with six Scottish mercenaries in kilts. (Take the B74.)

BANAGHER ★. There is a remarkable ancient carving on a small stone burial vault in the graveyard, depicting an ecclesiastic holding a cross and raising his other hand in blessing.

DERRY TO ARMAGH

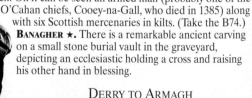

STRABANE. The town has long been a center of printing and publishing and was extremely active in the 18th century. It was here that John Dunlap learnt his trade (Gray's Printing Press); he went on to be the first man to print the American Declaration of Independence. Strabane is also the

birthplace
of the writer and
journalist Flann O'Brien ▲ *129*.

ULSTER HISTORY PARK (Culion). Like Craggaunowen ▲ *244*
and Ferrycarrig ▲ *180*, the park offers a number of life-size
reconstructions of different structural types to have been
erected in Ireland over the last six thousand years or more.
They include a Stone Age camp, late Stone Age megalithic
tombs, a *rath* ● *91*, a *crannóg* ● *90*, a Christian monastery
from the late Middle Ages ● *92*, Norman defenses and
Planter houses.

ULSTER AMERICAN FOLK PARK. Over the last two centuries the
port of Derry has witnessed the departure of many thousands
of emigrants. The second major exodus, when Catholics were
forced to leave during the Great Famine, is probably the most
famous ● *58*. But it should not be forgotten that in the 18th
century there were many Presbyterians whom King James had
encouraged to leave Scotland for the north of Ireland and
who then emigrated once more: 250,000 of them crossed the
Atlantic. The Ulster American Folk Park tells the story of all
these emigrants, beginning with the cottage of Thomas
Mellon, who left for America in the 1820's (it is one of his
descendants, Andrew Mellon, who created the park). It has
many reconstructed sites: typical Irish country dwellings of
the 19th century and the kind of homes they would have lived
in once they had arrived in America. One thought-provoking
creation is an Irish quayside rebuilt just as it was, from which
visitors can board a boat and disembark from the other side
onto an American quay of the same period. (Take the A505 at
Omagh.)

BEAGHMORE. On moorland at the edge of the Sperrin
Mountains, in County Tyrone, are some enigmatic circles of
standing stones. From the way they are laid out, it seems
possible that they were for some kind of fertility rite.
(Return to the A5.)

**IRISH AT THE
WHITE HOUSE**
Once their feet were
on American soil, the
Irish emigrants
quickly adapted to
their new life. Some
of them, such as
Ulysses S. Grant,
hero of the American
Civil War (above),
went on to reach the
highest echelons of
power: the north of
Ireland provided the
United States with a
dozen presidents.
Other emigrants such
as Robert Ross chose
more original ways to
achieve their
ambitions: he rode
into the White House
on horseback and set
fire to the Capitol
during the night of
August 24, 1814.

NEAR THIS SPOT
ON THE NORTH SIDE OF THE GREAT CHURCH
WAS LAID THE BODY OF
BRIAN BOROIMHE
SLAIN AT CLONTARF. A.D. MXIV.

THE STORY OF MACHA
Cruinnuig, the owner of much land in Ulster, forced his wife Macha, who could run as fast as the wind, to race against the horse of Conor, King of Ulster, during the annual gathering of Ulates. Macha was about to give birth and asked the king for a postponement, but he refused. She won the race and then gave birth to twins (*emain* in Gaelic). Before dying she cursed all the men of Ulster to

NAVAN FORT. This was the ancient capital of Ulster, seat of its kings. "Emain Macha" ("Macha's twins") was, according to legend, founded by Macha as her palace and refuge. It was here that the legendary King Conor MacNessa presided over the court of the Knights of the Red Branch, guarded by the young warrior Cú Chulainn. It is here, as well, that Deirdre, who killed herself at Dunseverick, near the Giant's Causeway, first saw her lover Naoise ▲ *314*.

This place also provided the framework for the tales of the great deeds of the warriors told in the *Tain*. What can be seen today is a mound on top of a hill, surrounded by an earth rampart and a ditch. Such a configuration suggests that the site is of ritual rather than defensive importance. The mound that tops the hill has been excavated, and successive occupations going back to 700 BC have been traced. The remains of five concentric circles of large wooden posts were found set around a central mast. In about 100 BC this odd structure seems to have been roofed over. It was subsequently filled with stones and the posts burned, probably in a huge ritual fire. What remained became covered with earth and grass, and forms the mound visible today. In the Interpretative Centre nearby, the eventful past of Navan Fort is brought alive with imaginative modern techniques. Other monuments and discoveries in the surrounding area indicate that Navan Fort was a place of religious significance. This might explain its diminishing importance once Saint Patrick brought his new religion to Armagh.

suffer the pains of childbirth, exempting only children, youths and Cú Chulainn.

ARMAGH

The name Armagh comes from the Irish "Ard Macha" ("hill of Macha"). It is the ecclesiastical capital of all Ireland. Like Dublin, it has handsome Georgian buildings. The architect Francis Johnston (1760–1829), a native of the city, left his mark on both places. Armagh is dominated by the two cathedrals, Catholic and Protestant, facing each other from adjacent hills.

THE MALL. The oval tree-lined green at the center of Armagh was once used as a racecourse. Prisoners also used to walk across it, from the Court House at one end to the prison at the

> "THERE IS A THROUGH-OTHERNESS ABOUT ARMAGH
> OF TOWER AND STEEPLE, UP ON THE HILL ARE THE ARGUING
> GRAVES OF THE KINGS AND BELOW ARE THE PEOPLE."
>
> W.R. RODGERS

other (now closed). These days, on summer evenings, people play cricket here. The Mall is bordered by some Georgian houses with fine façades, among them one housing the ARMAGH COUNTY MUSEUM (east side) and another, MUSEUM OF THE ROYAL IRISH FUSILIERS (north side), both full of town history. From the northern end of the square, College Hill leads to the OBSERVATORY founded in 1790 by Archbishop Robinson, who was also responsible for general improvements to the town's layout and appearance. There is also a Planetarium where interesting exhibitions are mounted.

ST PATRICK'S CATHOLIC CATHEDRAL.

The cathedral (below right), with its two symmetrical towers, was built between 1840 and 1873. Inside, it is entirely covered with mosaic decoration, giving it a Byzantine air. In the sacristy is a clock still awaiting collection by the winner of a lottery held to raise funds for completion of the building work after the Great Famine ● *58.*

ST PATRICK'S PROTESTANT CATHEDRAL.

Much restoration work was done to the medieval Church of Ireland cathedral late in the 19th century. It stands near to the spot where Saint Patrick founded his church in 447. Armagh was his first episcopal see. The chapterhouse contains some interesting pre-Christian carved figures, including one that is called *St Patrick* and another representing Queen Macha, her breasts bare. High up on the cathedral walls are grotesque carved heads. An exterior wall bears a tablet recording that Brian Boru ● *49* was buried nearby. The CATHEDRAL LIBRARY (1771) in Abbey Street has some interesting rare editions, among them a copy of *Gulliver's Travels* annotated by Swift himself, but it no longer has the *Book of Armagh* ▲ *151,* pawned for £5 in the 17th century.

ST PATRICK'S TRIAN.

The Interpretative Centre gives an account of Armagh's history and also has a children's display recreating Jonathan Swift's land of Lilliput. Swift spent time at Gosford Castle, about 6 miles to the southeast.

ARCHBISHOP'S PALACE.

The palace itself now houses the District Council Offices. In the grounds are the ruins of a Franciscan friary (1263) and the Palace Stables Heritage Centre which consists of the tackroom, carriage house and hayloft, with an audiovisual presentation.

"ROAD BOWLING"

The game, also called "bullet", originally came from Holland. It was once popular in many areas but is now only played in Cork and Armagh. It takes place on a road with plenty of bends. An iron ball weighing nearly two pounds is

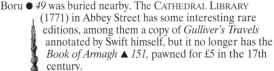

thrown along one-and-a-half miles of turns and curves. Whoever completes the course with the fewest throws is the winner. The bowler is preceded by a tactician who stands at the corners, legs

apart, and points out where the ball should be aimed in order to get round the bend. Games are held on summer Sundays. The championships take place in August.

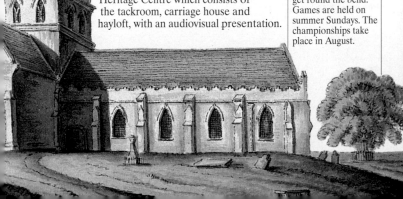

THE ORANGE ORDER
It was formed in 1795 after the Battle of the Diamond, near Loughgall, where Catholic Defenders fought with an

AROUND ARMAGH

LOUGHGALL. The village lies at the heart of Ireland's main fruit-growing region, best explored in May when the apple trees are in bloom. In Loughgall is a small museum dealing with the creation of the Orange Order here in 1795 ▲ *195*.

ARGORY AND ARDRESS HOUSES. About 3 miles northeast of Armagh, among the apple orchards (left), are two fine houses: ARGORY (1824), which is still lit by acetylene gas, and ARDRESS HOUSE, a small 17th-century country house enlarged in the 18th century and decorated with stuccowork by Michael Stapleton representing the four seasons ● *106*.

organized group of Protestants devoted to hounding Catholics out of the area. The latter, the "Peep O'Day Boys", seem to have evolved into the new Orange Order. The color orange was chosen in memory of William of Orange (William III), who had fought the Catholics, and the stated aim of the Order was to support the king and his heirs as long as they in turn supported the Protestants. It was officially dissolved in 1820, but survived by adopting a system of lodges, in the Masonic tradition, and is still active today.

LOUGH NEAGH. The counties of Armagh, Antrim, Derry and Tyrone all border Lough Neagh, the largest lake in the British Isles. It is approximately 18 miles long and 11 miles wide. Ten rivers flow into it and one, the Bann, flows out northward. The banks cannot be walked, but to the south is PEATLANDS PARK, a peat-bog nature reserve which can be visited on a small railway and offers information on the ecological, economic and social significance of turf in Ireland ■ *36*. Lough Neagh has enormous numbers of wild fowl, especially duck in winter, and ARBOE is one of the best points from which to observe the birds. For those more interested in ancient remains, there is also a tall CELTIC HIGH CROSS at Arboe. Near Portadown is OXFORD ISLAND. This has the Lough Neagh Discovery Centre ◆ *385* for those wishing to explore further. At Toomebridge, to the north, are the largest eel fisheries in Europe.

MOY. The ruins of the Charlemont star fort, built in 1602 by Mountjoy, Queen Elizabeth's Lord Deputy, overlook the River Blackwater. On the other side is the village of Moy where one of the biggest horse fairs in Ireland used to be held, attended by bloodstock agents from all over Europe.

BENBURB. In 1615 Sir Richard Wingfield built a castle here, and it still stands overlooking the Benburb Valley Park, which lies along the banks of the River Blackwater. The Benburb Valley Heritage Centre is housed in a 19th-century linen-weaving workshop and concentrates on the industrial and social history of the area.

The cows at Argory are *moils*, a rare old Irish breed ■ *42*.

The loughs, islands and wooded scenery of the Lake
District of County Fermanagh make it a romantic and
mysterious place. The waters are a challenge to the
fisherman's skill, but promise a rewarding catch. For others
they simply provide enchanting scenery. County Cavan,
which touches the southern end of Upper Lough Erne, is also
famous for its lakes and woodland.

ENNISKILLEN

The county town of Fermanagh is the town of Enniskillen, set
strategically on an island in a narrowing of Lough Erne.
MAIN STREET. The principal thoroughfare winds its way
through the town under several different names, as though it
were imitating the course of the River Erne. Along it stand
large business
buildings (note the
pointed forged-iron
pickets that stick
out along the lower
windows to
persuade cattle and
loafers to keep their
distance on busy
fair days), also the
COURT HOUSE, the
PRESBYTERIAN
CHURCH and the
offices of the local
paper, *The
Impartial Reporter*.
THE HILLS. On one
hill stands the Town
Hall, which has
niches displaying statues to represent the town's two British
regiments: the Inniskilling Dragoons and the Royal
Inniskilling Fusiliers. On another hill stand the Catholic
CHURCH OF ST MICHAEL, with a window dedicated to Saint
Molaise, and the Methodist church. On Church Street is the
Protestant CATHEDRAL OF ST MACCARTIN, much of it 17th
century.
BUTTER MARKET. Down the hill on the north shore of the
island is the old BUTTER MARKET, now occupied by craft
workshops. Among the more unusual items offered are flies
for trout fishing ◆ *356*, casts of sculptures and religious
artefacts, both pagan and Christian.
ENNISKILLEN CASTLE. Near to Castle Bridge is the Watergate.
It was built in 1612 by Sir William Cole, to whom the town
had been given after the Tyrone rebellion. He used the castle
of the Maguires (local Irish chiefs renowned for their
excesses) as the basis for his own building. In the keep is the
MUSEUM OF THE ROYAL INNISKILLING FUSILIERS. The COUNTY
MUSEUM, with which it is associated, along with the Heritage
Centre, shop and café, is housed in the same complex. The

KEY POSITION
A statue of Major
General Galbraith
Lowry Cole
(1772–1840), erected
in 1857, surveys the
isle of Enniskillen.
From high on his
Doric column set in
the middle of Fort
Hill gardens, he
overlooks the
meandering River
Erne. There are 107
steps to climb,
winding up the inside
of the column, before
one reaches the stone
general brandishing
his sword.

Siege of Enniskillen
in 1594.

325

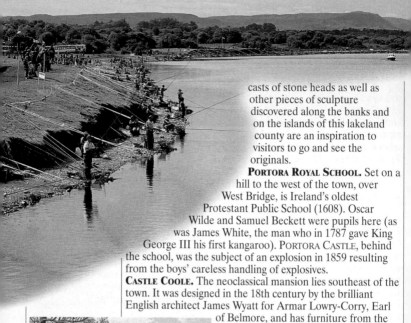

casts of stone heads as well as other pieces of sculpture discovered along the banks and on the islands of this lakeland county are an inspiration to visitors to go and see the originals.

PORTORA ROYAL SCHOOL. Set on a hill to the west of the town, over West Bridge, is Ireland's oldest Protestant Public School (1608). Oscar Wilde and Samuel Beckett were pupils here (as was James White, the man who in 1787 gave King George III his first kangaroo). PORTORA CASTLE, behind the school, was the subject of an explosion in 1859 resulting from the boys' careless handling of explosives.

CASTLE COOLE. The neoclassical mansion lies southeast of the town. It was designed in the 18th century by the brilliant English architect James Wyatt for Armar Lowry-Corry, Earl of Belmore, and has furniture from the period and marvelous plasterwork.

Castle Coole is the most splendid example of a neoclassical country house in Ireland. Completed in 1798, the house is built from pure Portland stone. It was given to the National Trust in 1951, and they have recently completed an expensive course of restoration and redecoration.

EARTHLY PARADISE
In May the islands on Lough Erne are covered in bluebells and celandines. At this time, trout fishermen arrive to spend patient days on their boats casting with real mayflies, blown by the wind onto the water, to tempt their prey. This kind of fly-fishing is called "dapping"
◆ 357.

LOWER LOUGH ERNE

DEVENISH ISLAND ★. Lower Lough Erne, north of Enniskillen, has a number of holy islands. Devenish Island, green and deserted, lies at a widening of the lough near its southern end. On it is one of the finest monastic sites in Northern Ireland. As with most monastic settlements, there is a ROUND TOWER (12th century), used as a lookout. It has interesting windows and a remarkable cornice decorated with a frieze. In the 1970's the foundation of a second round tower was discovered, probably of earlier date. Nearby are the walls of the ORATORY OF ST MOLAISE, which no doubt once held the remains of the saint who established the monastery in the 6th century. Judging from its decoration, it is 12th century, and it once had a stone roof which collapsed about two hundred years ago. Unlike some monasteries, this one flourished in the Middle Ages, despite Viking raids. Down the hill, toward the landing stage, is TEAMPULL MOR ("big church") which has a lovely window clearly dating it from the 13th century, although it was enlarged about one hundred years later. On the island's highest point sits the ABBEY CHURCH OF ST MARY. A priory was built here for Augustinians in the 15th century, with a tower and cloister to the north. A CROSS with intricate carving, possibly also 15th century, stands nearby, outlined against the sky. Lastly there is a small MUSEUM, with a display of Roman coins and a detailed history of the monastery.

TULLY CASTLE. Just after Inishmacsaint ("plain of sorrel island") the colonial fortified dwelling comes into view. It was built in 1613 and is one of a number of residences built by English and Scottish colonials drawn to the area for its rich and fertile soil. Tully and Monea (take the B81 toward Enniskillen) were links in a defensive chain that included Crom, Portora, Enniskillen, Archdale, Crevenish and Caldwell. Unfortunately most of these fortified dwellings were burned down in devastating fires. (Beyond Monea on the B81, turn left after Derrygonnelly onto the road to Lough Navar.)

CLIFFS OF MAGHO. The 1,000-foot cliffs in the Navar Forest Park offer a magnificent view over Lough Erne as far as the Atlantic, taking in both Boa Island and Castle Caldwell.

BELLEEK. The village is situated on the Erne at the point where it becomes a river once again. Since 1857 a special porcelain has been made here. It is a fine and delicate lustreware.

CASTLE CALDWELL. Visitors may be lucky enough to see terns nesting in the nature reserve. Less elusive is the stone violin carved at the gateway to the ruined castle in memory of a drunken violinist who was drowned nearby, and is accompanied, not surprisingly, with a verse warning of the incompatibility of boating and boozing.

BOA ISLAND. The road runs through Boa Island at the northern end of Lough Erne over bridges at either side. In Caldragh cemetery, hidden among untended greenery, is the extraordinary two-faced statue known as the Janus Figure (right). Next to it is a smaller statue called "Lusty Man".

WHITE ISLAND. Further north, on the east bank (boat from Castle Archdale), White Island is known for seven enigmatic and unsettling statues and a mask dating from between the 8th and 10th centuries. They were found in 1928 and are displayed on the wall of an ancient church. Most of the figures are Christian but one is a *sheela-na-gig* ▲ 244.

BELLEEK PORCELAIN
John Caldwell Bloomfield created a particular type of pottery made in Belleek that has earned an

international reputation for its fine decoration and delicate glaze. Caldwell Bloomfield decided to go into the ceramics business in 1857, when he realized that all the necessary raw materials were available locally (felspar, kaolin, flint, clay, schist and turf). A visit to the workshops can be arranged.

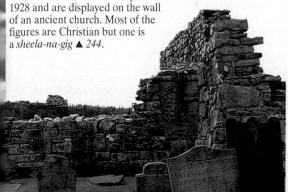

"I let the boat drift
. . . past the boathouse
at the mouth, and out
into the lake. It was
only the slow growing
distance from the ring
of reeds round the
shore that told that
the boat moved at all
on the lake. More
slowly still, the light
was going from the
August evening.**"**
   John McGahern,
      High Ground

A visit to the Marble
Arch Caves includes a
boat trip on an
underground lake.

UPPER LOUGH ERNE

Upstream from Enniskillen lies the shallower Upper Lough
Erne, a labyrinth of water and wooded islands whose
appearance varies with the changing skies. Herons stand like
statues amid the waterside irises. Great crested grebe bob on
water disturbed by passing boats and dive beneath the surface
where rudd and bream ■ *44* are lurking. The meanderings of
the upper lough also conceal unusual statues (Innishkeen and
Cleenish graveyards) as well as ancient tombstones carved
with chilling motifs: coffin, hourglass and skull (Galoon
Island). The old Ballyconnell–Ballinamore canal has been
reopened so that boats can now get from Lough Erne to the
Shannon ▲ *200,* ◆ *359.*

LISNASKEA. The 1,000-acre estate of NEW CROM CASTLE
(1838) is open to visitors. In the village is CASTLE BALFOUR, a
fortified dwelling dating from 1618, and also a CELTIC CROSS.
To south and west the Lake District continues. The serene
and enchanting countryside extends into County Cavan
(Lough Oughter, left) and further west to County Leitrim
(Lough Allen).

WESTERN COUNTY FERMANAGH

FLORENCE COURT. The three-story country house was built in
the 18th century by Lord Mount Florence, and the wings of
handsome arcades were added later. The interior is very fine,
especially the rococo stuccowork. In the park is a magnificent
yew tree, from which the species Irish Yew, also called the
Florence Court Yew, was propagated.

MARBLE ARCH. The awe-inspiring series of
caves are encrusted with magnificent
stalagmites and stalactites. Experienced
speleologists can also explore other more
difficult caves, of which there are many in
County Fermanagh.

LOUGHS MACNEAN. The upper and lower
loughs are places to catch pike and crayfish.
Further north, LOUGH MELVIN is famous for
its plentiful salmon and no less than five
varieties of trout: brown, sea, *sonaghan,*
gillaroo (Irish trout) and *Salmo trutta ferox*
■ *44.*

PRACTICAL
INFORMATION

Goats on the Burren.

Kinvarra.

Sean O'Faolain, novelist and short story writer, was born and raised in Cork. He studied at the National University of Ireland and then left Ireland to attend Harvard University, finally returning in 1933 to settle as a writer. Today he is probably best known for his short stories. Much of his writing is inspired by his experiences in Ireland and several of his works are concerned with the frustrations of living within provincial Irish society. However, the following excerpt is taken from his autobiography "Vive Moi!" which was published in 1964.

❝I had no idea how near the mountains of West Cork are to Cork City. The Pass of Keimaneigh, which marks their southern spur, high above Bantry Bay, is only forty-one miles away. A bare thirty miles out you already feel them closing in when you top the little hillock this side of the village of Inchageelah and its long, lean lake, so indented and twisted that it seems to the traveller beside it not one lake but many. You feel their near presence a bare fifteen or twenty miles out if you take the unfrequented back roads through Kilmurry and Teerelton . . . Beyond the first foothills, across the loose stone walls of the road, the outcropping rock, the sparse, windtorn trees, the first few tiny fields excavated painfully by generations of cottiers out of a hard, infertile, sweat-making land softened only by the reed-edged lake, I saw the smoke-blue mountains now quite near. On their peaks white clouds, larger far than themselves, rose into the blue sky. I heard over my head a lark trilling invisibly. When I saw and felt all this, and knew that all about me people spoke an ancient tongue, that I could as yet only partly interpret, I experienced the final obliteration of time that turns a moment into eternity. In that moment the crude photograph at whose runic symbols I had gazed so often in the poems of Tomás Rua – the old ruined chapel near the ancient rocks, edging the sea – became clear as a mirror. Remounting my bicycle with a pounding heart, I passed through my mirror into reality. I pedalled on past the village, on beside its lake, now appearing, now disappearing, past small white cottages, through the village of Beal-atha-'n-Ghaorthaidh, after which I came on the Lee again, now a mere rocky stream, until I came to the farm and farmhouse, called Tuirín Dubh, where I was to stay. It was not a picturesque house – little in these parts except the scenery is picturesque. It was a plain, cement-fronted, slated house of two stories. I saw an uncombed garden in front, red with fuchsias and old cottage roses. I saw a long stone loft and byres of uncemented stone to its left; a new corrugated-iron barn and more byres directly opposite . . . Of all our expeditions the most favoured by Eileen and by me was to the source of the Lee, beyond the small leaden lake of Gougane Barra, which is backed by a long, dark, dead-end valley or *coom*, known in Irish as Coom Ruadh, or the Red Coom, in English as Valley Desmond. All our symbols were concentrated in this glen. Near the edge of the lake, surrounded by steeply rising slopes or mountain faces, there is a tiny hermit island, now joined by a causeway to the mainland; on this drop of land there is a ruined chapel, beside a discreet little modern chapel in Romanesque style, almost hidden by the mountain ash and the rhododendrons that

The Burren plateau.

hang down over the dark water and are darkly reflected in it. There is also a small square cloister of "cells" where, we believed, hermit monks once slept. Here, a thousand years ago, the patron saint of Cork, Finnbarr, lived and prayed. . .

Only in one or two farmhouses about the lake, or in the fishing hotel at its edge – preoccupations of work and pleasure – does one ever forget the silence of the valley. Even in winter, when the great cataracts slide down the mountain face, the echoes of falling water are fitful: the winds fetch and carry them. In the summer a fisherman will hear the tinkle of the ghost of one of those falls only if he steals among the mirrored reeds under the pent of the cliffs, and withholds the plash of his oars. Tiny muted sounds will then awe and delight him by the vacancy out of which they creep, intermittently. We loved this valley, lake, ruined chapel and rude cloister because of their enclosure, their memories, and their silence. Many times then and in after years we entered the silent deadened

coom to climb the mountain beyond. Once we got lost there in a summer fog, aiming for the minute loch up there called the Lake of the Speckled Trout, dark as ink and cold as ice water, visited otherwise only by mountain sheep. When we reached the top of the coom, after some tough climbing, the fog lifted and we came on another valley, and a vast view westward across other mountaintops far over the sunset sea. On those fortresses what could touch us? We enjoyed among them what I may well call a juvenile fantasy of

grown desire, planning tiny cottages on either side of this lost valley or that, facing one another, so that by day we would descend to the lake and be together there and by night see, each, the other's beckoning light across the darkness of the glen. **"**

Barry Lyndon.

The Field.

Beautiful countryside and Irish skies. Wide open spaces, strong winds, local color, beer, Irish whiskey and song. The Emerald Isle simply lends itself to being portrayed on the big screen.

IRELAND AS SEEN BY AMERICANS

"MAN OF ARAN"

In the early 1930's, Robert Flaherty, the American director of Irish extraction – considered by some to be the "father of documentary"– who filmed *Nanook of the North* (1922) in the north of Canada and *Moana* (1926) in the Islands of Samoa – headed for Galway and then on to Inishmore. He would undoubtedly have read J.M. Synge's *123* plays *Riders to the Sea* (1904) and *The Aran Islands* (1907). He remained in the Aran Islands for two years and during that time directed the "poetic documentary" *Man of Aran* for Michael Balcon of Gaumont Films (UK). Flaherty selected his cast from local people and created an "ideal" Irish family: mother (Maggie Dirrane), father ("Tiger" King) and son (Mikaleen Dillane). They were the embodiment of the virtues of courage and tenacity in the face of hardship and the cruel sea. The spectacular tempest scenes were filmed at Bungowla Point, between Inishmore and the Islands of Brannagh. The shark fishing was specially

reconstructed for the film. *Man of Aran* was a huge success in the US and was awarded the Golden Lion at the Venice Film Festival in 1934. Today it is a cinema classic and many who visit the Aran Islands expect to see them exactly as portrayed in the film. You can see the famous cliffs, the *currachs* which braved the treacherous Atlantic Ocean, and, at Kilmurvy, the houses where the Flahertys would have lived.

"THE QUIET MAN"

Twenty years later another American director, also of Irish extraction, arrived in Innisfree with a script by F.S. Nugent. John Ford (Sean O'Fearna) made *The Quiet Man* in 1952, with Maureen O'Hara and John Wayne in the leading roles. The movie tells the story of an Irish community settled in America which dreams of finding its roots and returning to its homeland. The story ends with a wedding, but only after many heated arguments, numerous brawls and several large whiskeys. Set in the past, this movie gives an image of Ireland untouched by the

20th century, one that would influence people for years to come: it was an idealized, picture-postcard Ireland. Even today the roadsigns along the way to Innisfree are reminiscent of the John Ford movie. Take a *Quiet Man* tour around Cong and judge for yourself whether or not it is as glorious as the film.

"THE DEAD"

American director John Huston lived near Galway, in the Republic, for many years. In 1987 he adapted James Joyce's short story *The Dead* (taken from Joyce's collection *The Dubliners*) for the screen. Shot in Valencia, suburb

of Los Angeles, this was to be the last movie John Huston made before he died. Huston's Californian "Dublin" was a success thanks to set designer Stephen Grimes and costume designer Dorothy Jeakins, who in common with the exiled Joyce when he first wrote the piece had to rely upon their powers of imagination. Thus, though using a variety of styles and diverse means, the poetic Flaherty, the truculent John Ford and the ironic John Huston have one thing in common – a dream of Ireland.

The Dead.

Cal.

In the Name of the Father.

IRELAND AS SEEN BY THE IRISH

Though small, the Irish movie industry is nevertheless extremely important. Working within restricted budgets and often with limited technical resources Irish movie-makers from Sidney Olcott to Bob Quinn have attempted to make themselves heard.

THE ORIGIN

Irish movies date from 1910 when the Irish-Canadian Olcott made the first Irish fiction movie *The Lad from Old Ireland* using (even then) the theme of an emigrant who leaves Ireland to make his fortune in America and returns to save his family from poverty. In 1916, J.M. Sullivan founded the Film Company of Ireland, whose biggest success was

Knocknagow (1917). This movie portrayed the confrontations between the Irish and the British, giving moving descriptions of rural Ireland often taken from popular fiction, a common practise at that time.

THE RENAISSANCE

For many years Irish movies were made almost exclusively for a domestic market, and it was not until the 1980's – and the setting up of funding, by the Irish Film Fund, for movies of a more "political" nature – that Irish movies (often co-productions with UK companies) gained international distribution. These include *Cal* (1984), directed by Pat O'Connor and based on a novel by Bernard MacLaverty, which explores the tensions between Catholics and Protestants in 1970's Belfast; Neil Jordan's *The Crying Game*

(Oscar for best screenplay 1993), which tells the story of a bizarre romantic intrigue concerning an IRA terrorist; and the films of Jim Sheridan – *My Left Foot* (1989), *The Field* (1990) and the extraordinarily moving *In the Name of the Father* (1993) with Daniel Day-Lewis and Pete Postlethwaite, which vigorously denounces methods used by certain members of the British secret services against suspected IRA terrorists. There is also Thaddeus O'Sullivan's *December Bride*, portraying life within a rural community in northeast Ireland at the turn of the century; Margo Harkin's *Hush a Bye Baby*, made in Derry, in which a movie-maker denounces the hypocrisy of

women's roles within a Northern-Irish Catholic society in the 1980's; and Joe Comerford's *Reefer and the Model*, a bitter and funny tale describing the ideological, political and social stalemate of today's Irish society. These movies produced in 1988 and 1989 began a new trend in Irish cinema and also give a more realistic impression of Ireland. Other recent cinema successes in a lighter vein are those by novelist Roddy Doyle, whose ironic humor delighted all those who saw *The Commitments* (1990), directed by Alan Parker, and *The Snapper* (1993), directed by Stephen Frears, both of whom are British directors. Sign of the times, perhaps, that the rural world has now given way to that of suburbia.

IRELAND AS SEEN BY THE ENGLISH

"ODD MAN OUT"

In the movie *Odd Man Out* (1947), with a plot based on a Graham Greene novel and James Mason in the leading role, Carol Reed exposes the horrors of secrecy within a Belfast society. Carried along by the impressive cinematography of Robert Krasker, this movie anticipates *The Third Man* which

Reed filmed in Vienna soon after.

"RYAN'S DAUGHTER"

In 1970, David Lean made his epic *Ryan's Daughter* using a script by Robert Bolt. Starring Sarah Miles, Robert Mitchum and Trevor Howard, it was filmed on the Dingle Peninsula in County Kerry, in a village completely recreated for the purpose by set designer Stephen Grimes. This movie is

set in Ireland during the 1916 uprisings.

"BARRY LYNDON"

In 1975, Stanley Kubrick (a New Yorker who emigrated to Britain) produced *Barry Lyndon*, based on William M. Thackeray's novel of the same name. Ryan O'Neal starred as the unscrupulous rake whose career unfolds during the second half of the 18th century.

◆ USEFUL INFORMATION

Enormous numbers of tourists visit Ireland each year from all over the world. Whether they come for the scenery, the friendly people, the traditions, Ireland's rich and varied history, the pubs, the Fastnet race or simply some Irish "blarney", all are charmed by this fascinating country.

WHERE TO FIND INFORMATION BEFORE YOU LEAVE

UK:

BORD FÁILTE (IRISH TOURIST BOARD)
150 New Bond Street
London
W1Y 0AQ
Tel. (0171) 493 3201

NORTHERN IRELAND TOURIST BOARD
11 Berkeley Street
London
W1X 5AD
Tel. (0171) 493 0601

US:

BORD FÁILTE (IRISH TOURIST BOARD)
757 Third Avenue
New York
NY 10017
Tel. (212) 418 0800

IRISH TOURIST OFFICE
345 Park Avenue
New York
NY 10154
Tel. (212) 418 0800
or (800) 223 6470

FORMALITIES

PETS
All animals must undergo a quarantine period of a minimum of six months when entering the Republic or Northern Ireland from anywhere outside the UK.

FOOD REGULATIONS
The strict health regulations in Ireland forbid meat- and dairy-derived products to be brought into the country from anywhere outside the UK.

DOCUMENTS
◆ A valid passport (unless you are an EC citizen).
◆ Driving license (or international driving license if you are not a UK citizen).
◆ If you are traveling in your own vehicle check whether you need to take out extra insurance cover for the areas you are intending to visit (standard UK insurance policies usually cover travel in Northern Ireland, but not the Republic). You will also need to display a country of origin plaque on the rear of the vehicle.
◆ Form E111 (if traveling from the UK) to entitle you to medical treatment under the NHS; this is available from most post offices.

WHAT TO TAKE

◆ Warm clothing is essential — be prepared to wear lots of layers (even during the summer the evenings can get chilly), a raincoat and umbrella to protect you from the "soft" Irish weather and stout shoes should you wish to attempt the Irish terrain on foot.
◆ A pair of binoculars for spotting Irish seabirds.
◆ An electrical adaptor if traveling from the US.
◆ A box of watercolors to capture that stunning Irish light.

TELEPHONE

◆ REPUBLIC: from the US dial 011 353 + local code (drop the zero) + number. From the UK dial 00 353 + code + number.

◆ NORTHERN IRELAND: from the US dial 011 + 44 + local code + number. From the UK dial local code + number.

POINTS OF INTEREST: GETTING MARRIED IN IRELAND

Romantic and straightforward . . . there are certain requirements, however:
◆ One of the couple must be resident in the area for at least 14 days. On the 15th they may then apply to the local Registry Office (civil state) and get married 8 days later — a total of 23 days.
◆ Their partner need only be resident for 8 days and on the 8th day to confirm their intention to marry eight days later — a total of 16 days.
◆ The bans must be published in an Irish newspaper.

FOR INFORMATION CONTACT
◆ Register of Marriages
31 Molesworth Street, Dublin 2
Tel. (01) 767 3218
◆ Also contact the appropriate embassy for validation details.
◆ For those who desire a religious ceremony, get in touch with the local church.

SOME APPROXIMATE HOLIDAY PRICES

You may prefer to book accommodation for the first night only and purchase open vouchers for the rest of your stay. These can be exchanged at other B&Bs or guesthouses.

BED & BREAKFAST

Bed and breakfast	$18–30/£14–23* per night

MANOR HOUSES AND SUPERIOR HOTELS

Per night	$155–243/£45–89

Fine dining prepared by top European chefs; full Irish breakfast; car with unlimited mileage. All accommodation can be pre-booked or purchase open vouchers and book first night only.

STATELY HOMES, CASTLES AND DELUXE HOTELS

3 to 6 nights $280–505/£186–336*.   7 nights $275–495/£183–330* per night

Price includes car with unlimited mileage and full Irish breakfast – pick up and drop off to and from the airport can be arranged.

TOURS OF IRELAND

11- to 13-day tour of southern Ireland	$968–1,747/£260–345
14-day tour of southern Ireland	$1,178–1,917/£310–425

Accommodation provided in Bed & Breakfasts.

GOLF ◆ 354

Golfing holidays $740–880/£172–396 * (3 nights) $1275–1747/£275–595 * (6 nights)

Prices vary depending on the facilities. Tour operators specializing in golfing holidays may have arrangements with golf clubs: booking through them may allow you to play on some of the best and most popular golf courses in Ireland, many of which are closed to the public.

COARSE FISHING OR SALMON AND TROUT FISHING ◆ 356

Full board + tuition (4 days)	$594/£340–400 *

Pike fishing tends to be the least expensive. Tour operators specializing in fishing holidays will organize transport, hotels, fishing permits, guides and fishing boats on your behalf.

SHANNON CRUISE BOAT ◆ 358

Per person (min. 4 people.)	from $120–195/£80–130*
	(without rental car)

Completing the appropriate form (available from your travel agent) can save you losing any time making arrangements once you arrive. Transfers from the airport can be arranged.

RENTING A COTTAGE

Per person (min. 4 people) 1 wk $165–277/£110–185 * **	2 wks $192–493/£128–329 * **

Cottages are often in groups of six or eight, thus allowing you the option of staying among friends while remaining relatively private. Choose your destination before departing.

HORSE RIDING ◆ 351

8-day trails (6 days riding; 4–7 hours riding per day)	$680–1,440/£513–230 *
8-day riding holiday (5 days riding; 4 hours per day)	$850–1,095/£566–730

Horses, accommodation, farmhouse dinners, picnic lunches are all inclusive. The luggage is taken separately by car. Transfers direct from the airport are available for an extra charge.

*Average price per person
** There may be a supplementary charge for Christmas and Easter

TOUR OPERATORS

Many tour operators offer complete holidays in Ireland. This enables you to organize every detail of your stay before departure. The above table gives an idea of the prices you might expect to pay for different types of holidays.

More detailed information is available each year through the Irish Tourist Board (Bord Fáilte) or the Northern Ireland Tourist Board.

TO MAKE ADVANCE RESERVATIONS

Permits, transport and various activities can be individually booked before you leave. For information contact:

IN IRELAND
◆ Central Reservation Service
Tel. (00 353 1) 284 1765
Fax (00 353 1) 284 1751

IN THE UK
◆ Central Reservation Service
Tel. (0171) 839 8417

FROM THE US
◆ To reserve tickets in Ireland:
Tel. (011 353 1) 284 1765

CLIMATE

The Irish climate is mild, influenced by the prevailing southwesterly winds and by the warm currents of the north-Atlantic drift.

TEMPERATURES
◆ January and February are the coldest months, with average temperatures of 30°F to 45°F. July and August are the warmest months with average temperatures of 57°F to 61°F (highest average temperatures of 63°F to 68°F).

SUNLIGHT
May and June tend to be the sunniest months with an average of 5 to 6½ hours of sunlight a day. In the extreme southeast, however, there can be more than 7 hours per day.

RAIN
April is generally the driest month, although in the south of Ireland June tends to be the driest of all. December and January are usually the wettest months. Dublin and the surrounding area is the least rainy part of Ireland (an average of 30 inches per year), and the west of Ireland tends to be the wettest, with a yearly average rainfall of of 40 to 50 inches.

SNOW
Snowfalls are rare, except in the mountainous areas.

WIND
Between June and September the winds are at their least forceful, with strong winds blowing from November to March. The wind is strongest on the south, west and north coasts.

WATER TEMPERATURES
Water temperatures vary from coast to coast, from 45°F in the northeast to 50°F in the southwest in winter and from 55°F to 59°F in summer for those respective areas. Taking into consideration the latitude of Ireland, these temperatures are very high.

SAILING AND WINDSURFING

With its variety of sea and lake conditions, different sailing areas, extensive coastlines and numerous harbors, Ireland has much to offer to the sailing enthusiast or to those wishing to learn.

IRELAND SAILING ASSOCIATION
3 Park Road, Dun Laoghaire, Co. Dublin
Tel. (01) 280 0239 Fax (01) 280 7558

IRISH CRUISING CLUB
Hon. Sec. Mr Cromack P. McHenry
9 Heidelberg, Ardilea, Dublin 14
Tel. (01) 288 4733

INTERNATIONAL SAILING CENTRE
5 East Beach, Cobh, Co. Cork
Tel. (021) 811 237 Fax (021) 811 527

IRISH NATIONAL SAILING CENTRE
115 Lower Georges Street, Dun Laoghaire, Co. Dublin
Tel. (01) 280 6654 Fax. (01) 280 3712

SAIL IRELAND AND YACHTING INTERNATIONAL CHARTERS
Trident Hotel Marina, Kinsale, Co. Cork
Tel. (021) 772 927 Fax (021) 774 170

ATLANTIC ADVENTURES
Frances Street, Kilrush, Co. Clare
Tel. (065) 52133 Fax (065) 51720

THE GREAT PILGRIMAGES

CROAGH PATRICK, Co. Mayo ▲ 279, the last Sunday of July. Thousands of pilgrims, often barefoot, climb the rocky path to the top of this isolated peak (known locally as "The Reek"). Mass is celebrated in a little oratory at the summit, where there is a magnificent view over the bay of Clew with its string of islands. A lively pilgrimage.
LOUGH DERG, Station Island ▲ 294, Co. Donegal, between June 1 and August 15. At prayer in one of the island's lakeside caves, Saint Patrick is said to have seen visions of purgatory. Since the 12th century, pilgrims have spent three days and three nights praying on this small island in the middle of the lake. Pilgrims arrive barefoot and eat only one meal a day, consisting of bread and black tea. A fervent pilgrimage.
KNOCK, Co. Mayo ▲ 283, all year round. On the site where, in 1879, the Virgin Mary appeared with Saint Joseph and Saint John the Evangelist. It was consecrated by the pope in 1979 and has a basilica and two chapels.
DOWNPATRICK, Co. Down ▲ 306, not truly a pilgrimage, but a site associated with three well-known Irish saints: Saint Brigid, Saint Columcille and Saint Patrick (who died in nearby Saul). Their relics allegedly lie under the modern cenotaph, near the cathedral.

ANNUAL EVENTS

March
◆ St Patrick's Day (March 17) ● *71*: Irish national holiday

April
◆ Celtic week, Tralee, Co. Kerry ▲ *239*: grand gathering of Celtic musicians, singers and dancers from all over Europe

May
◆ The Lord Mayor's Show (May 7), Belfast: bands and floats
◆ *Fleadh Nua*, Ennis, Co. Clare: festival of traditional Irish music and dance ▲ *245*

June
◆ Bloomsday (June 16), Dublin ▲ *173*
◆ Strawberry Festival, Enniscorthy ▲ *180*
◆ Budweiser Irish Derby, The Curragh, Co. Kildare: European classic, one of Ireland's best-known racetracks
◆ March of Castlebar festival: annual gathering of ramblers. Walks and evening entertainment

July
◆ Murphys Irish Open Golf Championship, Co. Kilkenny (end of June/beginning of July)
◆ Orange Day (July 12): public holiday in Northern Ireland ● *71*
◆ Galway Arts Festival, Co. Galway
◆ Horseracing in Galway ▲ *261*
◆ O'Carolan harp and traditional music festival, Keadue, Co. Roscommon

August
◆ Kerrygold Horse Show, Dublin: international showcase of Irish horses, race meetings
◆ Puck Fair, Killorglin, Co. Kerry ▲ *231*
◆ Parade of the old order of Hibernians (August 15), Belfast and various other places
◆ Connemara Pony Show, Clifden, Co. Galway ▲ *266*
◆ Rose of Tralee Festival, Co. Kerry ▲ *239*
◆ *Fleadh Cheoil na hÉireann*, Co. Tipperary: the largest annual gathering of folk musicians (venue may vary)
◆ *Ould Lammas Fair*, Ballycastle, Co. Antrim ▲ *311*

September
◆ All-Ireland Hurling finals, Dublin (Croke Park, first Sunday in September) ● *82*
◆ All-Ireland Gaelic Football finals, Dublin (Croke Park, third Sunday in September) ● *82*
◆ Clarenbridge Oyster Festival, Co. Galway, with the international women's oyster opening competition
◆ Galway International Oyster Festival

October
◆ Cork Film Festival ▲ *225*
◆ International Trade Fair and Ballinasloe Festival, Co. Galway
◆ Gourmet Festival, Kinsale, Co. Cork ▲ *223*.
◆ Wexford Opera Festival
◆ Dublin Theatre Festival (first two weeks of October)
◆ Cork Jazz Festival

November
◆ Belfast International Festival, three-week drama and music festival

Other events

◆ Small trade fairs, various markets and animal auctions happen regularly in most towns and villages.
Examples of some of these are: Bantry, Co. Cork (first Friday of the month); Cork Cornmarket (Saturday), Kenmare, Co. Kerry (the day varies); Castletownbere, Co. Cork (first Thursday of the month); Ashford, Co. Wicklow (Monday); Roundwood, Co. Wicklow (Sunday afternoon). Contact the local tourist office for further information.

PUBLIC HOLIDAYS
◆ IN THE REPUBLIC OF IRELAND: January 1 and 2, March 17 (St Patrick's Day national holiday), Good Friday, Easter Sunday, Easter Monday, May 1, first Monday in June, first Monday in August, last Monday in October, December 25, 26 and 27.
◆ IN NORTHERN IRELAND: January 1 and 2, March 17, Easter Sunday and Easter Monday, May 1, last Monday in May, July 12 (Orange Day – national holiday), last Monday in August, December 25, 26 and 27.

BY AIR

FROM THE UK

Flights are available from many airports throughout the UK, including London, Birmingham, Bristol, Edinburgh, Glasgow, Liverpool and Manchester, to Belfast, Dublin, Shannon, Cork, Knock and Waterford. Prices vary greatly and can range from as little as £84 for a super apex return fare from London to Dublin to £282 for a business class ticket. Many operators also offer a fly-drive option.

◆ AER LINGUS
223 Regent Street
London, W1R 0AJ
Tel: (0181) 899 4747
or (0181) 569 4001

◆ BRITISH AIRWAYS
PO Box 10
London Heathrow Airport
Hounslow, Middlesex
TW6 2JA
Tel. (0181) 897 4000
or (0345) 222 111

◆ BRITISH MIDLAND
Donington Hall
Castle Donington
Derby
DE74 2SB
Tel. (0345) 554 554

◆ LOGANAIR
Trident House
Renfrew Road
Paisley
PA3 4EF
Tel. (041) 889 3181
or (061) 832 9922

◆ MANX AIRLINES
Isle of Man
(Ronaldsway Airport)
Ballasalla
Isle of Man
Tel. 0624 824 313

◆ RYAN AIR
Barkat House
116–18 Finchley Rd
London NW3 5HT
Tel. (0171) 435 7101
Discount student fares are available all year round.

CONTACT:

◆ CAMPUS TRAVEL
Tel. (0171) 730 3402

◆ STA TRAVEL LTD.
74 Old Brompton Rd
London SW1
Tel. (0171) 937 9921

FROM THE US

Flights are available from New York and Boston direct to Shannon and Dublin airports. Aer Lingus is the only airline offering flights to the Republic of Ireland. Alternatively it is possible to fly to the UK and then take a connection to Ireland. Prices range from between $378 and $1378 for a standard to business class ticket to $2,990 for a first class ticket.

◆ AER LINGUS
Tel. (212) 557 1110
or (800) 223 6537
(outside New York)

BY FERRY

Ireland is linked to Britain by a variety of ferry routes, including crossings from Swansea to Cork, Pembroke or Fishguard to Rosslare Harbour and Holyhead to Dún Laoghaire and Dublin. Prices vary depending on the time of year. Ferry companies frequently offer promotional faresaver packages alongside their standard tariff. Length of crossing varies from approximately two hours for the fastest crossing from Holyhead to Dún Laoghaire to eleven hours from Liverpool to Belfast.

◆ B&I LINE LTD
Reliance House
Water Street
Liverpool L2 8TP
Tel. (0151) 227 3131,
(0171) 734 7512/4681
Operate services from Holyhead to Dublin, Pembroke to Rosslare and organize tour packages.

◆ P&O EUROPEAN FERRIES
Cairnryan,
Stranraer
Wigtownshire
DG9 8RF
Tel. (05812) 2760
Services include crossings from Cairnryan to Larne. P&O also organize a variety of tour packages.

◆ STENA SEALINK LINE
Charter House
Park Street
Ashford, Kent
TN24 8EX
Tel. (01233) 647 047
(Car ferry and Sea Lynx)
or (01233) 647 033
(holidays)
Stena Sealink operate services from Holyhead to Dún Laoghaire, Fishguard to Rosslare and organize tour packages.

◆ SWANSEA CORK FERRIES
Ferry Port, King's Dock, Swansea
SA1 8RU
Tel. (0792) 456 116
Fax (0792) 644 356
Crossings from Swansea to Cork.

Aer Lingus

Aer Lingus is the national Irish airline.

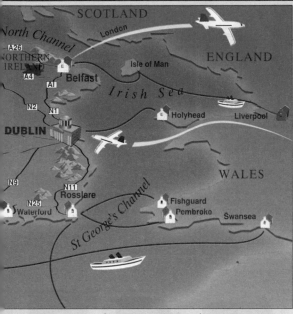

service throughout the summer months.

STUDENT TRAVEL
A Travelsave Stamp is available to holders of an International Student Identity Card at a cost of £8. This entitles the bearer to a discount of 50 percent off usual single adult fares on mainline trains, long distance buses and B&I Line ferries between Britain and Ireland.
For information contact:
◆ CAMPUS TRAVEL
52 Grosvenor Gardens,
London SW1 0AG
Tel. (0171) 730 3402

BY TRAIN
Traveling by a combination of train and ferry is a relatively fast, comfortable and economic way to travel to Ireland. A rail service connects all parts of Britain to all ports for shipping services to Ireland. This then connects with the Irish Rail service to stations throughout Ireland. Prices start as low as £42 for a supersaver fare.
◆ BRITISH RAIL INTERNATIONAL
International Rail Centre,
Victoria Station, London
SW1V 1JY
Tel. (0171) 834 2345 (information)
or (0171) 828 0892 (bookings)
or ask for

information at any designated British Rail station or tour operators throughout the UK.

BY COACH
Coach services are available between the UK and Ireland. These are organized by various private operators and also by the national Irish bus company Bus Éireann. Services run from various towns throughout the UK, including Birmingham, Bristol, London, Cardiff, Reading, Fishguard and Newport to Athlone, Ballina, Cork, Donegal, Ennis, Galway, Killarney,

Letterkenny, Limerick, Rosslare, Skibbereen, Sligo, Tralee, Waterford, Westport and Wexford.
Fares may cost as little as £15 for a single ticket to Dublin or £38 for a single fare to Cork.
◆ NATIONAL EXPRESS
Eurolines
52 Grosvenor Gdns
Victoria
London SW1
Tel. (0171) 730 0202
◆ NATIONAL EXPRESS
Digbeth Coach Station
Birmingham
Tel. (0121) 622 4373
◆ BUS EIREANN
Irish Bus Booking Office, Busáras
Store Street
Dublin 1
Tel. (01) 366 111
◆ SLATTERYS COACH SERVICE
162 Kentish Town Road
London, NW5
Tel. (0171) 482 1604 or (0171) 485 1438.
Most routes operate daily throughout the year although there is a more frequent

TOUR OPERATORS

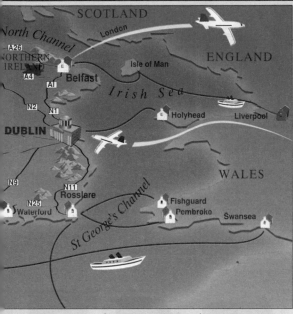

Many companies offer a variety of holiday programs throughout Ireland.
◆ AER LINGUS HOLIDAYS
Tel. (0181) 569 4001
◆ ANGLERS WORLD
Tel. (0246) 221 717
◆ B&I LINE HOLIDAYS
Tel. (0151) 236 8325
◆ CIE TOURS INTERNATIONAL
Tel. (0181) 667 0011
◆ CLIFF SMARTS ANGLING
Tel.(01536) 724 226
◆ DA STUDY TOURS
Tel. 0383 882 200
◆ DRIVE IRELAND
Tel. (0151) 231 1480
◆ SHAMROCK GOLF
Tel. (0151) 734 2344
◆ TIME OFF
Tel. (0171) 245 0055

GETTING AROUND BY CAR

Going by car is an enjoyable way to explore Ireland (except, of course, when traveling on the major routes where traffic is heavy) and is sometimes the only way to reach remote corners, inaccessible by public transport. Drivers tend to be extremely courteous, particularly in the more rural areas. Drivers often make some friendly gesture of greeting to each other when passing.

Watch out for obstacles, though: cows, sheep and donkeys are prone to wandering across the roads unexpectedly. The road system is relatively antiquated (except in Northern Ireland) and the condition of roads can be poor in places, so traveling from one place to another may take longer than anticipated.

MAPS

◆ Road maps are available from Bord Fáilte and Northern Irish Tourist Board
◆ Michelin Map of Ireland No. 405 (1:1,000,000)
◆ Ordnance Survey and Bartholomew series of maps (1:250,000) are available in five sections covering the whole of Ireland.

INTERNAL AIRWAYS

Flights are available between Dublin and Sligo, Knock, Shannon, Cork and Killarney.

DISTANCES BY ROAD AND AVERAGE LENGTH OF JOURNEY		
Dublin–Galway	135 miles	4 hours
Dublin–Belfast	102 miles	3 hours
Dublin–Donegal	137 miles	4 hours
Rosslare–Sligo	201 miles	5¾ hours
Dublin–Killarney	191 miles	5½ hours
Dublin–Cork	159 miles	4½ hours
Cork–Galway	129 miles	3¾ hours
Cork – Athlone	114 miles	3½ hours

THREE TIME-SAVING FERRY ROUTES

◆ Tarbert, Co. Kerry, to Killimer, Co. Clare, crossing the Shannon estuary.
◆ Ballyhack, Co. Wexford, to Passage East, Co. Waterford.
◆ Strangford to Portaferry, Co. Down (Northern Ireland), crossing the Strangford Lough.

DRIVING CODE IN IRELAND

◆ Drive on the left, give way to the right
◆ Speed limits:
  – Built-up areas: 30 mph
  – Major roads: 50 mph
  – Freeways: 70 mph
◆ Wearing seatbelts is compulsory
◆ Children under the age of twelve must sit in the rear seats of the vehicle
◆ Breathalizing tests are in force
◆ Wearing a crash helmet is compulsory for motorbike riders

An Pasáiste PASSAGE EAST

WARNING

In Belfast and Northern Ireland in general, no parking in areas marked "Control Zone". Any vehicle found in these zones will be treated as suspect and will be liable to attract police intervention.

BORDERS

To cross the border between the Republic and Northern Ireland stick to the main roads and head for the main border posts shown on most maps.

TRAVELING AROUND IRELAND ◆

ROAD SIGNS

It is easy to lose your way in Ireland. The main routes are well signposted but the minor route signposts are less reliable. You will find all sorts of signposts side by side: older ones are white with the place names in black and written in Gaelic or Gaelic and English and with distances in miles or in miles and kilometers . . . or other combinations. More recent signposts (white lettering on a green background for main roads and white lettering on a blue background for freeways) are written in Gaelic and English and the distances in kilometers.

In Northern Ireland the signposts are in English only and the distances in miles.

CAR RENTAL

◆ Many tour operators offer various fly-drive options allowing the car rental to be arranged when making the initial booking (◆ 335). Most of the larger car-rental companies have branches all over Ireland, and usually one in each major airport. There are also smaller companies and it is wise to compare prices between the different companies. Atlas Car Rentals at Gate 1 in the arrival hall at Dublin Airport offers extremely good deals.
Tel. (01) 844 4859.
◆ The following international car-rental companies have branches in

Ireland, with reservation desks in various airports throughout the Republic and Northern Ireland.
◆ Avis at Johnson & Perrott, Emmett Place, Cork
Tel. (021) 273 295
◆ Budget Rent-a-Car Ballygar, Co. Galway
Tel. (0903) 24668
◆ Hertz Rent-a-Car PO Box
23, Ferrybank, Wexford
Tel. (053) 23511
◆ Murrays Europcar Car Rental
Baggot Street Bridge Dublin 4
Tel. (016) 686 1777
COSTS
Expect to pay around Ir£50 per day when renting a medium-sized car with third-party insurance and unlimited mileage for

three to seven days during the main tourist season.
Should you intend to travel between the Republic and Northern Ireland you must inform the rental company when making the booking. Rental companies:
UK
◆ Hertz/Rent-a-Car
Tel. (0181) 679 1799
◆ Avis
Tel. (0181) 848 8733
Budget
Tel. (0800) 2766 000
US
◆ Hertz/Rent-a-Car
Tel. (800) 654 3131
◆ Avis
Tel. (800) 331 1212
◆ Budget
Tel. (800) 527 0700

GETTING AROUND BY BICYCLE

Exploring Ireland by bicycle provides a quicker way of getting around than walking or hiking — but bear in mind the relentless winds and frequent hills.
BIKE RENTAL
The two main stores are Raleigh Rent-a-Bike which has branches throughout

the Republic and Northern Ireland, and The Bike Store Ltd.
COSTS
Rental costs around Ir£8 per day and Ir£35 per week for a mountain bike (you will be expected to leave a deposit of one week's hire plus a surcharge should you wish to return the bike to a different branch).

ADDRESSES

◆ Raleigh Rent-a-Bike, Raleigh House, Kylemore Road, Dublin 10
Tel. (01) 626 1333
◆ The Bike Store Ltd. 58, Lower Gardiner Street, Dublin 1
Tel. (01) 284 4768
◆ Bike-It, 4, Belmont Road, Belfast
Tel. (0232) 471 141

IN CASE OF ACCIDENTS
Two useful contacts:
Tel. 999
for the emergency services,
and the
Irish Motorist Bureau 3–4 South Frederick Street, Dublin 2
Tel. (01) 679 233
who, for insurance purposes, must be notified of any road accident.

BUS ÉIREANN
Ulsterbus Goldline

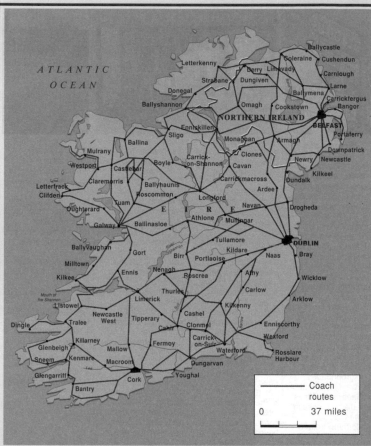

ATLANTIC OCEAN

Ballycastle
Letterkenny · Coleraine · Cushendun
Strabane · Derry · Limavady · Carnlough
Donegal · Dungiven · Larne
Ballyshannon · Omagh · Cookstown · Ballymena · Carrickfergus · Bangor
NORTHERN IRELAND · BELFAST
Enniskillen · Portaferry
Sligo · Monaghan · Armagh · Downpatrick
Ballina · Carrick-on-Shannon · Clones · Newry · Newcastle
Mulrany · Boyle · Cavan · Kilkeel
Westport · Castlebar · Carrickmacross · Dundalk
Letterfrack · Claremorris · Ballyhaunis · Ardee
Clifden · Roscommon · Longford · Navan · Drogheda
Oughterard · Tuam · E I R E · Athlone · Mullingar
Galway · Ballinasloe · Tullamore · DUBLIN
Ballyvaughan · Gort · Birr · Kildare · Naas · Bray
Milltown · Ennis · Nenagh · Portlaoise · Athy · Wicklow
Kilkee · Roscrea · Carlow
Mouth of the Shannon · Thurles · Kilkenny · Arklow
Listowel · Limerick · Cashel · Enniscorthy
Dingle · Newcastle West · Tipperary · Clonmel · Wexford
Tralee · Cahir · Carrick-on-Suir
Killarney · Fermoy · Waterford · Rosslare Harbour
Glenbeigh · Mallow · Dungarvan
Sneem · Kenmare · Macroom · Youghal
Glengarriff · Cork
Bantry

— Coach routes

0   37 miles

REPUBLIC OF IRELAND
BY TRAIN
Traveling by train between Dublin and other major cities in the Republic is relatively quick and easy, the longest journey (Dublin to Tralee) taking only four hours. However, as train routes fan out from Dublin, traveling between other cities without traveling via Dublin can prove difficult.
◆ Irish Rail/Iarnród Éireann
Connolly Station
Dublin 1
Tel. (01) 366 222
BY BUS
Traveling by bus is an excellent way of getting around Ireland. The national company Bus

Éireann offers regular services between all cities and most major towns and villages outside Dublin. It lays on extra services during peak tourist season to numerous other destinations.
◆ The approximate cost of a standard class one-way fare:
Cork to Killarney: Ir£8
Galway to Killarney: Ir£13
Galway to Belfast: Ir£15.80
Limerick–Shannon: Ir£3.40
Sligo to Derry: Ir£10
Wexford to Dublin: Ir£7
◆ Bus Éireann
Broadstone, Dublin 7
Tel. (01) 366 111

TRAVELCARDS
◆ Irish Explorer (train) 5 days' travel in a 15-day period: Ir£60, Ir£30 (for the under 16's)
◆ Irish Explorer (train and coach outside of Dublin) 8 days' travel in a 15-day period: Ir£85, Ir£42 (for the under 16's)
◆ Travelsave Stamps.
A student travel pass (you must show your International Student Identity Card) entitles the traveler to up to 50% reductions on long-distance journeys by coach, train and Irish Ferries: Ir£8.
◆ USIT
19, Aston Quay
Dublin 2
Tel. (01) 677 8117

NORTHERN IRELAND
BY TRAIN
The railway network in Northern Ireland is limited to three lines. A 7-day unlimited travel card is available at a cost of Ir£25.
◆ Northern Ireland Railways
28, Wellington Place
Belfast
Tel. (0232) 899 411
BY BUS
There is a regular and frequent coach service between all the major cities in Northern Ireland. A 7-day unlimited travel card is available, as for the train service.
◆ Ulsterbus
Great Victoria Street
Belfast
Tel. (0232) 320 011

POST

MONEY

IN THE REPUBLIC
The local currency is the "punt" or Irish pound (Ir£), which is divided into 100 pence, with Ir£5, Ir£10, Ir£20, Ir£50 and Ir£100 notes and 1p, 2p 5p, 10p, 20p, 50p and Ir£1 coins.

RATES OF EXCHANGE
£1=Ir£0.98,
$1=Ir£0.65

BANKS
Open Monday to Friday, 10am to 12.30pm and 1.30pm to 3pm. In Dublin banks are open until 5pm on Thursdays. Money can also be changed at the airport or in bureaux de change. UK notes are accepted in Ireland at the value of their Irish equivalents.

IN NORTHERN IRELAND
The local currency is the Northern Ireland pound which has the same value as the British pound. British currency is accepted.

RATES OF EXCHANGE
$1=£0.64

BANKS
Open Monday to Friday 10am to 3.30pm (frequently closed between 12.30pm and 1.30pm in smaller towns and villages).

AUTOTELLERS
There are a growing number of autotellers (Allied Irish Bank, Bank of Ireland and Ulster Bank).

NOTE: The two currencies are not interchangeable: the punt is only valid in the South, and the Northern Ireland pound in the North.

TELEPHONE

TELEPHONING FROM THE REPUBLIC OF IRELAND
◆ To call the UK from the Republic dial 00 44 + local code (minus the 0) + the number you require.
◆ To call the US from the Republic dial 00 1 + local code + number you require.

TO CALL THE REPUBLIC OF IRELAND
◆ From the US: dial 011 353 + local code (drop the zero) + number.
◆ From the UK: dial 00 353 + code + number.

TELEPHONING FROM NORTHERN IRELAND
◆ To call the UK from Northern Ireland dial 00 44 + local code (minus the 0) + number you require.
◆ To call the US from Northern Ireland dial 00 1 + local code + number you require.

TO CALL NORTHERN IRELAND
◆ From the US: dial 011 + 44 + local code + number.
◆ From the UK: dial local code + number.

THE COST OF A TELEPHONE CALL			
	local	long dist.	internat.
Republic	(3 mins)	(3 mins)	(3 mins)
	20p	Ir£1.60	Ir£2.40
N. Ireland	(3 mins)	(3 mins)	(5 mins)
	15p	30p	£1.78

THE CLOCK
The Republic of Ireland and Northern Ireland are at Greenwich Mean Time (GMT) except between September 25 and October 23 when Ireland is one hour ahead of GMT.

SHOP OPENING TIMES

REPUBLIC OF IRELAND
Shops open 9am to 5.30pm or 6pm, Monday to Saturday, closing at 1pm on Wednesday. Larger town centers often have late-night opening on Thursday and Friday. Grocers and newsagents open on Sunday morning.

NORTHERN IRELAND
Shops open 9am to 5.30pm, Monday to Saturday, in Belfast. Elsewhere, shops usually have half-day closing one weekday and may also close at lunchtime. There is late-night opening in the larger towns.

MAIL

FROM THE REPUBLIC
A letter to the UK costs 32p and a postcard 28p. An airmail letter to the US costs 52p and a postcard 38p. Available from post offices, some shops and even in pubs in rural areas.

FROM N. IRELAND
Postcards and letters to the UK cost 25p 1st class and 19p 2nd class. A letter to the US costs 37p, a postcard 25p. Available from post offices and shops displaying the sign "We sell stamps".

CONVERSION TABLE								
HAT SIZES								
Ireland/UK	6 7/8	7	7 1/8	7 1/4	7 3/8	7 1/2	7 5/8	7 3/4
US	6 7/8	7	7 1/8	7 1/4	7 3/8	7 1/2	7 5/8	7 3/4
MEN'S CLOTHING								
Ireland/UK	36	38	40	42	44	46		
US	36	38	40	42	44	46		
WOMEN'S CLOTHING								
Ireland/UK	10	12	14	16	18	20		
US	8	10	12	14	16	18		
WEIGHTS AND MEASURES								

• 1 mile = 1.6 km • 1 pound = 0.450 kg • 1 gallon = 4.55 l • 1 pint = 0.57 l
• 1 acre = 0.4 hectare • 1 yard = 0.91 meter

The Irish are famed for their hospitality. Wherever you go you are sure of a warm welcome. In many traditional Bed and Breakfasts (B&Bs) the owners live on the premises and run the business themselves. You will be given a comfortable room and offered a full cooked breakfast – a satisfying introduction to Irish cooking.

RESTAURANTS

LOCAL CUISINE

The food in Ireland is wholesome and served in generous portions, and as high-quality products are readily available Irish cooking can be delicious. Beef and lamb are particularly tasty as the animals are often raised on open grassland. Fish is easily available, as is seafood in general (try the Dublin prawns and Atlantic lobsters), and shellfish (Galway oysters, with their slightly sour taste go extremely well with a pint of *Guinness*).
Meals are usually served with potato (traditionally the staple food of Ireland) and a selection of other vegetables.

Dairy produce is an important part of the Irish diet: butter, salted and creamy, appears on the table at most meals; a variety of cheeses, some of them fairly strong: Milleens, St Killian, Cashel Blue, Ardrahan . . . also highly recommended are desserts or puddings such as apple tart, gooseberry or rhubarb crumble, served with custard or cream. Another Irish specialty worth looking out for is *carrigeen moss* (seaweed).

MEALS

The usual custom in Ireland is to eat three substantial meals a day. Breakfast usually consists of fruit juice, fruit, cereal or porridge followed by a fried breakfast of eggs, bacon, tomatoes, mushroom, sausages, or sometimes kippers or black pudding, and accompanied with tea or coffee and toast or soda bread ● *85* with butter and marmalade or jam. Certainly enough to keep you going until dinner time. Traditionally the main meal is served at mid-day but frequently lunch is just a light snack. Dinner is usually eaten between 7pm and 8.30pm.

WHERE TO EAT

◆ There are numerous classic Irish restaurants and many hotels have restaurants which are open to the general public. Expect to pay from around Ir£40 for a basic dinner for two with house wine.

◆ More than 360 restaurants offer a set menu consisting of three courses for Ir£7, Ir£8.50 or Ir£12, depending on which main course you choose (the set menu is often restricted to lunchtime and early evening). For a list of these restaurants see *Dining in Ireland,* available from most tourist offices.
◆ Many pubs offer pub lunches and serve basic food (dish of the day, soup and bread, salad) for very reasonable prices (around Ir£5).
◆ Coffee shops usually serve food all day (and prices are generally lower than in traditional restaurants).
◆ Farmhouses often serve dinner, but only for overnight guests and it will need to be ordered in advance (Ir£12).

TIPS

Service is not usually included (except in the more expensive hotels and restaurants) and it is customary to leave a 10 percent tip.

IN NORTHERN IRELAND

The cost of eating out in Northern Ireland is much lower than in the Republic. A guide to restaurants, *Where to Eat*, is available from tourist offices. Look for the label *A Taste of Ulster*, to guarantee good-quality traditional food.

CAMPING

Camping on public land is generally forbidden in Ireland, but there are more than one hundred well-equipped campsites which are approved by the tourist authority. Expect to pay around Ir£5 per night for a pitch.

WHERE TO STAY

◆ There are more than 150 tourist offices in the Republic, some of which are open all year round and some which operate only during the summer months. Most tourist offices are open from 9am to 6pm Monday to Friday and have the facility to rent you self-catering accommodation for a small fee. The larger tourist offices also provide other reservation services for activities such as golf, horseriding and fishing, and some may even be able to rent you a cottage.

Any establishment booked through the tourist office is approved by them and is listed in the Tourist Office's *Accommodation Guide*. They also display a green cloverleaf sign.
◆ The Northern Ireland Tourist Office has a similar guide entitled *Where to Stay*. There are approximately fifty tourist offices in Northern Ireland, which have the same opening hours and offer the same facilities as those in the Republic.

AVERAGE PER-NIGHT PRICES FOR A DOUBLE ROOM, BREAKFAST INCLUDED, AT PEAK SEASON	
Hotel (good rating)	Ir£65
Guesthouse	Ir£50
Farm/Bed & Breakfast	Ir£30
Manorhouse	Ir£120
Paying guest	Ir£120
Cottage (4–5 pers. for a week)	Ir£250

HOTELS AND GUESTHOUSES

Hotels and guesthouses are classified by the Tourist Office from 1-star (*) to 5-star (*****).
◆ The distinction between hotel and guesthouse can be difficult to ascertain as it is sometimes based on small details of hotel rules and service. The guide *Be Our Guest*, published by the Irish Hotel Federation and available from tourist offices lists both types of accommodation and gives prices and other useful information.

MANORHOUSES

Many impressive country manors have been turned into hotels and guesthouses and have become popular places to stay, providing comfortable rooms and excellent food. Twenty-eight of these establishments, considered to be the best of their kind, along with five restaurants, have set up the Association of Irish Country Houses

and Restaurants, Arbraccam Glebe Navan, Co. Meath. Tel. (046) 23416. Fax (046) 23292. Guidebook: *Blue Guide*, available from most tourist offices.

BED & BREAKFAST

Here Irish hospitality is at its best. Ranging in style from huge old houses to tiny cottages you are

guaranteed basic comfort and a friendly welcome.
◆ Farmhouses are not always quite what they sound. They are usually B&Bs on a farm and may be recently built and not

attached to a working farm. Needless to say the settings are usually delightful. A specialized guide entitled *Farmhouse Holidays*, published by the Tourist Office, gives details, photos and a short description of each of these. Reservations essential in high season.

PAYING GUESTS

◆ Castles and country manors provide a luxurious way to spend your stay and enjoy the relaxed lifestyle of an Irish country squire. Whatever the case, choose from horseriding, croquet, tennis, badminton, or fishing in the estate's private stretch of river. Rooms, breakfast and dinner included. Booking essential.

The Hidden Ireland Kensington Hall Grove, Dublin 6 Tel. (01) 668 6578 has compiled a list of 37 establishments who take paying guests. Illustrated guide available from most tourist offices.

SELF-CATERING

The illustrated guide entitled *Self Catering*, published by the Tourist Office, lists a range of approved self-catering accommodation.

YOUTH HOSTELS

Ideal for those on a restricted budget at only Ir£6 to Ir£14 per person per night. There are two chains of hostels, one in the south and one in the north, and the hostels are often located in magnificent settings.
◆ *An Oige* – Irish Youth Hostel Association, 61, Mountjoy St, Dublin 7 Tel. (01) 830 4555 (50 youth hostels in the Republic and 6 in the North);
◆ Independent Holiday Hostels of Ireland, USC Village, Belfield, Dublin 4 Tel. (01) 260 1634 (112 youth hostels throughout Ireland).

The pub is an important feature of Irish life. The 10,500 pubs scattered all over Ireland provide the setting for much socializing and Irish culture. People gather to gossip, do business, quench their thirst and even to hear music — either in the form of organized traditional music or sometimes completely impromptu. There are various "singing pubs" where local musicians and singers gather to play traditional music.

WHAT TO ORDER

A whole variety of beverages are available, but the local brews come highly recommended. These invariably include two key ingredients, both 100-percent Irish: mineral water from a nearby source and locally grown barley. Once the barley grain has sprouted, it is dried and turned into malt. Local malts are then used in the production of a range of whiskeys and beers.

THREE DIFFERENT TYPES OF BEER ● 77

Three types of draught beer are available by the pint or the "glass" (half pint)
◆ lager, at Ir£1.90 a pint (*Harp* leads the market);
◆ bitter, at Ir£1.90 a pint (*Smithwick's*, brewed in Kilkenny ▲ 187, is the most popular);
◆ stout, a dark, rich brew, at Ir£1.80 a pint (*Guinness* is probably the most famous, with its carefully drawn dark body and head of white foam; others include *Murphy's*, brewed in Cork, and *Beamish*).

WHISKEY ● 78

Forty percent proof, pure malt whiskey, made from grain dried in closed barns, triple distilled and allowed to age for a minimum of three years produces a light, smooth-tasting whiskey. Served at room temperature, without ice or water, a whiskey usually costs Ir£1.65. There are various different brands and everyone has their own favorite. Many of them are sold under the *Irish Distillers* label: *Jameson, Paddy, Powers, Tullamore, Bushmills* (distilled in the village of the same name, in Ulster ▲ 315).

★ THE "SINGING PUBS" OF DOOLIN

County Clare is famed for its music and in Doolin, an uninteresting seafront looking toward the Aran Islands, the music is as intoxicating as the whiskey. Its three singing pubs have some of the best folk musicians performing every evening at around 9.30pm. People from all over Ireland go to listen, play or even take lessons from the local experts.
◆ *O'Connors* Tel. (065) 74168
◆ *McDermott's* (no telephone)
◆ *McGann's* Tel. (065) 74133

IRISH COFFEE

Irish coffee is a drink concocted largely for the tourist trade, but is delicious nonetheless. In a medium-sized glass mix one part whiskey to two parts sweetened black coffee. Float cream on the top using a teaspoon. Sip the coffee through the layer of cream.

"GUINNESS" AND WHISKEY: USEFUL ADDRESSES

◆ GUINNESS HOPSTORE Crane St, Dublin 9 Tel. (01) 453 6700 Museum, shop, tastings. Open Mon. to Fri., 10am–4.30pm. *Entrance Ir£2.*

◆ JAMESON HERITAGE CENTRE Midleton, Co. Cork Tel. (021) 613 594 Open 10am—6pm Mar. to Nov. Guided tours. *Entrance Ir£3.50.*

◆ WHISKEY CORNER Bow Street, Dublin Tel. (01) 872 5566 Open Mon. to Fri., tours at 3.30pm. *Entrance Ir£3.*

◆ OLD BUSHMILLS DISTILLERY Bushmills, Co. Antrim Northern Ireland Tel. (02657) 31521 Open each morning, Mon. to Fri. from 9am. *Guided tour (Ir£2)*

LICENSING HOURS

IN THE REPUBLIC OF IRELAND
◆ Monday to Saturday
10.30am–11.30pm May to September,
10.30am–11.00pm October to April
◆ Sunday 12.30–2pm and 4–11pm
IN NORTHERN IRELAND
◆ Monday to Saturday 11.30am–11pm
◆ Sunday 12.30– 2pm and 7–10pm

A LITERARY TOUR OF DUBLIN PUBS

Dublin is considered to be the city of marvelous pubs and literary genius. Once the home of three Nobel prizewinners (Samuel Beckett ●131, George Bernard Shaw ●125 and William Butler Yeats ●122), there are many other writers, from Jonathan Swift ●119, to Brendan Behan ●130, who have lived in this amazing city. In homage to them there is a guided tour of the Dublin pubs they once patronized. In the evenings, actors provide an accompaniment of songs and recitations of selected extracts.

Pubs included in the tour are:
◆ *The Bailey*, 2, Duke Street, closely associated with James Joyce's *Ulysses* ●121;
◆ *Davy Byrne's*, 21, Duke Street, in which Leopold Bloom, the hero of *Ulysses* has "a gorgonzola sandwich washed down with a glass of burgundy";
◆ *McDaid's*, Harry Street, frequented by Brendan Behan;
◆ *The Long Hall*, South Great George Street, has no literary connections, but is rightly included as it is the most beautiful pub in Dublin, with its carved wood and exquisite mirrors;
◆ *Toner's*, 139, Lower Baggot Street, in memory of Yeats;
◆ *The Palace*, 21, Fleet Street, a traditional Irish pub;
◆ *Mulligan's*, 8, Poolbeg Street, an equally classic Irish pub.

INFORMATION AND RESERVATIONS
Colm
Tel. (01) 284 1765
or the Tourist Office
14, Upper O'Connell Street, Dublin
Tel. (01) 284 1765

A WELL-KNOWN IRISH PUB SONG: "MOLLY MALONE"

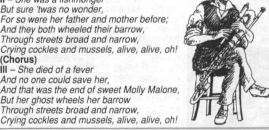

I – *In Dublin's fair city*
Where girls are so pretty
I first set my eyes on sweet Molly Malone,
As she wheeled her wheel barrow
Through streets broad and narrow
Crying cockles and mussels, alive, alive, oh !
Chorus: *Alive, alive, oh ! A live, a live oh !*
Crying cockles and mussels alive, alive, oh !
II – *She was a fishmonger*
But sure 'twas no wonder,
For so were her father and mother before;
And they both wheeled their barrow,
Through streets broad and narrow,
Crying cockles and mussels, alive, alive, oh!
(Chorus)
III – *She died of a fever*
And no one could save her,
And that was the end of sweet Molly Malone,
But her ghost wheels her barrow
Through streets broad and narrow,
Crying cockles and mussels, alive, alive, oh!

TOASTS, LIMERICKS AND IRISH BLARNEY

TOASTS
Legend has it that those who kiss the Blarney Stone ▲ 216 will receive the gift of eloquence, a quality long associated with the Irish. The original stone is set in the wall of Blarney Castle. As this stone is set 20 feet from the top of the wall and virtually impossible to reach, a substitute has been provided. Kissing the Blarney Stone is not for the fainthearted: set out slightly from the castle wall, it requires you to lean out backward, holding onto a small railing with someone securing your ankles — don't look down, it is a very long drop.
BLESSINGS
An old pub tradition, derived from a Gaelic practise, now virtually disappeared.
May the road go swift and narrow/May the wind be behind you

May the sun warm your face/May the rain fall softly on your fields/And until we meet again/May God hold you in the palm of his hand.
LIMERICKS
These are five-line, nonsense verses (popularized by Edward Lear in the 19th century). The form may come from the chorus "Will you come up to Limerick", supposed to follow each verse as it was improvised by each member of a party.
An old lady from near Fermanagh/Whose thoughts were terribly narrow/At the end of her paths/She did build two bird baths/To prevent mortal sins among sparrows.

TWO USEFUL WORDS
Sláinte: Cheers
Slán: Goodbye

347

◆ IRISH TRADITIONS:
FROM FOLK MUSIC TO FOLKLORE

In which other country are you equally likely to come across someone playing tin-whistle, a rock star, a group of people arguing furiously over a game of bowls and a bearded leprechaun, all dressed in green?

TRADITIONAL MUSIC

◆ *Comhaltas Éireann Ceoltóirí ● 72* is the official body responsible for the promotion of traditional Irish music and dance. Live folk music has a huge following, and each year, between March and August, the *Comhaltas* organizes around fifty of the major traditional music festivals (*fleadhs*) which brighten up Ireland's social calendar.

◆ The *Fleadh Cheoil na hÉireann*, which takes place over the last weekend in August (theoretically, in a different town each year) is perhaps the most impressive of them all. It attracts a huge number of spectators and participants (including some of the best Irish musicians) who come to support, perform or simply to have a good time. Weather permitting this is held mainly outdoors. The atmosphere is informal and music carries on all weekend.

◆ The *Fleadh Nua* in Ennis, at the end of May, is smaller but just as lively.

◆ The *Fleadh Amhran & Rince* (*Ould Lammas Fair*) held at Ballycastle, Co. Antrim, toward the middle of June, specializes in traditional song and dance and attracts enthusiasts from Northern Ireland.

◆ The *Comhaltas Ceoltóirí Éireann* also organizes music evenings at its own center in Dublin, the *Culturlan na hÉireann. Comhaltas Ceoltóirí Éireann* 35, Belgrave Square, Monkstown, Co. Dublin Tel. (01) 280 0295

MUSICAL INSTRUMENTS

Two of the essential instruments in traditional Irish music are those marvels of simplicity, the *bodhrán* (pronounced *bore-ron*) and the tin whistle *● 72*. The *bodhrán* is a large hand-held drum made from goatskin stretched over a beech frame. The drum is held in one hand by the crossed wooden bar underneath and the taut skin is then struck with a small drumstick (originally this would have been a bone) to make little drumrolls. The tone can be altered by using the underneath hand as a damper on the back of the skin. Thus the sound produced can range from muted to bright. Suppliers to music specialists: Roundstone Musical Instruments Roundstone, Co. Galway Tel. (095) 35875 Fax (095) 35980 Prices: Ir£30 to Ir£90.

◆ The tin whistle, a small pipe made of brass, is the

least sophisticated of all instruments. Prices: Ir£2 to Ir£10.
MANUFACTURERS
VIOLINS
(Around Ir£1,800)
◆ Martin Faherty Unit 3, Shandon Crafts, Shandon, Cork Tel. (021) 302 368
◆ Kevin Sykes 4, Newcastle Road, Galway Tel. (091) 66488
◆ John Flavey Passage East, Co. Waterford Tel. (051) 382 406
UILEANN PIPES
(Around Ir£1,800)
◆ Des Geary 40, Wolftone Square, Bray, Co. Wicklow Tel. (01) 286 6192
HARPS
(Ir£400 to Ir£2,000)
◆ Paddy Cafferky Lisduff, Craughwell, Co. Galway Tel. (091) 46265
◆ Larry Egar Ardmuire, Herbert Pk, Gardiner's Hill, Cork Tel. (021) 504 832

ROCK MUSIC ● 73

In the 1980's Irish rock music achieved international status thanks to such bands as the *Pogues* and *U2*, and Sinead O'Connor. In recognition of the talent of all these Dublin musicians the Tourist Office (14, Upper O'Connell Street) has compiled a tour which follows their progress throughout the city.

◆ *Bad Ass Cafe* 9–11, Crown Alley Tel. (01) 712 596 A very popular cafe-restaurant where Sinead O'Connor was once a waitress.

◆ *The Baggot Inn* Dandelion Market, where *U2* gave their first performances.

◆ Windmill Lane studio, where *U2* once recorded. This has become a kind of temple to their glory, and unruly fans have covered the outside walls in graffiti.

◆ Bono, lead singer of *U2*, is the owner of the well-established nightclub *The Kitchen*, located in Temple Bar, behind the Clarence Hotel, on Essex Street Tel. (01) 677 6178

MUSIC MAGAZINES
Hot Press (bi-monthly) is the Irish rock magazine.
CONCERT HALLS
The Point Depot (East Link Bridge, North Wall Quay), *The National Stadium, The Royal Dublin Society* and *The Olympia Theatre* are all in the center of Dublin.

There are the Irish who you can see and those who you cannot, but who, nonetheless, lead colorful lives and who are able to influence the fate of those unable to see them. These are the "little people": fairies, leprechauns . . . though the leprechaun is the only truly mischievous one of them all. Bearded and dressed

IRISH LEPRECHAUN

in green, his likeness can be found in most souvenir shops and he is the most active of all the fairy-folk. He possesses a pot of gold, buried at the end of the rainbow. The only way to steal his pot of gold is by fixing him with an unblinking stare. Some other "little people" resemble humans and come among them just to cause confusion. Banshees are the bringers of bad news, announcing a death by wailing down the chimney. The little people live in mounds and *raths* (pre-Christian tumuli): to avoid attracting bad luck you must take care never to remove

even the tiniest clod of earth from these places. Hawthorn bushes are purported to be fairy hideouts and so should never be pulled up for the same reason.

FOR INFORMATION
◆ There are various publications, including *Folktales of the Irish Countryside*, Danaher (Mercier); *Legends of Irish Witches and Fairies*, P. Kennedy (Mercier); *Superstitions of the Irish Country People*, Padraic O'Farrell (Mercier).
Or contact:
◆ Irish Folklore University College, Belfield, Dublin 4
Tel. (01) 706 8216
Fax (01) 706 1166

AN INTRODUCTION TO GAELIC

There are certain areas of Ireland, the *Gaeltacht* ● *68*, where Gaelic is still the first language.
For further information:
◆ Gael Linn
29, Cearnog Mhuirfean, Dublin 2
Tel. (01) 676 7283
Fax (01) 676 7030
will supply details of conversation courses at all levels in some of these areas. Costs are in the region of Ir£100 for a week's course of daily three-hour conversation classes, with some evening activities.
Listings are available from local tourist offices.

IRISH SPORT ● *82*

HURLING AND GAELIC FOOTBALL
These sports are played by over 300,000 enthusiasts throughout the provinces of Munster, Leinster, Connacht (Republic) and by a few in Ulster.
EVENTS
Each year these events attract crowds of up to seventy thousand spectators to Dublin's Croke Park Stadium.
◆ The All-Ireland Football finals, third Sunday in September.
◆ All-Ireland Hurling finals, first Sunday in September.
◆ The regional finals and national semi-finals, which have a very enthusiastic following, take place in July or August (see local press on Wednesday and Saturday for details)
SUPPLIERS OF HURLING EQUIPMENT
◆ Connolly Brothers Clare, Galway, Co. Galway
Tel. (091) 98303

Manufacturers and suppliers of hurling sticks (around Ir£10) and balls (around Ir£6).
◆ Ashcraft Mount Usher, Co. Wicklow
Tel. (040) 286 6954
ASSOCIATION
Gaelic Games Association Croke Park, Dublin 3
Tel. (01) 836 3222
ROAD BOWLING
▲ *323*
This takes place each weekend and on summer evenings along the smaller roads of County Cork (about nine thousand people play), and those of Armagh (about three thousand people play).

◆ The annual championship is held in both Cork (early July) and Armagh (late July).
ASSOCIATION
Bol Chumann na hEireann, Anngrove Carrigtuohilll , Co. Cork
Tel. (021) 883 249
publishes a yearly calendar of events and also supplies bowls.

GRAYHOUND RACING
These take place at night during the week at twenty different greyhound tracks throughout Ireland. There are usually eight races of about a mile long. Bets can be placed either through a mutual betting system (with a minimum stake of 50p), or through an

approved bookmaker (minimum stake of Ir£5).
GRAYHOUND TRACKS
These are located at the following sites: Dublin (Shelbourne Park and Harold Cross), Cork, Limerick, Tralee, Waterford, Youghal, Galway, Clonmel, Enniscorthy, Mullingar, Longford, Thurles, Newbridge, Dundalk, Lifford, Kilkenny, Navan, Belfast and Derry. Admission: Ir£3.
CALENDAR AND INFORMATION
Bord na gConn Irish Greyhounds Board 104, Henry Street, Limerick
Tel. (061) 316 788
Fax (061) 316 739

Horseracing and showjumping have an excellent following and the Irish pride themselves on breeding some of the world's best thoroughbreds. Horseriding is also enjoyed by many amateurs and pony-trekking provides an ideal way to explore the countryside.

HORSERACING

The racing calendar is packed with events: 250 races are run on twenty-seven different racetracks, two in Northern Ireland, and four, the most renowned, just outside Dublin. The most popular racecourses are around Dublin.

THE MOST POPULAR RACECOURSES

◆ The Curragh, Co. Kildare – 29 miles southwest of Dublin
◆ Punchestown, 22 miles southwest of Dublin;
◆ Leopardstown, virtually in the town, 6 miles from the center.
◆ Fairyhouse, Co. Meath – 12½ miles to the northwest.

FLATRACING AND STEEPLECHASING

The flatracing season runs from mid-March to the beginning of November, and steeplechases run throughout the year.
◆ The flatracing classics are held at the Curragh in mid-May, the 1,000 Guinea and the 2,000 Guinea races offering prizes of Ir£200,000 apiece, and the Irish Derby at the end of June with a first prize of Ir£600,000.
◆ The most renowned steeplechase is the Irish Grand National, which is run at Fairyhouse at the beginning of April
◆ Equal in status is the Punchestown festival, a three-day race meeting which takes place at the end of April. There are usually six or seven races each day, a mixture of hurdles and steeplechases.

POINT-TO-POINT RACING

Point-to-points are very popular in Ireland, particularly in County Cork (where approximately sixty point-to-point races are held each year). Most of them take place on Sundays between the beginning of January and the end of May. The course is cross-country and so includes such natural obstacles as stone walls, small streams, and hedges. These races are usually organized by the various hunting committees, and tend to have a fairly high profile on the Irish calendar of sporting events.

FOR FURTHER INFORMATION CONTACT:

◆ Irish Racing Board, Leopardstown Racecourse, Foxrock, Dublin 18
Tel. (01) 289 2888
Fax (01) 289 2019

BETTING

Betting is taken on all races, either through the Tote betting system or — and this is certainly much more entertaining to watch — through bookmakers or "bookies", who take individual bets (with a minimum stake of Ir£1).

ON THE BEACH: THE LAYTOWN RACES

On the precise spot where, a century ago, Tara's pin was found ▲ 159, on a six-mile stretch of sandy beach, one hundred riders compete over seven flatraces each year. Eccentric and archaic it may be, but it is sanctioned by the official Irish racing calendar. The race meeting held at Laytown (Co. Meath), is the only one in Ireland, and probably the only one in the world, whose precise date depends on a complete variable – in this instance: the sea. There must be sufficient low-tide in the evenings to permit the officials to construct the course in the morning (marking it out with white poles with red flags) and to allow time for the sand to stabilize before the horses and their riders compete. The ideal conditions usually occur some time around the end of July or the beginning of August.

FESTIVAL MEETINGS

Very lively and popular, they are part festival and part race meeting. There are about a dozen, among which the most highly regarded are:
◆ Killarney Festival (mid-July),
◆ Galway Festival (end July),
◆ Listowel Festival (end September),
◆ Christmas Festival at Leopardstown (following Christmas).

PONY-TREKKING AND HORSERIDING

There are 150 riding centers approved by the Association of Riding Establishments (AIRE) and by the Irish Tourist Office. Any of these will be able to supply you with good horses.

◆ **AIRE**
11, Moore Park, Droichead Nua, Co. Kildare
Tel. (045) 31584
These approved centers are recommended because they are guaranteed to be of a certain standard. The animals are usually a mixture of horses and Connemara ponies which, though small can be ridden by

adults. Local tourist offices, hotels and local inhabitants should point you in the right direction should you have any trouble locating one of these stables.

◆ A one-hour lesson either for beginners or more experienced riders costs between Ir£10 and Ir£15.

◆ A two-and-a-half hour hack costs in the region of Ir£25 and depending on the area may include a gallop along deserted beaches.

TRAIL-RIDING

Trail rides are available in some of the most beautiful areas (Donegal, Connemara, Kerry, Wicklow, Sligo).

◆ Small parties accompanied by an experienced guide depart for six days and nights (five to seven hours in the saddle each day) throughout the summer months. A picnic is provided for the midday stop. Dinner and overnight accommodation is provided at a guesthouse or hotel. Luggage is transported separately, by car.

◆ The longest-established, most spectacular and varied trail-ride is the Connemara Trail. Taking six days, it runs from Oughterard to Clifden, inland through Connemara, alternating bogland ■ *32* crossing with rides along deserted railway tracks. The final day is spent riding over the long stretches of beach in the bay of Mannin where the sand is mixed with white coral.

A different option allows you to explore Connemara by the coastal route. Expect to pay around Ir£780 for full-board with excellent accommodation.
FOR INFORMATION CONTACT:
Mr Willie Leahy, Aille Cross, Loughrea, Co. Galway
Tel. (091) 41216
Fax (091) 42363

◆ Killarney Reeks Trail operates along the same lines but in a landscape of a very different character: six days in the mountains of Macgillycuddy's Reeks, the highest in Ireland, and then down into the green and romantic Killarney countryside, with its lakes and forests such as Glencar and others.

There are magnificent views of the sea and large sandy beaches perfect for a long canter (Ross Beach and Waterville). Accommodation is in hotels, guesthouses or Bed & Breakfasts. Expect to pay between Ir£500 and Ir£700, depending on the type of accommodation.
FOR INFORMATION CONTACT:
Mr D. O'Sullivan, Killarney Riding Stables, Ballydowney, Killarney, Co. Kerry
Tel. (064) 31686
Fax (064) 34119.

SOME EXCELLENT RIDING CENTERS
(Addresses ◆ *363*)

◆ Boro Hill Houses Equestrian and Holiday Centre (twenty-five horses and ponies) specialize in riding holidays for children unaccompanied by their parents.

◆ Brennanstown Riding School (fifty horses and ponies) is located very close to Dublin.

◆ Clonshire Equestrian Centre (fifty horses and ponies) is located in a big hunting area.

◆ Devil's Glen Holiday and Equestrian Village (forty horses).

◆ Green Glen's Horse Village (thirty horses) is on the premises of the Millstreet international competition organizers, which take place in August and October. Treks arranged taking you into the counties of Cork and Kerry.

◆ Laragh Trekking Centre (eight horses) is situated in the Glendalough National Park. Accommodation available on site in a lovely house.

◆ Bansha House and Stables (twelve horses) is highly recommended by the Tourist Office and AIB Bank for the high standards of accommodation and awarded the grade "Green Tourism". Hunts arranged.

◆ Ladestown House Riding and Trekking (twenty horses and ponies) is right in the heart of rural Ireland.

◆ HORSES HORSESHOWS AND HUNTING

THE SHOWCASES OF IRISH HORSES

◆ The national Irish Hara ▲ 182, Irish National Stud Tully, Co. Kildare Tel. (045) 21617 Fax (045) 22129 *Entrance Ir£ 4.*

◆ The Dublin Horse-Show (Royal Dublin Society showgrounds, beginning of August) attracts competitors from all over the world along with the finest Irish competition horses. You can see the best Irish thoroughbreds on show at the five-day event. National and international showjumping.

◆ Millstreet International Show, in the pastoral setting of Co. Cork, during the last two weeks of August, is in the same vein but on a smaller scale.

◆ Ballinasloe, October Fair in County Galway is one of the oldest of its kind in Europe.

CONNEMARA PONIES

◆ Connemara Pony Breeder's Society, Hospital Road, Clifden, Co. Galway Tel. (095) 21863 Fax (095) 21005 Founded in 1923, it monitors the development of the breed, and lists and inspects approved pedigree Connemara ponies from two years old. The Connemara Pony Show takes place under the Society's vigilant eye each year

◆ Clifden Connemara Pony Show, Co. Galway, in mid-August. This top-quality show is of interest to specialists and amateurs alike. High-spirited, frisky ponies with gleaming coats, groomed manes and tails, and freshly shod hooves are shown by their owners, who sometimes present a rather stiff and awkward picture alongside their spry ponies. Meanwhile, other activities are in full swing. There are all sorts of different competitions, and experts are attracted from all over the world. A good two-year-old Connemara pony can fetch as much as Ir£1,500 to Ir£2,000.

◆ Connemara Pony Fair takes place in October at Maam Cross, Co. Galway and at Clifden, Co. Galway.

HUNTING

Although it may be a somewhat exclusive sport elsewhere, in Ireland hunting remains a popular and convivial pastime, one that has been practiced for many generations. First and foremost comes foxhunting, although there are also stag hunts and harriers. Hunting is a fast and potentially hazardous activity; participants are taken cross-country over various obstacles, which are almost impossible to avoid: double banks in the south, stone walls in the west, ditches and streams in the east. To take part it is best to be a fit, experienced rider. After the hunt, people usually retire to the local pub, which can prove as interesting as the hunt itself. More than thirty-five committees organize fox hunts (see local tourist office), some of which may be open to non-members, depending on availability. On average a hunt permit, or "cap fee" costs Ir£70. You will also need to add the cost of hiring a horse for the day (Ir£80). To make reservations contact the hunt secretary. Some hunt committees have become veritable institutions and are considered to be leading lights in this field. These include:

◆ Scarteen Hunt,
◆ Galway Blazers,
◆ Limerick Hunt,
◆ Meath Hunt,
◆ The Dunraven Arms Hotel, which is possibly the only hotel in Ireland to have its own pack and arrange hunts for its clients.

SPORT AND LEISURE

Legend has it that the Scottish colonialists introduced golf into Ireland at the beginning of the 17th century. In 1889 there were seven golf clubs; ten years later this number had increased to twenty (sixteen in the north of Ireland and four in the south). In 1891 the Golf Association of Ireland, the first of its kind, was set up, giving a boost to this sport. Today there are 250 golf clubs in Ireland (175 of which have eighteen-hole courses) and more than 170,000 golfers.

THE ATMOSPHERE

Golf is no longer the serious sport it used to be. Nowadays it is a more lighthearted pastime. A round of golf may often have the air of a pleasant stroll and the clubhouses can be good meeting places.

COMPLETE GUIDES TO GOLFING IN IRELAND
The Golfers Guide, in the Republic and the *Guide to Golf* in Northern Ireland are available in most local tourist offices.

THE SITES

◆ The links courses have given Irish golf its reputation. These are coastal, extremely windy, and subject to quirks of nature such as dunes and sand holes which, made worse by the wind, make the game more challenging and put golfers' nerves to the test. Links courses are playable all year round since any rainfall drains away through the sand.

GOLF TUITION

Hundreds of professional and ex-professional golfers, all belonging to the Irish Professional Golfers Association and affiliated to the various different clubs, offer coaching at all levels. Reservations are essential. Expect to pay Ir£15 for a thirty-minute lesson.

◆ There is a steadily increasing number of parkland courses, particularly in the center and the east, though even these, set among the gentle rolling hills, have their own particular difficulties. Here you can detect the signature of the great international golfers (Robert Trent Jones, Jack Nicklaus, Nick Hawtree or Arnold Palmer).

A ROUND OF GOLF

Booking is required although, in most cases, a telephone call a day or two in advance will suffice. A round of golf on any of the internationally acclaimed courses will need to be booked well in advance as these are extremely busy, particularly at weekends.

THREE OF IRELAND'S MAJOR GOLFING EVENTS

IRISH OPEN GOLF CHAMPIONSHIP
End of June, at Mount Juliet (Co. Kilkenny) designed by Jack Nicklaus. All the great international golfers compete.
Golfing Union of Ireland
81, Eglinton Road Dublin 4
Tel. (01) 269 411
Fax (01) 269 5368

JAMESON INTERNATIONAL GOLF CHALLENGE
Early October, in the southwest, on some very prestigious courses: Ballybunion, Waterville and Killarney. Open to amateurs. Whiskey tasting to keep you in the right spirit
Abbey Tours Unit 1 Lower Bridge Street Dublin 8
Tel. (01) 679 9144

BLACK BUSH TOURNAMENT
Held in Northern Ireland. This annual tournament attracts more than a thousand competitors from all over the world to play on the superb links of the north coast: Royal Portrush, Portstewart, Castlerock and Ballycastle.

Belm

Achill Isla

Clifden
Connemara
Golf Club

Aran Isla

Ballybuni
Golf Cl
Golf Chumann
Ceann Sibeal
Trale
Dingle
Dooks Golf Club
Waterville
Golf Club
Ken
Waterville
Glenga
Castletownbere

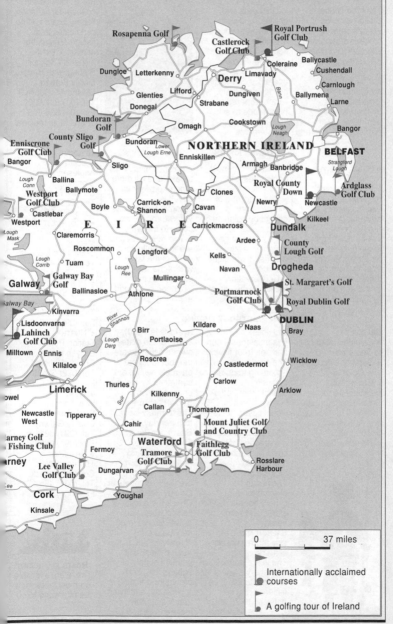

GOLFING TOUR OF IRELAND
Each of these eighteen-hole championships
has its own peculiarities. These courses are
not necessarily the best known, and some
may be unfamiliar to many. They are all
relatively easy to get into.

INTERNATIONALLY ACCLAIMED COURSES
Most of these golf links are exceptionally
windy. Their age-old reknown may make
them difficult to get into for anyone who is
not a member, especially at weekends.
Always reserve well in advance.

Rosapenna Golf

Royal Portrush
Golf Club

Castlerock
Golf Club

Coleraine

Ballycastle

Cushendall

Dungloe   Letterkenny   **Derry**   Limavady

Carnlough

Glenties   Lifford   Dungiven   Ballymena

Larne

Donegal   Strabane

Bundoran
Golf

Omagh   Cookstown

Lough
Neagh

Bangor

Enniscrone
Golf Club

County Sligo
Golf

Bundoran
Lower
Lough Erne

NORTHERN IRELAND

BELFAST

Bangor

Enniskillen

Armagh   Banbridge

Strangford
Lough

Sligo

Ardglass
Golf Club

Lough
Conn   Ballina

Ballymote

Clones

Royal County
Down

Newry   Newcastle

Westport
Golf Club   Castlebar

Carrick-on-
Shannon

Cavan

Kilkeel

Westport

Boyle

E   I   R   E

Carrickmacross   **Dundalk**

Lough
Mask   Claremorris

Roscommon   Longford

Ardee   County
Lough Golf

Drogheda

Lough
Corrib   Tuam

Kells

St. Margaret's Golf

Galway Bay
Golf

Lough
Ree   Mullingar

Navan

Galway

Ballinasloe   Athlone

Portmarnock
Golf Club

Royal Dublin Golf

alway Bay   Kinvarra

River
Shannon

Kildare   Naas   **DUBLIN**

Lisdoonvarna
Lahinch
Golf Club

Birr   Portlaoise

Bray

Milltown   Ennis

Lough
Derg

Roscrea

Killaloe

Castledermot

Wicklow

Thurles

Carlow

Limerick

Kilkenny   Arklow

owel

Callan

Newcastle
West   Tipperary

Thomastown

Cahir

Mount Juliet Golf
and Country Club

arney Golf
Fishing Club

Fermoy   **Waterford**

Faithlegg
Golf Club

arney

Lee Valley
Golf Club   Dungarvan

Tramore
Golf Club

Rosslare
Harbour

Cork

Youghal

Kinsale

| 0 | 37 miles |

🚩 Internationally acclaimed
● courses

🚩 A golfing tour of Ireland

◆ Fishing

Ireland has 8,700 miles of fishing rivers, 1,554 square miles of lakes and 3,110 miles of coastline and offers a wide range of excellent angling opportunities in some of the cleanest rivers, lakes and seas in Europe. The quality and variety of fish along with the beautiful setting make angling in Ireland a truly pleasurable sport.

Useful information

The Irish Tourist Board compiles various detailed brochures supplying information on the different angling areas and types of fishing, suitable accommodation, legislation and by-laws, angling permits or tickets and licenses and where to locate boats and ghillies. You can thus arrange your complete angling holiday before traveling. Some specialist tour operators offer entire holiday programs, either prepared or tailor-made to suit your individual requirements.

Coarse fishing

◆ Season: all year round
◆ Permit: none required, but check that the waters are not subject to private regulations
◆ A complete guide to the different areas for particular types of angling, compiled by the Central Fisheries Board and published by Gill & McMillan, is available from most bookstores and tackle stores.
◆ Pike, the king of this category, is caught by spinning or using bait. The largest pike to be caught in a lake weighed thirty-eight pounds.
◆ Conservation measure: the use of live fish as bait is prohibited; it is illegal to take and kill more than one pike per day; it is recommended that you return all your catch to the water.
◆ The best locations are the shallower parts of the lake where the weeds are plentiful, in the Shannon basin and adjoining lakes.

Salmon and trout fishing

Season
◆ Salmon: January 1 to September 30
◆ Sea trout: January 1 to October 12
◆ Brown trout: February 15 to September 30 (best mid-April to mid-June and August to September).
◆ Rainbow trout: April 1 to September 30

Licenses
Essential for salmon and sea-trout fishing. The cost varies according to duration and number of districts required. A license costing Ir£25 would cover all areas for the full season, while a single district, full season license costs Ir£12 and one-day license for all districts costs Ir£3. These can be purchased from fishery boards, tackle stores and some hotels.

Salmon and sea-trout angling permits
These are payable to the fishery owners for the right to fish their fisheries and cost between Ir£20 and Ir£70 per day (the average is Ir£30). Some of the state-owned fisheries are free but most are privately owned or controlled by a club or association.

Brown trout permits
These rarely exceed Ir£5 per day.

Best locations
The courses of Connemara and Mayo are renowned for their fishing, as are the Erriff rivers in County Galway. Check the quality of fishing when you arrive. Brown trout may be a rarity elsewhere but in Ireland there is a plentiful supply of fighting fish, and brown trout fishing is a pleasant, satisfying and reasonably inexpensive sport.

Fisheries
For all information concerning fisheries, fishery boards, state certificates and fishing regulations contact: Central Fisheries Board, Balnagowan House, Mobhi Boreen, Glasnevin, Dublin 9 Tel. (01) 837 9206 Fax (01) 836 0060 or one of its regional offices
◆ East:
as above
◆ South:
Anglesea Street, Clonmel, County Tipperary Tel. (052) 23624 Fax (052) 23971
◆ Southwest:
1, Neville Terrace, Macroom, County Cork Tel. (026) 41221 Fax (026) 41223
◆ Northwest:
Abbey Street, Ballina, Co. Mayo Tel. (096) 22623 Fax (096) 70543
◆ North:
Station Road, Ballyshannon, County Donegal Tel (072) 51435 Fax (072) 51816
◆ West:
Weir Lodge, Earl's Island, County Galway Tel. (091) 63118 Fax (091) 66335
◆ Shannon:
Thomond Weir, County Limerick Tel. (061) 455 171 Fax (061) 326 533

Boats and guides
These are available on most lakes for a fee of around Ir£40.

THE ART OF DAPPING

Dapping (angling using aquatic or terrestrial insects) was developed by the Irish. You will need a light fishing rod a minimum of 13 feet long, a monofilament line or

blow line, a dapping reel or spinning reel and a small fishhook (size 8 to 10). The insect is attached to the hook and dapped dry along the crest of the wave. The season begins in May once the mayflies (*Ephemera danica*) hatch and then continues for the rest of the season using terrestrial insects such as daddy-long-legs and grasshoppers. The best places for dapping are limestone lakes where the fish can detect the bait easily through the clear, clean water. For those wishing to learn the art of dapping contact one of the following:

◆ Clonanav Angling School, Ballymacaberry, Clonmel, Co. Waterford Tel. and Fax (052) 36141 A residential introductory course taught by a family of enthusiasts.
◆ School of Casting, Salmon and Trout Fishing Pontoon, Lough Conn, Co. Mayo Tel. and Fax (094) 56120

SEA ANGLING: FROM GREY MULLET TO SHARK

There are thirty coastal centers in Ireland offering various different options. You can:
◆ Go out on a charter boat to fish for hake, pollack, bass (May 15–June 15, strict control regulations), whiting, grey mullet, cod, gurnard, eel and various types of flat fish.
◆ Take a small fishing boat out to catch fish such as hake, pollack, cod, ray, skate and dogfish.
◆ Go out on the high seas in a fishing boat (around Ir£25 per person) to fish for cod, skate, conger, ling, coalfish, turbot and blue shark. The coastal center at Kinsale, County Cork, on the south coast probably has the best reputation of all the coastal centers offering shark-fishing trips. Many companies hire boats from them for this type of fishing. One such company is Tamar Sea Angling Denis Quay 6 Tel. (021) 774 190 Fax (021) 772 664.

ARTIFICIAL FLIES
The artificial flies which are used as bait are often extraordinary creations. They are available from any fishing tackle store. Two veritable artists in this field make and sell artificial flies of exceptional quality and are well worth a detour:
◆ Alice Comba Old Church Street, Cahir, Co. Tipperary Tel. (052) 42348 A pioneer in this predominantly male domain, Alice Comba was first introduced to the trade by her father. She makes very traditional flies for the purists, and has also branched out to make other, decorative objects from them, including feathery earrings.
◆ Frankie McPhilipps Butter Market, Enniskillen, Co. Fermanagh, Northern Ireland Tel. (0365) 324499 Eminent specialist who produces a type of fly called the "rogan fly", much favored by experts.

◆ INLAND WATERWAYS

With the introduction, in 1994, of a 45-mile canal linking the Shannon, in the Republic, and the Erne in Northern Ireland, the two major navigation networks amalgamated into one. This waterway is over 336 miles long and runs from Killaloe, Co. Clare, in the south, to Belleek, County Fermanagh, in the north. Its alternating lakes and rivers are dedicated to the joys of pleasure sailing and fishing, with no commercial traffic. Further to the east, approximately half-way along its 78-mile length, the Grand Canal joins up with the Barrow, a quiet river flowing into the sea on the south coast of Ireland.

USEFUL BOOKS

The Shell Guide to the Shannon, Gill & McMillan; *Official Navigation Guide*, EraMaptec; *The Shannon-Erne Waterway*, Woolthound Press.

EIGHT COMPANIES APPROVED BY THE IRISH TOURIST BOARD FOR THE SHANNON AND THE ERNE

You are recommended to choose from the 430 boats owned by one of these eight companies approved by the IBRA

IN THE REPUBLIC

◆ Athlone Cruisers (offices in Athlone and Carrick-on-Shannon) Jolly Mariner Marina, Athlone, Co. Westmeath
Tel. (0902) 72892
Fax (0902) 74386

◆ Carrick Craft (offices in Carrick-on-Shannon and Banagher), PO Box 14, Reading, RG3 6TA, UK
Tel. (0734) 422 975
Fax (0734) 451 473

◆ Derg Line (based in Killaloe, Co. Clare)
Tel. (061) 376 364
Fax (061) 376 205

◆ Emerald Star Line (offices in Carrick-on-Shannon, Portumna and Belturbet), 47, Dawson Street, Dublin 2
Tel. (01) 679 8166
Fax (01) 679 8165

◆ Shannon Castle Line (based in Williamstown Harbour, Co. Clare), Dolphin Works, Ringsend, Dublin 4
Tel. (01) 660 0964
Fax (01) 689 091

◆ Silver Line (based in Banagher,

Co. Offaly)
Tel. (0509) 51112
Fax (0509) 51632

◆ Tara Cruisers Carrick-on-Shannon
Tel. (078) 20736
Fax (078) 21284

◆ Ballykeeran Cruisers, Ballykeeran, Athlone, Co. Westmeath
Tel. (0902) 85163
Fax (0902) 85431

IN NORTHERN IRELAND

◆ Aghinver Boat Company
Tel. (0365) 631 400
Fax (0365) 631 968

◆ Belleek Charter Cruising
Tel. (0365) 658 027
Fax (0365) 658 793

◆ Carrybridge Boat Company
Tel. (0365) 387 651
Fax (0365) 325 511

◆ Erincurrach Cruising
Tel. (0365) 641 507

◆ Erne Marine
Tel. (0365) 348 267
Fax (0365) 348 866

◆ Lakeland Marina Ltd.
Tel. (0365) 631 414
Fax (0365) 631 960

◆ Lochside Cruisers Ltd.
Tel. (0365) 324 368
Fax (0365) 325 209

◆ Manor House Marine
Tel. (0365) 628 100
Fax (0365) 28000

◆ Erne Shannon Canal Boats
Tel. (0365) 748 712
Fax (0365) 748 493

SHANNON–ERNE WATERWAY

THE SHANNON ▲ *200*
Two hundred and seventeen miles long, its source is at Derryland, Co. Cavan, and it is swelled in places by small interior waters: Lough Ree (5 miles long by 4 miles wide) and Lough Dert (25 miles by 3 miles). The Shannon is navigable over 137 miles, including its two lakes. Six sluice gates regulate navigation. Botanists, photographers, bird-watchers and archeologists all find plenty to interest them in this historic conservation area.

SHANNON–ERNE LINK
The sailing is spectacular right from the start since, to reach the first small lake (Scur), the eight sluice gates need to be passed through. Constructed in 1860, and abandoned almost immediately, the canal has been closed until recently. The sluice gates are now electronically operated but all the other structures and fittings have been repaired in keeping with traditional techniques.

THE ERNE ▲ *325*
The Erne is made up of two lakes, the Lower Lough Erne (26 miles long), where the wind blows in from the ocean, and the Upper Lough Erne, which is shallower and covered with tiny islands over its 16-mile length. Speed boats and various types of motor boats are available for rent to sail on the lakes. Costs vary greatly according to type and size of boat. Reserve in advance either through a tour operator before you leave or call direct. In peak season these tend to get very booked up.

BOAT HIRE
Boats are usually hired per week, but weekend or several days' hire is often available. A good grade boat with six berths would cost around Ir£990 in peak season (inclusive of hot and cold water, shower, equipped kitchen, bedding, cards, radio and dinghy). A week's fuel would cost around Ir£70 and sluice-gate toll Ir£1. Fishing dinghies which can be attached to the side of the boat (remember to arrange the appropriate fishing permits and pay attention to any fishing regulations that might be in force ◆ *356*), and bicycles are optional extras.
◆ No license is required for sailing a boat but there is a minimum age requirement of 21. Basic instructions will be given to you before leaving.
◆ The average speed of a cruise is around 5 mph.
◆ Meteorological conditions are very changeable and currents on the lakes can be as strong as those at sea.

THE GRAND CANAL AND THE BARROW

In contrast to the River Shannon this is a reasonably straight stretch of water, with sluice gates dating back to the 18th century. The scenery is pastoral: lush meadows, animals grazing on the hillsides, historic villages — 68 relaxing miles.
◆ The boats on the Grand Canal and the Barrow tend to be different to those of the Shannon: rounder and flatter, as the waters here are shallower, but the process of hiring and operating them is the same. Expect to pay around Ir£780 for the hire of a barge with six berths for a week during high season.

Two approved companies share the market:
◆ Celtic Canal Cruisers Tullamore, Co. Offaly
Tel. (0506) 21861
Fax (0506) 51266
◆ Lowtown Cruisers Ltd.,
Robertstown, Naas, Co. Kildare
Tel. (045) 60532
Fax *idem*

BOAT TRIPS, ON-BOARD REFRESHMENTS AND EVENINGS ON THE WATER

There are delightful trips available either in launch boats or barges, which tend to last around one-and-a-half hours at a cost of about Ir£5 a head.
ON THE SHANNON AND ERNE BASIN
◆ Lough Key
Departs hourly from Boyle in summer.
Lough Key Boat Tours
Tel. (079) 62214
◆ Lough Ree
Departs from Athlone starting at 11am.
Shannon Holidays
Tel. (0902) 72892

◆ To Banagher
Silver Line Cruisers
Tel. (0509) 51112
◆ Lough Derg
Depart Killaloe, boat-trip and snacks
Derg Marina
Tel. (061) 376 364
Depart Dromineer, through Shannon Sailing
Tel. (067) 24295
◆ Shannon River
Derg Line Cruisers
Tel. (061) 376 364
◆ Lough Erne
Depart from Belturbet
Turbot Tours Ltd.
Tel. (049) 22360

TAKE TEA ON THE RIVER BARROW
Depart from New Ross ▲ *188*.
Charming, with beautiful views and good food, the route varies according to the tides. Tea (Ir£5), lunch (Ir£12), and dinner (Ir£25). Booking essential.
◆ Galley
Cruising Restaurant
Tel. (051) 21723
Bridge Quay
New Ross

OTHER EXCURSIONS
◆ Lake Corrib
Depart from Cong or Oughterard
◆ Killarney lakes
▲ *234*
Depart from Ross Castle
◆ Lough Gill
Depart from Parke's Castle ▲ *285*

Little Skellig (County Kerry). *The Twelve Bens (County Galway).*

The Irish have always roamed freely around their countryside and even today walkers enjoy few restrictions – a Keep Out sign is a rare sight. In 1978 the Long Distance Walking Routes Committee (the National Tourist Council) was set up. Since then 620 miles of footpaths and twenty designated walks have been marked out and more are being developed. These trails follow towpaths, *boreens* (small paths), roads once used for driving farm animals, "butter" routes once taken by farmers carrying their wares to market, and even ancient "coffin" routes, once routes to the local graveyard.

EXPLORING THE BOGS

Muddy perhaps, but a little mud is a small price to pay for the opportunity to appreciate these unspoiled havens of peace and tranquility. Walking on the bogs can be a strange experience as in places the ground seems to quake and quiver as if you were walking on a waterbed. It is best not to go out alone and to always stick to the paths. The following bogs are national natural reserves which are attached to the Wildlife Service of Public Works Office. However, there are many others and all are of equal interest.

POLLARDSTOWN FEN, COUNTY KILDARE (563 acres) The largest remaining calcareous, spring-fed fen in Ireland.
◆ Contact James Kenna, National Bogland Centre, Lullymore, Rathangar, Co. Kildare Tel. (045) 60133
CLARA BOG, COUNTY OFFALY (1,150 acres) Raised bogland with undulating hummock.
◆ Contact Cecil Potterton, Ardkill Fram, Carbury, Co. Kildare Tel. (0405) 53009
SLIEVE BLOOM MOUNTAINS, COUNTY LAOIS (5,250 acres)

Several flat bogs. Marked paths.
◆ Contact Outdoor Education Centre Roscrea Road, Birr, Co. Offaly Tel. (0509) 20339
KNOCKMOYLE SHESKIN, COUNTY MAYO (3,935 acres) Studded with pools.
◆ Contact Wildlife Service
CEADE FIELDS, COUNTY MAYO (2,500) Spectacular cliffs. Of great archeological interest.
◆ Contact Ballycastle Information Centre
BORD NA MONA An organization which controls the industrial mining of

the bogs. Bog Railway train tours run from Bord na Mona along a track once used to transport the peat across a section of the Bog of Allen to Shannonbridge, 6 miles away.
◆ Center for enviromental research Newbridge, Co. Kildare Tel. (045) 31201
◆ Clonmacnois and West Offaly Railway Blackwater Works Shannonbridge Tel. (0905) 74114 Train tours last forty-five minutes and go on the hour from 10am to 5pm April to October. Price: Ir£2.85 per adult.

BIRD SANCTUARIES

SALTEE ISLANDS, Co. WEXFORD, guillemots, puffins, gannets.
WEXFORD HARBOUR AND SLOBS, in summer, feeding terns; in winter,

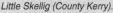

Greenland white-fronted geese.
NORTH BULL, Co. DUBLIN, waders, ducks, brent geese, short-eared owls.
IRISH WILDBIRD CONSERVANCY Ruttledge House

8, Longford Place, Monkstown, Co. Dublin Tel. (01) 284 4407
THE SKELLIGS, Co. KERRY, 20,000 pairs of breeding gannets, also puffins and manx. Landing is forbidden.
CAPE CLEAR BIRD OBSERVATORY, Co. CORK, Breeding birds include chough, black guillemot; major seabird

movements offshore, especially Jul.–Aug.; rarities seen late autumn, booking essential.
HORN HEAD, Co. DONEGAL, on the sheer cliffs, the largest colony of breeding razorbills in Ireland.
LOUGH SWILLY, Co. DONEGAL, late autumn 1,500 whooper swans.

The Wicklow Mountains (County Wicklow).

The Dunloe Gap (County Kerry).

USEFUL ADDRESS
◆ Long Distance
Walking Routes
Committee
Cospoi, 11th Floor
Hawkins House,
Hawkins Street,
Dublin 2
Tel. (01) 873 4700

MAPS AND GUIDE BOOKS

◆ State maps on a scale of 1:50,000 are published by Ordnance Survey, Phoenix Park, Dublin and Ordnance Survey of Northern Ireland
◆ *Irish Walk Guides* (in three volumes: *South West, West and North West, East and South East*), Gill and McMillan
◆ *Walking the Ulster Way*, Alan Warner, Appletree Press, Belfast

MARKERS
Yellow lettering on a black background.

Turn left | Straight ahead | Turn right

THE MAIN TRAILS

THE WESTERN WAY
120 miles (highest point 1,300 feet). Starting at Oughterard, Co. Galway it leads to Ballina, Co. Mayo via the Connemara mountains and Newport.

THE CAVAN WAY AND THE LEITRIM WAY
Approximately 60 miles (highest point 1,230 feet). Dowra (Co. Leitrim) is at the center of a star with arms leading toward Drumshambo (Co. Leitrim), Bellcoo (Co. Fermanagh), Manorhamilton (Co. Leitrim) with the option of taking the Ulster Way from Blacklion.

TAIN TRAIL AND ULSTER WAY
The Tain Trail, approximately 20 miles long (highest point,1,200 feet), is named after the Celtic epic poem *Tain Bo na Cuailigne*. It leads to the pretty and relatively unknown

Cooley Peninsula, to the north of Dublin. The Ulster Way, 430 miles long, goes right around the north of Ireland via the Mourne Mountains, the Antrim coast, the Giant's Causeway, and the lake country of Fermanagh.
◆ The Sports Council for Northern Ireland House of Sports, Upper Malone Road, Belfast, BT9 5LA

THE KILDARE WAY
(Grand Canal Towpath, Barrow Towpath, Royal Canal Towpath) 130 miles spreading from Kildare, mainly along canal towpaths. (Highest point 301 feet).

THE SLIEVE BLOOM WAY
38 miles long (highest point 1,300 feet). A complete circuit starting from Glenmonick Forest car park. In a mountainous area, in the middle of Ireland, between Birr and Mountmellick. Attractive and unspoiled, wooded and boggy in places. A path leads to the monastic site of Clonmacnois ▲ *203.*

WICKLOW WAY
82 miles (highest point 1,850 feet). The first to be established, it runs from Marley Park, to the south of Dublin, through the Wicklow Mountains, continues from glen to glen following old turf paths and roads once used to move livestock, as far as Aghavannagh, from where one can see Glendalough ▲ *178,* and finally arrives in the green and pleasant lower ground of Clonegal, Co. Carlow. The route is uneven and varied. On a clear day, you can even see the Welsh Mountains on the other side of the English Channel. . . The most attractive waterfall in Ireland, the Powerscourt Falls, is passed on route. Beware: the weather, changeable due to the altitude, can make walking conditions difficult.

THE KERRY WAY
134 miles (highest point 1,808 feet). Loop around Killary via Glencar, Glenbeigh, with a

possible detour to Valentia Island or to Waterview, then Sneem, Kenmare . . . The lushness of the scenery around the lakes contrasts dramatically with the austere rocky mountains, with the the vast Atlantic in the background.

THE DINGLE WAY
95 miles (highest point, 1,800 feet). Goes from Tralee to Castlegregory via Dingle and Cloghan. Rich Finistere scenery.

THE BURREN WAY
27 miles (highest point 850 feet), leads from Ballyvaughan to Liscannor via Doolin and the spectacular Cliffs of Moher ▲ *242.* The delicate flora (gentian, cranesbills, dryas) contrasts with the rugged gray reliefs of the karstic mountains. Stone route markers.

THE ARAN ISLANDS WAY
These three islands ▲ *270* still maintain a traditional Celtic way of life. See the stone forts, remains of early Christian tombs, ruined churches and, of course, the sea.

◆ SHOPPING

From clothing to crystal and pipes to pottery, Ireland produces many excellent quality goods. Internationally famed for its tweeds, linen and crystal, it has many other items of interest including whiskey, handmade cheeses, Celtic jewelry, local pottery and other crafts. These can be purchased from stores and craft shops all over Ireland.

KNITWEAR FROM THE ARAN ISLANDS AND DONEGAL

The Aran sweaters, worn by the local fishermen, were traditionally made from untreated, and thus waterproof, yarn. Both handknitted and machine-made versions are now readily available.

HAND-KNITTED
These sweaters are the best quality and most durable, but expect to pay around Ir£ 70–90.

MACHINE-MADE
Machine-made garments are much cheaper, but less hardwearing, not so warm and generally of a lesser standard. The different styles of cabling have been passed down through the generations and each has their own meaning.

Supposedly, the unfortunate victims of shipwrecks were easily identifiable by the patterns on their sweaters.

BLACKBERRY STITCH is a pattern of three points in one, and represents the holy trinity.

MOSS STITCH is a symbol of wealth. HONEYCOMB STITCH represents good luck (the sighting of a swarm of bees before going to sea was considered to be a lucky omen).

The DOUBLE ZIGZAG represents marriage.

LEARN TO KNIT AN ARAN SWEATER
Mrs Hegarty of the National Knitting Centre, Donegal will teach you to knit and design your own Aran

sweater (Ir£15 for three hours of tuition).
◆ National Knitting Centre
Lisfannon, Buncrana, Co. Donegal
Tel. (077) 62355
Fax (077) 62357

TWEED

Donegal is famous for its tweed, and some of the best Irish tweed is woven here. The most prestigious of the classic Irish tweeds is that which bears the Magee label. Produced by the same family for many generations and made using the colors of the Irish countryside, these tweeds frequently appear in the collections of many of Ireland's top couturiers. The factory is in the center of Donegal and is open to the public. Tweed is sold at around Ir£17 a yard.
◆ Magee & Co., Donegal City
Tel. (073) 210 050.
Open 9am to 6pm.
Closed Sunday.
Also in Donegal, another smaller tweed manufacturer is McNutts, which produces beautiful tweed available by the length (around Ir£12 a yard) or as ready-to-wear clothes (around Ir£100 for a lovely jacket).
◆ McNutts of Donegal, Downings, Co. Donegal
Tel (074) 55643.
Open 9am to 6pm.
Closed Sat. morning, Sun. and throughout the winter.
The Foxford Woollen

Mills was founded by a Sister of Charity at the end of the 19th century to provide work for poor young girls in the area. It produces slightly less expensive tweeds
◆ Foxford Woollen Mills, Foxford, Co. Mayo
Tel. (094) 56756.
Open 10am to 6pm.
Closed Sun. morning.

CRAFT SHOPS

Tweed articles such as caps, scarves (around Ir£10), and fishermen's hats (around Ir£18), can be found in many different craft shops thoughout Ireland, along with all kinds of Irish craftwork: crystal from Waterford, Galway or Tyrone; porcelain china from Arklow or Belleck, damask linen, Connemara marble, from Connemara, Celtic jewelry, straw crosses of Saint Brigid, pottery . . .

ADDRESSES
◆ Blarney Woollen Mills, 21–3, Nassau Street, Dublin 2
Tel. (01) 710 068
◆ Blarney Woollen Mills, Blarney, Co. Cork
Tel. (021) 385 280
◆ Dublin Woollen Mills, 41, Ormond Quay, Dublin 1
Tel. (01) 770 301
◆ Quills, The Square, Killarney, Co. Kerry
Tel. (064) 32277
Also in branches in Kenmare and Sneem, Co. Kerry
◆ Carraig Donn Lodge Road, Westport, Co. Sligo
Tel. (098) 25566
Also in Kilkenny.

KAPP & PETERSON PIPES

For more than 200 years these beautiful curved pipes, favored by connoisseurs, have had the reputation of being the most elegant and best quality of their kind. Their latest range, is called the "Sherlock Holmes".
Prices: Ir£15–100 and upward)
◆ Kapp & Peterson 117, Grafton Street Dublin 2
Tel. (01) 671 4652

NICOLAS MOSSE POTTERY

This rustic-style ware is handpainted with "naive" floral or animal patterns using a 19th-century sponging technique.
◆ Nicolas Mosse Pottery Bennettsbridge, Co. Kilkenny
Tel. (056) 27105
Fax (056) 27491

HANDWEAVER
Avoca Handweavers Killmacanogue Bray, Co. Wicklow
Tel. (01) 286 7466

TAILOR
Kevin and Howlin 31, Nassau Street Dublin 2
Tel. (01) 677 0257

USEFUL ADDRESSES

★ SPECIAL INTEREST

▭ CREDIT CARDS

○ RESTAURANT

◑ PUB FOOD

🏛 LUXURY HOTEL

🏠 BED & BREAKFAST
  OR GUEST HOUSE

Ｃ TOWN CENTER

⤷ ISOLATED

◠ QUIET

⩞ PANORAMA

⌇ SWIMMING POOL

⊤ TERRACE

♣ GARDEN

⚵ REDUCTIONS FOR
  CHILDREN

♫ MUSIC

Ｐ PARKING

◆

LEINSTER

DUBLIN CITY

▲142

PRACTICAL
INFORMATION

AMERICAN EMBASSY
42, Elgin Road, Dublin 4
Tel. (01) 668 8777
Fax (01) 668 9946

BRITISH EMBASSY
33, Merrion Rd, Dublin 4
Tel. (01) 269 5211

TOURIST OFFICES
◆ DUBLIN TOURISM
14, Upper O'Connell St,
Dublin 1
Tel. (01) 284 1765
Fax (01) 284 1751
Open July–Aug, Mon.–
Sat. 8.30am–8pm, Sun.

◆ NOTE

◆ All addresses are
followed by a map
reference.

PUBS

Pubs throughout Ireland
are generally open until
11pm (11.30pm in
summer), Monday to
Saturday and close for
a few hours on Sunday
afternoon.
Prices under Ir£2 or£2
are not listed.
The sign "Pub grub" is
displayed in some pubs
serving basic meals
◆ 344.

RESTAURANTS

These prices are only a
guide; they give the
average price of a meal
(set menu or main
courses).
Many restaurants take
last orders at 9pm.

10.30am–2pm; Jun.
15–30 and Sept. 1–15,
Mon.–Sat. 8.30am–6pm;
Mar.–Jun. 15, Mon.–Sat.
9am–5pm; Sept.15–
Feb., Mon.–Fri. 9am–
5pm, Sat. 9am–3.30pm

◆ NORTHERN IRELAND
TOURIST BOARD
16, Nassau St, Dublin 2
Tel. (01) 679 1977
Open Mon.–Fri. 9am–
5.30pm, Sat. 10am–5pm

◆ TEMPLE BAR
INFORMATION CENTRE
18, Eustace St,
Temple Bar, Dublin 2
Tel. (01) 715 717
Open Jun.–Sept., Mon.–
Fri. 9am–7pm, Sat.
11am– 7pm, Sun. noon–
4pm; Oct.–May, Mon.–
Fri. 9.30am–6pm, Sat.
noon–6pm

TRANSPORT
◆ IRISH RAIL
IARNRÓD ÉIREANN
35, Lower Abbey St,
Dublin 1
Tel. (01) 366 222
CONNOLLY STATION
Tel. (01) 703 2358
*For information on trains
to Belfast, Sligo,
Wexford and Rosslare.*

ACCOMMODATION

◆ This selection of Bed
& Breakfasts and Guest
Houses is by no means
exhaustive as there is
an enormous number of
Bed & Breakfasts and
places taking paying
guests throughout
Ireland.
◆ The prices indicated
are generally per
person for a night.
◆ A double room is less
expensive than two
single rooms.
◆ Many rooms with en-
suite bathrooms are
available.

CULTURE

◆ Protestant churches
(Church of Ireland),
often the oldest of Irish
churches, are only open
during services; outside
service times, ask the
vicar for the key.
◆ The Office of Public
Works (OPW) sells a
Heritage Card, at a cost

HEUSTON STATION
Tel. (01) 703 2132
*For information on trains
to Cork, Galway,
Limerick, Tralee and
Waterford.*

◆ DART (DUBLIN AREA
RAPID TRANSPORT)
Travel Centre,
35, Lower Abbey St,
Dublin 1
Tel. (01) 366 222
Open Mon.–Fri.
9am–5pm, Sat.
9am–1pm
*Dublin's express railway
network.*

◆ BUS ÉIREANN
Central Bus Station,
Store St, Dublin 1
Tel. (01) 366 111

◆ DUBLIN BUS
(BUS ÁTHA CLIATH)
59, Upper O'Connell St,
Dublin 1
Tel. (01) 873 4242
*For transport within the
greater Dublin area.*

CULTURE

ABBEY THEATRE
26, Lower Abbey St,
Dublin 1
Tel. (01) 878 7222

---

of Ir£10, which offers
unlimited access to all
National Heritage sites
and is valid for one
year.
◆ The organization
Heritage Island has
compiled a list of
approximately sixty
historic and cultural
sites. These can be
found in the Heritage
Island guide, which is
available for a price of
Ir£5, and includes a
VIP card entitling the
bearer and anyone
accompanying them to
a discount of up to
twenty-five percent on
admission to any of the
sites listed.
Available from Heritage
Island and from most
tourist offices.
HERITAGE ISLAND
37, Main Street,
Donnybrook, Dublin 4
Tel. (01) 260 0055
Fax (01) 260 0058

Box office: Mon.–Sat.
10.30am–7pm
*Part of the National
Theatre. Box office is
open Mon. –Sat.
10.30am–7pm. Tickets
Ir£8–13. Student
standby (Ir£5) available
1 hour before
performance Mon. and
Thur.*

BANK OF IRELAND
2, College Green,
Dublin 2
Tel. (01) 615 933 ext.
2265
Open Mon.–Fri. 10am–
4pm, Thur. 10am–5pm
*Guided tour (30 mins.)
Tue. 10.30am, 11.30am
and 1.45pm, except
public holidays.*

**CHESTER BEATTY
LIBRARY**
20, Shrewsbry Rd,
Dublin 4
Tel. (01) 269 2386
Open Tue.–Fri. 10am–
5pm, Sat. 2–5pm
*Guided tours Wed. and
Sat. at 2.30pm.*

CHRIST CHURCH
Christ Church Place,
Dublin 8
Tel. (01) 677 8099

Open 10am–5pm
Closed Dec. 26.
Ir£1 (donation)

CITY HALL
Cork Hill, Dublin 2
Tel. (01) 679 6111
Open Mon.–Fri.
9am–5pm

CUSTOM HOUSE
Custom House Quay,
Dublin 1
Tel. (01) 873 4555
Closed to the public.

DUBLIN CASTLE
Dame St, Dublin 2
Tel. (01) 677 7128
State Apartments open
Mon.–Fri. 10am–
12.15pm and 2–5pm;
Sat.–Sun. and public
holidays 2–5pm
Closed Dec. 24–26 and
Good Friday.
Ir£1.75

**DUBLIN ZOO
& ZOOLOGICAL
SOCIETY OF IRELAND**
Phœnix Park, Dublin 8
Tel. (01) 677 1425
Open Mar–Oct.,
Mon.– Sat.
9.30am–6pm, Sun.
10.30am–6pm;
Nov.–Feb., Mon.–Sat.
9.30am–4pm,
Sun. 10.30am–4pm
Ir£1.80–4.20

**DUBLIN'S WRITERS
MUSEUM**
18–19, Parnell Square
North, Dublin 1
Tel. (01) 872 2077
Open 10am–5pm, Sun.
11am–6pm
80p–Ir£2.50

DUBLINIA
St Michael's Hill,
Dublin 8
Tel. (01) 679 4611
Open May–Sept.
10am–5pm; Oct.–Apr.,
Mon.–Sat. 11am–4pm,
Sun. 10am–4.30pm
Ir£2.90–3.95

FOUR COURTS
Aras Ui Dhalaigh,
Inns Quay, Dublin 7
Tel. (01) 872 5555
Open 10.30am–4pm

GUINNESS BREWERY
St. James's Gate,
Crane St, Dublin 8
Tel. (01) 453 6700
Open Mon.–Fri.
10am–4pm
Closed public holidays.
*Located in Crane Street,
the Guinness Hop*

*Store houses the
World of Guinness
Exhibition. Audiovisual
display and the
Guinness museum.
Entrance fee includes a
free Guinness tasting.*
Ir£2

KILMAINHAM GAOL
Inchicore Rd, Dublin 8
Tel. (01) 453 5984
Open May–Sept.
10am–6pm; Oct.–Apr.
Opening times not
available
Ir£1–2

LEINSTER HOUSE
Dáil, Éireann,
Kildare St, Dublin 2
Tel. (01) 678 9911
*Open for visits by prior
written application.*

MARINO CASINO
Malahide Rd, Dublin 3
Tel. (01) 833 1618
Open Jun.–Sept.
9.30am–6.30pm; during
the winter months by
appointment only.
60p–Ir£1.50

MARSH'S LIBRARY
St Patrick's Close,
Dublin 8
Tel. (01) 454 3511
Open Mon., Wed., Fri.
10am–12.45pm and
2–5pm, Sat.
10.30am–12.45pm
Ir£1

**MUNICIPAL ART
GALLERY**
Parnell Square North,
Dublin 1
Tel. (01) 741 903
Open Tue.–Fri.
9.30am–6pm, Sat.
9.30am–5pm, Sun.
11am–5pm

**NATIONAL BOTANIC
GARDENS**
Glasnevin, Dublin 9
Tel. (01) 837 4388
Open Jun.–Sept.,
Mon.–Sat. 9am–6pm,
Sun. 11am–6pm;
Oct.–May, Mon.–Sat.
10am–4.30pm, Sun.
11am–4.30pm
Closed Christmas

**NATIONAL
GALLERY
OF IRELAND**
Merrion Square West,
Dublin 2
Tel. (01) 661 5133
Open Mon.–Sat.
10am–5pm, Thur.
10am–8.15pm, Sun.
2–5pm

*Guided tours by prior
arrangement: book at
least two weeks in
advance. Tour prices
start at Ir£20.*

**NATIONAL MUSEUM
OF IRELAND**
Kildare St, Dublin 2
Tel. (01) 661 8811
Open Tue.–Sat.
10am–5pm, Sun.
2–5pm

**NATURAL HISTORY
MUSEUM**
Merrion St, Dublin 2
Tel. (01) 661 8811
Open Tue.–Sat. 10am–
5pm, Sun. 2–5pm
Closed Christmas and
Good Friday

NEWMAN HOUSE
85–6, St Stephen's
Green South, Dublin 2
Tel. (01) 475 7255
Open Jun.–Sept.,
Tue.–Fri. 10am–
4.30pm, Sat. 2–4.30pm,
Sun. 11am–2pm
75p–Ir£1

NUMBER TWENTY NINE
Lower Fitzwilliam St,
Dublin 2
Tel. (01) 702 6165
Open Tue.–Sat.
10am–5pm, Sun. 2–5pm
Closed Good Friday and
two weeks before
Christmas

**POWERSCOURT
TOWN HOUSE**
South William St,
Dublin 2
Tel. (01) 679 4144
Open Mon., Tue., Wed.,
Fri., Sat. 8am–6pm
Thur. 8am–5pm

ROTUNDA HOSPITAL
O'Connell St,
Dublin 1
Tel. (01) 873 0700
*Visits by prior
arrangement only.*

**ROYAL COLLEGE
OF SURGEONS**
123, St Stephen's
Green, Dublin 2
Tel. (01) 478 0200
Closed to the public.

**ROYAL HOSPITAL OF
KILMAINHAM (MODERN
ART MUSEUM)**
Inchicore Rd, Dublin 8
Tel. (01) 671 8666
Open Tue.–Sat.
10am–5.30pm,
Sun. noon–5.30pm
*Guided tours on
request.*

ROYAL IRISH ACADEMY
19, Dawson St, Dublin 1
Tel. (01) 478 5466
Open Mon.–Fri.
9.30am–5.30pm
*Guided tours only, by
reservation.*

ST AUDOEN'S CHURCH
Usher's Quay, Dublin 1
Tel. (01) 679 1855
Open 8am–6pm

ST MARY'S ABBEY
Meetinghouse Lane,
Dublin 1
Tel. (01) 872 1490
Open Jun. 15–Sept. 15,
Wed. 10am–5pm
40p–Ir£1

**ST MARY
PRO-CATHEDRAL**
83, Marlborough St,
Dublin 1
Tel. (01) 874 5441
Open 8am–7pm

ST MICHAN'S CHURCH
Church Street, Dublin 1
Tel. (01) 872 4154
Open Nov.–Mar 15
10am–12.45pm
and 2–4.45pm
50p–Ir£1.20

**ST PATRICK'S
CATHEDRAL**
St Patrick's Close,
Dublin 8
Tel. (01) 475 4817
Open Mon.–Fri. 9am–
6pm, Sat. 9am–5pm,
Sun. 10am–4.30pm
Ir£1

**ST WERBURGH'S
CHURCH**
Werburgh St, Dublin 1
Tel. (01) 478 3710
Open Mon.–Fri.
10am–4pm
*Collect the keys from
8, Castle Street.*

TAILOR'S GUILD HALL
Back Lane, Dublin 8
Tel. (01) 454 4794
Open Mon.–Fri.
9.30am–4.30pm

TRINITY COLLEGE
Trinity College, Dublin 2
Tel. (01) 677 2941
– The Book of Kells
(reference library)
Tel. (01) 702 2320
Open Mon.–Fri. 9.30am–
5.30pm, Sun. noon–5pm
Closed public holidays.
Ir£2.50
– Dublin Experience
Tel. (01) 702 1177
Open May–Sept.
10am–5pm
Ir£1.50–2.75

365

WATERWAYS VISITORS' CENTRE
The Waterway Building, Grand Canal Quay, Dublin 2
Tel. (01) 677 7510
Open Jun.–Sept. 9.30am–6.30pm, Sept.–Jun. Wed.–Sun. 12.30–5pm
Exhibition showing the construction and operation of Ireland's canals and waterways.
60p–Ir£1.50

IRISH WHISKEY CORNER
Smithfield, 77, Bow St, Dublin 7
Tel. (01) 872 5566
One tour daily at 3.30pm. Visits can also be organized in advance.
Ir£3

PUBS/RESTAURANTS

AN BÉAL BOCHT
Charlemont St, Dublin 2
Tel. (01) 475 5614
Traditional music
♫

BAD ASS CAFÉ ★
9, Crown Alley, off Temple Bar, Dublin 2
Tel. (01) 671 2596
Open noon–midnight
Huge warehouse converted into American-style pizza house.
Ir£6.50–8.50
⌨ ◑ 夫

THE BAILEY
2, Duke St, Dublin 2
Tel. (01) 677 3055
Open Mon.–Sat. 12.15–2.30pm
Ir£5
⌨ ○ ◑

BÀTON ROUGE
119, St Stephen's Green, Dublin 2
Tel. (01) 475 1181
Open noon–3pm and 6pm–12.30am
Ir£9.95–16
⌨ ○ C

BEWLEY'S ORIENTAL CAFÉ ★
78–9, Grafton St, Dublin 2
Tel. (01) 677 6761
Open Sun.–Thur. 7.30–1am, Fri.–Sat. 7.30am–2am
The largest of three outlets (others at Westmoreland Street and South Great George's Street).

An institution in Dublin. The potato soup is highly recommended.
Ir£3
⌨ C

BRAZEN HEAD
20, Lower Bridge St, Dublin 2
Tel. (01) 677 9549
Dublin's oldest pub (1198).
♫

LA CAVE
28, South Anne St, Dublin 2
Tel. (01) 679 4409
Open 12.30pm–3am or later, Sun. 6pm–2am
French restaurant. Elegant and romantic.
Ir£10.95
⌨ ○ ♫

CLARENCE HOTEL TEA ROOM
6–8, Wellington Quay, Temple Bar, Dublin 2
Tel. (01) 677 6178
Due to reopen July 1995.

THE COMMONS RESTAURANT
Newman House, 85–6, St Stephen's Green, Dublin 2
Tel. (01) 780 530
Open Mon.–Fri. 12.30–2.15pm and Mon.–Sat. 7–10.15pm
Ir£16–28
⌨ ○

COOKE'S CAFÉ ★
14, South William St, Dublin 2
Tel. (01) 679 0536
Ir£7–13.95
⌨ ○

DAVY BYRNE'S
21, Duke St, Dublin 2
Tel. (01) 671 298
"NIce quiet bar. Nice piece of wood in that counter. Nicely planned. Like the way it curves there." James Joyce, "Ulysses".

DOBBINS
15, Stephen's Lane, Dublin 2
Tel. (01) 613 321
Ir£14.50–25
⌨ ○

EAMONN DORAMS DUBLIN & NEW YORK
Crown Alley, Temple Bar, Dublin 2
Tel. (01) 679 9114

Open 11am–2.30am
Ir£5–15
⌨ ○ ◑ ♫

FITZERS
National Gallery, Leinster Lawn, Merrion Square West, Dublin 2
Tel. (01) 661 4496
Open Mon.–Wed., Fri.–Sat. 10am–5pm, Thur. 10am–8pm, Sun. 2–4.30pm
Ir£4.25–8
⌨ ○

GALLAGHERS BOXTY HOUSE
20–1, Temple Bar, Dublin 2
Tel. (01) 677 2762
Ir£4.95–16
⌨ ○ ♫

HUGHES ★
19, Chancery St, Dublin 2
Tel. (01) 679 5186
Open Mon.–Fri. 9am–11pm
⌨ ◑ ♫

INTERNATIONAL BAR
23, Wicklow St, Dublin 2
Tel. (01) 677 9250
Open Mon.–Sat. 10.30am–11pm, Sun. 12.30–2pm, 4–11pm
Another Dublin institution. Mostly rock bands with blues nights. Comedy improvisation on Mon. and Wed. nights.

IRISH FILM CENTRE
6, Eustace St, Dublin 2
Tel. (01) 677 8788
Open Mon.–Wed. 9.30am–11.30pm, Thur.–Sat. 12.30–11.30pm. Bar open until 2am, Thur.–Sat.
This two-screen cinema center which specializes in art movies has a cafeteria serving delicious food. Eclectic menu includes a wide choice of vegetarian dishes. Ideal place to eat either before or after the performance.

KILKENNY KITCHEN
6, Nassau St, Dublin 2 (On the second floor of the Kilkenny Design Centre)
Tel. (01) 677 7066
Open Mon.–Sat. 9am–6pm
Closed Christmas
Cheap cafeteria, tends to get busy at lunchtime.
Ir£4–8
⌨

KING'S INN
42, Bolton St, Dublin 1
Tel. (01) 872 5909
C ♫

LOCKS RESTAURANT
1, Windsor Terrace Portobello, Dublin 8
Tel. (01) 543 391
Ir£25
⌨ ○ ⬓

LONGFIELD NUMBER TEN
10, Fitzwilliam St, Dublin 2
Tel. (01) 676 1367
Open 8–10.30am, 12.30–2.30pm and 7–10pm
Ir£22
⌨ ○

THE LOWER DECK
1, Portobello Harbour, Dublin 8
Tel. (01) 475 1423
Open 11.30am–midnight
◑ ♫

McDAID'S
3, Harry St, Dublin 2
Tel. (01) 679 4395
This pub was once frequented by Brendan Behan who used to write here.
⌨ ◑

MITCHELL CELLARS
21, Kildare St, Dublin 2
Tel. (01) 668 0367
Open Fri.–Tue. 12.15–2.30pm, Thur. 5–9pm
Closed Sat. (Jun.–Aug) and Christmas
Ir£6.75–12
⌨ ○ C

MULLIGAN'S
8, Poolbeg St, Dublin 2
Tel. (01) 677 5582
*Said to serve the best
Guinness in Dublin,
outside the brewery
itself.*
◑

O'DONOGHUES ★
15, Merrion Row,
Dublin 2
Tel. (01) 676 2807
*Pub with traditional and
folk music daily.*
♫

**THE OLD DUBLIN
RESTAURANT**
90–1 Francis St,
Dublin 8
Tel. (01) 542 028
Open Mon.–Fri.
12.30–2.30pm and
Mon.–Sat. 7–11pm
Closed Sun. and public
holidays.
Ir£12–19
▭ ○

THE PALACE BAR
21, Fleet St,
Dublin 2
Tel. (01) 677 9290
♫

**PERIWINKLE
SEAFOOD BAR** ★
Powerscourt
Townhouse Centre,
South William St,
Dublin 2
Tel. (01) 679 4203
Open Mon.–Sat.
11.30am–5pm
Ir£3–10
○

**RESTAURANT
PATRICK GUILBAUD**
46, James St, Dublin 2
Tel. (01) 676 4192
Closed Sun. and Mon.
French cuisine.
Ir£15–35
▭ ○

ROLY'S BISTRO
7, Ballsbridge Terrace,
Dublin 4
Tel. (01) 668 2611
Closed Dec. 24–7 and
Good Friday
Ir£10–20
▭ ○

RYAN'S
28, Parkgate St, Dublin 8
Tel. (01) 671 9935
Open Mon.–Fri. 12.30–
4pm, Tue.–Sat. 7.30–
10pm, food: 5–7.30pm
*Dublin's finest example
of a Victorian pub.*
Ir£6–12
▭ ◑

SLATTERY'S
129, Capel St, Dublin 4
Tel. (01) 872 7971
Open 7am–11pm, Sun.
noon–11pm
*Particularly well-known
for its traditional music
as well as its rock and
blues nights.*
◑ ♫

TANTE ZOC'S
1, Crow St
Tel. (01) 679 4407
Opn Mon.–Sat.
noon–3pm,
6pm–midnight
*Popular Cajun/Creole
restaurant with live jazz
every Thursday. Good
prices. Reserve in
advance.*
Ir£3–10
♫

THE TERRACE CAFÉ ★
Temple Bar Hotel,
Fleet St,
Dublin 2
Tel. (01) 677 3333
Open 7am–10.30pm
Ir£7–12.95
▭ ◑ ♫

**THE TOWER
RESTAURANT**
1st floor,
Ida Tower Craft,
Pearse St,
Dublin 2
Tel. (01) 677 5655
Open Mon.–Fri.
8.30am–5.30pm
Ir£3.95
○

THE WEXFORD INN ★
26, Wexford St,
Dublin 2
Tel. (01) 478 0391
♫

ACCOMMODATION

THE CLARENCE HOTEL
6–8, Wellington Quay,
Temple Bar, Dublin 2
Tel. (01) 677 6178
Fax (01) 677 7487
*Due to reopen August
1995. Central, lively
position. Taken over by
U2. "The Kitchen"
nightclub and "The
Garage" bar are both
trendy and fairly tacky.
Hotel comfortable and
luxurious. Expensive.*

ELEGANT IRELAND
15, Harcourt St,
Dublin 2
Tel. (01) 475 1665
Fax (01) 575 1012
*Agency with
approximately forty*

*luxurious houses and
castles available for
rent.*

FATIMA GUEST HOUSE
17, Upper Gardener St,
Dublin 1
Tel. (01) 874 5410
Fax (01) 872 7674
Ir£15–16.50
▭ ⌂ Ⓒ Ⓟ

**GEORGIAN HOUSE
HOTEL** ★
20–1, Lower Baggott St,
Dublin 2
Tel. (01) 661 8832
Fax (01) 661 8834
*A fine period building,
5 minutes from St
Stephen's Green. Good
seafood restaurant.*
Ir£52.80–83.60
▭ Ⓟ

**KINLAY HOUSE
YOUTH HOSTEL**
2–12, Lord Edward St,
Christ Church, Dublin 2
Tel. (01) 679 6644
*Well-located in Temple
Bar area. Comfortable.
Breakfast, towel, linen
and soap included.
Lockers, laundry and
bike rental available.*
Ir£7.50–16.50
▭

MOUNT HERBERT ★
7, Herbert Rd,
Ballsbridge, Dublin 4
Tel. (01) 668 4321
Fax (01) 660 7077
*Three-star guesthouse.
Welcoming.*
Ir£31–50
▭ ⌂ ○ ⌂ ☆ ⛪ Ⓟ

**THE SHELBOURNE
HOTEL FORTE
GRAND** ★
27, St Stephen's Green,
Dublin 2
Tel. (01) 676 6471
Fax (01) 661 6006
*Five-star, luxurious
hotel. Ireland's most
distinguished address.*
Ir£100–125
▭ ⌂ Ⓒ Ⓟ

**STEPHENS HALL
HOTEL** ★
14–17, Lower
Leeson St, Dublin 2
Tel. (01) 661 0585
Fax (01) 661 0606
*Three-star hotel.
Tastefully decorated
suites with fully-
equipped kitchens. In
the heart of Georgian
Dublin.*
Ir£80–110
▭ ⌂ ○ Ⓒ Ⓟ

**WESLEY HOUSE
GEORGIAN**
113, Anglesea Rd,
Ballsbridge, Dublin 4
Tel. (01) 681 201
Guesthouse.
Ir£25
▭ ⌂ ☆ Ⓟ

SHOPPING

**BLARNEY WOOLLEN
MILLS**
21–3, Nassau St,
Dublin 8
Tel. (01) 671 0068
Open Mon.–Sat.
9am–6pm,
Thur. 9am–8pm,
Sun. 11am–6pm
*Stocks woolen
sweaters.*

**DONEGAL TWEED
SHOP**
St Stephen's Green
Shopping Center,
Dublin 2
Tel. (01) 478 3941
Open Mon.–Sat.
9.30am–6pm,
Thur. 9.30am–8pm
*A range of tweed
garments.*

**McCONNELL
& NELSON**
38, Grafton St, Dublin 2
Tel. (01) 677 4344
Open Mon. 9am–1pm,
Tue.–Fri.
8.30am–5.30pm, Sat.
9am–1pm
*Smoked salmon, fresh
fish.*

COUNTY DUBLIN

PRACTICAL
INFORMATION

TOURIST OFFICES
◆ (H-6) 1, Clarinda Park
North, Dún Laoghaire,
Tel. (01) 280 8571
Fax (01) 284 1751
Open 9am–5.15pm

◆ (H-6) St Michael's
Walk, Dún Laoghaire,
Tel. (01) 284 4768
Fax (01) 280 6459
Open 8.30am–10pm

CULTURE

JAMES JOYCE MUSEUM
(H-6) Sandycove,
Tel. (01) 2809265
Open May–Sept.,
Mon.–Fri. 10am–1pm
and 2–5pm, Sun.
2–6pm; Apr. and Oct.
Mon. Fri. 10am–1pm,
2–5pm
Ir£1–1.90

MALAHIDE CASTLE
(H-6) Malahide
Tel. (01) 845 2655
Open Mon.–Fri.
10am–1pm and 2–5pm,
Sat. (Apr.–Oct. only)
11am–1pm and
2–6pm
*The home of the
Fry Model Railway
Tel. (01) 845 2758*
Ir£1.90–2.50

**NATIONAL MARITIME
MUSEUM** (H-6)
Old Mariner's Church,
Haigh Terrace,
Dún Laoghaire,
Tel. (01) 280 0969
Open Easter–Sept.,
Thur.–Sun.
2.30–5.30pm;
Oct., Sat.–Sun.
2.30–5.30pm
80p–Ir£1.50

PUBS/RESTAURANTS

CLARETS RESTAURANT
(H-6) 63, Main St,
Blackrock,
Tel. (01) 288 2008
Ir£13.95–22.95
▢ ○ **C**

KING SITRIC (H-6)
East Pier, Howth
Tel. (01) 832 5235
Closed Sun. and
public holidays.
▢ ♫

**NA MARA
RESTAURANT**
(H-6) 1, Harbour Rd,
Dún Laoghaire,
Tel. (01) 280 6767
Open noon–2.30pm
and 7–10.30pm
Closed Sun. and
public holidays.
Ir£11.75–23
▢ ○ ♨

**NEWBRIDGE HOUSE
& ITS TRADITIONAL
FARM** (H-6)
Donabate
Tel. (01) 843 6534
Open Tue.–Fri.
10am–5pm, Sat.
11am–6pm, Sun.
2–6pm; Nov.–Mar.
Sat.–Sun. 2–5pm.
*Beautifully located
within a 300-acre
park.*
Ir£1.65–2.90

**THE OLD
SCHOOLHOUSE** (H-6)
Swords
Tel. (01) 840 2846
Closed Sun.
Ir£10.95–12.95
▢ ○ **P**

ACCOMMODATION

PORT VIEW HOTEL ★
(H-6) Marine Rd, Dún
Laoghaire
Tel. (01) 280 1663
Fax (01) 280 0447
*Located 15 minutes
from the center of
Dublin. Comfortable
and reasonably priced
hotel offering a 75
percent reduction for
children under 10 years.*
Ir£25–58.50
▢ **C** ♫ **P**

COUNTY KILDARE

PRACTICAL INFORMATION

TOURIST OFFICE
(G-6) The Market House,
Kildare
Tel. (045) 22696
Open daily Jun.–Aug
10am–1pm, 2–6pm
Sept.–May,Fri.
10am–1pm, 2–6pm

CULTURE

CASTLETOWN HOUSE
(H-6) Celbridge ▲ *182*
Tel. (01) 628 8252
Open Apr.–Sept.,
Mon.–Fri. 10am–6pm,
Sat. 11am–6pm, Sun.
2–6pm; Oct., Mon.–Fri.
10am–5pm, Sun.
2–5pm, Nov.–Mar.
Sun. 2–5pm
Ir£2–2.50

**IRISH NATIONAL STUD
& JAPANESE GARDENS**
(G-6) Tully, Kildare
Tel. (045) 21617
Open 14 Mar.–Oct.
9.30am–6pm
Ir£3–4

ACCOMMODATION

**THE KILDARE HOTEL
& COUNTRY CLUB**
(H-6) Straffan
Tel. (01) 627 3333
Fax (01) 627 3312
Closed Good Friday
*Luxury 5-star hotel with
2 restaurants, 18-hole
golf course, river and
coarse fishing, tennis
courts and swimming
pool.*
From Ir£125
▢ ○ ♫

COUNTY KILKENNY

PRACTICAL INFORMATION

TOURIST OFFICE (F-8)
Rose Inn St, Kilkenny,
Tel. (056) 21755
Fax (056) 63955
Open May–Jul.,
Mon.–Sat. 9am–6pm,
Sun. 11am–5pm

CULTURE

BLACK ABBEY (F-8)
Kilkenny
Tel. (056) 21279
Open 7am–7pm
*Expect to give a
donation.*

**BUTLER GALLERY,
KILKENNY CASTLE**
(F-8) Kilkenny
Tel. (056) 61106
Open Feb.–Oct. 10am–
7pm; Nov.–Feb., Tue.–
Sun. 10.30am–5pm

DUNMORE CAVES (F-7)
Ballyfoyle
Tel. (056) 67726
Open Jun. 15–Sept. 15
10am–7pm; Sept. 15–
Oct. 14am–6pm; Mar.
15– Jun. 15, Tue.–Sat.
10am–5pm, Sun. 2–5pm
Guided tour.
60p–Ir£1.50

JERPOINT ABBEY (G-8)
Thomastowny
Tel. (056) 24623
Open Jun. 15–Sept. 15
9.30am–6.30pm; Sept.
15–Oct. 15 10am–1pm
and 2–5pm; Apr. 15
–Jun. 15, Tue.–Sun.
10am–1pm and 2–5pm
Ir£1.50

KILKENNY CASTLE
(F-8) Kilkenny
Tel. (056) 21450
Open Jun.–Sept. 10am–
7pm; Oct.– Mar.,

Tue.–Sat.
10.30am–12.45pm
and 2–5pm, Sun.
11am–12.45pm and
2–5pm; Apr.–May,
10.30am–5pm
Closed Christmas and
Good Friday
Ir£1–2

ROTHE HOUSE (F-8)
Parliament St,
Kilkenny
Tel. (056) 22893
Open Jul.–Aug, 9.30am–
6pm; Sept.– Jun.,
weekends 10am–5pm
60p–Ir£1.50

**SMITHWICKS
BREWERY**
(F-8) Parliament St,
Kilkenny
Tel. (056) 21014
July–Aug. open
Mon.–Fri. 3pm
*Tours (40 mins.) by
appointment. Tickets
available from the
tourist office.*

**ST CANICE'S
CATHEDRAL** (F-8)
Church's Lane, Kilkenny
Tel. (056) 64971
Open Easter–Sept.,
Mon.–Sat. 9am–1pm
and 2–6pm, Sun. 2–6pm;
Oct.–Easter, Mon.–Sat.
10am–1pm and 2–4pm
Ir£1

PUBS/RESTAURANTS

**EDWARD LANGTON'S
PUB & RESTAURANT ★**
(F-8) 69, John St,
Kilkenny,
Tel. (056) 65133
Restaurant Mon.–Sat.
noon–3pm and
5.30–10.30pm,
Sun. noon–3pm
*Won many awards for
best pub in Ireland.*
Restaurant Ir£15–18.50
Lunch Ir£5
Dinner Ir£12.50–16.50
▢ ○ ◑ **C** ♫

JOHN CLEERE (F-8)
Parliament St, Kilkenny
Tel. (056) 62573
Open 4.30–11.30pm
Traditional Irish music.
C ♫

KYTELER'S INN (F-8)
Kieran St, Kilkenny
Tel. (056) 21064
Open Mon.–Sat. until
6pm, Sun until 2pm.
Closed Christmas and
Good Friday
Ir£5.75–11.75
▢ ◑ **C** **P**

LADY HELEN MCCALMONT (G-8)
Mount Juliet,
Thomastown
Tel. (056) 24455
Open 7–9.30pm
Ir£16–33
▭ ○

LAUTRECS
9, St Kieran St, Kilkenny
Tel. (056) 62720
Open 5.30–1am daily
The only wine-bar in Kilkenny. Dark, cavernous setting. Good late-night bar.

TYNAN'S BAR (F-8)
Bridge House,
2, John Bridge, Kilkenny
Tel. (056) 21291
▭

COUNTY LAOIS

PRACTICAL INFORMATION

TOURIST OFFICE (F-7)
James Fintan Lawlor
Ave., Portlaoise
Tel. (0502) 21178
Open May–Sept.
Mon.–Sat. 9am–6pm

CULTURE

EMO COURT & GARDENS
(F-6) Emo
Tel. (0502) 26110
– House open Mar. 15–
Oct. 15., Mon. 2–6pm,
or by appointment.
– Gardens open end
Mar.–Oct.
10.30am–5.30pm
Situated two miles from Emo on the Dublin–Cork–Limerick road.
Ir£1–2–2.50

COUNTY LONGFORD

PRACTICAL INFORMATION

TOURIST OFFICE
(F-5) Main St, Longford
Tel. (043) 46566
Open Jun.–Sept.,
Mon.–Sat. 10am–1pm
and 2–6pm

CULTURE

CORLEA BOG EXHIBITION CENTRE
(F-5) Near Kenagh,
Ballymahon,
Tel. (043) 22386

(in summer)
Tel. (01) 661 3111
(in winter)
Exhibition of relics found in the bogs dating from AD 148.

COUNTY LOUTH

PRACTICAL INFORMATION

TOURIST OFFICE
(H-4) Market Square,
Dundalk
Tel. (042) 35484
Fax (042) 38070
Open Jun.–Sept.,
Mon.–Fri. 9am–6pm,
Sat. 10am–5.30pm;
Oct.–May, Mon.–Fri.
9.30am–5.30pm

CULTURE

ST PETER'S CHURCH
(H-5) West St, Drogheda
Open daily
8.30am–8.30pm

PROLEEK DOLMEN
(H-4)
Situated 3 miles from
Dundalk on the road to
Newry

LOUTH COUNTY MUSEUM (H-4)
Jocelyn St, Dundalk
Tel. (042) 27056
Open Tue.–Sat.
10.30am–5.30pm,
Sun. 2–6pm
50p–Ir£1

MONASTERBOICE (H-5)
West St, Drogheda
Tel. (041) 37070
6 miles to the northwest
of Drogheda
Information available from the Drogheda tourist office.

MELLIFONT ABBEY
(H-5) 5 miles northwest
of Drogheda
Tel. (041) 26459
Open Jun. 15–Sept. 15,
9.30am–6.30pm; Sept.
15–Oct. 10am– 5pm;
May–Jun. 15, Tue.–Sat.
9.30am–1pm and 2–
5.30pm, Sun. 2–5.30pm
Ir£1

PUBS/RESTAURANTS

PJ'S (H-4)
Carlingford
Tel. (042) 73106
Entertaining pub, with a storytelling publican.
♫

ACCOMMODATION

ARD NA MARA ★
(H-4) P. Monk,
Irish Grange
Tel. (042) 76280
Ir£12.50–13
⌂ 🄲 ⌂ 🄿

CARLINGFORD HOUSE
(H-4) Carlingford
Tel. (042) 73118
Ir£15
⌂ ⌂ 🄲 ⌂ 🄿

THE HIGHLANDS (H-4)
Mr McCarthy, Irish
Grange
Tel. (042) 76104
Ir£12–24
⌂ ⌂ 🛉 🄿

BALLYMASCANLON HOTEL (H-4) Dundalk
Tel. (042) 71124
Fax (042) 71598
Closed Christmas
Activities: golf, squash, tennis, health club.
Ir£50–73
▭ 🏛 ○ 🗗·· ⌂ 🛉
♣ 🄿

MCKEVITT'S VILLAGE HOTEL ★ (H-4)
Market Sq, Carlingford
Tel. (042) 73116
Two-star family hotel.
Activities: walking, horseriding, golf, fishing.
Ir£22–36
▭ 🄲 ⌂ ♫ 🄿

MOURNE VIEW (H-4)
Carlingford
Tel. (042) 73551
Activities: sailing, horseriding, golfing.
Ir£14–17
⌂ 🄿

COUNTY MEATH

PRACTICAL INFORMATION

TOURIST OFFICE
(H-5) Via Slane,
Newgrange
Tel. (041) 24274
Open Easter–Oct.
10am–7pm

CULTURE

DOWTH (H-5)
Northeast of Newgrange
Closed to the public.

HILL OF TARA INTERPRETATIVE CENTRE (H-5)
Navan, Co. Meath
Tel. (046) 25903

Open Jun. 15–Sept.
9.30am–6.30pm; May–
Jun. 15 9.30am–5pm;
Oct. 10am–5pm
40p–Ir£1

KNOWTH (H-5)
Slane
Tel. (041) 24824
Open May–Oct.
9.30am–6.30pm
50p–Ir£1.50

KELLS' MONASTERY & GRAVEYARD (G-5)
Kells
Tel. (046) 40151
Open Jun.–Sept.,
Mon.–Fri. 10am–1pm
and 2–5pm
Guided tours.

LOUGHCREW TUMULUS
(G-5)
3 miles to the south of
Newtown on the Earl
Tree Rd.
Contact Basil Balfe
Tel. (088) 590987.

NEWGRANGE (H-5)
Slane
Tel. (041) 24488
Open Jun.–Sept.
9.30am–7pm; Nov.–Feb.
10am–4.30pm; Mar, Apr.
and Oct. 10am–5pm;
May 9.30am–6pm
The area around Slane boasts some forty prehistoric tombs, Newgrange being the most visited. Well worth the queues. Bring a sweater: it is chilly inside, even in summer. Reserve in advance.
Ir£1–2

TRIM CASTLE (G-5)
Trim
Tel. (046) 37111
Reopening 1995.

PUBS/RESTAURANTS

DUNDERRY LODGE (H-5)
Dunderry Robinstown,
Navan
Tel. (046) 31671
Open Tue.–Sat.
7.30–9.30pm, Sun.
12.30–2.30pm
Closed at Christmas
Ir£13.50–20
▭

ACCOMMODATION

BOYNE VIEW (H-5)
Mr. Hevey, 1, Boyne
View, Slane
Tel. (041) 24121
Ir£15
⌂ 🗗·· ⌂ �⁄ 🄿

COUNTY OFFALY

PRACTICAL INFORMATION

TOURIST OFFICES
◆ (E-6) Clonmacnois
Tel. (0905) 74134
Open Apr.–Oct.,
Mon.–Thur. 9am–6pm,
Fri.–Sun. 10am–6pm

◆ (F-6) Rosse Row, Birr
Tel. (0509) 20110
Fax (0509) 20660
Open May–Sept.
9.30am–5.30pm

CULTURE

BIRR CASTLE DEMESNE (F-6) Birr
Tel. (0509) 20056
Open 9am–1pm and
2–6pm
*Private home of the
Earl of Rosse. Summer
exhibitions (May to
Sept.). Don't miss the
telescope, the world's
largest (1845–1917).*
Ir£1.30–3.20

CLARA BOG (F-6)
Clara (Tullamore, Tourist
Office, Co. Westmeath)
Tel. (0506) 52617
*Entrance free, guided
tours organized
throughout the August
festival.*

CLONMACNOIS & WEST OFFALY RAILWAY (E-6)
Clonmacnois
Tel. (0905) 74114
Open Easter–Oct.
10am–5pm
*Tours of the bog mining
areas by train (45 mins)
hourly on the hour.*
Ir£2–3

PUBS/RESTAURANTS

FLYNNS COMMERCIAL HOUSE ★ (E-6)
Main St, Banagher
Tel. (0509) 51312
Ir£3.75–5
▭ ◑ ◪ ☼ ▣

J.J. HOUGH ★ (E-6)
Main St, Banagher
◪ ♫

THE VINE HOUSE ★
(E-6) West End,
Banagher
Tel. (0509) 51463
Last orders 9.30pm
Ir£10–15
▭ ○ ◪ ⌂ ♫

ACCOMMODATION

ASHLING ★ (E-6)
B. Mahon, Banagher
Tel. (0509) 51228
*Activities: walking,
fishing.*
Ir£13–15
⌂ ⌂ ♨ ▣

BROSNA LODGE HOTEL ★
(E-6) Main St, Banagher
Tel. (0509) 51350
Fax (0509) 51521
*Two-star hotel. Recently
refurbished. Beautiful
surroundings and wide
range of local activities:
walking, fishing, golfing
horse riding.*
Ir£20–24
○ ◪ ⌂ ☆ ♨

COUNTY ARMS HOTEL
(F-6) Station Rd, Birr
Tel. (0509) 20791
Fax (0509) 21234
*Three-star hotel. Fine
example of Georgian
architecture. Peaceful
location. Activities:
golfing, fishing, indoor
swimming pool.*
From Ir£33
▭ ○ ◐•• ⌂ ♫ ♨
▣

CRANK HOUSE ★
(E-6) Main St, Banagher
Tel. (0509) 51458
Fax (0509) 51676
Thurnesse Hostel.
Ir£6
○ ◪ ⌂

DOOLY'S HOTEL ★
(F-6) Emmet Sq., Birr
Tel. (0509) 20032
Fax (0509) 21332
*Comfortable, 3-star
hotel. Modernized
historic coaching inn.
Activities: golf, fishing.*
Ir£29–50
⌂ ○ ◐ ◪ ▣

COUNTY WATERFORD

PRACTICAL INFORMATION

TOURIST OFFICES
◆ (E-9) Community
Office, Ardmore
Tel. (024) 94444
Open Jun.–Sept.
10am–8pm

◆ (F-9) Mary St,
Dungarvan,
Tel. (058) 41741
Open Jun. 15–Sept.,
Mon.–Sat. 10am–6pm

◆ (F-9) Railway Square,
Tramore
Tel. (051) 381 572
Open Jun.–Sept.,
Mon.–Sat. 10am–6pm

◆ REGIONAL TOURIST
ORGANISATION FOR
THE SOUTHEAST (F-9)
41, The Quay, Waterford
Tel. (051) 75823
Fax (051) 77388
Open Jul.–Aug,
Mon.–Sat. 9am–6pm,
Sun. 10am–5pm;
Sept.–Jun., Mon.–Sat.
9am–6pm

CULTURE

CELTWORLD (F-9)
Tramore
Tel. (051) 86166
Fax (051) 90146
Open Jul.–Aug
10am–10pm; Apr.–May,
Mon.–Fri. 10am–5pm,
Sat.–Sun. 11am–6pm;
Jun. and Sept.
10am–6pm
Ir£2.95–3.95

CHRIST CHURCH CATHEDRAL (F-9)
Cathedral Square,
Waterford
Tel. (051) 74119

HISTORIC SEASIDE VILLAGE (E-9)
Ardmore
Tel. (024) 94444

HOLY TRINITY CATHEDRAL (F-9)
Waterford
Tel. (051) 75166
Open Mon.–Sat. 8am–
7pm, Sun. 7am–6.30pm

LISMORE CASTLE GARDENS (E-9)
Lismore
Tel. (058) 54424
Open Apr.–Sept.
1.45–4.45pm
Ir£1–2

REGINALD'S TOWER MUSEUM (F-9)
Greyfriars Heritage
Centre, Waterford
Tel. (051) 73501
Open Easter–Sept. 15,
Mon.–Fri. 11am–1pm
and 2–6pm, Sat.
11am–3pm
*Due to reopen
June 1995.*

WATERFORD CRYSTAL GALLERY (F-9)
Waterford
Tel. (051) 73311
Open Mon.–Fri.
8.30am–5pm,
Sat.–Sun. 10am–5pm
Ir£2 (guided tour)

PUBS/RESTAURANTS

BELLS 66 (F-9)
Granville Hotel,
The Quay, Waterford
Tel. (051) 55111
Restaurant 7–9.30pm
Ir£8
▭ ○ ◪ ♨

DWYER'S OF MARY ST
(F-9) 5, Mary St,
Waterford
Tel. (051) 77478
Open Mon.–Sat. 6–10pm
Closed Dec. 25–6
and Good Friday
Ir£12–18
▭ ○ ◪ ♫

GEOFF'S (F-9)
9, John St, Waterford
Tel. (051) 74787
Open 10am–11.30pm

MULLANES (F-9)
15, New Gates St,
Waterford
Tel. (051) 73854
◪ ♫

THE PULPIT BAR
(F-9)
John St, Waterford
Tel. (051) 79184
▭

THE STRAND HOTEL
(F-9) Dunmore East
Tel. (051) 383 174
Closed Nov.–Easter
Restaurant 6–10pm
Ir£15
▭ ○ ◐•• ⌂ ⩔ ▣

T. & DOOLANS (F-9)
37–8, Georges St,
Waterford
Tel. (051) 72764
◪ ♫

ACCOMMODATION

BLACKWATER LODGE HOTEL (F-9)
Upper Ballyduff,
Waterford
Tel. (058) 60235
Fax (058) 60162
Closed Oct.–Jan.
*Activities: fishing,
hunting. This hotel has
the largest private
salmon fishery in
Ireland.*
Ir£27–31
▭ ◐

◆
GOLF

◆ 354

ARDGLASS GOLF CLUB
(I-4) Castleplace,
Ardglass, Co. Down
Tel. (0396) 841 219
Fax (0396) 841 841
Par 70, 5,741 yards,
green fee £13–16.
Coastal terrain. Club
pro: K. Dorrian.
*The difficulties begin
right from the 1st hole,
which involves clearing
a rough inlet of the sea
to get to the 2nd.*

BALLYBUNION
GOLF CLUB (C-7)
Co. Kerry
Tel. (068) 27146
Fax (068) 27387
Par 71, green fee Ir£30
(old course only) or
Ir£40 for both. Club pro:
T. Higgins.
New course: 18-hole.

BUNDORAN GOLF CLUB
(E-3) Bundoran,
Co. Donegal
Tel. (072) 4102
Par 70, 6,328 yards,
green fee Ir£12–14.
Club pro: D. Robinson.
Seaside links.

CASTLEROCK
GOLF CLUB (H-1)
Circular Rd, Castlerock
Co. Derry
Tel./Fax (0265) 848 314
Par 73, 6,687 yards,
green fee £13–£25.
Club pro: B. Kelly.
*The 4th hole of this links
course, with its "dog-leg"
layout, is very testing.*

CONNEMARA GOLF
CLUB (B-5)
Ballyconneely,
Clifden, Co. Galway
Tel. (095) 23502
Fax (095) 23662.
Par 72, 7,108 yards,
green fee £16. Pro on
request.
*Difficult, windy seaside
links. Booking essential.*

COUNTY LOUTH
GOLF CLUB (H-5)
Baltray, Drogheda,
Co. Louth
Tel. (041) 22329
Fax (041) 22969
Par 74, 6,780 yards,
green fee Ir£27–33. Club
pro: P. McGuirk.
*At the mouth of the River
Boyne. Traditional links.*

COUNTY SLIGO
GOLF CLUB (E-3)
Rosses Point, Co. Sligo
Tel. (071) 77186
Fax (071) 77460
Par 71, 6630 yards,
green fee Ir£15–20. Club
pro: L. Robinson.
*Superb seaside links
course. Some extremely
difficult uneven greens.*

DOOKS GOLF CLUB
(B-8) Glenbeigh,
Co. Kerry
Tel. (066) 68205
Par 70, green fee Ir£15
*Traditional style, tricky
links course on the Ring
of Kerry.*

ENNISCRONE
GOLF CLUB (D-3)
Enniscrone, Co. Sligo
Tel. (096) 36297
Fax (096) 36657
Par 72, 6624 yards,
green fee Ir£15. *Links.
Some extremely
challenging blind holes.*

FAITHLEGG GOLF
CLUB (F-9)
Faithlegg,
Co. Waterford
Tel. (051) 82688
Fax (051) 82664
Six miles from
Waterford. Par 72, 6,950
yards, *green fee Ir£22.
New parkland course.*

GALWAY BAY GOLF
AND COUNTRY CLUB
(D-6) Renville,
Oranmore, Co. Galway
Tel. (091) 90500
Fax (091) 90510
Par 72, green fee Ir£25.
Club pro: C. O'Connor
Jr., Ireland's major
professional golfer.
Windy parkland course.

GOLF CHUMANN
CEANN SIBEAL
DINGLE (A-8)
Ballyferriter
Tel. (066) 56255
Fax (066) 56409
Par 72, 6,417 yards.
green fee Ir£18. Club
pro: D. O'Connor.
*The most westerly golf
course in Europe, in a
stunning setting.*

LAHINCH GOLF
CLUB (C-6)
Co. Clare,
Tel. (065) 81003
Fax (065) 81592
Par 72, 6696 yards,
green fee Ir£25–30.
Club pro: R. McCavery.

LEE VALLEY GOLF
CLUB AND COUNTRY
CLUB (D-9)
Clashanure,
Ovens, Co. Cork
Tel. (021) 331 721
Fax (021) 331 695
Par 72, green fee Ir£20.
Club pro: B. McDaid.
*Eight miiles from Cork,
on the road to Killarney.
Parkland course in a
beautiful setting.*

MOUNT JULIET
GOLF AND COUNTRY
CLUB (F/G-8)
Thomastown,
Co. Kilkenny
Tel. (056) 24725
Fax (056) 24828
Par 72, 7,000 yards,
green fee Ir£57.
Club pro: K. Mongan.
*Ten miles south of
Kilkenny. Beautiful
parkland course
designed byJack
Nicklaus. Difficult.*

PORTMARNOCK
GOLF CLUB (H-6)
Co. Dublin,
Tel. (01) 846 2968
Fax (01) 846 2601
Par 72, 7,761 yards,
green fee Ir£40–50.
Club pro: J. Purcell.
Second course: 9 holes.

ROSAPENNA
GOLF CLUB (F-1)
Downings,
Co. Donegal
Tel. (074) 55301
Fax (074) 55128
Par 70, green fee
Ir£12–15. *Links.* Club
pro: S. Byrne.
*A series of spectacular
holes (2 to 10), along
the bay of Sheephaven.*

ROYAL COUNTY DOWN
GOLF CLUB (I-4)
Newcastle,
Co. Down
Tel. (03967) 23314
Fax (03967) 26281
Par 71, 6,968 yards,
green fee £40– £45,
Club pro: K. Whitson.
*Second course:
18 holes.*

ROYAL DUBLIN
GOLF CLUB (H-6)
Bull Island,
Dollymount,
Dublin 3
Tel. (01) 336 346
Fax (01) 336 504
Par 73, 6,828 yards,
green fee Ir£35–45.
Club pro: C. O'Connor.

ROYAL PORTRUSH
GOLF CLUB (H-1)
Bushmills Rd,
Portrush, Co. Antrim
Tel. (0265) 822 311
Fax (0265) 823 139
Par 72, 6,771 yards,
green fee £30–35.
Club pro: D. Stevenson.
*Second course:
18 holes.*

ST MARGARET'S
GOLF CLUB (H-6)
Skephubble, Co. Dublin
Tel. (01) 864 0400
Fax (01) 864 0289
Par 71, 6,533 yards,
green fee Ir£25–30.
Club pro: Paul Henry.
*Three miles from Dublin
Airport. 18-hole
parkland course.*

TRAMORE GOLF CLUB
(F-9) Newtown Hill,
Tramore, Co. Waterford
Tel./Fax (051) 86170
Par 78, green fee
Ir£12–17. Club pro: P.
McDaid.
*Inland course in a
beautiful setting.*

WATERVILLE
GOLF CLUB (B-9)
Waterville
Tel. (0667) 4102
Fax (0667) 4482
Par 74, 7856 yards,
green fee Ir£30. Club
pro: L. Higgins.
*Internationally
acclaimed course, one
of the longest in Europe.*

WESTPORT GOLF CLUB
(C-4) Westport, Co. Mayo
Tel. (098) 25113
Fax (098) 27217
Par 73, 6,949 yards,
green fee Ir£15–18.
Club pro: A. Melia.
*At the foot of Croagh
Patrick. The difficulties
of this parkland course
begin after the 9th hole.*

CLIFF HOUSE HOTEL
(E-9) Ardmore,
Co. Waterford
Tel. (024) 94106
Fax (024) 94496
*Activities: golfing,
horseriding, fishing.*
Ir£14–34
□ ⊡•• ⌂ **P**

GRANVILLE HOTEL ★
(F-9) Granville Hotel,
The Quay, Waterford
Tel. (051) 55111
Fax (051) 70307
Closed Christmas
*Waterford's most
prestigious hotel
overlooking the River
Suir. Golfing and fishing
can be arranged.*
Ir£41.50–62
□ �🏛 ○ **C** ⚒

COUNTY WESTMEATH

PRACTICAL INFORMATION

TOURIST OFFICE
◆ (F-5) The Castle,
Market Square, Athlone
Tel. (0902) 94630
Open Jun.–Aug,
Mon.–Sat. 9am–6pm;
Apr.–May, Sept.–Oct.
Mon.–Sat. 9.30am–1pm
and 2–6pm

CULTURE

ATHLONE CASTLE
(F-5) Athlone
Tel. (0902) 92912
Open Easter–Sept.,
Mon.–Sat. 10am–6pm,
Sun. 11am–4.30pm
80p–Ir£2.50

PUBS/RESTAURANTS

CROOKED WOOD HOUSE
(F-5) Crooked Wood,
Mullingar
Tel. (044) 72165
Open Tue.–Sat.
7.30–9.30pm,
Sun. 12.30–2pm
Closed Nov.
Ir£12–17
□ ⚒

GREVILLE ARMS HOTEL
(F-5) Pearse St,
Mullingar
Tel. (044) 48563
Open daily 7am–9pm.
*Offers good,
reasonably-priced food
in its luxurious red pub.
Also a more-expensive
hotel restaurant.
Restaurant: Ir£2–5
Hotel: from Ir£28*

COUNTY WEXFORD

PRACTICAL INFORMATION

TOURIST OFFICES
◆ (G-8) County Museum,
Enniscorthy Castle,
Enniscorthy
Tel. (054) 34699
Open Jun.–Sept.,
Mon.–Sat. 10am–6pm

◆ (G-8) Crescent Quay,
Wexford
Tel. (053) 23111
Open Jun.–Sept., Mon.–
Sat. 9am–6pm; Sun.
9am–5pm; Oct.–May,
Mon.–Fri. 9am–12.45pm
and 2–5.15pm

◆ (G-8) The Quay,
New Ross
Tel. (051) 21857
Open Jun.–Sept.
9am–1pm and 2–6pm

◆ (H-9) Rosslare Harbour
(Kilrane)
Tel. (053) 33622
Open 6.30–9.30am
and 1–10.30pm

CULTURE

ENNISCORTHY CASTLE
(G-8) Enniscorthy
Tel. (054) 35926
Open Mon.–Sat. 10am–
6pm, Sun. 2–5.30pm
30p–Ir£1.50

IRISH NATIONAL PARK
(G-8) Ferrycarrig
Tel. (053) 41733
Open Mar.–Oct.
10am–7pm, last
admission 5pm
Ir£3

**THE JOHN F. KENNEDY
ARBORETUM** (G-8)
New Ross
Tel. (051) 88171
Open May–Aug
10am–8pm; Oct.–Mar.
10am–5pm; Apr. and
Sept. 10am–6.30pm
40p–Ir£1

**JOHNSTOWN CASTLE
GARDENS** (G-8)
Murrintown
Tel. (053) 42888
– Gardens: open
9am–5.30pm
– Agricultural Museum:
open Jun.–Aug, Mon.–
Fri. 9am–5pm, Sat.–
Sun. 2–5pm; Apr.–May,
and Sept.–mid-Nov.,
Mon.– Fri. 9am–
12.30pm and 1.30–5pm,

Sat.–Sun. 2–5pm; mid-
Nov.–Mar, Mon.–Fri.
9am–12.30pm and
1.30–5pm

MARITIME MUSEUM
(G-9) Kilmore Quay,
Kilmore
Tel. (053) 29655
Open May–Sept.
noon–6pm; Oct.–Apr. by
appointment
50p–Ir£1

**WEXFORD WILD FOWL
RESERVE** (H-8)
North Slob
Tel. (053) 23129
Open 16 Apr.–Sept.
9am–6pm; Oct.–15 Apr.
10am–5pm

PUBS/RESTAURANTS

**GALLEY CRUISING
RESTAURANT** (G-8)
New Ross
Tel. (051) 21723
Open Easter–Oct.
12.30pm-7pm
*Floating restaurant
along the River Barrow.*
Ir£11–20

THE GOAL BAR (G-8)
72, South Main St,
Wexford
Tel. (053) 23727
*Country, rock and
traditional music almost
every night, sometimes
karaoke evenings.*
Ir£3–4.50
□ ◑ ♫

MOONEYS ★ (G-8)
12, Commercial Quay,
Wexford
Tel. (053) 24483
◑ ♫

TIM'S TAVERN (G-8)
51 South Main St,
Wexford
Tel. (053) 23861
Open lunchtime
noon–5pm; dinner
6.30–9.30pm
*This award-winning
venue is more a
restaurant than a pub.
Traditional music Wed.
and Sat.
evenings.*
Ir£15
◑

THE WREN'S NEST ★
(G-8) Crescent Quay,
Wexford
Tel. (053) 22359
*Traditional music Tue.
and Thur. Small and
cozy. Reasonably
priced meals.*
◑ ♫

ACCOMMODATION

KILRANE HOUSE ★
(H-9) Kilrane,
Rosslare Harbour
Tel. (053) 33135
Ir£15–16
□ ⊡•• **P**

ST JUDE (G-8)
Munfin, Enniscorthy
Tel. (054) 33011
Ir£13–15
⌂ ⊡•• ⚒ **P**

COUNTY WICKLOW

PRACTICAL INFORMATION

TOURIST OFFICES
◆ (H-7) Parade Ground,
Arklow
Tel. (0402) 32484
Open Jun.–Aug,
Mon.–Sat. 10am–6pm

◆ (H-7) Rialto Centre,
Fitzwilliam St, Wicklow
Tel. (0404) 69117
Open Jun.–Sept.,
Mon.–Sat. 9am–6pm;
Oct.–May, Mon.–Fri.
9.30am–1pm and
2–5.30pm

◆ (H-6) Unit 2,
Florence Rd, Bray
Tel. (01) 286 7128
Open 10am–6pm

CULTURE

**AVONDALE HOUSE &
PARNELL MUSEUM** (H-7)
Rathdrum
Tel. (0404) 46111
Open 11am–6pm
Ir£1–2

**GLENDALOUGH
VISITORS' CENTRE**
(H-7) Glendalough,
Tel. (0404) 45325

Open Jun.–Aug. 9am–
6.30pm; Oct. 15.– Mar.
15, 9.30am–5pm; Mar.
15–May and Sept.–Oct.
15, 9am–6pm
*Guided tours on
request.*
60p–Ir£1.50

MARITIME MUSEUM
(H-7) St Mary's Rd,
Arklow
Tel. (0402) 32868
Open Mon.–Fri.
10am–5pm
Ir£1

**MOUNT USHER
GARDENS** (H-7)
Ashford
Tel. (0404) 40116
Open Mar. 15–Oct.,
Mon.–Sat. 10.30am–
6pm, Sun. 11am–6pm
Ir£1.80–2.80

**POWERSCOURT
ESTATE & WATERFALL**
(H-6)
Enniskerry
Tel. (01) 286 7676
Open May–Sept.
9am–7pm; Oct.–Apr.
10.30am–dusk
Ir£1.70–2.80

RUSSBOROUGH HOUSE
(H-6) Blessington
Tel. (045) 65239
Open Easter–Oct.
11am–1.15pm and
2–3.30pm
*Two miles south of
Blessington.*
Ir£1–2.50

**WICKLOW MOUNTAINS
NATIONAL PARK** (H-7)
Information point,
Upper Lake,
Glendalough
Tel. (0404) 45425
Open May–Aug. 10am–
6pm; Sept., Sat.–Sun.
10am–6.30pm
Guided walks.

PUBS/RESTAURANTS

THE MEETINGS ★
(H-7) Avoca
Tel. (0402) 35226
Open Mon.–Fri.
11.30am–9pm, Sat.–
Sun. 11.30am–8.30pm
Ir£3–11
▭ ◑ ⌂ ♨ ▣

THE OLD RECTORY
(H-7) Wicklow
Tel. (0404) 67048
Open Sun.–Thur. 8–9pm,
Fri.–Sat. 7.30–9pm
Reserve in advance.
Ir£23
▭ ○ ♫

RATHSALLAGH HOUSE
(G-7) Dunlavin
Tel. (045) 53112
Closed Christmas
Ir£17
▭ ○ ♨

ROUNDWOOD INN ★
(H-6) Roundwood
Tel. (01) 281 8107
Closed Sun. and Mon.
Ir£14–18
▭ ◑

ACCOMMODATION

**ENNISCREE LODGE
HOTEL** (H-6)
Glencree Valley,
Enniskerry
Tel. (01) 286 3542
*Hotel with 10 bedrooms
overlooking the
Glencree Valley
From Ir£33.50*
▭⋯ ⌂ ⌂ ▣

**THE GLENDALOUGH
HOTEL** (H-7)
Glendalough
Tel. (0404) 45135
*Recently refurbished,
1880's hotel situated in
the Wicklow Valley.
Hotel restaurant, good
but limited menu at The
Tavern. Horseriding,
fishing, walking, cycling.
Ir£33–43*
▭ ♨

SHOPPING

AVOCA HANDWEAVERS
(H-6) Avoca Village
and Kilmacanogue,
Kilmacanogue
Tel. (0402) 35105
Open 9.30am–5.30pm
Tweeds, woolens.

◆

MUNSTER

**COUNTY
CLARE**

PRACTICAL
INFORMATION

TOURIST OFFICE
◆ (D-7) Clare Rd, Ennis
Tel. (065) 28366

Open Jun.–Sept., 9am–
6pm; Oct.–May, Tue.–
Sat. 9.30am– 5.30pm

◆ (C-7) Main St, Kilkee
Tel. (065) 56112
Open Jun.–Sept.,
10am–1pm and 2–6pm

◆ **SHANNON AIRPORT** (D-
7)
Tel. (061) 471664
Open Mon.–Fri.
6am–7pm, Sat.–Sun.
6am–9pm
*In winter, open for
aircraft arrivals.*

◆ **TRAFFIC AND TOURISM
DIVISION OF SHANNON
DEVELOPMENT** (D-7)
Shannon Town Centre,
Shannon
Tel. (061) 361 555
Open Mon.–Fri.
9.30am–5.30pm
*Information on counties
Clare, Limerick, the
north of Kerry, and the
north of Tipperary, and
southern Offaly.*

CULTURE

AILLWEE CAVE (D-6)
Ballyvaughan
Tel. (065) 77036
Open Mar.–Oct.
10am–6.30pm
Ir£2.20–3.85

**BUNRATTY CASTLE
& FOLK PARK** (D-7)
Bunratty
Tel. (061) 361 511
– Castle: open Apr.–Oct.
9.30am–6.30pm
– Gardens: open
Jun.–Aug 9.30am–
6.30pm; Sept.–May.
9.30am–5.30pm
Closed Dec. 23–7
and Good Friday
*Medieval banquets
each evening at 5.45pm
and 9pm, Reserve.
Tel. (061) 360 788
Ir£4*

**BURREN DISPLAY
CENTRE** (D-6)
Kilfenora
Tel. (065) 88060
Open Mar.–Oct.
9.30am–6pm;
Sept.–Feb. 9.30am–5pm
Ir£1–2

**CLARE HERITAGE
CENTRE** (D-6)
Corofin
Tel. (065) 37955
Open Mar. 15–Oct.,
9.30am–6pm;
Mon.–Sat. 10am–6pm
75p–Ir£1.75

CLIFFS OF MOHER
(C-6) Moher
– Visitors' Centre
Tel. (065) 81171
Open Mar.–Oct.
10am–6pm
– O'Brien Tower
Tel. (061) 361511
Open Mar.–Nov.
9am–7pm; Dec.–Feb.
10am–5pm
50–75p

**CRAGGAUNOWEN
PROJECT** (D-7)
Quin
Tel. (061) 367 178
Open Easter–Sept.
9am–6pm
Ir£1.80–3.10

**DYSERT O'DEA
CASTLE** (D-7)
Dysert O'Dea
Tel. (065) 37722

ENNIS ABBEY (D-7)
Ennis
Tel. (065) 29100
Open Jun.–Sept.
9.30am–6.30pm
*50p–Ir£1
The abbey is sometimes
open at Easter, for
confirmation:
Tel. (01) 661 3111*

**MONEEN
CHURCH** (B-7)
Moneen,
Tel. (065) 845 008

KNAPPOGUE CASTLE
(D-7) Quin
Tel. (061) 368 102
Open Apr.–Oct.
9.30am–5pm
*Situated six miles
southeast of Ennis.*

KILLINABOY CHURCH
(D-6) Killinaboy
Tel. (065) 37623
Open 8am–9pm

QUILTY CHURCH (C-7)
Quilty
Tel. (065) 84014

ST FINGHIN CHURCH
(D-7) Quin
Tel. (065) 25649

**SCATTERY ISLAND
INFORMATION
CENTRE**
(C-7) Merchants Quay,
Kilrush
Tel. (065) 52139
Open Jun. 15–Sept. 15
9.30am–6.30pm
*Exhibition on the
history of the
6th-century monastery
and the surrounding
area.*

PUBS/RESTAURANTS

BARRTRA SEAFOOD RESTAURANT (C-6)
Miltown Malbay Rd, Lahinch
Tel. (065) 81280
Closed Oct.–Apr.
Ir£9–14
⊡ ○ ◑ ⛷

MACCLOSKEYS (D-7)
Bunratty House Mews, Bunratty
Tel. (061) 364 082
Open Tue.–Sat. 7–10pm
Closed Dec. 20– Jan.25
Medieval banquets.
Ir£17–26
⊡ ○ ◙

MCDERMOTT'S ★
(C-6) Doolin
Tel. (065) 74700
Open 10.30am–midnight
◙ ◑ ♫

MCGANN'S ★ (C-6)
Doolin, Upper Village
Tel. (065) 74133
Open 10am–midnight
Music every evening in summer, weekends only in winter. Irish stew £3.
◙ ◑ ♫

O'CONNOR'S PUB ★
(C-6) Doolin, Lwr Village
Tel. (065) 74168
Traditional music all year round. Also a B&B.
◙ ◑ ⌂ ♫

ACCOMMODATION

DOOLIN HOSTEL ★
(C-6) Doolin, Lwr Village
Tel. (065) 74006
Quiet and modern. Tennis court. Laundry £2.50. Sheet 50p. Bicycles £5 per day. Accepts Visa.
Ir£6.50–7.50

SHOPPING

BURREN FISH PRODUCTS (C-6)
Lisdoonvarna
Tel. (065) 74432
Open Mon.–Sat. 8.30am–6pm, Sun. 10am–6pm
Salmon smokehouse.

CORK CITY (D-9)

PRACTICAL INFORMATION

AIRPORT
Cork Airport, Cork
Tel. (021) 313 131

Regular bus service Ir£2.20. Taxi Ir£6

TOURIST OFFICE
Grand Parade, Cork
Tel. (021) 273 251
Open Jul.–Aug., Mon.–Sat. 9am–5pm, Sun. 2–5pm; Sept.–Jun., Mon.–Sat. 9am–6pm

CULTURE

CORK ART SOCIETY
16, Lavetts Quay, Cork
Tel. (021) 277 749
Open Tue.–Sat. 10.30am–2pm and 3–5.30pm

CORK PUBLIC MUSEUM
Fitzgerald Park, Cork
Tel. (021) 270 679
Open Mon.–Fri. 11am–1pm, Sun. 3–5pm
Closed public holidays. Entrance free Mon.–Fri., 50p Sun.

THE CRAWFORD MUNICIPAL ART GALLERY
Emmett Place, Cork
Tel. (021) 273 377
Open Mon.–Fri. 10am–5pm

HOLY TRINITY CHURCH
Father Matthew Quay, Cork
Tel. (021) 270 827

HONAN CHAPEL
University College, Cork
Tel. (021) 276 871
Open Mon.–Fri. 9.15am–6.30pm
In the heart of the university.

ST ANNE'S ANGLICAN CHURCH
Shandon, Cork
Tel. (021) 501 672
Open Mon.–Sat. 10am–4.30pm
Ir£1–2

ST FINBARR'S CATHEDRAL
Bishop St, Cork
Tel. (021) 963 387
Open Jun.–Aug, Mon.–Sat. 10am–1pm and 2–5.30pm; Sept.–May, Mon.–Sat. 10am–1pm and 2–5pm

ST MARY'S CATHEDRAL
Sharman Crawford St, Cork
Tel. (021) 304 325
Open 8am–6pm

TRISKEL ARTS CENTRE
Tobin St, Cork
Tel. (021) 277 300
Open Mon.–Sat. 10.30am–5.30pm
Exhibitions, theater, concerts.

PUBS/RESTAURANTS

AN BODHRÁN ★
42, Oliver Plunkett St, Cork
Tel. (021) 274 544
Folk music: Tue: 9.30pm
Ir£1.25–2.45
◑

AN PHŒNIX
3, Union Quay, Cork
Tel. (021) 964 275
Open Mon.–Sat. noon–11pm, Sun 4–11pm
Closed Christmas and Good Friday
Folk music Sun., Mon., Wed., blues on Tuesdays in the dark pub, upstairs, rock music and heavy metal.
◙ ♫

AN SPAILPÍN FÁNACH
28, South Main St, Cork
Tel. (021) 277 949
One of Cork's most popular pubs. Live music Sun.–Fri.
Ir£4.50
◑ ♫

THE ARBUTUS LODGE
Montenotte, Cork
Tel. (021) 501 237
Closed Dec. 24–30
Ir£14.50–21.50
⊡ ○ ♣ ▣

CLIFFORD'S
18, Dyke Parade, Cork
Tel. (021) 275 333
Closed Christmas
Ir£12.50–28
⊡ ○ ◙

DONKEY'S EARS
4, Union Quay, Cork
Tel. (021) 964 846
Open Mon.–Sat. 1–11pm, Sun. 4–11pm

Closed Christmas
Loud live music: rock, hip-hop, funk and reggae.
◙ ♫

IVORY TOWER RESTAURANT ★
The Exchange Buildings, 35, Princes St, Cork
Tel. (021) 274 665
Open Mon.–Sat. noon–4pm and 6–11pm; Sun. 6–11pm.
Closed Tue. and Christmas
Delicious food. Three-course set-menu for Ir£15. Highly recommended.
○ ♟

THE LOBBY BAR
1, Union Quay, Cork
Tel. (021) 311 113
◑ ♫

MICHAEL'S BISTRO
4, Mardyke St, Cork
Tel. (021) 275 887
Closed Sat. lunchtime, Sun., Christmas
Ir£9–15
⊡ ○ ◙

REIDY'S VAULT BAR ★
Western Rd, Cork
Tel. (021) 275 751
Ir£1.5–8
⊡ ◑ ♫

ACCOMMODATION

JURYS HOTEL
Western Rd, Cork
Tel. (021) 276 622
Fax (021) 274 477
Closed Dec. 24–27
Deluxe hotel on a quiet 5-acre riverside site; 5 minutes walk from the center of town. Two restaurants and a pub.
Ir£70–90
⊡ 🏛 ○ ◑ ◙ ▣

KILLARNEY GUEST HOUSE ★
Western Rd, Cork
Tel. (021) 270 290
Closed Dec. 24–26
In the city center. Excellent breakfasts.
Ir£20–24
⌂ ▣ ⊡

ST KILDA GUEST HOUSE
Western Rd, Cork
Tel. (021) 273 095
Closed Dec. 24, 25, 26
Ten minutes from the center of town. Modern hotel with 26 rooms.
Ir£16–48
⊡ ⌂ ◙ ♟ ▣

SHOPPING

SHANDON BELL
Shandon St, Cork
Tel. (021) 397 686
Open Mon.–Fri.
9am–5.30pm
China, pottery.

COUNTY CORK

PRACTICAL INFORMATION

TOURIST OFFICES

◆ (D-10) Emmett Place, Kinsale
Tel. (021) 772 234
Fax (021) 774 438
Open Apr.–Oct., Mon.–Sat. 9.30am–6pm, Sun. 11am–5pm

◆ (E-9) HERITAGE CENTRE, Market House, Market Square, Youghal
Tel. (024) 92390
Open Jun.–Sept., Mon.–Sat. 10am–6pm

◆ (E-9) HERITAGE CENTRE, Midleton
Tel. (021) 613 702
Open Apr.–Oct. 9.30am–6pm

◆ (C-9) Main St, Glengarrif
Tel. (027) 63084
Open Jul.–Aug, Mon.–Sat. 10am–6pm

◆ (D-9) The Old Yacht Club, Cobh
Tel. (021) 813 301
Open Mon.–Fri. 9.30am–5.30pm, Sat.–Sun. 11am–5.30pm

◆ (D-10) 9, Rossa St, Clonakilty
Tel. (023) 32226
Open Jun.–Sept., Mon.–Sat. 10am–6pm

◆ (C-10) The Square, Bantry
Tel. (027) 50229
Open Jun.–Sept., Mon.–Sat. 10am–6pm

CULTURE

BANTRY HOUSE
(C-10) Bantry
Tel. (027) 50047
Open Jul.–Aug 9am–7pm; Sept.–Jun. 9am–6pm
Ir£1.75–3

BLARNEY CASTLE
(D-9) Blarney
Tel. (021) 385 252
Open Jun.–Aug, Mon.–Sat. 9am–7pm, Sun.

9.30am–5.30pm; May and Sept., Mon.–Sat. 9am–6.30pm, Sun. 9.30am–5.30pm; Oct.–Apr., Mon.–Sat. 9am–dusk, Sun. 9.30am–dusk
Ir£1–3

CEIM HILL MUSEUM
(C-10) near Union Hall, Skibbereen
Tel. (028) 36280
Open 10am–7pm
Ir£2

CHARLES FORT (D-10)
Kinsale
Tel. (021) 772 263
Open Jun. 15–Sept. 15 9am–6pm;
Apr. 15–Jun. 15, Tue.–Sat. 9am–4.30pm, Sun. 11am–5.30pm;
Sept. 15–Oct. 15., Mon.–Sat. 9am–5pm, Sun. 10am–5pm
60p–Ir£1.50

CLOYNE CATHEDRAL
(E-9) Cloyne
Open May.–Sept. 10am–6pm
Ir£1 (tour)

DESMOND CASTLE
(D-10) Kinsale
Tel. (021) 774 855
Open Jun.–Sept. 15 9am–6pm;
Sept. 15– Oct., Mon.–Sat. 9am–5pm, Sun. 10am–5pm
40p–Ir£1

FOTA WILDLIFE PARK
(E-9) Fota Island, Carrigtuohill
Tel. (021) 812 678
Open Apr.–Oct., Mon.–Fri. 10am–6pm, Sun. 11am–6pm
Ir£1.90 –3.30

GOUGANE BARRA NATIONAL PARK (C-9)
Information: Kenmare Tourist Office.
Tel. (064) 41233

JAMESON HERITAGE CENTRE (E-9)
Midleton
Tel. (021) 613 594
Open 10am–6pm
Ir£3.50

MICHAEL COLLINS MEMORIAL CENTRE
(D-10) Clonakilt
Information: Clonakilty Tourist Office.
Tel. (023) 33226

THE QUEENSTOWN PROJECT (D-9)
Cobh
Tel. (021) 813 591
Open Feb.–Sept., 10am–6pm
Ir£2–3.50

REGIONAL MUSEUM
(D-10) Fitzgerald Park, Kinsale
Tel. (021) 772 044
Open Jun.–Sept. 11am–1pm and 2.15–5pm; Oct.–May on request.
20–50p

RIVERSTOWN HOUSE
(D-9) Glanmi
Tel. (021) 821 722
Open May–Aug, Thur., Fri. and Sat. 2–6pm; Sept.–Apr. by appointment.
Ir£2

THE ROYAL GUNPOWDERMILLS
(D-9)
Ballincollig
Tel. (021) 874 430
Open Apr.–Sept. 10am–6pm
Ir£1.50–2.50

ST COLMAN'S CATHEDRAL (D-9)
Cobh
Tel. (021) 811 430
Open 7am–8.30pm

ST MARY'S CHURCH
(E-9) Youghal
Open 9am–1pm and 2–6pm

ST MULTOSE'S CHURCH (D-10)
Kinsale
Tel. (021) 77220

WEST CORK REGIONAL MUSEUM (D-10)
Clonakilty
Tel. (023) 33226
(Clonakilty Tourist Office)
Open Mon.–Sat. 10.30am–12.30pm and 2–5.30pm, Sun. 3–5pm.
50p–Ir£1

YACHT CLUB OF KINSALE (D-10)
Kinsale
Tel. (021) 772 196

PUBS/RESTAURANTS

AHERNE'S SEAFOOD BAR (E-9) 163, North Main St, Youghal
Tel. (024) 92424
Ir£12.50–21.50
▭ ○ ◑ 🏛 ⚘ 🄿

BLAIR'S COVE RESTAURANT (B-10)
Durrus
Closed Nov.–Mar. 15 and Mon.
Ir£23
▭ ○ ⌂

BLAIR'S INN (D-9)
Cloghroe, Blarney
Tel. (021) 381 470
Open noon–midnight
Closed Christmas and Good Friday
Ir£5–7.50
▭ ◑ ⌸ ♫ ⚘ 🄿

THE BLUE HAVEN ★
(D-10) Pearse St, Kinsale
Tel. (021) 772 209
Good value lunchtime menu. One of the best restaurants in Kinsale. Also, small hotel from Ir£30
◑ 🄲 ♫

CHEZ JEAN-MARC (D-10)
Lower O'Connell St, Kinsale
Tel. (021) 774 625
Closed Sun.
Ir£18
▭ ○ 🄲

COURTYARD RESTAURANT (D-10)
Kieran's Folk House Inn Gardwell, Kinsale
Tel. (021) 772 382
Closed Jan.–Mar and Nov.
Ir£8–12.50
▭ ○ ◑ 🄲 ♫

LONGUEVILLE HOUSE & PRESIDENT'S RESTAURANT (D-9)
Mallow
Tel. (022) 47156
Closed Dec.–Mar
Ir£7–26
▭ ○ ◑ 🄲 ⌸ ⌂ 🄿

MAN FRIDAY ★ (D-10)
Scilly, Kinsale
Tel. (021) 772 260
Ir£28
▭ ○ 🄲

375

MARY ANN'S BAR ★
(C-10) Castletownshend
Tel. (028) 36146
Closed Sun. (Jul.–Aug),
Sun.–Mon. (Sept.–Jun.)
Ir£19.95
▱ ○ ⌂

MOBY DICK'S (E-9)
Market Square, Youghal
Tel. (024) 92756
◑ ♫

THE SPANIARDS INN ★
(D-10) Kinsale
Tel. (021) 772 436
Open 12.30–3pm
Ir£2.95–6.50
◑ ▣ ♫

ACCOMMODATION

**ASSOLAS COUNTRY
HOUSE ★** (D-8)
Kanturk,
Tel. (029) 50015
Open Mar. 12–Oct.
Golf.
Ir£13–40
▱ ♛

**BALLYMALOE
HOUSE ★** (E-9)
Shanagarry, Midleton
Tel. (021) 652531
Closed Dec. 24–26
*Award-winning
restaurant. Activities:
walking, tennis,
horseriding, fishing,
golfing.*
Ir£25–56
▱ ○ ♛ ▣

**CASTLETOWNSHEND
GUEST HOUSE** (C-10)
Castletownshend, near
Skibbereen
Tel. (028) 36100
*Activities: golfing,
horseriding, fishing.
Self-catering houses
can be organized.*
Ir£25–33
⌂ ⚲

ELMWOOD HOUSE
(C-10) 6, Slip Lawn,
Bantry
Tel. (027) 50087
Ir£10–12.50
⌂ ▭·· ⌂ ♛

**INNISHANNON HOUSE
HOTEL** (D-9)
Innishannon
Tel. (021) 775121
*Built in 1720 on the
banks of the Bandon
River, this is one of the
most romantic hotels in
Ireland, Activities:
golfing, horseriding,
fishing.*
Ir£38–95
▱ ♜ ▭·· ⌂ ♛ ⚲

THE MILLS INN ★
(C-9) Macroom,
Ballyvourney
Tel. (026) 45237
*One of Ireland's oldest
inns. Recommended.
Fishing, riding, golf,
bicycle rental, walks.*
Ir£18–27
▱ ◑ ▭·· ⌂

SHOPPING

**STEPHAN PEARCE
POTTERY** (E-9)
Shanagarry
Tel. (021) 646 807
Open Mon.–Fri.
8am–5.30pm,
Sat. 10am–5.30pm,
Sun. noon–5.30pm
Pottery.

COUNTY KERRY

PRACTICAL
INFORMATION

TOURIST OFFICES
◆ FARRANFORE AIRPORT
(C-8) Farranforey
Tel. (066) 64399
Open 9.30am–5pm

◆ CLOGHANE AND
BRANDONE GALLERY
& INFORMATION CENTER
(B-8) Cloghane
Tel. (066) 38277
Open Jul.–Aug
10am–8pm, Sept. and
Jun. 10am–5pm
Exhibitions.

◆ (B-9) Main St,
Kenmare
Tel. (064) 41233
Open Mar.–Sept.,
Mon.–Sat. 9.30am–7pm,
Sun. 11am–5pm

◆ TOWN HALL (C-9)
Killarney
Tel. (064) 31633
Fax (064) 34506
Open Jul.–Aug,
Mon.–Sat. 9am–8pm,
Sun. 10am–1pm and
2–6pm; Jun. and Sept.,
Mon.–Sat. 9am–7pm;
Oct.–May, Mon.–Sat.
9.30am–6.30pm

MISCELLANEOUS

SLATTERY'S TRAVEL
(B-8) 1, Russell St,
Tralee
Tel. (066) 26277
Closed Nov.–Mar
Caravan hire.

CULTURE

ARDFERT CATHEDRAL
(B-8) Ardfert
Tel. (01) 661 3111
Open 15 Jul.–Sept. 15
9.30am–6.30pm
60p–Ir£1.50

CRAG CAVE (C-8)
Castleisland
Tel. (066) 41244
Open Mar.–Oct.,
Mon.–Sat. 10am–7pm
Ir£2.50–3

**DERRYNANE NATIONAL
HISTORIC PARK** (B-9)
Caherdaniel
Tel. (0667) 75113
Open Apr.–Oct.,
Mon.–Sat. 9am–5pm,
Sun. 11am–6pm
60p–Ir£1.50

**DUNQUIN
INTERPRETATIVE
CENTRE** (A-8) Dunquin
Tel. (066) 56371
Open Jul.–Aug
10am–7pm; Easter–Jun.,
Sept. 10am–6pm; Oct.,
Sat.–Sun. 10am–6pm
Ir£1–2.50

GALLARUS ORATORY
(A-8) Two miles south of
Kilmalkedar
Tel. (066) 55143

**"IONAD AN
BHLASCAOID MHOIR"
(BLASKET CENTRE)**
(A-8) Dunquin
Tel. (066) 56444
Open Easter–Sept.
10am–6pm
Ir£4–8

**KILLARNEY NATIONAL
PARK** (C-9)
Killarney
Tel. (064) 31947
Open Jul.–Sept. 15
9.30am–7pm

**MUCKROSS HOUSE
& GARDENS** (C-9)
Killarney
Tel. (064) 31440
Open Jul.–Aug.
9am–7pm; Mar. 15–Jun.,
Sept.–Oct. 9am–6pm;
Nov.–Mar. 15
9am–5.30pm. Closed
Christmas
Ir£1.45–3

ROSS CASTLE (C-9)
Killarney
Tel. (064) 35851
Open Jun.–Aug
9am–6.30pm; May and
Sept. 9am–6pm; Oct.
9am–5pm
Ir£1–2

STAIGUE FORT (B-9)
Castlecove
Tel. (066) 51188

PUBS/RESTAURANTS

AN CAFE LITEARTHA
(B-8) Dyke Gate,
Dingle
Tel. (066) 51388
◑ ▣

**THE ARMADA
RESTAURANT &
AN REALT BAR** (B-8)
Strand St, Dingle
Tel. (066) 51505
Open 6–9.30pm
Ir£8–16
▱ ○ ◑ ♫

**BOSTON'S BAR
& RESTAURANT ★**
(A-9) Knightstown,
Valentia Island
Tel. (066) 76140
Closed Nov.–Easter
Ir£16
▱ ○ ◑ ♫

THE DANNY MANN INN
(C-9) New St, Killarney
Tel. (064) 31640
Closed Christmas
Ir£11
▱ ○ ◑ ▣
♫ ▣

DICK MACK (B-8)
Dingle
Tel. (066) 51960
▣

**DOYLE SEAFOOD
BAR & TOWNHOUSE**
(B-8)
John St, Dingle
Tel. (066) 51174
Open Nov.–Mar,
Mon.–Sat. eve
Ir£16
▱ ○ ▣

EILEEN CREEDON (C-9)
Kilgarvan
Tel. (064) 85373
Ir£4
◑ ▭·· ♫

FÁILTE PUB (C-9)
College St, Killarney
Tel. (064) 31893
Open Mon.–Sat.
6.30–10pm, Sun.
12.30–3pm
Ir£8.40–14.85
▱ ○ ◑ ▣ ♫

THE HUNTSMAN (B-9)
Waterville
Tel. (066) 74124
Open Mon.–Sat.
10.30am–4pm and
6–9.30pm
Half-board can be
arranged.
Ir£12
◑ 🏠 ♫

THE ISLANDMAN ★
(B-8) Main St, Dingle
Tel. (065) 51803
Ir£4.95–12.50
🖭 ○ ○

KATE KEARNEY'S ★
(C-9) Dunloe Gap
Tel. (064) 4416
Open 6.30–9pm
Ir£11.50
🖭

KIRBY'S BROGUE INN
(B-8) Rock St, Tralee
Tel. (066) 23357
Ir£6–9
○ ◑ ◑ ⓒ ♫

LORD BAKER'S ★
(B-8) Main St, Dingle
Tel. (066) 51277
Ir£16.50
○ ◑ ⓒ

MAGUIRE'S (B-9)
Cahirciveen
Tel. (066) 72049
♫

MÁIRE DE BARRA (B-8)
Strand St, Dingle
Tel. (066) 51215
Closed Christmas and
Good Friday
Ir£5
◑ ⓒ ♫

O'CONNOR'S ABBEY TAVERN (C-8)
Abbey Dorney, 3 miles
from Tralee
Tel. (066) 35145
⚘ ♫

PACKIE'S (B-9)
Kenmare
Tel. (064) 41508
Open Mon.–Sat.
5–10pm. Closed
Nov. 15–Easter
Ir£8–17
🖭 ○ ⓒ

PARK HOTEL KENMARE RESTAURANT (B-9)
Kenmare
Tel. (064) 41200
Open 1–1.45pm
and 7–9pm
Closed Nov. 15–Dec. 23
and Jan. 2–Easter
Ir£8–36
🖭 ○ ♠♠

SCEILIG RESTAURANT
★ (C-9) High St,
Killarney
Tel. (064) 33062
Ir£5–9
🖭 ○ ⓒ

THE SHEBEEN BAR
(B-9) Cahirciveen
Tel. (066) 72361
Open 10am–midnight
Ir£3.15
◑ ♫

ACCOMMODATION

BAMBURY'S GUEST HOUSE ★ (B-8)
Mail Rd, Dingle
Tel. (066) 51244
New house. Peaceful
and spacious. Two
minutes from city center.
Ir£13–20
🖭 ⬆ ⓒ 🏠 ℗

THE BENAGH RESTAURANT B&B
(B-8) Cluain Searrach,
Cloghane
Tel. (066) 38142
Ir£12–15
⬆ ○ 🖭⋯ 🏠 ℗

CARAGH LODGE ★
(B-8) Caragh Lake
Tel. (066) 69115
Closed Oct. 13.–Apr. 13
Victorian fishing lodge
in an 8-acre park.
Superb gardens. Golf
and beaches nearby.
Horseriding, walking,
fishing.
Ir£44–90
🖭 🏛 🖭⋯ 🏠 ♠♠ ℗

GREAT SOUTHERN HOTEL ★ (B-9)
Parknasilla
Tel. (064) 45122
Activities: golfing,
horseriding, fishing,
tennis, bicycle hire.
Ir£15–79–225
🖭 ○ 🏛 🖭⋯ 🏠 ♠♠
☇ ℗

HAWTHORN HOUSE ★
(B-9) K. & T. Murphy,
Shelburne St, Kenmare
Tel. (064) 41035
Closed Christmas
Ir£18–22
🖭 ⬆ ⓒ 🏠 ℗

◆

ARAN ISLANDS

HOW TO GET THERE

ARAN ISLANDS (C-6)
Co. Galway
Flights to Inishmore,
Inisheer and Inishmaan
with Aer Arann.
– Flights from
Connemara Airport,
daily 9.30am, 11am,
4pm and 5pm,
information Connemara
Airport, Caisleán,
Inverin
Tel. (091) 93034
or (091) 93054
Fax (091) 93238
Flight 6 mins.
Ir£20–33 (A-R)
– Flights from Galway
Airport, Mon.–Sat. 9am,
more flights during the
summer months,
information Galway
Airport, Galway
Tel. (091) 55437
or (091) 55480
Fax (091) 52273

INIS MÓR (INISHMORE) (C-6)
Aran Islands,
Co. Galway
– Ferry from Galway,
May–Sept., information
Aran Ferries, Tourist
Office, Eyre Square,
Galway, Co. Galway
Tel. (091) 68903/92447
Crossing 90 mins.
– Ferry from Rossaveal
(Connemara),
information Aran
Ferries, Clynagh,
Carraroe, Co. Galway.

INIS MEÁIN (INISHMAAN) (C-6)
Aran Islands, Co. Galway
– Ferry from Rossaveal,
information Island
Ferries Teo, Clynagh,
Co. Galway
Tel. (091) 61767
– Ferry from Doolin,
Apr. 15–Sept.,
information Doolin
Ferries Company, The

Pier, Doolin, Co. Clare
Tel. (065) 74455
or (065) 74466

INIS OÍRR (INISHEER)
(C-6) Aran Islands,
Co. Galway
5 miles northwest of
Doolin (Co. Clare).
– Ferry from Rossaveal,
contact Island Ferries
Teo, Clynagh, Co.
Galway
Tel. (091) 61767
– Ferry from Doolin,
Apr. 15–Sept., contact
Doolin Ferries
Company, The Pier,
Doolin, Co. Clare
Tel. (065) 74455/74466

PRACTICAL INFORMATION

TOURIST OFFICES
◆ ARAN ISLANDS (D-6)
Victoria Place, Eyre Sq,
Galway, Co. Galway
Tel. (091) 63081
Fax (091) 65201
Open 9am–6.45pm

◆ (C-6) Kilronan,
Inishmore, Co. Galway
Tel. (099) 61263
Open Jun.–Aug.
10am–7pm

CULTURE

IONAD ARAN HERITAGE CENTRE
(C-6) Aran Island
Heritage Centre,
Inishmore Island,
Co. Galway
Tel. (099) 61355
Open Jun.–Sept.
10am–7pm; Apr., May
and Oct. 11am–5pm
Information on the
history and geology of
the island.
Ir£1–2

ACCOMMODATION

KILMURVEY HOUSE ★
(C-6) Kilronan, Aran
Islands, Co. Galway
Tel. (099) 61218
Guesthouse and pub.
Ir£13–17

🖭 ⬆ 🖭⋯ 🏠 ♠♠ ℗

PUBS/RESTAURANTS

DÚN AONGHASA RESTAURANT (C-6)
Kilronan,
Aran Islands,
Co. Galway
Tel. (099) 61104
Organizes lobster picnics.
Ir£6–10
🍴 ○ ☂

ARANMORE ISLAND

HOW TO GET THERE

ARANMORE ISLAND
(E-1) Co. Donegal
– Ferry from Burtonport,
departs Mon.–Sat.
from 8.30am, Sun. from
11am; information:
C. Bonner, Aranmore
Ferry, An Forbartha,
Aranmore
Tel. (075) 21532
Crossing 20 mins.

ACCOMMODATION

GLEN HOTEL (E-1)
Aranmore Island,
Co. Donegal
Tel. (075) 20505
Ir£14–15.20
🏠

BARTRAGH ISLAND

HOW TO GET THERE

BARTRAGH ISLAND
(D-3) Co. Mayo
In the bay of Killala.
– On foot or by car at low tide
– Local private boat at high tide; information
Tel. (096) 32644
Excellent venue for salmon fishing, bird sanctuary.

BERE ISLAND

HOW TO GET THERE

BERE ISLAND (B-10)
Co. Cork
Near Castletown, in the bay of Bantry.
*– Ferry from Castletown, Jul.–Aug,
Ten ferries per day;
Sept.–Jun., 5 ferries per day; for information contact:*
C. Harrington
Tel. (027) 75009
Crossing takes 15 mins.

PRACTICAL INFORMATION

LIGHTHOUSE (B-10) Bere Island,
Co. Cork
Tel. (027) 75077
or (027) 75011

ACCOMMODATION

HARBOUR VIEW (B-10)
Harbour View,
Bere Island, Co. Cork
Tel. (027) 75011
Ir£13–17
🏠 ◑

CLEAR ISLAND

HOW TO GET THERE

CLEAR ISLAND
(C-10) Co. Cork
Eight miles from Baltimore (Co. Cork)
*– Ferry from Schull ,
Jun.–Aug, 1 ferry per day, departs 2.30pm;
information: K. Molloy*
Tel. (028) 28138
Ir£6
*– Ferry from Baltimore,
Jul.–Aug, 3 ferries per day; May, Jun. and Sept., Mon.–Fri., 2 ferries per day,
Sat.–Sun., 1 ferry per day; information*
Tel. (028) 39135
Crossing 45 mins.
Ir£7

CULTURE

HERITAGE CENTRE
(C-10) Clear Island,
West Cork
Tel. (028) 39153
or (028) 39135
Open Jun.–Aug
2–6pm, or by appointment.

CLARE ISLAND

HOW TO GET THERE

CLARE ISLAND (C-4)
Co. Mayo
Fifteen miles from Westport and 4 miles to the northwest of Roonagh, at the entrance to Clew Bay.
*– Ferry from Roonagh Quay, Louisburgh,
May–Sept., frequent service from 10.30am;
Oct.–Apr. 1 ferry per day, contact C. O'Grady*
Tel. (098) 26307
Crossing 20 mins.

DEVENISH ISLAND

HOW TO GET THERE

DEVENISH ISLAND (F-3)
Lower Lough Erne,
Co. Fermanagh
Tel. (0365) 22711
*– Ferry from Tory point,
3 miles to the north of Enniskillen, Apr.–Sept.,
Tue.–Sat. 10am–7pm,
Sun. 2–7pm*
Ir£2

DURSEY ISLAND

HOW TO GET THERE

DURSEY ISLAND (B-10)
Co. Cork
*– Cablecar from Dursey Sound, 9 trips daily,
6 passengers per car,
9am–8pm, contact
P. Sheehan*
Tel. (027) 73017
50p–Ir£2

GARINISH ISLAND

HOW TO GET THERE

GARINISH ISLAND (C-9)
Glengarriff, Co. Cork
Tel. (027) 63081/63116
Fax (027) 63298
Open Apr. 26–Sept.,
Mon.–Sat. 9.30am–5pm,
Sun. 1–6pm; Oct.–Sept.
15, Mon.–Sat. 10am–
3.30pm, Sun. 1–6pm
Regular crossings to Glengarriff
Ir£5

CULTURE

ILNACULLIN GARDENS
(C-9) Garinish Island,
Glengarriff, Co. Cork
Tel. (027) 63040
Open Jul.–Aug, Mon.–
Sat. 9.30am– 6.30pm,
Sun. 11am– 7pm; Apr.–
Jun. and Sept., Mon.–
Sat. 10am–6.30pm,
Sun. 1–7pm; Mar. and
Oct., Mon.–Sat. 10am–
4.30pm, Sun. 1–5pm
Ir£1–2

INISHTURK ISLAND

HOW TO GET THERE

INISHTURK ISLAND
(B-4) Co. Mayo
Situated 8 miles to the southwest of Roonagh Quay, near Louisburgh.
*– no regular crossings,
information at Cleggan and Roonagh Quay.*

MACDARA'S ISLAND

HOW TO GET THERE

MACDARA'S ISLAND
(C-5) Carna, Co. Galway
*– Ferry from Clifden,
July 16 only, 10am–6pm,
information Clifden Tourist Office*
Tel. (095) 21163
Crossing takes1 hour
Pilgrimage: July 16

PRACTICAL INFORMATION

MACDARA'S ISLAND'S HOUSE (C-5)
MacDara's Island,
Carna, Co. Galway
Tel. (095) 21379

RATHLIN ISLAND

HOW TO GET THERE

RATHLIN ISLAND (I-1)
Co. Antrim
Six miles from
Ballycastle and 14
miles from the Argyll
peninsula
– Ferry from
Ballycastle, Easter–
Sept., 10.45am and
4pm, contact Rathlin
Ferry Company
Tel. (02657) 63917,
Rathlin Ferries
Tel. (02657) 63907
£1.75–3
– Post boat, Mon.,
Wed. and Fri. 10.30am.
Crossing 40 mins.

CULTURE

**RATHLIN ISLAND BIRD
SANCTUARY** (I-1)
Rathlin Island,
Co. Antrim
Information: L. McFaul,
South Cleggan, Rathlin
Island,
Tel. (02657) 63935
– Ballycastle Ferry,
1 ferry per day,
10.30am

SHERKIN ISLAND

HOW TO GET THERE

SHERKIN ISLAND
(C-10) Co. Cork
– Ferry from Baltimore,
information
V. O'Driscoll
Tel. (028) 20125
Crossing 10 mins.
– Ferry from Schull,
information K. Molloy
Tel. (028) 28138

SKELLIG ISLANDS

HOW TO GET THERE

SKELLIG ISLANDS
Co. Kerry (A-9)
– Ferry from
Portmagee, 9am–2pm,
Ir£15
– Two-hour tour of the
islands (Great Skellig
and Little Skellig).
Boat leaves from
Valentia Island,
2.30pm. Contact:
Skellig Heritage
Centre.
Ir£20

CULTURE

**SKELLIG HERITAGE
CENTRE** (A-9)
Valentia Island,
Co. Kerry
Tel. (066) 73306
or (066) 76124
Fax (066) 76333

TORY ISLAND

HOW TO GET THERE

TORY ISLAND (F-1)
Co. Donegal
– Ferries from Bunbeg
and Magheraroarty
daily during the
summer, information:
E. O'Neachtain
Tel. (074) 35502,
frequent crossings
(45 mins.).

ACCOMMODATION

TORY ISLAND HOTEL
(F-1) Co. Donegal
Tel. (074) 35920
Fax (074) 35920
Ir£14–30

WHIDDY ISLAND

HOW TO GET THERE

WHIDDY ISLAND (C-9)
Co. Cork
– Private boat from
Bantry, on request,
contact N. O'Leary
Tel. (027) 50310
Crossing 10 mins.

WHITE ISLAND

HOW TO GET THERE

WHITE ISLAND (F-3)
Lower Lough Erne,
Co. Fermanagh
– Ferry from Castle
Archdale Marina,
Jun.–Sept., Thur.–Sat.
10am–7pm, Sun.
2–7pm.
£2

INISFAIL ★ (C-8)
Beaufort
Tel. (064) 44404
Activities: golfing.
Ir£12–14
🅿

**MUCKROSS PARK
HOTEL ★** (C-9)
Lakes of Killarney
Tel. (064) 31938
Closed Jan. 1–Mar. 13
*Golfing, horseriding,
walking, fishing.*
Ir£35–60
🏛 ○ ⌂ 🛏 ⚒ 🅿

SILLERDANE LODGE ★
(C-9) Coolnoohill,
Kilgarvan
Tel. (064) 85359
*Activities: golfing,
horseriding, walking,
fishing.*
Ir£13.50
🅿

SHOPPING

CLEO IRELAND LTD
(B-9) 2, Shelbourne St,
Kenmare
Tel. (064) 91410
Open Mon.–Sat.
9.30am–8pm, Sun.
11am–6pm
Closed Dec.–Mar
Local crafts.

THE FISHERIES (B-8)
Killorglin
Tel. (066) 61106
Open 9am–1pm
Salmon smokehouse.

COUNTY LIMERICK

PRACTICAL INFORMATION

TOURIST OFFICES
◆ (D-7) Arthur's Quay,
Limerick
Tel. (061) 317522
Open Jul.–Aug 9am–
7pm; Sept.–Jun., Mon.–
Sat. 9.30am– 5.30pm

◆ THE THATCH COTTAGE
(D-7) Main St, Adare
Tel. (061) 396255
Open Jul.–Aug 9am–
7pm; May–Jun. and
Sept. 9am–6pm

CULTURE

CASTLE MATRIX
(D-7) Rathkeale
Tel. (069) 64284
Open May–Sept., Mon.–
Wed. and Sat 11.30am–
5pm, Sun. 1–5pm
Ir£3

DESMOND CASTLE (D-7)
Adare
Open Easter–Aug 9am–
6pm; Sept. 9am–5pm
40p–Ir£1

GLIN CASTLE (C-7)
Glin
Tel. (068) 34112
Open May 10am–noon
and 2–4pm, or by
appointment.
Ir£1.50–2.50

HUNT MUSEUM (D-7)
Foundation Building,
University of Limerick,
Limerick
Tel. (061) 333 644
Open Mon.–Sat.
10am–5pm
Ir£1–2

KING JOHN CASTLE
(D-7) Limerick
Tel. (061) 411 201
Open May–Oct.
9.30am– 4.30pm; Nov.–
Apr., Sun. 11am–4pm
Ir£1.40–3.30

**LOUGH GUR
INTERPRETATIVE
CENTRE** (D-8)
Lough Gur
Tel. (061) 85186
Open May–Sept.
10am–6pm
Ir£1–1.85

**ST MARY'S
CATHEDRAL** (D-7)
Limerick
Tel. (061) 338 697
Open 8.45am–1pm
and 2.15–5pm

PUBS/RESTAURANTS

THE MUSTARD SEED
(D-7) Adare
Tel. (061) 396 451
Open Tue.–Sat.
7–10pm
Closed Feb.
*Elegant restaurant in
one of the prettiest
villages in Ireland.*
Ir£24–25
▭ ○ ▭ ⌂ 🎵 🛏

ACCOMMODATION

ADARE MANOR HOTEL
(D-7) Adare
Tel. (061) 396 566
*Gothic mansion in 840
acres of parkland. Once
home of the earls of
Dunraven it is now a
5-star deluxe hotel with
golf course, fishing,
shooting and horse
riding. Expensive.*
Ir£95–220
▭ ○ 🏛 🛏 🅿

ALEXANDRA GUEST HOUSE ★
(D-7)
J. & M. Devane,
O'Connell Ave., Limerick
Tel. (061) 318472
Ir£14–16.50
▭ ⭐ 🅲 ♠

COUNTY TIPPERARY

PRACTICAL INFORMATION

TOURIST OFFICES
◆ (E-8) Castle St, Cahir
Tel. (052) 41453
Open May–Sept.,
Mon.–Sat. 9.30am–6pm,
Sun. 11am–5pm

◆ (E-8) Community
Office, Tipperary
Tel. (062) 51457
Open Mon.–Sat.
9am–7pm

◆ (E-8) Town Hall,
Cashel
Tel. (062) 61333
Open May–Sept.,
Mon.–Sat. 9am–6pm,
Sun. 10am–1pm

CULTURE

CAHIR CASTLE (E-8)
Cahir
Tel. (052) 41011
Open Jun. 15–Sept. 15
9am–7.30pm; Apr.–Jun
15 and Sept. 15–Oct. 15
10am–6pm;
Oct. 15–Mar. 10am–
1pm and 2–4.30pm
60p–Ir£1.50

SWISS COTTAGE (E-8)
Cahir
Tel. (052) 41144
Open May–Sept.
10am–6pm; Oct.–Nov.,
Sun. 10am–4.30pm;
Apr., Tue.–Sun.
10am–1pm and 2–5pm
60p–Ir£1.50

ROCK OF CASHEL
(E-8) Cashel
Tel. (062) 61437
Open Jun. 15–Sept. 15
9am–7.30pm; Mar. 15–
Jun. 15 9.30am–5.30pm;
Sept. 15–Mar. 15
9.30am–4.30pm
Ir£1–2

HOLYCROSS ABBEY
(E-7) Thurles
Tel. (0504) 43118
Open 8.45am–9.30pm

ORMOND CASTLE (E-8)
Tipperary
Tel. (051) 640 787
Open Jun. 15–Sept.
9.30am–6.30pm
60p–Ir£1.50

PUBS/RESTAURANTS

**THE SPEARMAN
RESTAURANT** ★ (E-8)
97, Main St, Cashel
Tel. (062) 61143
Ir£9.95–10.95
▭ 🅞 🅲

**GURTHA LOUGHA
HOUSE** ★ (E-7)
Ballinderry, Nenagh
Tel. (067) 22080
One sitting 8pm
Closed Christmas and
Feb.
Ir£22–40
▭ 🅞

ACCOMMODATION

THE CHESTNUTS ★
(E-8) J. & P. O'Halloran,
Kilkenny Dualla Rd,
R 691, Dualla, Cashel
Tel. (062) 61469
Ir£13–15
▭·· 🏠 ♠

◆

CONNACHT

GALWAY CITY (D-6)

PRACTICAL INFORMATION

TOURIST OFFICE
ARAN ISLANDS
Victoria Place,
Eyre Square, Galway
Tel. (091) 63081
Open 9am–6.45pm

CULTURE

CITY MUSEUM
Spanish Arch, Galway
Tel. (091) 67641
Open 10am–1pm
and 2.15–5.15pm;
winter Wed. and Fri.
30–60p

GALWAY ART CENTRE
65, Dominick St,
Galway
Tel. (091) 65886
Open Mon.–Sat.
10am–5.30pm

LYNCH'S CASTLE
Shop St, Galway
Headquarters of the
Allied Irish Bank, tours
during opening hours.

**NORA BARNACLE'S
HOUSE**
Bowling Green, Galway
Tel. (091) 64743
Open May 15–Sept. 15,
Mon.–Sat. 10am–5pm
Ir£1

**ST NICHOLAS'
CATHEDRAL**
Above the bridge at
Salmon Weir, Galway
Open 8am–9pm

**ST NICHOLAS'
COLLEGIATE CHURCH**
Next to Shop St, Galway
Open 9am–6pm;
winter 9am–5.30pm

PUBS/RESTAURANTS

**MCDONAGH'S FISH
RESTAURANT**
22, Quay St, Galway
Tel. (091) 65809
Open Mon.–Sat. noon–
10pm, Sun. 6–10pm
Ir£6–7
▭ 🅞

McSWIGGANS ★
3, Eyre St, Wood Quay,
Galway
Tel. (091) 68917
Ir£6.95
▭ 🅞 🅲 ♣ ♫

NIMMOS RESTAURANT
Spanish Arch, Galway
Tel. (091) 63565
Open 12.30–3pm and
7–11pm
Ir£2–14.50
▭ 🅞 ♫

O'MAILLES
30, Prospect Hill,
Galway
Tel. (091) 64595
Ir£3.95
♫

T. NAUGHTON & CO.
17, High St, Galway
Tel. (091) 68820
Closed Sun.
▭ 🅞

TAFFE'S
19-21, Shop St, Galway
Tel. (091) 64066
◑ 🅲 ♫

ACCOMMODATION

**ARDILAUN HOUSE
HOTEL** ★
Taylors House, Galway
Tel. (091) 21433
Ir£40–95
▭ ⭐ ▭·· 🏠 🅿

**BRENNANS YARD
HOTEL** ★
Lower Merchants Rd,
Galway
Tel. (091) 68166
Fax (091) 68262
Ir£55–120
▭ ⭐ ◑ 🅲 ♣ 🅿

**GLYNSK HOUSE
HOTEL** (C-5)
Cashel, Connemara
Tel. (095) 32279
Ir£20–25
▭·· 🏠 ⚖ ♣ 🅿

**GUIDER'S OSTERLY
LODGE** ★
142, Lower Salthill,
Galway
Tel. (091) 23794
Fax (091) 27881
Ir£16–20
▭ ⭐ ♣ 🅿

NORMAN VILLAS
86, Lower Salthill,
Galway
Tel. (091) 21131
Closed Christmas
Information: D. Keagh.
Ir£6–8
⭐

QUAY STREET HOUSE ★
10, Quay St,
Galway
Tel. (091) 68644
Ir£5.90–7.50
▭ 🄲

SHOPPING

CHARLIE BYRNE'S
BOOKSHOP
4, Middle St, Galway
Tel. (091) 61766
Open 10am–6pm

GALWAY BAY
SEA FOODS
New Docks, Galway
Tel. (091) 63011
Open Mon.–Sat.
9am–1pm and 2–6pm
Salmon smokehouse.

THE GRAINSTORE
Lower Abbeygate St
Galway
Tel. (091) 66620
Open Mon.–Sat.
10am–6pm
Art gallery.

HARTMANN JEWELLERS
29, William St, Galway
Tel. (091) 62063
Jewelry.

KENNY'S BOOKSHOP
High St, Galway
Tel. (091) 62739
Open Mon.–Sat.
9am–6pm
Books.

MULLIGAN
5, Middle St Court,
Middle St, Galway
Tel. (091) 64961
Traditional Irish music.

O'MAILLES
Dominick St, Galway
Tel. (091) 62696
Open Jul.–Aug,
Mon.–Sat. 9am–9pm;
Sept.–Jun., Mon.–Sat.
9am–6pm
Tweed and Aran.

THE WINDING STAIR
AN STAIGHRE BISE
4, Mainguard St, Galway
Tel. (091) 61682
Crafts and antiques.

COUNTY GALWAY

PRACTICAL INFORMATION

TOURIST OFFICES
◆ KELLER'S TRAVEL
AGENCY (E-6)
Ballinasloe
Tel. (0905) 42131

Open Mon.–Fri.
8.30am–6pm, Sat.
8.30am–5.30pm

◆ (B-5) Market St
Clifden
Tel. (095) 21163
Open May–Sept., Mon.–
Sat. 9am–5.45pm, Sun.
noon–4pm

◆ (D-6) Promenade
Salthill
Tel. (091) 63081
Open 9am–6.45pm;
Oct.–May, 9am–5.45pm

◆ (D-6) Thoor Ballylee
Gort
Tel. (091) 31436
Open Easter–Sept.
10am–6pm

BOAT TRIPS

LOUGH CORRIB
CRUISE (C/D-5)
K. McDonagh, Furbo
Hill, Furbo
Tel. (091) 592 447
Tours 1.30pm, 2.30pm
and 4.30pm

CULTURE

AUGHNANURE
CASTLE (D-6)
Aughnanure,
Oughterard
Tel. (091) 82214
Open 9.30am–6.30pm
60p–Ir£1.50

CLONFERT CATHEDRAL
(E-6) Clonfert
*Collect keys from house
opposite.*

CLONTUSKERT PRIORY
(E-6) Four miles to the
south of Ballinasloe
*Abbey is situated in a
private field. Ask for
permission from farmer
to cross his land.*

CONNEMARA
NATIONAL PARK (C-5)
Renville House,
Letterfrack
Tel. (095) 41054
Open Jul.–Aug 9.30am–
6.30pm; Jun. 10am–
6.30pm; May and Sept.
10am–5.30pm

*Visitors' center in the
park.*
Ir£1.50

COOLE PARK (D-6)
Gort
Tel. (091) 31804
Open Jun. 15–Aug
9.30am–6.30pm;
Apr. 15–Jun. 15,
Sept. 10am–5pm
70p–Ir£1

DUNGUAIRE CASTLE
(D-6) Kinvarra
Tel. (091) 37108
Open May–Sept.
9.30am–5pm
*Medieval banquets at
5.45pm and 8.45pm.*
Ir£1.80

KILMACDUAGH
MONASTERY (D-6)
Three miles from Gort,
Tel. (091) 31436 (Gort
Tourist Office)
*Contact C. Finnegan,
Kilmacduagh
Tel. (091) 31391.*

KYLEMORE ABBEY (C-5)
Letterfrack
Tel. (095) 41113
Open Easter–Oct.
10am–6pm
Ir£1–1.50

PORTUMNA CASTLE
(E-6) Portumna
Tel. (0509) 41658
Open Jun.–Sept. 15
9.30am–6.30pm
40p–Ir£1

TEACH AN PHIARSAIGH
(PATRICK PEARSE'S
COTTAGE) (C-5)
Rosmuck
Tel. (091) 74292
Open Jun. 15–Sept. 15
9.30am–6.30pm
40p–Ir£1

THOOR BALLYLEE
(D-6) Gort
Tel. (091) 31436
Open Apr.–Sept.
10am–6pm
*From Gort take the N18,
turn right after 3 miles.*
Ir£2.50

PUBS/RESTAURANTS

AN CRUISCÍN LÁN
(C-6) Spiddal
Tel. (091) 83148
Open 10.30am–9pm
Ir£4–10
◐ ▭•• 🏠 🄿

AUGHRIM SCHOOL
HOUSE (E-6)
Aughrim
Tel. (0905) 73936

Open Tue.–Sat.
6.30–9.30pm, Sun.
12.30–3pm
Ir£9.50–16.50
▭ ○ ▭•• 🏠 ⚥

BURKE'S (C-5)
Mount Gable House,
Clonbur
Tel. (092) 46175
♫

DALY RORY P. ★
(C-5) Portfinn Lodge,
Leenane
Tel. (095) 42265
Open Jul.–Sept.
noon–3pm
Ir£12–19
▭ ○ 🏠 ▭•• 🄿

DRIMCONG HOUSE ★
(D-5) Moy Cullen
Tel. (091) 85115
Open Tue.–Sat.
7–10.30pm
Closed Christmas–Mar.
Ir£8.50–24
▭ ○ ⚥ ♫

KYLEMORE ABBEY
RESTAURANT (C-5)
Letterfrack
Tel. (095) 41113
Open 9am–6pm
Closed Oct.–Easter
Ir£3.85
▭ ○ 🏠

MORAN'S OF THE
WEIR ★ (D-6)
Kilcolgan
Tel. (091) 96113
Ir£9–15
▭ ○ 🏠 ▭••

O'DOWDS SEAFOOD
BAR & RESTAURANT
(C-5) Roundstone,
Connemara
Tel. (095) 35809
Ir£6.50–10
▭ ○ ◐ 🏠 ▭•• ⚥ 🄿

O'GRADY SEAFOOD
RESTAURANT (B-5)
Market St, Clifden
Tel. (095) 21450
Closed Sun.–Mon.
and Nov.–Mar
Ir£8–17
▭ ○ 🏛 🄲 ⚥

PADDY BURKES (D-6)
Clarinbridge
Tel. (091) 96226
Ir£8–15.50
▭ ○ ▭•• 🏠

TI HUGHES ★ (C-6)
Spiddal
Tel. (091) 83447

TY AR MOR (D-6)
Barna Pier
Tel. (091) 592 223

Open noon–1pm
Ir£4–8.50

ACCOMMODATION

CASHEL HOUSE HOTEL ★ (C-5)
Cashel
Tel. (095) 31011
In an oasis of calm. Beautiful gardens. Tennis court. Horse riding. Good food.
Ir£50–63

CURRAREVAGH HOUSE (C-5) Oughterard, Connemara
Tel. (091) 82312
Fax (091) 82731
A charming country mansion beside Lough Corrib. Fishing, boats and tennis courts; golf and riding nearby.
Ir£44–55

HAYDENS HOTEL (E-6)
Dunlo St, Ballinasloe
Tel. (0905) 42347
Ir£28–48

LOUGH CORRIB HOSTEL ★ (C-5)
Camp St, Oughterard, Connemara
Tel./Fax (091) 82634
Ir£5.50

MARY KINNANE (C-5)
Letterard, Cashel, Connemara
Tel. (095) 32383
Ir£13.50–15

SÁILÍN ★ (C-6)
Spiddal,
Tel. (091) 83308
Ir£15

THE WHITE HOUSE ★ (C-5) Carna
Tel. (095) 32275
Ir£12–20

SHOPPING

CONNEMARA FISHERIES (C-5)
Dooras, Connemara
Tel. (092) 48113
Open Mon.–Fri. 10am–5pm, Sat. 10am–1pm
Salmon smokehouse.

GERARTY'S (C-5) Carna, Connemara
Tel. (095) 32239
Typical Irish products, coffee shop, bicycle rental and bureau de change.

ROUNDSTONE MUSICAL INSTRUMENTS (C-5)
I.D.A. Craft Centre, Roundstone
Tel. (095) 35808
Open 8am–7pm
Traditional Irish instruments: tin whistles, bodhráns.

COUNTY LEITRIM

PRACTICAL INFORMATION

TOURIST OFFICE (F-4) The Quay, Carrick-on-Shannon, Tel. (078) 20170
Open Jun.–Sept., Mon.–Sat. 9am–8pm, Sun. 10am–2pm

CULTURE

PARKE'S CASTLE (E-3) Lough Gill, Tel. (071) 64149
Open Easter–Oct. 10am–5pm
Four miles from Lough Gill.
60p–Ir£1.50

COUNTY MAYO

PRACTICAL INFORMATION

TOURIST OFFICES
◆ (D-3) Cathedral St, Ballina
Tel. (096) 70848
Open May–Sept. 10am–5.30pm

◆ (D-4) Knock, Co. Mayo
Tel. (094) 88193
Open May–Sept. 10am–6pm

◆ (D-4) Linen Hall St, Castleba
Tel. (094) 21207
Open Easter–Sept. 15, Mon.–Sat. 9.30am–6pm

◆ (C-4) The Mall, Westport
Tel. (098) 25711
Open Jul.–Aug 9am–6.45pm; Sept.–Jun., Mon.–Fri. 9am– 5.15pm

◆ (C-4) The Sound, Achill Island
Tel. (098) 45384
Open Jul.–Aug, Mon.–Sat. 10am–5.30pm

CULTURE

CONG'S ABBEY (D-5) Cong
Tel. (01) 661 3111
Open Jun.–Sept. 15 9.30am–6.30pm
40p–Ir£1

CÉIDE FIELDS (D-3)
Ballycastle
Tel. (096) 43325
Open Jun.–Sept. 9.30am–6.30pm, Mar. 15–May 10am–5pm, Oct. 10am–5pm
Ir£2

◆

◆

HORSERIDING

BANSHA HOUSE AND STABLES (E-8)
Bansha, Co. Tipperary
Tel. (062) 54194
Fax (062) 52499

BORO HILL HOUSE EQUESTRIAN AND HOLIDAY CENTRE (G-8)
Clonroche, Enniscorthy, Co. Wexford
Tel. (054) 44117
Fax (054) 44266

BRENNANSTOWN RIDING SCHOOL (H-6)
Hollybrook, Kilmacanogue, Bray, Co. Wicklow
Tel. (01) 286 3778
Fax (01) 282 9590

(D-7) **CLONSHIRE EQUESTRIAN CENTRE**
Adare, Co. Limerick
Tel. (061) 396 770
Fax (061) 396 541

HOLY TRINITY CHURCH (C-4)
Westport
Tel. (01) 661 3111
(OPW, Dublin)

GRANUAILE HERITAGE CENTRE (C-4)
Louisburg
Tel. (098) 66195
Open Easter–Oct., Mon.–Sat. 10am–6pm, Sun. 11am–6pm; Nov.–Easter, Mon.–Fri. 10am–6pm
Ir£1–2

OUR LADY'S SHRINE (D-4) Knock
Tel. (094) 88100
Open Jul.–Aug 10am–7pm; May–Oct. 10am–6pm
Folk Museum open 10am–7pm
50p–Ir£1.50

WESTPORT HOUSE (C-4) Westport
Tel. (098) 25430
Open Jul.–Aug 2–6pm
Entrance to house and zoo:
Ir£3–6

DEVIL'S GLEN HOLIDAY AND EQUESTRIAN VILLAGE (H-7)
Ashford, Co. Wicklow
Tel. (0404) 40637
Fax (0404) 40638

GREEN GLEN'S HORSE VILLAGE (C-8)
Millstreet Town, Co. Cork
Tel. (029) 70039
Fax (029) 70306

LADESTOWN HOUSE RIDING AND TREKKING STABLES (F-5) Mullingar, Co. Westmeath
Tel. (044) 48218
Fax (044) 42755

LARAGH TREKKING CENTRE (H-7)
Glendalough, Co. Wicklow
Tel. (0404) 45282
Fax (0404) 45204

382

PUBS/RESTAURANTS

ECHOES (D-5)
Main St, Cong
Tel. (092) 46059
Open Mon.–Sun.
5–10pm
Ir£12–18
⬚ O 🅲 ⚡

ENNISCOE HOUSE (C-4)
Castlehill
Tel. (096) 31112
Open Mar. 15–Oct. 15.
8–9pm
Ir£18–20
⬚ O

HOBAN'S (C-4)
The Octagon, Westport
Tel. (098) 27249
♫

THE HUMBERT INN
(D-4) Castlebar
Tel. (094) 21349
Open noon–3pm
◑ 🅲 ♫

MATT MOLLOY'S (C-4)
Bridge St, Westport
Tel. (098) 26655
⬚ 🅲 ♫

THE QUAY COTTAGE
(C-4) The Harbour,
Westport
Tel. (098) 26412
Ir£8
⬚

ACCOMMODATION

**ASHFORD CASTLE
HOTEL** ★ (D-5) Cong
Tel. (092) 46003
(Toll free US only:
Tel. 800 346 7007)
*Luxurious 13th-century
castle set on the shores
of Lough Corrib. Winner
of best hotel in Ireland
from 1989 to 1994. Golf,
horseriding, fishing,
tennis.*
Ir£78–95
⬚ 🏛 ⚜

**BREAFFY HOUSE
HOTEL** ★ (D-4)
Castleba
Tel./Fax (094) 22033
*Stone-built mansion
house set in parkland
estate. Quiet and
friendly; 38 rooms. Golf.*
Ir£38
⬚ ⬚⋯ 🏠 ⚜

**WESTERN STRAND
HOTEL** (C-3)
Belmullet
Tel./Fax (097) 81096
Tennis, golf, walking.
Ir£10–13
⬚ O 🅲 ♫

SHOPPING

EAGLE ISLE (D-3)
Doohama, Ballina
Tel. (097) 86829
Open Mon.–Sat.
10am–7pm
Salmon smokehouse.

**FOXFORD
WOOLLEN MILLS** (D-4)
Foxford
Tel. (094) 56104
Open Jun.–Sept.,
Mon.–Sat. 10am–6pm,
Sun. 2–6pm; Oct.–May,
Mon.–Sat. 10am–5pm,
Sun. 2–5pm
Tweeds, woolens.

HACKETT & TURPIN
(C-3) Carrow Teige,
Belmullet
Tel. (097) 88925
Open 9am–6.15pm
Clothing.

COUNTY
ROSCOMMON

PRACTICAL
INFORMATION

TOURIST OFFICES
◆ COURTHOUSE (E-4)
Market St, Boyle
Tel. (079) 62145
Open May–Sept., Mon.–
Sat. 10am–5.30pm

◆ (E-5) Harrison Hall,
Roscommon
Tel. (0903) 26342
Open Jun.–Sept.,
Mon.–Sat.
10am–5.30pm

CULTURE

BOYLE ABBEY (E-4)
Boyle
Tel. (079) 62604
Open Jun. 15–Sept. 15
9.30am–6.30pm
70p–Ir£1

CLONALIS HOUSE
(E-4) Castlerea
Tel. (0907) 20014
Open Jun.–Sept.,
Tue.–Sun. noon–5pm
Ir£2

**LOUGH KEY FOREST
PARK** (E-4)
Boyle
Tel. (079) 62214
*Attractions, playground,
forest walks.*
Ir£1–4

STROKESTOWN PARK
(E-4) Strokestown
Tel. (078) 33013
– House: open

Jun.–Sept. 18, Tue.–
Sun. noon–5pm
– Museum: open Mar.–
Nov. 11am–5pm
Ir£1–2 (park), *Ir£2.50*
(museum), *Ir£3* (house)

PUBS/RESTAURANTS

BOGSIDE INN (E-4)
Derrynadoey,
Knockvicar, Boyle
Tel. (078) 47155
Open 10am–midnight,
winter 11am–11.30pm
⬚⋯ ♫

COUNTY SLIGO

PRACTICAL
INFORMATION

TOURIST OFFICE
(E-3) Aras Reddan,
Temple St, Sligo
Tel. (071) 61201
Fax (071) 60360
Open Jul.–Aug,
Mon.–Sat. 9am–8pm,
Sun. 10am–6pm;
Oct.–Jun., Mon.–Fri.
9am–5pm

CULTURE

**CARROWMORE
MEGALITHIC
CEMETERY**
(E-3) Carrowmore
Tel. (071) 61534
Open May–Sept.
9.30am–6.30pm
Ir£1

DEER PARK (E-3)
Lough Gill
*Five miles from Sligo to
the north of Lough Gill.*

**DRUMCLIFF
MONASTERY** (E-3)
Drumcliff
Tel. (071) 63133

HAZELWOOD DEMESNE
(E-3).
*Private property owned
by the Korean Saehen
society. Closed to the
public.*

LISSADELL HOUSE (E-3)
Drumcliff
Eight miles to the north
of Sligo.
Tel. (071) 63150
Open Jun.–Sept. 15
10.30am–12.15pm
and 2–4.50pm
50p–Ir£2

SLIGO'S ABBEY (E-3)
Sligo
Open Jun.–Sept. 15
9.30am–6.30pm
40p–Ir£1

**SLIGO ART GALLERY
& COUNTY
MUSEUM**
(E-3) Sligo
Tel. (071) 42212
Open Jun.–Sept.,
Tue.–Sat. 10.30am–
12.30pm and
2.30–4.30pm;
Oct.–May, shorter
opening hours.

PUBS/RESTAURANTS

**KNOCKMUL
DOWNEY**
(E-3) Markree Castle,
Collooney
Tel. (071) 67800
Closed Christmas and
Feb.
Ir£8–22
⬚ O ⚜

McLYNN'S (E-3)
Old Market St,
Sligo
Tel. (071) 42088
🅲

THE MOORINGS (E-3)
Rosses Point
Tel. (071) 77112
Ir£8–15
⬚ O

THE THATCH (E-3)
Ballisodare
Tel. (071) 67288
◑ ♫

ACCOMMODATION

**COOPER'S HILL
HOUSE** (E-3)
Riverstown
Tel. (071) 65108
Fax (071) 65466
Open Mar.–Oct.
Ir£42–48
⬚ O 🏠 🅿

ULSTER

COUNTY ANTRIM

PRACTICAL INFORMATION

TOURIST OFFICES

◆ DUNLUCE CENTRE (H-1)
Dunluce Ave, Portrush
Tel. (01265) 824 444
or (01265) 44723
Open Jul.–Sept. 9am–
9pm, Jun. 9am–5pm,
Easter–May 9am–5pm,
Oct.–Easter, Sat.–Sun.
noon–5pm

◆ GIANT'S CAUSEWAY
CENTRE (H-1)
44, Causeway Head Rd,
Bushmills, Giant's
Causeway
Tel. (012657) 31855
Open Jul.–Aug 10am–
7pm, Jun. 10am–6pm,
Sept.–May 10am–5pm
*Two miles to the north of
Bushmills, on the
B146.*

◆ SHESKBURN HOUSE (I-1)
7, Mary St, Ballycastle
Tel. (012657) 62024
Open Jul.–Aug, Mon.–
Fri. 9.30am–5pm,
Sat.10am–6pm,
Sun. 2–6pm;
Sept.–Jun., Mon.–Fri.
9.30am–5pm

◆ FERRY TERMINAL (I-2)
Larne Harbour
BT401XB
Tel. (01574) 260 088
Open Jul.–Aug, Mon.–
Wed. 9am–5pm, Thur.–
Sat. 9am–5.30pm;
Sept.–Jun., Mon.–Sat.
10am–4pm

CULTURE

CARRICK-A-REDE BRIDGE (H-1)
Ballintoy
*Seasonal bridge
(Apr.–Sept.), installed
by salmon fishers,
linking the mainland to
a small island.*

CARRICKFERGUS CASTLE (I-3)
Carrickfergus
Tel. (1960) 351 273
Open Apr.–Sept.,
Mon.–Sat. 10am–
5.30pm, Sun.
2–5.30pm; Oct.–Mar,
Mon.–Sat. 10am–
3.30pm, Sun. 2–3.30pm
£1.25–2.50

DUNINENY CASTLE (I-1)
Ballycastle
*Currently closed to the
public.*

DUNLUCE CASTLE (H-1)
Dunluce Rd
Tel. (012657) 31938
Open Tue.–Sat. 10am–
4pm, Sun. 2–4pm
75p–£1.50
*Two and a half miles to
the south of Bushmills.*

DUNSEVERICK CASTLE
(H-1) Causeway Rd,
Bushmills
*Between Bushmills
and Ballintoy. Ruins.*

THE GIANT'S CAUSEWAY (H-1)
Bushmills
Tel. (012657) 31582
*Two miles to the north
of Bushmills,
on the B146.*

IRISH LINEN CENTRE & LISBURN MUSEUM
(I-3) Market Sq., Lisburn
Tel. (01846) 663 377
*Open Mar.–Sept.,
Mon.–Sat. 9.30am–
5.30pm, Sun.
2–5.30pm; Oct.–Mar,
Mon.–Sat. 9.30am–
5pm, Sun. 2–5pm
Late opening Thursday
until 9pm.*

KNIGHT RIDE & HERITAGE PLAZA
(I-3) Antrim St,
Carrickfergus
Tel. (01960) 366455
Open Jun.–Aug, Mon.–
Fri. 10am–9pm, Sat.
10am–6pm, Sun. noon–
6pm; Sept., Mon.–Sat.
10am–6pm, Sun. noon–
6pm; Apr.–May, Mon.–
Sat. 10am–6pm, Sun.
noon–6pm; Oct.–Mar,
Mon.–Sat. 10am–5pm,
Sun. noon–5pm
£1.25–2.50
*Monorail tour showing
the history of the city.*

OLD BUSHMILLS DISTILLERY (H-1)
Bushmills
Tel. (012657) 31521

Open 9am–12.30pm
and 1.30–3.30pm
£2 (Children: free)

PUBS/RESTAURANTS

COUNTRY HOUSE HOTEL (I-2)
20, Doagh Rd, Kell
Tel. (01266) 891 663
*From Ballymena, take
the 436 for 2 miles then
the B59, toward Doag,
for 3½ miles.*

DUNADRY HOTEL (I-3)
2, Islandreagh Drive
Dunadry
Tel. (01849) 432474
Health club and gym.
£10–18

GROUSE INN (H-2)
2, Springwell St,
Ballymena
Tel. (01266) 45234
Closed Sun.
£12

HARBOUR BAR (H-1)
5, Harbour Rd, Portrush
Tel. (01265) 825047
*Restaurant closed
Sun. (Apr.–Dec.).*
£5–6.50

HILLCREST COUNTRY HOUSE (H-1)
306, White Park Rd,
Bushmills, Giant's
Causeway
Tel. (012657) 31577

MAGHERABOY HOUSE HOTEL (H-1)
41, Magheraboy Rd,
Portrush, Co. Antrim
Tel. (0265) 823 507
£8–9

RAMORE RESTAURANT
(H-1) The Harbour
Portrush
Open Tue.–Sat.
6.30–10.30pm
£12–25

SWEENEY'S WINE BAR
(H-1) 6b, Seaport Ave.,
Portballintrae
Tel. (012657) 31279

THE KING'S HEAD ★
(I-3) Lisburn Rd,
Tel. (01232) 667 805

ACCOMMODATION

CUSHENDUN'S CAVE HOUSE (I-1)
Cushendun
Tel. (802) 667 4254
*Access via a grotto,
holiday houses in a
former convent.*

LONDONDERRY ARMS ★ (I-2)
20, Harbour Rd,
Carnlough BT44OEU
Tel. (01574) 885 255
Fax (01574) 885 263
*Built in 1848, by Lady
Londonderry, as a
coaching inn. Her great
grand son, Sir Winston
Churchill, inherited it in
1921. The O'Neill family
have owned and
managed the hotel
since 1946. Activities:
golfing, horseriding,
walking, fishing,
waterskiing.*
£45–86

THE BUSHMILLS INN ★
(H-1) 25, Main St,
Bushmills BT578QA
Tel. (012657) 32339
Fax (012657) 32048

Hotel and restaurant at the home of the world's oldest distillery. Activities: golfing, horseriding, fishing and a secret library.
£48–74
☐ ○ ⌂ **C** ⌂ ⚘
⚘ **P**

THE CAUSEWAY HOTEL (H-1)
Giant's Causeway, Bushmills BT578 SU
Tel. (012657) 31226
Fax (012657) 32552
£25–32
☐•• ⌂ ⚘ ⚲

COUNTY ARMAGH

PRACTICAL INFORMATION

TOURIST OFFICES
◆ OLD BANK BUILDING
(H-3) 40, English St, Armagh BT617BA
Tel. (01861) 527 808
Open Mon.–Sat. 9am–6pm, Sun. 1–6pm

CULTURE

ARCHBISHOP'S PALACE STABLES HERITAGE CENTRE
(H-3) Armagh
Tel. (01861) 522 722
Open Apr.–Sept., Mon.–Sat. 10am–7pm, Sun. 1–7pm; Oct.–Mar, Mon.–Sat. 10am–5pm, Sun. 2–5pm
£1.60–2.65

ARDRESS HOUSE (E-3)
Annaghmore
Tel. (01762) 851 236
Open Jul.–Aug, Fri.–Wed. 2–6pm; Apr.–Jun. and Sept., weekends and public holidays 2–6pm
Four miles from Portadown, on the road to Moy.
£2.20

ARMAGH COUNTY MUSEUM (H-3)
The Mall East, Armagh
Tel. (01861) 523 070
Open Mon.–Fri. 10am–5pm, Sat. 10am–1pm and 2–5pm

ARMAGH PLANETARIUM (H-3)
College Hill, Armagh
Tel. (01861) 523 689
Open Apr.–Dec., Mon.–Fri. 11.30am–5pm, Sat.–Sun. 1.30–5pm;

Jan.–Mar, Mon.–Fri. 11.30am–5pm, Sat. 1.30–5pm
£2.50–3.50

LOUGH NEAGH DISCOVERY CENTRE
(H-3) Oxford Island, Lough Neagh
Tel. (01762) 322 205

NAVAN FORT & CENTRE (H-3)
Killkylea Rd, Armagh
Tel. (01861) 525 550
Open Apr.–Sept., Mon.–Sat. 10am–7pm, Sun. 11am–7pm; Oct.–Mar, Mon.–Sat. 10am–5pm, Sun. 11am–5pm
£2.10–3.75

PEATLANDS PARK (H-3)
Peatlands Park, Milltown
Tel. (01762) 341 199
Open 9am–6pm

MUSEUM OF THE ROYAL IRISH FUSILIERS (H-3)
Armagh
Tel. (01861) 522 911
Closed for repairs.

ST PATRICK'S PROTESTANT CATHEDRAL (H-3)
Abbey St, Armagh
Tel. (01861) 523 142
Open Apr.–Oct. 10am–5pm, Nov.–Mar 10am–4pm

ST PATRICK'S CATHOLIC CATHEDRAL
(H-3) Cathedral Rd, Armagh
Open 8.15am–8pm

ST PATRICK'S TRIAN
(H-3) Armagh
Tel. (01861) 527 808
Open Apr.–Sept., Mon.–Sat. 10am–7pm, Sun. 1–7pm; Oct.–Mar, Mon.–Sat. 10am–5pm, Sun. 2–5pm
Folk museum.
£1.50–3

PUBS/RESTAURANTS

HEARTY'S FOLK COTTAGE ★ (H-4)
Glass Drummond, Crossmaglen
Tel. (01693) 861 916

Open Sun. 2–7pm (*Sunday coffee*), or by reservation
☐ ☐•• ⌂ ♫ ⚘

WHEEL & LANTERN
(H-3) Market St, Armagh
Tel. (01861) 522 288
Open Mon.–Sat. 10am 5pm
Closed Wed. and Sun.
Situated in the Lennox store.

BELFAST (I-3) (CO. ANTRIM)

PRACTICAL INFORMATION

AIRPORT
Information
Tel. (08494) 22888

TOURIST OFFICES
◆ BELFAST CITY AIRPORT
Sydenham Bypass, Belfast
Tel. (01232) 457 745
Open 3.30am–10pm

◆ NORTHERN IRELAND RAILWAY
Central Station, East Bridge St, Belfast BT13PB
Tel. (01232) 899 411
Open 6.30am–11pm

◆ ST ANNE'S COURT
59, North St, Belfast
Tel. (01232) 246 609
Fax (01232) 312 424
Open Jul.–Aug, Mon.–Fri. 9am–6.30pm, Sat. 9am–5.15pm, Sun. noon–4pm; Sept.–Jun., Mon.–Sat. 9am–5.15pm

TRANSPORT
◆ CITY BUS
Main Water Rd, Belfast, Co. Antrim
Tel. (01232) 246 485

◆ ULSTERBUS
Great Victoria St, Belfast, Co. Antrim
Tel. (01232) 333 000

CULTURE

BELFAST CASTLE
Antrim Rd, Belfast
Tel. (01232) 776 925
Open Mon.–Sat. 9am–10.30pm, Sun. 9am–6pm

BELFAST ZOO
Antrim Rd, Belfast
Tel. (01232) 776 277
Open Apr.–Sept. 10am–5pm
£2.05–4.10

GRAND OPERA HOUSE
Great Victoria St, Belfast
Tel. (01232) 249 129
Open Mon.–Fri. 9.30am–5.30pm

CITY HALL
Donegall Square, Belfast
Tel. (01232) 320 202
Book in advance for guided tours.

BOTANIC GARDENS
Belfast
Tel. (01232) 324 902
Open Mon.–Fri. 10am–5pm, Sat. 1–5pm, Sun. 2–5pm

LINEN HALL LIBRARY
17, Donegall Square, Belfast
Tel. (01232) 321 707
Open Mon.–Sat. 9.30am–5.30pm, Sun. 9.30am–4pm

OLD MUSEUM
Tel. (01232) 235 053
Open Mon.–Sat. 10am–5.30pm

ROYAL ULSTER RIFLES MUSEUM
War Memorial Building, Swaring St, Belfast
Tel. (01232) 232 086
Currently closed to the public.

ST GEORGE'S CHURCH
High St, Belfast
Tel. (01232) 231 275
Open 9.30am–1pm

ST MALACHY'S CHURCH
Alfred St, Belfast
Tel. (01232) 321 713
Open 7.30am–5.30pm

ULSTER MUSEUM
Botanic Gardens, Stranmilis Rd, Belfast
Tel. (01232) 381 251
Open Mon.–Fri. 10am–5pm, Sat. 1–5pm, Sun. 2–5pm

PUBS/RESTAURANTS

BEWLEY'S ORIENTAL CAFÉ
Donegall Arcade, Belfast
Tel. (01232) 234 955
Open Mon.–Sat. 8am–5.30pm, Thur. 8am–8.30pm
☐

BITTLE'S BAR ★
70, Upper Church Lane, Belfast
Tel. (01232) 311 088
Closed Sun.
◐ ♫

THE CLARENCE
18, Donegall Square East, Belfast
Tel. (01232) 238 862
Open Mon.–Thur. noon–6pm, Fri. noon–8pm
£7–10
🍴 ○

THE CROWN LIQUOR SALOON ★
49, Great Victoria St, Belfast
Tel. (01232) 249 476
Pub food Mon.–Sat.
£6–7
🍴 ◑

DUKE OF YORK
3, Commercial Court, Belfast
Tel. (01232) 241 062
Open Mon.–Fri. noon–2pm, Sat. noon–5pm
♫

KITCHEN BAR
16, Victoria Square, Belfast
Tel. (01232) 324 901
Open for snacks:
11.30am–2.30pm
£4
🍴 ◑ 🄲 ♫

KELLY'S CELLARS
30, Bank St, Belfast
Tel. (01232) 324 835
Pub food 11.30am–4pm
£2–5
🍴 ◑ 🄲 ♫

LA BOHÈME ★
103, Great Victoria St, Belfast
Tel. (01232) 240 666
Closed Sun. and Christmas
£11–15
🍴 ○ 🄲

LARRYS PIANO BAR
21, Bedford St, Belfast,
Tel. (0232) 325 061
Open Tue.–Sat.
5pm–1am
Restaurant Fri.–Sat.
evening.
£16
🍴 ○ ♫

LAVERY'S GIN PALACE
12, Bradbury Pl., Belfast
Tel. (01232) 327 159

Three bars open until 1am, discotheque.
£1–2.50
◑ ♫

MADDENS
74, Berry St, Belfast
Tel. (01232) 244 114
◑

MORNING STAR
17, Pottinger's Entry, Belfast
Tel. (01232) 323 976
Open Mon.–Sat.
11.30am–9pm
🍴 ◑ ♫

NICK'S WAREHOUSE
35, Hill St, Belfast,
Tel. (01232) 439 690
Closed Sun.
Wine bar.
£3.50–4.80
🍴 ○ ◑ ♫

PAT'S BAR
19, Prince's Dock St, Belfast
Tel. (01232) 744 524
◑ ♫

ROBINSON'S
38, Great Victoria St, Belfast
Tel. (01232) 790 909
On three floors, discotheque (Thur., Sat.), restaurant, pub.
£3–10
🍴 ○ ◑

ROSCOFF
7, Lesley House, Shaftesbury Sq., Belfast
Tel. (01232) 331 532
Closed Christmas, Easter, and July 12
£14.50–21.50
🍴 ○ 🀄

ROTTERDAM BAR ★
54, Pilot St, Belfast
Tel. (01232) 746 021
◑ 🕾 🏠 ♫ 🅿

SAINTS & SCHOLARS ★
3, University St, Belfast
Tel. (01232) 325 137
£5–9
🍴 ○ ◑ ♫

STORMONT HOTEL ★
587, Upper Newtownards Rd, Belfast
Tel. (01232) 658 621
£15–18
🍴 ○ ◑

ACCOMMODATION

DUKES HOTEL
65, University St, Belfast BT71HL
Tel. (01232) 236 666

Activities: gym, sauna, waterskiing, windsurfing, golfing, horseriding, fishing.
£76.50–96
🏨 ○ ◑ 🄲 🀄

EUROPA HOTEL
Great Victoria St, Belfast BT27AP
Tel. (01232) 327 000
Fax (01232) 327 800
£94–130
🏨 ○ ◑ 🄲 🀄

OAKHILL COUNTRY HOUSE ★
59, Dunmurry Lane, Belfast BT179JR
Tel. (01232) 610 658
Closed for 15 days before Christmas
£140
🏨 🕾 🏠 🚶 🅿

PEARL COURT
11, Malone Rd, Belfast BT96RT
Tel. (01232) 666 145
Open 7am–11pm, Sun. 8am–11pm
£40 for 2 persons.
🛏 🄲 🏠

COUNTY DERRY

PRACTICAL INFORMATION

TOURIST OFFICES
◆ BENONE TOURIST COMPLEX (H-1)
53, Benone Ave., Seacoast Rd, Magilligan
Tel. (01504) 750 555
Open Jun.–Sept.
9am–10.30pm

◆ (G-2) 8, Bishop St, Derry
Tel. (01504) 267 284
Open Jul.–Sept., Mon.–Sat. 9am–6pm, Sun. 10am–6pm; Oct.–Jun., Mon.–Thur. 9am–5.15pm, Fri. 9am–5pm

◆ TOWN HALL (H-1)
The Crescent, Port Stewart
Tel. (01265) 832 286
Open Jun.–Sept., Mon.–Sat. 10.30am–4pm

CULTURE

AMELIA EARHEART COTTAGE (H-2)
Ballyarnett
Tel. (01504) 354 040
Open Mon.–Fri.
9am–4pm

BANAGHER OLD CHURCH (G-2)
Maghermore
Two miles to the southwest of Dungiven.

DUNGIVEN PRIORY & O'CAHAN TOMB (H-2)
Dungiven
To the east of Dunvigen (A5), pedestrian access.

THE GUILDHALL (G-2)
Derry
Tel. (01504) 365 151
Open 9am–5pm
Visits by appointment.
For information contact: City Marketing Dept.

HEZLETT HOUSE (G-2)
Derry
Tel. (01265) 848 567
Open Jul.–Aug, Fri.–Wed. 1–6pm; Apr.–Jun. and Sept., weekends and public holidays 1–5pm
70p–£1.40

MARTELLO TOWER (H-1) Magilligan Strand
At the end of the beach, in a military surveillance zone.

MUSSENDEN TEMPLE (H-1) Mussenden Rd, Castlerock
Tel. (01265) 848 728
Open Jul.–Aug noon–6pm; Apr.–Jun; Sept. Sat.–Sun. noon–6pm

ST COLUMBA'S CATHEDRAL (CHURCH OF IRELAND) (G-2) Derry
Tel. (01504) 262 746
Open Mon.–Sat. 9am–5pm

TOWER MUSEUM *(G-2)*
Union Hall Pl., Derry
Tel. (01504) 372 411

Open Jul.–Aug,
Mon.–Sat. 10am–5pm;
Sept.–Jun., Tue.–Sat.
10am–5pm
£1–2.50

PUBS/RESTAURANTS

**BROWN TROUT GOLF
& COUNTRY INN ★**
(H-2) 209, Agivey Rd,
Mullaghmore,
Aghdowey
Tel. (01265) 868 209
Open Jun.–Sept.
7am–9.30pm
£9–14
▭ O ◑

MACDUFF'S ★ (H-1)
112, Killeague Rd,
Blackhill, Coleraine
Tel. (01265) 868 433
Open Tue.–Sat.
7–9.30pm
£18–19
▭ O ◙

THE MARKET INN ★
(H-2) 27, St Patrick St,
Draperstown
Tel. (01648) 28250
Open Tue.–Fri.
noon–3pm
£3–4
◑ ◙ ♫

METRO BAR (G-2)
3, Bank Place, Derry
Tel. (01504) 267 401
Open noon–2.30pm
▭ ◑ ◙

MORELLI'S ★ (H-1)
57, The Promenade,
Portstewart
Tel. (01265) 832 150
Open May–Sept.
9am–11.30pm,
Oct.–Apr. noon–8pm
*Serves snacks, self
service.*
£5

SCHOONERS ★ (G-2)
59, Victoria Rd, Derry
Tel. (01504) 311 500
Open Mon.–Thur.
12.30–2.30pm and
5.30–9pm, Fri.–Sun.
5.30–10pm
£11–12
▭ O ◙

ACCOMMODATION

**BEECH HILL COUNTRY
HOUSE HOTEL ★** (G-2)
32, Ardmore Rd, Derry
BT473QP
Tel. (01504) 49279
Fax (01504) 45366
Closed Christmas
£52.50–100
▭ ⌂ ▥ O ▭⁚⁚ ⚐
▣

WATERFOOT HOTEL
(G-2) Caw Roundabout,
14, Clooney Rd, Derry
Tel. (01504) 45500
£47–62
▭ O ▥ ⌂ ▣

COUNTY DONEGAL

PRACTICAL INFORMATION

TOURIST OFFICES
◆ (F-2) Derry Rd,
Letterkenny

Tel. (074) 21160
Fax (074) 25180
Open Jun.–Aug, Mon.–
Sat. 9am–8pm, Sun.
10am–6pm; Sept.–May,
Mon.–Fri. 9am–5pm

◆ (G-1) Inishowen
Tel. (077) 74933

◆ (E-2) Main St,
Dungloe
Tel. (075) 21297
Open Jun.–Sept., Mon.–
Sat. 10am– 5.30pm,
Sun. 10am–1.30pm

◆ (F-2) Quay St,
Donegal
Tel. (073) 21148
Fax (073) 22763
Open Easter–Sept.,
Mon.–Sat. 9am–8pm,
Sun. 9am–6pm; Oct.–
Easter, Mon.–Sat.
9am–6pm

CULTURE

**COLMCILLE HERITAGE
CENTRE** (E-2)
Colmcillel
Tel. (074) 37044
Information: M. Egan.
50p–Ir£1

DOE CASTLE (F-1)
On the N56, just before
Creeslough
Tel. (074) 24613
*Contact: Donegal
County Museum.*

DONEGAL CASTLE
(F-2) Donegal
Tel. (073) 22405
Due to reopen 1995.

**DONEGAL COUNTY
MUSEUM** (F-2)
Letterkenny
Tel. (074) 24613

Open Tue.–Fri.
11am–12.30pm and
1–4.30pm, Sat. 1–4pm

**FOLK MUSEUM
CENTRE** (E-2)
Glencolumbkille
Tel. (073) 30017
Open Easter–Oct.,
10am–6pm
Guided tour.
75p–Ir£1.50

**THE GLEBE HOUSE
& GALLERY** (F-2)
Church Hill,
Co. Donegal
Tel. (074) 37071
Open for exhibitions
Closed Fri.
60p–Ir£1.50

GLENVEAGH CASTLE
(F-2) Church Hill
Tel. (074) 37090
Open Jun.–Sept.
10am–7.30pm;
Apr. 23–May, Oct–Nov.
6, 10am–6.30pm
Ir£1

**GLENVEAGH NATIONAL
PARK** (F-2)
Church Hill
Tel. (074) 37088
Open 10am–6.30pm
60p–Ir£1.50

**GRIANAN OF AILEACH
CHURCH** (G-1)
*For information contact
the local tourist office*
Tel. (077) 62600

**LETTERKENNY
CATHEDRAL** (F-2)
Letterkenny
Tel. (074) 21021

MILITARY MUSEUM
(G-1) Dunree Fort
Tel. (077) 61817
Open Jun.–Sept.,
Mon.–Fri. 10am–6pm,
Sat.–Sun. noon–6pm
75p–Ir£1.50

**VINTAGE CAR
MUSEUM**
(G-1) Buncranal
Tel. (077) 61130
Open Jun.–Sept., 10am–
8pm; Oct.–May, Sun.
and by appointment.
50p–Ir£1.50

PUBS/RESTAURANTS

**AN GRADAM FEASA
RESTAURANT** (E-2)
Foras Cultuir Uladh,
Glencolumbkille
Tel. (073) 30213
Closed Oct.–Jan.
Ir£3.50–7
▭ O

BRIDGE BAR (G-1)
Rathmeltonl
Tel. (074) 51119
Ir£3.50
▭ ◑ ♫

**CASTLE MURRAY
HOUSE ★** (E-2)
Dunkineely
Tel. (073) 37022
Closed Christmas and
Mon.–Thurs. in winter
Ir£15–20
▭ O

HUDIE BEAG'S (F-1)
Bunbeg, Gweedore
Tel. (075) 31016
♫

KEALY'S (G-1)
Greencastle,
Tel. (077) 81010
Ir£10–16
▭ O

LEO'S PUB (F-1)
Crolly
Tel. (075) 48143
♫

NANCY'S (E-2)
Ardaral
Tel. (075) 41187
◑

THE PIPER'S REST
(E-2) Main St,
Kilcarl
Tel. (075) 38205
◑ ♫

RATHMULLAN HOUSE
(G-1) Lough Swilly,
Rathmullan
Tel. (074) 58188
Open Apr.–Oct.
Ir£8–17
▭ O ▥ ▣

**ST JOHN'S
RESTAURANT**
(G-1) Fahan, Inishowen
Tel. (077) 60289
Open Tue.–Sat.
6–10pm. Closed
Christmas, Good Friday
Ir£20
▭ Q ⚐

ACCOMMODATION

**CAMPBELL'S (PIER
HOUSE) ★** (E-1)
Burtonport
Tel. (075) 42017
Ir£14–18
◙ ⌂ ⚏ ⚑ ▣

**CARA'S
TRADITIONAL
THATCHED HOSTEL**
(E-2) Kilca
Tel. (073) 38368
Ir£5
▣

CORNER HOUSE (E-2)
Cashel, Glencolumbkille
Tel. (073) 30021
Ir£13
⌂ 🏠 🄳 🄲 ⌂ 🅿

DERRYLAHAN HOSTEL
(E-2) Derrylahan, Kilcar
Tel. (073) 38079
Ir£5–7
🄳•• 🏕 🅿

FERNBANK (G-1)
Redcastle
Tel. (077) 830 322
Ir£15
🏠 🄳••

GREENHAVEN ★ (E-2)
Portnoo Rd, Ardara
Tel. (075) 41129
Ir£14.50–16
🄳 ⌂ 🄳•• ⌂ 🏕 ⛷
🅿

MACGRORY HOTEL
(G-1) Culdaff
Tel. (077) 79104
Ir£14
🄳 🄳 ⌂ 🎵 🅿

OSTÁN THORAÍ (F-1)
Tory Island
Tel. (074) 35920

THE PIER BAR (E-2)
Killybeg
Tel. (073) 31386
Ir£15
🏠 🄲 ⛷ ✄

RATHMULLAN HOUSE
(G-1) Lough Swilly,
Rathmullan
Tel. (074) 58188
Ir£35–55
🄳 🏛 🅿

SHANDON HOTEL ★
(F-1) Marble Hill Strand,
Portnablagh
Tel. (074) 36137
Ir£35–41
🄳 🄾 🏛 🅿

SHOPPING

**DONEGAL CRAFT
VILLAGE** (F-2)
Ballyshannon Rd,
Donegal
Tel. (073) 22015
Various craft shops.

**J. & A. KANE
CERAMIC'S** (F-1)
Moyra Rectory,
Main Rd, Falcarragh
Tel. (074) 35330
Open Jun.–Sept.,
China, jewelry.

**JOANNA O'KANE
CERAMICS** (G-2)
Cavancor Studios,
Ballindrait, Lifford

Tel. (074) 41143
*Open Mon.–Sat.
noon–6pm, Sun. 2–6pm
Porcelain museum on
the history of the house,
open Easter–Aug.*
Ir£1–2

**McNUTTS OF
DOWNINGS**
(F-2) Downings,
Letterkenny,
Co. Donegal
Tel. (074) 535400
Tweeds.

STUDIO DONEGAL (E-2)
Kilcarl
Tel. (073) 38194
Open 9am–6pm
*Handwoven
fabrics.*

THE TWEED FACTORY
(E-2) Kilcar
Tel. (073) 38002
Open 9am–6pm
*Typical Irish products,
tea shop and tourist
information.*

COUNTY DOWN

PRACTICAL
INFORMATION

VISITORS' CENTERS
◆ (H–3) GATEWAY
200, Newry Rd,
Banbridge BT323NB,
Tel. (018206) 23322
Fax (018206) 23114
Open Jun.–Sept.,
Mon.–Sat. 10am–8pm,
Sun. noon–6pm;
Oct.–May, Mon.–Sat.
10am–5pm,
Sun. noon–5pm

◆ (I-4) 74, Market St,
Downpatrick BT3 06LZ
Tel. (01396) 612 233
Fax (01396) 612 350
Open Jun.–Aug, Mon.–
Sat. 9.30am–5pm, Sun.
2–5pm; Sept.–May,
Mon.–Sat. 9.30am–5pm

◆ (I-3) 34, Quay St,
Bangor BT205ED
Tel. (01247) 270 069
Fax (01247) 274 466
Open Jul.–Aug
9am–5pm, Sat.

10am–1pm and 2–5pm,
Sun. 2–6pm; Sept.–
Jun., Mon.–Thur.
9am–1pm and 2–5pm,
Fri. 9am–1pm and
2–4.30pm

**PORTAFERRY
FERRY TERMINAL**
(I-3) Portaferry
Tel. (01396) 881 637
*Portaferry–Strangford
crossing, Mon.–Fri.,
leaves 7.30am–10.30pm,
returns 7.45am–
10.45pm, ferries every
30 mins.*
£3

CULTURE

**BRONTË HOMELAND
VISITORS CENTRE**
(I-4) Former
Drumballyroney Church
and School House,
Rathfriland
Tel. (018206) 31152
Open Mar.–Oct.,
Tue.–Fri. 11am–5pm,
Sat.–Sun. 2–6pm
50p–£1

CASTLE WARD (I-3)
Strangford, Downpatrick
Tel. (01396) 881 204
– Castle: open
May.–Aug, Fri.–Wed.
1–6pm; Easter 1–6pm;
Apr. and Sept.–Oct.,
Sat.–Sun. 1–6pm
£1.30–2.60
– Park open from
dawn until dusk
£3.60 (per vehicle)

**DOWNPATRICK'S
CATHEDRAL** (I-4)
Downpatrick
Tel. (01396) 614 922
Open Mon.–Fri.
10am–1pm and 2–5pm,
Sat.–Sun. 2–5pm

DUNDRUM CASTLE
(I-4) Dundrum
Open Apr.–Sept.,
Tue.–Sun. 10am–6pm;
Oct.–Mar by
appointment.
*Contact Historic
Monuments Branch
(Belfast)
Tel. (01232) 235 000*
40–75p

**EXPLORIS SEA
AQUARIUM** (I-3)
The Rope Walk,
Portaferry
Tel. (012477) 28062
Open Mon.–Fri.
10am–6pm, Sat.
11am–6pm, Sun.
1–6pm
£2–3

IRISH LINEN TOUR (H-3)
The Linen Homelands,
200, Newry Rd,
Banbridge
Tel. (018206) 23322
Open May–Sept.,
Wed.–Sat.
*One-day tour 9.30am to
4pm.*
£12

**MOUNT STEWARD
& TEMPLE OF THE
WINDS** (I-3)
Newtownards
Tel. (01277) 88387
– House: open
May–Sept., Wed.–Mon.
1–6pm; Apr. and Oct.,
weekends 1–6pm;
Easter 1–6pm
£1.65–3.30
– Gardens: open
Apr.–Sept. 10.30am–
6pm; Mar, Sun. 1–5pm;
Oct., weekends.
10.30am–6pm
£1.35–2.70

**NENDRUM MONASTIC
SITE & MUSEUM** (I-3)
Mahee Island,
Strangford Lough
– Site: entrance free
– Museum: open
Apr.–Sept., Tue.–Sat.
10am–1pm and 1.30–
7pm, Sun. 2–7pm
50p

ROWALLEN GARDENS
(I-3) Saintfield
Tel. (01238) 510 131
Open Apr.–Oct.,
Mon.–Fri. 10.30am–
6pm, Sat.–Sun, 2–6pm;
Nov.–Apr., Mon.–Fri.
10.30am–4.30pm
£1.75–2.50

**SCRABO COUNTRY
PARK** (I-3)
203a, Scrabo Rd,
Newtownards
Tel. (01247) 811 491
Open 11am–6.30pm
Closed Fri.

THE SILENT VALLEY
(I-4) Head Rd, 3 miles
to the north of Kilkeel
Open May–Sept. 10am–
6.30pm, Oct.–Apr.
10am–4pm
*Contact: Department of
Environment, Eastern
Supply, Sub Division
Westland House, Old
Westland Rd, Belfast
Tel. (01232) 746 181*

**ULSTER FOLK AND
TRANSPORT MUSEUM**
(I-3) Cultra, Holywood
Tel. (01232) 428 428
Open Jul.–Aug, Mon.–

Sat. 10.30am–6pm,
Sun. noon–6pm;
Apr.–Jun. and Sept.,
Mon.– Fri. 9.30am–
5pm, Sat. 10.30am–
6pm, Sun. noon–6pm;
Oct.–Mar, Mon.–Fri.
9.30am–4pm, Sat.–Sun.
12.30–4.30pm
£2.20–3.30

PUBS/RESTAURANTS

ADELBODEN LODGE ★
(I-3) 38, Donaghadee
Rd, Groomsport
Tel. (01247) 464 288
Open Mon.–Sat.
noon–midnight
£15–25
▭ ○ ◑ ⬛ ⌇

BURRENDALE HOTEL ★
(I-4) 51, Castlewellan
Rd, Newcastle
Tel. (013967) 22599
Open Mon.–Sat.
7–9pm, Sun. 5–8pm
£9–16
▭ ○ ◑ ⬛ ▣

**CASTLE ESPIE COFFEE
ROOM** ★ (I-3)
78, Ballydrain Rd,
Comber
Tel. (01247) 872 517
Open Mon.–Sat.
10.30am–5.30pm,
Sun. 11.30am–5pm
◑ ⬛ ⌇

**DEANE'S ON THE
SQUARE** ★ (I-3)
Station Sq., Helen's Bay
Tel. (01247) 852 841
Open Tue.–Sat.
7–9.30pm, Sun.
12.30–2.30pm
£16.50–19
▭ ○ ↦ ⌂

DUFFERIN ARMS ★
(I-3) 35, High St,
Killyleagh
Tel. (01396) 828 229
Restaurant Mon.–Wed.
5.30–9pm, Thur.–Sat.
5.30–9.30pm
£8–9
▭ ○ ◑ ♫

**DUNDONALD
OLD MILL** ★ (I-3)
231, Belfast Rd,
Dundonald
Tel. (01232) 480 117
Open Mon.–Sat.
10am–5.15pm,
Sun. 11am–5.15pm
£4
▭

THE GEORGE ★ (I-3)
10, Estate Rd,
Clandeboye, Bangor
Tel. (01247) 853 311

Open Mon.–Sat. noon–
3pm, Fri.–Sat. 7–9pm
£25
▭ ○

HILLSIDE ★ (I-3)
21, Main St,
Hillsborough
Tel. (01846) 682 765
Open 7–9.30pm
Closed Sun. except for
pub food
£21
▭ ○ ◑

**RED FOX COFFEE
SHOP** ★ (I-3)
6, Main St, Hillsborough
Tel. (01846) 682 586
Open Tue.–Sat.
10.15am–2pm and
3–5pm
Afternoon teas.

RITCHIE'S ★ (I-3)
3, Ballynahinch St,
Hillsborough
Tel. (01846) 683 601
Open 12.30–2.30pm
Closed Sun.
£2–4.50
▭ ○

WHITE GABLES HOTEL
★ (I-3) 14, Dromore Rd,
Hillsborough
Tel. (01846) 682 755
Restaurant Mon.–Fri.
12.30–2.30pm and
7–9pm, Sat. 7–9.30pm
£5–12
▭ ○

ACCOMMODATION

BAYVIEW (J-3)
Mrs. Patton,
187, Harbour Rd,
Ballyhalbert
BT221BP
Tel. (01247) 758 908
*Evening meals on
request.*
£12.50
⌂ ↦ ⌂ ⚕ ⌇ ▣

CHESTNUT INN (I-4)
Castlewellan
Tel. (013967) 78247
*Activities: disco,
horseriding. Golf
course, forest parks,
Dundrum bay beaches
nearby.*
£18–35 (for 2 persons)
⬛ ⌂ ♫

CULLODEN HOTEL ★
(I-3) Craigavad, Cultra
Tel. (01232) 425 223
Fax (01232) 426 777
Closed Christmas
*Activities: golfing,
horseriding, fishing.*
£106–172
▭ ⛪ ○ ♫ ⚕ ▣

**KILLYLEAGH CASTLE
TOWERS** (I-3)
Killyleagh BT309QA,
Tel. (01396) 828 261
*Apartments for rent:
– £100–350 per week,
– £50–200 per
weekend (3 days),
Sept.–Jun. only.*

**O'HARA'S ROYAL
HOTEL** (I-3)
26, Quay St, Bangor
Tel. (01247) 271 866
£12.50–20
Restaurant open
7–9.30pm, Sun. 5–9pm.
£12–12.50
▭ ○ ◑ ▣

PORTAFERRY HOTEL ★
(I 3) 10, The Strand,
Portaferry BT22 1PE
Tel. (012477) 28231
Fax (012477) 28999
Closed Christmas
*Award-winning
restaurant. Excellent
rooms. Golfing,
horseriding, hiking,
fishing.*
£45–80
▭ ⛪ ○ ↦ ⌂ ♫
⌇ ▣

COUNTY FERMANAGH

PRACTICAL INFORMATION

TOURIST OFFICE (F-3)
Wellington Rd,
Enniskillen
Tel. (01365) 323 110
Open Jul.–Aug,
Mon.–Fri. 9am–6.30pm,
Sat. 10am–6pm, Sun.
11am–5pm; Jun. and
Sept., Mon.–Fri.
9am–5.30pm, Sat.
10am–6pm, Sun.
11am–5pm; Oct.–May,
Mon.–Fri. 9am–5pm

CULTURE

CASTLE COOLE (F-3)
Enniskillen
Tel. (01365) 322 690
Open Jun.–Aug,
Fri.–Wed. 2–6pm;
Apr., May, Sept.,
weekends and public
holidays 2–6pm
£1.20–2.40

**FERMANAGH
HERITAGE CENTRE
& MUSEUM**
(F-3) Enniskillen
Tel. (01365) 325 000
Open Tue.–Fri.
10am–5pm, Sat.–Mon.
2–5pm
50p–£1

**FLORENCE COURT
HOUSE** (F-3)
Tel. (01365) 348 249
Open Jun.–Aug,
Wed.–Mon. 1–6pm;
Apr., May, Sept.,
weekends and public
holidays 1–6pm
£2.40

**FORTHILL PARK
& COLE
MONUMENT** (F-3)
Enniskillen
Tel. (01365) 325 050
Open May–Sept.,
Mon.–Fri. 11am–6pm,
Sat.–Sun. 2–6pm
50p

**MARBLE ARCH
CAVES**
(F-3) Marlbank Scenic
Loop Rd,
Florence Court
Tel. (01365) 348 855
Open 11am–5pm
£2–4

MONEA CASTLE (F-3)
Ten miles northwest of
Enniskillen

**NEW CROM CASTLE
& CROM ESTATE** (G-4)
Newtownbutler
Tel. (01365) 738 174
Open Apr.–Sept. 2–6pm
Parking £2.50

PUBS/RESTAURANTS

**BLAKE'S OF THE
HOLLOW** ★ (F-3)
6, Church St,
Enniskillen
Tel. (01365) 322 143
Closed Sun.
◑ ♫

**HOLLANDER
RESTAURANT** (F-3)
5, Main St,
Irvinestown
Tel. (01365) 621 231
£8–11
▭ ○ ◑ ⬛

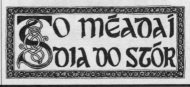

ACCOMMODATION

MANOR HOUSE COUNTRY HOTEL (F-3)
BT94 1HY Killadeas
Tel. (01365) 621 561
Fax (01365) 621 545
Five and a half miles to the north of Enniskillen. Activities: tennis, shooting, sailing, waterskiing, golfing, horseriding, fishing.
£50–75

TULLYHONA GUESTHOUSE (F-3)
G. Armstrong,
59, Marble Arch Rd,
Florence Court
Tel. (01365) 348 452
Seven miles southwest of Enniskillen.
£15–17

SHOPPING

BELLEEK POTTERY
(F-3) Belleek
Tel. (01365) 651 501
Open Mon.–Fri.
9am–6pm

COUNTY TYRONE

PRACTICAL INFORMATION

◆ (G-3) 1, Market St,
Omagh
Tel. (01662) 247 831
Fax (01662) 240 774
Open Easter–Sept.,
Mon.–Sat. 9am–1pm
and 2–5pm;
Oct.–Easter, Mon.–Fri.
9am–1pm and 2–5pm

◆ SION MILLS
TOURIST OFFICE (G-2)
151, Melmount Rd,
Sion Mills, Strabane
Tel. (016626) 58027
Open Jun.–Sept.,
Mon.–Thur.
9.30am–5pm

CULTURE

ARDBOE CROSS
(H-3)
On the east bank of Lough Neagh, on route B73.

THE ARGORY (H-3)
Derrycaw Rd, Moy,
Dungannon, Co. Tyrone
Tel. (018687) 84753
Open Jul.–Aug,
Wed.–Mon. 2–6pm;
Apr.–Jun. and Sept.,
weekends and public
holidays 2–6pm
£1.10–2.20
(£1 per car)

BENBURB CASTLE & CENTRE (H-3)
10, Main St, Benburb
Tel. (01861) 548 187

BENBURB VALLEY PARK HERITAGE CENTRE (H-3)
89, Milltown Rd,
Tullymore Etra, Benburb,
Dungannon
Tel. (01861) 549 752
Open Easter–Sept.,
Tue.–Sat. 10am–5pm,
Sun. 2–5pm
£1–2

GRAY'S PRINTING PRESS (G-2)
49, Main St,
Strabane
Tel. (01504) 884094
Open Apr.–Sept.
2–5.30pm Closed Thur.,
Sun. and public
holidays.
70p–£1.40

SPERRIN HERITAGE CENTRE (G-2)
274, Glenelly Rd,
Cranagh, Gortin
Tel. (016626) 48142
Open Easter–Sept.,
Mon.–Fri. 11am–6pm,
Sat. 11.30am–6pm
Sun. 2–7pm
On the B47, 9 miles to the east of Plumbridge.
80p–£1.80

THE ULSTER HISTORY PARK (G-3)
Cullion, Omagh
Tel. (016626) 48188
Open Apr.–Sept.,
Mon.–Sat. 10.30am–
6.30pm, Sun. 11.30am–
7pm, public holidays.
10.30am–7pm;
Oct.–Mar, Mon.–Fri.
9am–5pm
£1.50–2.50

THE ULSTER AMERICAN FOLK PARK (G-3)
Camphill, Omagh
Tel. (01662) 243 292
Open Easter–Sept. 15,
Mon.–Sat.
11am–6.30pm,
Sun. and public holidays
11.30am–7pm;
Sept. 15–Easter,
Mon.–Fri. 10.30am–5pm
£1.50–3

WELLBROOK BEETLING MILL (H-3)
Cookstown
Tel. (016487) 51735
Open Wed.–Mon.
2–6pm
Guided tour on request
70p–£1.40

PUBS/RESTAURANTS

GREENMOUNT LODGE
(G-3) Mrs. Reed,
58, Greenmount Rd,
Gortaclare, Omagh
Tel. (01662) 841 325
Open Fri.–Sat. 7–9pm
Reservation essential.
£12.50–17.50

MELLON COUNTRY INN ★ (G-3)
134, Beltany Rd,
Omagh
Tel. (016626) 61224
£6–17.50

ROSAMUND'S COFFEE SHOP (G-3)
Station House,
Augher
Tel. (016625) 48601
Open Mon.–Sat.
9am–5pm
£2–3.15

ROYAL ARMS HOTEL ★ (G-3)
51, High St,
Omagh
Tel. (01662) 243 262
Local whiskey.
Restaurant £10–12

ACCOMMODATION

GRANGE LODGE COUNTRY HOUSE ★
(H-3) N. Brown,
7, Grange Rd,
Dungannon BT71 1EJ
Tel. (018687) 84212
or (018687) 22458
Fax (018687) 23891
One mile from the M1 (junction 15). Activities: golfing, fishing. Dinner available to guests by prior arrangement.
£35–55

APPENDICES

Abbreviations:

BF: Bord Fáilte (Tourist office), Dublin
BN: Bibliothèque nationale, Paris
NGI: National Gallery of Ireland, Dublin
NITO: Northern Ireland Tourist Office, Belfast
NLI: National Library of Ireland, Dublin
NMI: National Museum of Ireland, Dublin
OPW: Office of Public Works, Dublin
UM: Ulster Museum, Belfast

When the city is not mentioned, it is Paris or the surrounding area.

Illustrators:

Yvon Le Corre: 11, 15, 87, 133, 161, 178, 179, 181, 186, 193, 197, 198, 199, 202, 204, 216-217, 220, 221, 223, 224, 225, 227, 228–9, 230, 236, 237, 238, 239, 242-243, 251, 252–3, 260–1, 264–5, 268, 271, 272–3, 274–5, 276–7, 280–1, 283, 288–9, 294–5, 296–7, 298–9, 307, 312, 314–5, 319, 320–1, 327, 331

Cover:
Anne Bodin
Jean-Marie Guillou
Jean Chevallier

Spine:
Jean-Marie Guillou

Back cover:
Maurice Pommier
Jean-Marie Guillou

10 Jean Chevallier, François Desbordes, Catherine Totems, 11 Yvon Le Corre,

◆ LIST OF ILLUSTRATIONS

Maurice Pommier
14, 15 Alban Larousse

Nature:
18–19 Gilbert Houbre,
Jean Chevallier
20–1 Jean Chevallier,
François Desbordes
22–3 François
Desbordes,
Jean Chevallier,
Claire Felloni
24–5 Gilbert Houbre,
François Desbordes,
Pascal Robin
26–7 Jean Chevallier
28–9 François
Desbordes,
Frédérique Schwebel,
Gilbert Houbre,
Jean Chevallier,
Frédéric Bony
30–1 François
Desbordes,
Claire Felloni,
Jean Chevallier,
Dominique Mansion
32–3 Anne Bodin,
Claire Felloni
34–5 Claire Felloni,
Dominique Mansion,
Bernard Duhem,
Jean Chevallier,
François Desbordes
36–7 François Place
38–9 Jean Chevallier,
Gismonde Curiace,
Frédéric Bony
40–1 François
Desbordes,
Jean Chevallier,
Claire Felloni,
Dominique Mansion
42–3 François
Desbordes
44–5 François Place,
Pascal Robin
46 Denis Clavreul,
Jean Chevallier,
Anne Bodin

Arts and traditions:
74 Jean-Marie Guillou
83 Anne Bodin

Architecture:
Jean-Marie Guillou
Roger Hutchins
Maurice Pommier
Claude Quiec
Catherine Totems
Tony Townsend

Itineraries:
174 illustration Gallimard
201, 232 Jean Chevallier
233 Jean Chevallier,
François Desbordes
317 Maurice Pommier
324 Alban Larousse
327 Pascal Robin
Rest Maurice Pommier
except: 331 Yvon Le
Corre

Maps:
Vincent Brunot
Eric Gillion
Claire Cormier
Jean-Marc Lanusse
Alban Larousse
Catherine Totems

Computer graphics:
Paul Coulbois
Patrick Alexandre
Kristof Chemineau
Martine Frouin-
Marmouguet
Patrick Merienne

**We should like to
thank the following
people for their
help:**
Bord Fáilte
Patricia Desseine
Dublin Corporation
Lucian Freud
Irene Halpin, de la
Crawford Municipal
Art Gallery
Valérie Hardy
Pierre Joannon
Kenny's Bookshop
Liebig
Simon Lincoln, of the
Irish Architectural
Archives
Bernard Marck
Melanie McDonagh
Marie McFeely, of the
National Gallery of
Ireland
John and Rhona McKay
Peter Murray, of the
Crawford Municipal
Art Gallery
National Monuments
(Northern Ireland), for
the architectural
reconstructions on
pages 92–3 and 96–7
Northern Ireland Tourist
Office
Patricia O'Gorman
RCA
Bill Rolston
John Clement Ryan, of
Irish Distillers Ltd.
Eileen Tweedy
Lize Martine Van
Gelderen
Anne Yeats

We have tried
unsuccessfully to trace
the heirs or publishers of
certain documents. An
account has been
opened for them at our
publishing house.

ACKNOWLEDGEMENTS
Grateful acknowledgment
is made to the following
for permission to reprint
previously published
material:

◆ DEVIN-ADAIR,
PUBLISHERS, INC.:
Excerpt from *Tarry Flynn*
by Patrick Kavanagh
(The Pilot Press Ltd.,
London, 1948), copyright
by Devin-Adair,
Publishers, Inc. All rights
reserved. Reprinted by
permission of Devin-
Adair, Publishers, Inc.,
Old Greenwich, CT
06870.

◆ FABER AND FABER, INC.
AND FABER AND FABER
LIMITED: Excerpt from
*Over Nine Waves: A
Book of Irish Legends* by
Marie Heaney, copyright
© 1994 by Marie Heaney.
Rights in Canada
administered by Faber
and Faber Limited,
London. Reprinted by
permission.

◆ FARRAR, STRAUS &
GIROUX, INC.: Excerpts
from *The Connor Girls*
and *My Mother's Mother*
from *A Fanatic Heart* by
Edna O'Brien, copyright
© 1984 by Edna O'Brien.
Reprinted by permission.
(In the UK by permission
of Weidenfeld and
Nicolson).

◆ FARRAR, STRAUS &
GIROUX, INC AND FABER
AND FABER LIMITED:
Excerpt from "The Strand
at Lough Beg" from
*Selected Poems 1966-
1987* by Seamus Heaney,
copyright © 1976, 1979,
1990 by Seamus Heaney.
Rights in Canada from
Field Work administered
by Faber and Faber
Limited, London.
Reprinted by permission.

◆ THE GALLERY PRESS:
Excerpt from *Aristocrats*
by Brian Friel (1980).
Reprinted by permission
of The Gallery Press,
County Meath, Ireland,
and the author.

◆ HARCOURT BRACE &
COMPANY AND THE HOGARTH
PRESS: Excerpt from *The
Diary of Virginia Woolf,
Vol IV: 1931-1935*, edited
by Anne Olivier Bell,
copyright © 1982 by
Quentin Bell and
Angelica Garnett. Rights
in Canada administered
on behalf of the estate by
The Hogarth Press,
London. Reprinted by
permission of Harcourt
Brace & Company and
The Hogarth Press.

◆ NORTHWESTERN
UNIVERSITY PRESS AND LEILA
VENNEWITZ: Excerpt from
Irish Journal by Heinrich
Böll, translated by Leila
Vennewitz, copyright
© 1967 by Leila
Vennewitz. Reprinted by
permission of
Northwestern University
Press and Leila
Vennewitz.

◆ RANDOM HOUSE, INC.
and THE ESTATE OF JAMES
JOYCE: Excerpt from
Ulysses by James Joyce,
copyright © 1934,
copyright renewed 1962
by Lucia and George
Joyce. Rights in Canada
administered by The
Estate of James Joyce,
Sean Sweeney, Trustee.
Reprinted by permission
of Random House, Inc.
and The Estate of James
Joyce, Sean Sweeney,
Trustee.

◆ THE SAMUEL BECKETT
ESTATE and THE CALDER
EDUCATIONAL TRUST,
LONDON: Excerpt from
First Love by Samuel
Beckett, translated by
Samuel Beckett, Calder &
Boyars Limited, London.
Copyright © Samuel
Beckett 1970.
Reproduced in the UK by
permission.

◆ SIMON & SCHUSTER, INC.:
"The Lake Isle of
Innisfree" from *The
Poems of W.B. Yeats: A
New Edition*, edited by
Richard J. Finneran (New
York: Macmillan, 1983).
Reprinted by permission.

◆ THE SOCIETY OF
AUTHORS: Excerpt from
Sixteen Self Sketches by
Bernard Shaw (Constable
& Company Limited,
London 1949). Reprinted
by permission of The
Society of Authors on
behalf of The Bernard
Shaw Estate.

◆ VIKING PENGUIN: Excerpt
from "Gold Watch",
copyright © 1980 by
John McGahern (first
appeared in *The New
Yorker*), from *High
Ground* by John
McGahern. Reprinted by
permission of Viking
Penguin, a division of
Penguin Books USA, Inc.

◆ WALKER AND COMPANY:
Excerpt from *At Swim-
Two Birds* by Flann
O'Brien, copyright
© 1951, 1966 by Brian
Nolan. Reprinted by
permission of Walker and
Company, 435 Hudson
St., New York, NY 10014,
1-800-289-2553. All
rights reserved.

Words in brackets give the anglicized version of the Irish term.

◆ GENERAL ◆

◆ ABHAINN (AVON, OWEN): river
◆ ÁRD (ARD): place name meaning high
◆ ÁTH (ATH): ford crossing
◆ BAILE (BAL, BALLY): town
◆ (BAILEY): castle courtyard
◆ BALLA: wall
◆ BÁDHÚN: castle enclosure
◆ BÁN: white
◆ BEAG: small
◆ BÉAL (BAL, BEL): estuary
◆ BEAN, pl. MNÁ: woman,
◆ BEANN (BEN): mountain peak
◆ BÓITHRÍN (BORREEN): path
◆ BUN: end of a road, mouth of a river
◆ CAIRN: stone tumulus
◆ CAISEAL, CAISLEÁN (CASHEL): castle
◆ CARRAIG, CORRIG (CARRICK): rock
◆ CATH: battle
◆ CATHAIR (CAHER): fortified enclosure
◆ CEANN (KEN, KIN, CAN): cap
◆ CEILP (KELP): burned kelp used as fertilizer
◆ CILL (KILL): church
◆ CIST: stone tomb
◆ CLOCHÁN, pl. CLOCHÁIN: dry-stone beehive hut
◆ CLOCHAR (CLOGHER): convent
◆ CLOCH (CLOGH): rock
◆ CLUAIN (CLON): meadow
◆ CNOC (KNOCK): hill, used in the names of approximately two thousand towns and villages
◆ CRANNÓG: artificial island on a lake with a good defense position
◆ CÚL: back, support
◆ CURRACH: primitive boat made from animal skin stretched over a wood frame
◆ DAIR, DOIRE (DERRY, DARE): oak, oak grove
◆ DEARG: red
◆ DOMHNACH:(DONAGH): large church
◆ DROIM: mountain peak
◆ DROIMNEACH : drumlin
◆ DÚN: fortress
◆ EANACH: marsh
◆ EAS (AS, ESS): waterfall
◆ ÉIRINN (ERIN): poetic synonym for Ireland
◆ EISCIR: esker
◆ FEAR, pl. FIR: man
◆ FEART (FERT): tomb or burial mound
◆ FERNAGH (FERNEY, FERNANE): alder woods

◆ GALLÁN: raised stone
◆ GAELTACHT: Irish-speaking areas
◆ GLEANN: glen, valley
◆ GORT: field
◆ GRIANÁN: palace, summerhouse
◆ INIS, ENNIS: island
◆ INSE: bogland
◆ LIOS (LISS, LIS): clay fort
◆ LOUGH: loch
◆ MÁ, MÁIGH: plain
◆ MAINISTIR: monastery
◆ MÓIN: mound
◆ MÓR: large
◆ MULLACH: rounded promontory
◆ POTEEN or POITÍN: illegal alcoholic drink distilled from potatoes
◆ RÁTH: circular fort
◆ RINN, (REEN): peak
◆ ROS: promontory or wood
◆ SCEILG (SCELLIG, SKELLIG): rock, peak
◆ SEAN: old
◆ SHEELA-NA-GIG: female figure with exaggerated features seen on sculptures all over Ireland
◆ SLIABH (SLIEVE): mountain
◆ SRÁID, (STRAD): road
◆ TEACH, pl. TITHE: house
◆ TEAMPULL: church
◆ TÍR: country
◆ TOBAR (TUBBER): source, well
◆ TOCHAR (TOGHER): artificial track over bogland
◆ TRÁIGH, TRÁ: strand or shore
◆ TULACH (TULL, TULLY): small hill
◆ TURLACH: temporary lakes
◆ UACHTAR (OUGHTER): upper

◆ DAILY LIFE ◆

◆ AMÁRACH: tomorrow
◆ AN BANC/SIOPA: bank
◆ AR OSCAILT: open
◆ BAILE: town
◆ BODHRÁN: drum
◆ BORD FÁILTE: tourist office
◆ BRÚ ÓIGE: youth hostel
◆ CEOL AGUS ÓL: music and drink
◆ CONAS TÁ TÚ: how are you? (Response: TÁ MÉ GO MAITH: I'm well)
◆ DIA DHUIT: hello
◆ DIA SIS MHUIRE DHUIT: hello (response to Dia dhuit)
◆ DÚNTA: closed
◆ FÁILTE: welcome
◆ FÓGRA: notice
◆ GÉILL SLÍ: do not enter
◆ GO RAIBH MAITH AGAT : thank you
◆ INNIU: today

◆ LEITHREAS: toilets
◆ NÍL/NÍ HEA: no
◆ NÁ CAITEAR TOBAC: no smoking
◆ OÍCHE MHAITH: good night
◆ OIFIG AN PHOIST: post office
◆ SLÁN: goodbye
◆ TÁ/SEA: yes

DAYS OF
◆ THE WEEK ◆

◆ DÉ LUAIN: Monday
◆ DÉ MÁIRT: Tuesday
◆ DÉ CÉADAOIN: Wednesday
◆ DÉARDAOIN: Thursday
◆ DÉ HAOINE: Friday
◆ DÉ SATHAIRN: Saturday
◆ DÉ DOMHNAIGH: Sunday

◆ CULTURE ◆

◆ COMHALTAS CEOLTÓIRÍ ÉIREANN: cultural institute founded to promote traditional music and dance
◆ CONRADH NA GAEILGE: Gaelic league for the promotion of the Irish language
◆ FLEADH CEOIL: music festival
◆ NAOMH: saint
◆ OGHAM: primitive writing using a series of hatch marks.
◆ SEANCHAÍ: storyteller
◆ SHEBEEN: illegal drinking den
◆ SHELTA: dialect spoken by the tinkers, or "travellers"
◆ SIAMSA TÍRE: folk theater of Ireland
◆ STABHT: stout (drink)
◆ YOLA: ancient dialect formerly spoken in Forth and Bargy, Co. Wexford

◆ SPORT ◆

◆ G.A.A.: Gaelic Athletic Association founded in 1884 for the promotion of Irish sport (hurling and Gaelic football)
◆ IOMÁNAÍOCHT: hurling
◆ PEIL: Gaelic football

◆ POLITICS ◆

◆ ÁRAS AN UACHTARÁIN: residence of president, Phoenix Park, Dublin
◆ DÁIL ÉIREANN: deputy chamber
◆ FIANNA FÁIL: main political party in the Republic of Ireland, splinter group of moderates from Sinn Féin, opposed to the

1921 treaty with England
◆ FINE GAEL: the other party which is a splinter group from Sinn Féin, in favor of the 1921 treaty
◆ GARDAÍ SÍOCHÁNA: police (Irish Republic, lit. guardians of the peace)
◆ SEANAD ÉIREANN: high chamber of Irish legislation
◆ SINN FÉIN: "ourselves alone", political branch of the Irish Republican Army
◆ TAOISEACH: prime minister
◆ TEACHTA DÁLA: member of the Irish party

MYTHS AND
◆ LEGENDS ◆

◆ ARD RÍ: supreme sovereign of the Irish Gaelic people
◆ BEAN SÍ (BANSHEE): lit. woman fairy, a spirit whose wail announces a death in the family
◆ BRUGH NA BÓINNE: burial site of the legendary kings of Ireland in the valley of the Boyne
◆ CÚ CHULAINN: legendary hound, hero of the Ulster myth cycle.
◆ DIARMAIT AND GRÁINNE: one of Ireland's best known love stories. It tells of the legendary flight across Ireland of two lovers: Gráinne, daughter of Cormac MacAirt, King of Tara, and her lover Diarmait, and their pursuit by Finn.
◆ OISÍN (OSSIAN): bardic warrior of the Fenian cycle
◆ TARA: ancient capital of the Ard Rí, the country's most important political and liturgical center
◆ TÍR NA-NÓG: "land of eternal youth", beyond the Gaéls
◆ TUATHA DÉ DANANN: literally "people of the goddess Anu or Danu", divine mother of the gods and goddess of fertility. Said to have landed in Greece around 1900 BC, the Tuatha are supposed to be the fourth of six legendary races to have invaded Ireland.

BIBLIOGRAPHY
AND INDEX

ESSENTIAL
◆ READING ◆

◆ BANVILLE (J.) Ghosts, Secker and Warburg, London, 1993
◆ CROOKSHANK (A.) and THE KNIGHT OF GLIN: Watercolours of Ireland, Barrie & Jenkins, London, 1994
◆ HERITY (M.) and EOGAN (G.): Ireland in Prehistory, Routledge & Kegan Paul, Boston, 1976
◆ JOYCE (J.): Dubliners, Alfred A. Knopf, New York, 1991
◆ KEANE (M.) Good Behaviour, Sphere Books, London, 1982
◆ SOMERVILLE and ROSS: Experiences of an Irish R.M., Everyman's Library, London
◆ TREVOR (W.): The Stories of William Trevor, Penguin, Harmondsworth, 1983
◆ TREVOR (W.): A Writer's Ireland – Landscape in Literature, Thames & Hudson, London, 1984
◆ YEATS (W.B.): The Poems, Everyman's Library, London, 1992

GENERAL
◆ INTEREST ◆

◆ BÖLL (H.) TRANS. VENNEWITZ (L.): Irish Journal, McGraw-Hill Book Co., New York, 1967
◆ DONLEAVY (J.P.): A Singular Country, Ryan, Peterborough, 1989
◆ DONLEAVY (J.P.): J.P. Donleavy's Ireland in All her Sins and Some of her Graces, Michael Joseph, Rainbird, London, 1986
◆ FITZGIBBON (C.): The Irish in Ireland, David & Charles, London, 1983
◆ HILL (I.): Northern Ireland, Blackstaff Press, Belfast, 1986
◆ GOFF (A.): Walled Gardens, Scenes from an Anglo-Irish Childhood, Eland, London, 1994
◆ LORD KILLANIN and DUIGNAN (M.V.): The Shell Guide to Ireland, Ebury Press, London, 1962
◆ LAVELLE (D.): Skellig – Island Outpost of Europe, The O'Brien Press, Dublin, 1976
◆ LEHAN (B.): Dublin, Time Life, Amsterdam, 1978
◆ McCABE (B.) and LE GARSMEUR (A.): W.B. Yeats – Images of Ireland, Little, Brown & Co., Boston; Toronto; London, 1991
◆ McCABE (B.) and LE GARSMEUR (A.): James Joyce – Reflections of Ireland, Little, Brown & Co., Boston; Toronto; London, 1993
◆ McCARTHY (J.): Joyce's Dublin, A Walking Guide to

Ulysses, Wolfhound Press, Dublin, 1986
◆ MANNING (O.): The Dreaming Stone, Evans Brothers, London, 1950
◆ MARTINEAU (H.): Letters from Ireland, John Chapman, London, 1852
◆ NEWBY (E.): Round Ireland in Low Gear, Collins, London, 1987
◆ O'BRIEN (E.): The Beckett Country: Beckett's Ireland, Black Cat Press, Monkstown, Co. Dublin in assoc. with Faber and Faber, London, 1986
◆ O'FAOLAIN (S.): An Irish Journey, Longmans Green & Co., London, 1949
◆ ROLT (L.T.C.): Green and Silver, George Allen & Unwin, London, 1949
◆ SOMERVILLE (E.) and ROSS (M.): Through Connemara in a Governess Cart, W.H. Allen & Co., London, 1893
◆ YOUNG (A.): A Tour in Ireland, Irish University Press, Dublin, 1970

◆ NATURE ◆

◆ The Book of the Burren, Tir Eolas, Newtownlynch, 1992
◆ D'ARCY (G.): Birds of Ireland, Appletree Press, Belfast, 1986
◆ FEEHAN (J.): The Landscape of Slieve Bloom, Blackwater Press, 1979
◆ MITCHELL (G.F.): The Shell Guide to Reading the Irish Landscape, Country House, Dublin, 1986
◆ WALSH (W.): An Irish Florilegium II – Wild and Garden Plants of Ireland, Thames & Hudson, London, 1988
◆ WEBB (D.A.): An Irish Flora, Dundalgan Press, Dundalk, 1943
◆ WHITTOW (J.B.): Geology and Scenery in Ireland, Penguin, Harmondsworth, 1974

HISTORY AND
◆ LANGUAGE ◆

◆ BARDON (J.): A History of Ulster, Blackstaff Press, Belfast, 1992
◆ DE BREFFNY (B.) ED.: The Irish World – The History and Cultural Achievements of the Irish People, Thames & Hudson, London, 1986
◆ BRENNAN (P.): The Conflict in Northern Ireland, Longman, France, Paris, 1991
◆ BROWN (T.): Ireland. A Social and Cultural History, Fontana, Glasgow, 1981
◆ COFFEY (T.M.): Agony at Easter, Macmillan, New York, 1969
◆ CURTIS (E.): History of Medieval Ireland from 1086 to 1513, Methuen, London, 1938

◆ EDGEWORTH (M.), ED. BUTLER (H.): Tour in Connemara in 1833, Constable, London, 1950
◆ FLOWER (R.): The Irish Tradition, Clarendon Press, Oxford, 1947
◆ FOSTER (R.F.): Modern Ireland 1600–1972, Penguin, London, 1988
◆ FOSTER (R.F.) ED.: The Oxford Illustrated History of Modern Ireland, Oxford University Press, London, 1989
◆ HUSSEY (G.): Ireland today, Penguin Books, 1995
◆ LECKY (W.E.H.): A History of Ireland in the Eighteenth Century, Longmans Green & Co, London, 1912
◆ LEE (J.J.): Ireland 1912–1985. Politics and Society, Cambridge University Press, Cambridge, 1989
◆ LYONS (F.S.L.): Ireland since the Famine, Collins-Fontana, Glasgow, 1973
◆ MOODY (T.W.), MARTIN (F.X.) and BYRNE (F.J.): A New History of Ireland, 10 vols., Oxford University Press, London, 1976
◆ MOODY (T.W.), MARTIN (F.X.) and BYRNE (F.J.): The Oxford Illustrated History of Ireland, Oxford University Press, Oxford, 1989
◆ PAKENHAM (T.): The Year of Liberty, Hodder & Stoughton, London, 1969
◆ DE PAOR (L.): Divided Ulster, Penguin, Harmondsworth, 1970
◆ SHAW (G.B.S.): The Matter with Ireland, Rupert Hart-Davis, London, 1962
◆ SPENSER (E.) ED. RENWICK (W.L.): A View of the Present State of Ireland, Eric Partridge, Scholastic Press, 1934
◆ THOMSON (D.): The Great Hunger, Hamish Hamilton, London, 1962

ART AND
◆ HERITAGE◆

◆ Ancient Monuments of Northern Ireland, 2 vols., Her Majesty's Stationery Office, Belfast, 1975
◆ BRENNAN (M .): The Stars and the Stones – Ancient Art and Astronomy in Ireland, Thames & Hudson, London, 1983
◆ DELARGY (J.H.): The Gaelic Storyteller, Cumberlege, London, 1945
◆ EOGEN (G.): Knowth and the Passage-tombs of Ireland, Thames & Hudson, London,1990
◆ EVANS (E.E.): The Personality of Ireland, Cambridge University Press, Cambridge, 1973
◆ FITZGIBBON (T.): A Taste of Ireland in food and pictures, Pan Books, London,1970
◆ GRAVES (R.): The White Goddess, Faber and Faber, London,1948

◆ HEANEY (M.): Over Nine Waves, Faber and Faber, London, 1994
◆ LAING (L.): Celtic Britain and Ireland AD 200–800, Irish Academic Press, Dublin, 1990
◆ O'DANACHAIR (C.): Folktales of the Irish Countryside, Mercier Press, Dublin and Cork, 1976
◆ O'KELLY (M.J.): Newgrange – Archeology, Art & Legend, Thames & Hudson, London,1988
◆ O'RIORDAIN (P.): Antiquities of the Irish Countryside, Methuen, London,1955
◆ O'RIORDAIN (P.) and DANIEL (G.): New Grange, Thames & Hudson, London,1964
◆ O'NEILL (T.): Life and Tradition in Rural Ireland, Dent, London,1977
◆ SÚILLEABHÁIN (S.): A Handbook of Irish Folklore, Education Company, Dublin, 1942; Singing Tree Press, Detroit, 1970
◆ SÚILLEABHÁIN (S.): Irish Wake Amusements, The Mercier Press, Cork, 1967
◆ SHAW-SMITH (D .): Ireland's Traditional Crafts, Thames & Hudson, London, 1986
◆ WILDE (LADY J.): Ancient Legends, Mystic Charms and Superstitions of Ireland, London, 1888

ART AND
◆ ARCHITECTURE ◆

◆ ARNOLD (B.): Irish Art; A Concise History, Thames & Hudson, London, 1977
◆ ARNOLD (W.) and MORRISON (R.): The Historic Hotels of Ireland, Thames & Hudson, London, 1988
◆ DE BREFFNY (B.) and MOTT (G.): Castles of Ireland, Thames & Hudson, London, 1992
◆ DIXON (H.): An Introduction to Ulster Architecture, Ulster Architectural Heritage Society, 1975
◆ FINLAY (I.): Celtic Art: An Introduction, Faber and Faber, London, 1973
◆ GUINNESS (D.): Georgian Dublin, Batsford, London, 1979
◆ GUINNESS (D.) and O'BRIEN (J.): Great Irish Houses and Castles, Weidenfeld and Nicolson, 1992
◆ GUINNESS (D.) and RYAN (W): Irish Homes and Castles, Thames & Hudson, London, 1971
◆ HARBISON (P.): Irish Art & Architecture – From Prehistory to the Present, Thames & Hudson, London, 1993
◆ HENRY (F.): Early Christian Irish Art, Three Candles, Dublin, 1963
◆ HENRY (F.) ED.: The Book of Kells, Thames & Hudson, London, 1988

◆ Leask (H.-G.): *Irish Castles*, Dudalgan Press, Dundalk, 1986
◆ Leask (H.-G.): *Irish Churches and Monastic Buildings*, Dudalgan Press, Dundalk, 1987
◆ McLaren (D .) and Marsden (S.): *In Ruins – The Once Great Houses of Ireland*, Collins, London, 1980
◆ Megaw (R.) and Megaw (V.): *Celtic Art – From its Beginnings to the Book of Kells*, Thames & Hudson, London, 1991
◆ Morrison (R.) and Fitz-Simon (C.): *The Irish Village*, Thames & Hudson, London, 1986
◆ Rothery (S.): *Everyday Buildings of Ireland*, College of Technology, Bolton Street, Dublin, 1975
◆ Rowan (A.): *North West Ulster – The Buildings of Ireland*, Penguin, Harmondsworth, 1979
◆ Stalley (R.A.): *Architecture and Sculpture in Ireland 1150–1350*, Gill and Macmillan, Dublin, 1971
◆ White (J.): *The National Gallery of Ireland*, Thames & Hudson, London, 1968

◆ Painting ◆

◆ Bodkin (T.): *Four Irish Landscape Painters*, The Talbot Press, Dublin, 1920
◆ Butler (P.): *Irish Watercolours and Drawings*, Weidenfeld & Nicolson, London, 1990
◆ Pyle (H.): *J.B. Yeats in the National Gallery of Ireland*, The National Gallery of Ireland, Dublin, 1986
◆ Yeats (J.B.): *Life in the West of Ireland*, Maunsel & Co., Dublin, 1912

◆ Literature ◆

◆ Beckett (S.): *All that Fall*, Faber and Faber, London, 1957
◆ Beckett (S.): *First Love*, Calder & Boyars, London and New York, 1973
◆ Beckett (S.): *More Pricks than Kicks*, Calder & Boyars, London, 1970
◆ Behan (B.): *Borstal Boy*, Hutchinson, London, 1958
◆ Behan (B.): *The Hostage*, Methuen, London, 1958; Grove Press, New York, 1959
◆ Behan (B.): *Richard's Cork Leg*, Eyre Methuen, London, 1973
◆ Bell (A.O.) ed. and McNeille (A.) assist.: *The Diary of Virginia Woolf Volume Four 1931–1935*, Harcourt Brace Janovich, New York and London, 1982
◆ Böll (H.) trans. Venneuitz (L.): *Irish Journal*, Secker &

Warburg, McGraw-Hill Book Co., New York, 1967
◆ Bowen (E.): *A Day in the Dark*, Jonathan Cape, London, 1965
◆ Bowen (E.): *Seven Winters. Memories of a Dublin Childhood, Irish University Press*, 1972
◆ Deane (S.) ed.: *The Field Day Anthology of Irish Writing*, 3 vols., Field Day Publications, Derry, 1991
◆ Donaghue (D.): *Warrenpoint*, Jonathan Cape, London,1991
◆ Donaghue (D.): *We Irish*, The Harvester Press, Brighton, 1986; Alfred A. Knopf, New York, 1987
◆ Donleavy (J.P.): *The Gingerbread Man*, Neville Spearman, London, 1962
◆ Doyle (R.): *Paddy Clarke Ha Ha Ha*, Secker & Warburg, London, 1993
◆ Doyle (R.): *The Snapper*, Secker & Warburg, London, 1990
◆ Edgworth (M.): *Castle Rackrent*, Macmillan London, 1970
◆ Friel (B.): *Aristocrats*, Gallery Press, 1983
◆ Friel (B.): *Translations*, Faber and Faber, London, 1982
◆ Gogarty (O. St. J.): *As Ireland was Going Down Sackville Street*, Harcourt, Brace & World, New York, 1937
◆ Gregory (Lady), ed. Murphy (D.J.): *Journals 1916–1930*, Colin Smythe, Gerrards Cross, 1978, 1987
◆ Heaney (M.): *Over Nine Waves, A Book of Irish Legends*, Faber and Faber, London and Boston, 1994
◆ Heaney (S.): *Door into the Dark*, Faber and Faber, London, 1969
◆ Heaney (S.): *Field Work*, Faber and Faber, London and Boston, 1969
◆ Heaney (S.): *Station Island*, Faber and Faber, London, 1984
◆ Heaney (S.): *Sweeney Astray*, Field Day Theater Co., Derry, 1983
◆ Heaney (S.): *Wintering Out*, Faber and Faber, London, 1972
◆ Joyce (J.): *Finnegans Wake*, Faber and Faber, London, 1939
◆ Joyce (J.): *Portrait of the Artist as a Young Man*, Alfred A. Knopf, New York, 1991
◆ Joyce (J.): *Ulysses*, Everyman's Library, London, 1992
◆ Kavanagh (P.): *Collected Poems*, Martin Brian & O'Keefe, London, 1972
◆ Kavanagh (P.): *Self Portrait*, 1964
◆ Kavanagh (P.): *Tarry Flynn*, The Pilot Press, London, 1948
◆ Keane (M.): *The Knight of Cheerful Countenance*, Virago Modern Classics, London, 1993

◆ Keane (M.): *The Rising Tide*, Virago Books, London, 1984
◆ Keane (M.): *Time after Time*, Sphere Books, London, 1984
◆ Kinsella (T.) trans.: *The Táin*, Dolmen Editions, Ireland, 1969
◆ Lavin (M.): *The Shrine and Other Stories*, Houghton Mifflin, Boston, 1977
◆ Longley (M.): *Poems 1963–1983*, Penguin, Harmondsworth, 1986
◆ McGahern (J.): *Among Women*, Faber and Faber, London, 1990
◆ McGahern (J.): *High Ground*, Faber and Faber Ltd, London, 1985
◆ Mahon (D.): *Selected Poems*, Viking/Gallery in assoc. with Oxford University Press, Oxford, 1991
◆ Moore (B.): *The Lonely Passion of Judith Hearne*, Little Brown, Boston, 1955
◆ Moore (B.): *Lies of Silence*, Bloomsbury, London, 1990
◆ Moore (G.): *A Drama in Muslim*, Boni & Liveright, New York, 1922
◆ Moryson (F.): *An Itinerary, Vol. III* James MacLehose and Sons, Glasgow, 1908
◆ Muldoon (P .): *Why Brownlee Left*, Faber and Faber, London, 1980
◆ Muldoon (P.): *Selected Poems 1968–1983*, Faber and Faber, London
◆ O'Brien (E.): *Mrs. Reinhardt and Other Stories*, Jonathan Cape, London, 1978
◆ O'Brien (E.): *Returning*, Penguin Books, London, 1983
◆ O'Brien (F.): *At Swim-Two-Birds*, MacGibbon & Kee, London, 1966
◆ O'Casey (S.): *Drums under the Window*, Macmillan, London, 1945
◆ O'Casey (S.): *Juno and the Paycock*, Macmillan London Ltd, London, 1972
◆ O'Connor (F.): *An Only Child*, Macmillan, London, 1961
◆ O'Faolain (S.): *No Country for Young Men*, Allen Lane, London, 1980
◆ O'Faolain (S.): *Foreign Affairs and Other Stories*, Penguin, Harmondsworth, 1986
◆ O'Faolain (S.): *Vive Moi!*, 1964
◆ Paulin (T.): *Ireland and the English Crisis*, Bloodaxe, Newcastle-upon-Tyne, 1984
◆ Paulin (T.): *The Liberty Tree*, Faber and Faber, London, 1982
◆ Paulin (T.): *A State of Justice*, Faber and Faber, London, 1977
◆ Shaw (G.B.S.): *The Complete Plays of Bernard Shaw*, Odhams Press, London, 1934

◆ Shaw (G.B.S.): *Sixteen Self Sketches*, Constable & Co., London, 1949
◆ Stephens (J.): *The Crock of Gold*, Macmillan, London, 1946
◆ Strabo trans. Jones (S.L.): *Geography*, London and New York, 1930
◆ Swift (J.), *Satires and personal writings*, Oxford University Press, London 1958
◆ Swift (J.), ed. Davis (H.) et al.,: *Prose Works*, 14 vols., Basil Blackwell, Oxford, 1939–68
◆ Synge (J.M.): *The Aran Islands*, Maunsel & Roberts Ltd, Dublin; and London, 1921
◆ Synge (J.M.S.): *The Autobiography of J.M. Synge*, Dolmen Press, Dublin; Oxford University Press, London, 1965
◆ Thackeray (W.M.): *The Irish Sketch Book*, Smith, Elder & Co., London, 1892
◆ Thackeray (W.M.): *The Memoirs of Barry Lyndon Esq.*, John Murray, London, 1911
◆ Trevor (W.): *Mrs Eckdorf in O'Neill's Hotel*, Penguin, Harmondsworth, 1985
◆ Trevor (W.): *The New Fiction from Ireland and Other Stories*, Bodley Head, London, 1986
◆ Wilde (O.): *The Works of Oscar Wilde*, Collins, London, 1948
◆ Yeats (W.B.): *Collected Plays*, Macmillan, London, 1934
◆ Yeats (W.B.), ed. Donoghue (D.): *Memoirs*, Macmillan, London, 1988

◆ Journals ◆

◆ *Analecta Hibernica*, Dublin
◆ *Archeology Ireland*, Dublin
◆ *Archivium Hibernicum*, Maynooth, Co. Kildare
◆ *Collectanea Hibernica*, Dublin
◆ *Irish Economic and Social History*, Belfast
◆ *Irish Geography*, Dublin
◆ *Irish Historical Studies*, Dublin
◆ *Irish Literary Supplement*, New York
◆ *Irish Review*, Cork
◆ *Irish University Review*, Dublin
◆ *Journal of the Cork Historical and Archeological Society*, Ballin College
◆ *Linen Hall Review*, Belfast
◆ *Studia Hibernica*, Dublin

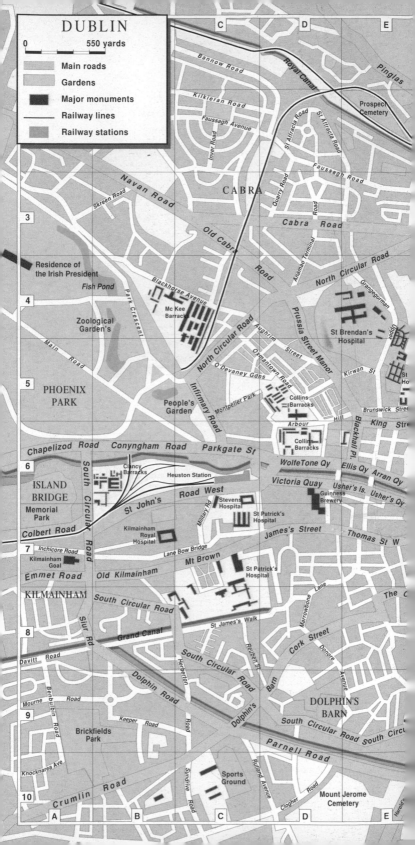